Knowing, Learning, and Instruction
Essays in Honor of Robert Glaser

D1213981

Knowing, Learning, and Instruction

Essays in Honor of Robert Glaser

Edited by
Lauren B. Resnick

LEA LAWRENCE ERLBAUM ASSOCIATES, PUBLISHERS
1989 Hillsdale, New Jersey   Hove and London

Lawrence Erlbaum Associates, Inc., Publishers
365 Broadway
Hillsdale, New Jersey 07642

CTAL

LB

1051

. K715

1989

Library of Congress Cataloging-in-Publication Data

Knowing, learning, and instruction : Essays in honor of Robert Glaser
  / edited by Lauren B. Resnick.
      p. cm.
    Includes bibliographies and index.
    ISBN 0-8058-0068-9. — ISBN 0-8058-0460-9 (pbk.)
    1. Educational psychology—Congresses. 2. Learning—Congresses.
  3. Teaching—Congresses. I. Glaser, Robert, 1921–
  II. Resnick, Lauren B.
  LB1051.K715   1989
  370.15—dc19   89-30180
                                                              CIP

Printed in the United States of America
10 9 8 7 6 5 4 3 2 1

Contents

List of Contributors

Ellen Ahwesh
*Learning Research
and Development Center
University of Pittsburgh*

Miriam Bassock
*Learning Research
and Development Center
University of Pittsburgh*

Isabel L. Beck
*Learning Research
and Development Center
University of Pittsburgh*

Carl Bereiter
*Ontario Institute for Studies
in Education*

Jeffrey Blais
*Learning Research
and Development Center
University of Pittsburgh*

Jeffrey Bonar
*Learning Research
and Development Center
University of Pittsburgh*

Ann L. Brown
*University of California,
Berkeley*

John Seely Brown
*Xerox Palo Alto Research
Center*

Michelene T. H. Chi
*Learning Research
and Development Center
University of Pittsburgh*

Allan Collins
BBN Laboratories

Rochel Gelman
University of Pennsylvania

Terry R. Greene
*Learning Research
and Development Center
University of Pittsburgh*

James G. Greeno
University of California, Berkeley

Joyce Ivill-Friel
*Learning Research
and Development Center
University of Pittsburgh*

Walter Kintsch
University of Colorado

Jill H. Larkin
Carnegie-Mellon University

Gaea Leinhardt
*Learning Research
and Development Center
University of Pittsburgh*

Alan Lesgold
*Learning Research
and Development Center
University of Pittsburgh*

Margaret G. McKeown
*Learning Research
and Development Center
University of Pittsburgh*

Mary L. Means
*Learning Research
and Development Center
University of Pittsburgh*

Pearla Nesher
University of Haifa, Israel

Susan E. Newman
Xerox Palo Alto Research Center

Annemarie S. Palincsar
Michigan State University

Charles A. Perfetti
*Learning Research
and Development Center
University of Pittsburgh*

Lauren B. Resnick
*Learning Research
and Development Center
University of Pittsburgh*

Marlene Scardamalia
*Ontario Institute for
Studies in Education*

James F. Voss
*Learning Research
and Development Center
University of Pittsburgh*

Preface

Writing the preface of a book is always a time of particular pleasure for an author or editor. It marks the end of a period of labor that, if one is fortunate, has resulted in some degree of new understanding and mastery. It is also an occasion to reflect on the efforts of those who have made the venture possible and to express thanks and recognition. I have multiple reasons to welcome this moment of reflection, for this volume honors Robert Glaser, a close colleague for many years. Initial planning for this volume also marked the 20th anniversary of the Learning Research and Development Center (LRDC), an institution Glaser founded and has led over the course of an influential career. Finally, publication of this volume recalls a conference at which the papers included here were first presented, a meeting of unusual intellectual liveliness at which issues of fundamental importance to the cognitive science of instruction were debated.

It is difficult to know where to begin in saying why a *festschrift* for Bob Glaser seemed a virtual necessity. His scholarship is extensive, and his influence on both the science of learning and the development of a field of application for this science has been immense. Bob has shown laboratory and experimental psychologists how their work could make a difference in the world and has lured several into new careers. He has taught educators to demand and to build a scientific base for their efforts.

Reviewing nearly 40 years of Bob's publications, I was struck by an extraordinary combination of continuity—several themes mark his work from the beginning to the present—and of responsiveness to new trends and promising ideas. Bob began his publishing life as a student of measurement theory and human performance. A behavioral psychologist, he entered the arena of education as an advocate and analyst of programmed instruction, teaching machines, and the theory that gave birth to them. He is now a leading proponent of cognitive science, espousing a view of the human being as thinker that many consider a radical departure from the behaviorist view. Contrary to what one might expect, this major shift in scientific perspective was accomplished without an abrupt break either in scholarly productivity or in fundamental research and social commitments. Across the behavioral-cognitive dividing line, Bob has maintained a continuing set of core questions and preoccupations. These include the nature of aptitudes and individual differences, the interaction of knowledge and skill in expertise, the roles of testing and technology in education, and training adapted to individual differences.

On each of these topics, Bob has written influential papers and edited widely read collections. At each stage of his career, most recently in a chapter for the 1989 *Annual Review of Psychology* (Glaser & Bassok, in press), he has demonstrated extraordinary ability to locate the key issue, to identify the seminal idea, to consider the best work being done, and to formulate an emerging set of problems that would mobilize and organize the work of many others. He did this in the late 1950s for programmed instruction (Glaser & Lumsdaine, 1960), showing how the basic idea introduced by Skinner could penetrate and energize all forms of education and training. He extended the principles of behavioral analysis to individualized education, first developing the notion of *individually prescribed instruction* as a means of organizing an entire elementary school to permit individual progress in accordance with the best learning principles of the time. Subsequently, he supported younger colleagues (myself included) in developing variants and extensions of individualized education. Finally, he gave all of these programs theoretical advocacy under the label *adaptive education* (Glaser, 1977), a term that for Bob encompassed a vision of an educational system devoted to teaching all students rather than selecting an able few for success.

In the course of these years, Bob took a leading position on two issues that continue to be at the forefront of educational development—testing and technology—always relating these to his central vision of educational possibilities. In 1963 he published a paper introducing the idea of *criterion referenced testing,* testing to determine exactly what students know and can do, not how they compare with other students (Glaser, 1963). Such testing is a central requirement for any educational system that aims to adapt instruction to all students. Testing aimed at supporting instruction rather than certifying (or denying) ability has remained a continuing interest, one now informed by cognitive analysis of aptitudes and abilities. A recent paper on the integration of instruction and testing (Glaser, 1986), for example, outlines a research program in testing that puts diagnostic testing tied to specific instructional interventions at the heart of the venture. Bob maintains an active personal and collaborative research program on instructional testing (e.g., Glaser, Lesgold, & Lajoie, 1987).

As early as the 1960s, well before educational technology became a popular field for research and development, Bob saw possibilities for using computers to enhance and enrich the instructional process (Cooley & Glaser, 1969). Some of his most recent research pursues this vision in the context of today's enlarged computing capabilities. He is, for example, developing and studying computerized discovery laboratories that can help students appreciate the structure of a field of knowledge by actively exploring it instead of trying to absorb the prepackaged messages of others (e.g., Shute, Glaser, & Raghavan, in press).

Much of Bob's current work on cognitive analyses of learning derives from his long-standing interest in individual differences (Glaser, 1977). Early on, he saw the possibilities for understanding such differences through empirical studies of the cognitive processes involved in various kinds of aptitude tests (e.g., Pellegrino & Glaser, 1979; Gitomer, Curtis, Glaser, & Lensky, 1987). As his aptitude studies proceeded, he became increasingly impressed with the role of knowledge differences in aptitudes (Glaser, 1984). This led to a companion line of research on the nature of expertise in specific academic disciplines and technical domains (e.g., Chi, Feltovich, & Glaser, 1981) and, subsequently, on differences in how people acquire knowledge in particular domains of expertise (Chi, Bassok, Lewis, Reimann, & Glaser, in press). Not surprisingly for someone whose theoretical and applied lines of work have always been intertwined, and for someone who has always been more interested in how to improve human competence than in how to select people of already developed ability, Bob's research on aptitudes and knowledge acquisition led him to explore the nature of learning and thinking skills and how these might be taught. A conference on this topic that he organized with Susan Chipman and Judith Segal resulted in a pair of widely influential volumes (Chipman, Segal, & Glaser, 1985; Segal, Chipman, & Glaser, 1985).

Over and beyond his own major contributions to research in these areas, the capacity to detect emerging trends in scholarship, to give them voice and shape, and to support and encourage the work of many others in order to build a science has marked Bob's leadership to an unusual degree. Nowhere is this more evident than in the institution—LRDC—that he founded and continues to co-direct today. The words that Bob wrote about establishing LRDC describe it even now:

> The problem . . . is to provide a functional entity that affords the climate, the organization, and the facilities for maximizing fruitful interaction between the scientific study of learning and educational practice, so that the

development of educational models grows out of, and feeds back into, the findings of behavioral science. This Center, therefore, is designed to function as a research and development facility which proceeds from basic research findings and new knowledge through practical availability. Its operational parts provide for exploratory theoretical research, for basic and specific development, for design and proving, for training of personnel to implement new developments, for field investigations to monitor and follow up innovations, for demonstration in a variety of operating institutions, and for systematic dissemination. The Center also includes a system for feeding from the field to the laboratory the results of practical experience and the real problems encountered there. (Glaser & Gow, 1964)

Thanks to Bob Glaser's continuing efforts, it is clear today that a research and development institute of the kind he initially envisaged can thrive and lead the way both in scholarship and in developing strong connections between scholarly research and educational practice. LRDC has changed over the more than 20 years of its existence, responding to shifting problems and opportunities. In the early years, applied work in the schools and, to a lesser degree, in technical training dominated; but a line of fundamental research on learning and the conditions that foster it was always maintained. When opportunities to develop a new, cognitively based science of learning and thinking relevant to education arose, LRDC undertook an increasingly large program of fundamental research; but its lines of application to education were always kept strong. Today, because cognitive science has developed to a point where direct applications to education and training are feasible, and with new theoretical issues beginning to shape the field of cognition and instruction, the center is again adapting its agenda. Throughout its existence, however, the commitment to fundamental science in interaction with practical problems of learning and education has remained.

When the University of Pittsburgh's President, Wesley W. Posvar, made funds available to celebrate the center's 20th anniversary—at the same time marking the University's 200th anniversary—it was not difficult for me and Bob Glaser, as LRDC's co-directors, to decide that a conference in which the most current and innovative research on cognition and instruction was presented and discussed was the right way to celebrate. It was considerably more difficult for me to persuade Bob to let me organize the conference and edit a volume of conference papers as a festschrift in his honor. He did not want to be left out of the fun. No paper by Bob appears in this collection, but that is only because we could not find a graceful way for someone to contribute a paper to his own festschrift! Indeed, the chapters speak to a set of issues that he has helped articulate and that drive his own work. And Bob was very much a participant in what turned out to be an intense, week-long set of discussions that probed new questions and opened new agendas for many who were there. To convey the intensity of those discussions in cold print seems impossible. Yet some of the excitement of the ideas that were shared will be apparent to those who read the chapters assembled here.

Bringing a book of this complexity to publication requires the help of many individuals. I want particularly to thank my LRDC colleagues, not all of whose work could fit in this volume. Their vital interest in this project provided further evidence of the center's intellectual camaraderie and the pride we take in each other's work. Very special thanks go to Michelle von Koch, who served as editor and severe but friendly critic of most chapters in the volume, including my own. Her understanding of the substantive issues was uncanny, and her wisdom about communicating complex ideas went well beyond the usual help one expects even from a skilled writer and editor.

REFERENCES

Chi, M. T. H., Bassok, M., Lewis, M. W., Reimann, P., & Glaser, R. (in press). Self-explanations: How students study and use examples in learning to solve problems. *Cognitive Science.*

Chi, M. T. H., Feltovich, P., & Glaser, R. (1981). Categorization and representation of physics problems by experts and novices. *Cognitive Science, 5,* 121–152.

Chipman, S. J., Segal, J. W., & Glaser, R. (Eds.). (1985). *Thinking and learning skills: Research and open questions* (Vol. 2). Hillsdale, NJ: Lawrence Erlbaum Associates.

Cooley, W. W., & Glaser, R. (1969). The computer and individualized instruction. *Science, 166,* 574–582.

Gitomer, D. H., Curtis, M. E., Glaser, R., & Lensky, D. B. (1987). Processing differences as a function of item difficulty in verbal analogy performance. *Journal of Educational psychology, 79,* 212–219.

Glaser, R. (1963). Instructional technology and the measurement of learning outcomes: Some questions. *American Psychologist, 18,* 519–521.

Glaser, R. (1977). *Adaptive education: Individual diversity and learning.* New York: Holt, Rinehart & Winston.

Glaser, R. (1984). Education and thinking: The role of knowledge. *American Psychologist, 39,* 93–104.

Glaser, R. (1986). The integration of instruction and testing. In E. Freeman (Ed.), *The redesign of testing in the 21st century: Proceedings of the 1985 ETS Invitational Conference* (pp. 45–58). Princeton, NJ: Educational Testing Service.

Glaser, R., & Bassok, M. (in press). Learning theory and the study of instruction. In *Annual Review of Psychology.* Palo Alto, CA: Annual Reviews, Inc.

Glaser, R., & Gow, J. S., Jr. (1964). The Learning Research and Development Center at the University of Pittsburgh. *American Psychologist, 19*(11), 854–858.

Glaser, R., Lesgold, A. M., & Lajoie, S. (1987). Toward a cognitive theory for the measurement of achievement. In R. R. Ronning, J. Glover, J. C. Conoley, & J. C. Witt (Eds.), *The influence of cognitive psychology on testing and measurement* (pp. 41–85). Hillsdale, NJ: Lawrence Erlbaum Associates.

Glaser, R., & Lumsdaine, A. A. (1960). *Teaching machines and programmed learning: A source book*. Washington, DC: National Education Association.

Pellegrino, J. W., & Glaser, R. (1979). Cognitive correlates and components in the analysis of individual differences. *Intelligence, 3,* 187–214.

Segal, J. W., Chipman, S. F., & Glaser, R. (Eds.). (1985). *Thinking and learning skills: Relating instruction to research* (Vol. 1). Hillsdale, NJ: Lawrence Erlbaum Associates.

Shute, V., Glaser, R., & Raghavan, K. (in press). Inference and discovery in an exploratory laboratory. In P. L. Ackerman, R. J. Sternberg, & R. Glaser, (Eds.), *Learning and individual diferences*. San Francisco: W. H. Freeman.

Robert Glaser

Born January 18, 1921, Providence, Rhode Island. Married Sylvia Lotman, 1945: children—Ellen Glaser DiBenedetti, Karen Glaser; grandchildren—Abraham and Jenya DiBenedetti.

Education

B.S., City College of New York, 1942; M.A., Indiana University, 1947; Ph.D., Indiana University, 1949.

Professional Experience

1963–Present Director, Learning Research and Development Center
1972–Present University Professor of Psychology & Education, University of Pittsburgh

1983 Visiting Professor, Southern Illinois University School of Medicine
1982 Visiting Professor, Central Institute of Educational Research, China
1982 Visiting Professor, Japan Society for the Promotion of Science
1981 Visiting Professor, Central University of Venezuela, Caracas
1975 Visiting Professor, University of Heidelberg
1975 Visiting Professor, University of Goteborg
1974 Distinguished Visiting Scholar, Educational Testing Service
1964–1972 Professor of Education, University of Pittsburgh
1957–1972 Professor of Psychology, University of Pittsburgh
1956–1957 Associate Professor of Psychology, University of Pittsburgh
1952–1956 Senior Research Scientist, American Institutes for Research
1950–1952 Research Assistant Professor, University of Illinois
1949–1950 Assistant Professor of Psychology, University of Kentucky
1948–1949 Instructor, Indiana University

Honors

1975–Present Member, National Academy of Education
1958–Present Fellow, American Association for the Advancement of Science
1957–Present Fellow, American Psychology Association

1989 Member, The Royal Norwegian Society of Sciences and Letters
1987–1989 Editor, the new *Educational Researcher*
1987 American Psychological Association's Distinguished Scientific Award for the Applications of Psychology
1985 Honorary Doctor of Science Degree, University of Goteborg, Sweden
1984 Honorary Doctor of Science Degree, Indiana University
1981–1985 President, National Academy of Education

1981   E. L. Thorndike Award for Distinguished Psychological Contributions to Education
1980   Honorary Doctor of Science Degree, University of Leuven, Belgium
1979–1985   Associate Editor, *American Psychologist,* American Psychological Association
1979–1980   President, Division on Evaluation and Measurement, American Psychological Association
1977   Outstanding Faculty Award, Council of Graduate Students in Education, University of Pittsburgh
1976   American Educational Research Association Award for Distinguished Research in Education
1975   John Simon Guggenheim Fellowship
1972   University Professor, University of Pittsburgh
1971–1972   President, American Educational Research Association
1971–1972   President, Division of Educational Psychology, American Psychological Association
1970   Award for Outstanding Research in the Field of Instructional Materials, American Educational Research Association/American Educational Publishers Institute
1969–1970   Fellow, Center for Advanced Study in the Behavioral Sciences
1966–1968   Vice-President, Division of Learning and Instruction, American Educational Research Association
1961   Special Citation for Outstanding Services to Education in the Commonwealth of Pennsylvania

1

Introduction

Lauren B. Resnick
Learning Research and Development Center
University of Pittsburgh

This book appears at a moment of new challenges and opportunities for instructional theory. A maturing cognitive science now provides stronger theoretical and methodological frameworks for the study of knowledge and learning than have been available heretofore. We can now approach questions of instruction with a solid base of information about how knowledge and process interact to produce competent performance and with a flexible array of methods for examining learning in those disciplines—practical or academic—we might wish to teach. Current cognitive theory emphasizes three interrelated aspects of learning that, together, call for forms of instructional theory very different from those that grew out of earlier associationist and behaviorist psychologies. First, learning is a process of knowledge *construction,* not of knowledge recording or absorption. Second, learning is *knowledge-dependent;* people use current knowledge to construct new knowledge. Third, learning is highly tuned to the *situation* in which it takes place.

Constructivism.   Cognitive theories tell us that learning occurs not by recording information but by interpreting it. Effective learning depends on the intentions, self-monitoring, elaborations, and representational constructions of the individual learner. The traditional view of instruction as direct transfer of knowledge does not fit this constructivist perspective. We need instead instructional theories that place the learner's constructive mental activity at the heart of any instructional exchange, that treat instruction as an intervention in an ongoing knowledge construction process. This does not mean, however, that students can be left to discover everything for themselves. Instruction must provide information for learners' knowledge construction processes. It must constrain those processes so that they will result in knowledge that is both true and powerful—*true* in the sense of describing the world well or according well with the theories of a discipline and *powerful* in the sense of being lasting and finding diverse occasions for use. At the same time, instruction must stimulate active knowledge construction processes among people who may initially doubt their own ability for or right to do independent thinking. Where necessary, instruction must also directly teach knowledge construction strategies.

Knowledge-Dependent Learning.   In an influential article, Robert Glaser (1984) assembled extensive evidence suggesting that both reasoning and learning are knowledge-driven. Those who are knowledge-rich reason more profoundly. They also elaborate as they study and thereby learn more effectively. Knowledge thus begets knowledge. Since that 1984 article, more evidence of the knowledge-dependence of thinking and learning has appeared. New research, some of it discussed in this volume (see Voss, Blais, Means, Greene, & Ahwesh, chap. 7; Chi & Bassok, chap. 8), has documented processes by which people elaborate items of knowledge and devise relationships among them that enable formulation of wider arguments and explanations. This research often highlights marked individual differences in people's tendency and ability to engage in these elaborative processes. Such differences may depend partly on prior knowledge and partly on habits of engaging with intellectual questions. The phenomenon of knowledge-dependent learning poses urgent questions for a theory of instruction. If learning depends on elaboration and extension of prior knowledge, should instruction expend its resources directly adding to that knowledge so people can reason and elaborate more effectively or on teaching them to reason and interpret information so they can more easily acquire new knowledge for themselves? Is it possible to teach reasoning without knowledge or knowledge without reasoning? If not, if the two are inextricably linked, how is it possible to break the cycle in which the knowledge-rich become still richer and the knowledge-poor remain poor?

Situated Knowledge. Traditional instructional theory assumes that knowledge and skill can be analyzed into component parts that function in the same way no matter where they are used. This assumption is the foundation for the building-from-the-bottom approach that characterizes most current school and technical instruction. Complexity, which overloads humans' limited attentional capacities, is initially avoided in favor of teaching separate components that presumably can be combined later without difficulty. Such instruction typically begins with basic elements or the facts of a knowledge domain. These are taught and practiced to some reliable level of performance. It is assumed that students will later be able to use these basics as the starting point for thinking and reasoning processes and for building more complex concepts and skills.

Cognitive theory today offers strong reasons to consider such bottom-up instruction suspect. First, we know that human memory for isolated facts is very limited. Knowledge is retained only when embedded in some organizing structure. Thus, students who learn many separate facts are unlikely to retain their knowledge beyond the period of test-taking—a much noticed, worrisome feature of the current educational system. Second, we now recognize that skills and knowledge are not independent of the contexts—mental, physical, and social—in which they are used. Instead, they are attuned to, even part of, the environments in which they are practiced. A new challenge for instruction is to develop ways of organizing learning that permit skills to be practiced in the environments in which they will be used. Such contextualized practice is needed both to tune skills and knowledge to their environments of use and to provide motivation for practicing abilities that in isolation might seem purposeless or meaningless.

Responding to these questions and challenges, cognitive scientists are examining and developing various new approaches to instruction. The chapters in this volume explore theory and data relevant to several constructivist methods of helping people create correct and powerful forms of knowledge; they examine the problem of cultivating more powerful processes of knowledge construction; and they probe the question of how to contextualize learning. I consider each of these before introducing the individual chapters.

BOOTSTRAPPING KNOWLEDGE CONSTRUCTION

The fact that learning depends heavily on what people already know poses a fundamental problem for instruction. Without special intervention, the knowledge rich would grow greatly in knowledge, the knowledge poor very little. Those most in need of instructional help, therefore, need special boosters for their knowledge construction efforts—extra help in identifying critical elements of their own knowledge and in learning from what others may tell or show them. It may be helpful to recast the traditional instructional question of how to convey information as a problem of *cognitive bootstrapping*—beginning a climb without firmly established prior knowledge, yet behaving as if one had the knowledge. Current cognitive instructional theory suggests various approaches to bootstrapping knowledge construction.

Texts That Support the Construction of Situation Models

Theories of mental models (Gentner & Stevens, 1983; Johnson-Laird, 1983) are central to cognitive science's search for ways of characterizing the relationship between thinking and the external reality to which thought and its symbols refer. To learn *about* something, to come to understand it, is, in current cognitive science parlance, to construct a mental model. How can we best assist learners in their process of constructing powerful and accurate mental representations of situations?

Many events, situations, and phenomena of interest to the curious and attentive person cannot be directly experienced, so deliberate instruction has an especially large role to play in helping people extend their knowledge. Instruction can make available historical events, situations that no longer exist but are of continuing cultural interest and importance. Or, the material of instructional interest may be contemporary, but so geographically removed or socially inaccessible that it cannot be directly experienced. Such is the case, for example, with events in other countries or activities of a social group to which one does not have access.

Written texts are among the time-tested ways of providing information that cannot be directly experienced. Considerable attention has been devoted to discovering how to make texts more effective as instructional vehicles. In the past most such research has focused on structural features of texts (e.g., organizational structure, grammatical complexity, vocabulary) or on adjuncts to texts (e.g., questions or headings) that might affect the ways in which they were read. Today, however, researchers are not only asking what general characteristics of texts enhance learning, but also exactly what kind of information is presented in them and what prior knowledge is presupposed. This research focuses explicitly on how to develop texts that facilitate learners' construction of particular kinds of *situation models* (see Kintsch, chap. 2 in this volume). Different situation models may be enhanced by different kinds of text designs, and the effectiveness of these designs will interact with the knowledge that the learner has available as a starting point for constructing a new model (Beck & McKeown, chap. 3 in this volume). Related research extends the notion of facilitative instructional presentations to include teachers' explanations and students' responses to them (see Leinhardt, chap. 4 in this volume).

Tapping Implicit Knowledge

People do not come as empty vessels to learning. In almost any domain, even beginners carry with them ideas of how things work and frameworks for interpreting new information. These ideas may come from everyday experience, which forms the basis for a large repertoire of mental models that correspond to frequently encountered physical and social phenomena. Most often these models remain implicit. People are sometimes unaware of having them but, nevertheless, use them as frameworks for interpreting situations and acting in them.

Sometimes implicitly held models contain core principles and constraints that can effectively help people to learn a formal system. This is the case in mathematics, where research has revealed that children and unschooled adults gain substantial knowledge about basic principles of number and arithmetic from informal experience (Gelman & Greeno, chap. 5 in this volume; Resnick, 1986). These principles, however, are rarely invoked in the course of school arithmetic learning. Substantial evidence now exists that children attempt to construct calculation procedures on the basis of examples that do not adequately constrain their constructions (VanLehn, 1985). As a result, they invent systematic but incorrect procedures that have come to be known as *buggy algorithms* or *malrules*. Research is beginning to explore the idea that mathematics learning can be enhanced by instruction that taps children's implicit models of the number system, bringing these principles into discussion and explicitly linking them to the formal mathematics being taught. Students of cognition and instruction face the challenge of identifying for many domains the implicit principles that might play this constraining role in learning and devising ways to make school learning as sensitive to these principles as possible.

Implicitly held mental models can also contradict new ideas being taught and interfere with learning. There is substantial and growing evidence that in many fields of science (perhaps most dramatically in physics) basic scientific concepts are in fundamental epistemological conflict with many commonplace everyday conceptions. As a result, people's everyday conceptions of natural phenomena do little to support, and may actually hinder, learning modern scientific constructs. In many domains of knowledge, learning new theoretical systems may require individual mental reorganizations of knowledge similar to the reorganizations that sciences themselves undergo. Much attention is currently focused on the potential role of contradiction in making people aware of their implicit models and in stimulating reformulation of them. According to current instructional theories, recognition of contradictions can be provoked either by confrontations with data that disconfirm a current belief, or by confrontations with contradictory beliefs and predictions of others, especially peers. Some investigators now recognize, however, that contradiction of current beliefs may lead to discomfort with one's own present conceptions, without necessarily leading one *toward* a more scientifically appropriate new construct (e.g., Johsua & Dupin, 1987). A current challenge is to find various ways to bootstrap new theory construction without ignoring the existence and power of prior conceptions.

Objectifying Theoretical Constructs

Theoretical systems are difficult to learn, partly because they refer to entities with no direct correspondents in sensory experience. Learning mathematics, physical and social sciences requires an understanding of such theoretical systems. Theoretical systems in physics, for example, include entities such as forces, vectors, and inertia that serve to explain phenomena but cannot actually be observed. In economics the concept of a market imposes order upon observations of supply, demand, and price fluctuations, but the market itself cannot be directly seen. In mathematics, too, entities such as numbers and operations are mental constructions, not perceptible phenomena. Instruction in domains in which theoretical entities play a central role requires attention to helping students construct not only mental models of situations, but also mental models of theories. Ordinary inductive processes cannot be relied on for constructing theoretical models, because the entities that comprise these models cannot be directly observed.

One promising approach to bootstrapping learners' construction of theoretical constructs is creating means of *objectifying* constructs, that is, building physical displays that allow explicit representation of key theoretical constructs. Such displays afford public and, therefore, discussable referents for key theoretical constructs (see Nesher, chap. 6 in this volume). It becomes possible, then, to manipulate these objects, observe the effects, and apply processes analogous to inductive learning to the problem of building theoretical constructs. In exploring the possibilities for objectifying theoretical constructs, cognitive scientists have been borrowing ideas from mathematics, where there has traditionally been an interest in creating concrete or graphic representations of basic entities in the mathematical system (cf. Dienes & Golding, 1971). At the same time, they have been using the new representational capacities of computers to construct representations that behave as theoretical objects *would* under perfect theoretical assumptions. White (in press) and Roschelle (1987), for example, have created computer systems in which objects move in accordance with Newtonian principles, and graphical representations of vectors can be used to control or predict these motions. By supporting conversation about theoretical constructs that students do not yet fully understand, such programs allow students to enter a knowledge culture in which the target theoretical constructs play a role. The graphic displays ensure that individuals talk about the same thing, and that the object of their discussion behaves as it should within the to-be-learned theoretical system.

A related line of work has explored the role of analogies in helping students construct new explanatory systems. For certain topics (e.g., basic electricity), there has been extensive exploration of the strengths and weaknesses of different kinds of analogies. Each analogy highlights certain theoretical features and makes it difficult to appreciate others (cf. Gentner, 1983). Research on analogies in instruction makes it clear that simply presenting analogies is often insufficient to bootstrap theory construction. Analogies are instructionally effective only when the learner is prepared to accept the idea that two systems or situations are similar in some fundamental way. If students believe, for example, that a spring, with its obvious elasticity, and a board that appears solid and inelastic are fundamentally different, showing them a spring analogy will not help them understand that a board exerts an upward force on an object that rests on it. Clement (1987) has been exploring the role of "bridging analogies"—situations midway between a source and a target system—that can help students understand how two apparently different systems are, in fact, related. Effective use of analogies often requires extensive discussion and dialogic development of ideas. Through such talk, people tune and refine each other's mental models, creating a culturally shared set of representations and theories. Research on the process of tuning and refining theoretical models through discussion and explanation is increasingly attracting cognitive scientists' attention.

TEACHING PROCESSES OF KNOWLEDGE CONSTRUCTION

Except in the narrowest training environments in which the entire goal of instruction is to produce skill at repeated performance of the same task, educators usually aim to teach competencies that have wide applicability. It is obviously impossible, in the limited number of years and hours that students spend in classrooms, to teach every specific skill and piece of knowledge that people will require during their lives. Rather than trying to impart volumes of specific knowledge, it is often argued, instruction should cultivate general abilities that will facilitate learning throughout life and in variable settings. The search for teachable, general learning abilities is as old as the history of education. The issues of what such abilities are and how they are acquired have occupied the attention of psychologists in every phase of the discipline's history. Educational research has long addressed this question under the rubric of *transfer*. In a sense, transfer is the holy grail of educators—something we are ever in search of, that hope pretends lies just beyond the next experiment or reform program.

Two major theories of transfer, each with long historical traditions, have dominated this search (see Larkin, chap. 9 in this volume). One, known once as the theory of mental discipline, equated the mind to a set of general faculties that could be exercised like muscles. According to this view, if each faculty were optimally exercised, the mind would be optimally capable of acquiring new knowledge. Faculty psychology and mental discipline theory were educators' defense of such traditional subjects as mathematics and Latin, which were thought to train the mind, even though, as in the case of Latin, less and less justification for the subject as practical in its own right could be adduced. Early in this century, with the rise of associationism as a dominant psychological account of mental functioning, the theory of mental discipline began to lose favor. Exercising the faculties by studying such subjects as mathematics or Latin did not, on empirical investigation, prove to facilitate learning other subjects.

Early in this century, Thorndike and Woodworth (1901) proposed an alternative account of transfer: the theory of common elements. According to this theory, capability transfers from one task to another to the extent that the tasks share common elements. Most cognitive psychologists since Thorndike have assumed some variant of a common elements theory when considering the issue of transfer and skills for learning. They have sought the common elements for transfer in both basic processes, such as speed of encoding or basic reading abilities (see Perfetti, chap. 10 in this volume), and in items of knowledge ranging from shared stimulus-response pairs in associationist theories to shared aspects of knowledge structures and schemas in modern cognitive theories.

Recently considerable evidence from both cognitive studies of learning and developmental studies of cognitive self-management points to a feature of successful learning that goes beyond specific knowledge (cf. Glaser & Pellegrino, 1987). Successful learners tend to elaborate and develop self-explanations that extend the information in texts or other instructional material (see Chi & Bassok, chap. 8 in this volume). Weaker learners do not engage spontaneously in this kind of elaboration. Also important is a strong difference among learners in their tendency to *monitor* their own understanding as they work. Better learners seem to attend closely to and properly assess their own state of understanding, perhaps a prelude to their elaborative activity. Differences in individuals' self-monitoring and tendency to elaborate have been widely noted as distinguishing weaker from stronger readers, younger from older children, retarded from normal children, poor from good memorizers, and also people with greater from those with lesser knowledge of the topic being studied. These frequently noted disparities have given birth to the construct of *metacognition*—people's knowledge and monitoring of their own cognitive states and processes (Brown, Bransford, Ferrara, & Campione, 1983).

Substantial work now suggests that knowledge *about* cognitive processes (for example, knowledge about what good readers do) is probably less important than self-monitoring *of* those processes. Indeed, the habit of *meaning imposition*—the tendency to elaborate and seek relationships—has emerged in recent discussions (e.g., Resnick, 1987a) as a major candidate for explaining the strong tendency for good learners in one domain to be good in others as well. This notion of disposition to elaborate or of intention to learn represents an alternative (or auxiliary) to looking for generality and transfer in basic processes or in packages of knowledge that have wide applicability. According to this view, the observed generality and transfer to learning come from intentional efforts to find links among elements of knowledge, to develop explanations and justifications, and to raise questions.

It is frequently proposed that the processes of knowledge construction observed among the most successful learners might be directly taught to others. There has been a virtual explosion of laboratory and field intervention studies in which various cognitive skills and strategies are taught (see Chipman, Segal, & Glaser, 1985; Resnick, 1987a; Segal, Chipman, & Glaser, 1985). A pattern of findings is now beginning to emerge that sets the stage for a new approach to the problem of teaching knowledge construction abilities. The evidence suggests that it is relatively easy to teach and learn particular strategies such as memorizing, summarizing a text passage, identifying a particular kind of faulty argument, or estimating a numerical answer. When these strategies are learned and practiced in isolation, however, they are not very likely to be used spontaneously by students. In addition, most strategies require attainment of a certain level of specific knowledge in order to be used. For these reasons, when strategy training is embedded in the study of a particular subject matter, the strategies are much more likely to be used, at least for that discipline, although transfer to other subject matters is problematic. What is more, evidence is increasingly accumulating that people's use of strategies and knowledge to construct new knowledge depends heavily on whether they view themselves as being in charge of their learning, or whether they expect others—most often a teacher—to direct them. Psychologists now speak of the need to cultivate *intentional learning,* learning that is actively desired by and controlled by the learner (see Bereiter & Scardamalia, chap. 12 in this volume).

In a certain sense, a new kind of mental discipline theory is being formulated, one that situates learning ability in a combination of skills and dispositions for elaborative and generative mental work. The new attention to dispositions for mental activity, in turn, directs instructional theorists' attention to aspects of human functioning that have for many decades been treated as separate from cognition. Cognitive scientists have freely allowed that cognition must interact with motivational, emotional, and social aspects of a person's life. But there have been few serious efforts to study this interaction. For their part, social psychologists have largely treated motivation as mainly a motor for intellectual activity, something that determines how *much* activity there will be, but not what *kind* of activity. Research on social interaction conducted by sociologists, anthropologists, and linguists, as well as some psychologists, has become very sophisticated in accounting for patterns of language use and social status. But it has by and large proceeded without attention to the *content* of the interaction.

This situation is now beginning to change. A significant number of researchers, some of them directly concerned with instructional theory and practice, are now examining motivation linked to cognition, along with various aspects of socially shared cognition. Dweck and Elliot (1983) and Nicholls (1983), for example, have developed theories of individual differences in motivational patterns that link people's conceptions of success and failure and of themselves as learners directly to the kinds of elaborations and reasoning processes in which they are likely to engage. Psycholinguists (e.g., Clark & Wilkes-Gibb, 1986) have begun to show that the meaning is established through a social negotiation in which both parties in a dialogue try to establish what the other knows and then adjust communication to the partner's knowledge status. Other researchers are extending the study of reasoning to include the ways in which people argue with each other. All of this is leading to a revival of interest in the few social science theorists who in the past have tried to show the ways in which individual thought capacities might be rooted in social participation: Mead (1934), who viewed thought as a form of "conversation with the generalized other"; and Vygotsky (1978) who conceived of cognitive development as a process of internalizing concepts, values, and modes of thought that are initially practiced in social interaction with adults. Instructional theorists have begun to study ways of embedding learning in social communities in which elaboration and interpretation are regularly practiced, and to use forms of "scaffolding"—performances in which other people, or by extension, tools and devices, carry part of the performance load—as regular aspects of instruction (see Brown & Palincsar, chap. 13 in this volume). There seems good reason to believe that these lines of work represent early versions of what we will recognize a decade from now as a major new line of development in cognitive theory as a whole and in instructional theory in particular.

SITUATED LEARNING AS A FORM OF INSTRUCTION

How instructed knowledge relates to knowledge-in-use is a perennially troubling problem for education and for theories of instruction. Most of our thinking about education stems from an implicit assumption that skill and knowledge exist independently of the contexts in which they are acquired, that once a person learns something, she knows it no matter where she is. On this assumption, failure to use a particular piece of knowledge or skill is attributed to the individual's not recognizing its relevance to the situation or not being motivated to apply it. This assumption that knowledge is context-independent is deeply rooted in educational thinking and in cognitive science as a whole. It is essential to the idea that thinking can be understood as symbol-manipulation, which in turn underlies the whole venture of cognitive modeling of human thought by computer programs. It also underlies experimental psychology's tradition of laboratory research on learning and thinking. Only if one assumes that thought proceeds in the same ways in different environments can one expect to learn about thought in general by observing behavior in a very particular, often artificial environment. Finally, it justifies the venture of schooling as it is currently organized. If knowledge can be acquired in one context and then freely moved into another (as long as relevance is shown and motivation assured), it makes good sense to designate a particular environment—school—as a place that specializes in helping people learn.

Today, however, many questions are being raised about this assumption of context-independent thought and knowledge. Social scientists are asking whether cognitive abilities can be separated from the social and emotional contexts in which thought and action take place. Philosophers are questioning the assumption that thought can be fully understood as a symbolic process rather than as one in which mental activities interact directly with the material and social world (e.g., Dreyfus & Dreyfus, 1986; Searle, 1984). Cognitive scientists themselves (e.g., Winograd & Flores, 1986) are beginning to ask how they can study and characterize what has come to be called *situated knowledge*. Those concerned with education and instruction must do the same.

Comparing the ways in which people are expected to perform and learn in school with the ways in which mental competence is expressed outside school in various work and practical settings reveals several features that differentiate typical instructional settings from performance settings (Resnick, 1987b). In school and in most other instructional settings, people are expected to learn and perform individually. Yet in work and personal life, most mental activity is performed in the context of some shared task that allows mental work to be distributed over several individuals. Almost all real-world mental activity also involves the use of tools that expand people's mental power. These tools can be as complex as computer simulation programs or as simple as lists of frequently used calculations, but they are almost always present. In school, however, people are usually expected to perform without any props or crutches. This insistence on thought independent of tools seems to derive from the belief that mental capabilities are encapsulated within individual minds, a belief that sidesteps the important question of how programs of thought interact with the world. Closely related to the avoidance of tools in school is school's tendency to focus almost entirely on symbolic activities. This contrasts sharply with ordinary activity in which actions are intimately connected with objects and events, and people often use the objects directly in their reasoning.

Each of these features of schooling—its focus on individual cognition, its demand for tool-free performance, and its insistence on symbolic performances—is linked to schools' aspiration to teach competencies that are general rather than situation specific. These typical features of school, however, need not be taken as conditions necessary for learning. Before schools became so dominant in our society that even on-the-job training often came to resemble classroom teaching, most instruction took place in craft and trade apprenticeships. Although full-scale apprenticeships are not common today, studies of apprenticeships in developing countries, where many of the traditional forms still survive, provide a glimpse of how such training works (Greenfield, 1984; Lave, 1977). Apprentices spend numerous hours watching masters, journeymen, and older apprentices at work. From the beginning, they observe both the full process of production and the resultant product, and they may practice a few basic skills. When they achieve an acceptable level of competence in these basic skills, they attempt the entire process of producing a simple artifact on their own. This task, repeated until mastered, is not practiced as an exercise without economic significance; the apprentice's products may be offered for sale, although at a lower price than the master's work. When construction of one item is mastered, the apprentice begins to work on another, more complex one and, thus, proceeds through a curriculum that, while graded and sequenced, always exercises component skills in the context in which they will be used. There is very little direct instruction apart from the masters pointing out errors, but there is much learning through this graded, contextually embedded process. There is also considerable self-correction, made possible because the apprentices, through observation, have established criteria against which they can judge their own products.

Real apprenticeship has all but disappeared in industrialized countries, although the title is sometimes retained for entry level, trainee positions. Not only the rise of schooling but also the conditions of today's technical work have driven it out. High-technology work environments seem to preclude traditional apprenticeship activities. It may take hours or days to complete an equipment diagnosis, and some problems may not occur at all during the course of training. As a result, trainees cannot be exposed to the full range of conditions they will encounter as working technicians. In addition, the environment is dangerous and expensive if mishandled; it is not reasonable to allow trainees to make and then correct errors. Finally, neither the equipment's functioning nor the mental activity of an expert equipment diagnostician is visible, as are the master craftsman's physical activity and product; so observation alone is unlikely to support the desirable and necessary conceptual development that occurs in the craft shop.

Evidence is beginning to accumulate that traditional schooling's focus on individual, isolated activity, on symbols correctly manipulated but divorced from experience, and on decontextualized skills may be partly responsible for our schools' difficulty in teaching processes of thinking and knowledge construction. In a recent review of programs claiming to teach thinking skills, learning skills, or higher order cognitive abilities, several elements common to successful programs were identified (Resnick, 1987a). Most of the effective programs have features characteristic of out-of-school cognitive performances. They involve socially shared intellectual work, and they are organized around joint accomplishment of tasks, so that elements of the skill take on meaning in the context of the whole. Many of the programs also use procedures (e.g., modeling) that make usually hidden processes overt, and they encourage student observation and commentary. They also allow skill to build up bit by bit, yet permit participation even for the relatively unskilled, often as a result of the social sharing of tasks. Finally, the most successful programs are organized around particular bodies of knowledge and interpretation—subject matters—rather than general abilities. Treatment of subject matter is tailored to engage students in processes of meaning construction and interpretation that link symbols to their referents.

This kind of instruction adapts some of the features of traditional craft apprenticeship to instruction in thinking. It provides graduated and supported practice in cognitive skills in a situation of actual use. In the final chapter of this volume, Collins, Brown, and Newman have labeled such teaching *cognitive apprenticeship*. Several other chapters (Lesgold, Ivill-Friel, & Bonar, chap. 11; Bereiter & Scardamalia, chap. 12; Brown & Palincsar, chap. 13) discuss specific applications. There is much still to be learned about cognitive apprenticeship, including whether it is more effective than context-independent teaching at producing truly general learning abilities. But it is already clear that investigations of situated learning will play an important role as cognitive instructional theory continues to develop.

INTRODUCTION TO THE CHAPTERS

The chapters in this volume explore key questions about the nature of knowledge and analyze methods for assisting learners' knowledge construction. They examine the role of knowledge in reasoning and in learning, and consider ways in which skills and dispositions for learning might be taught. The chapters range across instructional disciplines, examining the enabling disciplines of reading and writing, the traditional subject matters of mathematics, science, and social science, and certain technical skills. They consider learners of all ages, from preschool children to adults.

In chapter 2, **Kintsch** explores the ways readers use text to create mental models of the situations to which texts refer. Kintsch points out that, in studying text understanding, psychologists have traditionally focused on comprehension of what he calls the *textbase,* that is, on the extent to which a reader or listener constructs a representation of the relationships among propositions that correspond to those stated or implied in the text. This representation *of* the text, he argues, must be distinguished from a representation of the situation described *by* the text. Complex relations hold between the processes of building a text representation and a situation representation. Readers must represent the text adequately in order to arrive at a representation of the situation that corresponds to the text, but they must also make inferences that go beyond textual propositions, especially when their goal is to solve problems or otherwise apply the information acquired rather than just recall the text. Under these conditions, Kintsch shows, recall of the text may be distorted in order to conform to readers' understanding of the problem situation.

Research on text understanding has traditionally included attention to both situation models and textbases, without clearly distinguishing between them. By insisting on this distinction, Kintsch highlights the problem of the relationships between symbols and their referents—for the textbase representation functions *within* the symbolic domain, whereas the situation model requires a representation of the *referents* of the textual propositions. In past research on text comprehension, this distinction has been difficult to draw, partly because the texts studied have had clear referents only in other purely verbal expressions of knowledge. In studying understanding of arithmetic story problems and of texts that support the construction of mental maps of a town, Kintsch has alternative measures of text understanding to those of verbal recall. As a result, he is able to explore more explicitly the relationships between construction of an intrasymbolic representation and a referential representation.

Beck and McKeown consider in chapter 3 the problem of designing instructional texts that recognize the knowledge-dependence of learning. Although they do not use Kintsch's terminology, their analysis of the problem starts from an assumption entirely in keeping with Kintsch's theory: The goal of a text is to assist the reader in developing a representation of a situation that goes beyond the textual information. Beck and McKeown insist on the need to compensate for children's relative lack of knowledge of both the topics that textbooks treat and the expository genre by providing texts that are optimally structured. They offer a number of criteria for such well-structured texts and show that most current textbooks fail to meet them. A particularly compelling aspect of this analysis is their detailing of the special problems of expository as opposed to narrative texts. Not only are children far less familiar with expository texts than narratives, but also the expository genre itself does not have the kind of single organizing macrostructure characteristic of narratives. As a result, children do not have fixed expectations drawn from genre knowledge about what will occur in the text, expectations that might help them to build a situation model. They are thus forced to rely on whatever they may already know about the topic and on what the text itself is able to supply.

The general thrust of Beck and McKeown's argument is that textbook writers are presented with a special burden. They must provide texts that are well-structured according to criteria that blend traditional rhetorical standards and critical inferences from a broad body of cognitive research on text understanding. Because they propose improvement in texts designed to teach reading skill rather than any specific subject matter content, they imply that a steady diet of well-structured expository texts will not only communicate effectively the specific content presented in those texts but will also produce an ability on the part of children to process adequately less well-structured texts. In other words, there is an implicit assumption that children will become less dependent on the quality of the text over time.

Leinhardt also is concerned in chapter 4 with finding powerful ways of communicating knowledge, while taking the knowledge construction processes of students clearly into account. She considers the role of the teacher, rather than the text, in this process. She examines both the teacher's explanations and the children's interpretations of them in the class. Her analysis makes it clear that no sharp line can be drawn between transmitting information and supporting mental constructions by learners. She shows that children rarely receive everything transmitted and that some children go at least a bit beyond what the teacher directly conveys. Yet the teacher's explanation clearly provides both an invitation to learning and information critical to students' constructive processes. It makes sense to think of Leinhardt's teacher as providing the text from which children must create their mental or situation models. Much as Kintsch shows that the kinds of models that readers create are constrained by, but not completely determined by, the form of the text, so Leinhardt shows that children construct variations on the model the teacher has presented.

Leinhardt raises a number of questions about the nature of good instructional explanations and good lessons (i.e., the combination of presentations, reviews of past work, practice exercises, and recitation). In her description of an expert teacher conducting a series of arithmetic lessons for a whole elementary school class, one is struck with the many tuning decisions that the teacher must make in the course of instruction, although the lesson series as a whole follows a largely preplanned agenda. Leinhardt does not attempt here to specify the rules that underlie these tuning decisions. Indeed, one has the impression that the knowledge guiding such decisions is, for the skilled teacher, highly implicit and likely to be difficult to explicate.

The next two chapters continue the discussion of mathematics learning. **Gelman and Greeno** take on the question of the origins of mental models of mathematics in chapter 5. In so doing, they focus on *implicit* knowledge—knowledge that people are not consciously aware of, that they cannot effectively talk about, but that guides their thinking, reasoning, and action. Gelman and Greeno's account focuses on acquisition of arithmetic knowledge that precedes formal schooling and proceeds without explicit instruction. How, they ask, can ordinary experience in the world produce focused learning? They propose that implicitly held knowledge of fundamental principles (of counting, for example) serves as a conceptual skeleton that gets learning started. These principles structure and constrain attention as the child experiences the very variable and ill-structured world. As a result, from varied experiences with counting words and objects, children are able to abstract a set of rules that allows them to quantify sets of objects reliably.

Regularities in children's counting behavior, especially their ability to invent correct variants of counting procedures and to detect errors in someone else's counting, provide evidence of this implicit knowledge of basic principles. Children's failure to apply consistently correct counting *procedures* should not necessarily be taken as evidence that they do not know the *principles*. Three kinds of competence are needed for correct performance on any given occasion. Gelman and Greeno distinguish *conceptual* competence, which is knowledge of the principles and constraints that are defining and essential, from *procedural* competence, which is knowledge of how to generate performance plans that honor the principles and constraints. They further distinguish both of these from *interpretative* competence, which is knowledge of how to interpret verbal instructions and physical displays to decide which of these plans is applicable on a given occasion. Even if conceptual and procedural competence is adequate, deficits in interpretative competence can produce failures or errors in performance.

Complementing Gelman and Greeno's focus on how mathematical knowledge may be constructed in the course of everyday experience, **Nesher** takes on the problem of deliberately organizing experience to foster mental model construction in chapter 6. In mathematics, as in other domains in which theoretical constructs do not have exact correspondents in ordinary experience, verbal and symbolic presentations risk becoming formulaic expressions without clear referents. Statements that, to those who already know about number or operations, have a clear referent are likely to be empty formalisms to beginners, even when couched in ordinary language rather than in the symbols and equations of formal mathematics. Nesher proposes a solution to this dilemma: the creation of a physical reference system designed specifically for pedagogical purposes.

This reference system, which she calls a *learning system,* is designed to be perfectly morphic, not to ordinary experience but to objects in the theoretical system of mathematical entities. With such a physical realization of a mathematical system to examine and manipulate, she proposes, it becomes possible for learners to talk about a system that is mathematically correct even when they do not yet know the mathematics involved. Because the objects in the learning system correspond perfectly to the theoretical objects (e.g., numbers, operations), talk about the objects in the learning system is mathematical talk, even though conducted in ordinary language. Thus a referent that is public and understandable is provided for the previously referentially empty formulas and notations of mathematics. The objectification of the theoretical world provided in Nesher's proposed learning system provides bridges from ordinary language to mathematical language and from physical experience to theoretical description. The constraints of the physical objects in the learning system correspond to the theoretical constraints in the number system and, thus, channel students' mental model constructions in the direction of a mathematically correct system.

Two chapters explore knowledge-based reasoning and learning, one in the social sciences and one in the physical sciences. In chapter 7, **Voss, Blais, Means, Greene, and Ahwesh** compare reasoning about economics problems among individuals having different amounts of formal education in economics and different amounts of practical experience with economics questions. The focus is on *informal reasoning,* that is, reasoning that proceeds by plausible argument and justifiable defense rather than by the formal deduction and proof that usually characterize reasoning in science and mathematics. The results show substantial disparities in measures of reasoning quality—for example, the extent to which long chains of reasoning were used; the extent to which counterarguments were generated and considered as the subject represented the problem veridically; the extent to which qualifications were specified; the extent to which alternative arguments were generated and supported by relevant reasons; and the extent to which the arguments were couched in terms of general economics principles. On the whole, college-educated subjects, whether or not they had formally studied economics, were better reasoners. They also gave evidence of more articulated knowledge of economics, a finding that held even for subjects who had not studied economics. This reflects on the degree to which formal instruction may bypass the economic problems considered in everyday life, and provides an example from the social sciences of a phenomenon well known in physical sciences and mathematics—the lack of connection between theoretical systems taught and everyday experience.

Chi and Bassok explore in chapter 8 the ways in which good and poor learners use their knowledge to gain new information when studying examples. They analyze the mental activities of students studying a physics textbook before attempting to solve the typical end-of-chapter problems; these problems are highly conventionalized yet rely on a fairly rich network of knowledge. Their analysis shows that successful students use text examples to elaborate a rich representation of the problem, including explanations of why variables are related in the way they are and why particular solution steps are carried out. These representations go well beyond the rather sparse material presented in the text examples, drawing on previously held knowledge and also on the explanatory material. Such elaborations are largely absent among the weaker students.

Both Voss's group and Chi and Bassok emphasize the correlation of reasoning skill with the extent of subjects' knowledge of the domain. Yet both sets of findings contain anomalies that are puzzling in the context of a theory that places specific knowledge at the heart of reasoning ability. Voss's group found that, although attending college improved reasoning, study of economics in particular did not. Chi and Bassok found that less successful students did not engage in self-explanation processes, even when, by common measures of retention, they had knowledge they could call upon in elaborative studying. Both sets of findings could be used to suggest that differences in elaboration abilities or habits, rather than differences in knowledge, produce the contrast between good and poor learners. Defending the knowledge-dependence view, Voss et al. point to the hypothesized mismatch between the content of economics courses and the everyday problems they asked subjects to solve. Similarly Chi and Bassok suggest that their finding could be an artifact of the standard recall measures that they used to compare their subjects' knowledge. Perhaps, they suggest, the less successful students have encoded their knowledge differently from the more successful; these qualitative differences would not have been detected by the kinds of knowledge tests used. In considering this possibility, Chi and Bassok discuss different possible meanings of understanding in a way that links their work on learning differences to the problems of characterizing knowledge and competence addressed in the earlier chapters by Gelman and Greeno and by Kintsch.

The tension between theories that stress the knowledge-dependence of learning and those that highlight process differences is evident again in a pair of chapters that address the question of transferable learning. **Larkin** adds a new thrust to the continuing search for transferable *knowledge* in chapter 9. Working within the common elements tradition, she attempts to identify knowledge that is specific enough to be recognized as appropriate to a particular situation and yet still has applicability in diverse contexts. Her chapter focuses on two types of strategic knowledge. Using as a guide an AI program (FERMI) that is capable of solving a wide variety of physical science problems, Larkin examines strategies such as decomposition of quantities and maintenance of invariance that can be applied to problems in such domains as hydrostatics and electricity if the system has sufficient domain-specific knowledge to identify correctly the quantities involved and the invariances required. Another common element for transfer, she proposes, is a strategy for generating subgoals. These kinds of strategic knowledge are not explicitly taught in science curricula. More direct attention to such intermediate level strategies, she proposes, could produce better transfer than has characterized most instructional experiments.

In chapter 10, **Perfetti** focuses on transferable *processes*. He argues that the important competencies that can be transferred are not specific elements of domain knowledge, but rather language comprehension abilities that are carried across domains. While admitting that knowledge of a text's topic contributes to language comprehension (a phenomenon that has been widely documented in research on reading comprehension), he claims that certain fundamental reading processes are relatively uninfluenced by topical knowledge. The core of his argument is that there is a distinction between achieving a *meaning* and an *interpretation* for text. The former—text meaning—resembles Kintsch's textbase or text representation. It stays close to the text itself and involves little inference beyond information directly provided by the text. Text *interpretation,* which requires inference and is more independent of the text, resembles Kintsch's *situation model.* Perfetti argues that constructing a *meaning* is highly dependent upon knowledge of the conventional symbols (words) and of the syntax of the language, but not upon knowledge of the situation to which the text refers. Furthermore, these processes of meaning construction are *impenetrable* (or *modular* as Fodor, 1983, would term them) by knowledge of the situation. They are carried out automatically, as it were. The impenetrable processes include word identification (lexical access) and sentence parsing.

Perfetti's insistence on impenetrability and noninhibitability of word recognition and sentence-parsing processes yields a very different picture of a transferable strategy from Larkin's. According to Perfetti, general reading ability transfers because the same words and the same syntactic forms are used in many texts *and* because the processes are automatic and impenetrable by specific knowledge. Larkin's components of general knowledge transfer because they can be *imposed* deliberately and interpretatively on more than a single situation. Larkin's elements of transfer would find use as part of Perfetti's interpretation process, as something that he allocates to the knowledge-dependent and, thus, nongeneral part of competence. The implications for instruction are correspondingly different. Both require that particular knowledge be acquired: knowledge of word meanings and sentence syntax for Perfetti; knowledge of powerful underlying quantitative or scientific concepts for Larkin. Cultivation of Perfetti's restricted but general written language competence, however, requires instructional focus on *automatic* (i.e., acquired impenetrability) word recognition and lexical access in the context of normal written sentence syntax, whereas cultivation of Larkin's powerful knowledge components requires focusing on deliberate analysis and reflection so that presented problems are reinterpreted and reanalyzed in light of the quantitative or scientific concepts.

The next three chapters consider problems of teaching complex skills and dispositions. **Lesgold, Ivill-Friel, and Bonar** discuss in chapter 11 the special problems of an intelligent tutoring system that combines contextualized practice with specialized coaching of skill components. The power of an intelligent tutor depends on its basic instructional plan as embodied in the analysis of the subject matter on which it is based, in the explanations it is able to offer, and in the connections it promotes among different parts of domain knowledge and on the quality and appropriateness of tuning rules for adapting the instruction to individual students. This chapter considers the nature of tuning rules, implemented as a special form of testing designed to *steer* instruction (cf. Glaser, 1986). Instructional steering, in contrast to many other forms of testing, is specific to a particular curriculum structure and pedagogical plan and is also highly local to a particular moment in a student's progress through a curriculum. Lesgold, Ivill-Friel, and Bonar address the issue of how to assess elementary components of a skill without isolating them from the complexity of the full performance. They note that, since knowledge is situation-specific, a component that appears to have been mastered by a student in one context may no longer be available or accessible in others. This situation-embeddedness of knowledge requires that a tutor's basic plan of instruction provide forms of situated practice that expose students to the many contexts in which a skill component will be required. The authors claim it also places particular strain on the instructional tuning process, because it calls into question many of the standard canons of test construction. They propose steps toward a new theory and practice of assessment explicitly designed to measure skill and knowledge embedded in complex performances.

Bereiter and Scardamalia consider in chapter 12 how instructional theory and practice would change if the cultivation of intentionality in learning were taken as a primary goal of education. They discuss at some length two key aspects of intentional learning: the extent to which the tendency to engage in this effortful activity depends on one's conception of knowledge and how it is acquired, and the ways in which the instructional situation can either promote or inhibit these tendencies. Even when teachers have more ambitious goals in mind, students who conceive of knowledge as collections of facts will engage strategies for learning that are primarily aimed at successful memorization. The authors report on research designed to reveal students' conceptions of knowledge and learning goals and to examine the effects of these conceptions on the ways in which they study, especially in open instructional environments where individual preferences can be exercised.

This research suggests that many children have a very impoverished conception of knowledge and learning that is greatly influenced by their experience of schoolwork as required activity with no specified relationship to knowledge and learning. The authors argue that the equation of learning with production of work turns learning into an incidental rather than an intentional process. They show that in traditional instruction the students' role is generally limited to providing answers, while the teacher makes the major decisions concerning required activities and their sequence. They argue for alternative forms of instruction in which students and teachers would jointly engage in knowledge construction, and in which teachers would progressively turn over the higher-level, metacognitive functions to the students.

In chapter 13, **Brown and Palincsar** develop the notion of collaborative knowledge construction as a primary form of instruction, thereby extending central concepts of the Vygotskian theory that thought is rooted in social experience. They consider alternative conceptions of the ways in which group activities may stimulate or support learning. These include providing motivational support, sharing both the thinking load and expertise (truly collaborative forms of cognitive interaction in which a task that no individual could have managed alone is performed by the group), setting up conflicts that spur further personal thought, and providing models of effective thinking and learning strategies.

The authors report a series of successful interventions that apply these principles to teaching reading and oral comprehension skills. In these programs, groups of children collaboratively construct interpretations of written or spoken texts. The teacher guides the process, sometimes models effective interpretation strategies, and systematically hands over cognitive management of the activity to the students. The Vygotskian notions that cognitive competence derives from an internalization of initially public activity and that children can perform certain tasks collaboratively that they are not yet able to perform on their own informs Brown and Palincsar's approach. Instruction proceeds most effectively when tasks fall in what Vygotsky called the *zone of proximal development,* that is, when it allows students to engage at their present level of competence and to be assisted in attaining a higher level, and when individual performance is "scaffolded" by collaborators.

Collins, Seely Brown, and Newman consider in chapter 14 how to organize instruction so that acquired knowledge is not isolated from the contexts in which it may come to be used. They note that the abstraction of knowledge from the settings of its use is a development peculiar to the organization of modern schooling. In other settings for learning, this separation does not occur. To develop this point, they contrast typical school learning with the learning that occurs in traditional apprenticeship, where coached practice in actual tasks of production, with decreasing degrees of support from the master, is the primary mode of instruction and learning. They pose the problem of developing apprenticeships for cognitive skills, suggesting that special techniques will be needed to externalize thought processes and to encourage the development of self-correction and self-monitoring skills. In these terms, they analyze three examples of successful cognitive apprenticeship. Two are models described in some detail in the chapters by Brown and Palincsar and by Bereiter and Scardamalia. The third is an approach to teaching mathematics problem-solving skill developed by Alan Schoenfeld (1985). Schoenfeld uses a combination of expert teacher modeling of problem-solving heuristics in which normally covert reasoning processes are spoken aloud and of extensive student practice in collaborative problem solving. He aims to build self-consciousness and self-confidence in problem solving through extended engagement in these activities. Expanding these models, Collins et al. propose a framework for the design of learning environments. This closing chapter, highlighting and interweaving themes raised throughout the volume, presents a challenge and a possible model for the future of cognition and instruction.

REFERENCES

Brown, A. L., Bransford, J. D., Ferrara, R. A., & Campione, J. C. (1983). Learning, remembering, and understanding. In J. H. Flavell & E. M. Markman (Eds.), *Cognitive development* (Vol. III of P. H. Mussen, Ed., *Handbook of child psychology*, pp. 77–166). New York: Wiley.

Chipman, S. F., Segal, J. W., & Glaser, R. (Eds.). (1985). *Thinking and learning skills: Vol. 2. Research and open questions*. Hillsdale, NJ: Lawrence Erlbaum Associates.

Clark, H. H., & Wilkes-Gibbs, D. (1986). Referring as a collaborative process. *Cognition, 22*, 1–39.

Clement, J. (1987). Overcoming students' misconceptions in physics: The role of anchoring intuitions and analogical validity. *Proceedings of the Second International Seminar on Misconceptions and Educational Strategies in Science and Mathematics*. Ithaca, NY: Cornell University.

Dienes, Z. P., & Golding, E. W. (1971). *Approach to modern mathematics*. New York: Herder & Herder.

Dreyfus, H. L., & Dreyfus, S. E. (1986). *Mind over machine*. New York: Free Press.

Dweck, C. S., & Elliot, E. L. (1983). Achievement motivation. In E. M. Hetherington (Ed.), *Socialization, personality, and social development* (Vol. IV of P. H. Mussen, Ed., *Handbook of child psychology*, pp. 643–692). New York: Wiley.

Fodor, J. D. (1983). *Parsing constraints and the freedom of expression*. Montgomery, VT: Bradford Press.

Gentner, D. (1983). Structure mapping: A theoretical framework for analogy. *Cognitive Psychology, 15*, 1–38.

Gentner, D., & Stevens, A. L. (Eds.). (1983). *Mental models*. Hillsdale, NJ: Lawrence Erlbaum Associates.

Glaser, R. (1984). Education and thinking: The role of knowledge. *American Psychologist, 39*, 93–104.

Glaser, R. (1986). The integration of instruction and testing. In E. Freeman (Ed.), *The redesign of testing in the 21st century: Proceedings of the 1985 ETS Invitational Conference* (pp. 45–58). Princeton, NJ: Educational Testing Service.

Glaser, R., & Pellegrino, J. W. (1987). Aptitudes for learning and cognitive processes. In F. Weinert & R. Kluwe (Eds.), *Metacognition, motivation, and understanding* (pp. 267–288). Hillsdale, NJ: Lawrence Erlbaum Associates.

Greenfield, P. M. (1984). A theory of the teacher in the learning activities of everyday life. In B. Rogoff & J. Lave (Eds.), *Everyday cognition* (pp. 117–138). Cambridge, MA: Harvard University Press.

Johnson-Laird, P. N. (1983). *Mental models*. Cambridge, MA: Harvard University Press.

Johsua, S., & Dupin, J. J. (1987). Taking into account student conceptions in instructional strategy: An example in physics. *Cognition and Instruction, 4*, 117–125.

Lave, J. (1977). Tailor-made experiments and evaluating the intellectual consequences of apprenticeship training. *Quarterly Newsletter of the Institute for Comparative Human Development, 1*, 1–3.

Mead, G. H. (1934). *Mind, self, and society*. Chicago: University of Chicago Press.

Nicholls, J. G. (1983). Conceptions of ability and achievement motivation: A theory and its implications for education. In S. G. Paris, G. M. Olson, & H. W. Stevenson (Eds.), *Learning and motivation in the classroom* (pp. 211–238). Hillsdale, NJ: Lawrence Erlbaum Associates.

Resnick, L. B. (1986). The development of mathematical intuition. In M. Perlmutter (Ed.),

Perspectives on intellectual development: The Minnesota Symposia on Child Psychology (Vol. 19, pp. 159–194). Hillsdale, NJ: Lawrence Erlbaum Associates.

Resnick, L. B. (1987a). *Education and learning to think.* Washington, DC: National Academy Press.

Resnick, L. B. (1987b). Learning in school and out. *Educational Researcher, 16*(9), 13–20.

Roschelle, J. (1987, May). *The Envisioning Machine: Facilitating students' reconceptualization of motion.* Paper presented at the Third International Conference on AI and Education, Pittsburgh, PA.

Schoenfeld, A. H. (1985). *Mathematical problem solving.* New York: Academic Press.

Searle, J. (1984). *Minds, brains and science.* Cambridge, MA: Harvard University Press.

Segal, J. W., Chipman, S. F., & Glaser, R. (Eds.). (1985). *Thinking and learning skills: Vol. 1. Relating instruction to research.* Hillsdale, NJ: Lawrence Erlbaum Associates.

Thorndike, E. L., & Woodworth, R. L. (1901). The influence of improvement in one mental function upon the efficiency of other functions. *Psychological Review, 8,* 247–261.

VanLehn, K. (1985). *Arithmetic procedures are induced from examples* (Tech. Rep.). Palo Alto, CA: Xerox PARC.

Vygotsky, L. S. (1978). *Mind in society.* Cambridge, MA: Harvard University Press.

White, B. Y. (in press). ThinkerTools: Causal models, conceptual change, and science education. *Cognition and Instruction.*

Winograd, T., & Flores, F. (1986). *Understanding computers and cognition: A new foundation for design.* Norwood, NJ: Ablex.

2

Learning From Text

Walter Kintsch
University of Colorado

Some texts (e.g., literary texts) are studied in their own right; other texts are merely media by which information is transmitted, as is the case when a student learns about geography from reading a chapter in a textbook, when someone solves a problem stated in verbal form, or when one learns to operate a computer from reading a manual. In these cases, the text itself is secondary. What matters most is how well the student learns geography, whether the problem can be solved correctly, or whether we know what to do with our computer. All too often we seem to "understand" the manual all right, but remain at a loss about what to do; more attention to the text as such would be of little help. The problem is not with the words and phrases, nor even with the overall structure of the text; indeed, we could memorize the text and still not know which button to press. The problem is with understanding the situation

Reprinted from *Cognition and Instruction,* Volume 3, Number 2, 1986.

described by the text. Clearly, understanding the text as such is not a sufficient condition for understanding what to do.

It is one thing to write a chapter in a geography book (or a verbal problem statement, an operating manual, etc.) that is easily comprehended and memorized, but another to write it in such a way that a given student is able to learn from it effectively. Current research on text comprehension has dealt primarily with the first problem. Interest in how people form mental models of situations is high, but we are only just beginning to understand the issues involved. This chapter describes a theoretical framework that deals with the distinction between understanding the text and learning from it. It reports two experimental studies that illustrate and explore this distinction. The first study is concerned with how grade school children understand simple word arithmetic problems. The second deals with how college students form mental maps from texts that they read.

The theoretical framework used here is that of van Dijk and Kintsch (1983). The portion of their theory that is relevant here concerns the distinction between a *textbase* and a *situation model*. The textbase is the mental representation of the text that a reader or listener constructs in the process of comprehension. This representation is built from propositions and expresses the semantic content of the text at both a local and a global level. More or less closely tied to it is the situation model, which is a mental representation of the situation described by the text. Thus, the textbase reflects the coherence relations among the propositions in a text and their organization, whereas the situation model may be a mental map of the country described by the text, an arithmetic structure derived from the text, or an operating procedure constructed from the information given in the text. These two mental representations are not independent of each other, but each has its own characteristics, and each supports some types of behavior but not others. In addition, different factors are important for constructing the textbase and the situation models. Some of these differences are discussed in the experiments reported in this chapter.

MEMORY REPRESENTATIONS OF TEXT: TEXTBASES AND SITUATION MODELS

If we view memory as the more or less permanent record of psychological processes, memory for discourse must reflect the manifold components that discourse processing involves. Perceptual acts, whether reading or listening, comprise analyses and computations at several different levels (e.g., from analyses of single visual features to the primal sketch and eventually to the full image). Similarly, it may be useful to distinguish several distinct levels of conceptual analysis: (a) the processes concerned with the parsing of the text; (b) the establishment of a coherent representation of the meaning of the text, both at the local and global levels; and (c) the integration of the text content into the comprehender's knowledge system. The latter may involve either the updating of an existing situation model or the construction of a new one on the basis of the information obtained from the text.

These processes are not independent, of course. Obviously, how the text is represented will have something to do with how the situation is interpreted. Conversely, as van Dijk and Kintsch (1983) argued, the comprehender's situation model affects such processes as pronoun identification at the parsing level or the determination of coherence relations at the textbase level. Nevertheless, the nature of the computations performed at each level is quite different. At the parsing level, we deal with sentences and clauses, and the resulting memory trace consists of the linguistic surface representation of the text. At the textbase level, the elements are propositions, which become organized into a microstructure and macrostructure. Some of the processes involved in the formation of situation models and the memorial representations they give rise to are described in this chapter.

It is not the case, however, that a full linguistic parse must precede the formation of the propositional textbase or that the construction of a situation model must wait for the completion of the textbase. Instead, it appears to be quite generally the case that textbases are formed without a complete linguistic analysis—especially when there are strong semantic constraints or when the syntax is overly complex. Similarly, situation models may be formed—especially when the situation is familiar or particularly well structured—without bothering about a coherent, well-organized textbase (e.g., Bransford & Franks, 1972). Later, an experiment is described in which subjects constructed a reasonably good textbase without being able to form an adequate model of the situation at all.

To clarify the distinction between the three levels of analysis described here, I list in Table 2.1 a few prototypical research studies at each of the three levels. The list of variables and studies could have been made many times longer for the first two categories, but not for the third. Note the nonindependence of these categories: Pronoun identification also depends strongly on the situation model (Reichman, 1981), and although Clark's (1979) study is concerned primarily with the surface form of the questions people ask, that form is directly determined by the model of the situation the person has in mind. However, such interactions do not invalidate the distinctions between levels that I have made; they merely illustrate the obvious point that processes at different levels communicate their results and take advantage of each other.

Although considerable progress has been made in the study of surface and

TABLE 2.1

Examples of Research Problems and Studies Concerned With Surface,
Textbase, and Situational Variables

Level	Experimental Variables	Literature
Surface	syntactic chunking	Jarvella (1971)
	pronoun identification	Clark & Sengul (1979)
	question form	Clark (1979)
Textbase	propositional priming	Ratcliff & McKoon (1978)
	free recall	Kintsch & van Dijk (1978)
	episode boundaries	Haberlandt, Berian, & Sandson (1980)
Situation	verification in linear arrays	Bransford & Franks (1972)
	plausible inferences	Reder (1980)
	sentence scrambling	Kintsch, Mandel, & Kozminsky (1977)

textbase processing, our understanding of how situation models are formed and how they are used is still in its infancy. Present deficiencies in this respect are both theoretical and empirical. An extensive database and a respectable body of theory exist in psycholinguistics (Clark & Clark, 1977). A great deal is also known about how textbases, including macrostructures, are formed (e.g., about eye movements in reading, bridging inferences, short-term memory constraints, hierarchical levels, etc.), and reasonable theoretical accounts thereof exist, at least at the level of first approximations (e.g., Kintsch & van Dijk, 1978). In contrast, much less is known about situation models: The empirical database is disjoint, highly incomplete, and still quite insufficient to support detailed processing models.

How can one study situation models? Especially, how can situation models be distinguished experimentally from textbases? One approach that is widely used today is to study the effects of knowledge on text processing or, conversely, the effects of text processing on knowledge. The latter approach has been taken recently by Mandl and Ballstaedt (1986), who investigated how a person's situation model about some general topic (e.g., volcanoes, dreams) is influenced and modified by reading a relevant text on that subject. How knowledge affects the way a person understands and recalls a text has been investigated by Mannes (1986; influenza), Perfetti (1985; football), Scardamalia (1985; bacteria), and Voss, Vesonder, and Spilich (1980; baseball). Two somewhat different experimental designs that can be used to disentangle textbases from situaton models are discussed later in this chapter. One case involves the study of word problems in arithmetic. We know what sort of model must be constructed to solve these problems, and we know from the texts that we give our subjects what sort of textbase is being constructed; these constraints greatly facilitate experimental comparisons between the two models. In the second case, we resort to an experimental setup where we have reason to believe that the situation model is qualitatively different from the textbase. We try to induce subjects to use a spatial image as their situation model to contrast it more easily with their propositional textbase.

WORD PROBLEMS IN ARITHMETIC

In solving a word problem, the information conveyed by the text must be transformed into a problem model suitable for doing arithmetic. Currently, there are some fairly strong theories about what that problem model[1] is like when a child solves the problem correctly (Kintsch & Greeno, 1985; Riley, Greeno, & Heller, 1983). When an error is made the nature of the error often gives us a clue as to how the problem was misconstrued. The recall protocols of children who read a word problem text without solving the problem reflect the structure of the textbase in the absence of a problem model. Thus, error data provide an indication of the problem model, and recall without problem solving specifies the nature of the textbase. It therefore becomes possible to predict what recall should be like when it is influenced both by the textbase and the problem model. When subjects recall the problem text after having solved the problem, specific distortions of the problem text should occur to make it match the problem model that the child was working with more closely. In other words, recall should become reconstructive, with the (known) problem model serving as the basis for the reconstruction. Thus, recall of word problems that have been solved should be jointly determined by the properties of the textbase that was constructed during initial reading and by the model that was constructed to solve the problem.

The interaction between text and problem solving is quite complex. On the one hand, the problem model (not the original linguistic formulation) determines how a problem will be recalled. On the other hand, the textbase, which is derived from the particular linguistic formulation used in the word problem, determines what sort of problem model will be constructed. This is demonstrated in the work of DeCorte, Verschaffel, and DeWin (1982), in which minor linguistic modifications greatly affected the students' ability to solve the problem. For instance, in the example:

---

[1]What van Dijk and Kintsch (1983) called *situation model* traditionally has been termed the *problem model* in the problem-solving literature; we follow this use of the term here. Note that the term *model* is not used here in the strict logical sense of Greeno (1985); Greeno's model might be regarded as a formal, abstract characterization of the psychological problem or situation model.

Problem 1:   Tom and Joe have 6 marbles altogether.
Tom has 4 marbles.
How many marbles does Joe have?

replacing "marbles" in Line 2 with "of these" results in a 14% increase in the solution frequency for first-grade students. The key words "of these" tell the subjects which arithmetic strategy is appropriate at this point. Specifically, the words indicate a subset (Kintsch & Greeno, 1985), and without these key words, the problem solver has to infer without direct linguistic support that Joe's marbles constitute a subset, which is a more demanding and error prone process.

It is not only the linguistic formulation of the problem that is important, however. Beyond that, one needs to understand the situation described in the problem. If a word problem involves a situation or action that students are familiar with, they find it easier to form an appropriate problem model than when there is no concrete, familiar structure. A well-known example reported by Hudson (1983) demonstrates this nicely. Hudson presented the same arithmetic problem in two forms that may be paraphrased as:

Problem 2:   There are 5 birds and 3 worms.
How many more birds are there than worms?
Problem 3:   There are 5 birds and 3 worms.
How many birds won't get a worm?

Problem 2 was solved correctly by 39% of Hudson's subjects, whereas the arithmetically equivalent Problem 3 was solved by 79%. In Problem 3, the linguistic expression allowed subjects to form a definitive situation model — birds eating worms — that provided them with the correct arithmetic structure to solve the problem. In Problem 2, however, the abstract relational term "more than" provided no such crutch.

What do students do when they are faced with a problem that is too complex to handle? One strategy is to turn a difficult problem into a simpler one that can be solved. Indeed, Riley et al. (1983) reported that incorrectly solved problems tend to be misrecalled as simpler problems. In an experiment by Dellarosa, Weimer, and Kintsch (1985), we followed up this interesting observation of Riley et al. to find out whether there is a relation between the answer produced in solving the problem and the form of the misrecall. The existence of such a relation provides experimental support for the claim made earlier that the problem model used for the solution of a word problem determines how it will later be recalled.

Dellarosa et al. worked with 30 second-grade students who were given extensive practice in solving and recalling word problems of the form used by Riley et al. The experimental data reported here are based on the last 24 prob-

TABLE 2.2
Examples of the Problems Based on Riley, Greeno, and Heller (1983)

Easy	*Hard*
Change 1	Change 5
Joe had 3 marbles.	Joe had some marbles.
Then Tom gave him 5 more marbles.	Then Tom gave him 5 more marbles.
How many marbles does Joe have now?	Now Joe has 8 marbles.
	How many marbles did Joe have
	in the beginning?
Combine 1	Combine 2
Joe has 3 marbles.	Joe and Tom have 8 marbles
Tom has 5 marbles.	altogether.
How many marbles do they have	Joe has 3 marbles.
altogether?	How many marbles does Tom have?
Compare 4	Compare 5
Joe has 8 marbles.	Joe has 8 marbles.
Tom has 5 marbles less than Joe.	He has 5 more marbles than Tom.
How many marbles does Tom have?	How many marbles does Tom have?

lems each student worked with: *change* (involving *give–take*), *combine* (involving *superset* or *part–whole* relations), and *compare* (involving *more than* or *less than*) were used, half of them in easy versions and half in versions that are known to be difficult for these subjects. Examples of easy and hard problems of each type are shown in Table 2.2.[2] Subjects solved four problems of each kind. They merely listened to one problem and then recalled it, whereas they solved another problem without recalling it; two problems were first solved and then recalled. Thus, there were 6 recall-only, 6 solve-only, and 12 recall-and-solve problems for each subject, plus some practice problems.

The solution frequencies shown in the first panel of Fig. 2.1 confirm that we were indeed successful in selecting hard and easy problems and that the latter were solved significantly more frequently than the former. More interesting are the recall results, given here in terms of the percentage of words from each problem that were correctly reproduced (essentially identical results are obtained if the analysis is based on the number of propositions recalled). When subjects only had to recall the problems but not solve them, there was no significant difference between the recall of the easy and hard problems, confirming that at the level of the textbase these problems were quite comparable. On the other hand, after solving the problems, subjects recalled significantly more easy problems than hard problems. Although the difficult problems were inherently no less recallable than the easy problems,

---

[2]In the notation of Riley et al. (1983), Change 1 and 5, Combine 1 and 2, and Compare 4 and 5 were used as easy and hard problems, respectively.

they were not recalled as well after a solution attempt had been made: The complexity of the problem model required for solving these problems confused the subjects. Thus, Fig. 2.1 provides some evidence that the subjects in this experiment did not recall the text directly, but rather they recalled the problem model they had formed from the text. This interpretation of Fig. 2.1 is, however, not the only one possible. Alternatively, it may merely be that the greater difficulty of the problem-solving process interfered more strongly with memory. Fortunately, the data reported by Dellarosa et al. (1985) are rich enough to exclude an interpretation in terms of generalized interference effect and to demonstrate clearly that the specific properties of the model that subjects construct in solving the problems are responsible for the observed recall distortions.

First, consider the tendency in recall to simplify problems, as reported by Riley et al. (1983), which is clearly present in our data as well. If the difficult version of the change problem was misrecalled, it was misrecalled 81% of the time as the easy version. Similarly, the difficult version of the combine problem was almost always (94%) changed to the easy form of the combine problem when it was misrecalled. The difficult compare problem was misrecalled as an easy problem of the same type 71% of the time. In the first two cases, the verbal structure was simplified, and this consequently changed the arithmetic structure of the problem (thus resulting in an incorrect solution). In the third case, however, the correct arithmetic structure was preserved when the problem was misrecalled. This serves to bring the linguistic form of the problem in line with the problem structure. The original "more than" is changed to "less than" (and the names are switched accordingly) because the problem is really a subtraction problem. Thus,

Problem 4:   Joe has 8 marbles.
              He has 5 more marbles than Tom.
              · How many marbles does Tom have?

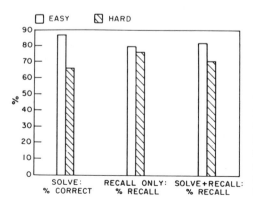

FIG. 2.1. Solving and recalling word problems. The first two columns show the percentage of correct solutions for easy and hard problems; the next four columns show the percentage of words recalled for problems that were recalled only and for problems that were both solved and recalled.

becomes

Problem 5: Joe has 8 marbles.
Tom has 5 marbles less than Joe.
How many marbles does Tom have?

Our data clearly replicate Riley et al. (1983) in that subjects tended to simplify the problems when they made an error in recall. Furthermore, when a problem was simplified, it was simplified to a problem of the same type. That is, a change problem remained a change problem, but it was just turned into a simpler version. However, it remains to be shown whether these recall changes are in fact related to solution performance (i.e., whether we are justified in attributing these changes to the distorting influence of the problem model).

To answer this question, we must clean up the error data a bit, and to make things clearer, we restrict our analyses to the contrast between the two easiest problems (which in our data are the easy versions of the change and combine problems) and the two hardest ones (the hard versions of the same problem types). (The intermediate problems yield intermediate results.) First of all, we separate errors into three classes: conceptual errors, where the wrong arithmetic operation has been performed; nonconceptual errors, where the result is either off by 1 or where the operation was right but the wrong numbers were used, as evidenced from the recall data; and a small residual group of unclassifiable errors. Figure 2.2 shows that the contrast between the easiest and hardest problems is much greater than Fig. 2.1 suggests if one looks only at conceptual errors: Nonconceptual errors occurred with a certain base rate independent of problem type, but conceptual errors were almost never made on the easiest problems, though very often on the hardest problems.

It is instructive to look at the nature of these conceptual errors. First, con-

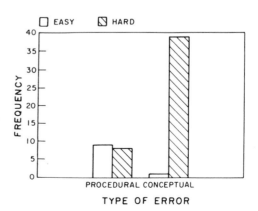

FIG. 2.2. The nature of errors for easy and hard problems.

sider those cases in which the hard combine problem was misrecalled as the easy combine problem. An example of the former is:

Problem 6:   Joe and Tom had 8 marbles altogether.
             Tom had 3 marbles.
             How many marbles did Joe have?

which tended to be transformed in recall to an easier version of a combine problem, such as:

Problem 7:   Joe had 8 marbles.
             Tom had 3 marbles.
             Joe and Tom had 8 marbles altogether.

Figure 2.3 shows the frequency of such misrecall when subjects merely recalled the problem and when they first solved and then recalled it. In the latter case, three conditions are distinguished: First, the solution was correct; second, any error was made; and third, a superset error was made (i.e., the cardinality of the superset was given as the answer, as in the example shown in Problem 7). When the difficult version of a combine problem was merely recalled, but not solved, simplification to the simple version occurred at a relatively low rate. However, when the problem was solved first and an error was made, this particular type of misrecall become much more likely. When the error was a superset error, the wording was recalled in conformity with that error in 73% of the cases. Clearly, the textbase of the problem was not being used as the basis for the recall; rather, the text was constructed from the problem model.

Figure 2.4 shows much the same pattern of results in those cases where the difficult version of a compare problem was misrecalled as an addition problem. The original form of the difficult compare problem is:

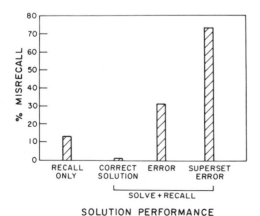

FIG. 2.3. Frequency of misrecall of Combine 2 problems as Combine 1 when the problems were only recalled, when they were solved correctly, when an error was made in solving the problem, and when a superset error was made.

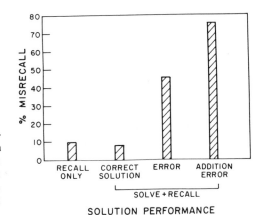

FIG. 2.4. Frequency of mis-recall of Compare 5 as addition problems when the problems were only recalled, when they were solved correctly, when an error was made in solving the problem, and when an addition error was made.

Problem 8:   Joe had 8 marbles.
                He had 5 more marbles than Tom.
                How many marbles did Tom have?

The second line of Problem 8 was misrecalled either as:

Problem 9:   Tom had 5 more marbles than Joe.

which turns it into an easier version of a compare problem, or as:

Problem 10:   Tom had 5 marbles.

which produces a combine structure. Either misrepresentation would lead the subject to perform an addition operation. This kind of misrecall occurred with a moderate base rate when the problem was only recalled but did not have to be solved or when it was recalled after it had been solved correctly. However, this form of misrecall became much more frequent when an error was made, and it became the dominant mode of recall when the error was an addition error.

A particularly interesting distortion occurred when the difficult version of the compare problem was changed linguistically to conform better to its underlying arithmetic structure (i.e., Problem 4 is transformed into Problem 5). Such misrecall was associated with correct solution rather than with errors, as shown in Fig. 2.5. Indeed, such misrecall occurred quite frequently even when the problem did not have to be solved, but it was relatively rare when an error was made. (Errors in this case tended to be addition errors, which induced quite a different pattern of misrecall, as we have already seen.)

Although recall can be reconstructive rather than reproductive, much current work on text recall has focused mainly on the reproductive aspects (e.g.,

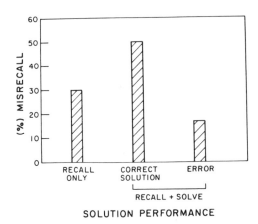

FIG. 2.5. Frequency of misrecall of Compare 5 problems as Compare 4 when the problems were only recalled, when they were solved correctly, and when an error was made in solving the problem.

Kintsch & van Dijk, 1978). What has been shown here is not just that recall can be reconstructive, but what the source of this reconstruction is (viz., the situation or problem model). Clearly, distiguishing between the textbase and the problem model as distinct levels of representation is theoretically necessary in view of these results.

When the word arithmetic problems were recalled after the solution, the problem model dominated the textbase. When the two diverged, as when subjects formed a deviant arithmetic structure when solving the problem, the problem model determined the form of recall, which therefore became highly reconstructive. However, some studies are reviewed in the next section showing that this is not necessarily so.

MENTAL MAPS AS SITUATION MODELS

With the word problems, we knew fairly well what the properties of the textbase as well as the problem model had to be, and we were therefore able to attribute certain observations to one or the other source. Another way of separating out textbase and situation model effects is to make the two very different qualitatively. Perrig and Kintsch (1985) achieved this by inducing subjects to construct a situation model in the form of a mental image in order to contrast it more easily with their propositional textbase.

Specifically, Perrig and Kintsch wrote a description of a town in two forms. In one case, the survey text, the layout of the town was described in geographical terms (e.g., "the church is north of the inn"). It was expected that subjects who read this text would use the geographical information it contained to form a mental image of a map of the town. In the second case, the route version, essentially the same geographical information was presented in a different form, as a series of instructions for driving through the town (e.g., "coming from the church, you make a left turn to reach the inn").

We hoped that the subjects who read this version would form a different situation model of the town in question, perhaps a list of procedures for finding the various places mentioned in the text. A priori, there were no reasons to expect one of these models to be easier to form than the other. One would, however, expect that if a subject formed a mental map, statements about this map would be easier to verify than informationally equivalent statements expressed in procedural terms, and vice versa. Indeed, such a finding might be considered a confirmation of the hypothesis that qualitatively different situation models had been formed in the two cases.

The texts used, however, were designed not only to yield qualitatively different situation models, but also different textbases. The route version was written to be more coherent than the survey version. In a route description, one step is causally and temporally linked to the next, whereas in the survey description, statements could sometimes be permuted without affecting the clarity of the text. The texts were presented to subjects on a screen, sentence by sentence (long sentences were sometimes divided). As a rough indicator of the semantic coherence of each text, the number of terms in each sentence that were repeated in the next sentence (argument overlap, in the terminology of Kintsch & van Dijk, 1978) were determined. On the average, sentences in the route text were connected by 2.50 common terms, whereas sentences in the survey text shared only 1.75 terms, thus confirming the greater coherence of the former. More coherent texts are known to be recalled better than less coherent texts (e.g., Kintsch, Kozminsky, Streby, McKoon, & Keenan, 1975). Hence, one may predict that the route text would be recalled better than the survey text. An additional factor that contributed to this prediction was the reader being addressed directly in the route text ("you are driving . . ."), which is also known to improve recall (Keenan, McWhinney, & Mayhew, 1977). Examples from both the route and survey text are shown in Table 2.3.

Perrig and Kintsch's (1985) first experiment did not quite yield the results anticipated, but for an interesting reason (see Fig. 2.6). The recall results

TABLE 2.3
Three Sample Sentences From the Route and Survey Texts

Route:	Survey:
Going left on Main, after a few blocks you see the Lutheran church on your right.	A few blocks north on Main is a Lutheran church on its east side.
Returning on Main Street to the other end, you come to the general store.	The general store is on the southern end of Main Street.

It is a social center of the town,
especially for the youth.

Note. The first two are locative sentences; the third, nonlocative, sentence is identical in both versions.

were as we predicted: The route text was recalled substantially (48%) better than the survey text. On a recognition test for statements from the text, this difference disappeared, and performance was statistically equivalent for the two texts. That, too, is exactly what would be expected. The better recall of the route text is due, presumably, to the tighter organization (coherence) of that text and hence is primarily a retrieval effect. It is well known in the memory literature that organization has powerful effects in recall, but either no or relatively small second-order effects in recognition (e.g., Kintsch, 1968).

The third type of test of interest here is the verification of inference statements about locations in the town. For instance, if the text mentioned that "the church is north of the inn" and "the inn is on the highway," a correct inference statement might be: "The highway is south of the church." The results of the verification test of such statements were not as predicted: There was no evidence that subjects had formed either a mental map or a procedural model of the town. They were unable to verify correctly either route or survey statements (average $d' = .52$). This result is quite interesting when taken in conjunction with the perfectly adequate recall performance: Obviously, Perrig and Kintsch's (1985) subjects had understood the text well enough to recall it (the percentage of propositions reproduced is not unusually low for descriptive texts of that length), but they had not understood it well enough to verify inferential statements about locations in the town with much more than chance accuracy. If we take the ability to infer new information from the information actually presented in the text as an indication that an adequate situation model had been formed, we must conclude from these results that our subjects had no (adequate) situation model, although they certainly had formed an adequate textbase, as is attested by their normal recall performance.

It is not very helpful to say that these subjects "understood" or "did not understand." Common-sense terms such as understanding and comprehension need to be replaced at this point with more precise theoretical terms (e.g., having formed a textbase or situation model).

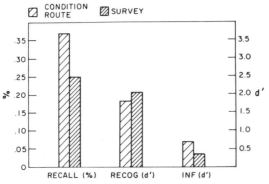

FIG. 2.6. Percentage of propositions recalled and d's for recognition and inference tests for the route and survey texts in Experiment 1.

Perrig and Kintsch (1985) performed a second experiment in which subjects had a better chance for forming an adequate situation model because the description of the town was simplified. In other respects, this second experiment was quite comparable to the first. Once again, the route text was more coherent than the survey text (an average of 2.35 cohesive elements between sentences vs. only 1.29 for the survey text). The results (Fig. 2.7) clearly replicate the first experiment as far as the textbase-related behavior goes. There was better recall (29%) for the route text, but no significant difference between the two texts in recognition. However, subjects did learn their way around the simpler town, and the average d' for verifying inference statements was a respectable 1.78. There was no overall difference between the route and survey texts in their effectiveness in this respect, nor was there any particular reason to expect such a difference. Note that this contrasts with the recall results, where a performance difference existed between the two versions of the text. The greater coherence of one of the texts yielded a better textbase but had no effect on the situation model that was constructed because, even in the less coherent version, coherence was sufficient to allow the construction of an adequate textbase, though not as good a textbase as in the other case.

The interaction between the form of the text and the form of the inference statement was quite significant, as shown in Fig. 2.8. Subjects verified inference statements better when they were in the same form as the original text. That is, subjects who read the survey text were better (and faster, too) when they verified survey statements rather than route statements, whereas the reverse was true for subjects who had read the route text. Thus, it appears to be the case that different situation models were formed in these two cases: a mental map of the town versus something like a sequence of procedures for getting around in the town. When subjects had to shift from one format to the other, their performance suffered and they were slowed down by the need to translate between these two representations.

The results are shown separately for male and female subjects in Fig. 2.8

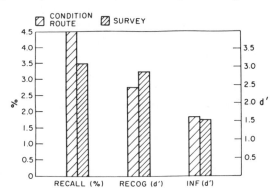

FIG. 2.7. Percentage of propositions recalled and d's for recognition and inference tests for the route and survey texts in Experiment 2.

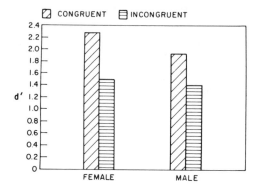

FIG. 2.8.   d′ values for inferences congruent and incongruent with the text for female and male subjects.

because of the presence of a triple interaction between the format of the text read, the format of the question, and sex. This interaction, which was quite surprising, is indicated in Fig. 2.8 by the size of the difference between the text-congruent and text-incongruent inferences, which was larger for females than for males. What is going on here is futher indicated in Fig. 2.9: Female subjects were just about as good on survey inferences as on route inferences, but they were always better when the inference was in the same form as the text they had read (Fig. 2.8). In other words, female subjects formed the kind of textbase that was invited by the nature of the text they read (hence, the congruency effects) and didn't much care whether they used a route or survey format. On the other hand, males demonstrated a strong bias in favor of mental maps, and they tried to form mental maps, even when the text invited a different format of representation. Hence, congruency effects were observed only when the males read the survey text (in which case they were very bad on route inferences) but not when they read the route text (they were still better, and faster, on survey inferences!). Therefore, the kind of situation model that is formed depends not only on the nature of the text, but also on the biases that readers have: Female subjects in the Perrig and Kintsch (1985) experiment simply did what the text suggested, but males insisted on using their favorite form of representation (spatial imagery), even when another form would have been more obvious. (Note that this was not a notably successful strategy either: The females did just as well with the survey texts as the males, but handled the route texts quite a bit better.)

The main point is that certain properties of a text (specifically, its coherence) affect recall but not inferencing. It follows from this observation that the mental structure or memory representation on which recall is based differs from the structure (representation) on which inferencing is based.[3] Are

---

[3]For a similar argument, see Tulving (1985), who concluded from such observations that several different memory systems exist.

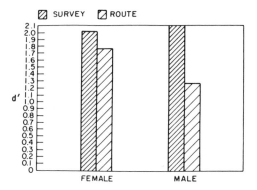

FIG. 2.9.   d′ values for survey and route inferences for female and male subjects.

there experimental variables that affect primarily the subject's ability to learn from a text (i.e., make inferences) rather than just the ability to recall the text? Weaver and Kintsch (1985) tried to achieve such an effect by instructing their subjects to concentrate on learning the map when they were reading the text. Specifically, subjects were asked to sketch a map as the text was presented sentence by sentence. Control subjects were allowed to study the text for an equivalent period of time. Both the survey and route texts from the earlier study were used. The recall results from this study are shown in Figure 10. The two groups of subjects produced almost the same number of words on the recall test, but there the similarity ends. The control subjects who read the text in the usual way for the most part reproduced what they had read. Only 24% of their output consisted of words not reproduced from the text (i.e., inferences and elaborations). Most of those (79%) were wrong, indicating that these readers knew that a great deal of location information had been given in the text, but they could not accurately remember it. The subjects who drew a map while the text was presented reacted quite differently: They reproduced fewer words and inferred more (35%), and what they inferred was overwhelmingly correct (82%). Much as the children who had solved word arithmetic problems, they reconstructed what they knew about the town, rather than reproducing the text they had read.

Indeed, Fig. 2.10 seriously underestimates the amount of reconstructive recall in the map-drawing condition: It is quite possible that propositions that we scored as reproductions because they appeared in the text were actually reconstructions. An analysis of the data in terms of the Kintsch and van Dijk (1978) model suggests that this was the case. Both the survey and route texts were analyzed propositionally, and the propositions were arranged in a hierarchical structure according to the model of Kintsch and van Dijk (1978). A computer program written by Young (1984) was used for that purpose. As a result of this analysis, a classification of all propositions in the texts in terms of their level in the text hierarchy was obtained. As is well known, level in the

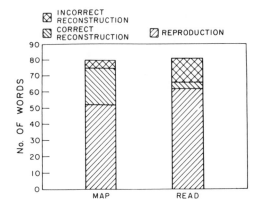

FIG. 2.10. Composition of recall in the map-drawing and reading conditions.

hierarchy correlates rather strongly with recall probability, presumably because higher level propositions are encoded better and because the hierarchy is used to guide the retrieval process in recall (these results are reviewed in van Dijk & Kintsch, 1983, pp. 44ff, 356ff). The levels effect is thus a textbase phenomenon, and if propositions are actually reconstructed rather than recalled (even though they may have appeared in the original text), one would not expect a levels effect for such propositions. Subjects in our map-drawing group could have reconstructed locative propositions from their mental map, but not the nonlocative, descriptive propositions that were also part of the text because the latter information is not contained in a mental map. Thus, one would expect a levels effect for nonlocative propositions (retrieved via the textbase), but not for locative propositions (reconstructed from the situation model) for the map-drawing subjects, whereas levels effects should be obtained for both types of propositions for the control subjects. Fig. 2.11 and 12 show that this was, indeed, the case. For the subjects who merely read the text, the usual levels effect was observed for both locative and nonlocative propositions (there were no Level 1 locative propositions in the text), whereas the map-drawing subjects showed a significant levels effect only for the nonlocative propositions. It seems that the locative propositions they produced on the recall test were at least in part reconstructed, rather than reproduced, from their textbase.

CONCLUSION

There is a complex interplay between the ability of subjects to remember a text as such and their ability to use the information conveyed by the text as a basis for action or further computation. The two studies reported here investigate this relationship. In the case of children who solved and/or recalled

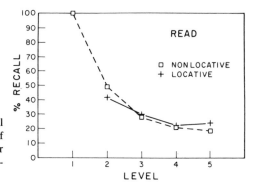

FIG. 2.11. Percentage of recall of propositions as a function of level in the textbase hierarchy for locative and nonlocative propositions in the reading conditions.

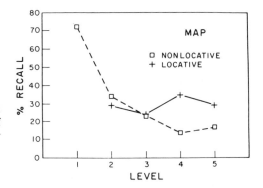

FIG. 2.12. Percentage of recall of propositions as a function of level in the textbase hierarchy for locative and nonlocative propositions in the map-drawing condition.

word arithmetic problems, the way in which the problem is worded strongly influenced the difficulty of problem solving. Two specific factors have been discussed here. It matters a great deal how closely the linguistic formulation matches the underlying arithmetic structure and how directly that structure is signaled by the text. Furthermore, the degree of constraint that the general situation in a word problem exerts with respect to the arithmetic structure determines the ease or difficulty with which subjects can derive the arithmetic problem structure from the verbal formulation. In some abstract problem formulations, the general situation is of very little help, but for problems embedded in concrete, familiar actions or events, the situational constraints can almost ensure the correct arithmetic interpretation.

Thus, although the text determines what problem model will be constructed and how it will be constructed, once that model exists, memory for the text depends more on the problem model than on the actual text itself. Once they had solved a problem, the children tended to recall it by reconstructing the text from their problem model, not by reproducing the original textbase.

In the map studies, a similar dichotomy was observed between remembering the text as such and what was learned from it. The former depended on how well the text was written (e.g., how coherent it was). The latter, however, turned out to be a function of the kind of encoding operation a reader performed. It was not enough to encode just the propositional structure of the text at both a local and a global level; such encoding merely ensured that the text could be recalled or recognized. To learn about the town so that correct spatial inferences could be made, it was necessary for subjects to encode the spatial relationships specified by the text in terms of a spatial map or in terms of a sequence of procedures for moving around.

As far as recall was concerned, subjects in the map studies behaved much like the children with the word problems: Once they had formed a good mental model of the spatial layout of the town, they reconstructed the text from that model, rather than reproducing what they had actually read.

Mental models have been found to play an important role in many ways (e.g., Gentner & Stevens, 1983; Johnson-Laird, 1983); clearly, they play an equally important role in text comprehension and memory. Van Dijk and Kintsch (1983) introduced the term situation model for the kind of mental model of a situation that is constructed from a text. It must be distinguished from another kind of mental model for the text itself (i.e., the textbase). As the present experiments show, both concepts are necessary to understand text comprehension and memory.

Instruction may be directed at either the textbase or the situation model. It is necessary, however, to be quite clear about which of these is the goal of instruction because different factors must be considered, depending on whether one wants students to comprehend and remember a text optimally or to learn something from that text. Current research on text comprehension provides some guidelines for how to achieve the first of these goals: Make the text coherent, use and signal a clear macrostructure, do not overload short-term memory, and so forth. It is possible to derive theoretically motivated readability analyses of texts if the goal is to optimize the comprehender's ability to construct an adequate textbase (Kintsch & Vipond, 1979; Miller & Kintsch, 1980). However, such analyses are not always appropriate. If the goal of instruction is to enable students to learn some subject matter on the basis of a text, it becomes necessary to consider how the student can construct from the text a mental model of the situation. As the data have shown, what sort of textbase is formed matters a great deal for the construction of a situation model, but the formation of a textbase is not a sufficient condition for the building of a situation model. Additional factors must be considered to enable efficient learning. Learning from text is not to be equated with remembering the text. Clearly, a great deal of further research will be required before we know as much about learning from text as we now know about the text memory itself.

ACKNOWLEDGMENTS

This article is based on a talk given at the Cognition and Instruction Symposium conducted at the University of Pittsburgh, July 1985.

The research reported here was supported by National Institute of Mental Health Grant MH 15872 and by National Science Foundation Grant BNS-83-09075.

REFERENCES

Bransford, J. D., & Franks, J. J. (1972). The abstraction of linguistic ideas. *Cognitive Psychology, 2,* 331-350.

Clark, H. H. (1979). Responding to indirect speech acts. *Cognitive Psychology, 11,* 430-477.

Clark, H. H., & Clark, E. V. (1977). *Psychology and language.* New York: Harcourt Brace Jovanovich.

Clark, H. H., & Sengul, C. J. (1979). In search of referents for nouns and pronouns. *Memory & Cognition, 7,* 35-41.

DeCorte, E., Verschaffel, L., & DeWin, L. (1982). Influence of rewording verbal problems on children's problem representations and solutions. *Journal of Educational Psychology, 77,* 460-470.

Dellarosa, D., Weimer, R., & Kintsch, W. (1985). *Children's recall of arithmetic word problems* (Institute of Cognitive Science Tech. Rep. No. 14). University of Colorado, Boulder.

Gentner, D., & Stevens, A. L. (Eds.). (1983). *Mental models.* Hillsdale, NJ: Lawrence Erlbaum Associates, Inc.

Greeno, J. G. (1985, July). *Comprehension and learning of subject matter.* Paper presented at the Institute on Cognition and Instruction, Learning Research and Development Center, University of Pittsburgh, Pittsburgh.

Haberlandt, K., Berian, C., & Sandson, J. (1980). The episode schema in story processing. *Journal of Verbal Learning and Verbal Behavior, 19,* 635-650.

Hudson, T. (1983). Correspondences and numerical differences between disjoint sets. *Child Development, 54,* 84-90.

Jarvella, R. J. (1971). Syntactic processing of connected speech. *Journal of Verbal Learning and Verbal Behavior, 10,* 409-416.

Johnson-Laird, P. N. (1983). *Mental models.* Cambridge, MA: Harvard University Press.

Keenan, J. M., McWhinney, B., & Mayhew, D. (1977). Pragmatics in memory: A study of natural conversation. *Journal of Verbal Learning and Verbal Behavior, 16,* 549-560.

Kintsch, W. (1968). Recognition and free recall of organized lists. *Journal of Experimental Psychology, 78,* 481-487.

Kintsch, W., & Greeno, J. G. (1985). Understanding and solving word arithmetic problems. *Psychological Review, 92,* 109-129.

Kintsch, W., Kozminsky, E., Streby, W. J., McKoon, G., & Keenan, J. M. (1975). Comprehension and recall as a function of content variables. *Journal of Verbal Learning and Verbal Behavior, 14,* 196-214.

Kintsch, W., Mandel, T. S., & Kozminsky, E. (1977). Summarizing scrambled stories. *Memory & Cognition, 5,* 547-552.

Kintsch, W., & van Dijk, T. A. (1978). Towards a model of discourse comprehension and production. *Psychological Review, 85,* 363-394.

Kintsch, W., & Vipond, D. (1979). Reading comprehension and readability in educational practice and psychological theory. In L. G. Nilsson (Ed.), *Perspectives on memory research* (pp. 329-365). Hillsdale, NJ: Lawrence Erlbaum Associates, Inc.

Mandl, H., & Ballstaedt, S. P. (1986). Assessment of concept-building in text comprehension. In F. Klix & H. Hagendorf (Eds.), *In memoriam Hermann Ebbinghaus: Symposium on structures and functions of human memory*. New York: Elsevier North Holland.

Mannes, S. (1986). *Text comprehension as a function of subject-matter knowledge*. Unpublished master's thesis, University of Colorado, Boulder.

Miller, J. R., & Kintsch, W. (1980). Readability and recall of short prose passages: A theoretical analysis. *Journal of Experimental Psychology: Human Learning and Memory, 6,* 335-354.

Perfetti, C. (1985, July). *Readability and learning from text*. Paper presented at the Institute on Cognition and Instruction, Learning Research and Development Center, University of Pittsburgh, Pittsburgh.

Perrig, W., & Kintsch, W. (1985). Propositional and situational representations of text. *Journal of Memory and Language, 24,* 503-518.

Ratcliff, R., & McKoon, G. (1978). Priming in item recognition: Evidence or propositional structure of sentences. *Journal of Verbal Learning and Verbal Behavior, 17,* 403-418.

Reder, L. M. (1980). Plausibility judgments versus fact retrieval: Alternative strategies for sentence verification. *Psychological Review, 89,* 250-280.

Reichman, R. (1981). *Plain speaking: A theory of grammar and spontaneous discourse* (BBN Tech. Rep. No. 4681). Cambridge, MA: Bolt, Beranek, and Newman.

Riley, M. S., Greeno, J. G., & Heller, J. I. (1983). Development of children's problem-solving ability in arithmetic. In H. P. Ginsburg (Ed.), *The development of mathematical thinking* (pp. 153-196). New York: Academic.

Scardamalia, M. (1985, July). *Intentionality in learning*. Paper presented at the Institute on Cognition and Instruction, Learning Research and Development Center, University of Pittsburgh, Pittsburgh.

Tulving, E. (1985). How many memory systems are there? *American Psychologist, 40,* 385-398.

van Dijk, T. A., & Kintsch, W. (1983). *Strategies of discourse comprehension*. New York: Academic.

Voss, J. F., Vesonder, G. T., & Spilich, G. J. (1980). Text generation and recall by high-knowledge and low-knowledge individuals. *Journal of Verbal Learning and Verbal Behavior, 17,* 651-667.

Weaver, C. A., & Kintsch, W. (1985). *Levels of understanding in text comprehension*. Unpublished manuscript.

Young, S. R. (1984). *A theory and simulation of macrostructures* (Institute of Cognitive Science Tech. Rep. No. 134). University of Colorado, Boulder.

3

Expository Text for Young Readers: The Issue of Coherence

Isabel L. Beck
Margaret G. McKeown
Learning Research and Development Center
University of Pittsburgh

Research over the past decade or so has brought important insights into complex cognitive processes, with reading chief among them. The cognitive perspective has changed the focus of reading research from analysis of what a reader can remember and recall to investigation of how the reader processes information to create a representation of a text's message.

Reading is no longer viewed as lifting the message from a text but as an active, complex process in which a reader applies information from various sources concurrently to construct meaning. Information on the printed page is only one of the reader's resources. Understanding a text also requires the reader to have knowledge of the topic in memory and to use that knowledge to organize, interpret, and integrate information. The effect of knowledge on comprehension is generally acknowledged to involve the theoretical notion of *schemata*, abstract mental structures that serve as frameworks with slots that may be filled by incoming text information (e.g., Anderson, Spiro, & Anderson, 1978; Bartlett, 1932; Rumelhart,

1980; Schank & Abelson, 1977; Thorndyke & Yekovich, 1980). If a reader lacks schemata relevant to the text being read, certain textual information that would fit into the slots may not be adequately understood.

In addition to knowledge of a topic, the reader must draw on semantic and linguistic knowledge to draw inferences and establish relations in a text (Beck & Carpenter, 1986; Perfetti, 1985). Understanding of even very simple utterances requires such knowledge. Consider the sentence, "The little girl sat on her uncle's knee." Comprehension of this statement entails speedy recognition that *her* refers to the little girl, and that to sit on someone's knee means to sit on the lap, thus the appropriate schemata preclude an image of the uncle lying on the floor with a child perched on his leg.

Another source needed in a reader's repertoire is knowledge of how text information can be organized into meaningful categories or prototypical structures. For example, in reading a narrative, the reader is apt to interpret certain information as a problem or conflict and other information as a plan to solve the problem, and he or she is apt to expect this information to be followed, in turn, by attempts to solve the problem and eventually by a resolution (Mandler, 1978; Stein & Trabasso, 1982).

Insights into the reading process gained from a cognitive perspective allow greater understanding of where and why the reading process might break down. For example, research has focused on the quality of knowledge readers bring to text (Chiesi, Spilich, & Voss, 1979; Pearson, Hansen, & Gordon, 1979; Spilich, Vesonder, Chiesi, & Voss, 1979), how readers access this knowledge and integrate various text and reader information (Bransford & Johnson 1972; Brown, Smiley, Day, Townsend, & Lawton, 1977), and how characteristics of text influence and make demands on the reading process (Anderson & Armbruster, 1984; Beck, McKeown, Omanson, & Pople, 1984; Clark & Haviland, 1977). Such advances in our understanding of cognitive processes provide a rich framework for investigations of instructional issues.

A traditional instructional concern in the reading field is the difficulty students have with subject-matter reading. This difficulty becomes particularly apparent around third or fourth grade when students are confronted with learning more subject-matter content through textbooks. Subject-matter texts are expository, and conventional wisdom holds that students' difficulty with them stems from an unfamiliarity with the expository genre. This unfamiliarity has been attributed in part to the fact that basal Readers, the mainstay of reading instruction in this country, have in the past been composed mostly of narrative selections and thus ill prepare students for this new type of prose. Therefore, it has been suggested that expositions be adequately represented in basal Readers to give students earlier experience with the expository genre in the course of reading instruction.

A look at recent editions of basal Readers shows that this suggestion has not gone unheard.

The expositions now found in basal Readers, therefore, are intended to serve the important function of providing experience with the expository genre that is presumed to benefit students' ability to read and learn from subject-matter textbooks. Because of this presumed function, we examined the expositions found in Grades 3 through 6 of recent editions of four basal Readers.[1] The intent was to assess their usefulness as an introduction to the expository genre in light of some insights into text processing that recent research in cognitive psychology offers. Because our intent was to evaluate the success of basal Readers' inclusion of expositions generally, the four programs are referred to separately, for convenience only, as Programs A, B, C, and D.

Two potentially problematic issues are salient in selecting or writing expositions for young readers. The one mentioned earlier, the genre's unfamiliarity, is the focus of this chapter. A second issue is that expositions often contain content that is new. Indeed, the customary function of expository text is to introduce new content. As Black (1985) has noted: "Expository texts are the ones that convey new information and explain new topics to people. In contrast, stories and other narrative texts mostly describe new variations on well-learned informational themes" (p. 249).

Although issues of content are not the present focus, a few words about content are in order, because issues of expository presentation for young readers are compounded by the typically unfamiliar content found in expositions. The content of expositions in basal Readers must be viewed in light of the fact that the books are anthologies of short selections that exhibit little, if any, content connection. The expository selections in basal Readers are predominantly taken from the science and social studies domains, but in the anthology format they appear without the sequential development that characterizes subject-matter textbooks. For example, a single third-grade Reader contains short, isolated expositions on content as diverse as diffusion and composition of white light, echolocation by bats, and the formation of fossils. Moreover, the lessons that accompany each selection give no more attention to providing the background knowledge that a third grader needs to understand such topics than they give to a simple story about visiting the zoo.

The point made here about the content of basal expositions is that it is often tough; it frequently calls for significant amounts of prerequisite knowledge. The lack of sequential development and brevity of the lessons

---

[1]The basal reading programs we examined are *Ginn Reading Program*, 1982; Harcourt, Brace, Jovanovich, *Bookmark Reading Program, Eagle Edition*, 1983; *Houghton Mifflin Reading Program*, 1983; *Macmillan Reading Series R*, 1983.

in Readers preclude their supporting the development of the schemata needed for comprehending a passage about white light or echolocation. Given the difficulty students face with such content, it becomes crucial that the content be structured so young readers are able to construct a coherent representation of the text.

AN ASPECT OF TEXT STRUCTURE: COHERENCE

Structure, generically, is how something is put together. There is a variety of perspectives from which to examine how expositions are put together. The issue of primary concern in our investigation was how comprehensibility is affected by an exposition's coherence, a construct we have used in past research. Coherence refers to the extent to which the sequencing or ordering of ideas in a text makes sense and the extent to which the language used in discussing those ideas makes the nature of the ideas and their relationships apparent. A coherent text all fits together, seems of a whole, because a train of well-expressed ideas appears in a manner that discloses their connections.

A large body of research is consistent with the notion that textual coherence directly affects comprehensibility. A number of aspects of text coherence have been shown to affect comprehension. Negative influences include the use of references that are ambiguous (Frederiksen, 1981), distant (Cirilo, 1981; Lesgold, Roth, & Curtis, 1979), or indirect (Haviland & Clark, 1974; Just & Carpenter, 1978); the inclusion of concepts for which the reader lacks requisite background (Chiesi et al., 1979; Pearson et al., 1979); indistinct relationships between events (Black & Bern, 1981; Kintsch, Mandel, & Kozminsky, 1977; Stein & Nezworski, 1978); and the inclusion of irrelevant events or ideas (Schank, 1975; Trabasso, Secco, & Van den Broek, 1984). The relationship between coherence and comprehensibility is also recognized by Anderson and Armbruster (1984) in their discussion of "considerate text."

We have used assessments of coherence in earlier research to guide revisions of narrative selections from basal Readers. Coherence of these narratives was strengthened by making connections within the text more apparent, filling potential knowledge gaps, and organizing and clarifying text events and states. These revisions were successful in making the stories more comprehensible for target-aged readers (Beck et al., 1984).

Although our earlier work dealt with narratives, the coherence of expository text may have an even stronger relationship to comprehensibility. Narratives, and indeed many human interactions, contain inherent structural elements of a goal or problem, attempts to attain the goal or solve the problem, and eventually, a resolution. The power of this overall organization, or macrostructure, is that it is familiar to readers and they expect it as they read (Mandler & Johnson, 1977; Rumelhart, 1975; Stein & Glenn, 1979; Thorndyke, 1977). Indeed, narrative structure's power in aiding comprehension is predictive; if the elements of the structure appear in a scrambled order, or if an element is omitted, comprehension suffers (Mandler, 1978; Stein & Glenn, 1978).

There are not inherent structural elements in expository prose as there are in stories, however; the author structures an expository text to fit its communicative purpose. Thus, structure derives from the purpose that the text is to serve. This has led to research on expository patterns that writers employ, to discover if there is some basic set of macrostructures.

In some of the earliest research in this area, Meyer (1975) identified the structures in expository text as cause/effect, comparison/contrast, problem/solution, description, and collection. Although these structures do describe patterns of expositions, they lack the power of story structure for two reasons. First, they do not uniquely characterize expository text; narrative text contains these patterns as well (Stein, 1986). Furthermore, most natural text exhibits a mix of these structures (Hiebert, Englert, & Brennan, 1983; Meyer & Freedle, 1984). Any given structure may exist at the sentence, paragraph, or passage level, but rarely does one structure characterize an entire text. For example, a piece about air pollution in a city might begin with what appears to be problem/solution structure; it might present air pollution as a problem and explore solutions to alleviate it. Yet, within the text, there could well be cause/effect structures that detail the sources of pollution and its particular consequences, and descriptive passages that tell how the buildings look because of the presence of pollutants.

Because of the ubiquity of narrative structure, the reader enters a narrative text expecting a specific structure and is able to use knowledge of that structure to organize what is read. However, in approaching an exposition, the reader's expectations can only be based on knowledge of the topic, because no overall expository structure exists. The reader, then, is more dependent on the coherence of the text being read to guide construction of a meaningful text representation.

Our use of coherence as a construct for examining expository text involved two broad categories of relationships. The first was the relationship of a part to the whole, the issue of how a specific section relates to the main topic of the selection. The other category was the relationships among the parts, whether, sentence by sentence and paragraph by paragraph, the selection provides an overall organization.

Relationship of Part to Whole

For a text to achieve coherence, all the parts (e.g., subtopics, sections, key concepts) should be relevant to the central topic. In our examination of expository selections, we found that coherence was often disrupted by the introductory passage and by internal passages within a selection that digressed to a new topic.

Introductory Material. The initial passage of a text should set a reader thinking in the direction of the topic. As readers begin a text, they expect the topic to be established (Kieras, 1985). If it is not revealed, the reader may focus on irrelevant ideas to the detriment of comprehension. Setting up the topic is especially important for expository texts, as they convey information for which readers likely have no prior framework.

Basal publishers often introduce expository material with a "catchy" scenario, which attempts to capture students' interest and create a link to the topic through a situation that they can easily relate to. The notion that students will pay attention to new information if their interest is piqued is intuitively compelling. The notion that new information is best communicated when it is linked to what is already known is confirmed by research (e.g., Beck, Omanson, & McKeown, 1982; Graves & Palmer, 1981; Langer, 1981; Pearson et al., 1979). However, the effectiveness of these notions depends on how well they are implemented. The known information must be considered in terms of how well it relates to the topic and whether it is appropriate for facilitating students' understanding of the new information. In our review of introductory materials, we found that the interest-piquing scenario tended to obscure or overwhelm the topic of the selection.

An introduction that obscures the topic appears in an 800-word, fourth-grade selection in Program A about subways, what subways are, how they were invented, how people use them, and more. Entitled *Subways on the Move,* it begins:

> It is Saturday morning. You are alone in the house when the phone rings. A friend of yours needs help. Her pet lizard has gotten out of the cage and is stuck behind the stove. You'd like to help, but there's no way to get to your friend's house. Your parents are out with the car, your bike has a flat, and it's too far to walk. What would you do?
>
> You would probably say that you'd wait for your parents to come home. But if you live in a big city you might not have to; you could take the subway. A subway would get you to your friend's house fast.

The selection then moves to describing subways as underground railroads used for city travel. The introduction does nothing to prepare children to think about the use and development of subways. Indeed, the scenario about the loss of a pet lizard may well obscure the central topic.

An introduction that overwhelms the topic appears in a fifth-grade selection whose purpose is to give students a sense of what psychologists do. The introductory material here creates a focus of its own. This selection in

Program D, *Exploring the Mind,* begins with a hypothetical scenario, which occupies about half the approximately 550-word selection, describing the various responses of children in a classroom to the news that a much anticipated field trip has been canceled.

> Mark, for instance, finds tears in his eyes. "Something always happens to spoil our fun," he blurts out between sobs.
> Ellen is disappointed, too. But she takes it out on Mark. "Cry-baby! Cry-baby!"
> Michael blames the teacher. "This always happens," he whispers. "If we could only have a different teacher, we'd have more fun. All she ever wants to do is work."

After about 100 more words detailing other children's reactions, the text finally notes that it is hard to know why people behave as they do and that a psychologist is a mind-scientist who explores why people are alike and different. Because the introduction takes up half the selection with explicit portrayals of typical child behavior, it is likely to distract students from the purpose of the article, not lead them to it. Students might think about who their classroom crybaby is or similar disappointments they have experienced rather than be stirred to wonder why people behave as they do.

Introductory material in a selection should establish a framework for subsequent text information, and there is evidence that a framework can influence what the reader remembers (Anderson, 1977; Bransford & Johnson, 1972). The kinds of introductions described here create an inappropriate framework and thus direct a reader's attention away from the main concepts.

Introducing a new topic with a catchy scenario, however, is not always inappropriate. Indeed, we found examples that were likely to establish an appropriate framework. One such introduction was found in a fifth-grade selection about Komodo dragons and other strange creatures. The approximately 1,000-word selection in Program A, entitled *Yes, There Really Are Dragons,* begins with a 45-word description of a boy escaping from a dragon's grasp, followed by a 40-word discussion of the role of dragons in stories. This leads to the statement that dragons are make-believe—"or are they?" The text then presents the notion that some creatures, thought to be legendary, really do exist, and it goes on to describe these creatures. The introduction will likely arouse reader interest, while building appropriate expectations. Children are familiar with and typically interested in tales of legendary creatures, and discussion of Komodo dragons is a relevant extension of legendary creatures.

Digressions. A second situation of coherence being disrupted was found where passages within a selection digressed to a new topic. These digressions are problematic in that they disrupt the flow of text ideas on a specific topic and draw attention to a new focus.

Support for the notion that digressions have a negative effect on comprehension comes from the work of Schank (1975) and Stein and Trabasso (1982). Although their work concerned narrative text, it is reasonable to hypothesize that comprehension suffers even more where expositions contain digressions, in that the narrative structure may help override irrelevant passages, but there is no such universal structure found in expositions.

In our analysis of digressions, we found not only passages that jumped to new topics but passages where discussion of some tangential theme was so extensive that it seemed a switch in topic. An example of a digression that jumps to a new topic occurs in a fourth-grade selection in Program A about volcanoes. The selection includes a description of the process of eruption and information about specific volcanoes. At one point, *Mountains From Beneath the Earth,* an approximately 950-word selection, mentions that many volcanoes are near each other in the Pacific Ring of Fire and that Japan is in the Ring of Fire. Then begins a discussion of Japan's most famous volcano, Mt. Fuji. In the midst of text about Mt. Fuji's volcanic characteristics, there appears a 60-word passage about Mt. Fuji as a summer resort and a problem with crowds on the mountain that was alleviated by the installation of a cable car. The text then returns to the topic of volcanoes, stating that in the past we had no means of predicting eruptions so whole cities were often destroyed. The reader gets two interruptive jolts, one between the description of Mt. Fuji's volcanic characteristics and the resort scenario, and another where the discussion jumps from cable cars to volcanic destruction.

A digression so extensive that it seems like a switch in topic occurs in Program A's poorly introduced selection about subways discussed earlier. About two-thirds of the way into this approximately 800-word selection, the text notes that Aztec ruins were discovered during excavation for the Mexico City subway. Then, in approximately 250 words, the text digresses to the building skills of the Aztecs, the discovery of Aztec culture by the Spanish, and the eventual defeat of the Aztecs at the hands of the Spanish. Introduction of the Mexican subway as an example in a general selection about subways is reasonable. An aside about Aztecs that comprises over one fourth of the selection, however, might well be taken to be the central topic.

Undoubtedly, Aztec history is fascinating. Yet, presenting it in the midst of an overview of subways does not facilitate comprehension of either topic. At times such asides are useful for sparking some student interest, but there are ways to present them that do not disrupt the coherence of a selection. They could be presented after the main text as part of a follow up to the topic. If presented within the text, they could be marked off in a separate box to indicate their divergence from the main focus (Anderson & Armbruster, 1984). A digression could also be folded into the text, if the reader is alerted that an aside is going to occur and if its relationship to the main topic is established. It is our conjecture that the digressions found in basal expositions disrupt coherence because brief, isolated selections in basal Readers do not afford enough space to introduce a side topic and adequately develop its relationship to the main topic; that is, connections are not developed so that the selection seems "of a whole," instead the digressions strike the reader as interrupting the flow of ideas.

Relationship Among Parts

Given that the purpose of expository text is to communicate information about a topic, selections should be organized to build toward an understanding of that topic. Individual statements should fit together logically to build the main points or arguments, and connections between points should be well developed and fairly explicit. Many selections examined in this investigation lack the degree of organization required to foster comprehension and learning. Instead, they present a loose collection of ideas that revolve around a topic. As the following examples demonstrate, this situation occurs to varying degrees and for different reasons. In our analysis, we found five general areas in which coherence was poorly provided for. The most pervasive problem was proliferation of subtopics. At the level of overall structure, we also discovered neglected opportunities to provide overarching concepts and to categorize the material discussed in a manner that facilitates comprehension and learning. Where headings appear within a selection, we found that they often misrepresent the nature of the material that follows. And finally, we found a tendency to disrupt the flow of ideas.

Too Many Subtopics. The most frequent impediment to a coherent presentation was the tendency to try to cover too many aspects of a given topic in a single selection. Rather than being organized around a few subtopics and aptly introducing, explaining, and linking them, selections offered a variety of subtopics, with only limited information about each. Explanations of the subtopics and development of relationships among them did not occur. This superficial treatment of ideas in instruction has been noted in other areas of the curriculum and has been dubbed "mentioning" (Durkin, 1984).

Consider the range of issues in a third-grade selection in Program C entitled *Your Busy Brain.* This roughly 900-word selection discusses the brain's physical appearance and protection by the skull; its function as a message center made up of nerve cells, including several examples of how messages are sent and received; its role in long- and short-term memory; its parts and what each controls; its activity during sleep in both involuntary movement and dreaming. Some conjectures about how we learn and a demonstration of how learning occurs are also presented through a scenario of an amusement park maze.

Each subtopic serves to support the notion that the brain is "busy," but to try to describe a set of diverse functions like neural impulse, memory, and dreaming in addition to the brain's physical appearance in a 900-word selection absolutely prohibits both supportive elaboration in the descriptions and development of the logical connections necessary for coherent presentation. A coherent text would present fewer aspects of the topic, deal with each in more depth, and draw clear connections among them.

Failure to State an Overarching Concept.   Another problem revealed by our analysis of the relationship among parts of an exposition is the failure of the structure to make explicit a general concept that is embodied by the content. For example, a sixth-grade selection in Program D entitled *Following the Western Star* has an implied conceptual framework—the idea that western expansion of U.S. territory involved groups of people with different aims, traveling in different ways. The text consists of three separately treated examples of westward movement: lone mountain men who moved west to make a living as trappers, prospectors who followed the California gold rush, and settlers who traveled west by wagon train. But no attempt is made to present them within the overall conceptual framework.

Opportunities to develop the concept of westward expansion exist within the selection but are neglected. The selection begins with a 60-word passage detailing Jefferson's purchase of the Louisiana territory. Then it jumps into the first example of westward movement, mountain men. The line of thought that is needed to establish the topic that the three examples illustrate is that the purchase of the Louisiana territory opened up settlement to the west to various groups who began to move to look for better opportunities. That line of thought is never established.

The selection is 1,200 words long, enough space to present the three examples and develop the relationship that ties them to the overall concept. Instead, the text uses space for minute details about the three examples. For instance, readers are told that mountain men sometimes traveled on ponies, sometimes on foot, and other times on mule back, and that wagon trains started off by 7 o'clock in the morning.

Because this development of the overarching concept never occurs, artificial transitions connect the examples. For instance, the text moves awkwardly from the discussion of mountain men to the subject of the gold rush.

Yet their time was not long. In the 1830's, due to one of the quirks of fashion, beaver hats disappeared from stores; then men wore silk hats. And mountain men were out of jobs.

But as always seemed to happen in the West, something else came along to change bad luck into good. On January 24, 1848, John Marshall, who was building a sawmill on the American River in California, noticed a shining stone in the water. He picked it up . . . and began the California Gold Rush!

From this selection, students may learn a little about what mountain men did, what the California gold rush was, and that wagon trains carried some people west. However, the opportunity is missed to begin to build their understanding of an important phenomenon in the history of their country—that the opening of the West offered great opportunities both for individuals and for the development of the nation. This missed opportunity is particularly unfortunate, as the concept of territorial expansion is recurrent in the course of social studies learning.

Available but Unused Frameworks.   In our review, we also found instances where categories of facts offered a useful framework for organizing the content but were used to little advantage. In a fourth-grade selection in Program C of approximately 700 words entitled *Look Who's Using a Tool,* animals are shown to use tools for three general purposes: to catch or prepare food, to make life easier, or to protect their families. Although this framework is available, the text does not present the examples as being of three kinds.

The text is organized as follows. In the introductory paragraphs two examples of tool use, those of an elephant using tree branches to scratch her back and to spank her calf, are described before the different uses for tools are labeled. Even after the mention of the different purposes, examples related to food and protection are intermingled rather than separated into two groups. Nine examples are presented. For the first six, food and protection examples alternate. Then three food examples are presented.

Because the examples of tool use are clearly presented, and the topic and specific content of the selection are at a fairly simple conceptual level, the lack of the available organizing device may not cause comprehension difficulties. However, clustering the examples according to the purposes of tool use could bolster learning in several ways. First, if the examples were grouped, it would be easier for the reader to see that animals use tools principally in connection with getting food. Second, if all the food examples and protection examples were separated, it might make it easier for a reader to remember the tool use for the specific animals discussed. Third, such categories might themselves serve as memory prompts for the material.

But most importantly, grouping examples by purpose would provide children with a model for organizing concepts or facts. Reading a selection that categorizes examples by subtopic might help children to develop tactics for organizing new information as part of their repertoires for comprehending future material that they read or study or write about.

Poor Use of Headings.   One organizing device often found in subject-matter textbooks is the use of headings to mark subtopics, and some expository selections in the basals also use such headings. There is value in using headings to organize material (Anderson & Armbruster, 1984). However, their mere presence does not upgrade coherence. Any potential benefit depends on their ties to the text that follows. This review uncovered instances of headings that served to aggravate a problematic relationship among parts of a text rather than to aid the organization of information.

The headings used in *Lighthouses,* for example, a fourth-grade selection in Program A about the history of lighthouses and the life of lighthouse families, do not accurately describe the information that follows them. In addition, all information that relates to a particular heading is not found within that section. A two-paragraph introduction sets up the topic of lighthouses and their role in helping sailors find their way. The rest of the text is presented under the five headings: "Kinds of Lighthouses," "Lighthouses in the past," "Life in Lighthouses," "Lighthouse Children," and "The Light."

The first evidence of a problem is that ideas related to the first two headings are confounded. The "Kinds of Lighthouses" section begins with a 100-word overview of how lighthouses were developed to replace bonfires that were once set on beaches—information that seems more suited to the notion of "Lighthouses in the Past." Following this passage, various kinds of lighthouses are described. Then the text returns to the topic of early lighthouses under "Lighthouses in the Past."

"Life in Lighthouses" describes children's experiences, "The [lighthouse] keeper might have been your mother or father . . . you would likely know much more about nature than mainland children would." Yet "Lighthouse Children," the subsequent heading, is hardly a departure from the topic under discussion. The final section, "The Light," describes different sources of illumination, from coal to wood to electricity. After this, with no change in heading, the text returns to the topic of children's lives, with a long passage about how children felt about growing up in lighthouses and the desire of many of them to become lighthouse keepers themselves.

These headings and their relationship to the text are a good indication of the selection's lack of an orderly, coherent organization. Headings help a reader build expectations about the kind of information to be gained from a text. Reader expectations influence what is understood and remembered from a text (Anderson, 1977). In this case, the information provided by the headings could lead the reader to develop inappropriate expectations which, in turn, can interfere with comprehension. The inappropriate use of headings has a further potential negative side effect; if children are misled by inaccurate headings, they miss an opportunity to develop an appreciation of their value in guiding attention.

Interruption of Connected Ideas.   Coherence is negatively affected when a stream of related ideas that comprise a unit of information, such as a description or an explanation, is interrupted. The interruption disrupts coherence because the reader must hold the first part of the unit in mind until arriving at the point in text where the rest of the unit occurs. The text, then, may be harder to understand, and the interrupted unit of information may be harder to recall (Black, 1985).

An example of interrupted units of information occurs in a third-grade selection in Program B entitled *Comets*. The selection begins, "About two or three times in your life, you may be able to see a comet. A comet is a beautiful sight as it crosses the sky like a rocket." From this beginning, it seems that a reader could reasonably expect to be told what a comet is. But the text fails to address this issue until about 45 words later. Instead, information on the length of the trail of light left by a comet and the path comets take follows.

When the description of comets begins, the text states that the *main part* of the comet is the head. From such an introduction a reader could well expect that other parts will be mentioned, but the fact that a comet consists of a head *and a tail* is not presented until the middle of the next paragraph, about 45 words later. Even then, the tail is never specifically described. Instead, the fact that a tail exists appears in an account of its formation as the comet nears the sun. A more effective organization might have been first to present the notion that a comet is made up of a head and a tail, and then to describe the parts.

Related to the notion that a comet's tail is formed by proximity to the sun is the notion that the tail disappears when a comet moves away from the sun. Surely this phenomenon is best noted in proximity to the account of the tail's formation. Yet the description of the comet's tail and the information about the tail's disappearance are separated by 33 words of text. The intervening text discusses the number of tails a comet may have and which way a comet's tail points.

In the rest of the selection, related facts and ideas that should be contiguously presented are separated by fairly lengthy passages about other content. The effect is that the relationships necessary for understanding the content become harder to discern. This negative outcome seems particularly likely because the content is unfamiliar to the readers; the selection may be their first encounter with these concepts. Hence, it is probable that, at most, students will grasp several unrelated facts about comets.

An Example of Coherent Presentation

We conclude our discussion with an example of a selection that presents the content in an orderly, coherent way. This fourth-grade selection in Program A of roughly 1,400 words describes the work of veterinarians in various settings.

Entitled *Animals Need Doctors, Too,* the selection sets up a global organization by stating that some vets care for pets, whereas others work in zoos, or animal parks, or on farms. These four settings are then used as subheadings to organize the selection. The information under each subheading is appropriate and is presented in an orderly way. Examples of a vet's duties in each setting are provided and are set up by general statements that explicitly state the concept to be considered. For instance, the section describing zoo veterinarians begins by stating that the vet goes on rounds each day and asks the zookeeper if there are problems. The next paragraph notes that sometimes there are problems and follows with examples of animal health problems that might be encountered in a zoo.

Appropriate transitions between the text sections provide relationships among the settings. For example, the section on zoo veterinarians follows the section on pet care and draws a connection by noting that zoo vets care for animals that are not as common as pets. Similarly, the final section on farm animals begins by stating that farm animals, as well as pets, zoo animals, and wild animals, need care. In this selection, the provision and orderly use of a global organization, the explicit statement of general concepts, and logically drawn relationships among the various concepts produce a coherent presentation of what vets do.

Albeit, the content of the veterinarian selection is not difficult nor wholly unfamiliar to students, and the organization is rather simple. This situation is characteristic of basal expository selections. Selections that deal with simpler, more familiar topics generally exhibit greater coherence, whereas those covering the more complex topics that expository passages are often designed to convey demonstrate little consideration for facilitating comprehensibility through a coherent presentation.

DISCUSSION

At the outset of this chapter we noted some conventionally held notions about the role ascribed to expository selections in basal Readers. Briefly, these notions are that students have difficulty with subject-matter textbooks because they are unfamiliar with the expository genre, that students' unfamiliarity is due in part to basal Readers having been comprised primarily of narrative selections, that including expositions in Readers will provide beneficial experiences with the genre, and that those experiences will benefit students' ability to read and learn from subject-matter textbooks. The question posed in our study was whether the expository selections in current basals do provide such beneficial experience. The answer, based on an examination of the coherence of these selections, is that they do not.

To the extent that these expository texts require young readers to establish relations and impose organization on the content themselves, they are likely to preclude adequate comprehension. This conclusion is based on research on the kinds of text characteristics that often cause readers difficulty (Black & Bern, 1981; Cirilo, 1981; Frederiksen, 1981; Haviland & Clark, 1974; Kintsch et al., 1977; Lesgold et al., 1979; Stein & Nezworski, 1978; Trabasso et al., 1984) and our experiences monitoring children's interactions with texts that exhibit such problems (Beck et al., 1984; Beck et al., 1982).

Certainly, the ability to deal with poor text presentations is an important part of a mature reader's repertoire. But it seems unlikely that this ability will develop from a diet of poorly organized, disjointed texts about unfamiliar topics. Rather, the ability to interact with less than optimal text presentations can more effectively develop with accumulated experience with coherently organized expository texts that can serve as models. Through exposure to such models, readers may build an understanding of the kind of information found in expository texts and how that information can be organized.

Implicit in the foregoing discussion is a contrast with other recommendations about how instruction about expository structure should be approached (Bartlett, 1978; McDonald, 1978; Meyer, Brandt, & Bluth, 1980). Such instruction is based on ideal models of prototypic structures, such as cause/effect and problem/solution, in the abstract. The point of instruction is not to enable students to categorize a selection as exhibiting a specific structural type, but to help them become sensitive to the type of information contained in expository text and to ways that information might be organized. In our view, a route to the goal is instruction about expository structure that is based on good models; that is, on well-organized texts.

In considering the kinds of experiences that could help prepare students for subject-matter learning, recall that the content of expository texts often is strikingly different from the story fare to which young readers are most accustomed. Notions of how best to prepare students for subject-matter learning should not be limited to considerations of structural characteristics of the expository genre. Building students' content knowledge can be a productive way to establish background that can facilitate subject-matter learning. And new content topics can be introduced through genres other than expositions. Biographies, historical fiction, and personal accounts of events and discoveries are formats that combine informational content with more familiar narrative structures. Indeed, it traditionally has been assumed that children build a background about historical events and figures through narrative readings of these types (Ravitch, 1985).

This chapter began by noting that the recognition of a reader's active role in constructing meaning in the reading process is important to any consideration of instructional problems. The difficulties of reading subject-matter texts can be viewed as an impetus to upgrading a reader's sources of information for dealing with expository text. The need for broad, rich resources arises because expository texts present new content in an unfamiliar genre. Expository text, then, is different enough from narrative text that the information young readers bring to the reading task may not be adequate to allow understanding of the texts.

Our examination of expository selections in basal Readers showed that the texts that are meant to provide young readers experience with a new genre are likely themselves to cause comprehension failure; these texts are quite often characterized by a lack of coherence. Clearly, if young readers are to develop the ability to handle expository texts, they need opportunities to interact with good models, with expository texts that are coherently organized.

ACKNOWLEDGMENTS

The research described in this paper was supported by the Center for the Study of Learning of the Learning Research and Development Center, University of Pittsburgh, supported by funds from the Office of Educational Research and Improvement (OERI), United States Department of Education. The opinions expressed do not necessarily reflect the position or policy of OERI, and no official endorsement should be inferred.

We acknowledge Robert Glaser's leadership in shaping the field of instructional psychology by bringing a cognitive perspective to the study of instructional issues. This work reflects the influence of those ideas which have provided rich resources for using instructional materials to understand aspects of learning and instruction.

REFERENCES

Anderson, R. C. (1977). *Schema-directed processes in language comprehension* (Tech. Rep. No. 50). Urbana, IL: University of Illinois, Center for the Study of Reading.
Anderson, R. C., Spiro, R. J., & Anderson, M. C. (1978). Schemata as scaffolding for the

representation of information in connected discourse. *American Educational Research Journal, 15,* 433–440.

Anderson, T. H., & Armbruster, B. B. (1984). Content area textbooks. In R. C. Anderson, J. Osborn, & R. J. Tierney (Eds.), *Learning to read in American schools* (pp. 193–224). Hillsdale, NJ: Lawrence Erlbaum Associates.

Bartlett, B. J. (1978). *Top-level structure as an organizational strategy for recall of classroom text.* Unpublished doctoral dissertation, Arizona State University. Cited in Meyer, B. J. F., Brandt, D. M., & Bluth, G. J. (1980). Use of top-level structure in text: Key for reading comprehension of ninth-grade students. *Reading Research Quarterly, 16,* 72–103.

Bartlett, F. C. (1932). *Remembering: A study of experimental and social psychology.* Cambridge, MA: Cambridge University Press.

Beck, I. L., & Carpenter, P. A. (1986). Cognitive approaches to understanding reading: Implications for instructional practice. *American Psychologist, 41,* 1098–1105.

Beck, I. L., McKeown, M. G., Omanson, R. C., & Pople, M. T. (1984). Improving the comprehensibility of stories: The effects of revisions that improve coherence. *Reading Research Quarterly, 19,* 263–277.

Beck, I. L., Omanson, R. C., & McKeown, M. G. (1982). An instructional redesign of reading lessons: Effects on comprehension. *Reading Research Quarterly, 17,* 462–481.

Black, J. B. (1985). An exposition on understanding expository text. In B. K. Britton & J. B. Black (Eds.), *Understanding expository text: A theoretical and practical handbook for analyzing explanatory text* (pp. 249–267). Hillsdale, NJ: Lawrence Erlbaum Associates.

Black, J. B., & Bern, H. (1981). Causal coherence and memory for events in narratives. *Journal of Verbal Learning and Verbal Behavior, 20,* 267–275.

Bransford, J. D., & Johnson, M. K. (1972). Contextual prerequisites for understanding: Some investigations of comprehension and recall. *Journal of Verbal Learning and Verbal Behavior, 11,* 717–726.

Brown, A. L., Smiley, S. S., Day, J. D., Townsend, M. A., & Lawton, S. C. (1977). Intrusion of a thematic idea in children's recall of prose. *Child Development, 48,* 1454–66.

Chiesi, H. L., Spilich, G. J., & Voss, J. F. (1979). Acquisition of domain-related information in relation to high and low domain knowledge. *Journal of Verbal Learning and Verbal Behavior, 18,* 275–290.

Cirilo, R. K. (1981). Referential coherence and text structure in story comprehension. *Journal of Verbal Learning and Verbal Behavior, 20,* 358–367.

Clark, H. H., & Haviland, S. (1977). Comprehension and the given-new contract. In R. O. Freedle (Ed.), *Discourse production and comprehension* (pp. 1–40). Norwood, NJ: Ablex.

Durkin, D. (1984). Do basal manuals teach reading comprehension? In R. C. Anderson, J. Osborn, & R. J. Tierney (Eds.), *Learning to read in American schools: Basal readers and content texts* (pp. 29–38). Hillsdale, NJ: Lawrence Erlbaum Associates.

Frederiksen, J. R. (1981). Understanding anaphora: Rules used by readers in assigning pronominal referents. *Discourse Processes, 4,* 323–348.

Graves, M. F., & Palmer, R. J. (1981). Validating previewing as a method of improving fifth and sixth grade students' comprehension of short stories. *Michigan Reading Journal, 15,* 1–3.

Haviland, S., & Clark, H. H. (1974). What's new? Acquiring new information as a process in comprehension. *Journal of Verbal Learning and Verbal Behavior, 13,* 512–521.

Hiebert, E. H., Englert, C. S., & Brennan, S. (1983). Awareness of text structure in recognition and production of expository discourse. *Journal of Reading Behavior, 15,* 63–79.

Just, M. A., & Carpenter, P. A. (1978). Inference processes during reading: Reflections from eye fixations. In J. W. Senders, D. F. Fisher, & R. A. Monty (Eds.), *Eye movements and higher psychological functions* (pp. 157–174). Hillsdale, NJ: Lawrence Erlbaum Associates.

Kieras, D. E. (1985). Thematic processes in the comprehension of technical prose. In B. K. Britton & J. B. Black (Eds.), *Understanding expository text: A theoretical and practical handbook for analyzing explanatory text* (pp. 89–107). Hillsdale, NJ: Lawrence Erlbaum Associates.

Kintsch, W., Mandel, T. S., & Kozminsky, E. (1977). Summarizing scrambled stories. *Memory & Cognition, 5,* 547–552.

Langer, J. A. (1981). Pre-reading plan (Prep): Facilitating text comprehension. In J. Chapman (Ed.), *The reader and the text.* London: Heineman.

Lesgold, A. M., Roth, S. F., & Curtis, M. E. (1979). Foregrounding effects in discourse comprehension. *Journal of Verbal Learning and Verbal Behavior, 18,* 291–308.

Mandler, J. M. (1978). A code in the node: The use of a story schema in retrieval. *Discourse Processes, 1,* 14–35.

Mandler, J. M., & Johnson, N. S. (1977). Remembrance of things parsed: Story structure and recall. *Cognitive Psychology, 9,* 111–151.

McDonald, G. E. (1978). *The effects of instruction in the use of an abstract structural schema as an aid to comprehension and recall of written discourse.* Unpublished doctoral dissertation, Virginia Polytechnic Institute and State University. Cited in Meyer, B. J. F., Brandt, D. M., & Bluth, G. J. (1980). Use of top-level structure in text: Key for reading comprehension of ninth-grade students. *Reading Research Quarterly, 16,* 72–103.

Meyer, B. J. F. (1975). *The organization of prose and its effects on memory.* Amsterdam: North-Holland.

Meyer, B. J. F., Brandt, D. M., & Bluth, G. J. (1980). Use of top-level structure in text: Key for reading comprehension of ninth-grade students. *Reading Research Quarterly, 16,* 72–103.

Meyer, B. J. F., & Freedle, R. O. (1984). Effects of discourse type on recall. *American Educational Research Journal, 21,* 121–143.

Pearson, P. D., Hansen, J., & Gordon, C. (1979). The effect of background knowledge on young children's comprehension of explicit and implicit information. *Journal of Reading Behavior, 11,* 201–209.

Perfetti, C. A. (1985). *Reading ability.* New York: Oxford University Press.

Ravitch, D. (1985, November 17). Decline and fall of teaching history. *The New York Times Magazine* (pp. 50–56, 101, 117).

Rumelhart, D. E. (1975). Notes on a schema for stories. In D. G. Bobrow & A. Collins (Eds.), *Representation and understanding: Studies in cognitive science* (pp. 211–236). New York: Academic Press.

Rumelhart, D. E. (1980). Schemata: The building blocks of cognition. In R. J. Spiro, B. C. Bruce, & W. F. Brewer (Eds.), *Theoretical issues in reading comprehension* (pp. 33–58). Hillsdale, NJ: Lawrence Erlbaum Associates.

Schank, R. C. (1975). The structure of episodes in memory. In D. Bobrow & A. Collins (Eds.), *Representation and understanding: Studies in cognitive science* (pp. 237–272). New York: Academic Press.

Schank, R. C., & Abelson, R. P. (1977). *Scripts, plans, goals, and understanding: An inquiry into human knowledge structures.* Hillsdale, NJ: Lawrence Erlbaum Associates.

Spilich, G. J., Vesonder, G. T., Chiesi, H. L., & Voss, J. F. (1979). Text processing of domain-related information for individuals with high and low domain knowledge. *Journal of Verbal Learning and Verbal Behavior, 18,* 275–290.

Stein, N. L. (1986). Knowledge and process in the acquisition of writing skills. In E. Z. Rothkopf (Ed.), *Review of research in education* (Vol. 13, pp. 225–258). Washington DC: American Educational Research Association.

Stein, N. L., & Glenn, C. G. (1978). *The role of temporal organization in story comprehension* (Tech. Rep. No. 71). Urbana, IL: University of Illinois, Center for the Study of Reading.

Stein, N. L., & Glenn, C. G. (1979). An analysis of story comprehension in elementary school children. In R. O. Freedle (Ed.), *Advances in discourse processing* (Vol. 2): *New directions in discourse processing* (pp. 53–120). Norwood, NJ: Ablex.

Stein, N. L., & Nezworski, T. (1978). The effects of organization and instructional set on story memory. *Discourse Processes, 1,* 177–193.

Stein, N. L., & Trabasso, T. (1982). What's in a story: An approach to comprehension and instruction. In R. Glaser (Ed.), *Advances in the psychology of instruction* (Vol. 2, pp. 213–267). Hillsdale, NJ: Lawrence Erlbaum Associates.

Thorndyke, P. W. (1977). Cognitive structures in comprehension and memory of narrative discourse. *Cognitive Psychology, 9,* 77–110.

Thorndyke, P. W., & Yekovich, F. R. (1980). A critique of schemata as a theory of human story memory. *Poetics, 9,* 23–47.

Trabasso, T., Secco, T., & Van den Broek, P. (1984). Causal cohesion and story coherence. In H. Mandl, N. L. Stein, & T. Trabasso (Eds.), *Learning and comprehension of text* (pp. 83–111). Hillsdale, NJ: Lawrence Erlbaum Associates.

4

Development of an Expert Explanation: An Analysis of a Sequence of Subtraction Lessons

Gaea Leinhardt
Learning Research and Development Center
University of Pittsburgh

Teaching is the art of transmitting knowledge in a way that ensures the learner receives it. This is accomplished by the careful manipulation of the circumstances of learning and by the essential simplification of complex material. To do this, the teacher must understand both the key concepts and procedures of the subject (subject-matter knowledge) and which aspects of the concepts and procedures are subtle or difficult to grasp (student-learning knowledge). By building on these two knowledge bases, the successful teacher can explain new material to students in a way that enhances students' knowledge acquisition.

The research described in this article examined the nature of an instructional explanation. This examination was done in the particular context of a series of expert mathematical lessons on subtraction with regrouping given to second-grade children. To analyze the lesson content, videotapes of the

Reprinted from *Cognition and Instruction*, Volume 4, Number 4, 1987.

complete episode were transcribed and then interpreted by means of semantic nets. The impact of these lessons was gauged by observing, interviewing, and testing a sample of students before, during, and after the instructional sequence. Student interviews conducted during the sequence were converted into semantic nets similar in format to those used for the teacher's lessons. Using the cumulative information from all the teacher's lessons and the additional information provided by interviews with the teacher, a planning net (VanLehn & Brown, 1980) for her explanation was constructed showing all the teacher's goals and actions for the entire lesson sequence.

Over the past three decades, a large amount of research has been done on instructional processes and their impact on student knowledge. However, there has been a noticeable dearth of material that examines a complete educational episode, that is, the instruction and learning of a particular piece of mathematical knowledge from beginning to end. Excellent studies of instructional techniques (Collins & Stevens, 1982; Rosenshine & Stevens, 1986; Slavin & Karweit, 1985), of teacher decisions (Borko & Niles, 1984; Calderhead, 1984; Shavelson & Stern, 1981), and of the impact of specific educational processes (Berliner, King, Rubin, & Fisher, 1981; Brophy & Good, 1986; Leinhardt, Zigmond, & Cooley, 1981) exist. Yet, few studies document how a specific piece of subject-matter content is taught and learned. In Shulman's (1986) sense, there is a lack of case literature. Recent examples of instructional-episode studies include Petitto's (1985) analysis of a long-division lesson, Lampert's (1986) analysis of multiplication, and Leinhardt and Smith's (1985) analysis of a fraction lesson.

An educational episode varies in length and can be seen as a detachable piece of instructional material—in this case, the teaching of subtraction with regrouping. Each such episode's objective is to move students toward competence in a specific area. The examination of subtraction with regrouping provides a unique opportunity to study a clearly defined educational episode. A core feature within a mathematics instruction episode is the explanation of new material, including its logical connection to prior knowledge. I hypothesize that an instructional explanation should have the following features:

1. Identification of the goal.
2. Signal monitors indicating progress toward the goal.
3. Examples of the case or instance.
4. Demonstrations that include parallel representations, some level of linkage of these representations, and identification of conditions of use and nonuse.

5. Legitimization of the new concept or procedure in terms of one or more of the following — known principles, cross-checks of representations, and compelling logic.
6. Linkage of new concepts to old through identification of familiar, expanded, and new elements.

An explanation can be completed within a single lesson or can extend over several lessons. The completion of an explanation in one sense marks the boundaries of an episode.

Subtraction with regrouping was chosen as a topic for study, not only because it is a clearly defined instructional episode, but also because it presents a unique set of challenges to the students and the teacher. It is of particular interest because it is usually the second major algorithm taught to students, the first being addition with regrouping. When expertly taught, it can provide the opportunity to learn a considerable amount about the nature of our number system.

Subtraction with regrouping also presents a unique set of problems to the student and teacher. When students first encounter a problem that has a smaller number at the top of the ones column than at the bottom, the natural tendencies are to subtract the smaller from the larger (i.e., the top from the bottom) because that is how subtraction is defined, to add one column and subtract the others, or to pursue another of the incorrect strategies documented as subtraction bugs by Brown and VanLehn (1980) in their analysis of systematic student errors. Unless students are armed with a regrouping algorithm, a negative accounting strategy, or the determination to use a count-on strategy (essentially ignoring the place value system), they will violate some mathematical constraint in their solutions.

From the perspective taken in this article, subtraction with regrouping is a procedure that requires the selective violation of some mathematical constraints. For example, it is possible to violate the restriction of only one digit per column while making notations, but it is not acceptable to violate the constraint of maintaining the value of the minuend or subtrahend when one uses the regrouping procedure. An expert explanation helps students understand the constraints and begin to master the difficult subtraction-with-regrouping algorithm. Spanning several mathematics lessons, the teacher in this study gradually provided the tools and logic for using the subtraction-with-regrouping algorithm. By studying the cognitive aspects of such expert explanations, we can begin to discern the critical features of an explanation.

The next section provides an overview of the method. Then, detailed descriptions of each of the first eight of Ms. Patrick's lessons on subtraction with regrouping are presented. In that section, semantic nets show the presented concepts and connections between them. Following each lesson description, evidence is presented of the student learning that occurred, including semantic nets showing the concepts and connections expressed by the students interviewed on that day. The cognitive aspects of the teacher's explanations are compared with the cognitive structure of the students' changing knowledge base. The next major section examines the differences in students' performance on tests and in the interviews before and after the entire instructional sequence. Finally, through an analysis of the teacher's lessons and of the concepts she expressed in interviews, a model of an expert explanation is offered.

METHOD

Teacher and Students

The teacher for this study, Ms. Patrick, and the 8 students were from a second-grade classroom in an all-Black, inner-city elementary school. Ms. Patrick was selected from a set of 12 experts who had been previously identified for a study of expert mathematics teaching. She was chosen because she was the only expert who was teaching subtraction with regrouping and because, in previous years, her students had performed especially well compared to other students in the district and their performances were relatively free of subtraction bugs after instruction. With the help of the teacher, students were selected to provide a mix of ability levels (2 high, 2 low, and 4 middle) and to ensure certain practical considerations for successful participation (i.e., frequency of attendance, likelihood of not transferring out, and expected degree of talkativeness).

Data Collection

The classroom was observed 28 times, including four full-day observations during the first week of school. Ten consecutive lessons on subtraction with regrouping were videotaped, 8 of which formed the data base for analyzing the lessons. Ms. Patrick was interviewed briefly immediately before and after each lesson and, after 5 of the lessons, video-based stimulated recall interviews with her were also conducted.

Each of the 8 students was interviewed twice during the instructional sequence, once by means of a video-based stimulated recall and once during class by means of a think-aloud protocol (Ericsson & Simon, 1980, 1984). All the students' in-class work and homework assignments were photocopied. The students were also tested and interviewed before and after the entire instructional sequence with instruments that measured their understanding of as well as performance on subtraction with regrouping.

Two types of preinstructional performance measures were collected: (a) a chapter pretest administered by the teacher and (b) a specially designed pre-unit interview administered by the researcher. The chapter pretest consisted of two-digit subtraction problems, some requiring regrouping, and word problems involving two-digit subtraction and addition. The students were instructed to circle all subtraction problems that required regrouping and these comprised 5 of the 14 items.

The pre-unit interview had two components, each with three tasks. The first component was designed to assess the students' skill in and understanding of the basic subtraction algorithm. This segment consisted of four subtraction problems, beginning with a single-digit problem and ending with a two-digit problem that required regrouping. The tasks were to read the problem aloud, calculate the answer, and then show the problem using base-10 blocks. The goals of the second component were to determine the level of the students' skill in and understanding of the addition-with-regrouping algorithm and to assess the students' knowledge of the relationship between written numbers and their value. It began with the students rolling special dice to generate numbers, which they were to write on paper and then display with base-10 blocks. Finally, the students were asked to add two of the numbers in both their numeric and blocks representations.

At the conclusion of the instructional sequence, the students' knowledge was assessed using a chapter posttest administered by the teacher and an interview similar to the pre-unit interview. The chapter posttest, like the pretest, contained 14 items, formatted in the same manner, with different problems.

The post-unit interview consisted of eight subtraction problems that were to be read aloud, calculated, and then demonstrated with base-10 blocks; students were also asked to link their block solution to the numeric solution at least once. This interview was designed to assess the students' skill with and knowledge of the subtraction-with-regrouping algorithm. The first three problems were similar to ones that the students had encountered during the unit. The last five problems were designed to test the students' ability to extend their knowledge beyond the instructional range. Each of these five problems was chosen for a specific reason: 567 minus 262, because it generates a zero in the answer; 253 minus 127, because it requires tens regrouping; 727 minus 483, because it requires hundreds but *not* tens regrouping; 625 minus 357, because it requires both tens and hundreds regrouping; and 402 minus 177, because it requires tens and hundreds regrouping and has a zero in the minuend. The problems were presented in order of increasing difficulty.

Data Analysis

Students' prechapter and postchapter tests were scored to generate a measure of their performance skill, and the data are presented in terms of percentage of items correct. Their pre-unit and post-unit interviews were transcribed and then scored in terms of percentage correct along two dimensions: (a) type of task (read, solve, show) and (b) location of items in the curriculum (i.e., in-range or out-of-range). These results are discussed later. First the actual lessons and the students' grasp of presentations are examined.

The lesson videotapes and interviews with the teacher and with students during the instructional sequence were transcribed and then analyzed using semantic nets that displayed concepts and their interconnections. A semantic net was constructed by reading the protocol of the videotaped lesson transcript (and supporting it with an interview transcript about the lesson) and creating nodes and links for every conceptual statement made. When new statements were made about items in existing nodes, the additional information was added, with a new node and a line linking it to the existing one. In this way, many relationships among concepts and their properties could be displayed in one location. The labels on the line links indicate the nature of the connections. For example, *is a* links two concepts where the first is a member of the larger class of the second (e.g., subtraction *is a* operation), and *has prop* links two concepts where the second is a property of the first (e.g., problem *has prop* answer/solution). When a concept or connection is erroneous, a hatch-marked line or node is used. Dashed lines or nodes are used to indicate implied concepts or connections.

These examples of semantic net language are taken from Fig. 4.3, the semantic net for Lesson 1. To understand its construction, consider the excerpts from the lesson transcript and the corresponding partial nets that were developed, as shown in Fig. 4.1.

The power of using a semantic net comes from its ability to display the connected concepts even when the concepts are presented at different times. In this study, semantic nets are used to document the concepts the teacher discussed in each lesson. Semantic nets have several advantages over lists of statements. Semantic nets can show the cumulative structure of ideas presented over a 20- to 40-min period. They can visually display the connections between concepts in a simple design that eliminates repetition

Semantic net:

Protocol:

The top number's smaller than the bottom so you were right. What kind of a problem is this? A fooler. (While teacher is inspecting a student correction of black board problem)

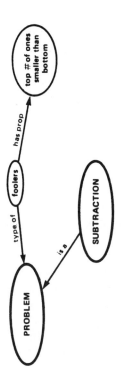

Now, since tens are always on this side [left] and ones are always on this side [right], I'm going to have my containers [of sticks] just like that. Tens here and ones there. (While teacher is setting up cans with grouped sticks and ungrouped sticks, just prior to student work with stick bundles.)

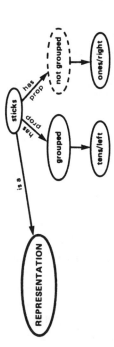

FIG. 4.1.   Construction of partial semantic nets from protocol.

of phrases, allowing researchers and others to readily "see" what was cognitively available in the lesson as a whole and how all the ideas were interrelated. When a series of lessons is converted into semantic nets, the nets can be compared to see the changing structure from lesson to lesson. Similarly, student knowledge as displayed in interviews can be converted into semantic nets and can then be compared to the teacher's nets (for corresponding lessons) to see which concepts and relationships the students grasped.

DESCRIPTIONS OF LESSONS

The eight videotaped lessons on subtraction with regrouping formed an instructional episode. Each lesson focused on a critical element and made connections to prior and future lessons. Each lesson is described by means of a summary of the activities that occurred and by a discussion of the concepts presented.

In the analyses, node-link diagrams display concepts and their connections as presented during the course of instruction. After each lesson description and its corresponding semantic net, results of student interviews on that day are presented and discussed using semantic nets. For each net, the concepts and links were empirically generated from the transcripts. The diagrams for all the lessons for both students and teacher follow the format shown in Fig. 4.2.

Fig. 4.2 shows the standard arrangement of the five basic nodes and links forming the core of all the semantic nets in this article. These represent the major concepts the teacher focused on during the instructional episode. SUBTRACTION has been placed at the center and is attached to the PROBLEM

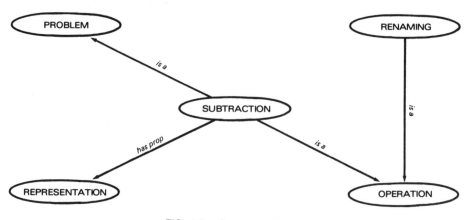

FIG. 4.2. Core semantic net.

node in the upper left. Subtraction is a problem, but it is also an OPERATION as shown in the lower right node. RENAMING, shown in the upper right, is also an operation, and learning to perform it was the object of these lessons. Finally, the net shows that subtraction problems can have multiple representations. The REPRESENTATION node is located in the lower left of the diagram.

The lessons examined in this study tended to focus on different parts of this diagram as the sequence progressed. For example, the first lesson emphasized representations whereas the second and third lessons tended to emphasize the renaming operation; the last set of lessons dealt rather extensively with different problem contexts. These five core nodes can be found in each semantic net for both the teacher's lessons and the students' midinstruction interviews. The core net permits us to compare across lessons as well as between a particular lesson and a student's grasp of its concepts and connections.

Lesson 1

The first lesson can be described as setting up a series of linkages between already existing knowledge and new knowledge, attaching new knowledge to old. Ms. Patrick first reviewed adding tens to units ($10 + 6 = 16$). She reviewed the method for two-digit subtraction without regrouping, adding at the end of this segment two fooler problems (i.e., those which required regrouping because the number in the ones column of the subtrahend was larger than the number in the ones column of the minuend). This review served to retrieve old skills and helped to make them accessible during instruction. She repeated the review three times using different representations of tens and ones. Moving from the concrete to the abstract, she first demonstrated with banded and loose popsicle sticks, then with felt strips and squares, and finally with two-digit numbers that were renamed and partitioned (i.e., $27 = 2$ tens and 7 ones, and $27 = 1$ ten and 17 ones).

During the lesson, Ms. Patrick cycled through several examples of subtraction using sticks while simultaneously writing the problems on the blackboard in a tens chart. (The tens chart consisted of a large cross with the word *tens* written in the upper left quadrant and the word *ones* in the upper right and with appropriate numerals inserted below.) In the examples, sticks were grouped into tens and ones, both of which were counted; amounts were "subtracted," "taken away," or "needed"; the partitioning operation resulted in a remaining set, which was the answer; and answers on the tens chart were checked against answers with sticks. The climax of this part of the lesson occurred at the end of this segment when Ms. Patrick gave the problem 26 minus 8 and asked the students to solve it using their sticks. The first student was stumped, but another, Baron, "invented" the solution

76

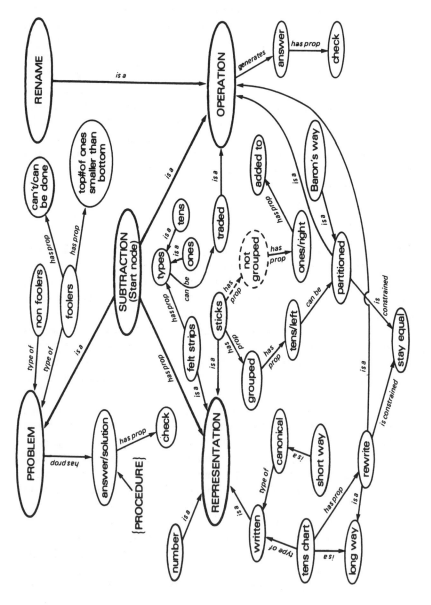

FIG. 4.3. Lesson 1, teacher.

of unbinding the sticks, as shown in Fig. 4.3. Interestingly, the children remembered the significance of the event and thereafter conceptually linked it to Baron. In this segment, the operational nature of subtraction emerged, practice was given, and concrete and written demonstrations were run in parallel, although not explicitly connected. This is shown in Fig. 4.3 by a convergence toward OPERATION. An example of an implied connection between demonstrations was the simultaneous writing of a 3 in the tens chart when three bundles of sticks were involved in a demonstration, even though Ms. Patrick did not specifically say, "We have three bundles of tens sticks, which is written as a 3 in the tens chart."

Throughout the lesson, Ms. Patrick orchestrated a build-up of excitement toward the resolution of this problem of how to solve subtraction problems in which the top number of ones was smaller than the number below it. She constructed for the children internally integrated islands of information but left open the small pieces of data that would have connected the concepts. For example, Ms. Patrick reviewed the notion that quantity can be represented by numbers, sticks, or felt strips, and added the notion that some representations could be renamed (or that there exist parallel operations that transform the initial state), although she did not quite say that a felt 10-strip could be renamed just like a number in the tens column.

The transcription of the teacher's planning protocol supports this interpretation of the first lesson:

> I'm going to drill with the children on how to add ten to one place numbers . . . some problems on the board . . . two-place subtraction . . . some foolers to warm up. Then I'm going to show them using the sticks again, move to the felt board and use 10-strips, and move from like more concrete to a little bit more abstract. They'll have some

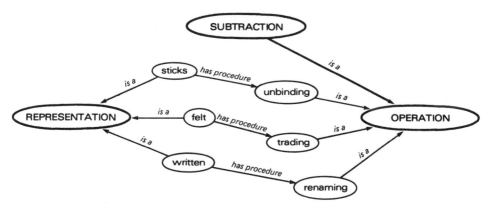

FIG. 4.4. Lesson 1, teacher–summary of operation.

papers, name numbers in a different way, to get used to renaming numbers that we'll need. This is all preliminary activities for regrouping in subtraction. If they're not too bored and fidgety, then I'm going to show them with the real problem straight to the abstract.

The teacher engaged in a set of activities that were designed to make available to her and to the students the tools that would be needed for the explanation. By the end of Lesson 1, several segments of knowledge had been presented, and these segments became the basis for constructing the semantic net.

Having described the surface characteristics of the lesson, we turn to a more conceptually driven description of the lessson content. In Fig. 4.3, the critical conceptual elements of Lesson 1 are displayed. (Names of key nodes appear in small capital letters within the discussion of each figure.) SUBTRACTION is a PROBLEM type that has two subtypes: NONFOOLERS and FOOLERS. Foolers are problems that have two properties. First, the TOP NUMBER IN THE ONES IS SMALLER THAN THE BOTTOM, and second, they CANNOT YET BE DONE but will soon be DOABLE by the students. All problems have ANSWERS or SOLUTIONS that can be CHECKED, and there are PROCEDURES associated with them. Subtraction is also an OPERATION, as shown in the lower right of the figure, and RENAMING, in the upper right corner, is also an operation. In the lower left corner are three REPRESENTATIONS Ms. Patrick used for subtraction problems: FELT STRIPS, STICKS, and WRITTEN. Each of these representations has associated properties and procedures.

Noteworthy here is the teacher's choice of referents for the lesson. To explain regrouping, she decided to use sticks and felt strips as well as numbers. The procedures associated with these concrete referents are similar in the sense that they both generate more *ones,* but they differ in the specific actions involved; and the actions, in turn, are driven by the nature of the concrete items. With sticks, the bundles of 10 can be unbundled to access ones that can then be moved around. In the case of felt strips, getting more ones can be achieved only by trading a felt strip for 10 single squares and these single squares must come from an outside supply (or "bank"). Using bundles of sticks for the initial demonstrations, then, was particularly suitable because of their self-contained procedural capability. Trading is a more complex procedure than partitioning, in part because of the temporary violation of equality involved.

The map shows how material was connected over the course of the lesson. The following excerpts from the lesson transcription show how the portion of the net on felt strips (connected to representations) was developed. It starts 31 min into the lesson, when Ms. Patrick says:

How many people saw something new that we learned right here? Did anybody notice anything new that we were able to do at the end of that part? Okay, we might try some more, and then you'll catch on. Something new's coming up here. I think Baron thought up a good idea, and it worked.

Now we are going to move from sticks to our, our FELT STRIPS. How much is this worth, Chuck? [10] This is worth a TEN. (holds up 10-strip)

How much is this worth right here, Terry? (holds up 1 square) A ONE. Remember that. Okay. I'm going to put a number on the board in picture form. (puts up five 10-strips and two squares)

Can you tell me what number . . . does that equal, Peter? [52]

Very good. That's 52. Now, 52 equals a certain number of tens and a certain number of ones.

Let's see if you can help me fill in the spaces here. (goes to horizontal write-out of problem, 52 = ___ tens and ___ ones) Fifty-two equals how many tens? Raise your hand. Peter. [5] Right. And how many ones, Tonia? [2] Two. Okay, that's usually the name for 52.

. . . Numbers can be called by different names and we are going to try to name 52 in a different way today, alright? You might say, "How are you going to do that?" But Baron helped us kind of get an idea of how we are going to do this.

Fifty-two is 5 tens and 2 ones because this side of the equal sign is the same—it's worth the same as this. (points to 52 and to right side) Now if we can get both sides of the equal sign to be worth the same, then it would be a different name for it . . .

So we're going to put 52 here again and we are going to try to find a different name.

Let's go over here. (points to display of felt strips) Remember what Baron said when she (another student) got stuck? He said she could take . . . the gum band . . . off to get more of what she needed.

Now let's say I needed more ones there. What could I do to get more ones from this picture, Lynn? [trade] Okay, what's it worth? [10]

Okay, so I can't just throw it away, can I? I have to kind of TRADE it so I'm going to trade it for 10 single squares. Now here's my 1, 2, 3, 4, 5, 6, 7, 8, 9, 10.

Now, I didn't really lose anything here because this is still worth that one I took away, right? (holds up a 10-strip) But now we have a new name for 52.

As can be seen, there was much more detail in the verbal description than appears in the net. However, the major components, felt strips and trading, are clearly indicated.

In summary, this lesson introduced renaming, partitioning, and trading operations. Students were taught that numbers and felt strips could be operated on, that both renaming tens for ones and trading tens for ones were operations, that both renaming and trading could be checked, and that the check required maintaining an equality of value across the operation. Figure 4.4 focuses on just the operaional portion of this first lesson and shows the parallel nature of UNBINDING, TRADING, and RENAMING. This would remain a core system for the rest of the eight lessons, both as a basis for legitimizing moves and as a basis for anticipating other moves. The students had been exposed to a long, detailed lesson. At the end of the lesson, they were supposed to know that foolers were doable and that trading, unbinding, and renaming were ways to get more ones. The full procedure connecting the renaming transformation to the problem of solving foolers, however, had not yet been spelled out.

Two students, Lynn and Rich, were interviewed after Lesson 1. Lynn was a student who grasped most of the lesson and who had come with some prior knowledge of the term *borrowing*. (Ms. Patrick had responded to Lynn's introduction of the borrowing label by telling the class that *borrowing* was another way of saying *renaming* and by further explaining in a supportive way that borrowing, like *carrying*, was an old-fashioned term. Thus, Ms. Patrick contextualized Lynn's vocabulary, while preserving the preferred lesson vocabulary.) During the stimulated recall, Lynn again pointed out that when the felt strips were traded, it was borrowing. (She did not volunteer this information for the banded sticks.) Lynn commented that taking the sticks apart was like making the lines on the felt strips. (She was referring to the nine lines of demarcation on the tens strip.) This was not quite accurate, but several other children in class displayed the same conceptual link, wanting to cut the felt strip rather than trade it and sensing that the partitioning notion associated with sticks was closer to the notion of cutting felt strips than to trading them. Lynn seemed to have grasped the key concepts of trading/borrowing and the parallelism of sticks and felt. What she lacked was automaticity in adding to units (thus she *computed* the addition of 10 to the units for each example worked) and in renaming two-digit numbers. She knew the material covered, but some parts were more readily accessible than others. A serendipitous note: For Lynn, at least, during the replay, concepts and their links were attached strongly to their actors in the actual lesson: "See that, June couldn't do that (26 minus 8), but I was thinking like Baron" (the boy who had suggested the solution of taking off the rubber bands.)

Figure 4.5 shows a net representing Lynn's knowledge as expressed in the stimulated recall after Lesson 1. The net shows that Lynn followed the STICKS portion of the lesson well and tied it to a notion of SUBTRACTION problems, not just to general or counting PROBLEMS. She added connections that were implied, but not present, in the original lesson. Lynn also caught the notion that problems have SOLUTIONS and that solutions can be CHECKED.

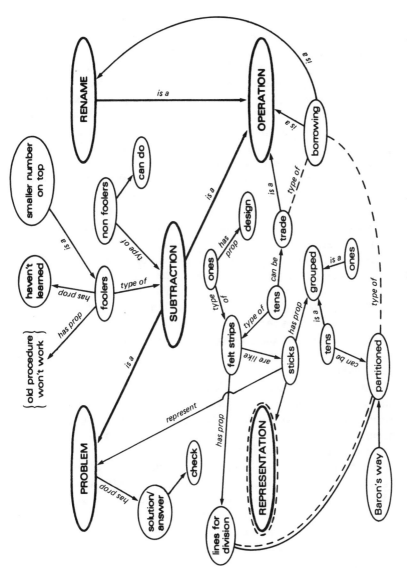

FIG. 4.5. Lesson 1, child-Lynn.

81

She recognized that FOOLERS had not yet been taught and that the old subtraction solution could not be applied when the problem had THE TOP NUMBER SMALLER THAN THE BOTTOM (in the ones column). Lynn's understanding of sticks was fairly complete. Sticks could be GROUPED, the TENS grouping could be PARTITIONED *and* Lynn considered partitioning as a type of BORROWING. This last is perhaps Lynn's most powerful contribution to the lesson material. It was never stated in the lesson, and the inference was not an obvious one. Lynn also seemed to realize that TRADING and RENAMING were similar operations; however, the interview was not deep enough to assure us of that. Missing from Lynn's interview is any discussion of the written REPRESENTATIONS or their connection to the concrete ones. Also missing is a description of checking for equal value as the process for checking solution correctness. Lynn's net is not as "neat" as the teacher's and some concepts seem oddly connected.

The second child whom we interviewed after the first lesson was Rich. Rich remembered the incident with Baron vividly and spontaneously told the interviewer about it. In Rich's representation (see Fig. 4.6), sticks could be not only grouped into TENS and ONES, PARTITIONED, and CHANGED, but partitioning was seen as a type of SUBTRACTION OPERATION that could result in a CORRECT ANSWER. This was a slight oversimplification because partitioning is only the first step in the solution; however, the important part for Rich was that he knew that the unbinding of the sticks was related to solving foolers. This is shown on the net by the connection between tens, partitioning, and answer in the bottom of the figure.

Rich was able to describe the nature of FELT STRIPS but not the operation of trading associated with them. However, Rich stated that the strips had a VALUE that could be expressed as a number. This idea had been implied, but not presented in the lesson. Rich was pleased to show the interviewer that he had command of the PROCEDURES that had been developed for RENAMING. He did not connect the five major nodes together by any verbal description, but he was generally less verbal than Lynn, so it is possible that Rich had made mental connections that he did not make explicit to us.

At the end of Lesson 1, two competent students followed most of the lesson's key elements and apparently developed connected concepts that were very similar to those presented by the teacher. Other than Lynn's apparent confusion about the demarcating lines on the felt strips being partitioning lines, we found no misconceptions. Both students clearly knew the characteristics of foolers and knew that the lessons were designed to teach solutions to such problems.

Lesson 2

The second lesson began with a quick review of trading felt strips. Ms. Patrick incorporated trading felt strips into a procedure for renaming

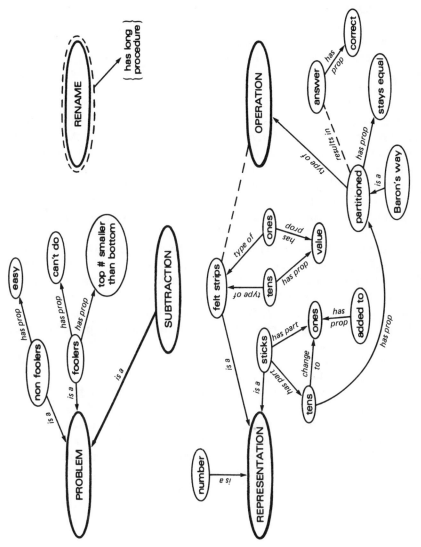

FIG. 4.6. Lesson 1, child–Rich.

83

numbers in a tens chart. She began with a display of felt strips, asking the students for the regular name of the five 10-strips and four squares. After a student responded with 54, she moved to the chalkboard and had the students fill in the number chart aloud, "54 equals 5 tens plus 4 ones." She moved back to the felt board to demonstrate trading. She reviewed the process of getting more ones by trading in a felt 10-strip for 10 felt squares. The next step was having the students fill in the new number chart, "54 equals 4 tens and 14 ones." Ms. Patrick repeated this demonstration twice with groups at the board, and then had the students practice it on four problems at their seats.

Ms. Patrick began to refine the renaming procedure. For example, for renaming 46, she taught the students to move directly to 3 tens and 16 ones, skipping the initial step of naming 46 as 4 tens and 6 ones. After having them do four problems as a group at the board, Ms. Patrick simplified the procedure further by introducing crossing out, the "short way."

After completing 10 examples of crossing out at the board, she wrote 82 minus 47 and told the students that fooler problems would no longer fool them. She led the class through the solution of 82 minus 47 and two more examples of subtraction problems that required regrouping. Ms. Patrick ended the presentation by telling the students that they now knew how to solve fooler problems. She explained to the class that the most important thing in solving a subtraction problem was to decide if the problem needed to have its top number renamed to get more ones. If more ones were needed, then they had to rename first, and then they would be able to subtract. In this way, she pulled foolers and the renaming procedure back into the mainstream of subtraction and added a constraint (the decision about whether to use renaming or not) that would inhibit overusing the regrouping procedure.

Figure 4.7 shows the net of the main body of the lesson. The renaming concept was expanded into an operative that paralleled the felt-strip trading. It generated more ones, retained the value, and answered foolers. In this lesson, Ms. Patrick emphasized that FELT STRIPS could be TRADED and that trading was a type of RENAMING. Renaming has the property that it generates MORE ONES, while it retains the EQUALITY of the number's value, and generates ANSWERS to FOOLERS. Further, several procedures were refined. The main point of the presentation was to SHORTEN the rename operation to its canonical form and to link that procedure to the concrete representation of felt and the problem of the foolers. RENAMING, in turn, was linked to WRITTEN forms of numbers as the principal REPRESENTATION system after the introductory part of the lesson that had reviewed felt strips. Another feature of this lesson was the notion that foolers COULD now be done. As

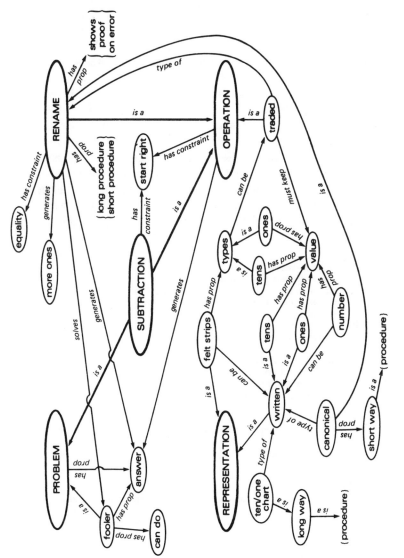

FIG. 4.7. Lesson 2, teacher.

85

Fig. 4.7 shows, there is a slight decrease in action around the representation node focusing now on felt and two written forms, and an expansion around the OPERATION node.

Throughout the first 2 days of subtraction, several computational procedures, as shown in Fig. 4.8 and 4.9, were introduced for handling renaming with different representation. On the nets, the presence of a procedure is noted by PROCEDURE enclosed in brackets. In Fig. 4.8 and 4.9, the procedures are laid out as a set of nested production systems that call on one another. In Fig. 4.9, the two parallel lists explicate the implied similarities across representations, and they also show how different the actual operations were from one another. This point is often lost when yokes are built between procedures in a concrete world and procedures in a numerical world.

After Lesson 2, a third student, Lem, was interviewed. He understood the process of trading tens for ones and knew that felt strips, numbers, and the tens/ones written form of representing quantities (chart) could all be used in subtraction. His concrete and computational knowledge were quite developed. In designing problems for the interviewer (something he did

Rename
    A.) If want to rename
        then write original number as tens and ones
        then write new number tens decremented by 1 ten
        then write new number ones incremented by ten

    B.) If want to rename
        then write new number as tens and ones

    C.) If want to rename (short)
        then cross out tens' number
        then decrement tens' number by 1
        then write new tens' number above old
        then cross off ones
        then increment ones by 10
        then write new ones' number above old

    D.) If want more ones
        then rename

Test. If want to check rename
        then add new tens to new ones if equal in value to old then checks
                or
        then count sticks or felt if equal in value to old then checks

Subtraction Foolers
    If want to subtract fooler
    then rename
    then subtract

FIG. 4.8. Procedures.

spontaneously), he was able to explicate the rules for generating a fooler, the rules for trading, and the constraint of maintaining equality when trading. His understanding of the regrouping algorithm was strong enough for him to correct all the interviewer's simulated errors in a solution of a fooler problem (81 minus 29). His corrections seemed to suggest a principled level of knowledge about the subtraction with regrouping procedure. For example, Lem articulated a constraint not mentioned in the lesson, namely that one could not subtract the top number from the bottom number, because it was "upside down." At the end of Lesson 2, Lem had learned everything from the teacher's lesson except for the connection between felt strips and written numerals.

Figure 4.10 shows the concepts that Lem had grasped by the end of Lesson 2 and his complex, intertwined network of ideas. FELT STRIPS, NUMBERS, and

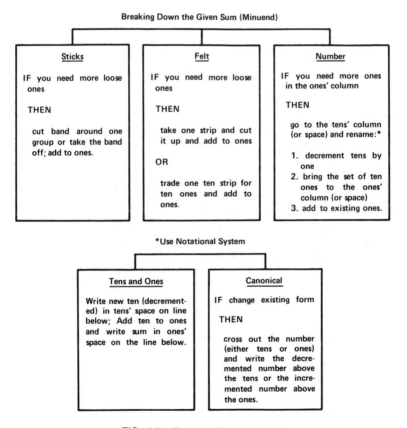

FIG. 4.9.   Rename-like procedures.

the TENS/ONES chart as a WRITTEN system all had the property that they could be part of SUBTRACTION. He realized that subtraction PROBLEMS had ANSWERS whether or not they were FOOLERS. Lem retained all the relevant information about foolers from the first lesson and formed a system of information around RENAMING in both the SHORT and LONG ways, although he was less comfortable using the short method. Lem's net looked very much like the teacher's, with the exception that Lem did not include a connection between felt strips and written numbers.

Lesson 3

Because Lesson 3 occurred on a Monday, Ms. Patrick began by asking the students to recall Friday's math lesson. For homework, Ms. Patrick had assigned problems that gave practice in the long form of renaming:

$$XY = X \text{ tens and } Y \text{ ones}$$
$$XY = (X - 1) \text{ tens and } (Y + 10) \text{ ones}$$

She undertook a rapid review of the renaming procedure at the blackboard, beginning with one example using a number sentence and ending with four examples using the cross-out (short way) method to which students responded chorally. At this point Ms. Patrick explicitly connected the trading of felt strips with the renaming procedure. Next, 6 students were called to the board to practice the abbreviated renaming procedure, and the class chorally corrected the answers.

Ms. Patrick was continually careful to ask students to explain *why* they had to regroup certain problems. After the six practice problems in renaming, Ms. Patrick inserted a subtraction problem that did not require regrouping (84 minus 61). The students easily recognized that they could subtract it without renaming. Once again, Ms. Patrick asked why this problem could be subtracted without renaming. This emphasis on understanding why something was done and on proving the legitimacy of various moves were hallmarks of the lessons. The *why* and proof behaviors moved the lessons beyond simple procedural exercises to a more conceptual level of instruction.

Ms. Patrick then had the class publicly practice 18 subtraction problems (both regular and regrouping). She called individual students to the board and then had the group chorally correct each solution. After the public practice, she had students do individual seat work. For this she passed out paper, had the students fold it into 16 parts, and began the practice segment

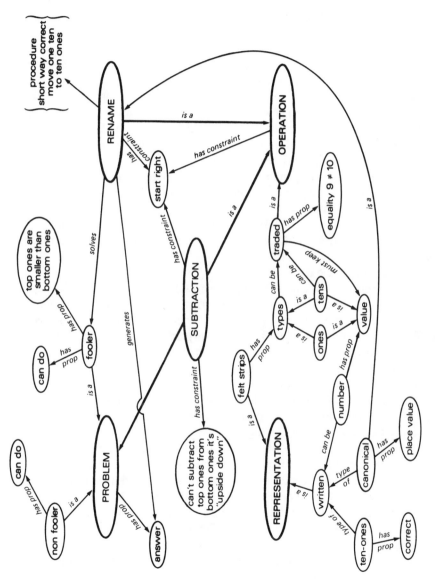

FIG. 4.10. Lesson 2, child–Lem.

89

by guiding them through a few problems. The students worked independently on several more problems, some of which required regrouping.

Figure 4.11 displays the semantic net of the lesson that emphasized RENAMING. Various properties of renaming were discussed, such as its relationship to ADDITION, the VALUE consistency, the two procedures, and constraints. The figure shows the places where renaming was connected to SUBTRACTION PROBLEMS. Some vocabulary words surrounding subtraction problems (e.g., DIFFERENCE and MINUS) were introduced. In comparing this figure to those for the previous two lessons, we can see that most of the action has migrated to the PROBLEM and RENAME nodes in the upper portion of the figure. Rename as a concept has been more clearly defined and its relationship to the operation of REGROUPING within ADDITION has been mentioned. The multiple representations have been narrowed to focus on the written procedure. In general, the figure is less dense than the figure for the first 2 days. This phenomenon is consistent with the activity-level description of the lesson.

After the third lesson, 3 children were interviewed using a stimulated recall format. The first child, Chuck, was the lowest performing child in the class. During the first 2 days, he had clearly been attentive, but his level of engagement was unclear.

Before turning to the figure that represents Chuck's explicit knowledge of math, we should note his more general characteristics. Like all the students, he was interested in our presence and in the videotaping procedures. He was a surprisingly nervous and tense child — surprisingly because his outward demeanor was placid. However, the first topic he discussed with the interviewer was the search for his lost homework over the weekend, and the second was his fear of getting answers wrong at the board. Chuck was pleased that he had mastered the long form of renaming and noted that this type of renaming (done on the homework) was different from the type of renaming (short way) done during the lesson.

The most notable feature of Chuck's interview was his language. More than any other child's, it seemed choppy and disconnected, with little or no external trace between topics or concepts. this is reflected in his semantic net shown in Fig. 4.12. There are several pairs of relations on the figure that do not connect to anything else. For example, he thought that ZEROS were unnecessary (a misapplication of the teacher's statement about leftmost zeros), that TEN was always NINE PLUS ONE, that basic facts generated CORRECT answers, and so on. Chuck's knowledge was sometimes wrong, and if correct, always brittle; he tended to overapply rules. Although Chuck clearly knew the long form of RENAMING, when faced with a nonfooler subtraction problem in the interview, he classed it as a "FOOLER" and started to regroup, before self-correcting and subtracting accurately. Chuck also recognized the importance of knowing the basic facts, although he some-

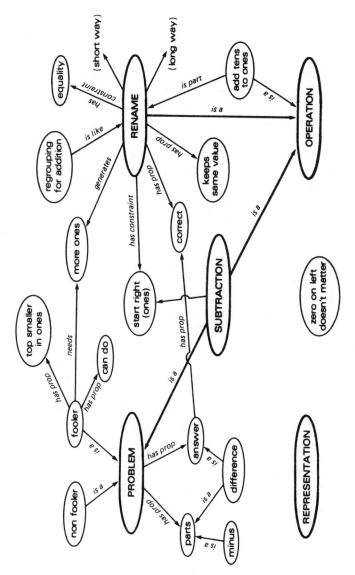

FIG. 4.11. Lesson 3, teacher.

times got them wrong. He frequently called SUBTRACTION (problems and operations) ADDITION, although he would perform the subtraction OPERATION correctly.

Terry was the second student interviewed after Lesson 3. She was another low-ability student. Her stimulated recall interview (see Fig. 4.13) revealed fairly accurate concepts about the OPERATIONAL aspects of SUBTRACTION and the role of RENAMING; however, the teacher's introduction of the term REGROUPING ("I thought that was for adding") had confused her. She used the ambiguous term AND as an operator for both ADDITION and subtraction. Terry, like Chuck, was overly sensitive to environmental cues and was convinced that public failure (her own) was stupid and that another child's need to count STICKS (i.e., slash marks) was BABYISH. She was deeply concerned about her own errors and was not consoled in the stimulated recall when we showed her doing work correctly. The net representing her thinking has the same disconnected quality as Chuck's. Three days into the lesson sequence she showed none of the connections between PROBLEM, solution, checking, and operation that were present in the teacher's presentation and in Lynn's *first* lesson representation. Terry did expound rather clearly on the transformation of a number — getting MORE ONES FROM the TENS — although she often misread NUMBERS by REVERSING them (reading 35 as 53 for example). The main feature of her net is sparseness.

By contrast, Willis's interview demonstrated that he had a somewhat more coherent conceptual net for lesson 3 (Fig. 4.14). Willis was very bright child but soft-spoken and somewhat terse in his responses. He reported SUBTRACTION as both a PROBLEM and an OPERATION. He linked the TRADE notions of FELT STRIPS with the RENAMING operation of WRITTEN numbers. He also grasped the aside about LEFT-MOST ZEROS.

Figure 4.14 shows the connection Willis made concerning the *purpose* of renaming, which was to alter a FOOLER by generating MORE ONES and make it DOABLE by normal subtraction operations. However, Willis's net does not resemble the teacher's because it focuses on aspects of the problems to be done rather than on constraints on the rename operation that the teacher emphasized. To some extent, Willis's thinking anticipated the next lesson (see Fig. 4.15), which shifted emphasis from the procedures to the class of problems the procedures help to solve.

Lesson 4

Ms. Patrick began Lesson 4 by applying the subtraction-with-regrouping algorithm to two "real-life" problems. She had the students calculate how old Dr. Martin Luther King would have been if he were alive, by subtracting 1929 from 1984. She worked through the problem orally at the board, utilizing individual and choral responses. Because this problem generated

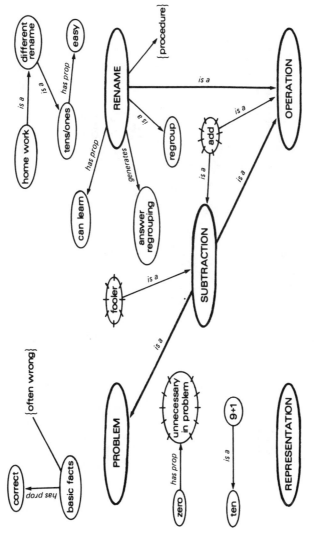

FIG. 4.12. Lesson 3, child–Chuck.

94

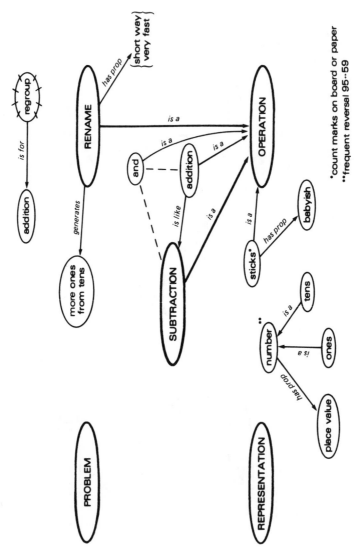

FIG. 4.13. Lesson 3, child—Terry.

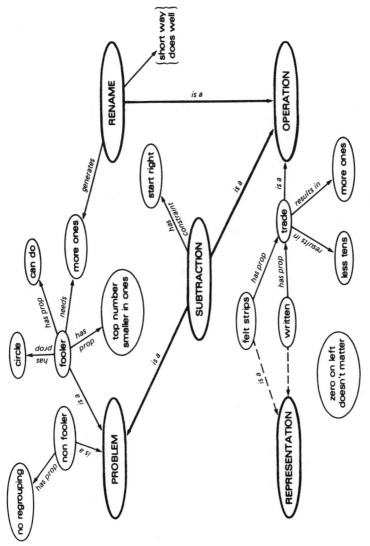

FIG. 4.14. Lesson 3, child—Willis.

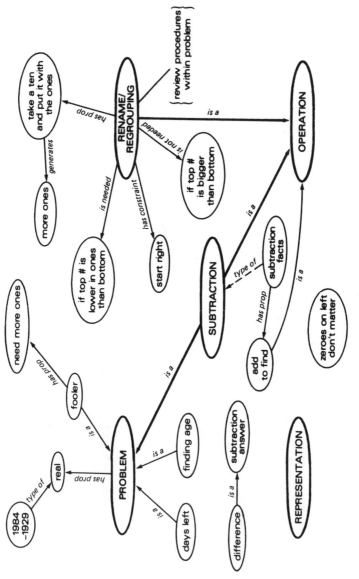

FIG. 4.15. Lesson 4, teacher.

two zeros to the left of the answer, Ms. Patrick reviewed the role of left-most zeros. The other applied problem was calculating how many days were left in the month (31 minus 17). Ms. Patrick moved into the next phase of her lesson by asking a student to recall two important things she had written on the board near the end of the previous lesson. After a student successfully recalled that learning basic facts and starting in the ones place were the important strategies, Ms. Patrick had the students work individually at their desks, correcting (as if they were the teacher) a ditto containing a hypothetical student's answers to 30 problems, 12 of which were wrong. Ms. Patrick recorded the number of errors they found and the students enjoyed playing teacher.

The next segment of the lesson began with a brief but thorough review of the subtraction-with-regrouping algorithm and the reasons for each step. Ms. Patrick also reviewed the meaning of the term *difference,* when a student was unable to respond to her query, "What's the difference?" Ms. Patrick then had the students practice doing subtraction problems, making use of the folded papers they had begun using in the previous lesson. When these four problems were completed, she had the students correct them orally.

Next, the class discussed the textbook's pictorial display of blocks – some loose and some in bars of 10. It showed how to solve subtraction-with-regrouping problems, both in blocks and in the numerical cross-out notation. The students practiced 20 of these problems, working individually at their desks for 20 min, while Ms. Patrick "traveled" and did some tutoring. (*Traveling* is a specific pedagogical behavior. See Leinhardt, 1977; Leinhardt, Weidman, & Hammond, 1987.)

Because this was primarily a review lesson, the concepts covered were relatively simple. Fig. 4.15 displays the semantic net of the lesson. This figure is similar to that of Lesson 3 (Fig. 4.11) in that almost all the nodes are now located at the top of the figure in association with PROBLEMS and RENAME. Although this was a review, several new features were added. Using ADDING TO FIND answers to SUBTRACTION FACTS problems was suggested as a method for solving them. The movement of a TEN TO THE ONES was verbally emphasized as a way of generating MORE ONES, which are needed to solve FOOLERS. ("Take a ten and put it with the ones . . . trot that ten over to the ones and add it on.") The circumstances under which renaming should and should not be employed were also emphasized in this lesson. (Ms. Patrick had a student explain that a problem needs to be renamed if "THE TOP NUMBER IS LOWER THAN THE BOTTOM NUMBER [in the ones column].")

During Lesson 4, two children, Lem and Nicki, were given in-class think-aloud interviews. During Lem's think-aloud interview, he showed considerable skill in utilizing the subtraction-with-regrouping algorithm (compared with his skill in Lesson 2) and he was able to explain the reasons for implementing it. He was now adept at using the short form of subtraction with regrouping and could even do some problems in his head. His proficiency in recalling subtraction facts was quite high, although near the end of the interview he had to struggle to retrieve the answer for 8 minus 3. At one point, he inverted the order of a subtraction statement, saying 2 minus 3 is 1 when he meant 3 minus 2 is 1 or perhaps 2 *from* 3 is 1, indicating a possible language problem. Like so many students, he had trouble responding to the request to read the *whole* problem, focusing instead on the columns (i.e., for 46 minus 38, he said the problem was 6 minus 8). He experienced some difficulty with a problem that had a zero in the ones place of the minuend; for another problem he began subtracting in the tens column before self-correcting to start in the ones. During this lesson, Lem demonstrated the ability to check his subtraction answers with addition, a skill not yet covered in the context of subtraction with regrouping, and he was also able to correct another student's error.

Lem's second interview (Fig. 4.16) showed some interesting changes when compared with his first interview (Fig. 4.10). The RENAME operation assumed considerable importance and clarity with several properties attached; the ANSWER node also became prominent. Lem reflected the shift in emphasis from the lower to upper portions of the net, a shift that occurred in Ms. Patrick's lessons as she moved from many REPRESENTATIONS to the focus on the written numeric task of SUBTRACTION. Lem also demonstrated associational skills both in terms of relating ADDING facts to subtraction (note the loop of subtraction, answer, CHECKING, and addition) in relating MONEY knowledge to key numbers that turned up in the lesson. Lem was able to verbalize an important but subtle portion of the lesson—namely, that FOOLER problems had the property of needing MORE ONES if they were to be solved using subtraction. Lem thought about his math; he didn't just do it.

Nicki was interviewed for the first time during Lesson 4. She was able to perform the renaming procedure correctly most of the time except when she overapplied the algorithm by occasionally renaming a problem that did not require renaming. She had trouble with one renaming problem when she incremented the tens rather than decrementing them. She could perform the entire subtraction-with-regrouping procedure on most occasions, except for the renaming errors and one sign interpretation error. Except for thinking that $10 - 8 = 18$ was correct, she successfully identified and corrected all the other errors on the ditto and many other student errors in class. Her skill in answering math-facts items was high, and she seemed to have a fluid sense of number. For example, she was unusually sensitive to reversible math facts embedded in various regrouping problems (e.g., in $94 - 36 = 58$ and $90 - 56 = 34$, she noticed that after regrouping, both these problems had 8, 3, and 5 in their tens columns). Essentially, she solved most

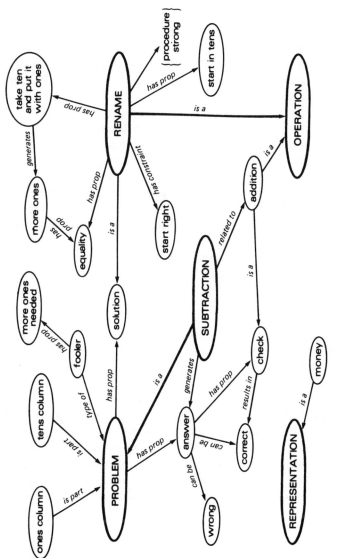

FIG. 4.16. Lesson 4, child–Lem.

99

problems correctly. She puzzled about notation issues. For example, she worried about the position for a single-digit answer to a two-digit subtraction problem, wondering if it should "go in the middle." Evidently she was insecure about the role of place in place value and its notation, and was slightly distracted by noncritical features of the problem.

Nicki's major difficulty was in reading. Many words in the textbook and on the board were difficult for her and she frequently asked the interviewer to tell her a word. By the end of Lesson 4, however, she felt comfortable with her ability to solve foolers, said she liked this new procedure, and thought it was easy.

Figure 4.17 is a net displaying the main elements of Nicki's knowledge after Lesson 4. The key feature is the weighting of her net toward the PROBLEM node. Both her RENAME and ANSWER nodes were somewhat sparse and not well connected to SUBTRACTION or problem. For example, the rename node does not connect through MORE ONES to fooler, and answer is not connected to problem or rename or check, as it was in Lem's. She retained both the BORROW and RENAME labels but her responses were not elaborate. She also understood the relevant distinction between FOOLERS and NONFOOLERS. Nicki's understanding and skill in utilizing the renaming PROCEDURE were strong. She knew the importance of renaming in the tens column first to generate more ones.

Lesson 5

This lesson was a review that began with a drill on subtraction facts using flash cards bearing problems of two-digit minus one-digit numbers. After flashing 53 cards, Ms. Patrick moved into a review of all the types of math skills the students had worked on that year. Then she passed out a work sheet with review problems requiring those skills; the students worked on this individually at their desks. The lesson had somehow led the children to overfocus on subtraction, as evidenced by their subtracting in addition problems. In the postlesson interview, the teacher understood the implications of the students' errors, found the phenomenon interesting, and was ready to do some repair work in future lessons. No children were interviewed for this review lesson, and no semantic net was constructed.

Lesson 6

This lesson began with a review of math facts and families, by having students generate two addition and two subtraction equations from sets of three numbers that Ms. Patrick had written on the board (e.g., for 9, 4, and 5, the equations were $5 + 4 = 9$, $4 + 5 = 9$, $9 - 5 = 4$, and $9 - 4 = 5$). Each student had an opportunity to solve 1 of the 16 problems.

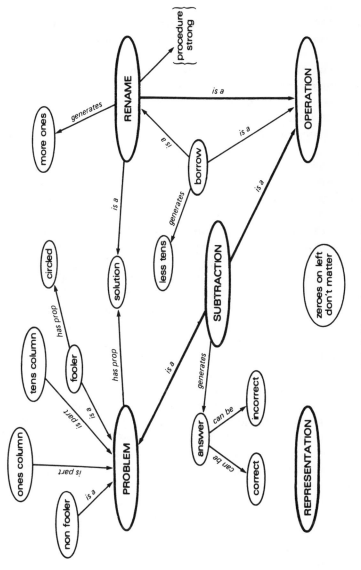

FIG. 4.17. Lesson 4, child–Nicki

Ms. Patrick introduced money as another concrete manipulative to demonstrate combining and trading tens and ones. The students practiced translating dimes and pennies into numeric values and trading dimes for pennies to calculate the trade of tens for ones. Utilizing the money to demonstrate regrouping, they then practiced some addition and subtraction problems, working first publicly at the board and then individually at their seats.

At this point, Ms. Patrick showed the children how to check their answers to subtraction problems by using addition. In this demonstration she again reviewed that the term *difference* meant the answer to a subtraction problem. The final segment of the lesson involved practicing a series of addition and subtraction problems that students worked individually at their seats.

Figure 4.18 is a semantic net representing the concepts and connections from Lesson 6. It shows the new REPRESENTATION Ms. Patrick used, MONEY, and its trading property, TRADING being an OPERATION that is like RENAMING. The lesson also heavily emphasized the relationship between SUBTRACTION and ADDITION. The following new concepts were introduced: the relationship between money and WRITTEN problems; addition as an operation that can be used to CHECK subtraction; addition as part–part JOINING to yield a whole BIGGER than the parts; and subtraction as part–whole separation, yielding a part SMALLER than the whole. Much time was spent on the idea that a set of THREE NUMBERS could be rearranged to generate four different problems. This property of PROBLEMS was expanded to show that it worked for larger two-digit numbers as well as for simple subtraction facts. This led to a discussion of the property of rewriting one problem in multiple ways and of the inverse relationship between addition and subtraction that allows addition to be a check on subtraction. The addition node, with its connections to the problem and operation nodes, indicates that this lesson provided both an expansion of the subtraction lessons as well as a reembedding of subtraction into the larger additive context.

Lesson 6 was packed with extensions of the basic work that had already been covered. Ms. Patrick felt that the lesson did not go well and blamed this failure on her use of so many concrete manipulatives. The observers felt that perhaps the lesson did not go well because of the introduction of money, a new, concrete representation for regrouping tens and ones. In the analysis of the lesson, there seemed to be a broader reason. Although the students certainly had no initial problem with money, Ms. Patrick introduced too much new material. She worked with the following *new* information in this lesson:

1. Creation of four problems from three numbers (5, 4, 9).
2. Using dimes and pennies as tens and ones.

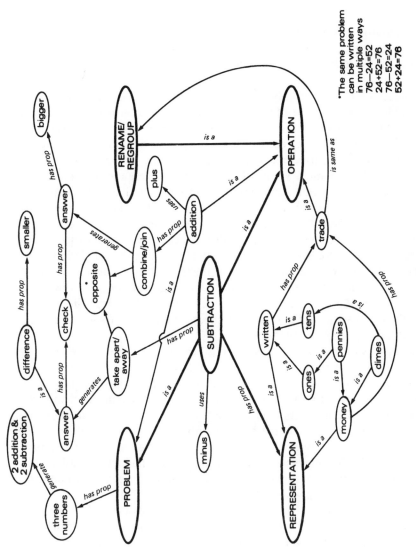

FIG. 4.18. Lesson 6, teacher.

*The same problem can be written in multiple ways
76—24=52
24+52=76
76—52=24
52+24=76

3. Trading dimes for pennies and vice versa.
4. Adding and subtracting money.
5. Adding as part–part joining, yielding wholes larger than parts.
6. Subtracting as part–whole separation, yielding parts smaller than the whole.
7. Addition as inverse of subtraction.
8. Rewriting problems from horizontal to vertical form.
9. Using addition as a check on subtraction.

The lesson went smoothly and students responded correctly most of the time. However, the focus of the lesson (adding and subtracting with money) was lost in the quantity and detail of other material. When students tried to work independently, they consistently ignored sign operators. Ignoring sign indicators is, of course, endemic to the American blocked curriculum (2 weeks of addition and 2 weeks of subtraction), where the students tend to focus on the operation from the first problem and use it to solve all subsequent problems on the exercise. However, Ms. Patrick, along with other good teachers, teach against this tendency and are usually successful. In reviewing the lesson, there was evidence that two goals competed: (a) the need to move the set of lessons on subtraction along to completion versus (b) the desire to cover all the nuances of the topic. Interestingly, Ms. Patrick clearly recognized that the conflict in goals had occurred, and during the replay of the tape, she said that she would have restructured the lesson to stop before discussing the notion of checking answers, if she had realized what was happening at the time.

Terry was interviewed in class during Lesson 6. She had some difficulty distinguishing between addition and subtraction operations and in responding to plus or minus signs with the correct procedure. At first, when working on generating two addition and two subtraction problems from three single-digit numbers, she focused on only one of the numbers and generated a problem using that number with any other two numbers. As the lesson progressed, however, she became quite skilled at the three-number task. When money problems were introduced, she had trouble using coins to calculate answers to subtraction-with-regrouping problems, although she knew that a dime was worth 10 pennies.

Figure 4.19 displays Terry's understanding of Lesson 6. She had three shaky areas. First, in counting pennies and dimes, she did not distinguish between counting the *number* of coins and counting the *value* of the coins. This is shown on the net as a property (COUNT TOGETHER BY ONES) connecting pennies and dimes. Of course, *countability* is an attribute of both pennies and dimes, and Terry correctly used that feature—thus treating money as chips; but counting numbers of coins was not the point of that exercise. It is quite possible that none of the other children distinguished between value

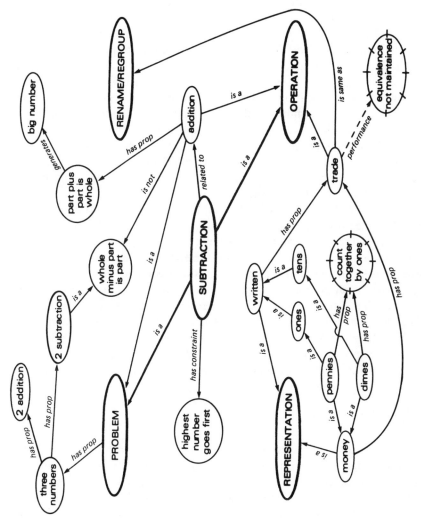

FIG. 4.19. Lesson 6, child—Terry.

105

and quantity, but they always counted value rather than quantity and so were not "caught." Terry knew DIMES are like TENS, and PENNIES are like ONES. She quickly switched to a combined count of tens and ones when asked to do so by the interviewer, but she did not start that way.

Her second shaky area was in trading for more pennies. Instead of trading in 1 dime for 10 pennies, she exchanged the dime for only the number of pennies she needed to solve the problem. This is a common error made with *manipulatives*. Again, when the question was posed more clearly (by the teacher), she quickly traded a dime for 10 pennies. As in her first interview (Fig. 4.13, Lesson 3), Terry still had some difficulty distinguishing between addition and subtraction problems. She used the term "and" to mean both minus and plus, although she easily grasped that SUBTRACTION is related to ADDITION as explicated in the lesson, and she generated for the interviewer sets of parallel facts (e.g., $5 + 4 = 9$, $4 + 5 = 9$, $9 - 5 = 4$, and $9 - 4 = 5$) with both small and large numbers. Terry's disregarding the sign operator seemed to occur because the part of the problem-solving routine that she used to select procedures was not part of her problem reading, but part of the total task environment (i.e., whatever procedure was used for the first one or two problems on the page).

In contrasting her second interview with her first, it seems that Terry's ideas had become more detailed and more elaborate. Furthermore, the net shows that she now had more connections between concepts. The relationship between adding and subtracting is a good example of these connections. In the first interview, she was troubled because she thought that regrouping was for addition and that renaming was for subtraction; but in the second, TRADING, REGROUPING, and RENAMING were all seen as equivalent. Further, the precise relationship between the role of the BIG NUMBER (whole) in ADDITION (i.e., the ANSWER) and in SUBTRACTION (i.e., the start place) was now quite clear to her.

Lesson 7

Lesson 7 was another review of the use of subtraction with regrouping, and this knowledge was practiced by working on a variety of addition and subtraction problems. Ms. Patrick began by reading a long, involved story problem. The students listened and chorally responded to her questions. Their tasks were first to determine whether the problems required addition or subtraction and then to calculate the answers. Following the story problem, she orally drilled the students on basic addition and subtraction facts. The next segment of the lesson reviewed transforming horizontal problems to their vertical form. This set of problems simultaneously reviewed two-digit addition and subtraction problems, some of which required regrouping. Ms. Patrick began this review by calling for choral responses to problems she presented on the board, and then she called groups of students to the board to work on more problems. After this public practice, she passed out a work sheet consisting of 14 two-digit, vertical addition and subtraction problems, some of which required regrouping. She had students begin to work on a few of these problems publicly, and then she had them work individually while she monitored and tutored.

Figure 4.20 displays Ms. Patrick's seventh lesson on SUBTRACTION with REGROUPING, which included an extension of the subtraction-with-regrouping procedure, namely REWRITING HORIZONTAL PROBLEMS VERTICALLY. The instruction on rewriting horizontal problems in vertical form, although it may appear to be primarily procedural, actually made use of the whole-part concepts associated with subtraction that she had discussed in Lesson 6. For example, by saying that the LARGER NUMBER GOES ON TOP, rather than that the *first* number goes on the top, she emphasized the attribute of the WHOLE number on which the students needed to focus. The net is sparse, showing that little new material was introduced.

Chuck was interviewed for the second time in class during Lesson 7. There were three examples within the think-aloud interview in which Chuck demonstrated that he knew when to regroup and could articulate the rule. Further, he was able to explain to the class a subtraction-with-regrouping problem step by step. His confusion about zeros as place holders had been resolved; he now knew that erasing zeros on the right was not permitted.

Figure 4.21 displays the knowledge Chuck expressed during the lesson. Compared with his earlier interview, some of his prior confusions seemed to have been resolved (see Fig. 4.12). He knew when to use ZERO. He knew when and how to RENAME. In class he followed the REWRITING and SIGN attention exercises. Unlike Lem, who insisted on understanding, Chuck's self-demands for understanding were minimal. Chuck still operated in a mild cloud of faith, so that if the teacher said something, he assumed it was "good" and for his benefit. The importance of STARTING IN THE ONES place was still being emphasized and when asked why the teacher told him that Chuck responded characteristically, "Oh, I think because, uh, you could start off, I think because you start off good that way." Chuck was attentive and tried to follow the lesson, but he was not absorbed. His net is still sparse and although more connected than before, it still has little islands of information that appear disconnected to the main structure of knowledge.

Lesson 8

Lesson 8 began with a review that responded to an error seen in several homework papers. Specifically, in a problem like 43 minus 9, some students had forgotten to subtract in the tens column (or perhaps to record in the

108

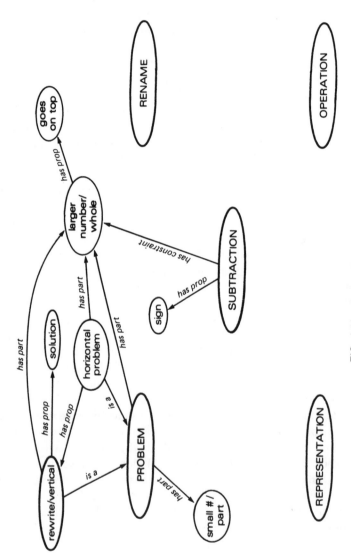

FIG. 4.20. Lesson 7, teacher.

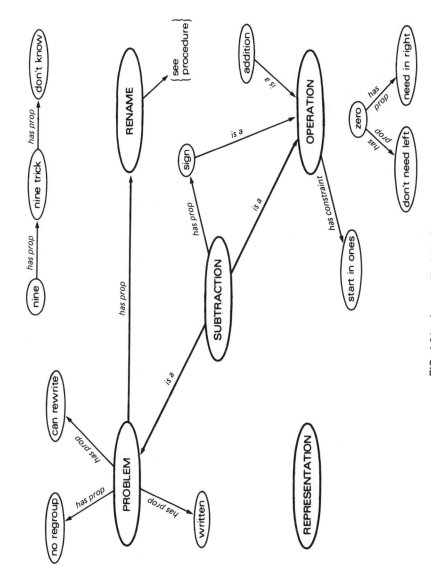

FIG. 4.21. Lesson 7, child—Chuck.

answer space) after regrouping and subtracting in the ones (i.e., their answer was 4 instead of 34). After discussing three problems, Ms. Patrick had the students practice their basic addition and subtraction skills with a game. The next segment of the lesson involved working on word problems to further develop their problem-solving skills. The students' tasks included (a) determining the facts of the problem, (b) selecting the correct operation, and finally (c) calculating the solution. After having the students practice several such problems orally, Patrick handed out a work sheet containing more word problems. They worked on the first few of these as a class and then continued to work individually at their desks.

Lesson 8 was a fairly complex lesson on problem-solving strategies. It was an expansion of a series of lessons on problem solving that had occurred throughout the year. The lesson dealt with a conceptual framework very different from that in the other lessons on subtraction with regrouping, namely, a framework based on problem-solving strategies. A semantic net for this lesson would have to build on that problem-solving framework; therefore, no net is presented. However, we have considered it here because it embedded subtraction with regrouping into yet another more complex mathematical environment.

Two students, Nicki and Lynn, were interviewed about Lesson 8. Nicki's interview occurred after the lesson in a stimulated recall. She was able to explain other students' errors in cases where they had neglected to complete the subtraction procedure after performing the regrouping step and, thus, had subtracted only in the ones column. She understood place value and knew that equality meant "equal things, equal size." She showed a good use of the counting-on strategy for solving subtraction facts, and she related the reversibility of addition and subtraction to the use of subtraction to find the missing addend in problems of addition. Vocabulary in this lesson, as in Lesson 4, was a difficult area for her. She did not know the meaning of terms such as *clue* or *label*. However, when simpler language was used, she showed skill at identifying the clues in a story problem, knowing which operation was needed, and describing the answer in terms of the units/objects involved. She converted story problems into numeric problems quickly and solved them, although she could not explicate the steps. She now understood that regrouping was not always used in subtraction. She had no trouble rewriting horizontal problems in vertical form and knew how and why it was done. Her skill in using subtraction with regrouping was high and was solidly embedded in her mathematical thinking.

The main features of Nicki's interview are displayed in Fig. 4.22. Nicki had a well-established understanding of the procedures for SUBTRACTION with REGROUPING, as well as most of the basic concepts. By this time, she had appropriately attached the subtraction-with-regrouping concepts to some of the relevant issues in the STORY PROBLEMS. For example, she recognized that

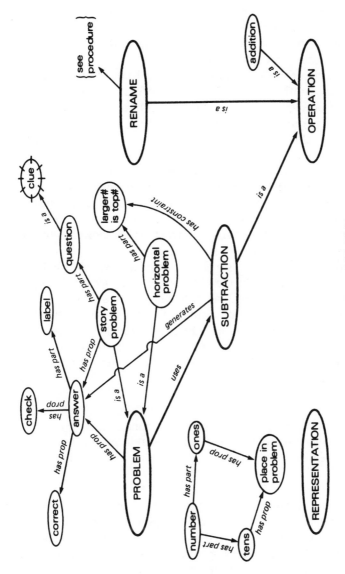

FIG. 4.22. Lesson 8, child—Nicki.

111

ANSWERS to story problems required using the same OPERATIONS used in the numeric problems. As to the meaning of the word CLUE, she had never heard it before and made the assumption, based on the contextual use of the word in the lesson, that clue meant the QUESTION asked in the story. She understood that in REWRITING HORIZONTAL PROBLEMS VERTICALLY, the LARGER NUMBER GOES ON TOP. She also had a firm grasp of the notions that answers could be CHECKED and could be proven CORRECT.

Lynn participated in an in-class think-aloud interview during Lesson 8. She was very proficient at picking out the clue words that determined whether the problem required addition or subtraction. (Note: Clues were quite different from simplistic "key words.")

Throughout this lesson, Lynn stayed one or two steps ahead of the teacher. She knew all the procedures and even the modified rules for thier use. the net for Lynn (Fig. 4.23) shows her knowledge skeletally because so much information was internalized in every statement or action. During the class she solved word problems correctly and ahead of the teacher. She knew when and how to regroup and no longer distinguished between fooler and nonfooler problems. As the net of her interview shows, Lynn integrated a considerable amount of information about PROBLEMS, NUMBERS, and SUBTRACTION. As with Nicki's net, the emphasis is on problems, their ANSWERS, their PARTS, and the fact that they can be CHECKED. Lynn's net also has a little NUMBER "island" that incorporates notions of PLACE VALUE that are quite similar to Nicki's. The commentary accompanying her thinking about the elements in story problems indicated a multilevel mental representation and a delightful appreciation of the content. The following quote shows Lynn's comments (in brackets) on parts of the teacher's oral reading of two story problems:

> Charles used 32 sticks to build a house . . . [Boy, that's a few sticks to be building a house.] . . . and 18 sticks to build a fence. [Small fence.] . . . LaTanya washed 22 dinner dishes. She dropped four . . . [ooo!] . . . of them and they broke. [Ooo! LaTanya's Mommy gonna git her.]

Interestingly, although Lynn often worried about a large number of things other than the lesson, she could always pick up the stream of content without missing anything. A partial list of Lynn's nonacademic concerns expressed in class included: going to sleep at night; finding a seventh step missing from a list; counting the letters in her name (20); and correcting the pronunciation of *qua* from *ka* to *kwa* (one of the syllables in one of her three names); worrying about dry skin and white "yuck" on her arms; sticks, ticks, and bugs; relative length of her finger nails and those of other family members; the different colors of her sweater under different lights; and

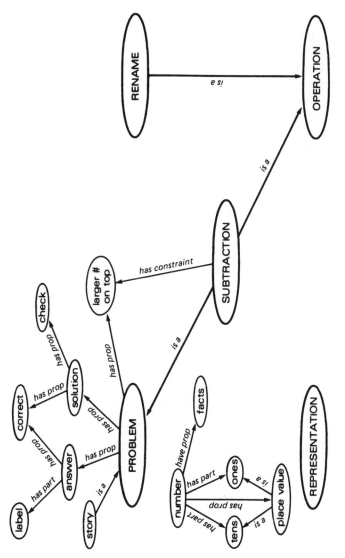

FIG. 4.23. Lesson 8, child—Lynn.

113

being too hot and deciding when to take off her sweater. In spite of these multiple competing interests, Lynn always followed the lesson. (See Leinhardt & Putnam, 1987, for a discussion of what this implies for the learning functions of the child.) By the end of Lesson 8, both Lynn and Nicki displayed high levels of competence and understanding of the subtraction-with-regrouping algorithm.

A comparison of the students' semantic nets for each lesson with those of the teacher provides some evidence of the impact of these lessons on the students' knowledge and on the structure of that knowledge. Despite the necessarily fragmentary nature of data gleaned from students during in-class think-aloud protocols and from video-based stimulated recalls, some trends emerged.

The higher ability students grasped more of the lesson content than did lower ability students, had fewer misconceptions, and were often able to provide more elaborate explanations for a concept or connection than was explicated in the lesson. Focusing on Lesson 3, for example, where three students were interviewed, we see that Willis, a high-ability student (see Fig. 4.14), had more of the presented concepts and connections (see teachers's net, Fig. 4.11) than did Chuck and Terry, two low-ability students (see Figs. 4.12 and 4.13). As can be seen from the semantic nets, Willis had no misconceptions, whereas Chuch and Terry each had one or more (see hatch-marked nodes on Figs. 4.12 and 4.13). Both lower ability students had meager, if any, concepts connected to the PROBLEM node, whereas Willis had considerable richness surrounding the notions of FOOLER and NONFOOLER problems. In fact, his net indicates an extra connection that does not appear on the teacher's net for that lesson, namely, that NONFOOLERS need NO REGROUPING. Most of the core concepts, however, were in place for all students, and the teacher's repetition and consistency helped even the weaker students become competent by the end of the lesson sequence.

RESULTS OF STUDENTS' PREINSTRUCTION AND POSTINSTRUCTION MEASURES

To assess the impact of these lessons on the students in a different way, we turn now to a discussion of the tests and interviews that were administered before and after the entire instructional episode.

Computational Test Performance

Prior to instruction, the students took a 14-term chapter pretest (see Table 4.1). Five items, Part A, were two-digit subtraction problems requiring no regrouping; 5, Part B, were subtraction problems requiring regrouping; and

TABLE 4.1
Percentage Correct on Chapter Pretest and Posttest

Problem Type (14 Items)	Pretest	Posttest
Part A Regular subtraction (5 items)	93	100
Part B Subtraction with regrouping (5 items)	0[a]	100
Part C Word problems with regrouping		
Addition (2 items)	94	88
Subtraction (2 items)	0	88

Note. N = 8 students.
[a]48% were correctly identified as foolers.

4, Part C, were word problems, 2 addition and 2 subtraction, both requiring regrouping. The posttest followed the same format and was given 2 weeks (10 instructional days) later.

On the pretest, 5 students got all 5 items of Part A correct. Three students missed 1 item. None of the 8 students could solve any of the items in Part B. On the word-problem portion, 7 students correctly answered the 2 addition problems; all 8 missed the subtraction problems. In all the subtraction errors, the students reversed the top and bottom numbers in the units column.

On the posttest, all 8 students got 5 out of 5 correct on Parts A and B. Of the 4 word problems in Part C, 5 students correctly answered all of them, 2 children correctly answered 3, and 1 child only got 2 correct. On any scale, the students' performances were impressive. In approximately 7 hr of instruction, students at all ability levels had gone from not knowing or understanding subtraction with regrouping to high levels of performance (computational skill).

In-Depth Interview Performance

In addition to the text-based pretest and posttest, the 8 students were interviewed before and after instruction in more depth. The first interview consisted of four subtraction items printed on cards ($8 - 5$, $10 - 7$, $28 - 16$, $34 - 17$) and two roll-the-dice-and-add problems that are not discussed in this article. The interview after instruction consisted of eight numeric problems ($28 - 16$, $34 - 17$, $42 - 18$, $567 - 262$, $253 - 127$, $727 - 483$, $625 - 357$, and $402 - 177$), the last five of which went beyond the instructional range of these second graders. On both interviews, there were three tasks for the numeric problems: read the problem aloud, compute the answer, and demonstrate the results with Dienes base-10 blocks. (For a description of Dienes base-10 arithmetic blocks, see Resnick & Ford, 1981,

p. 117.) On the second interview, an additional task was to link the numeric and block solutions verbally for at least one item.

The pre-unit interview results are shown in the top portion of Table 4.2. The first 4 students were somewhat weaker than the second 4. Chuck's inability to read the problems aloud was surprising. Another interesting outcome was that, in all but one case, the students were more successful at solving problems numerically than they were at showing how a problem could be solved with blocks. This seems to indicate that operating in the concrete world poses problems of its own and is not an *automatic* support for abstract thinking.

Table 4.2 also shows students' performance after instruction both on problems within the range of instruction and on transfer problems out of range. (The last two problems were two grade-levels beyond range.) As can be seen, most students (with the exception of Terry) could solve in-range problems and even weaker students solved nearly half the out-of-range problems. The out-of-range success demonstrates principled knowledge applied to tougher settings. As in the pre-unit interview, the students' ability to show the work with Dienes blocks was lower than their ability to solve the problem numerically.

It is important to describe what one can infer from the post-unit interview results and why. The post-unit interview results tell us a great deal about the quality of instruction and the way children learn from such instruction. The results are significant not only because of the students' successful perform-

TABLE 4.2
Student Performance on Interview Tasks: Percentage Correct by Task

Time	Problem Type	Task	Chuck	June	Nicki	Terry	Lem	Lynn	Willis	Rich
Prior to	Subtraction	Read	25	100	75	75	100	100	100	75
instruction	problems	Solve	0	100	50	75	75	75	75	75
	(4 items)[a]	Show	75	100	50	25	75	50	75	50
After	In-range	Read	67	33	67	67	33	100	67	100
instruction	problems	Solve	100	100	100	67	100	100	100	100
	(3 items)[b]	Show	33	67	100	0	67	100	67	33
		Link once[d]	+	NA	−	+	+	+	+	NA
	Out-of-	Read	40	0	80	60	60	100	100	80
	range	Solve	40	40	60	40	80	80	80	60
	problems (5 items)[c]	Show	40	0	20	0	60	40	0	0

[a]8 − 5, 10 − 7, 28 − 16, 34 − 17.
[b]28 − 16, 34 − 17, 42 − 18.
[c]567 − 262, 253 − 127, 727 − 483, 625 − 357, 402 − 177.
[d]The student "did it" (+), "did not do it" (−), or was "not asked" (NA).

ance on familiar items and tasks but also because of their relatively high performance on novel tasks and on problems that were more difficult than the ones they had hitherto encountered. The post-unit interview extended the range of items along two dimensions—task environment and task difficulty—by introducing a new representation (Dienes blocks) and by presenting problems in the familiar representation but at a level of difficulty beyond the scope of instruction (three-digit subtraction with regrouping).

Of the tasks in the postinstruction interview, the only completely familiar one was solving two-digit subtraction with regrouping using paper and pencil, a task on which all but one child performed perfectly (see Line 5 on Table 4.2). The other items placed the children in a novel task environment or else asked them to work at a more advanced level in a familiar task. The students had not been taught to (a) read the whole problem aloud, (b) use a base-10 block manipulative for calculation (other than their experience in the pre-unit interview), (c) describe correspondences (links) between representations, or (d) regroup in the tens, hundreds, or both for three-digit subtraction problems. Their moderate success on these four types of items implies some level of conceptual understanding beyond the mere computational performance skill displayed in solving two-digit subtraction-with-regrouping problems on paper.

One of the most striking indications of student understanding was the ability of some students to show problem solutions with base-10 blocks. The introduction of Dienes blocks for solving subtraction-with-regrouping problems actually presented a challenge to students on both previously mentioned dimensions: Using Dienes blocks was both an extension of the lessons (an increase in task difficulty) and another task (a different task environment). (Although felt strips had been demonstrated, the students had not handled them to develop solutions.)

One aspect of the students' relative facility with Dienes blocks is interesting because of the nature of the blocks themselves as a referent. To get more ones (or more tens) using the blocks, students had to make use of an outside "bank" (or supply) of the lower valued blocks. The presence of the bank actually caused some difficulty in the postinstruction interview for one student. Unlike the bundles of sticks used in Ms. Patrick's lesson, both felt strips and Dienes blocks carry this need for an outside bank. Ms. Patrick's bundles of sticks, on the other hand, were ideally suited to an initial demonstration of regrouping because the action of unbinding or partitioning the 10 to get more ones could be accomplished with the given bundle—there was no need for an outside bank.

Successful student manipulation of Dienes blocks after instruction would not by itself indicate student understanding. However, being able to learn the Dienes system easily would suggest understanding. There are many levels of understanding, and knowing how to use the Dienes system is indicative of a moderate level of understanding (Leinhardt, 1988). Being able to explain the relationship between the trading of felt strips (in class) and the cross marks of regrouping suggests considerable understanding. However, real understanding is characterized by the ability to make analogical connections between concepts in a way that was not directly taught, by recognizing core similarities across representations without explicit instruction on their common features, by flexibility in discussing a concept, and by the ability to verbally explain a complex idea. Such understanding develops incrementally and is enhanced by expert instruction. Clearly, most of Ms. Patrick's higher performing students and some of the lower performing ones gave evidence of good understanding.

CONCLUDING DISCUSSION

Over the course of eight lessons, Ms. Patrick had set up a strong conceptual framework for subtraction with regrouping. First, she demonstrated both the need for and possibility of subtracting the special types of problems she called foolers. Second, she moved laterally (in an intellectual sense) and developed the renaming procedure and the proof of legitimacy of its algorithm. (This proof rested on the fact that the value of the quantity in the minuend was unaltered by the notational transformation.) Third, she moved back to the initial fooler problem and showed how the new renaming procedure could be utilized. Finally, she demonstrated the utility of the procedure under a wide variety of conditions and included some examples where the procedure is *not* used (e.g., addition and subtraction without regrouping).

Tactically, Ms. Patrick overrehearsed the top children to guarantee the success of the lower children. Some educators may be concerned that approximately 40 to 80 min were "wasted" for certain children, but evidence from this study suggests that their time was not wasted. Although the top children took it easy on 1 or 2 days, they were not bored. They continued to work and to develop subtle changes in their mental representations while they remained available as *models* for the lower performing children. The range of differences in student understanding was not captured by the students' chapter posttest performance, where a ceiling effect was obtained. Rather, the differences emerged in the interviews that were held with students following instruction.

By the end of the lesson sequence, students at both the high and low ends of the ability-performance profile in our sample were able to perform the subtraction-with-regrouping algorithm fluidly. The low-ability students' performance on interviews and tests (see Chuck and Terry as examples) showed that they had reached a considerable level of mastery and that their earlier misconceptions were resolved, although the conceptual foundation for their skill was somewhat thin, as shown by their sparse nets and fragmented concepts. The higher ability students (see, e.g., Lynn and Lem) not only mastered the algorithm, they understood it well enough to extend their knowledge and to perform tasks and solve problems beyond the range of instruction. Let us now consider the features of Ms. Patrick's explanations that contributed to this successful learning by both high- and low-ability students.

Explanation as the Execution of a Plan

The series of lessons that have been described were designed to teach the skill of subtraction with regrouping. As part of getting the children to learn subtraction, this particular teacher felt that they should understand both the procedures and, to some extent, the underlying legitimacy of the mathematics employed. Ms. Patrick built an elaborate explanation that contained all the elements for an effective instructional explanation described in the introduction of this article, plus some additional features. She identified the goal of solving foolers; she consistently noted progress within and between the first three lessons by phrases such as "Did anybody notice anything new that we were able to do at the end of that part?"; she demonstrated examples in several representations (sticks, strips, etc.) and by the end of the third lesson connected them; she legitimatized the regrouping concept with all the representations, "proving" that value was not lost; and she connected the new procedure to more familiar ones in several ways—by giving fooler and nonfooler problems, by integrating familiar subtraction into the new procedure, and by recalling prior use of representations. Ms. Patrick did more than this, however. To capture some of the subtleties of her work, her explanation was analyzed in terms of its goal states and supporting actions. This resulted in a planning net for an explanation that resembles the structure of a more generic planning net developed for a lesson on understanding an algorithm (see Leinhardt & Greeno, 1986). This net is presented as a model of an expert explanation (see Fig. 4.24). As in other planning nets, the diagram displays goals and action plans for an event, in this case a series of lessons on subtraction with regrouping. Goals are in hexagons, actions in rectangles, and decision/test points in diamonds. Data used in developing this planning net came from statements in the teacher's interviews, and from events in the videotaped lessons.

At the top of Fig. 4.24, Ms. Patrick's three major goals appear in hexagons. They are CLARIFYING the subtraction procedure, LEARNING the subtraction-with-regrouping procedure, and UNDERSTANDING the nature of regrouping. These goal states are achieved as both a direct and an indirect consequence of many action systems and subgoals, some of which are

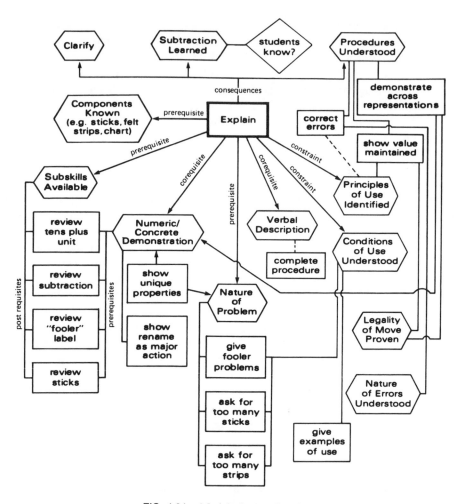

FIG. 4.24.   Model of an explanation.

shown in this figure. Not all the details are shown; however, this model demonstrates the key features of an explanation and how they were instantiated in this sequence of lessons.

The action of EXPLAINING subtraction with regrouping, shown in a rectangle just below the top three goal states, has as a consequence the complete or partial achievement of each goal. Explaining has a prerequisite goal that must be met, namely, that the COMPONENTS to be used in the explanation are already known. For example, as Ms. Patrick stated in the interview before her first lesson, she wanted to make sure the students remembered how to use sticks and felt strips. If a teacher or instructor attempts to explain something new by using an analogy or a new representation that must itself be learned, the lesson is unlikely to be of any major benefit to the hapless student who will likely lose sight of the principal objective. In meeting this goal of ensuring that the components are known, the teacher links older familiar information with the new as the demonstrations unfold.

Another prerequisite of the explanation is that the SUBSKILLS to be used in the performance of the procedure are available — some might even argue they must be available in automatic form. For example, for this series of lessons, the students needed to be able to add units to 10, know how to do two-digit subtraction without regrouping, recognize fooler problems, and count by tens (e.g., grouped sticks). If these skills have already been taught, they can be retrieved for use in the explanation process merely by asking for their use — activating them or taking them out of "cold storage." The performance of these retrieval actions results in their being in the goal state of having subskills available.

The actions that review subskills can also be seen as prerequisites for the goal of having the NUMERIC and CONCRETE representations demonstrated. For this goal there are separate procedures not shown in the figure (i.e., unbinding, trading, rewriting) that are associated with each representation (i.e., sticks, felt, number chart, and rewriting the numbers). Another corequisite goal for a good explanation is to have a clear and complete VERBAL description of the concepts or procedures provided. Further, each demonstration should include an identification of the UNIQUE feature of the representation that requires its particular solution procedure. For example, in teaching the students how to take 8 sticks from 26 sticks (consisting of two bundles of 10 sticks and 6 loose ones), Ms. Patrick led them to the discovery that the rubber band could be taken off one of the bundles of sticks, whereas the procedure for rewriting numbers involved subtracting 1 from the numeral in the tens place and adding 10 to the numeral in the ones place on the chart. Both these actions (unbinding and renaming) involved a manipulation of the tens and ones, but they were very different at the specific level. A good explanation points to this uniqueness.

Another prerequisite for an explanation is to have the students realize the NATURE OF THE PROBLEM, in this case to have them see why the normal subtraction procedure does not work, and if appropriate, where the contradiction is located. In this set of lessons, the teacher brought students to this goal state by embedding trick problems that she had labeled foolers in each of the representations that were being used — sticks, felt, and numbers. This is a way of identifying the dominant goal of an explanation and setting up signal monitors or pointers as progress is made toward the goal.

A constraint on the explanation is that the CONDITION and CIRCUMSTANCES

OF USE be identified. That is, the procedure needs to be recognized as one that is used only under specific circumstances. Subtraction with regrouping is used when a number in the minuend is smaller than the corresponding number in the subtrahend. Finally, the PRINCIPLES that permit the procedure to be used need to be identified, and the LEGALITY of the procedure needs to be proven. The action of producing intentional ERRORS or making use of student errors is often a key move in an explanation. In working through the corrections of such errors, the teacher can accomplish the goal of identifying and understanding principles of use.

In summary, an explanation can be seen as a critical component of instruction. The features of an explanation described earlier provide a frame for reviewing the content of this particular instructional sequence. The first feature in an explanation is explicating the goal of the lessons. Ms. Patrick did this by identifying a class of apparently unsolvable problems called foolers (Lessons 1 and 2). By the end of Lesson 1, a good deal of progress has been made toward the primary goal and was so stated. A second feature involves the use of parallel representations and their linkages. Ms. Patrick did this extensively during the first 3 days using felt strips, popsicle sticks, and three written systems. Although the linkage between them was not explicit, the teacher implied the connections, as her actions moved from one system (felt) to a corresponding system (written). Conditions and contexts for use were included in Lesson 2, when the rename procedure was re-embedded in subtraction. The conditions of use were further examined in Lesson 6, when a variety of problems (using addition and subtraction with and without regrouping) were given. Multiple contexts (money, vertical, horizontal, and word problems) were explored in the last few lessons. Both principles of use and checking were introduced in Lesson 1 — proof of equal value of number and sticks — and again in Lesson 4, when addition and subtraction were linked as inverses. Connecting old knowledge to new and identification of new elements were handled in Lesson 2 and in Lesson 7 (rewriting exercises).

As we worked through an analysis of each lesson, we noticed that the critical elements of the lesson were captured by each child interviewed on that day. For the weaker children, the enriching information was sometimes missed. But there was also considerable redundancy that served as a kind of cushion that could make the next lesson easier to follow. Thus, although the task of following the lesson became increasingly difficult for the weaker children, it was never impossible.

Educational and Scientific Importance

This study is a step in the development of a technique that interprets an actual lesson sequence in terms of the planned sequence, the teacher's evaluation of the lessons, the students' learning, and the established pedagogical theory about learning. The analyses using this multifaceted technique will have implications for both experts and student teachers as they plan appropriate elements for explanations and consider the mathematical concepts embedded in the instructional topics. In this article, student acquisition of a portion of subtraction knowledge has been described in the context of carefully documented instruction. Although there has been considerable research on teacher actions (through process–product research and ethnography, to mention only two), on student learning, and on student performance following instruction, the work reported here represents the beginning of a new approach that carefully documents the logical sequence of instruction and maps student learning onto each segment of that sequence. In this particular lesson sequence, we had a teacher who had crafted each segment with care and skill, and who moved children of varying ability from the limitation of being bound by rigid (though real and useful) constraints to the freedom to suspend an appropriate constraint (e.g., multiple digits per column), and thereby perform subtraction competently as well as understand the procedure.

ACKNOWLEDGMENTS

The research reported herein was supported by the Learning Research and Development Center, supported in part initially by funds from the National Institute of Education and subsequently by funds from the Office of Educational Research and Improvement (OERI), United States Department of Education. The opinions expressed do not necessarily reflect the position or policy of OERI, and no official endorsement should be inferred.

I thank Sharon Lesgold and Carla Weidman for their substantive contributions to the design and conduct of the field research, Joyce Fienberg for her research and editorial assistance, and Brad Hyland for his enormous and tireless artistic support in the preparation of this article.

REFERENCES

Berliner, D. C., King, M., Rubin, J., & Fisher, C. W. (1981). *Describing classroom activities.* Unpublished manuscript, Far West Laboratory for Educational Research & Development, San Francisco.

Borko, H., & Niles, J. (1984, April). *Teachers' strategies for forming reading groups: Do real students make a difference?* Paper presented at the meeting of the American Educational Research Association, New Orleans.

Brophy, J., & Good, T. L. (1986). Teacher behavior and student achievement. In M. C.

Wittrock (Ed.). *Handbook of research on teaching* (3rd ed., pp. 328-375) New York: Macmillan.

Brown, J. S., & VanLehn, K. (1980). Repair theory: A generative theory of bugs in procedural skills. *Cognitive Science, 4,* 379-426.

Calderhead, J. (1984). *Teachers' classroom decision making.* Eastbourne, East Sussex, England: Holt, Rinehart & Winston.

Collins, A., & Stevens, A. L. (1982). Goals and strategies of inquiry teachers. In R. Glaser (Ed.), *Advances in instructional psychology* (Vol. 2, pp. 65-119). Hillsdale, NJ: Lawrence Erlbaum Associates, Inc.

Ericsson, K. A., & Simon, H. A. (1980). Verbal reports as data. *Psychological Review, 87,* 215-251.

Ericsson, K. A., & Simon, H. A. (1984). *Protocol analysis: Verbal reports as data.* Cambridge, MA: MIT Press.

Lampert, M. (1986). Teaching multiplication. *Journal of Mathematical Behavior, 5,* 241-280.

Leinhardt, G. (1977). Evaluating an adaptive educational program: Implementation to replication. *Instructional Science, 6,* 223-257.

Leinhardt, G. (1988). Getting to know: Tracing students' mathematical knowledge from intuition to competence. *Educational Psychologist, 23,* 119-144.

Leinhardt, G., & Greeno, J. G. (1986). The cognitive skill of teaching. *Journal of Educational Psychology, 78,* 75-95.

Leinhardt, G., & Putnam, R. T. (1987). The skill of learning from classroom lessons. *American Educational Research Journal, 24,* 557-588.

Leinhardt, G., & Smith, D. A. (1985). Expertise in mathematics instruction: Subject matter knowledge. *Journal of Educational Psychology, 77,* 247-271.

Leinhardt, G., Weidman, C., & Hammond, K. (1987). Introduction and integration of classroom routines by expert teachers. *Curriculum Inquiry, 17,* 135-176.

Leinhardt, G., Zigmond, N., & Cooley, W. W. (1981). Reading instruction and its effects. *American Educational Research Journal, 18,* 343-361.

Petitto, A. L. (1985). Division of labor: Procedural learning in teacher-led small groups. *Cognition and Instruction, 2,* 233-270.

Resnick, L. B., & Ford, W. W. (1981). *The psychology of mathematics for instruction.* Hillsdale, NJ: Lawrence Erlbaum Associates, Inc.

Rosenshine, B. V., & Stevens, R. (1986). Teaching functions. In M. C. Wittrock (Ed.), *Handbook of research on teaching* (3rd ed., pp. 376-391). New York: Macmillan.

Shavelson, R. J., & Stern, P. (1981). Research on teachers' pedagogical thoughts, judgements, decisions, and behavior. *Review of Educational Research, 51,* 455-498.

Shulman, L. S. (1986). Those who understand: Knowledge growth in teaching. *Educational Researcher, 15*(2), 4-14.

Slavin, R. E., & Karweit, N. L. (1985). Effects of whole class, ability grouped, and individualized instruction on mathematics achievement. *American Educational Research Journal, 22,* 351-367.

VanLehn, K., & Brown, J. S. (1980). Planning nets: A representation for formalizing analogies and semantic models of procedural skills. In R. E. Snow, P. A. Frederico, & W. E. Montague (Eds.), *Aptitude, learning and instruction: Vol. 2. Cognitive process analysis and problem solving* (pp. 95-138). Hillsdale, NJ: Lawrence Erlbaum Associates, Inc.

5

On The Nature of Competence: Principles for Understanding in a Domain©

Rochel Gelman
University of Pennsylvania

James G. Greeno
University of California, Berkeley

It is now commonplace that a theory of instruction requires the three significant components identified by Glaser (e.g., 1976): a theory of the knowledge that we want students to acquire, a theory of the initial state of the learner, and a theory of the process of transition between the initial state and the desired state of knowledge to be achieved in instructional settings. In this chapter we review and integrate the research that we, with our students and associates, have done to characterize the initial knowledge states that learners bring to mathematics instruction. Previous work shows that children have significant implicit understanding of counting, number, and sets before they receive instruction (e.g., Gelman & Meck, 1986; Hudson, 1983; Resnick, 1986). Our models characterize this understanding in the form of schemata that can be used for generating plans for both performance of tasks and representations of information in texts and situations presented as problems.

Our studies and analyses of early mathematical competence emphasize relations between the content of the subject matter of mathematics and performance of tasks, a topic of concern for at least a decade now (Resnick, 1976). The structure of a subject such as mathematics clearly bears on the goals of instruction and plays a crucial role in the formulation of models that represent states of knowledge that we hope students will acquire.

Our analyses also highlight the relation between subject-matter principles and cognitive analyses of the initial state of the learner. We are concerned with the understanding of subject-matter principles that an individual initially brings to the task of learning more about the subject. Even in very young children, this initial understanding is principled—albeit in a limited and implicit way. Over time, presumably as a function of both informal and formal instruction, knowledge about the subject matter of the domain builds on this principled base. As the base expands, so does knowledge of the principles of the domain, including a more explicit or stateable understanding of the principles, the language, and/or the symbols that represent both the principles and entities of the domain and the organized body of domain-specific facts and algorithms that characterize the subject matter in question. Hence, despite the limits on the young child's understanding of mathematics, the presence of significant implicit understanding of fundamental mathematical principles in preschool and early elementary schoolchildren has implications for the design of curriculum and instruction in mathematics.

Some resist our proposal that early states of knowledge involve some principled understanding. We take this position, in part, because data show young children and infants respond to the environment in numerical ways before they have been given explicit number instruction. For example, infants respond to a set of disparate objects on the basis of their number even though they could respond instead to the particular color, shape, size, and so forth (e.g., Cooper, 1984; Starkey, Spelke, & Gelman, 1983; Strauss & Curtis, 1981, 1984). Such selective attention or disattention needs to be explained, especially because chimpanzees, members of a closely related species, do not respond, sometimes even after the benefit of extended training and feedback (Premack, 1976; Premack, Woodruff, & Kennel, 1978).

Our move to attribute implicit knowledge of some counting principles serves this end. It resembles Cheng and Gallistel's (1984) move to grant implicit knowledge of Euclidean principles to rats to account for their totally selective use of geometric, as opposed to landmark, information about the position of hidden food. Both positions assume that organisms can have structured representations that capture mathematical principles even though they cannot use the mathematical language or symbol system that members of a culture learn to use to re-present mathematical principles and facts. Still, given that Cheng and Gallistel's rats never will access their principles, our positions differ in important ways. Rats do not use a symbol system, be it the language of mathematics to *re-present* their implicit principled knowledge or otherwise; nor can they build new principles of geometry out of the ones already available. In contrast, children do develop symbol systems and can develop the ability to use the language of mathematics. They also can acquire new principles that go well beyond the skeletal-like ones they begin with. Therefore we develop the position that, in the child's case, early principled knowledge does more than structure selective attention and implicit use of principled knowledge. It enables the learning of the meaning of mathematical symbols and new principles.

The foregoing introduces the fact that cognitive scientists use the term *representation* in many ways. As Mandler (1983, 1984a) noted, its use is not restricted to the *stands-for* usage, one that dominates discussions of mathematical knowledge. Many use the term assuming there are organized bodies of mental structures that either render a body of learned knowledge coherent or make the acquisition of knowledge and skills coherent. Examples of this notion of representation include the proposal that a general schema structure can organize and/or support the learning of particular scripts, story grammars, and event or scene structures. Similarly, classification structures support the acquisition of categorically organized bodies of knowledge as well as inferences about novel cases; associative networks or clusters of distinctive features are said to make possible recognition of the familiar; and that action or sensorimotor schemata serve as mediators of coherent motor skills and plans (see Mandler, 1983, 1984b, for detailed examples).

Mandler also noted that these alternative uses of the notion of representation differ along many dimensions. She focused on one, whether the representation is potentially stateable or accessible. Her conclusion that sensorimotor representations are never accessed as such highlights the fact that one can attribute representations to organisms without granting them the ability to use symbols to represent these representations at a different level. Indeed, it is this consequence that underlies Mandler's argument that Piaget's account of what infants know and how they develop symbols out of sensorimotor representations must be wrong. For she shows that infants do have knowledge that can be accessed and/or be stated at a future time in development.

Our claim that preverbal children have principled knowledge of counting is consistent with Mandler's conclusion. For we take it for granted that knowledge of the principles is implicit at first. With time, and under the right conditions, knowledge of these is made explicit. Because the principles are potentially accessible, they *can* be modified or even incorporated into a particular symbol system.

But if we do not mean that the principles are neither stateable at first nor known in mathematical terms, what do we mean? The idea is that a skeletal set of principles is available to support the kind of selective attention and learning in the domain characterized by these principles. Initial representations serve as enabling devices. Learning would be exceedingly hard, if not impossible, were there no such conceptual skeletons supporting the growth and development of body parts (principles) and the accrual of the relevant body of knowledge. In the end, surely as a function of everyday experiences and "healthy" instruction, both the body and the skeleton will develop together. Eventually, the child will come to understand counting (and other principles of arithmetic) *at many levels,* enough that even the claim that she *re-presents* number and other mathematical concepts in the stands-for, symbolic sense is correct. Indeed, a major goal of mathematics instruction is to make students fluent speakers of the language of mathematics. Later we develop the theme that the road to this goal involves the acquisition of layers of representation. Successive layers feed off ones already available or acquired.

Granting the young principles does not mean we assume they know everything about these and related ones. There will be much for them to learn; but they are given a push in the right direction.

In this chapter we develop and extend our position that young children have implicit understanding of some counting principles (e.g., Gelman & Gallistel, 1978; Gelman & Meck, 1986; Gelman, Meck, & Merkin, 1986; Greeno, Riley, & Gelman, 1984), by using the Greeno et al. (1984) proposal that competent plans for counting reflect the ability of *procedural competence* to generate plans that honor the constraints dictated by the domain of knowledge as well as the constraints dictated by the task and setting. We assume that the ability to use these kinds of constraints depends on the nature of what we have called *conceptual competence* and *utilization competence,* respectively. Our proposal that competent plans for counting reflect multiple components of competence has implications regarding the interpretation of variable performance and an account of how early numerical understandings might develop.

First, we cover background issues and a summary of our previous work. Next, we extend the Greeno et al. analysis, especially with regard to the question of how to characterize competence involved in linguistic or symbolic interpretations of situations in the domain. After that, we take up topics related to the interpretation of variability in performance, that is, the competence–performance distinction. The end of the chapter includes suggestions about how competence models like ours contribute to a theory of active learning. We present and discuss some suggestions on how to develop links between our analyses of the initial states of learners and the theory of transition that is needed if we are to have a theory of instruction.

Because we believe our approach to modeling understanding of counting and arithmetic can be applied to other bodies of knowledge that are organized in terms of a set of principles and the entities to which those principles apply, we make an effort throughout the chapter to use examples from other domains to illustrate points.

WHY POSTULATE PRINCIPLES?

Fundamentally, we postulate principles to provide a basis for defining knowledge in a domain. In the case of counting, implicit knowledge of the stable-order principle underlies our understanding that one need not use the conventional count words of a language to count. As long as some ordered set of tags is used, be it comprised of verbal elements or not, and as long as one uses these in a way that honors the one–one principle, we can say they are using counting tags. In other words, the tags are counting tags if their use honors the constraints of the counting principles. Given this, if we grant people implicit knowledge we provide them a tool for identifying the many acceptable sets of tags used throughout the world. If the structure and use of a set fails to meet the constraints of the principles, as is the case for the alphabet in English, but not Hebrew, then the list is *not* a count list.

When counting a set, one does not have to point to each item, start at the beginning of a row, arrange items in a row, count anything in particular, and so forth. There are multiple ways to keep track of the number of items used in a count-on strategy (Fuson, 1982), just as there are multiple count strategies that can be used to solve a variety of arithmetic problems. All these count strategies are united by their function: They solve the problem of determining the cardinality of a set. They do not determine the cause of an object's acceleration or one's memory for places, or even the area covered by a particular object.

How are we able to determine that these disparate events are in the equivalence class of procedures for counting? What gives us license to say that a variety of distinct behaviors are all instances of the class of counting behaviors? What leads us to say that attributing cause and choosing a counting direction are not in the same class? Our answer is knowledge of the counting principles. Our representation of these principles serves to define what counting is and underlies our ability to identify members of the equivalence class of counting behaviors. Just as principles of syntax help define the class of acceptable utterances in a language, so do principles of counting help define the class of acceptable instances of counting.

The fact that principles define the equivalence class of counting behaviors is related to another characteristic they possess. They serve as the basis from which novel instances can be generated; they yield constraints that a planner must honor if a plan is to lead to counting. Whatever else the requirements of a novel setting, if the planner does not honor the constraints of the principles, the solution cannot be considered an example of counting. We return to the issue of generativity when we consider the kind of evidence one can use to attribute implicit knowledge of the counting principles to an individual.

A principle analysis of knowledge also provides a way of determining whether people have an implicit theory about a domain. The more their knowledge can be characterized in terms of the principles of that domain, the more we can say they have a theory. For theories are comprised of the principles of a domain and the entities governed or defined by these principles. We say people are experts in physics because their knowledge is organized in terms of formal principles of physics and the related entities. Similarly, we might say people have an understanding of number that takes them beyond the idea that numbers are what you count when they have acquired implicit understanding of the principles of a group defined in terms of the operation of addition on the positive and negative integers. For given the idea of number so defined, negative numbers and zero *are* numbers. It may not be possible to count zero things, but it is possible to say that zero is an identity element for addition.

Principles can do more than organize the knowledge already accrued in a domain: They also can help us search for and identify domain-relevant inputs. The problem of what a domain-relevant interpretation of the environment is, might seem like a nonexistent one. But, as Quine noted, when one points to an object in the environment and says "gavagai,"there are no a priori reasons to rule out the notion that this new word refers to the grass the object is sitting on, the color of that object, the number of parts that object has, the size of the object, the weight of the object, the way the object does or does not move, the item that should be counted first, and so on. (See Schwartz, 1979, for a review of the relevant philosophical literature here.) Nor is there any a priori reason to assume that the sound sequence, "tout" is a French word as opposed to the second entry in the English count list, "two."

If we grant learners some domain-specific principles, we provide them with a way to define a range of relevant inputs, the ones that support learning about that domain. Because principles embody constraints on the kinds of inputs that can be processed as data that are relevant to that domain, they therefore can direct attention to those aspects of the environment that need to be selected and attended to. They can also provide clues as to how to interpret a given utterance or set of utterances because they outline the use rules for the verbalizations (Gelman, 1986). Focus on that part of the input that is in fact relevant to learning more about the domain is of course a necessary step, but it is *not* sufficient. Knowing that the count words are the kinds of words one has to master to use symbols as tags does not guarantee that the learning will take place automatically. Indeed, in the case of the count words of English, everything we know about serial learning points to a protracted period of learning.

Spelke's work provides an example of the way principles—this time about the identification of objects—direct attention so that learning about the object's properties can then proceed. She proposes that infants expect the parts of an object to be connected and to move together. Therefore they should treat those parts of an occluded object that move together, at the same rate and along parallel paths, as parts of one continuous object. The fact that the parts have the same shape, color, and texture or that the nonoccluded objects constitute a good form should be irrelevant for *finding* those parts that go together to form one object. Once the objects are found, then such information can support the learning about the attributes of particular kinds of objects. It is not Spelke's view that such information is not used; rather that it does not serve as primitive clues for finding those parts that cohere to form an object or "thing." Until infants accomplish this, with the aid of principled assumptions, they will not be concerned about the color, shape, etc. of that thing. A series of experiments support these predictions (Kellman & Spelke, 1981; Spelke, 1988).

The idea that principles serve to direct attention is consistent with various constructivist theories of mind. Cognitive scientists' proposal that prior knowledge in a domain determines what and how other materials are interpreted and learned (Bransford & Johnson, 1972; Resnick, 1986) is another case in this class of argument. Piagetian theory that stimuli can serve as food for a particular cognitive activity only when there is a requisite structure with which to assimilate that stimulus is similarly related to this position. The common point in all these accounts is that the perceived order in a stimulus is often constructed on the basis of available structures. Sets of objects do not have to be counted; they can be stacked, put in the mouth, exchanged for something else, or even thrown around—as chimpanzees might prefer to do. Dienes blocks can hardly afford base rules to someone who has no understanding of number (Schoenfeld, 1986). And action-at-a-distance is only a problem for those who assume that physical causes are mediated by physical mechanisms.

From this point of view, it becomes clearer why we say that infants attend to number-relevant information from displays because their attention is directed by at least some implicit knowledge of some of the counting principles (or ones that are closely related). Similarly, we can explain why older children, when asked to find *N* things, seek out and find collections of *N*, ignoring item type, size, texture, and the like. The times they do attend to these other attributes are when they engage other principles. For example, causal principles function to direct attention to the size, substance, surface characteristics, weight, etc. of objects. For such considerations influence the choice of device for moving that object, decisions as to how fast the object will move, and so on.

There are two further reasons to maintain that understanding in a domain involves the implicit use of a domain's principles. The first is that we get an enriched analysis of the competence–performance distinction. We see later that this happens when we separate the notion of competence within a domain from competence for assessing a setting within which to display the domain-specific competence as well as competence for generating a plan of action that honors the constraints of both the domain's and the settings's requirements. Doing this leads to the realization that the ability to generate a competent plan of action depends on all three of these abilities. It also highlights the fact that once one has a competent plan of action, the plan still needs to be executed. Failure to execute the plan could be due to yet further variables, especially those that are traditionally associated with performance problems (e.g., Flavell, 1970). In sum, two issues need to be considered in treatments of competence. The first concerns the need to distinguish between competence that is required for the domain and a competent plan of action. A competent plan is required for correct performance in a specific task setting, so even if a child has the competence corresponding to all the counting principles, if she lacks some of the interpretative competence (discussed later) or planning competence needed to generate the requisite counting procedures for a given setting, she will not succeed. Such a child would generate incorrect plans for counting, in spite of the fact that she has counting-principle conceptual competence. Additionally, even if a child does generate a competent plan, skills required for execution might surpass her performance abilities. In this case, a different source of difficulty contributes to the variability of performance levels.

Second, our approach provides some clues as to how to account for self-initiated and self-guided learning of further knowledge within a domain. Because principles underlie selective attention to domain-relevant inputs, it follows that the mental structures involved serve to interpret environments. The same structures can provide at least a match–no match test of whether the environment and behavior does meet the constraints of the domain. Hence, the conclusion that our position allows for the development of a theory of self-initiated monitoring of the adequacy of stimuli and responses to same. If we add the assumption that those environments that set up structural isomorphs between the definition of domain-relevant stimuli and the ones presented in the environment are especially salient, we start to have a handle on the kind of mechanism that might support the learning of further facts and/or principles of the domain in question. Later we expand on these points.

What Counts as Evidence?: Clues From Language Acquisition

We say children have understanding of some of the principles that govern a domain of knowledge, even when they cannot state the principles, if their behavior reveals implicit or tacit use and understanding of the principles. Our attribution of principled understanding assumes that correct performances are not due simply to some ability to produce a chain of responses memorized by rote in the context of the task in question. Thus, we need evidence to rule out the rote-learning alternative. We turn to the study of language for an analogous case that provides such evidence.

First, when intending to talk, speakers produce sound sequences that are identifiable as utterances as opposed to melodies or other kinds of patterned sounds. This suggests the use of a speech planner constrained by the principles of phonetics, morphology, and syntax. Second, even though speakers sometimes produce ill-formed utterances, their utterances are almost always novel. To be sure, some phrases are used repeatedly, like "How are you?" and "Excuse me."; but, by and large, even beginning language users produce novel utterances that are recognized as acceptable instances of the language. This ability to generate novel utterances provides a major source of evidence that the speaker–hearer makes use of principles. For otherwise, it is hard to explain the ability to use and combine speech relevant units, be they phonemes, morphemes, words, or phrases.

Another indication that implicit principles of understanding guide the language user comes from error-detection data. "What did Frank buy and?" is not an acceptable sentence to speakers of English, even though they may have never encountered the entire string or the acceptable string within which it is embedded. Our ability to sort strings of words that are acceptable from those that are not provides yet another line of support for the conclusion that we have implicit, principled understanding of the rules of syntax that guide and constrain the selection and combination of words. For strings generated in accord with these constraints are possible instances of an utterance; those that violate these constraints are not. In the present example the *coordinate constraint* (Ross, 1967) is violated. When the string is altered to honor the constraint, as in "What did Frank buy and keep?," our implicit understanding of the rule that embodies the constraint leads us to accept the sentence. Implicit knowledge of such principles makes it possible for us to identify members of the equivalence class of responses that are judged acceptable.

To summarize, people are said to have principled knowledge of language because, in addition to being able to produce acceptable utterances, they produce novel utterances and can discriminate between novel acceptable and novel nonacceptable strings of words. Similar evidence led Greeno et al. (1984) to conclude that, at least by 5 years of age, children can be granted implicit knowledge of some principles of counting. Children readily respond to requests to count and produce behaviors that others recognize as instances of the potential class of counting behaviors. They do not label the objects or the attributes in a collection. Moreover, they can count in novel ways when given task requirements that require they do so, and they can tell the difference between correct and incorrect counts (see Gelman & Meck, 1986, for a recent review).

Still, one might object that such evidence is not as compelling for counting as it is for language. Certain patterns for counting are repeated over and over again—even though substitutes for these are permissible. For example, the principles of counting allow one to skip around, while tagging items in a linear array. Empirically, however, linear arrays are invariably counted from one end to the other, and for good reason. The tactic minimizes the likelihood of violating the one–one constraint. Because there are potent conventionalized counting sequences, it is necessary to show that child observers do discriminate between correct and incorrect count sequences even when nonconventional counts are involved. We return to a discussion of this requirement when we discuss *interpretative competence.* For not only does it constitute a requirement for the experimenter, it complicates the child's interpretation of a task. Subjects must be able to tell whether they are to set aside matters of convention or not.

Components of Competence

We characterize implicit understanding as a set of knowledge structures that imply the kinds of successful performances that children give. In formal analyses we derive plans for performing tasks that children perform and meaning structures that they understand. We consider the content of the knowledge structures and the results of the derivations (i.e., the plans and the meaning structures) as realistic psychological hypotheses, although we doubt very much that the methods we use in deriving the plans and meaning structures correspond to psychological mechanisms. We refer to the knowledge structures used in deriving plans and meaning structures as *competence,* following Chomsky (e.g., 1965), who introduced the term to refer to implicitly understood rules of syntax used in deriving correctly formed sentences.

We divide the competence that we postulate into two categories, which we call *operational* and *interpretive.* The distinction is principally for convenience. Some of the knowledge that we discuss is used mainly in generating plans for cognitive and physical activity; other knowledge is used mainly in generating interpretations of the situation. Most of our previous discussions have been about operational competence. Most of the new material in this chapter is about interpretive competence.

Figure 5.1 shows the main components of the framework that we have developed. As background, we review the components of this framework that are involved in the tasks of simple counting analyzed by Greeno et al. (1984).

Suppose the task setting contains a set of objects, and an interviewer asks, "How many are there?" For the moment, assume that interpretation of this question is not problematic (we discuss problematic cases later). A goal is set to find the number of objects in the set, and this is transmitted to the planner.

To plan the actions of counting, the planner has two main knowledge sources: action schemata and utilization propositions. The action schemata, which were called *conceptual competence* in Greeno et al. (1984), include structures that characterize the counting principles that Gelman and Gallistel (1978) concluded preschool children understand implicitly. The principles include three how-to-count principles—one–one, stable-

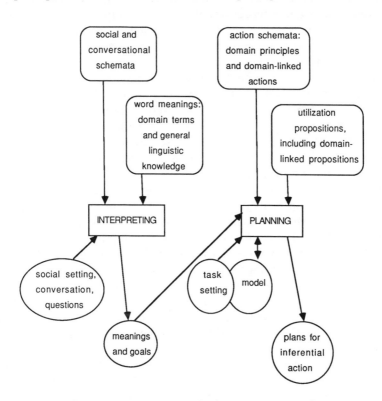

FIG. 5.1.   Components contributing to a competent plan.

order, and cardinality—and two conditions-of-application principles—item-irrelevance and order-irrelevance of objects. The three how-to principles capture the facts that counting requires tagging uniquely each item in a set of objects with a stably ordered list of tags, and the last tag in the list can be used to represent the number of objects in the set. The other two principles reflect the mathematically relevant consequences of the how-to constraints, namely, that any collection of discrete items can be counted, and that the order in which these are counted is irrelevant as long as the how-to principles are honored.

Two sets of schemata are included in the Greeno et al. (1984) characterization of conceptual competence. Schemata of *domain-specific* competence represent the constraints that the principles place on the generation of actions in a given setting. For example, schemata are included that specify that, in a count, tags must be applied to the items being tagged so that one and only one tag is applied to each item to be counted; a schema called KEEP-EQUAL INCREASE expresses this constraint.

The second part of conceptual competence has schemata such as PICK-UP, which characterize classes of behaviors that help satisfy the principles as specified. For example, the PICK-UP schema provides a means for satisfying some of the requirements specified in the domain-specific part of conceptual competence because it is one way to transfer items from the to-be-counted to the already-counted set as count tags. Such accomplishment-oriented schemata could be used for other purposes; hence, the fact that they serve this function in counting is surely learned. We refer to these schemata as *domain-linked* competence because they are recruited to satisfy requirements that arise from domain-specific competence but are not unique to counting. (See the next section for further discussion of domain linked vs. domain specific.)

Utilization propositions provide connections between features of the problem setting and goals of the planner. These propositions allow the planner to infer that some goals or subgoals can be achieved using features of the task setting. The planner includes a theorem prover that attempts to show that requisite conditions of actions can be satisfied in the setting. An example involves the arrangement of objects to be counted. If the objects are in a straight line, they can be counted by starting at one end and moving across the line. The position in the line at any time provides the information needed in remembering which objects have and have not been counted. Knowledge that a straight line of objects can be used to partition the set is a utilization proposition.

The planner that uses action schemata and utilization propositions to achieve goals contains *procedural competence*. The planner uses the knowledge sources of conceptual competence and utilizational propositions as well as general rules about the way to deal with action schemata. The planner has knowledge that recognizes a goal and searches for an action schema with a consequence that matches the goal. The planner also identifies requirements of schemata as subgoals that need to be the subject of further planning.

The claim that competence, as characterized, is sufficient to determine successful performance is buttressed by an analysis by Smith, Greeno, and Vitolo (1985), who implemented a program that constructs plans for counting using the information structures and procedures assumed in the competence analysis. Their program implements a planning procedure and generates plans for counting in various settings when given components of knowledge about actions and features of task settings corresponding to the action schemata and utilization propositions of Greeno et al.'s (1984) analysis. Smith et al. (1985) also showed that the system can generate novel plans for counting when new constraints are imposed on the procedure, such as requiring that a designated object be associated with a designated numeral. It does so for the cases given, without adding schemata to the description of conceptual competence.

Demarcating Domain-Specific From Domain-Linked Competence.
As discussed earlier, principle-driven models of understanding can be used to define domains as well as the nature of the equivalence class of behaviors in that domain. Based on a specified class of tasks that are judged to be in the domain of counting, we can determine those components of the competence that are necessary and sufficient to derive plans for correct performance. Judgments are required to determine whether a task involves counting and whether a specific performance of the task is correct, but these seem no more problematic than in the case of language where judgments are needed to determine whether strings of words are or are not grammatical.

As an example, we judge that counting includes settings where objects are arranged in a straight line and are tagged in a sequence from one end to another with corresponding increments in the numerals. Counting also includes settings where objects are moved into a designated location with an increment of the numeral string for each object. A third case that we need not judge as counting is construction of a set of tokens that is numerically equal to a set of objects—for example, creating a set of coins that is equal to a given set of books by placing a token in a bag corresponding to each book. Although, the last case involves a principle of one–one correspondence, it does not involve the principles of stable ordering and cardinality.

We say that a schema is part of domain-specific competence if it is included in the derivations of plans for all the tasks in the domain and if its removal allows derivation of plans that give incorrect performance. We say that a schema is *universal* in the domain if it is used in derivations for all the domain tasks and that a schema is *necessary* in the domain if its removal allows derivation of incorrect plans.

Of the 12 schemata that Greeno et al. (1984) specified as competence for counting, 8 are in domain-specific competence, according to these criteria. The domain-specific schemata include COUNT. COUNT relates the set of tags (actually, numerals because we assume enough of the count list is learned by 5 years of age) and the set of objects. It also specifies that the number of the set of objects is found by the procedure, MATCH, which creates a subset of tags (numerals) equal to the set of objects, and KEEP–EQUAL–INCREASE, which requires an addition to the set of tags (numerals) each time an object is counted. Counting-specific schemata also include INITIALIZE and INCREMENT, which include members in a subset of an ordered set, ASSIGN, which associates a property with an object, and RETRIEVE-FIRST and RETRIEVE-NEXT, which locate members of an ordered set. These 5 schemata are always involved in counting because counting always uses a set of ordered tags, in this case the numerals in English.

As an example of our method of demarcation, consider a task where the goal is to assemble a set of tokens that are equal to a given set of objects— for example, to put coins into a bag so the set of coins is numerically equal to a given set of books. Suppose the books are on a shelf, and the task is performed as follows: First, be sure the coin bag is empty; then start at one end of the row of books. With one hand, point to the first book and with the other hand, place a coin in the bag. Then point at the next book and drop another coin in the bag. Continue this until you have pointed to the last book in the row and dropped a coin in the bag for that book. Then stop.

We judge that this task does not involve counting; neither numerals nor another set of ordered tags is used. Further, there is no evidence that the cardinality value of the book as represented by the last tag in a stably ordered list was determined. (To support this judgment, consider an alternative method that finds the number of books by counting them first and then putting that number of coins into the bag. Our intuitions put the operations involving explicit determination and use of number in the category of counting, but not the procedure that merely matches two sets.) Even so, the procedure of creating the set of coins equal to the books is closely related to counting. This is reflected in an analysis of competence, which shows that many of the schemata of counting are used in planning this set of actions, including MATCH, KEEP–EQUAL–INCREASE, and other schemata for lower level actions. The top-level schema of counting, which we call COUNT, is not included in planning the action with the coins and books. Recall that COUNT is the schema that requires numerals and identifies the number of a set as the result of the operation of counting. If we were to include the books-and-coins task as an instance of counting, then the schema we call COUNT would not be a part of counting-specific competence.

Another example illustrates necessity of a schema by showing that its removal allows incorrect plans to be generated. In a constrained counting task, Gelman and Gallistel (1978) asked children to count a set of five objects arranged in a line. The children typically did, using the English count words as tags. The task of interest started when the experimenter pointed to the second object in the line and said, "Now count them again, but make this the 'one'." Then, the instruction was repeated, asking for the second object to be "the 'two'," "the 'three'," "the 'four'," and "the 'five'," after which the same five trial types were repeated for the fourth object in the line. Most 5-year-old children perform this task nearly perfectly, and we have argued that correct performance in this constrained task is strong evidence that children understand the principles of counting, because it is extremely unlikely that they would have learned a procedure for the task by watching other people perform it. Further, children cannot use the counting solutions they have already learned and must create new ones or variations on the ones they already know will work.

Three- and four-year-olds can err on the constrained task, especially with five items. Their incorrect performances can be interpreted using the analysis of competence. For example, if the second object is designated as "the 'three'," some children point to the first object and say "one," then say "two" without pointing to an object, then point to the second object and say "three." The third object is "four," the fourth object is "five," and the last object is "six." This performance can be generated if the schema called KEEP–EQUAL–INCREASE is omitted from the knowledge base of the planner. KEEP–EQUAL–INCREASE requires that each time a numeral is added to the set that has been used, an object must be added to the set that has been tagged. The fact that incorrect performance can be derived if KEEP–EQUAL–INCREASE is omitted supports its being a necessary part of competence for counting.

Counting-linked conceptual competence consists of schemata that are used in planning actions of counting in some but not all task settings. For example, schemata for moving objects into a designated location when they have been counted are not used for all counting procedures; therefore, we say they are counting-linked, rather than counting-specific. In our formal analysis, the actions of moving objects are recruited in planning to accomplish the goal of keeping a partition between counted and not-yet-counted objects. This goal is accomplished in different ways in different settings. For example, with objects in a line, the partition can be maintained by moving from one end of the line to the other, pointing to each object as it is counted. This does not mean that a different understanding of counting principles is elicited by objects that are moved from that elicited by objects that are in a line. The required understanding of counting is the same, but different resources are available for achieving one of the requirements implied by the counting principles. Different utilization principles apply to the different situations, enabling the planner to choose appropriate counting-linked actions.

As another example, if items to be counted are arranged in a circle rather than a line, the plan for counting requires marking the first item counted. This action is not required when the objects are in a straight line, although the procedure of pointing to the objects in turn is used by many children in this setting, as it is when there is a straight line of objects. The circle display introduces a setting-relevant problem, one that requires an action of explicitly marking the beginning and ending of the set. Unless the starting point is remembered correctly, one–one correspondence could be violated by stopping too soon or continuing too long with the counting procedure. Utilization propositions apply in the straight-line case to infer that counting is complete when the end of the line is reached, and for the circle case, to recognize that a test for completion is needed.

Some counting-linked actions can come to be used as if they are instances of schemata that are counting specific. For example, children learn a procedure for keeping track of counted objects in a line by pointing to them as they count. The schemata for this are the same as for keeping track of which numeral was used last and are probably assimilated to counting-specific competence, at least at some point in development, because young children appear to need them for all counting tasks involving 3-dimensional and 2-dimensional rows of objects. However, the actions of moving along a line of objects by pointing to them in turn are counting-linked actions only when objects are arranged in a straight line. Hence, the calling up of this knowledge is dependent on the setting and interpretative competence in that setting. So strictly speaking, such actions are not counting specific. Still, we believe they can function this way at times because they are isomorphic to a counting-specific schema.

We note an analogy between the ability to demarcate knowledge that is specific to a domain of procedures and the theoretical criterion that Chomsky (1965) called *descriptive adequacy*. Chomsky proposed that a grammar should account for relations of similarity among sentences of a language, for example, for the classes of sentences that are judged to be paraphrases of each other. The ability of the counting competence analysis to account for intuitions that a class of procedures should all be judged to be counting examples is a form of descriptive adequacy that has special utility in clarifying the boundaries of domain-specific and domain-general understanding.

Our analysis also clarifies the distinction between competence and performance. In fact, it reveals that there are two distinctions involved. First, there is the distinction between domain-specific competence and competence for generating competent plans of action for a specific task setting. A child might have the competence corresponding to all the counting principles but lack some of the utilization propositions or action schemata needed to generate competent plans that make possible correct counting procedures in a setting. Such a child would generate faulty plans for counting, in spite of having all the domain-specific competence, because he or she would lack knowledge that is outside the domain of counting that is needed for successful planning in the specific task setting.

A second distinction is between the generation of a competent plan and the successful execution of a plan. Successful execution of counting requires holding information in memory, attending to the objects to be counted, and other information-processing requirements. The scheme shown in Fig. 5.1 accounts for the construction of a plan of action, but not for the plan's execution. A child could generate a correct plan for counting but then forget where he or she is in the process of counting, or forget a component of the plan, or skip an object because he or she does not notice it is there. Such failures of execution would count as incorrect performance in a narrower sense than failures of competence outside the domain of counting principles. We have not considered requirements of execution in our earlier discussions, but we give some attention to them here and in the next sections.

EXTENSIONS OF THE ANALYSIS OF COMPETENCE

One goal of this chapter is to develop and extend our notions about the components of competence. As we worked with the Greeno et al. model, we recognized that failure due to the absence of knowledge of a principle should be distinguished from failure due to the lack of the domain-relevant knowledge, for example, that a partitioning schema and the English string of words, "one, two, three, four, five," and so forth can serve counting. Whereas the principles define the domain, the latter do not. Earlier, we discussed why one need not use the count words to count. A partitioning schema can serve many functions, including classification and any other procedure that is to be applied to all members of a set. Still, even though other ordered lists can serve as tags, the one that is chosen becomes numerically meaningful because it is used in a way that satisfies the constraints of the counting principles. Similarly, methods of partitioning take on counting-specific meaning because they serve to honor the one–one constraints. These considerations have encouraged us to subcategorize conceptual competence into counting competence and counting-linked competence.

An error due to a failure to consider whether items are arranged in a row as opposed to a circle seems a different kind of error than one due to a failure to use conversational rules for experimental settings. The latter should influence performance on any task; the former should have a more focused effect on the class of counting tasks. The distinction here is between interpretations of tasks that require domain-specific as opposed to domain-general knowledge, a distinction that leads us to embed our prior treatment of utilization competence in an extended analysis of interpretative competence.

The latter represents more than the ability to assess a setting in terms of counting requirements. It also includes a characterization of principles of communicative competence, the ingredients to which underlie the ability to classify and use social settings, appropriate conversational formats, and so on. Development of our model in a way that clarifies these qualitative differences follows.

Conceptual Competence for Counting

In the Greeno et al. model of counting, those schemata that specify the counting principles for the abstract mathematical knowledge of counting constitute one subset of the schemata we have called conceptual competence. Henceforth, we use the phrase counting competence to refer to such principled or definitional knowledge. The other subset of schemata included in the model of conceptual competence is now referred to as counting-linked competence.

Counting-linked competence is clearly domain relevant and, as we will see, can even serve as a source for learning further principles. These domain-linked schemata are not, however, definitional for counting. The English count words no more define counting than do the Greek or Hebrew alphabets or a sequence of hand configurations. And although partitioning between counted and uncounted objects is a central ingredient of counting procedures, if a partition were present because of a feature of the situation, then a counting procedure would not require actions to achieve partitioning. For example, if objects appear on a screen in a temporal sequence, counting can simply increment the numerals each time an object appears, without explicit recording of the partition between counted and uncounted objects.

As an example of a counting-linked action, consider the partitioning method of moving counted objects into a designated location. That method of partitioning is used in many contexts; for example, dishes that have been washed can be placed on a different counter from those that have not been washed. Until the planner recognizes that such a method of partitioning can serve the domain-specific constraints of counting competence, that partitioning carries no counting-linked meaning. But once so recognized it can be assimilated to the goals of a counting-competence plan, and, hence, it acquires the additional status of counting-linked. It does not then lose its status as a general ability for use with plans in other domains, anymore than does the alphabet when used to order books in a library. Rather, its embedding in a counting plan gives it one of its many potential meanings. The knowledge in the domain of counting is expanded by the attachment of the method to schemata counting competence.

The foregoing discussion contains the germs of a model of learning or an account of how conceptual competence could develop. Plans that use a method generates actions that help honor the one–one constraints. Such successes reinforce the planner's selection of the partitioning method for embedding in other plans designed to meet the constraints of a counting task. With use in the name of the counting goals, the partitioning method gets assimilated or attached to the counting principles and hence represented as part of counting-linked competence. We will return to a discussion of learning, and show that a similar analysis can be developed for how the counting words of English first become part of counting-linked competence and then embodiments of further principles of counting.

Competence for Understanding and Interpreting Situations

A significant extension of our previous discussions involves a treatment of children's interpretations of the tasks they are asked to perform. To do this, it is necessary to consider processes of *social interpretation* and *linguistic interpretation*. These interpretative processes deal with the interactive aspects of the setting. Greeno et al. (1984) discussed children's use of features of the task setting to achieve goals and called the general knowledge for that *utilization competence.* That discussion was concerned with children's assessments of such domain-relevant props as the arrangement of items in a line or a circle that provide resources for achieving goals that have been activated in the child's understanding of the task.

In subsequent analyses, we have considered children's processes of comprehending information in task situations and determining the goals they then try to achieve. This includes knowledge that supports correct understanding of the language used to describe situations and to ask questions, including general linguistic capability as well as knowledge of domain-relevant vocabulary, such as "how many?," "more," and so forth. It also includes knowledge about social roles and conversational conventions that can influence the child's understanding of important aspects of the task.

An Extended Model of Interpretative Competence.   The idea that children's interpretations of task requirements benefit from structures of competence is familiar and compelling. For, without them, there would be no basis from which to select and assess the domain-relevant information in a given task, be it verbal or otherwise. In Piagetian terms, there would be no possibility of assimilating the environment correctly because there would be no appropriate structure to project onto (interpret) the environment. Whereas correct understanding of some components of the task setting is intricately linked to conceptual competence, understanding of other features is not. The vocabulary of the domain and the arrangement of items in a setting are variables that are so linked. They are also the kind of variables featured in the Greeno et al. analysis of utilization competence. We can now call the related propositions counting-linked utilization propositions.

Gelman et al.'s (1986) analysis of why children failed Baroody's (1984) test of the order invariance principle did not focus on such domain-specific variables; instead it highlighted the abilities to interpret social and conversational contexts. Limits on these abilities can lead one to a misunderstanding of the intended meaning of an experimenter's question (Donaldson, 1978). For this reason, we see the need to extend our notions of interpretation requirements to include the ability of the child to converge on the goal the experimenter has in mind. To do this, the child must have the ability to assess correctly both the setting and the conversational frame.

Understanding the different classes of social settings, syntax, and rules of conversation are not dependent on conceptual competence for counting, although they do contribute to communicative competence (Hymes, 1967), and therefore, what we call *interpretative competence.* If children set a counting goal that takes account of the counting-relevant variables but is not the one the experimenter had in mind, they will not succeed. An interpretative error of this kind will generate a failure on a particular task, even if the child has the requisite conceptual competence of the domain, a correct interpretation of the domain-relevant features of a task, and adequate procedural competence.

To address these questions of interpretation, we have added to our analysis the components of competence in Fig. 5.1 called *social and conversational schemata* and schematic knowledge of *word meanings.* Social and conversational schemata feed children's understandings of the task, including the questions they try to answer. The general social setting creates a context for the interaction between the child and the interviewer. The child's understanding of this setting is constructed using social schemata that he or she has about interacting with adults. This understanding includes communication goals that the child understands as operating in the conversational interaction of the interview. The child's understanding also includes his or her interpretation of speech acts, based on schemata of conversational patterns such as being asked to give information that the questioner already knows.

In the context of the communicative interaction and the task setting, the interviewer presents domain-relevant information and asks questions about this information. Meanings of terms that refer to sets, numbers, and other domain-specific terms constitute further components of competence in the domain of counting. The process of interpreting the information presented linguistically includes a grammar that constructs meanings of phrases and sentences out of the meanings of words. Interpretation also includes setting goals for actions that can produce answers for questions.

An Example.   To illustrate our motivation for modifying our analysis of utilization competence, we turn to Baroody's (1984) study of the order-invariance counting principle. Baroody challenged our conclusion that pre-school children have implicit knowledge of the order-irrelevance principle. He suggested instead that they may have mastered a more restricted order-irrelevance rule, one that allows them to count the same row from either end and yet not appreciate that the cardinality of a set is preserved across any and all the different count orders. To assess this possibility, Baroody asked 5- and 6-year-old children to count a row of eight objects from left to right. This done, the experimenter covered the display and pointed to the place of the right-most item and said, "Could you make this the number one? (All children agreed they could.) We got eight (or whatever was the child's value) counting this way. What do you think we would get counting the other way?" The vast majority of the 5-year-olds responded with some value other than eight.

Gelman et al. (1986) suggested that the younger children in the Baroody experiment misinterpreted the experimenter's second question about cardinality. Perhaps the children did not treat the second question as a straightforward request for information about their knowledge of the conditions under which cardinal value is preserved and instead took it as a challenge to the correctness of their first answer. In the context of the present discussion, we can say their and the experimenter's interpretation of the goal differed. The experimenter intended they report the same cardinal value, if they believed the set size was the same; however, the younger children assumed they were supposed to find a goal that would allow them to give a different answer.

Support for this proposal comes from the demonstration that an altered question format led the younger children in Gelman et al. to do as well as an older control group. Instead of referring to their first count, Gelman et al. asked, "Could you count starting with the 'five'?" "What will you get?" or "How many will there be?" Further, children who participated in Gelman's Baroody Control condition and changed their answers did so in a systematic way. They either increased or decreased their previous answer by one, something they could have done if they were trying to find a numerical problem that required they change their answer. "Their problem" could well have been to add or subtract one (the number of items highlighted) from their previous answer.

Communicative Contexts of Experimental Interviews

Why assume that young children are especially prone to treat repeated questions in the same or slightly different form as challenges to initial answers? In point of fact, the experimental setting often violates the rule of everyday conversations, in the Baroody case, the rule that one not repeat what is known already by the listener (Clark & Lucy, 1975; Grice, 1975). A question about available information presents an especially flagrant violation of this rule. Yet, this is typically done in experiments with young children. Imagine the quandary of a child who knows not to say the obvious when shown five items and asked by an adult "how many?" She knows the experimenter knows the answer, so she has to violate the rule of conversation and state what she takes to be obvious, find something else less to talk about, or decide to remain quiet. But even if a child realizes that she is supposed to tell what anyone could know, there is a further hurdle. In many studies of cognitive development the same question is asked more than once, and often the repetition follows right on the heels of the first presentation of the question. There is nothing malicious about this. Researchers often want to know how children respond to irrelevant transformations of the arrays. Still, from the child's perspective, she must once again answer although everyone in the conversation knows the answer. Little surprise if the child tries to come up with another thing to say or changes her answer.

With experience, many children in this culture come to learn that the experiment, or a situation like it, is governed by its own rules of interaction, discourse, and question–answer formats and that it is one setting where they are supposed to tell what others might know (e.g., Goffman, 1974; Heath, 1981; Schieffelin & Ochs, 1986; Shatz, 1983; Siegel, Waters, & Dinwiddy, 1987). Because the experimental setting is hardly an everyday experience for any major culture or ethnic group of preschool children, we might expect the rules that apply here to be relatively late to develop— even for those who are encouraged to initiate talk and tell what they know (Elbers, 1986). Our task as experimenters then is to determine whether the answer was changed because of limits on interpretative competence or to a real failure in conceptual competence.

The foregoing analysis is supported by Rose and Blank (1974), who used either a one-question or two-question format to test conservation knowledge. In the former, children judged whether two rows of objects contained the same number or not but kept their decision to themselves; props served to remind them of it. Next, one row was transformed and the equivalence/nonequivalence question repeated. Children were then asked to answer and reveal their initial judgment. The two question format was like the standard conservation task. There was a reliable difference favoring the one-question format. Siegel et al. (1987) confirmed this finding and went on to show that 4- and 5-year-old children who "fail" the two-question conservation task probably do because they think they will please the experimenter. These authors had children this age watch puppets who either passed or failed conservation tests and indicate whether the puppets' answers served to "tell what they knew" or "please the experimenter." The children said that the nonconserving puppets were trying to please the experimenter and that the conserving puppets were telling what they knew.

Kintsch (chap. 2 in this volume) provides a different kind of example of how limits in children's arithmetic competence alter their interpretations of a text. The children who erred had the requisite level of reading competence. For, instead of answering the arithmetic problem presented in the text, they answered an earlier one—one known to be at a lower level in the hierarchy of knowledge about arithmetic problems. From our perspective, these children's interpretation of the arithmetic-relevant components of the text were erroneous because their arithmetic competence did not yet include schemata that they needed. They did the next best thing and answered an easier problem. This raises the question of how children interpret the domain-relevant content of the word problems.

Understanding Quantitative Language

Children's understanding of specific terms also influences their interpretations of the tasks used in interviews and experiments. Experimenters have been sensitive to the influence of children's understanding of specific terms in descriptions and questions. Thus, questions about quantitative comparisons are often presented in concrete terms, such as "Who would have more toys to play with?" rather than simply "Which is more?" Models of text processing have been developed that account for different amounts of success in solving problems in arithmetic (Briars & Larkin, 1984; Kintsch & Greeno, 1985; Riley, Greeno, & Heller, 1983). However, there has been no theory that connects hypotheses about representations of text with understanding of general mathematical concepts and principles. An analysis of competence in which representations of language about quantities and numbers are related to hypotheses about understanding of general concepts and principles is being developed by Greeno, Walter Johnson, and Adele Goldberg. (A preliminary report was in Greeno and Johnson, 1984.)

Effects of Wording on Children's Performance.   At one level it is obvious that children's ability to succeed in tasks certainly depends on their understanding of language that is used to describe the tasks and to ask questions. If questions were asked in English to a child who only understood Spanish, no one would be surprised if the child failed. Several research findings have shown, however, that effects of language understanding can be considerably more subtle than total lack of comprehension.

Markman and her associates have introduced an important set of phenomena involving influences of wording on interpretation (Markman, 1979; Markman & Seibert, 1976). Markman studied the effect of referring to sets of objects with collection terms, such as "forest" or "football team," rather than class terms, such as "trees" or "football players." Children were more successful on tasks involving class inclusion and other quantitative relations, if the conversation and questions included references to collections.

One of the tasks studied by Markman was class inclusion (Markman & Seibert, 1976). When children mistakenly say there are more of a subset than of the set that contains it, they are often said to lack understanding of the hierarchical structure of subset relations (e.g., Inhelder & Piaget, 1959/1964). This conclusion may not be warranted. Children tested with collection terms (e.g., "Here is a bunch of grapes; there are green grapes and there are purple grapes, and this is the bunch. Who would have more to eat, someone who ate the green grapes or someone who ate the bunch?") answered correctly more often than children tested with descriptions and questions stated entirely in class terms (e.g., "Here are some grapes, there are green grapes and there are purple grapes; who would have more to eat, someone who ate the green grapes or someone who ate the grapes?").

Tasks used in Markman's experiments included conservation of number, questions about the cardinalities of sets following counting, and other situations in which she found that collection terms facilitated performance. Markman's data fit with our hypothesis that interpretative competence plays a role in representation of the task. In subsequent studies, Fuson, Pergament, and Lyons (1985) and Fuson (1986) have failed to replicate some of Markman's findings, so there may be other factors in addition to the wording of descriptions and questions that influence the phenomena. However, as we show later in this section, the likely role of collection terms is to encourage representations involving references to sets, rather than to require them, which would be consistent with the phenomena occurring in some contexts and not in others. Our analysis provides a reason for expecting that the collection-term effect might be more robust in class-inclusion tasks than in other quantitative judgments, and this is consistent with Fuson's (1986) success in replicating that finding.

Another effect of linguistic factors on children's success was demonstrated by Hudson (1983). Hudson was interested in children's difficulty with questions about differences between cardinalities of sets. If children are shown pictures of two sets and are asked "How many more?"—for example, when shown five birds and two worms and asked "How many more birds are there than worms?" children often answer with the number of the larger set rather than the difference—that is, "five," rather than "three," in the case of five birds and three worms. This has often been interpreted as indicating that the children lack understanding of a concept of one-to-one correspondence. However, a different question leads to quite different results. For example, if the interviewer says, "The birds are going to race over and each one is going to try to get a worm. How many of the birds won't get a worm?" significantly more children answer correctly. It seems that children are able to compare the sets by forming sets with one-to-one correspondence and counting the remainder, when enough linguistic cues are provided.

Theoretical Framework.   The analysis that Greeno, Johnson, and Goldberg (in progress) are developing provides hypotheses about competence for understanding descriptions and questions about numbers and sets of objects.

Fig. 5.2 shows an expansion of some of the components of interpretive competence shown in Fig. 5.1. There are three main components of the new analysis: (a) Analyses of propositional representations and intensions provide hypotheses about understanding of language about numbers and sets; (b) analyses of actions performed to make inferences and answer questions include hypotheses about competence for decisions made in determining sets to be counted and performing counting activities; (c) analyses of actions performed to construct models based on propositions that provide concrete representations that can be used to facilitate reasoning include hypotheses about understanding relations between predicates in propositions and sets that can be constructed.

Propositional representations and intensions are analyzed using Montague grammar (Dowty, Wall, & Peters, 1981), a system that provides formal methods for deriving meanings of phrases and sentences from assumptions about meanings of individual words.[1] Different levels of under-

---

[1]We recognize that many concepts cannot be defined with reference to intensional and extensional components. However, number concepts are a different matter and set theoretic models of them are common. Hence, our choice of a Montague Grammar to model the understanding of mathematical terms seems reasonable.

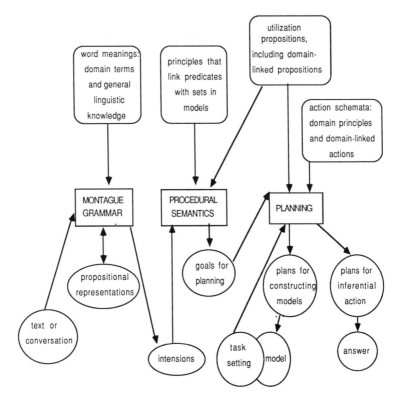

FIG. 5.2.   Expansion of interpretative competence for understanding language.

standing of mathematical concepts and principles are characterized as different meanings of words, especially numerals and words that refer to relations between sets. Depending on the specific assumptions that are made, propositions may include information about individual objects, sets of objects and their respective cardinalities, relations between sets such as subset and complementary sets, and numbers by which sets differ. We hypothesize that the different meanings of words that lead to different information in propositions correspond to different levels of understanding of principles that are implicit in children's comprehension of language about numbers and sets.

Given propositions about a situation, including a question, decisions about sets to be counted or other inferential actions determine a set of goals for planning actions that can provide an answer to the question. These goals constitute a link between the predicates in propositions and the objects, sets, and relations that are in the task situations. These goals are determined by procedures that are specified in the analysis, a version of procedural semantics in Johnson-Laird's (1983) sense. The difficulty or likelihood of setting the goals correctly depends on the information in the propositions and especially in the intensions that relate terms in the propositions to objects, sets, and relations in the situation. Analyses are provided of the trade-offs between complexity of information in propositions and complexity of procedures needed to determine the actions needed to answer questions.

When questions are asked about hypothetical situations, children can find answers either by operating on symbolic representations or by constructing mental or physical models of the situation and using the models in their reasoning. Greeno et al. (in progress) are analyzing processes of setting goals for the actions of constructing physical models using small blocks that correspond to objects and cards that blocks are placed on to correspond to different sets that are described. Construction of these models is analogous to the construction of mental models in other task situations, such as syllogistic reasoning (Johnson-Laird, 1983), and the analyses of procedures for setting the goals and for generating the plans for constructing models are further contributions to the study of procedural semantics.

These components of Greeno et al.'s current analysis are related to the components of understanding that vanDijk and Kintsch (1983) and Kintsch and Greeno (1985) have used in discussing text processing. VanDijk and Kintsch distinguished between forming a textbase of propositions and forming a situation model, and Kintsch and Greeno considered the formation of a problem model, a special case of a situation model for problem situations. Greeno et al.'s analysis of the propositional representations, based on word meanings, provides hypotheses about the competence underlying formation of the propositional textbase. When a text or conversation is about a situation that is present, the connection to that situation consists of the intensional mapping from terms to the situation, and goals for answering questions about the situation are interpreted as part of that connection. When descriptions and questions are about situations that are not present, Greeno et al. assume that models based on the descriptions will be constructed. Their analysis provides hypotheses about competence that underlies construction of problem and situation models.

Propositions and Intensions.   The basic finding from the analysis is a set of distinctions between different levels of understanding of terms, especially of numerals. At the simplest level, the meanings of numerals include reference only to individual objects and the results or arguments of counting operations. Implicitly, numerals are associated with sets in the process of counting, but this does not imply that the representations of meaning include explicit references to sets.

At a second level, numerals denote the cardinalities of sets, and reference to sets is included in the meanings of propositions that have numerals and other quantifiers, such as "some." These meanings reflect an understanding of numbers as the cardinalities of sets; in effect, when a child hears a phrase such as "three marbles," he or she understands that there is a set of marbles and that "three" denotes the cardinality of that set. We therefore say that the competence for understanding propositions that include reference to sets includes understanding of a principle that we call *linguistic cardinality*.

At a third level, numerals also denote the numerical differences between sets. At this level, the meaning of a sentence such as "Kay has two more marbles than Jay" includes reference to the set of Kay's marbles, the set of Jay's marbles, and a third entity, the numerical difference between the two sets. In this usage, numbers are properties of a relation between sets, and a child's concept of number must therefore be more complex than is needed for understanding numbers only as cardinalities of individual sets. We say that the competence for understanding propositions that include reference to set differences includes a principle of *linguistic numerical difference*.

Linguistic Cardinality for Representing Single Sets.   To illustrate the distinction between the first two levels, consider the sentence "Jay has three bowls." First, we show a propositional representation at the first level, where linguistic cardinality is not assumed.

1   "Jay has three bowls" $\Rightarrow \exists x \exists y \exists z [bowl\,(x) \land bowl\,(y) \land bowl\,(z) \land has\,(Jay,x) \land has\,(Jay,y) \land has\,(Jay,z) \land x \neq y \land x \neq z \land y \neq z].$

This logical notation is read, "There is an x, there is a y, and there is a z, such that x is a bowl, y is a bowl, z is a bowl. Jay has x, Jay has y, Jay has z. X and y are not the same, x and z are not the same, and y and z are not the same (i.e., x, y, and z are distinct objects). The important feature of the proposition for us is that it refers separately to the three objects that are Jay's bowls, rather than referring to the set of bowls.

In contrast, a propositional representation with linguistic cardinality is:

2   "Jay has three bowls" $\Rightarrow \exists X [3(X) \land \forall x(x \in X \rightarrow bowl\,(x)) \land \forall x(x \in X \rightarrow has\,(Jay,x))].$

By convention, we use capital letters for variables that have sets of objects as values and lower case letters for variables that have individual objects as values. The second logical form is read, "There is a set X, such that X's cardinality is 3, and for all x, if x is a member of X, then x is a bowl (i.e., all the members of X are bowls), and for all x, if x is a member of X, then Jay has x (i.e., Jay has all the members of X).

The derivation of these representations is based on assumptions about the meanings and semantic categories of the individual words in the sentences. The difference between 1. and 2. depends on the meaning of the word *three*. In the current analysis of Greeno et al., numeral terms are in the same semantic category as determiners, such as *a* and *the*. The meaning of "Jay has a bowl" includes reference to a bowl—that is, for "Jay has a bowl" to be true, there must be an object that is a bowl that Jay has. The meaning of "Jay has three bowls" is analogous. For "Jay has three bowls" to be true there has to be something that "three bowls" denotes and that Jay has. In *1*, the something is three individual bowls, and the meaning of three includes references to three individual objects. In *2*, the something is a set of objects with cardinality *3*, and the meaning of three includes reference to that set.

Propositions are descriptions of situations, and the intensions of terms in a propositional representation are mappings from situation indices to the objects that terms denote. Intensions exist for the terms in a proposition for situations, where the proposition is true. For example, suppose that there is a world containing five ceramic bowls, a, b, c, d, and e, and two persons, j and k. Suppose that Jay is the name of person *j*, and Kay is the name of person *k*. Further suppose that in one situation, person *k* has bowls *a, b, c,* and *d*, and that person *j* has bowl *e*. Then person *k* gives two of her bowls to person *j*, creating another situation in which person *k* has bowls *a* and *b*, and person *j* has bowls *c, d,* and *e*. The intensions of some terms in propositions about this world would be:

3 $^\wedge$Jay: $[<s*> \rightarrow j]$

            $^\wedge$Kay: $[<s*> \rightarrow k]$

            $^\wedge$bowl: $[<s*> \rightarrow \{a,b,c,d,e\}]$

            $^\wedge$has: $\lceil <s_1> \rightarrow \{(j,e),(k,a),(k,b)(k,c)(k,d)\} \rceil$

                      $\lfloor <s_2> \rightarrow \{(j,c),(j,d),(j,e)(k,a)(k,b)\} \rfloor$

The symbol $<s_1>$ is the index for the first situation, and $<2_2>$ is the index for the second situation. $<s*>$ is shorthand for all the situations in the model. The first line says that the denotation of the term *Jay* is the individual object *j*, in all the situations. The third line says that the denotation of the term bowl is a set of objects, $\{a,b,c,d,e,\}$, and this also applies in all the situations. The last entry says that the denotation of *has* is a set of pairs. In situation $<s_1>$, the pairs are (j,e), (k,a), (k,b), (k,c), and (k,d), that is, *j* has *e*, *k* has *a*, *k* has *b*, *k* has *c*, and *k* has *d*. In situation $<s_2>$, the pairs are not the same as in $<s_1>$. In $<s_2>$, *j* has *c*, *j* has *d*, *j* has *e*, *k* has *a*, and *k* has *b*.

To map a propositional representation onto a situation, the variables in the proposition must be assigned values that make the proposition true.

The sentence "Jay has three bowls" is true in situation $<s_2>$, though not in situation $<s_1>$. An assignment that makes formula 1 true in $<s_2>$ is $x = c$, $y = d$, and $z = e$. The intensions of terms in 1. are a subset of the intensions shown in 3.

To apply the second propositional representation, there has to be another entity, because the set of bowls that Jay has in referred to in the proposition. The set is $\{c,d,e\}$, and that set has to be added to the model to apply formula 2 to the situation. If the assignment $X = \{c,d,e\}$ is made, then formula 2 is true in situation $<s_2>$, though not, of course, in situation $<s_1>$. This also enables the numeral 3 to have a denotation in the model:

4 $$\hat{\ }3: [<s_2> \to \{\{c,d,e\}\}]$$

The denotation of a numeral is a number, and, as is standard in mathematical treatments, a number is the set of sets of objects that have that number of objects. There are many sets of objects that have three members, but we only list those that are distinguished as the values of variables or the denotations of other terms.

An important feature of this formulation is that numerals have denotations when we include the principle of linguistic cardinality in competence for understanding language, but they do not when we exclude the principle of linguistic cardinality. Understanding of linguistic cardinality therefore corresponds to somewhat more explicit understanding of the concept of number than in the competence for procedures of counting that Greeno et al. (1984) analyzed. Even so, this understanding is still primarily implicit, compared to fully explicit understanding that people have if they have studied the set-theoretic axioms for number and can state and explain them in an appropriate language.

Another important feature of understanding, according to this analysis, is that the understanding is not just a change in the representation, but that it includes the entity that the representation is about. There is a symbol in the representation that denotes the set of three objects, but there also is a set of three objects in the model that the symbol denotes. By assuming a difference in the meanings of numerals, we also assume a difference in the way that children conceptualize situations, such that the abstract structures corresponding to terms in the language are present in the situations to which the language refers.

Another example of linguistic cardinality in understanding involves language that has been used in experimental tasks. An experimenter places five toy blocks on a table and says to a child, "Here are some blocks." (The experimenter will also say, "Count the blocks," but we delay discussion of understanding goals and procedures until the next subsection.) Let a,b,c,d, and e denote the blocks in the situation. Then the propositional representation based on competence with linguistic cardinality is:

5   "Here are some blocks" $\Rightarrow \exists X[\forall x(x \in X \rightarrow$
block $(x)) \wedge \{a,b,c,d,e\} = X]$.

There is a set X, such that the members of X are blocks, and the set $\{a,b,c,d,e\}$ is the set X. The assignment of X's value is included in the propositional representation $X = \{a,b,c,d,e\}$. The intension of the other term in the proposition is:

6    $^\wedge$block :$[<s_1> \rightarrow \{a,b,c,d,e\}]$.

Without linguistic cardinality, the translation of the sentence is:

7   "Here are some blocks" $\Rightarrow \exists v \exists w \exists x \exists y \exists z[$block $(v) \wedge$
block $(w) \wedge$ block $(x) \wedge$ block $(y) \wedge$ block $(z) \wedge$
$(a = v) \wedge (b = w) \wedge (c = x) \wedge (d = y) \wedge (e = z)]$.

Again, the assignments of values for the variables are in the proposition, $a = v$, $b = w$, and so on, and the intension of block is:

$$^\wedge\text{block} :[<s_1> \rightarrow \{a,b,c,d,e\}],$$

the same as 6. The difference in the two representations is that in 5, with linguistic cardinality, there is a reference to the set $\{a,b,c,d,e\}$ as the value of a variable, whereas in 7 there is no symbol that denotes the set. This does not mean that the concept of set is completely absent in the understanding of someone without linguistic cardinality, as is emphasized by the fact that 6 describes the intension of *block* in both versions. The concept of set is somewhat more explicit if linguistic cardinality is included in competence.

The preceding account of the contrast between a nonlinguistic and linguistic principle of cardinality illustrates our general position regarding the nature of counting-principle competence in very young children. Recall, we cautioned the reader against interpreting our attribution of initial competence as one that granted the child the ability to represent the English count words in mathematical terms. This section should make clear three of our points. First, it is possible to grant the young some counting-specific competence, without granting them full competence. Second, the learning of linguistically related principles can be based on this competence. Finally, the acquisition process involves acquiring layers of representations. Just how much this must be the case becomes clear in the next section.

Linguistic Cardinality and Relations Between Sets.   A consequence of having references to sets is that relations between sets can be represented in propositions derived with linguistic cardinality. An example is, "Jay had eight bowls; then he lost two of them; now six of them are left." In the second and third sentences, "them" refers anaphorically to the set of eight bowls that Jay had. "Two of them" and "six of them" denote subsets of that set of eight bowls, and "left" indicates that the set denoted by "six of them" is a complement of the set that "two of them" denotes. With linguistic cardinality, a translation includes predicates that denote relations between sets. If there are sets of objects in the task situation, these predicates denote the pairs of sets that have the relations—that is, the set of two lost bowls are a subset of the initial eight bowls, the set of six bowls that are left is another subset of the initial eight bowls, and the two lost bowls and the six remaining bowls are complementary sets.

Another relation between sets that can be cued linguistically is that of disjoint sets, denoted by the term *more,* as in "Kay had four books; then she bought five more books." With linguistic cardinality, "more" can relate the books Kay bought to the books she had by an implicit anaphoric reference.

If competence does not include the principle of linguistic cardinality, then propositional representations will lack references to sets. Individual sentences such as "Jay had eight bowls" will be represented (recall formula *1*), but anaphoric reference such as "of them," "left," and "more" cannot be translated into propositions, because the objects they refer to are not in the representations. If there are physical objects in the situation, or if the child creates a mental model of objects, then sets of those objects provide denotations of the relational terms, and coherent representations can be constructed. This result provides an interesting example of a way in which physical or mental models enable language to be understood when the listener's or reader's lexical knowledge is inadequate in some important ways.

Numerical Comparisons Between Sets.   A third meaning of numerals that Greeno et al. (in progress) propose involves reference to differences between sets. Consider a situation with pictures of five birds and two worms. An interviewer says, "Here are some birds and some worms. There are three more birds than worms." In this case "three" is not the cardinality of any specific set of birds. Rather, it is the magnitude of a relation between the set of birds and the set of worms. Understanding the meanings of numerals as properties of relations, rather than only of sets, involves another principle that we call *linguistic set difference.*

Let $\{b_1, \ldots, b_5\}$ denote a set of pictures of five birds, and let $\{a_1, a_2\}$ denote a set of pictures of two worms. Then, with the principles of linguistic cardinality and set difference, a translation of a comparative sentence is:

8   "There are three more birds than worms" $\Rightarrow \exists Y[\forall y(y \in Y \rightarrow$
     $worm\ (y)) \wedge (\{a_1, a_2\} = Y) \wedge \exists\Delta\exists X[3(\Delta) \wedge (more(X, Y) = \Delta)$
     $\wedge\ \forall x(x \in X \rightarrow bird\ (x)) \wedge (\{b_1, \ldots, b_5\} = X)]]$.

Δ is a variable that takes a relation between sets as its value. Formula 8 says that there is a set Y, the members of Y are worms, Y is the set $\{a_1, a_2\}$. Further, there is a difference relation Δ and a set X; the magnitude of the difference is 3; the difference relation is more (X, Y); the members of X are birds; and X is the set $\{b_1, \ldots, b_5\}$. Assignments of variables that make the sentence true in the situation are $Y = \{a_1, a_2\}$; $X = \{b_1, \ldots, b_5\}$; and $\Delta = \{(\{b_1, \ldots, b_5\}, \{a_1, a_2\})\}$. The intensions of terms are:

9          $^\wedge bird$: $[<s_1> \rightarrow \{b_1, \ldots, b_5\}]$
           $^\wedge worm$: $[<s_1> \rightarrow \{a_1, a_2\}]$
           $^\wedge more$: $[<s_1> \rightarrow \{(\{b_1, \ldots, b_5\}, \{a_1, a_2\})\}]$
           $^\wedge 3$: $[<s_1> \rightarrow \{\{(\{b_1, \ldots, b_5\}, \{a_1, a_2\})\}\}]$

The denotation of *more* is the set of pairs of sets in which the first set has more members than the second set. The denotation of *3* is the set of pairs of sets in which the sets differ by three.

If the principle of linguistic set difference is not included in the domain-specific part of competence, a translation of "three more birds" might be obtained using the meanings of *three* and *more* that we discussed previously. These meanings are inappropriate for comparison of sets; they would apply correctly for a text such as "There are two birds on the bird feeder; then some more birds came and there were three more birds on the bird feeder." If "There are three more birds than worms" is translated using only the principle of linguistic cardinality, the result is:

10   "There are three more birds than worms" $\Rightarrow \exists Y[\forall y(y \in Y \rightarrow$
      $worm\ (y)) \wedge (\{a_1, a_2\} = Y) \wedge \exists X\{3(X) \wedge more\ (X, Y) \wedge$
      $\forall x(x \in X \rightarrow bird\ (x)) \wedge (\{b_1, \ldots, b_5\} = X)]]$.

This translation is analogous to the translation of "Kay bought three more books," where "more" means that the books Kay bought are different from those she had before. Of course, *10* is semantically incorrect; it says that X has cardinality three, but it identifies X as a set with five members.

Setting Goals for Inferences

In experimental tasks, children often show their understanding by answering questions for which they have to make inferences. In this section we turn to the process of setting goals for actions that result in inferences. We consider situations where there are objects and where propositions describe or ask questions about properties of the objects, including abstract properties such as cardinalities or relative sizes of sets. The processes that we detail, again using results of the ongoing analysis by Greeno et al., construct relations between the propositions and actions that are performed on objects in the situation. Analyses of these processes and the principles that underlie them are part of the theory of procedural semantics, as Johnson-Laird (1983) has discussed.

Associating Cardinalities with Sets.   First, we consider a phenomenon involving the principle of linguistic cardinality. Some objects are shown to a child—for example, five blocks. The experimenter says to the child, "Here are some blocks; count the blocks." Then, after the child has finished, the experimenter asks, "How many blocks are there?"

Performances of children observed by Schaeffer, Eggleston, and Scott (1974) and by Gelman and Gallistel (1978) suggested that young children misinterpret either the intent of a "how many" question or have not yet incorporated a linguistic representation of cardinal numbers into their arithmetic understanding of the phrase. Gelman and Gallistel's subjects counted a given set up to six times in a row. Many of them recounted the objects when asked, "now, how many?" even though they had just counted and answered the same question. Schaeffer et al. (1974) report a similar tendency for children with some but limited ability to "make x." When asked to count x and, while the experimenter's hand covered the display, indicate how many there were, these children recounted on a majority of their trials. One might take these recounting tendencies as evidence that the children lacked any understanding of the principle of cardinality. The argument would go as follows. If children have a firm grasp of cardinality, they should use the result of the prior counts to answer the question and should not have to count the objects a second time. We can think of two alternative accounts.[2]

First, the tendency to recount may be due to the social and conversa-

---

[2]In some settings young children do not recount when asked, "How many?." Instead, they simply repeat the last tag they hear (Fuson, Pergament, & Lyons, 1985; Ginsburg & Russell, 1981). This suggests a third possibility. Young children may not interpret "how many" in cardinal terms. They may think it means "count" or "say some number word". In the latter case, the best candidate is the last said, simply because it is most likely to be the one in short-term memory. This and the previous option emphasize the possibility that the children had not yet learned a principle of linguistic cardinality; the first option emphasizes the role of conversational rules in interpretative competence. Research is needed to choose between these. Still, these are all accounts that implicate limits on how children use language, be it number specific or not. Once again, our analysis shows how children could have implicit knowledge of the counting principles before they develop more extensive knowledge of them.

tional setting, (as we pointed out earlier in a related discussion). The child is asked repeatedly how many objects there are. In ordinary conversation, individuals do not ask for information they already have, and the child has just finished determining publicly how many there are. A possible interpretation by the child is that he or she might have counted incorrectly, in which case it would be appropriate to count the objects again, to be sure.

A second explanation is related to the first and involves the child's representation of the situation. Earlier we used translations of the sentence "Here are some blocks" to illustrate the principle of linguistic cardinality. The translations are formulas 5 and 7. The instruction, "Count the blocks," requires setting a goal for the action of counting. According to Greeno et al.'s (1984) analysis of counting, the goal of counting includes reference to a set, but that reference could easily be constructed in the process of transferring information from the situation to the planning system. (Recall that the set of blocks is present in the situation as the denotation of the term block, shown in formula 6.) Thus, cognizance that there is a set of blocks could remain implicit in the process of counting, rather than have the somewhat more explicit form of a reference to the set in the child's propositional representation.

The hypothesis that young children understand cardinality, even if they misinterpret questions about "How many," is supported in results of a study by Gelman (in progress). Children who seem to lack a cardinality rule when first asked simply to count do much better on a subsequent task. In that task they are introduced to a set of x dolls and told the value of x— for example, "here are four dolls." Then, the dolls are put away and they are asked to get the same number if, say, flags or umbrellas, so each doll will have one. Such data suggest that children acquire an ability to understand the way cardinality maps onto the different count words before they understand that a request to answer "How many?" is a request to use that newfound understanding.

A reasonable conjecture is that, if a child's representation is like 5, including a reference the set of blocks, it is more likely that he or she will modify that propositional representation, after the blocks have been counted, than it is if the child's representation is like 7. The conjecture is based simply on the fact that less processing is involved. To change 5, the child would simply add the proposition that X, or the set $\{a,b,c,d,e\}$, has cardinality five, resulting in the representation

11      $\exists X[5(X) \land \forall x(x \in X \to block\ (x)) \land (\{a,b,c,d,e\} = X)]$,

which is a translation of "Here are five blocks." To change 7, more cognitive work would have to be done. There is no reference in 7 to anything that has the property 5, because 7 only has references to individual objects. Indeed, the most natural way to include the result of counting in 7 would be to add a reference to the set of objects to the representation so that 5 could be included as a property of something.

Young children may not interpret "How many?" in cardinal terms. They may think it means "Count," or "Say some number word." In the latter case, the best candidate is the last said, simply because it is most likely to be the one in short-term memory. This and the second option aforementioned emphasize the possibility that the children had not yet learned a principle of linguistic cardinality; the first option emphasizes the role of conversational rules in interpretative competence. Research is needed to choose between these. Still, these are all accounts that implicate limits on how children use language, be it number specific or not. Once again then, our analysis shows how children could have implicit knowledge of the counting principles before they developed more extensive knowledge of them.

In a previous section we discussed one of Markman's effects of varying the use of class terms and collection terms. We turn now to our account of why this variation in language points to an explanation of recounting with reference to interpretative competence. In one experiment, Markman (1979) presented sets of toys, such as blocks, to 3- and 4-year-old children in two conditions. To children in the *class condition* the experimenter said, "Here are some blocks; count the blocks," and to children in the *collection condition* the experimenter said, "Here is a pile of blocks; count the blocks in the pile." After the child counted the blocks, the experimenter asked "How many are there?" In the class condition in Markman's study, children recounted on about one-half of the trials, whereas when collection terms were used, recounting occurred on fewer than 10% of the trials. In a subsequent study by Fuson et al. (1985), a different group of 3- and 4-year-olds answered "How many?" by giving the last numeral used in counting on about three-fourths of the trials when class terms were used, and on 60% of the trials when collection terms were used. We think the discrepancy in findings is due to the ambiguity of the situation. To show why, we first discuss Greeno et al.'s analysis of the meaning of collection terms.

In analyzing the meaning of *a pile of blocks,* Greeno et al. (in progress) use the concept, developed by Massey (1976), of composite objects, which are not the same as sets. Composite objects contain other objects as parts, whereas sets contain individual objects as members. Examples that clarify this distinction are sentences such as "Tom, Dick, and Harry carried the piano upstairs." A group of men did the carrying, acting as a whole, and the logic of sets fails to capture that kind of relation.

Massey used the notation +( ) to denote composite objects, so that +(Tom, Dick, Harry) denotes the composite object, made up of Tom, Dick, and Harry, not the set whose members are Tom, Dick, and Harry, which would be denoted {Tom, Dick, Harry}. Let the blocks shown to a child be denoted *a,b,c,d,* and *e.* Also, assume that competence does not include the principle of linguistic cardinality. If it did, then a set would be represented and the collection term would probably be redundant. Then, using Massey's notation, the translation of "Here is a pile of blocks" is:

12   "Here is a pile of blocks" $\Rightarrow \exists u[pile\ (u)\ \wedge$
            $\exists v \exists w \exists x \exists y \exists z[block\ (v)\ \wedge \ldots \wedge block\ (z)\ \wedge$
            $made\text{-}of\ (u,v)\ \wedge \ldots \wedge made\text{-}of\ (u,z)\ \wedge$
            $(\ +(a,b,c,d,e) = u)];$

that is, there is an object *u,* such that *u* is a pile, and there are objects *v, w, x, y,* and *z,* and objects *v, . . ., z* are blocks, and *u* is made of *v, . . ., z,* and *u* is the composite object $+(a,b,c,d,e)$. Assignments that make the formula true are *v* = *a,* *w* = *b, . . ., z* = *e,* and *u* = $+(a,b,c,d,e)$. Intensions of terms in the representation are:

13   $^\wedge block$: $[<S_1> \rightarrow \{a,b,c,d,e\}]$
     $^\wedge pile$: $[<S_1> \rightarrow +(a,b,c,d,e)]$
     $^\wedge made\text{-}up$: $[<S_1> \rightarrow \{(+(a,b,c,d,e),\ a),\ (+(a,b,c,d,e),\ b),\ . . .,$
                $(+(a,b,c,d,e),\ e)\}]$

Formula *12,* with a collection term, does not include reference to the set of blocks, and therefore modifying *12* to include the result of counting would not be as easy as modifying *5* to get *11.* On the other hand, the representation does include the composite objects, and the parts of that object are the members of the set that is counted. This might encourage *some* children to create a representation of the set and add it to the propositional representation. The matter is subtle, however, and untangling it probably will require research on the general question of children's understanding of terms that denote composite objects in contexts other than those involving numbers. Understanding the conditions in which children tend to recount sets also requires clarifying the effect of the social and conversational context involved when an experimenter asks a question directly about the result of their counting.

Questions About Amounts of Difference.   Another finding that implicates the role of language in reasoning about quantity is Hudson's (1983) result, showing that, if young children are asked "How many more . . . are there than . . . ?", they often respond with the number in the larger set, but, if they are asked "How many . . . won't get a . . . ?", they usually give the amount of the difference between the sets.

The principle of linguistic set difference provides an interpretation of Hudson's finding. First, consider the representation of the question when competence includes linguistic cardinality and set difference. If the pictures of birds are $b_1, \ldots, b_5$, and the pictures of worms are a_1, a_2, then the translation of the question is:

14   "There are how many more birds than worms" $\Rightarrow$
            $\exists Y[\forall y(y \in Y \rightarrow worm\ (y)) \in (\{a_1, a_2\} = Y) \wedge$
            $\exists \Delta \exists X[?(\Delta) \wedge (more\ (X, Y) = \Delta) \wedge \forall x(x \in X \rightarrow$
            $bird\ (x)) \wedge (\{b_1, \ldots, b_5\} = X)]]$.

Greeno et al. (in progress) analyze the declarative statement "There are how many more birds than worms," rather than the question, "How many more birds are there than worms?" to avoid the difficult but irrelevant problem of analyzing the syntax of questions. "How many" is treated as a numerical determiner, just like numerals, except that the number is translated as ?, indicating that a number is to be treated as a goal. Except for this change, formula *14* is the same as *8*, the translation of "There are three more birds than worms." The assignments are $Y = \{a_1, a_2\}$, $X = \{b_1, \ldots, b_5\}$, and $\Delta = \{(\{b_1, \ldots, b_5\}, \{a_1, a_2\})\}$, and the intensions are:

15          $^\wedge bird$: $[<s_1> \rightarrow \{b_1, \ldots, b_5\}]$
            $^\wedge worm$: $[<s_1> \rightarrow \{a_1, a_2\}]$
            $^\wedge more$: $[<s_1> \rightarrow \{(\{b_1, \ldots, b_5\}, \{a_1, a_2\})\}]$
            $^\wedge ?$: $[<s_1> \rightarrow \{\{(\{b_1, \ldots, b_5\}, \{a_1, a_2\})\}\}]$

The interpreter can set a goal to find the numerical amount of the difference between $\{b_1, \ldots, b_5\}$ and $\{a_1, a_2\}$, and several methods are available, including finding the difference between the cardinalities of the two sets, if the child knows about subtraction.

If competence does not include the principle of linguistic set difference but does include cardinality, a translation of the question is:

16   "There are how many more birds than worms" $\Rightarrow$
            $\exists Y[\forall y(y \in Y \rightarrow worm\ (y)) \wedge (\{a_1, a_2\} = Y) \wedge$
            $\exists X[?(X) \wedge more\ (X, Y) \wedge \forall x(x \in X \rightarrow bird\ (x)) \wedge$
            $(\{b_1, \ldots, b_5\} = X)]]$.

Recall that this results from a meaning of "more" that would be appropriate in a different context, such as "How many more birds flew onto the roof?" This meaning of "more" is like "other than" or, technically, "disjoint." *16* can be applied to the situation with the assignments $Y = \{a_1, a_2\}$ and $X = \{b_1, \ldots, b_5\}$ resulting in the intensions:

17          $^\wedge bird$: $[<s_1> \rightarrow \{b_1, \ldots, b_5\}]$
            $^\wedge worm$: $[<s_1> \rightarrow \{a_1, a_2\}]$
            $^\wedge more$: $[<s_1> \rightarrow \{(\{b_1, \ldots, b_5\}, \{a_1, a_2\})\}]$
            $^\wedge ?$: $[<s_1> \rightarrow \{\{b_1, \ldots, b_5\}\}]$

Given this representation, the interpreter would set a goal of finding the number of objects in the set $\{b_1, \ldots, b_5\}$, and the answer would be "five," the typical response of preschool children.

To derive *16* and *17*, Greeno et al. assume that competence includes cardinality. If competence did not include cardinality, the question "How many more birds than worms?" could also be interpreted to lead the children to answer with the number of birds, rather than the difference. The point, however, is that linguistic cardinality is not sufficient to provide a correct interpretation of "How many more?" questions. The principle of linguistic set comparison is also needed; that is, numbers must be understood as properties of differences between sets, as well as properties of individual sets.

Qualitive Comparisons Between Sets. Next, we consider two of Markman's findings that involve comparisons of sets: the facilitation of number conservation (Markman, 1979) and the facilitation of class inclusion (Markman & Seibert, 1976) when collection terms are used.

In the number conservation experiment, the interviewer presented two rows of toy soldiers in one-to-one correspondence and asked which row had more. Then the interviewer spread one of the rows out and repeated the question. In the class condition, the interviewer said, "These are your soldiers and these are my soldiers. What's more: my soldiers or your soldiers, or are they both the same?" In the collection condition, the interviewer said, "This is your army and this is my army. What's more: my army or your army, or are they both the same?" In four problems of this kind, presented to 4- and 5-year-olds, children in the class collection were correct on an average of 1.46 problems, whereas children in the collection condition were correct on an average of 3.18 problems. Again, Fuson (1986) failed to replicate this finding, and, as in the cases of the recounting finding and others, further empirical work is needed to characterize the conditions in which the effect occurs. We provide an analysis that we hope clarifies the theoretical situation, here as well.

We begin with the version of conceptual competence that has the principle of linguistic cardinality and the concept of differences between sets. Rather than "These are my soldiers and these are your soldiers," we analyze "These are Jay's soldiers and these are Kay's soldiers," to avoid the complexities of indexical terms. Also, we avoid the need to analyze possessive terms by considering the equivalent sentences with relative clauses, "These are some soldiers such that Jay has them," and similarly for Kay.

Let the soldiers that are called "Jay's soldiers" be denoted $a_1, \ldots, a_7$, and let the soldiers called "Kay's soldiers" be denoted $b_1, \ldots, b_7$. Then with linguistic cardinality included in competence, the sentences corresponding to "These are Jay's soldiers" and "These are Kay's soldiers" are translated to:

18   "There are some soldiers such that Jay has them" $\Rightarrow$
$\exists X[\forall x(x \in X \to soldier\ (x)) \land \forall x(x \in X \to$
$has\ (Jay, x)) \land (\{a_1, \ldots, a_7\} = X)].$

"There are some soldiers such that Kay has them" $\Rightarrow$
$\exists Y[\forall y(y \in Y \to soldier\ (y)) \land \forall y(y \in Y \to$
$has\ (Kay, y)) \land (\{b_1, \ldots, b_7\} = Y)].$

Assignments of variables are $X = \{a_1, \ldots, a_7\}$ and $Y = \{b_1, \ldots, b_7\}$. Suppose that Jay's soldiers are placed on [one] card C_1 and Kay's soldiers are placed on [another] card C_2. Then, the intensions are:

19    $^\land soldier$: $[<s_1> \to \{a_1, \ldots, a_7, b_1, \ldots, b_7\}]$
     $^\land Jay$: $[<s_1> \to C_1]$
     $^\land Kay$: $[<s_1> \to C_2]$
     $^\land has$: $[<s_1> \to \{(C_1, a_1), \ldots, (C_1, a_7), (C_2, b_1), \ldots,$
          $(C_2, b_7)\}]$

Then a question is asked: "Which is more: Jay's soldiers or Kay's soldiers, or are they the same?" Again avoiding analysis of question syntax, Greeno et al. analyze the sentences: "Jay has more soldiers than Kay," "Kay has more soldiers than Jay," and "Jay has the same soldiers as Kay," with "the same" translated as equal and interpreted as having an equal number. If the principle of linguistic-set difference is included along with linguistic cardinality, the translation of comparative sentences is:

20   "Jay has more soldiers than Kay" $\Rightarrow$
$\exists Y[\forall y(y \in Y \to soldier\ (y)) \land \forall y(y \in Y \to has\ (Kay, y)) \land$
$\exists \Delta \exists X[(\Delta = more\ (X,Y)) \land \forall x(x \in X \to soldier\ (x)) \land$
$\forall x(x \in X \to has\ (Jay, x))]],$

and the corresponding formulas with more (Y,X) and equal (X,Y). When the interpreter sets goals based on these sentences, the meaning of Δ as a numerical difference between sets results in setting goals to compare the cardinalities of the sets, and this leads to the correct answer.

If competence does not include linguistic set differences but includes cardinality, the demonstrative sentences lead to the same representation as 18 and 19, but the comparative sentences are:

21   "Jay has more soldiers than Kay" $\Rightarrow$
$\exists Y[\forall y(y \in Y \to soldier\ (y)) \land \forall y(y \in Y \to has\ (Kay, y)) \land$
$\exists X[more\ (X,Y) \land \forall x(x \in X \to soldier\ (x)) \land$
$\forall x(x \in X \to has\ (Jay, x))]],$

and the corresponding formulas with more (Y, X) and equal (X, Y). Recall that the meaning of more in this reading is the same as "other than," which would make either "Jay has more soldiers than Kay" or "Kay has more soldiers than Jay" correct, and would make "Jay has the same soldiers as Kay" incorrect, assuming that "the same" is understood as meaning identical soldiers. On the other hand, the situation would be somewhat confusing for a child because a presupposition of the question is that only one of the three alternatives is correct. We can only guess how a child might respond, but one possibility could be to consider the numbers of objects in the sets and answer on the basis of those.

If competence does not include linguistic cardinality, then the representations of "These are Jay's soldiers" and "These are Kay's soldiers" include references to individual objects, rather than to sets. Lacking reference to sets of soldiers could correspond to the stage of understanding that Piaget called graphical collections, which are spatially defined and might well lead to a spatial interpretation of "more" in the question "Which is more?" Of course, the sets of objects are present, and, if the child interprets more and equal numerically, he or she could set goals for counting the sets of objects, and the correct answer could be given without having references to sets in the propositional representation.

Markman (1979) found that use of collection terms improved the performance of preschool children on number conservation tasks. If we assume that collection terms such as *army* denote composite objects in Massey's (1976) sense, and let the two armies be denoted $+(a_1, \ldots, a_7)$ and $+(b_1, \ldots, b_7)$, then the translations of sentences corresponding to "This is Jay's army" and "This is Kay's army" are:

22      $\exists u[army\ (u) \wedge has\ (Jay,\ u) \wedge (+(a_1, \ldots, a_7) = u)]$;
        $\exists v[army\ (v) \wedge has\ (Kay,\ v) \wedge (+(b_1, \ldots, b_7) = v)]$.

The comparative sentence corresponding to "Jay's army is more than Kay's army" is:

23          $\exists v[army\ (v) \wedge has\ (Kay,\ v) \wedge \exists u[more\ (u,v) \wedge$
            $army\ (u) \wedge has\ (Jay,\ u)]]$.

It would not be surprising if references to the composite objects would lead some children to consider the comparisons numerically. However, it would also not be surprising if they did not. A case could be made that understanding armies, piles of blocks, and so on as composite objects might even emphasize their spatial extents, rather than their cardinalities, but that would predict the opposite effect from the one Markman (1979) obtained. As with the phenomenon of recounting, understanding of the role of collective nouns on number conservation probably requires research on the general question of children's understanding of collective nouns.

On the other hand, an analysis of language used in class inclusion tasks suggests that a facilitating effect of collection terms should be a relatively robust phenomenon. In number conservation tasks and others in which two separate sets are compared, the collections can be compared in ways, such as the size of the spaces they occupy, that allow the numerically smaller collection to be judged greater. Calling attention to the collections, if the terms are interpreted as composite objects, does not necessarily result in comparisons based on numbers. In class inclusion tasks, however, the numerically smaller set, the subset, corresponds to a part of the composite object. Therefore, calling attention to the collection should facilitate the correct judgment that the whole is greater than a part, whether the collection is interpreted as a set or a composite object.

Consider the following task, used by Markman and Seibert (1976). A set of toy blocks was presented, including 10 blue blocks and 5 red blocks. In the class condition, the interviewer said, "Here are some blocks. These are blue blocks, and these are red blocks. Who would have more toys to play with, someone who owned the blue blocks or someone who owned the blocks?" If competence includes linguistic cardinality and linguistic set difference, the representation will include references to the set of blocks, the set of blue blocks, the set of red blocks, and the difference between the set of blocks and the set of blue blocks. Correct performance depends on determining the denotations of terms correctly. Specifically, the symbol for the set of blocks has to denote the set that includes all the blocks. A procedure that then assures a correct answer determines the cardinalities of the compared sets and judges which set is "more" according to which of their cardinalities is the larger number.

If competence does not include linguistic cardinality and linguistic set difference, the representation of propositions will be much less complete. Intensions can still be constructed correctly, but a more complex set of inferences is needed for that to occur, and it is reasonable to expect that children would make errors in assigning terms to sets of objects in the situation. The standard finding in class inclusion questions suggests that children have a bias to assign distinct denotations to different terms; that is, when "blue blocks" has been mapped to a set of objects, the mapping of "blocks" to objects tends to be to a set of objects distinct from those used in the first mapping. The representation with symbols that denote sets and set differences makes such mappings less likely, because there is specific information in the representations to guide construction of the correct mappings.

Use of collection terms may provide especially reliable facilitation of performance in class inclusion because they are consistent with the whole–

part relations that are crucial for correct judgments in the situation. Reference to the "pile" of blocks, for example, requires a denotation that includes all the blocks, whether the collection term is interpreted as a set or as a composite object. Therefore, information that prevents the incorrect mapping of "the blocks" to the subset different from the blue blocks is included in the propositions when collection terms are used.

ON VARIATION

Variation per se Does Not Rule Out a Competence Model

Many assume that a behavior is principle governed if it, or ones judged to be in an equivalence class with it, is produced error free, in all settings calling for it. Briars and Siegler (1984) and Fuson and Hall (1983) articulated this position most clearly in their accounts, based on a learning-by-association theory, of the development of counting skills. This class of theories characterizes the acquisition process as the gradual accrual of reinforced habits of behavior in response to particular settings. The proposal is that children learn to count first primarily by rote and hence without understanding. Gradually the young learn, in a piecemeal way, various component counting skills, such as reciting the count list, pointing to objects, repeating the last count word in a list and so on. This happens as a function of their being reinforced for repeating response patterns they encounter in their environment. As more and more of these component skills are reinforced for use together, they are also associated in memory. Eventually, given enough cases of such learning, children induce the generalizations common to the habits they have formed for different tasks and components within those tasks. It is only then that they can be said to have an understanding of the principles of counting—the test of which is their ability to apply them without variability and transfer them to novel situations, that is, to ones for which they have not already acquired a habit. Such an account of learning is much like Hull's (1937) and Anderson's (1983). All predict that how well children do on particular tasks is a function of how much experience they have had with them. The younger the children, the less experienced they are and, therefore, the more likely they are to err—even on tasks they have already encountered. Novel tasks should present formidable barriers to success.

The previous account assumes that variable performance, either within or between tasks, can be traced to how much successful experience a child has had with a task. Children should do well on the tasks they have practiced and poorly on those they have not. It should be clear why this position leads to the conclusion that children cannot be granted conceptual understanding of a domain unless their performance is consistently correct and unless they succeed on a wide variety of tasks that are reasonably defined as relevant to that domain. Note that the conclusion also presumes that the conceptual competence hypothesis predicts essentially no variability in performance, either within or across tasks in a domain.

Although it is true that variability in performance is readily explained by the no-principle model, it is *not* true that the principle-first model is ruled out by this criterion. This criterion by itself is actually neutral in its ability to discriminate between the two classes of models. For, to assume that the presence of conceptual competence in a domain guarantees successful performance on any tasks therein is to maintain that conceptual competence is sufficient for the successful execution of the kind of behavior required in any given task setting. But this is not the case. First, conceptual competence does not contain recipes for successful behaviors. The fact that infants can respond categorically to speech sounds before they can make these sounds helps make this point. What conceptual competence does do is provide those constraints the planner must honor if it is to generate a successful plan of action. In the case of counting, additional cognitive components, including domain-linked knowledge, procedural competence, and interpretative competence, are all needed to derive competent plans for action. Once derived, these plans have to be executed without error and, as we noted earlier, this too is a matter of no small consequence. Hence, competence models like ours are consistent with—indeed predict—variability in just the way it is observed. We develop this conclusion and then turn to the question of how then to distinguish between the two models.

To review, conceptual competence does not contain instructions for putting the counting principles into practice. It provides domain-relevant constraints that the planner must honor for it to assemble a potentially successful plan for counting. But even should the planner take all the constraints of conceptual competence in the domain into account, there is still no guarantee that a complete plan can be assembled for a given task in a given setting. For this to happen, the planner must also take into account certain classes of variables that contribute to the correct interpretation of the setting and task—including some that are domain specific and some domain general.

Domain-specific variables are ones like the quantitative vocabulary used in a problem or the instructions, the props that can be used to solve the problem, and the type or arrangement of items. Domain-general variables include the kind of social setting for the task as well as interpretations of the kinds of conversations that take place in that setting. If all the task requirements are correctly interpreted, be they domain specific or domain general, and, if all these are honored in concert with the constraints of the counting principles, then the stage is set for the assembly of a successful plan. But success at this point does not guarantee accurate performance.

On the assumption that a successful plan is actually generated, the stage is finally set for the potential execution of a performance. But even now there is still room for error. Just as speech errors can occur as a consequence of output problems that occur in the postplanning stage (Fromkin, 1973) so errors are possible in the execution stage of a successful plan. As indicated earlier, this is especially so in the initial efforts at execution.

The point should be clear now: Our model of how individuals generate competent plans of action is at least as consistent with the fact that the young produce errors and variable levels of performance as are association theory accounts. Additionally, our model offers a classification scheme of the sources of variability. One can ask whether failure or errors occur because a child lacks the requisite conceptual competence, has made an interpretative error, has a faulty planner, or encounters problems in the execution of an acceptable plan. Before concluding that an error on the output side means there is no conceptual competence, one must consider whether any of these other contributors to the planning and execution processes are the culprits. In addition to conceptual competence, there are other conditions for correct performance. Hence, the facts of variability in their own right do not rule out a principle-first account of counting—or, for that matter, any other domain.

Ways to Distinguish the Two Classes of Models

If variability per se cannot distinguish the principle first from the principle after, what criteria can? We have introduced some in various places throughout the chapter. Here, we pull these together and focus on the kinds of analyses that might be appropriate.

As indicated, a principle-first model implies generativity. If children are able to generate some plans of action they have not used before, we can grant them implicit knowledge of conceptual competence. In the abstract, this clear prediction separates the two models. For there would be no account of how children could succeed if they did have some principled understanding from which to generate novel solutions. In actuality, novel tasks involve novel settings and children could fail because the setting is problematic. Still, there seems a clear prediction to make. And if either lack of familiarity with, or knowledge of, a setting presents an impediment, then task variations designed to let children come to understand the critical ingredients of the setting also should reveal their competence. Like Wilkinson (1984), Gelman and Meck (1986) found that one way to do this is to let children answer a question a second time. To illustrate, consider one of the Gelman and Meck (1986) tasks.

The task in question required children to determine whether a puppet counted correctly or not. Of particular interest was their ability to say that a novel, but acceptable, counting procedure was acceptable. For example, the puppet started a count in the middle of a row, continued to one end, and then went to the remaining items. In addition to presenting children with novel counting acts, such trials require the ability to recognize that the intended meaning of the question put to them is something like "Is this a possible way to count?" and not "Is this the usual way to count rows of items?." A child who simply answers on the basis of convention is guaranteed to err, even if he or she knows that place of starting a count is irrelevant.

Briars and Siegler (1984) found that 3-year-olds treated these kinds of trials as error trials; Gelman and Meck (1983) did not. Consider some of the differences in the details of task settings and question–answer formats in these two studies. Gelman and Meck (1983) asked children to explain their judgments and allowed the experimenter to use an interactive testing mode. Briars and Siegler (1984) did neither. As a result, some of the Gelman–Meck trials were presented a second time. On the assumption that the interaction with and conversation about the puppet's knowledge could have encouraged children to by-pass the conventional, in a further study Gelman and Meck (1986) looked at whether the effect of allowing repeated questioning was especially pronounced on such ambiguous trials. It was. Children improved mainly on ambiguous trials, and, the younger they were, the more they did so. (Because scoring criteria required validating evidence for the judgment of success, the result is not due to young children's tendencies to change answers with repeated trials.)

The preceding suggests that before denying them the ability to generate a novel plan, we might also want to give children a chance to work by themselves on a problem, without external feedback. DeLoache, Sugarman, and Brown (1985) did this with positive results, in a study of young children playing with an array of stacking cups. As Wilkinson (1984) noted, any position that denies children knowledge of the principles has to predict that there will be no improvement in performance as a function of repeated self-initiated attempts at the problem. In contrast, a conceptual competence model, be it about number, knowledge, size relations, and so forth, gains support from such data.

Our idea that principles both help to organize the search of the environment for domain relevant inputs and guide learning, points to other predictions that follow uniquely from a conceptual competence model. For one, children should be able to select those inputs that are most suited to the domain. When asked to find N things, they should be able to seek out and find a collection of items, and, while doing so, they should be able to ignore an item's size and weight. In contrast, when asked to balance something, they should pay more attention to the size of the object before them. Or when asked to find a DAX, they should look for an object they have yet to learn a name for, and so on.

These selective attention predictions are related to another criterion that could be used to distinguish the models, learning rates. If principled constraints direct attention to stimuli that are most relevant to the domain, then learning tasks that teach to these kinds of stimuli should be easier than ones that do not. In contrast, if children bring no bias to interpret one stimulus–response pairing as more privileged than another, there should be no difference in the two kinds of conditions. This design logic prevails in the animal learning literature. Learning models that postulate biological constraints as mediators of which responses (e.g., a bird's flying versus pecking) will be most readily associated with different classes of stimuli (e.g., shock versus color) are contrasted with association models that follow the standard assumption that all stimuli and responses are equipotential in the absence of a particular conditioning history (see Rozin & Schull, 1987 for a recent review). A related design is discussed later, when we show how the constraints of principles in different domains help children learn the difference between words that function as labels and words that make up a count list. The logic of the aforementioned kind of learning studies resembles that which underlies the view that children will transfer their learning more broadly if what they learn is tied to or based on existing structures of knowledge (Brown & Reeve, 1987; Case, Sandieson, & Dennis, 1986; Inhelder, Sinclair, & Bovet, 1974; Lampert, 1986).

The Smith et al. (1985) simulation points to another way to assess our position. Recall that these authors asked what parts of the Greeno et al. (1984) model they had to alter to produce a model that would simulate performance on novel tasks. They succeeded by altering procedural and utilization (interpretative) competence, while leaving conceptual competence as it was. On the other hand, the models of interpretative competence discussed in an earlier section did have to expand conceptual competence to include, for example, the cardinal linguistic principle. Findings like these add support to the idea that one can separate conceptual competence from other domains of skills that influence the production of a successful plan of action. More importantly, they point to a line of work that can assess the consequences of deficits of different kinds. For one can ask, in a very precise way, what the consequences are of deleting a particular set or subset of schemata or propositions, general versus domain-specific knowledge, and so on. The outcomes of interest are the kind of behavior that is simulated and its classification by experts or novices as a case of counting or not, and the reason why, if not.

This is not an exhaustive list of ways that one can assess different models. It begins the discussion of the need to develop more precise ways of evaluating the different predictions of different models if we are to avoid accepting or rejecting models on the grounds of criteria that do not allow us to discriminate between them.

The Competence–Performance Distinction Reconsidered

Some will think we have complicated the notion of competence. For there is the view that competence models are nothing but implicit knowledge structures for a given domain, be the domain syntax, space, logic, or ornithology. We do not take this perspective but prefer instead the idea that competence in a domain is being able to generate competent plans of action that honor the constraints of the principles of knowledge in that domain. Otherwise the plans could not yield examples of behaviors that are in the equivalence class of the target area. For procedural competence to generate all and only those plans that meet this criterion requires that consider more than the constraints of conceptual competence. It also must be constrained by domain-relevant interpretations of the setting. This could not happen if conceptual competence were not driving the attention to and learning about those aspects of the environment that are suitable stimuli.

What emerges from the present analysis of conceptual competence is the idea that principles provide guidelines for behavior. They constrain the range of stimuli one should attend to, the kinds of things one should learn to expand knowledge of a domain, and the class of behaviors one can suitably organize to meet goals of action that are recognized as relevant to the domain in question. They do not, however, come packaged with recipes for successful outputs.

With the foregoing in mind, we propose that traditional views of the competence–performance distinction be modified to deal with the fact that successful behaviors depend on competent plans of action. We believe theories of the mind should be theories of how the mind governs action as well as pure thoughts; they have to deal with the fact that actions are often part and parcel of thinking. This is especially true in the problem-solving domain, and, hence, models of competence that fail to address the question of how conceptual competence links to behavior must be viewed as incomplete. Thus, it hardly makes sense to pit competence against performance. The focus should be the difference between domain-specific and domain-independent variables as contributors to competent plans for performance. Domain-specific competence is a *sine qua non* for successful problem solving with a domain. Although necessary, it is not sufficient. We have seen that other competences, ones we refer to as domain general, are also involved in the production of a competent plan. Given this, the question is what contributes to the successful execution of that plan and thus successful performance.

TOWARD A MODEL OF ACTIVE LEARNING: SOME SPECULATIONS

Recent discussions have highlighted the way the young participate actively in their own learning (Brown, Bransford, Ferrara, & Campione, 1983; Gelman & Brown, 1986; Resnick, 1986). Young learners often ignore what an adult tries to get them to do; they focus on what they find interesting; they monitor, on their own, their progress through a solution; they self-correct, or at least start a trial over again without obvious external feed-back; and they keep at a problem until they find a better solution than one they have achieved, even if this means going from an error-free solution to one that is error prone. Especially compelling examples of such self-initi-ated and active involvement are provided by Karmiloff-Smith and Inhel-der's (1974/75) case study of children learning to balance blocks and Brown and Reeve's (1987) analyses of how toddlers become progressively more sophisticated in stacking cups that are ordered in size. Children persist at these activities and move through more and more sophisticated levels of solutions without any external feedback. There is no denying the obvious supporting role that others can play. But any model of learning must also deal with the fact that children do not simply absorb the material we put in front of them. A model must account for their selective attention and motivation, their self-generated learning activities, and their ability to make progress without benefit of others telling them the solutions. Analy-ses of competence like ours contribute some essential components of such an account.

Principles Direct Attention and Support Organized, Coherent Storage of Data

Earlier we proposed that infants attend to number-relevant information from displays because their attention is directed by implicit knowledge of at least some components of pertinent mathematical principles. Gelman (1986) developed this argument, that is, that domain-specific principles can help the young organize the search of their environment for domain-rele-vant inputs. The idea is that principles provide clues regarding the way environments are used to serve a particular goal or function. Because numerals are used by others in a way that satisfies the counting principles, and because color terms and the alphabet entries are not, the child who has implicit counting principles available can at least sort these different classes of verbal items into those that have something to do with counting and those that do not.

If principles direct attention to environments that are suited to their goals, then learners are at least in the position to collect information that relates to them. But there is more to developing skill and further competence at counting than finding and remembering an appropriate class of stimuli. In the case of counting, one needs to acquire knowledge about those actions that serve the goals of the counting principles, the kind of actions that will have to become part of domain-linked knowledge. We note that the environment is made up of behaviors of others, as well as objects and their attributes. If we assume that counting competence can serve to highlight these relevant behaviors, those that will satisfy constraints on the planner, we have a beginning account of this kind of learning. In our discussion earlier of the partitioning schema, we invoke this very account when we suggest that such a schema might become attached to conceptual competence because it characterizes a class of actions that can satisfy the one–one constraints.

If the planner is systematically constrained to use a class of action schemata that satisfy the constraints, it also is in a position consistently to generate plans that work, that is, that are reinforced either by an observer or because the requisites of conceptual competence have been met. This outcome, in turn, sets the stage for such plans being used again and therefore learned as solutions that do meet the constraints of the principles. If success continues, they can become attached to domain-specific knowledge and hence become domain linked. In this way, a class of actions, say, partitioning, which can take on counting meaning when used in the context of counting. We suggest that learning-by-doing can most readily led to the build up of further knowledge in a domain when the actions selected by the planner satisfy constraints of the principles in a domain. For this provides a way to accumulate those behaviors that share a common feature and hence contribute to the development of a representation of the class of such behaviors as well as the settings within which the instances can function. This is a good outcome, as far as we are concerned. For, we are inclined to a learning model that builds both a domain-linked representation of a more general partitioning schema as well a representation of at least some of the plans that use it. The advantage of allowing the latter is that the planner need not generate de novo plans for familiar settings. The Greeno et al. (1984) model gives the planner no such option; yet, it is obvious that plans that honor the counting constraints are learned and even preferred (Gelman & Meck, 1986). There are reasons to prefer to count rows from one end to the other rather than from, say, the middle. The risk of violating the constraints of the one–one principles is minimized.

Some might suggest the learning of relevant behavioral components could occur by imitation. But, given that the determination of what to imitate is also controlled by the nature of available representations (Aronfreed, 1968; Piaget, 1951), a learning-by-imitation count has to articulate these. If we allow that the schemata of counting competence could underly the ability to imitate acts that meet the counting constraints, then we have one route to the acquisition of domain-linked procedures that are imitated.

A mechanism of imitation-plus-reinforcement is often invoked to explain how children learn what the count words are. To appreciate the problem a beginning language learner faces in the absence of implicit principles, ponder the fact that the exact same set of stimuli can serve as inputs for the learning of count words, color terms, and the names of the objects. A parent could have a picture book and point to each successive picture while saying "tree, flower, doggie, house," or "one, two, three, four," or "green, white, brown, red." The child has to learn that each of these lists present different kinds of words. What might keep the child from assuming that a count word can be used as a name or vice versa? Better yet, why not assume that the object *tree* has more than one name? We suggest that it is the presence of principles that provides children with clues about the constraints the use of the terms must meet.

It has been suggested that the initial learning of labels for objects benefits from assumptions children make about three implicit principles. First, they assume that an object as a whole rather than any of its parts, attributes, surrounds and so forth is the referent (Soja, Carey, & Spelke, 1985; Spelke, 1988). Second, they assume that once an object in a class has been assigned a label, that label applies to other objects at the same level in that class (Markman & Hutchinson, 1984; Waxman & Gelman, 1986). Finally, they assume that unique object kinds each are assigned unique names; different objects are not given the same labels (Markman, 1986). Contrast these assumptions with the potential use of number words, given implicit knowledge of the counting principles.

One way to satisfy the stable-order principle is to use a list to tag items. If the principle is part of competence, it can serve to direct attention to ordered lists of words. Indeed, it might make these salient. But this principle, by itself, cannot tell the child how to use the list. This depends on the availability of further principles. During counting, the same words must be used with different objects (the item-indifference principle) at different times. If they were used with different objects in a given set, then the one–one principle would be violated. Thus, the child who takes advantage of implicit principles for both counting and labelling has implicit use rules regarding the way a term can or should be used over time. A label must be used with the same object every time; a count word need not. Further, the same label must be used for members of the same class, even when more than one is present at a given time; the same count word cannot be used under such a condition.

Our claim is not that children are unable to learn to sort these different classes of verbal materials if they lack principles for identifying labels and count words. Without them, however, learning should depend fully on an associative process and, therefore, be more difficult than principle-aided efforts. Further, the initial ability to use a given class of words should be more variable across children. Landau and Gleitman (1985) and Gelman and Meck (1986) offer preliminary data to support such an account of why young children have difficulty learning to use color words, words that are surely ubiquitous in their environments.

Our account of how children learn the count words is incomplete. For children have to do more than identify correctly the class of count words and use the first three in the list. They have to master the list. Because the learning of long lists is a formidable task even for adults, we might expect that mastery is attained over a long course. This is likely to be especially true in English because the base rule that serves to generate entries is not transparent until the list gets up to the 20s and 30s (Fuson & Hall, 1983). Given the mind's penchant for imposing its own order on difficult inputs like lists, we might even expect young children to fix on somewhat idiosyncratic lists when they count. Errors, like saying the number after 29 is 20/10 or after 999 is 990/10, occur often enough to get reported (Hartnett & Gelman, 1987; Miller & Stigler, 1987); so do the private or idiosyncratic lists like 1-2-11-8 that some 2-year-olds use (the one here was brought to our attention by a friend on behalf of her young granddaughter).

Despite the fact that the idiosyncratic lists are rule governed and/or serve the requirements of the stable-ordering principle, their continued use will produce communication problems. Rule governed or not, they have to be discarded and replaced with the conventional count lists, let alone the kinds of linguistic representations we discussed earlier. Presumably, the desire of both adults and children to communicate with each other serves as one contributor to this development. For, on the basis of volunteered reports to Gelman, adults are bewildered by the child who looks at a set of four objects and insists there are eight or refuses to include "two" in his count list. (Indeed, we often discover another idiosyncratic count list when the claim that the child cannot count yet is discussed.) On the assumption that children give up what does not communicate and try to find what does, they eventually should adopt the conventional list, especially because it is likely that the adult who thinks the child has made an error will provide it, just as they correct children who mislabel (R. Brown, 1973).

Our suggestions regarding the acquisition of a domain-linked partitioning schema also apply to how the count words start to take on meaning, even if they do not become the subject of a conversation. When actions

like pointing and number word use meet the constraints of counting competence, they can be reinforced because they are consistent with the requisites the planner has to monitor. If they meet these, then there is no need
for the child to count in a different way. As a result, the very same solution
and words might be used again, and again. Such an account allows that
what look like conventional counting procedures might even be invented
and added to the child's knowledge about counting in a way that overlaps
with that of the more mature counter. In other words, whether or not
someone reinforces a child's use of conventional procedures, the simple
fact that he or she honors constraints can serve to reinforce their use. We
note that a similar analysis could be developed for the acquisition of mathematical terms and the meaning of numerals. Indeed, it is implicit in the
different versions of the models for understanding previously developed.
This argument is made explicit in the next section.

Constraints Provide the Planner With Monitoring Potential

Young children have a ubiquitous tendency to persist until they get something right. To do this they must have capacity to monitor (of course
without awareness) the relationship between their outputs and the target
they aim for. Our model of planning provides a hint as to how to characterize this. Because the planner has to determine whether a chosen procedure meets the requisites dictated by the principles, it can serve as a
potential source of feedback to children learning to count or solve a novel
problem. For, if the requisite conditions are not met, the planning effort or
execution of a plan can be rejected or aborted. This means that the child
can start again—without being told to do so by an external agent.

The plans that we assume are constructed from competence schemata
could serve as cognitive templates for actions. The importance of a cognitive schema in an early stage of skill acquisition was recognized by
Bruner and Koslowski (1972) and Fitts (1964) and has been confirmed in
recent research by Pirolli (1987). A learning mechanism that is responsive
to the extent to which a plan and the output from it honor requisites of
competence could, in turn, use the template (more generally, the representation) to monitor the success or failure of performance. Such representations could serve three functions.

First, the plan for an action sequence might be incomplete, leaving some
actions in the sequence unspecified, but specifying the goal or subgoal that
the missing actions should achieve. This would enable trials of actions that
could be evaluated according to their local effects and obviate the need to
wait for the outcome of the complete action sequence and an analysis to
determine whether a given component was successful or not. Second, plans
based on competence schemata could serve as a basis for confirmation that

an action sequence has been performed successfully. This would occur when the significant features of performance match the plan. A learning mechanism could use such occasions to reinforce the action sequence that was performed.

A third function of competence schemata in learning could be to identify features of an action sequence that are responsible for incorrect performance. As discussed previously, the incorrect performance could be signaled by negative feedback from the environment (e.g., by a teacher) or by the learner's own comparison of his or her performance with the plan. The plan includes attachments of component actions to the subgoals that they are intended to achieve. When an action sequence is unsuccessful, comparison of the performance with the individual's plan could allow some narrowing of the possibilities for changing components to correct the error. Lacking the kind of template that plans could provide, the problem of assigning blame for failures is often insuperable, but with a representation of component subgoals, there could be a considerable easing of this task.

These potential roles of plans based on competence schemata in acquiring correct procedures all depend on the availability of plans to a learning mechanism to allow determination of the features of the actions and results that matched the plan and the features that did not. For this to occur, there must be representations of intended actions and performance in a form that allows the necessary comparisons to occur. Recent analyses of computational systems by Smith (1983) have identified reflection as a strong computational capability. To compute reflectively, a system must be able to use information about the state of its own symbolic environment under interpretation as data; that is, it must be able to evaluate and modify the expressions that represent and determine its own actions, as well as the intended meanings of those expressions in the world that it is acting in. Reflective computation in this sense has not yet been accomplished in electronic computers, but the considerations we have discussed here make it plausible that it is a feature of human cognitive functioning, responsible for important achievements of learning in principled domains. Piaget reached a similar conclusion, discussing how our ability to reflect on our representations allows us to learn more about the structures involved (Piaget, 1970, 1975).

There are reasons for expecting that representations of intentions do not persist after individuals have become expert, but instead go underground in cognitive structures, even if they are present during earlier phases of learning. In Fitts's (1964) and Anderson's (1983) terms, we would say that the process of representing plans dissipates during the phase of automatization. Perhaps this corresponds to the phenomenological and empirically documented shift from having to think about what one does to performance that is accomplished without attention (e.g., Schneider & Shiffrin,

1977). This would be consistent with our view that the representation of intended actions in the form of plans is important for learning in an intermediate phase of acquisition, when the skill still needs to be corrected and made reliably correct.

Growth of New Conceptual Competence

If procedures reflect conceptual competence, these can serve as inputs for the development of further competence. For example, in the case of counting from left to right, the child could set up a correspondence between two orders, the tags and the spatial position of items, leading to coordination of the idea of an ordinal position in an array of objects with the ordered list of numerals. Learning that depends on the detection and storage of such structural correspondences would be strongly facilitated by structures of competence that include ordering as an explicit feature. Indeed, Gelman and Meck (1986) conclude that just such learning went on in their analysis of some of the solutions children produced in a novel task setting. They conclude that some children were able to learn about the ordinal meaning of number words because they detected the correspondence between the order of an item in the count list and the spatial order of items in linear arrays. If so, the ability to detect a structural isomorph between what one's principles allow and what is present in a setting becomes a candidate mechanism for learning new principles or at least components of new principles.

Analyses of different forms of competence suggest hypotheses about the nature of competence that may be acquired in conceptual growth. The analysis by Greeno, Johnson, and Goldberg described earlier emphasizes changes in understanding that are based on acquiring new meanings of words. An interesting conjecture is that changes in knowledge of word meanings develops as a function of domain-specific use conditions and settings. This idea has an obvious relation to Vygotsky's (1962) theory of cognitive development. The existence now of methods for conducting detailed and formal analyses of different components of knowledge, including principles that may be understood implicitly, makes it possible to formulate the idea in more precise terms.

As an example, consider the meanings of numeral terms. One important transition involves acquisition of word meanings like those shown earlier, where the meaning of a numeral used as a determiner includes information that a set exists. A possible source of this transition is in the conceptual competence that children have for counting. Gelman and Gallistel (1978) and Greeno et al. (1984) argued that children's competence for counting includes implicit understanding of cardinality, including the principle that numbers are properties of sets. In the conceptual competence for counting, this principle functions in several ways; for example, the set of objects to be counted has to be partitioned into the subset that has been counted and the subset that remains to be counted, and counting is complete only when all members of the set are in the counted subset. The important fact is that, in counting, the objects have to be treated as a set, but that feature is incorporated in the constraints on actions and is therefore embedded in the structure of the actions rather than explicitly available as a feature that is accessible to other reasoning. The suggestion that emerges is that acquisition of word meanings with references to sets could involve abstraction and explication of features that are implicit in the actions and plans of counting. In an early stage, numeral terms might denote counting procedures that include set-theoretic features implicitly, and later, the denotations of numeral terms would include those features explicitly.

Another transition would involve acquiring the meaning of numerals as denoting differences between sets in contexts involving comparisons. A hypothesis about learning the principle of linguistic set differences is suggested by Greeno et al.'s (in progress) hypothesis that understanding set differences involves a new meaning of numerals. Understanding about differences between sets could develop after children have learned about differences between cardinal numbers as part of their instruction in arithmetic, where they learn to add and subtract. This conjecture is consistent with the fact that children come to understand such sentences as "There are three more birds than worms" after they have studied arithmetic in school for some time. In data collected by Riley and reported by Riley, Greeno, and Heller (1983), word problems involving questions of "How many more?" and "How many less?" were solved correctly by 80% of the children who were near the end of second grade, but by only 25% of the children who were near the end of first grade.

CONCLUSIONS

The studies and analyses reviewed in this chapter contribute to a characterization of young children's understanding of concepts and principles of mathematics and provide some suggestions for a theory of learning in mathematics and other subject-matter domains. We have not developed suggestions here that directly apply to the practice of instruction. The results and ideas that we have developed, however, raise some issues about instruction that we mention briefly in conclusion.

Assessment of Understanding.   The accumulating results of research on children's understanding in mathematics and other domains has the clear implication that, if tests of children's knowledge are limited to their performance of procedures that they have been taught, we will fail to obtain data that adequately reflect their understanding. It is now a firm conclusion for many domains that children understand significant principles that are not reflected in their performance of the tasks that are commonly used in instruction and standard tests. It is important for instructional research to develop and analyze methods of assessment that more adequately capture children's understanding. A significant feature of performance that reflects understanding is its *generative* character; to assess understanding, we need to present opportunities to respond to novel situations. Research and development on new methods of assessment will require major advances in basic scientific knowledge and theory about the characteristics of that understanding, beyond results that are already available. Still, theoretical concepts and methods are available to support the research that is needed.

Our analyses of conceptual understanding build representations upon representations upon representations of beginning levels of conceptual competence. They highlight the need to avoid assessments of an all-or-none kind of understanding. Instead, they point to assessments that identify the level of understanding a child already has as well as those he or she may be reaching (cf. A. Brown, chap. 13 in this volume). This is no less true regarding the understanding of number words than it is regarding the understanding of advanced principles of mathematics. The reason for this emerged in our analyses of linguistic principles of domain-specific competence. An amazing amount of development goes into the achievement of a linguistic version of a mathematical principle.

Instruction that Activates Understanding.   It is a major problem that many students learn procedures for manipulating symbols without relating them to the underlying concepts and principles. (The now well-known "bugs" of elementary arithmetic, see Brown & Burton, 1978, provide striking examples.) Efforts to teach children the meanings of the procedures, for example, by using manipulative materials, such as place-value blocks, have not been as successful as might be expected (e.g., Resnick & Omanson, in press). The results of research on competence suggests a dimension of meaningful learning that has not been emphasized. It should be possible, at least in principle, to analyze the problem of learning as a transformation of competence. We suggest that children's competence can play a crucial role in supporting learning in subject-matter domains by guiding attention to relevant features of the environment and recruiting new procedures that are linked meaningfully to general structures of competence. Apparently this does not happen in much school instruction, particularly in mathematics. Designs of curriculum and instruction that connect new information and tasks with the concepts and principles of the domain that children already understand, and that extend and explicate that understanding, would constitute major improvements. The kinds of instruction discussed by Ann Brown and by Collins and John Seely Brown in this volume indicate directions that are relevant and promising.

The Social Settings of Instruction and Learning. The importance of understanding the social settings in which instruction and learning occur, and working to make those settings more appropriate is widely recognized. It is emphasized by results and interpretations that have emerged in research reviewed here as well as elsewhere in this volume. An aspect that is especially salient in relation to competence is the importance of creating a social setting in which students play active roles as agents of understanding, in which their current competence is relevant to the group's shared concerns for the subject matter and its efforts to reach better understandings of concepts and principles, as well as procedures. We consider Lampert's (1986) discussion of conversational teaching as a relevant and promising example of work that can provide significant progress on this crucial problem.

ACKNOWLEDGMENTS

Prepared on the basis of talks given by each of us at the July, 1985 symposium on Cognition and Instruction at the Learning Research and Development Center, University of Pittsburgh, which was held in celebration of LRDC's 20th Anniversary and to honor Robert Glaser.

The research was supported in part by NSF Grants BNS 81-04881 and BNS 85-19575 to Rochel Gelman and by NSF Grant BNS 8310708 to James Greeno. We thank Alan Schoenfeld and Randy Gallistel, both for listening as we worked and reading earlier drafts of this chapter. Finally a special note of gratitude to Noreen Greeno, who graciously put up with our round-the-clock writing sessions in Berkeley.

REFERENCES

Anderson, J. R. (1983). *The architecture of cognition.* Cambridge, MA: Harvard University Press.

Aronfreed, J. (1968). *Conduct and conscience: The socialization of internalized control over behavior.* New York: Academic Press.

Baroody, A. J. (1984). More precisely defining and measuring the order-irrelevance principle. *Journal of Experimental Child Psychology, 38,* 33–41.

Bransford, J. D., & Johnson, M. K. (1972). Contextual prerequisites for understanding: Some investigations of comprehension and recall. *Journal of Verbal Learning and Verbal Behavior, 11,* 717–726.

Briars, D. J., & Larkin, J. H. (1984). An integrated model of skill in solving elementary word problems. *Cognition and Instruction, 1,* 245–296.

Briars, D. J., & Siegler, R. S. (1984). A featural analysis of preschoolers' counting knowledge. *Developmental Psychology, 20,* 607–618.

Brown, A. L., Bransford, J. D., Ferrara, R. A., & Campione, J. C. (1983). Learning, remembering, and understanding. In J. H. Flavell & E. M. Markman (Eds.), *Handbook of child psychology: Vol. 3. Cognitive development* (4th ed., pp. 420–494). New York: Wiley.

Brown, A. L., & Reeve, R. A. (1987). Bandwidths of competence: The role of supportive contexts in learning and development. In L. S. Liben (Ed.), *Development and learning: Conflicts or congruence?* (pp. 173–223). Hillsdale, NJ: Lawrence Erlbaum Associates.

Brown, J. S., & Burton, R. (1978). Diagnostic models for procedural bugs in basic mathematical skills. *Cognitive Science, 2,* 155–192.

Brown, R. (1973). *A first language: The early stages.* Cambridge, MA: Harvard University Press.

Bruner, J. S., & Koslowski, B. (1972). Visual preadaptive constituents of manipulatory action. *Perception, 1,* 3–14.

Case, R., Sandieson, R., & Dennis, S. (1986). Two cognitive developmental approaches to the design of remedial instruction. *Cognitive Development, 1,* 293–333.

Cheng, K., & Gallistel, C. R. (1984). Testing the geometric power of an animal's spatial representation. In H. Roitblat, T. G. Bever, & H. Terrace (Eds.), *Animal cognition* (pp. 409–423). Hillsdale, NJ: Lawrence Erlbaum Associates.

Clark, H. H., & Lucy, P. (1975). Understanding what is meant from what is said: A study in conversationally conveyed requests. *Journal of Verbal Learning and Verbal Behavior, 14,* 56–72.

Chomsky, N. (1965). *Aspects of the theory of syntax.* Cambridge, MA: MIT Press.

Cooper, R. G., Jr. (1984). Early number development: Discovering number space with addition and subtraction. In C. Sophian (Ed.), *The origins of cognitive skills.* Hillsdale, NJ: Lawrence Erlbaum Associates.

DeLoache, J. S., Sugarman, S., & Brown, A. L. (1985). The development of error correction in young children's manipulative play. *Child Development, 56,* 928–939.

Donaldson, M. (1978). *Children's minds.* New York: Norton.

Dowty, D. R., Wall, R. E., & Peters, S. (1981). *Introduction to Montague semantics.* Dordrecht: D. Reidel.

Elbers, E. (1986). Interaction and instruction in the conservation experiment. *European Journal of Psychology of Education, 1,* 77–89.

Fitts, P. M. (1964). Perceptual motor skill learning. In A. W. Melton (Ed.), *Categories of human learning.* New York: Academic Press.

Flavell, J. H. (1970). Developmental studies of mediated memory. In H. W. Reese & L. P. Lipsitt (Eds.). *Advances in child development* (Vol. 5). New York: Academic Press.

Fromkin, V. A. (1973). *Speech errors as linguistic evidence.* The Hague: Mouton.

Fuson, K. C. (1982). Analysis of the counting-on solution procedure in addition. In T. P. Carpenter, J. M. Moser, & T. A. Romberg (Eds.), *Addition and subtraction: A cognitive perspective.* Hillsdale, NJ: Lawrence Erlbaum Associates.

Fuson, K. C. (1986, November). *Effects of collection terms on class inclusion and number tasks.* Paper presented at the meeting of the Psychonomics Society, New Orleans.

Fuson, K. C., & Hall, J. W. (1983). The acquisition of early number word meanings: A conceptual analysis and review. In H. P. Ginsburg (Ed.), *The development of mathematical thinking.* New York: Academic Press.

Fuson, K. C., Pergament, G. G., & Lyons, B. G. (1985). Collection items and preschoolers' use of the cardinality rule. *Cognitive Psychology, 17,* 315–323.

Gelman, R. (1986). First principles for structuring acquisition. Presidential address, Division 7 of the American Psychological Association. *Newsletter of Division 7, APA,* Fall.

Gelman, R., & Brown, A. L. (1986). Changing views of cognitive competence in the young. In N. Smelser & D. Gerstein (Eds.), *Discoveries and trends in behavioral and social sciences* (pp. 175–207). Commission on Behavioral and Social Sciences and Education, Washington, DC: NRC Press.

Gelman, R., & Gallistel, C. R. (1978). *The child's understanding of number.* Cambridge, MA: Harvard University Press.

Gelman, R., & Meck, E. (1983). Preschoolers' counting: Principles before skill. *Cognition, 13,* 343–359.

Gelman, R., & Meck, E. (1986). The notion of principle: The case of counting. In J. Hiebert (Ed.), *The relationship between procedural and conceptual competence* (pp. 29–57). Hillsdale, NJ: Lawrence Erlbaum Associates.

Gelman, R., Meck, E., & Merkin, S. (1986). Conceptual competence in the numerical domain. *Cognitive Development, 1,* 1–29.

Ginsburg, H., & Russell, R. L. (1981). Social class and racial influences on early mathematical thinking. *Monographs of the Society for Research in Child Development, 46* (6, Serial No. 193).

Glaser, R. (1976). Cognitive psychology and instructional design. In D. Klahr (Ed.), *Cognition and instruction* (pp. 303–316). Hillsdale, NJ: Lawrence Erlbaum Associates.

Goffman, E. (1974). *Frame analysis.* Cambridge, MA: Harvard University Press.

Greeno, J. G., & Johnson, W. (1984). *Competence for solving and understanding problems.* Paper presented at the International Congress of Psychology, Acapulco, Mexico.

Greeno, J. G., Johnson, W., & Goldberg, A. (in progress). *Competence for understanding language and reasoning with mental models.*

Greeno, J. G., Riley, M. S., & Gelman, R. (1984). Conceptual competence and children's counting. *Cognitive Psychology, 16,* 94–143.

Grice, H. P. (1975). Logic and conversation. In P. Cole & J. I. Morgan (Eds.), *Speech acts: Syntax and semantics* (Vol. 3). New York: Academic Press.

Hartnett, P., & Gelman, R. (1987, April). *Inducing further numerical principles given some knowledge of principles of counting and addition.* Paper presented at the meeting of the Society for Research in Child Development, Baltimore.

Heath, S. E. (1981). Questioning at home and school: A comparative study. In G. Spindler (Ed.), *Doing ethnography: Educational anthropology in action.* New York: Holt, Rinehart, & Winston.

Hudson, T. (1983). Correspondences and numerical differences between disjoint sets. *Child Development, 54,* 84–90.

Hull, C. L. (1937). Mind, mechanism and adaptive behavior. *Psychological Review, 44,* 1–32.

Hymes, D. (1967). Models of the interaction of language and social setting. *Journal of Social Issues, 23,* 2:8–28.

Inhelder, B., & Piaget, J. (1959/1964). *The early growth of logic in the child.* New York: Harper & Row.

Inhelder, B., Sinclair, H., & Bovet, M. (1974). *Learning and the development of cognition.* Cambridge, MA: Harvard University Press.

Johnson-Laird, P. N. (1983). *Mental models: Towards a cognitive science of language, inference and consciousness.* Cambridge, MA: Harvard University Press.

Karmiloff-Smith, A., & Inhelder, B. (1974/75). If you want to get ahead, get a theory. *Cognition, 3,* 195–212.

Kellman, P. J., & Spelke, E. S. (1981). Perception of partly occluded objects in infancy. *Cognitive Psychology, 15,* 483–524.

Kintsch, W., & Greeno, J. G. (1985). Understanding and solving word arithmetic problems. *Psychological Review, 92,* 109–129.

Lampert, M. (1986). Knowing, doing and teaching multiplication. *Cognition and Instruction, 3,* 305–342.

Landau, B., & Gleitman, L. (1985). *Language and experience: Evidence from the blind child.* Cambridge, MA: Harvard University Press.

Mandler, J. M. (1983). Representation. In J. H. Flavell & E. M. Markman (Eds.), *Handbook of child psychology: Vol. 3. Cognitive development* (4th ed., pp. 420–494). New York: Wiley.

Mandler, J. M. (1984a). *Stories, scripts and scenes: Aspects of schemata theory.* Hillsdale, NJ: Lawrence Erlbaum Associates.

Mandler, J. M. (1984b). Representation and recall in infancy. In M. Moscovitch (Ed.), *Infant memory.* New York: Plenum.

Markman, E. M. (1979). Classes and collections: Conceptual organization and numerical abilities. *Cognitive Psychology, 11,* 395–411.

Markman, E. M. (1986). How children constrain the possible meanings of words. In U. Neisser (Ed.)., *The ecological and intellectual basis of categorization.* Cambridge, England: Cambridge University Press.

Markman, E. M., & Hutchinson, J. E. (1984). Children's sensitivity to constraints on word meaning: Taxonomic vs. thematic relations. *Cognitive Psychology, 16,* 1–27.

Markman, E. M., & Seibert, J. (1976). Classes and collections: Internal organization and resulting holistic properties. *Cognitive Psychology, 8,* 561–577.

Massey, G. J. (1976). Tom, Dick, and Harry, and all the king's men. *American Philosophical Quarterly, 13,* 89–107.

Miller, K., & Stigler, J. (1987). *Counting in Chinese: Cultural variation in a basic cognitive skill.* Unpublished manuscript. University of Texas at Austin.

Piaget, J. (1951). *Play, dreams and imitation in childhood.* New York: Norton.

Piaget, J. (1970). Piaget's theory. In P. H. Mussen (Ed.), *Carmichael's manual of child psychology:* (Vol. 1). New York: Wiley.

Piaget, J. (1975). *L'équilibration des structures cognitives: Problème central du dévèlopment.* Études d' épistemologie génètique (Vol. 33). Paris: Presses Universitaires de France.

Pirolli, P. L. (1987). A model of purpose-driven analogy and skill acquisition in programming. *Proceedings of the Cognitive Science Society Conference.*

Premack, D. (1976). *Intelligence in ape and man.* Hillsdale, NJ: Lawrence Erlbaum Associates.

Premack, D., Woodruff, G., & Kennel, K. (1978). Conservation of liquid and solid quantity in chimpanzee. *Science, 202,* 991–994.

Resnick, L. B. (1976). Task analysis in instructional design: Some cases from mathematics. In D. Klahr (Ed.), *Cognition and instruction* (pp. 51–80). Hillsdale, NJ: Lawrence Erlbaum Associates.

Resnick, L. B. (1986). Cognition and instruction: Recent theories of human competence and how it is acquired. In B. L. Hammonds (Ed.), *Psychology and learning: The master lecture series* (Vol. 4 pp. 123–187). Washington, DC: American Psychological Association.

Resnick, L. B., & Omanson, S. F. (in press). Learning to understand arithmetic. In R. Glaser (Ed.), *Advances in instructional psychology* (Vol. 3). Hillsdale, NJ: Lawrence Erlbaum Associates.

Riley, M. S., Greeno, J. G., & Heller, J. I. (1983). Development of children's problem-solving ability in arithmetic. In H. P. Ginsburg (Ed.), *The development of mathematical thinking.* New York: Academic Press.

Rose, S. A., & Blank, M. (1974). The potency of context in children's cognition: An illustration through conservation. *Child Development, 45,* 499–502.

Ross, J. R. (1967). *Constraints on variables in syntax.* Unpublished doctoral dissertation, Massachusetts Institute of Technology, Cambridge.

Rozin, P., & Schull, J. (1987). The adaptive-evolutionary point of view in experimental psychology. In R. C. Atkinson, R. J. Herrstein, G. Lindzey, & R. D. Luce (Eds.), *Handbook of experimental psychology*. New York: Wiley-Interscience.

Schaeffer, B., Eggleston, V. H., & Scott, J. L. (1974). Number development in young children. *Cognitive Psychology, 16*, 28-64.

Schieffelin, B. B., & Ochs, E. (1986). Language socialization. *Annual Review of Anthropology, 15*.

Schneider, W., & Shiffrin, R. (1977). Controlled and automatic human information processing: I. Direction, search and attention. *Psychological Review, 84*, 1-66.

Schoenfeld, A. H. (1986). On having and using geometric knowledge. In J. Hiebert (Ed.), *Conceptual and procedural knowledge: The case of mathematics* (pp. 225-264). Hillsdale, NJ: Lawrence Erlbaum Associates.

Schwartz, S. (1979). Natural kind terms. *Cognition, 7*, 301-315.

Shatz, M. (1983). Communication. In J. Flavell & E. M. Markman (Eds.), *Handbook of child psychology: Vol. 3. Cognitive development* (4th ed., pp. 420-494). New York: Wiley.

Siegel, M., Waters, L. J., & Dinwiddy, L. S. (1987). *Misleading children: Causal attributions for inconsistency under repeated questioning*. Unpublished manuscript, University of Queensland, Australia.

Smith, B. C. (1983). *Reflection and semantics in a procedural language*. (Report MIT/LCS/TR-272). Laboratory for Computer Science, Massachusetts Institute of Technology.

Smith, D. A., Greeno, J. G., & Vitolo, T. M. (1985). *Competence for procedures of counting*. Unpublished manuscript, University of Pittsburgh.

Soja, N., Carey, S., & Spelke, E. S. (1985, April). *Acquisition of scientific knowledge: The problem of reorganization*. Paper presented at the meeting of the Society for Research in Child Development, Montreal.

Spelke, E. S. (1988). Where perceiving ends and thinking begins: The apprehension of objects in infants. In A. Yonas (Ed.), *Perceptual development in infancy: Minnesota Symposium in child development* (Vol. 20). Hillsdale, NJ: Lawrence Erlbaum Associates.

Starkey, P., Spelke, E. S., & Gelman, R. (1983). Detection of intermodal correspondences by human infants. *Science, 222*, 179-181.

Strauss, M. S., & Curtis, L. E. (1981). Infant perception of numerosity. *Child Development, 52*, 1146-1152.

Strauss, M. S., & Curtis, L. E. (1984). Development of numerical concepts in infancy. In C. Sophian (Ed.), *The origins of cognitive skills*. Hillsdale, NJ: Lawrence Erlbaum Associates.

vanDijk, T. A., & Kintsch, W. (1983). *Strategies of discourse comprehension*. New York: Academic Press.

Vygotsky, L. S. (1962). *Thought and language*. Cambridge, MA: MIT Press.

Waxman, S., & Gelman, R. (1986). Preschooler's use of superordinate relations in classification. *Cognitive Development, 1*, 139-156.

Wilkinson, A. C. (1984). Children's partial knowledge of the cognitive skill of counting. *Cognitive Psychology, 16*, 28-64.

6

Microworlds
In Mathematical Education:
A Pedagogical Realism

Pearla Nesher
University of Haifa
Haifa, Israel

This chapter argues that school learning is different to some extent from the spontaneous learning of the child in his natural environment. It does not intend to underestimate the extent of learning that takes place outside school; rather, it emphasizes the role of schools in designing a learning environment, which is the heart of any instructional theory and activity. I regard instruction as a goal-directed, intentional, and conscious activity and therefore amenable to rational analysis and critical consideration.

The chapter looks at the rationale for constructing an instructional environment especially designed for learning mathematics. Although the discussion specifically focuses on mathematics learning by young children, many of the underlying assumptions apply to learning any other formal language. It begins with a close examination, from a pedagogical point of view, of a specific knowledge domain—elementary mathematics, its entities, and representation. An attempt is then made to demonstrate that a simple distinction between the world and its' representation, one often made, is not sufficient for dealing with instructional questions. A *learning system,* rigorously defined as a four-argument relation, is then elaborated to demonstrate the structure and function of an intentionally designed instructional environment. A major distinction is made between illustrations (exemplifications) and applications. The distinction is drawn along four dimensions: concrete illustrations (the reference), the role of ordinary language, the sense of the mathematical language, and the role of applications in the teaching of mathematics. Finally, an attempt is made to see these elaborations in a broader perspective, relating this essentially educational work to the framework of other researchers' work in cognitive science and artificial intelligence.

The reader may find some resemblance between the term *learning system* and the terms *microworlds* or *learning environments,* which are used freely in artificial intelligence and more recently in education (Papert, 1980). Because the latter terms have not been rigorously articulated, I purposely avoid them. I prefer introducing the term *learning system* and define it so that it will not be too freely used. However, before my systematic exposition of a *learning system,* I use the term microworld more loosely.

WHAT ONTOLOGY BEST SERVES
THE LEARNING OF MATHEMATICAL LANGUAGE?

The ontological status of the mathematical knowledge that concerns us here requires discussion. The analysis begins with natural numbers, because those seem to be the most confusing with respect to the ontological question. Clarifying their nature makes it easier to understand other kinds of numbers (e.g., rational, decimal, irrational) or other entities in mathematics, such as relations, operations, and functions.

This discussion should not be regarded as a philosophical attempt to resolve the controversy between the different schools within the philosophy of mathematics (Benacerraf & Putnam, 1985; Kitcher, 1983). Rather, the arguments here aim to clarify educational issues. Different approaches to the teaching of arithmetic correspond to different conceptions about the sense and the reference of mathematical language, and the microworld approach, in particular, seems to correspond best to a certain kind of realism.

The theoretical system here addresses two main pedagogical needs: (1) the need for a young child to construct knowledge through interaction with the environment, and (2) the need to arrive at mathematical truths. The system can best be termed *pedagogical realism.*

Number Words as Contrasted to Numerals

In discussing the question "What are numbers?," I first distinguish between the linguistic signs and what they symbolize. Further, I distinguish between *number words,* such as "five" or "seven," and the *numerals* 5 or 7. The number words are part of ordinary language (OL), but the numerals are part of the symbolic language of mathematics (ML). People usually think that both refer to the same entity, but I believe they refer to different entities. Number words are usually used in ordinary language as *concept signs,* quantitative qualifiers of objects that are specified by their class term, such as "children" in the case of "three children." Note that in such cases the objects are never individually specified. In saying "Dan, Ruth, and Ron went to the playground," there is no need to mention "three children" explicitly. A general class term (children) is accompanied by the quantifier (three) to indicate the quantity of the objects referred to.

Numerals, on the other hand, are used to name numbers as objects. The claim is that the numeral 9, for example, is a name for a specific and unique number that has a number of properties to be learned at school, such as being the square of 3, or 1 less than 10, or greater than 5 by 4. These are all characteristics only of the number 9. Thus, this numeral is the name of an abstract mathematical object—the number 9.

The use of number signs in both cases (number words and numerals) seems to be different from an ontological point of view. Although a numeral serves as a *name* for an abstract *object* in mathematical language, a similar number word is used as a predicate in ordinary language. It is suggested, then, that each individual number is an abstract object that can be characterized by its own properties within the mathematical system. For example:"5 is a prime number, but 6 is not." Note that even if one has the image of 5 as a multitude of elements, in the language of mathematics one speaks about 5 in the singular: "5 *is* an odd number" and not "5 *are* an odd number."

One could argue that conceiving of numbers as abstract objects is a result of the long development of the conception of number (Nesher, P., 1986; Nesher & Katriel, 1986). Clearly, the child's first acquaintance with numbers occurs in his use of ordinary language. In aiming to teach the symbolic language of mathematics, a shift must occur by which the child learns the notion of number as a mathematical *entity* on which he has to act within a mathematical system. Two sets of examples illustrate this point. If we consider, first, the child's conception of number when he enters school, we find that he has mostly learned and used sentences such as those in Set I:

Set I:
(a) John ate five (5) cookies.

(b) John is five (5) years old.
(c) I live at 5 Franklin Street.

In these sentences, numbers are used as predicates to other objects that are *not* numbers (i.e., cookies, years, and a house name). Yet it is the intention of school teachers to instruct the child in uses appearing in Set II sentences:

Set II:
(d) 5 = 2 + 3.
(e) 5 > 3.
(f) 5 is a prime number.

From the grammatical point of view, the number word and numeral 5 in the Set I sentences do not appear in the nominative clause of the sentence but in the predicate. The number name is used in an adjectival manner to modify other objects. Only in Set II do the numerals become the subjects of the sentence; they always appear in the nominative clause and they are *predicated*. In Set II, sentence (e), "Five is greater than three," for example, "five" is the subject of the sentence that is predicated by "is greater than three." In calling the reference of the nominative clause the "object," we are following Frege's distinction between "concept" and "object" (Frege, 1892a) that is central to this discussion. The two notions are mutually exclusive (in a given sentence) and mark the sharp distinction between names that designate definite single objects and predicates that designate concepts capable of having many, few, or no objects in their extension. This is similar to Quine's (1960) distinction between singular and general terms.

Sense and Reference of Mathematical Expressions

If one accepts the tradition that regards the mathematical symbols as elements of a language, one can expect to have another distinction within this language system between sense and reference (Frege, 1892b). Consider a given sentence that expresses a thought. It consists of a name (or an extended phrase that functions as an identification of an object) and a predicate that describes the identified object. In the sentence, "Ruth's dress is beautiful," the identified object is "Ruth's dress," and it is predicated by the word "beautiful." The thought is a combination of both the name's and the predicate's senses, and this is what we understand is expressed by the sentence. The relation between the sentence and its sense is one of *expressing* thoughts. A different relation inherent to language, however, that of *referring* or designating. Via the referring relation, it is possible to identify objects and relations in the world described by the language (Nesher, D., 1986).

These characteristics are also true of numbers, mathematical operations, and relations as part of mathematical language. They have sense as a function of expressing and a reference as a function of designating. For example, the phrase $3 + 2$ is a complex name for the number 5. Both have the same *reference,* which is the (abstract) number 5, yet $3 + 2$ differs from 5 in its *sense,* which is expressed here by the operation sign $+$. Therefore, they differ in the thought that each conveys. If we consider the following expressions, all having the same reference, the number 4: $2 + 2, 2 \times 2, 2$ to the power of 2, we see that each expresses a distinct mathematical thought or sense because of its different operation sign.

Operation signs formally determine a unique substitution of a simple name for a complex name. This is the idea behind such exercises as $2 + 3 = $ _____. However, this substitution, which is possible because both the simple and the complex names have the same reference, does not sufficiently explain the use of many complex names for one reference. It is only the sense that prevents these complex names from being redundant. In elementary schools, we sometimes find exercises that try to deal explicitly with the operations, relying on the knowledge of the reference of the simple complex names, as in the following example by Wirtz, Morton, and Sawyer (1962):

Find the rule:

$$(2,3) \rightarrow 5$$
$$(2,3) \rightarrow 6$$
$$(2,3) \rightarrow 8$$

The different senses of the symbolic language of mathematics comprise its essence and should become the gist of understanding mathematics. In a way, the senses of new relations that *could not* be expressed in ordinary language are embedded in the new symbolic language to become a tool for expressing notions that are impossible to express without them.

One simple example illustrates: Try to write in mathematical form, "One-fourth of a number decreased by 5." This expression is ambiguous as it stands, and only the symbolic language of mathematics can remove the ambiguity by expressing it as either: $\frac{1}{4} X - 5$ or $\frac{1}{4} (X - 5)$.

Another example is found in the use of the world "is." The ordinary language word "is" is expressed in mathematical language in four distinct senses (having four different symbols):

"is" in the case of equality: $=$
"is" in the case of class membership: ϵ
"is" in the case of entailment: $\supset$
"is" in the case of existence: $\exists$

The various senses of the word "is" do not cause any trouble in everyday life. In ordinary language one can understand an ambiguous sentence because of its context. Mathematical phrases, on the other hand, are context independent and have a unique, nonambiguous reference. In mathematics it is difficult to find one name for two objects; although it is possible to have different names for the same referent, they will differ in regard to the thoughts they express, their cognitive purpose, and their sense. Otherwise, one would always obtain the trivial expression of the form "A = A."

One can argue that the story does not end here, that the + sign itself implies different senses, such as those known in the educational literature (Carpenter, Moser, & Romberg, 1982; Nesher & Katriel, 1977; Vergnaud, 1982) as "static" (combine), "dynamic" (change), or "comparing." I address this question when dealing with different classes of applications versus different senses of the operations in mathematics.

The Truth of Mathematical Sentences

The educational enterprise strives to teach young children the rules of formation of mathematical language sentences; the sense of different sentences in mathematics, including new symbols that do not appear in ordinary language; and truths about such new sentences that are unique to mathematics and involve the question of reference.

Let us briefly probe the question of mathematical truth. Mathematical language, like other languages, is descriptive and always purports to express something true. As a matter of fact, all phrase substitutions in mathematical language are performed in such a manner as to retain their truth-value. In such substitutions we are interested in expressing a new thought. Much of our teaching in mathematics pertains to the discovery of new expressions that maintain the truth-value of a sentence. To refer to the truth-value of a sentence is to judge the thought it expresses as false as well as true.

The question of arriving at mathematical truths is a deep philosophical one that I cannot resolve here but present, instead, Russell's formulation of the correspondence theory of truth. Russell (1912) asserts that truth and falsehood are properties of beliefs that depend on something that lies outside the belief itself. Thus, truth consists in some form of a *correspondence* between belief and fact. Tarski's notorious example (1949) explains, "The sentence *snow is white* is true if, and only if, snow is white" (p. 54). Note that the first part describes a sentence (the underlined), whereas the second part describes the fact in the world. Thus, though the notion of truth is tied to an expressed thought or belief, by no means can it be determined only by it. An independent system of facts is needed against which the belief can be tested. Correspondence, however, is not the only possible theory of truth. Russell, in the same chapter, also discusses a theory of truth that consists of *coherence*. There, the mark of falsehood is the failure to cohere in the body of our beliefs.

Significant questions are "How can the child arrive at a true mathematical sentence?" or "How can he know which numeral (or operation) to put in the blank space?" The answer to the latter has nothing to do with syntactic rules, but with knowledge about abstract numbers and their characteristics. To write that $2 + 3 = 6$ is syntactically as good as writing that $2 + 3 = 5$; the only difference is that in the first case we obtain a false sentence and in the second a true one. There are two main possibilities for the young child to arrive at the true sentences. One is to learn and memorize the true facts of mathematics as presented by an expert in the field and later to refer to the memory as the criterion of truth of a given sentence. The second is for teachers to provide the child with some tool for verification of the truth of mathematical sentences via experimentation in a concrete world (assumed to be analogous to the mathematical world).

Advantages and disadvantages are present in each of these two alternatives. In accepting the first approach, it seems that one directly addresses abstract numbers as the objects of mathematics. This procedure relies heavily on authoritarian methods of imposing knowledge. It does not enable the child to realize that the truths of arithmetic are objective and necessary, and not the teacher's invention. The logical deduction that is the soul of mathematics is lost in this pedagogical approach. The second approach, using manipulative materials as the source for verification, is committed to introducing arithmetic as an empirical science rather than a deductive one. Karl Popper (1968) writes: "As far as calculus is applied to reality, it loses the character of a logical calculus and becomes a descriptive theory *which may* be empirically refutable; and so far as it is treated as irrefutable, i.e., as a system of *logically* true formulae, rather than a descriptive scientific theory, it is not applied to reality" (p. 210).

This summarizes, in fact, the main dilemma in teaching mathematics at an early age, before the child reaches the stage of formal operations. Clearly, the child cannot reach conclusions about the truths of mathematical sentences with methods as rigorous as those applied by a pure mathematician. Although mathematicians can demonstrate the truth of a given sentence by proving its coherence within the entire mathematical system, young children cannot. Thus, if the young child is to gain some knowledge about truths in mathematics not based on authoritative sources, he should rely on the correspondence theory of truth rather than on the coherence theory of truth.

Designing a concrete world in which the child can fully examine the truth of mathematical sentences via a state of events is the major task for any theory of mathematical instruction in the early grades.

PROPOSAL FOR A LEARNING SYSTEM (LS)

Equipped with the distinction between ordinary language and its designation and mathematical language and its designation, we now consider how elementary schoolchildren can be taught to arrive at the truth-value of mathematical sentences. We must develop an approach that allows the teacher to communicate mathematical notions without employing ostention (i.e., without directly displaying or pointing to mathematical entities) and without reliance on the method of formal deduction. In this section, I describe a learning system (LS) whose components are devised to move the young learner from the unknown to the known within these limitations.

The Structure of the LS

The LS is based on two components: (1) an articulation of the unit of knowledge to be taught, based on the expert's knowledge, referred to as the *knowledge component* of the system, and (2) an illustrative domain, homomorphic to the knowledge component and purposely selected to serve as the *exemplification component.* Note that the notion of *microworld,* which seems to be a natural choice of term here, is sometimes identified merely with the exemplification component and sometimes with the entire LS. I, therefore, have introduced the term LS to ensure that microworld is seen to encompass both components.

The *knowledge component* is articulated in this case not by mathematicians alone but by experts who can tailor the body of knowledge to the learner's particular constraints (age, ability, etc.) and to a learning sequence. They should, of course, know the subject matter, and, equally important, they must also know the psychology of the child and the psychology of learning.

For the *exemplification component* to fulfill its role, it must be familiar to the learner. The child should be acquainted with the exemplifying objects and be able to use familiar language to describe and communicate the relations among these objects. He should intuitively grasp truths within this component. Familiarity, however, is not sufficient. The selection of the exemplification component should ensure that the relations and the operations among the objects are amenable to full correspondence to the *knowledge component* to be taught and yet be *unknown* to the child. (Otherwise, what is the child going to learn?)

On the surface, the demands for familiarity and newness appear to be contradictory. But some aspects of the system are familiar and serve as anchors to develop an understanding of a new system relation and a new language. For example, one can use the known colors of the Cuisenaire Rods (Gattegno, 1962) and their observable lengths to point out new relations and new operations among natural numbers.

It is possible, at this point, to formulate the gist of the *learning system:* The LS has a component *familiar* to the child from previous experience, by which he is going to learn *new concepts* and relationships, as defined by the expert in the knowledge component. The system becomes a *learning system*, once the *knowledge component* and the *exemplification component* are tied together by a set of well-defined correspondence (mapping) rules. These rules map the objects, relations, and operations in one component to the objects, relations, and operations of the other component. This correspondence holds between the languages that describe each of them in a manner that Suppes (1974) calls the logical consequence: "One sentence is a logical consequence of a second just when the first sentence is satisfied in any model in which the second is satisfied" (p. 104).

As noted later, this definition is sufficient for describing the relationship between an event and its analogy or a realm and its representation but cannot sufficiently describe an LS. In an LS a relation of logical consequence should hold twice: once between the objects and the language that describes them in each component and once between the two components.

Let us look more closely into this last claim by examining the relationships among the following four components: the mathematical objects and the relations to be learned, the mathematical language, the objects and the relations in the exemplification component, and the language that describes the objects and the relations of the exemplification component.

Because the child knows neither the mathematical objects nor the mathematical language, their homomorphism to the exemplification component does not yet help him. He can play within the exemplification component without realizing that it was meant to be homomorphic to anther object. It is, however, possible to let the child manipulate the exemplification component until he can distinguish and recognize *new relationships* within this component, defined mostly by the experts. Familiarity with these new relations will serve as the basis for learning new concepts that will later be coded by the mathematical language.

Two examples illustrate the last point: first, an LS for teaching the additive relationship within triplets of natural numbers. This example, purposely selected because it is simple and well known, should facilitate a demonstration of the various aspects of the LS. The second example presents an LS designed to demonstrate multiplication of positive rational numbers.

LS for the Additive Relationship Among Triplets of Natural Numbers

The knowledge component includes the natural numbers, the + and − operations, and the = relation. The exemplification model is the set of Cuisenaire Rods. The Cuisenaire Rods are wooden rods whose cross sections are 1 square centimeter and whose lengths vary in 1 cm steps. Each rod length is color coded. The shortest rod is 1 cm long and is white. The longest is 10 cm long and is orange. The objects in this model, the rods, are isomorphic to the natural numbers in mathematics. Their isomorphism can be demonstrated by applying a special version of Peano's Axioms to the rods, as shown next.

The primitives are: "the white," "rod," and "the follower in the stairs."

The five postulates have the form:

p1. The white is a rod.

p2. The follower in the stairs of any rod is a rod.

p3. No two rods have the same follower in the stairs.

p4. The white is not the follower of any rod.

p5. Any property that belongs to the white, and also to the follower in the stairs of every rod that has the property, belongs to all rods.

Note the parallelism of these axioms to the original ones presented in Appendix A. Such an isomorphism between the set of natural numbers and the rods exemplification makes possible the extension of knowledge of relationships among numbers via the rods model. Propositions about numbers that are derived from the Peano system of primitives and postulates can be fully derived isomorphically for the rods model.

After choosing the objects, there is still a need to define the actions in the exemplification component that are to be isomorphic to the +, −, and = in the knowledge component. One interpretation for the + sign in the exemplification component can involve placing two rods "end to end," and the − sign for placing and aligning two rods "side by side"; the = sign can be exemplified by selecting a third rod that, together with the two rods already operated on, forms a specific "three rod configuration" that is characterized by its two equal lengths on both lines of the rods (see Fig. 6.1).

With such an LS, the children can start from what they know. They are already acquainted with the colors of the rods and can distinguish among them, although they may not yet distinguish among the various numerals, operations, and relations. From their comprehension of ordinary language, they are able to understand the description of the actions *to put end to end* or *to put side by side*. From this, children are able to discover triplets of rods that form the three-rod configurations that fulfill, in the expert's view, the mathematical additive relationship. Note that the definition of "end to end," and the insistence of marking it later with the plus (+) sign, could not be the child's invention but must originate with the expert.

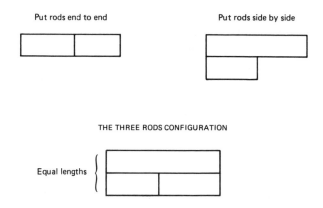

FIG. 6.1.   The exemplification of the additive relation.

Although the child can discover many relationships within the exemplification model, the expert must ensure that the child's knowledge of mathematics will converge on the standard conventions. The expert selects an exemplification model on the assumption that specific definitions of objects, operations, and relations in that domain will yield all the true mathematical sentences that appear as a result of dealing with that exemplification. Once the LS was defined as in Fig. 6.1, it was assured that all the facts of adding natural numbers in this model were true. Thus, the teacher (the expert) knows ahead of time that there are logical consequences to this specific definition of the rods' configuration. Yet for the children, the naive learners, the only requirement before learning is that they become acquainted with colors and lengths of wooden rods and understand the teacher's ordinary language explanations.

From this point onwards, the children, who until now played with the rods to build structures such as houses or bridges, are instructed to probe the special relations embedded in the *three-rod configuration* (Fig. 6.1). These relations should be new to them (therefore constituting a learning goal). The children are then instructed to distinguish and describe the relations they conceive in the rods' configuration, first in natural language and then by employing the numerals and the mathematical signs $(+, -,$ and $=)$. By this process, we expect children to use the symbolic language for relations they have already conceptually realized and understood. This can be promoted further by asking them to go in the opposite direction, to build a rod configuration for a given phrase described in the formal language. If it is not certain that the children have grasped the meaning of the various formal symbols, the teacher can always go back to the well-articulated ordinary language expressions that describe the exemplification that are supposed to be understood by the children.

The constant transitions back and forth between the rod configurations, the articulated natural language, and the formal description for each relationship in the knowledge domain should strengthen the child's understanding of the sense of the formal language. It should be clear that, by this process, the child learns the mathematical language in the specific sense defined by the selection of the exemplification component for this LS. This is the child's first encounter with mathematical language, and the child's mathematics learning just begins here.

The Sequence of Learning

The sequence of learning *within the LS* is then expected to be that:

1. Children become acquainted with the exemplification component to distinguish various relations within it. For example, that the smallest rod is the white one, that the green rod is longer than the red one, that there are only 10 different kinds of rods, that all the rods that are colored the same have the same length, and so forth.

2. Children are instructed (using subsets of phrases from ordinary language) to realize specific configurations within the exemplification component that were rigorously defined by the expert. For example, when one puts two rods *end to end,* one can always find a third rod that will complete it in a special configuration—the three-rod configuration (see Fig. 6.1).

3. Children are then instructed to describe new configurations in the exemplification component with a *new language*—the mathematical language. Thus, "putting end to end" is replaced by the + symbol, for example.

4. Children move freely between the exemplification component and the symbolic language in a way that enables them to receive a problem in formal language (i.e., $2 + 3 = ?$), to build the exemplification for it, to figure out the answer in the exemplification model, and then to move back to the formal language to supply the formal answer.

5. Children acquire proficiency with the new mathematical language and learn the characteristics of the objects and relations described by this language. They gain, in particular, control over the truth-value of the sentences expressed in mathematical language without the immediate support of the exemplification component.

Note that the position of the expert and the naive learner with respect to the same LS is quite different. The expert prepares the LS as follows: He or she starts with awareness of the mathematical domain and the formal language that he would like to teach. After an analysis of that knowledge component, he searches for an exemplification component that will be understood by the child and whose relations will be analogous to those of the knowledge component, which are the instruction target. He or she will communicate initially with the aid of ordinary language and must plan the subset of the ordinary language that describes, in an articulated manner, the objects and relations in the exemplification component. Later he will replace the ordinary language with the formal language.

Schematically, the order for the *expert* is described in Table 6.1. The expert starts with the mathematical relationships and language he wants to convey and then searches for the corresponding exemplification relationships and language. For the learner, the path is quite different. The learner must start with the exemplification component, which is familiar to him. New configurations and relations based on this exemplification are described to him in familiar ordinary language. Only later is mathematical language employed to describe the new configurations with the hope that, by combining the use of formal language and an understood environment, he or she will obtain a mental image of the mathematical objects and relations (Gentner & Stevens, 1983; Holyoak, 1985; Johnson-Laird, 1980). This last step is never assured and cannot be tested by the preceding process. Only the proper and fluent use of the mathematical language can be observed.

TABLE 6.1

The order for the expert:

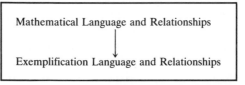

The order for the learner:

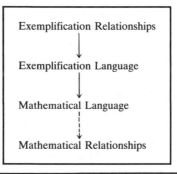

Schematically, the learner's path is presented in Table 6.1. First, he is engaged in the exemplification relationships and language. Then he is introduced to the mathematical language, in the hope of his arriving at an understanding of the abstract mathematical objects and relationships.

This method for enabling the learner to proceed from what he knows to what he does not know is also compatible with learning theories, such as Piaget's, which demand that the child's interaction with his environment and reflection on his acts form a basis for reflective abstraction. The limitations imposed on this environment, as in an LS, enhance the child's reflections on his own activities.

Although the learner's knowledge is restricted to the given model, he still can learn the characteristics of the additive relationship and gain a mental model for them. For example, when dealing with (natural) numbers, he can learn that the sum is always greater than each of the two addends, that the additive relation among three numbers is unique, that a missing addend can be found either by subtracting or by adding (with the same result), that the order of the addends is inconsequential, and so forth. All these mathematical truths can be observed and learned and not just verbally imitated. The LS makes it easier to comprehend the entire system of relations rather than isolated bits of it. The restricted reference within the exemplification component seems to foster such comprehension.

Typically, an LS does not consist merely of *objects* but embodies a system of relationships that are the target of the instruction and comprise the learning unit. Once the mapping between the knowledge component and the exemplification component has been established, the learner is free to probe either component and discover new relationships, all of which are true within both components of the LS.

To fulfill this last requirement, the exemplification component in an LS cannot simply be an illustrative device. The definitions of the configurations and the articulated set of mapping rules between the exemplification component and the knowledge component should be incorporated as the essence of the LS. Sometimes those who design exemplification models assume that, once they have laid out the mapping between the objects of the knowledge and exemplification components, they have completed the design of the illustration. It is then up to the user to determine the rest of the correspondence. Moreover, they believe that forming the specific configurations in the exemplification component is either unimportant or can be done by the learner. My claim is that rigorously defining the operations and the conditions for the truth-value of the knowledge component in the exemplification component is the main goal in introducing an LS.

Imagine that the wooden rods were introduced as objects that exemplify only the knowledge objects (the natural numbers 1 to 10), without any rigorous definition of the + sign. In this case, the child could take two

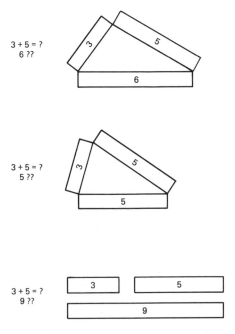

3 + 5 = ?
6 ??

3 + 5 = ?
5 ??

3 + 5 = ?
9 ??

FIG. 6.2.   Alternative three-rod configurations.

objects and arrange them as in Fig. 6.2. How can the child find out how much 3 + 5 is, for example? If the rods have not been put in a specific configuration, the same two rods can yield different answers for the + operation with the same numbers, depending on the layout of the rods. One could argue that the child can find out the result by counting. But then he is dependent on his present knowledge of counting, and, if he counts incorrectly, there is no way for him to discover his error. The exemplification in this case cannot help him. Thus, the requirement for an exemplification is not merely to serve as a concrete display, for the child's activity, but also as a feedback system that allows him to find out for himself when he is right or wrong. This brings us back to the means of arriving at the truth-value of mathematical sentences.

Assuming that the child cannot arrive at a truth-value via the methods of the coherence theory of truth, that is, using the chains of logical deductions starting from Peano's axioms, one must conclude it is necessary to design a method derived from the correspondence theory of truth. This means that one requires an independent fact in the world to judge whether a sentence given in mathematical language is true or false. For example, to find out if 2 + 3 equals 5, the child must have a way of arriving at 5 by using rod lengths (as suggested by the additive configuration). The rods serve as an independent check for the true numerical answer. This function can be fulfilled in the exemplification component only if the configuration for each symbol in the mathematical language is rigorously defined not merely for the objects of mathematics. Functioning as a model, the exemplification component of an LS must fulfill the requirements described by Suppes (1974); it must be simple and abstract to a greater extent than the phenomena it intends to model. It must connect all the parts in a way that enables the child to test the coherence and consistency of the entire system and thus form the basis for his ability to judge for himself the truth-value of a given mathematical sentence.

We now have an LS in which there are two components, each having its own particular sense and reference. The sense of the + sign is *not* "putting rods end to end" and the reference of the numeral 3 is *not* the green wooden rod. The + sign and the numeral 3 have sense and reference within the mathematical domain. The exemplification component is only a pedagogical device that serves as a "dummy reference" on which to build a sense that is analogous to the mathematical sense. Thus, a child who cannot cope with the abstract notions of mathematics can learn, by means of this device, the sentences of arithmetic and can verify their truth according to the correspondence theory of truth: The arithmetic sentences that are written in the symbolic language can be verified for their truth-value by their correspondence to the independent dummy reference in the exemplification component. Yet, *the sense* of the mathematical sentences will be as accurate and rigorous as if the child had directly approached the true abstract reference of mathematics. The different uses of language within the LS are presented schematically in Fig. 6.3.

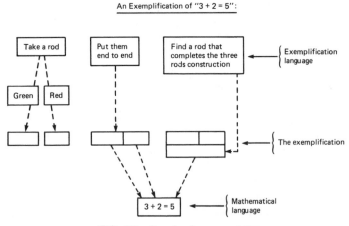

FIG. 6.3.   Levels of representation.

LS for Multiplying Positive Rational Numbers

A second sample LS provides a sense of the flavor of the creative enterprise confronting the educator who seeks to devise simple and clear learning systems. Although this may not necessarily be the best exemplification for this particular unit of learning, it is an easy one to describe and clearly illuminates the structure of an LS.

Let two rational numbers be represented by k/n and l/m, where k, n, l, and m are natural numbers (I purposely omit zero). Let k and l be the numerators and n and m be the denominators. Multiplication of the two rational numbers is defined as follows:

$$\frac{k}{n} \times \frac{l}{m} = \frac{k \cdot l}{n \cdot m}$$

This comprises the knowledge component. One possible exemplification for this unit of knowledge can be defined as follows: For a rational number k/n, a fixed area of a transparent square is divided into n equal strips, of which k are colored (see Fig. 6.4). A similar square can represent the rational number l/m. The multiplication operation is then defined as placing two such squares one above the other with one rotated by 90°.

Note that the isomorphism between the exemplification component and the knowledge component, as far as multiplication of positive rational numbers is concerned, is insured by this definition. The learner can take any two rational numbers, find their exemplification (i.e., find two squares that are divided into strips and colored according to the specific given digits) then act according to what has been defined as multiplication in the exemplification component (i.e., put one over the other in 90° rotation and "read" how many parts are doubly colored relative to the total number of parts in the new configuration). This LS is less elegant than the rods because the number that we reach by multiplication has a different shape than the numbers that are the factors, which might cause some difficulty when dealing with division. This problem casts doubt on whether this exemplification is sufficiently simple for a young child, and it illustrates the difficulty of finding exemplifications that convey a full topic with sufficient simplicity and consistency.

A Unit of Learning

When choosing an exemplification component for a specific knowledge component, apart from the question of simplicity, the question of the size and extent of the learning unit arises. We must answer this question to decide how to sequence the learning. In choosing the exemplification, one clearly must analyze the entire knowledge domain to find a consistent

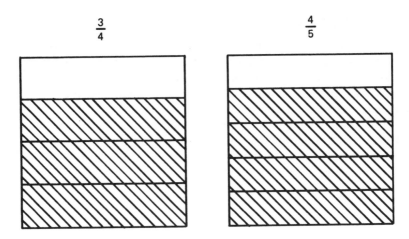

$$\frac{3}{4} \qquad \frac{4}{5}$$

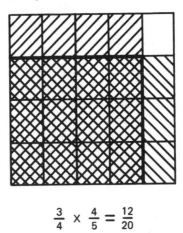

Put one square over the other in 90 degree rotation.

$$\frac{3}{4} \times \frac{4}{5} = \frac{12}{20}$$

FIG. 6.4. Exemplification for rational numbers multiplication.

exemplification for it. Yet this entire domain cannot be taught at once and should be broken into units of learning. I define the minimal learning unit as the minimal number of constraints in the exemplification component needed to specify the intended operations in the knowledge component within an LS that will simultaneously enable the child to learn the newly introduced constraints *and* freely probe the consequences of these constraints. These constraints define the syntax of the exemplification component that makes it isomorphic to the knowledge component. Within these constraints, however, the learner can operate spontaneously and discover mathematical truths. For example, once the child has learned the syntax of the configurations for addition and subtraction in rods (see Fig. 6.3), he can realize for himself all the number facts or the relation between addition and subtraction in the additive configuration.

This definition of a unit of learning is essential if the teacher is to avoid the pitfall of using units too small to render a programmed instruction format. In programmed instruction, the learning goals as well as the tasks are well ordered after a careful task analysis, and the student does not progress without mastering a prerequisite level. This usually does not leave much room for free exploration and discovery beyond the planned sequence. It also, I believe, does not capture the true structure of knowledge. For example, I suggest that the unit of learning in our first example of an LS is the *additive relation*, which includes an understanding of the part–whole scheme that underlies addition and subtraction in natural numbers (Nesher, Greeno, & Riley, 1982), rather than addition and subtraction as two different mathematical operations. More generally, a unit of knowledge should represent a portion of knowledge that cannot be further dissected without losing its essential concepts. This constitutes a minimal unit of knowledge. The additive relation is such a unit that should not be cut into smaller units. Finding these units of learning is a major task for the experts who design instruction.

APPLICATIONS, LEARNING SYSTEMS, AND ILLUSTRATIONS; TWO APPROACHES TO THE TEACHING OF MATHEMATICS

Having an exemplification as a simple abstract model that serves as a basis for building the sense and reference of the mathematical language and finding out truths *within* mathematics does not solve the problem of learning to apply this language in a variety of situations.

Two objections can readily be made to the introduction of an LS as well as against any other artificially structured pedagogical device: (1) the system does not take into consideration the child's previous spontaneous experience in his natural environment; and (2) the concentration on one artificial device does not lead the child to transfer concepts to situations where mathematics can be applied.

In response to the first objection, every exemplification should be based on elements already familiar to the child from his previous experience. For example, the choice of Cuisenaire Rods takes into account the child's acquaintance with colors, lengths, and constructive play with wooden blocks. Similarly, in suggesting the LS for multiplying rational numbers, the learner's acquaintance with equal partitioning, shading, 90° rotation, and so forth is taken into account. Thus, the child's previous experience in his natural environment *and* at school are of benefit.

The second criticism requires a more lengthy response. First of all, "application" should not be confused with "experience." Experience, even in the Piagetian sense of "interaction with the environment," can refer not only to the interaction with the surrounding situations (applications) but, as I have tried to show in the preceding section, to a specially constructed model devised to constitute the child's experience in the school environment.

Also, a distinction can be drawn between applications and illustrations (or exemplifications). The latter is used to promote the *learning* and the *understanding* of something unknown to the learner: a new concept, a new relation, a new theorem, for instance. The former is the use of these mathematical concepts, relations, or theorems in domains outside of mathematics. This distinction does not refer to the kind of objects to be manipulated, but to the role they play in the sequence of instruction.

The importance of teaching applications in mathematics instruction has long been debated among mathematicians as well as among mathematics educators (Kline, 1970). However, I do not think that this is the issue. The significance of applications is not debatable, as Frege (1892b) pointed out in the last century: "Why can arithmetical equations be applied? Only because they express thought . . . Now it is applicability alone which elevates arithmetic from game to rank of a science" (p. 187). The first part of this quotation is at the heart of the argument. That mathematics can be applied in the sciences as well as in everyday life, such as in measuring with a wide variety of scales, merely clarifies that it is an abstract language, rigorously articulated, describing thoughts that lie beyond and that are independent of any particular application. The debate, then, should focus on how this abstract language should be learned, and when in the process of learning mathematics the applications should be introduced.

I present now two opposing approaches to the teaching of mathematics in the primary grades. The first is the LS approach (although it could also be called the structural or the microworld approach), and the second is the natural-environmental approach (or the applicational approach). Although the two pedagogical approaches differ with regard to the role they assign to applications in the sequence of learning, they also differ on other deeper dimensions that should be considered in their evaluation. These are (a) the choice of the concrete illustration by which the new concepts and objects of mathematics are first presented, (b) the role of natural language in the teaching of the new symbolic language, (c) the sense and reference that is assigned to the new learned language, and (d) the manner and timing of learning the applications of the new language.

There are representatives of both approaches among school programs. For example, of the programs of the "new math" (in the 1950s and 1960s), the Nuffield Project (1966) and in many parts of the School Mathematics Study Group (SMSG, 1965) took the environmental approach; whereas the Gattegno program (1962) and the Dienes Program (1960) took the LS approach. The contrast is sharpest if we look at the extremes. In fact, many program designers, not being aware of this issue, employ both approaches in the same text in an eclectic manner. In regard to programs now found at schools, "real math" (Willough, Bereiter, Hilton, & Rubinstein, 1981, 1985) can probably be considered for the most part an environmental program, whereas most computer simulations and tutorials can be considered LS programs. Now let us examine more carefully each of the dimensions that distinguish the two major pedagogical approaches.

Concrete Illustration.   The natural-environmental approach uses all the concrete objects and illustrations available in the child's immediate and natural environment. The core notions are "spontaneous" and "abstraction," and the belief is that the more diverse the examples the child is confronted within his spontaneous experience, the sooner the abstraction of the mathematical notion will occur. No special efforts should be made for teaching applications, because the child is exposed to many applications in the course of learning the new concepts, and the transfer is assumed to be immediate.

The LS approach, on the other hand, suggests one (or more) good exemplifications that can be assumed to be the best choice for illustrating the homomorphism of the entities and relations in the knowledge domain to be learned and the selected illustrations. Although the natural-environmental approach emphasizes the richness of the illustration, the structural approach emphasizes elaborated and detailed isomorphism and the mapping between the exemplification component and the knowledge component.

That different roles can be attributed to the same illustrative objects also reveals different beliefs about the nature of the mathematics. Supporters of the LS approach make a commitment to a pedagogical realism. They assume that the exemplification component is merely a "dummy reference" for the true reference of the mathematical objects and relations. The supporters of the applicational approach, on the other hand, consider the physical illustrations embedded in the various applications the reference of the mathematical sentences.

The Role of Language in Teaching Mathematical Language.   The environmental approach employs ordinary language with no restriction (except that it be understood by the child). Accuracy is stressed only in regard to the formal language of mathematics, and the use of this language is sometimes delayed to avoid premature formalization. Ordinary language descriptions of acts in real-world situations are considered a legitimate part of mathematics (see Nuffield, 1966, for a generic example).

In contrast, for the LS approach, there exists an intermediate stage between ordinary language and the formal mathematical language. This approach generally uses an exemplification language whose terms are taken from ordinary language to be understood by the child. However, it is a well-controlled subset of ordinary language; all the terms are unambiguously defined, and each is analogical to the mathematical term and symbol to be learned.

This surface difference covers a deeper distinction concerning the role of ordinary language in teaching mathematics. There is no debate regarding the need to use ordinary language for communication in mathematical activities; the core of the controversy lies in the role of ordinary language in facilitating the learning and understanding of mathematical language. The LS approach claims that one cannot articulate the new notions of mathematics by means of ordinary language because it is ambiguous in many respects, as suggested earlier. Note the following example: The word "more" can correspond to two quite different mathematical symbols, as in

> Eight is five *more* than a certain number
> Five and a certain number is *more* than eight

In moving into the symbolic language of mathematics, the term *more* will be translated into two different symbols:

$$8 = n + 5$$
$$5 + n > 8$$

There is a further problem: If a one-to-one translation between the ordinary language and the mathematical language is not possible, then not only is it difficult to attach one mathematical symbol to a given word in the ordinary language, but there also may be some cases of contradictory meaning. If, for example, the meaning of the minus sign $(-)$ is equated in many textbooks for young children with "lost," "left," "less," and so forth, then a problem of the following formulation becomes "illegal":

> On Friday, three children from the first grade and five children from the second grade left school earlier than usual. How many children altogether left school early that day?

In this example, the word "left" guides the child, who relies on verbal cues to subtract, but this would lead to a mathematical error (for a more detailed discussion on "verbal cues" as distractors, see Nesher & Teubal, 1974).

Thus, if the only devices for the explanation of the new symbols of mathematics are left to ordinary language, as evidently occurs in the natural-environmental approach, one should also take its pitfalls into consideration. The LS approach does not rely on ordinary language for its explanation but rather articulates a subset of it to accompany the exemplification component. In our generic example, expressions of the kind "Put rods end to end," "Put rods side by side," "Build stairs," for example, were part of the subset of natural language habitually employed in teaching elementary arithmetic with the exemplification of rods. Yet, the emphasis in the instruction is on the articulated configurations rather than on the wording. Only later, when the sense of the mathematical language in its abstract mode is mastered, will various applications, including those that produce misleading surface cues, be introduced.

The Sense of a Formal Expression.   For the proponents of the environmental approach, the sense of mathematical operation lies in the various clusters of applications. For example, the plus sign (+) has the sense of *combine, change,* and *compare* (see Carpenter et al., 1982, for further explanation of these terms). Ohlsson (1986) also defined the different clusters of rational number applications as their sense. For those supporting the LS approach, however, the sense of a mathematical symbol is the distinct thought it conveys within the mathematical system. All other sets of related applications are only applications. In the teaching of *applications* one must take into consideration the various clusters, or sets of applications and what makes them easy or hard; but these are not the senses of the formal language. In mathematical language the + sign has but one abstract sense that makes it applicable to many situations.

The Learning of Applications.   In the environmental approach, applications are part of the process of learning a new concept. The mathematical language is learned via many applications that appear throughout the learning process. This approach assumes that situations for applications abound and are easily understood by the child. The learning of mathematical operations is grounded in these applications. The LS approach assumes that application should be learned separately and purposely, once the child has become acquainted with the mathematical sense in a more abstract environment, as in the LS. Nor does it assume that the skeleton of

TABLE 6.2
Contrasting the Environmental and the LS Approaches

The Environmental Approach	*The LS Approach*
Application	Exemplification
↓	↓
Ordinary language	Exemplification language
↓	↓
Mathematical language	Mathematical language
	↓
	Applications

one illustration will prepare the child to use the mathematical language in a variety of applicative situations that are remote from the exemplification model. Therefore, a special effort is made to teach applications, guided by analysis of various clusters of applications.

CONCLUDING REMARKS

This chapter examines issues concerning the design of mathematics instruction in schools. More generally, it probes the question of how young children can learn a formal language, such as mathematics. The examination consists of more than the pedagogical approaches; it penetrates epistemological questions concerning the nature of the knowledge to be taught. Now, it seems appropriate to present my approach, which is essentially an educational one first formulated in my dissertation (P. Nesher, 1972), in the framework of recent works in cognitive science and artificial intelligence.

Delving into questions of knowledge has traditionally been the prerogative of philosophy, particularly epistemology. Mental representation and acquisition of knowledge, on the other hand, have been dealt with in the field of cognitive psychology. In the last two decades, however, a new research trend has emerged that also occupies itself with questions of knowledge, artificial intelligence. Furthermore, researchers in education are concerned with questions related to knowing, especially the acquisition of knowledge. Obviously, each discipline adopts a different angle when dealing with the study of knowledge.

Whereas philosophers are concerned with questions of sources of knowledge, evidence, and truth, cognitive scientists are mainly interested in questions of the representation of knowledge within human memory. Their agenda involves understanding higher mental activities, such as thinking, reasoning, and problem solving. Their intention is to formulate a descriptive theory that predicts human behavior in real time. Scientists dealing with similar questions from the point of view of artificial intelligence, however, are concerned with completely different questions. Their problem is to understand human knowledge so as to create computers as sophisticated as human beings that can replace human beings in a greater variety of activities. Their agenda is to improve the performance of computers rather than to supply a descriptive theory of the human mind; they study human knowledge as a model of performance to be imitated.

Educational researchers consider these questions quite differently. Their agenda is to facilitate the acquisition and construction of knowledge by the younger members of society. As opposed to scholars of cognitive science and artificial intelligence who are interested mainly in the performance of experts who are already skilled in various domains, educators are interested in naive learners, or novices, and how they develop into experts. The educational question, then, is what are the facilitators and impediments in extending knowledge and in acquiring proficiencies? It should be understood, of course, that although the particular agenda of these disciplines differ, their research efforts are parallel and can be mutually enriching.

What is the lesson for education from the study of artificial intelligence and cognitive science? Two major trends have a bearing. The first concerns epistemological assumptions about the structure of knowledge, and the second deals with the nature of representation.

The Epistemological Assumption

Although in the 1950s and 1960s researchers in artificial intelligence believed in the possibility of imitating human behavior by means of natural language (see attempts to produce a mechanical translation, Bar-Hillel, 1964), later efforts in the 1970s and 1980s abandoned this overall strategy and proposed a completely different agenda concentrating on the study of intelligent performance within restricted domains (Schank & Abelson, 1977; Sleeman & Brown, 1982; Winograd, 1975; Winston, 1975).

This shift, besides leading to more successful results in the use of computers for restricted problems, was in fact a shift in the epistemological approach to knowledge itself. The assumption behind this shift suggested that *knowledge is domain specific* and that intelligent behavior is domain dependent. It was understood that any discussion about knowledge should be connected to specific episodes within specific realms of knowledge. This, of course, encouraged the research on the performance of experts who best represent learnedness in specific domains. Simulation of expert performance became a way to examine theories about knowledge structure in a given domain. Work in cognitive science in the last two decades adopted epistemological assumptions about the nature of human knowledge and its mental representation in human memory similar to those developed in the field of artificial intelligence. I refer here to the theories concerning schemata, semantic nets, scripts, and the like, each of which is anchored within a *specific domain* or *episode* (Anderson, 1976, 1980; Anderson, Greeno, Kline, & Neves, 1981; Collins & Quillian, 1972; Kintsch, 1974; Kintsch & Greeno, 1985; Norman & Rumelhart, 1975; Schank & Abelson, 1977; Winston, 1975).

Educators too must learn from this shift and deal with their questions within a content domain. They should attend to learning problems within a given restricted knowledge domain, taking into account its *specificity* as part of a more general learning theory. Such an approach has been taken in the work discussed in this chapter, by first analyzing the knowledge domain and then employing the results of this analysis in assuming a position on mathematical instruction.

The Nature of Representation

Issues of knowledge representation have been extensively studied within the fields of artificial intelligence and cognitive science and should also be considered carefully by educators. In the effort to teach a computer to work intelligently within a specific domain, many aspects of the relations between the real world and its representation have been studied and tested by computer simulations. Questions about representation have led to the notion of the *microworld* as a representation for restricted domains that can be used to test theories describing the real world (DiSessa, 1977; Papert, 1980). Similarly, efforts have been made to understand the power of analogies (Gentner & Stevens, 1983; Holyoak, 1985). Microworlds have several advantages: They enable a connection between the physical experience and the formalisms; they allow direct access to the formal theories without any distortion from practical considerations; they enable mathematical thinking to be easier and more creative (Papert, 1980). Underlying all these considerations is the distinction made between the two realms— the real world and its mapped representation (see also Resnick, 1982, and VanLehn & Brown, 1978, concerning attempts to find adequate representations for subtraction).

The goal for education here is to find alternative, instructionally more efficient representations for the worlds to be learned. In observing a growing child, it is appealing to think that spontaneous learning is the most efficient learning. Yet, this observation should not lead to an erroneous enshrined conception when it comes to the learning of formal systems. It is possible that the human mind, creative as it is, can design learning environments that will promote learning via suitable representations in a manner superior to the natural environment. I do not suggest that the artificial representation can replace the child's intuitions from his everyday experience. On the contrary, I suggest enriching the child's intuitions that are needed for formal learning by connecting the child's experience in the natural environment with school experience in more formal systems, in the form of various learning systems. Designing such LSs is the most challenging role of modern pedagogy.

Equipped with the two assumptions that education should share the nature of knowledge and the nature of representation with artificial intelligence and cognitive psychology, note how education also differs from these two disciplines. In education, two distinct kinds of relations need to be considered: the relation between the world and its representation, and the relation between the already known system of knowledge and the novel one. This can be seen as a four-place relation that takes into account the known world, the representation of the known world, the novel world to be learned, and the representation of the novel world. The educational consideration is the four-place relation in which each argument has a necessary role in the process of learning. The "novel" world is not really a novel one for the expert, only for the learner. How a child progresses from his known world and its representation to the as-yet unknown is uniquely an educational question. Overoccupation with the kind of expert system that predominates in artificial intelligence and cognitive psychology might blur the real educational concern, which attends to the slow progression by the learner in the accumulation of knowledge.

This chapter takes into consideration the assumption that knowledge is domain specific and presents the analysis of a specific domain, elementary mathematics. Later, it offers a framework for an LS similar to a microworld. This framework corresponds to a realistic conception of mathematical language and entities. Thus, those who tend to employ a microworld as a pedagogical device rely on what I have termed *pedagogical realism*. This approach has an independent reference, or dummy-reference, on which the child can verify the truths of a subject-matter domain, such as mathematics, according to the correspondence theory of truth. The seemingly useful alternative approach, the natural-environmental approach, conceals a number of difficulties that the LS is said to avoid.

REFERENCES

Anderson, J. R. (1976). *Language, memory and thought*. Hillsdale, NJ: Lawrence Erlbaum Associates.

Anderson, J. R. (1980). *Cognitive psychology and its implications*. San Francisco: W. H. Freeman.

Anderson, J. R., Greeno, J. G., Kline, P. J., & Neves, D. M. (1981). Acquisition of problem-solving skill. In J. R. Anderson (Ed.), *Cognitive skills and their acquisition*. Hillsdale, NJ: Lawrence Erlbaum Associates.

Bar-Hillel, Y. (1964). *Language and information*, Reading, MA: Addison-Wesley.

Benacerraf, P., & Putnam, H. (Eds.). (1985). *Philosophy of mathematics* (2nd ed.). Cambridge University Press.

Carpenter, T. P., Moser, J. M., & Romberg, T. A. (1982). *Addition and subtraction: A cognitive perspective*. Hillsdale, NJ: Lawrence Erlbaum Associates.

Collins, A. M., & Quillian, M. R. (1972). Experiments on semantic memory and language comprehension. In I. W. Gregg (Ed.), *Cognition and learning*. New York: Wiley.

Dienes, Z. P. (1960). *Building up mathematics*. New York: Humanities Press.

DiSessa, A. A. (1977). On learnable representations of knowledge: A meaning for the computational metaphor. MIT, AI Laboratory, LOGO Memo 47.

Frege, G. (1892a). On concept and object. In *Translations from the philosophical writings of Gottlob Frege*. Translated and edited by P. Geach & M. Black (1952). Oxford: Basil Blackwell.

Frege, G. (1892b). On sense and reference. In *Translations from the philosophical writings of Gottlob Frege*. Translated and edited by P. Geach & M. Black (1952). Oxford: Basil Blackwell.

Gattegno, C. (1962). *Modern mathematics with numbers in colours*. Reading, England: Lamport Gilbort.

Gentner, D., & Stevens, A. L. (Eds.) (1983). *Mental models*. Hillsdale, NJ: Lawrence Erlbaum Associates.

Holyoak, K. J. (1985). The pragmatics of analogical transfer. *The Psychology of Learning and Motivation, 19,* 59–87.

Johnson-Laird, P. N. (1980). Mental models in cognitive science *Cognitive Science, 4,* 1, 71–115.

Kintsch, W. (1974). *The representation of meaning in memory*. Hillsdale, NJ: Lawrence Erlbaum Associates.

Kintsch, W., & Greeno, J. G. (1985). *Understanding and solving arithmetic word problems* (draft).

Kitcher, P. (1983). *The nature of mathematical knowledge*. Cambridge, England: Oxford University Press.

Kline, M. A. (1970). Logic vs. pedagogy. *American Mathematical Monthly,* 264–282.

Nesher, D. (1986). *Epistemological investigation: Is metalanguage possible? Evolutionary hierarchy vs. logical hierarchy of language*. Proceedings of the Eleventh International Wittgenstein Symposium, Austrian Ludwig Wittgenstein Society.

Nesher, P. (1972). *From ordinary language to arithmetical language in the primary grades* (What does it mean to teach '2 + 3 = 5'). Doctoral dissertation, Harvard University. Dissertation Abstracts International, 1976, *36,* 7918A–7919A, University Microfilms No. 76-10, 525.

Nesher, P. (1986). Linguistic precursors of number in children. In S. Strauss (Ed.), *Ontogeny and historical development*. Norwood, NJ: Ablex.

Nesher, P., Greeno, J. G., & Riley, M. S. (1982). The development of semantic categories for addition and subtraction. *Educational Studies in Mathematics, 13,* 373–394.

Nesher, P., & Katriel, T. (1977). A semantic analysis of addition and subtraction word problems in arithmetic. *Educational Studies in Mathematics, 8,* 251–269.

Nesher, P., & Katriel, T. (1986). Learning numbers: A linguistic perspective. *Journal for Research in Mathematics Education, 17,* 2, 100–112.

Nesher, P., & Teubal, E. (1974). Verbal cues as an interfering factor in verbal problem solving, *Educational Studies in Mathematics, 6,* 41–51.

Norman, D. A., & Rumelhart, D. E. (1975). *Explorations in cognition*. San Francisco: W. H. Freeman.

Nuffield Mathematics Project. (1966). *I do and I understand,* New York: Wiley.

Ohlsson, S. (1986). *Sense and reference in the design of interactive illustrations for rational numbers* (draft). LRDC, University of Pittsburgh.

Papert, S. (1980). *Mindstorms children, computers, and powerful ideas,* New York: Basic Books.

Popper, K. A. (1968). *Conjectures and refutations: The growth of scientific knowledge*. New York: Harper & Row.

Quine, W. V. (1960). *Word and object*. Cambridge, MA: The MIT Press.

Resnick, L. B. (1982). *Syntax and semantics in learning to subtract*. In P. T. Carpenter, J. M. Moser, & A. T. Romberg (Eds.), *Addition and subtraction: A cognitive perspective*. Hillsdale, NJ: Lawrence Erlbaum Associates.

Russell, B. (1912). *The problems of philosophy* (1952 ed.). Cambridge, England: Oxford University Press.

Russell, B. (1971). *Introduction to mathematical philosophy*. New York: Simon & Schuster.

Schank, R. C., & Abelson, R. (1977). *Scripts, plans, goals and understanding.* Hillsdale, NJ: Lawrence Erlbaum Associates.

Sleeman, D., & Brown, J. S. (1982). *Intelligent tutoring systems.* New York: Academic Press.

S.M.S.G. (School Mathematics Study Group). (1965). *Mathematics for the elementary school.* Book K, Teachers Commentary, Unit No. 51. New Haven, CT: Yale University Press.

Suppes, P. (1974). The semantics of children language. *American Psychologist, 29,* 2, 103–115.

Tarski, A. (1949). The semantic conception of truth. In H. Feigl & W. Sellars (Eds.), *Reading in philosophical analysis* (pp. 52–85). New York: Appelton-Century-Crofts.

VanLehn, K., & Brown, J. S. (1978). Planning nets: A representation for formalizing analogies and semantic models of procedural skills (Tech. Rep. 1). University of Pittsburgh, LRDC.

Vergnaud, G. (1982). A classification of cognitive tasks and operations of thought involved in addition and subtraction problems. In T. P. Carpenter, J. M. Moser, & T. A. Romberg (Eds.) *Addition and subtraction: A cognitive perspective* (pp. 39–60). Hillsdale, NJ: Lawrence Erlbaum Associates.

Willough, S. S., Bereiter, C., Hilton, P., & Rubinstein, J. H. (1981, 1985). *Real Math.* La Salle, IL: Open Court.

Winograd, T. (1975). Frame representations and the declarative procedural controversy. In Bobrow & Collins (Eds.), *Representation and understanding,* New York: Academic Press.

Winston, P. (1975). "Learning structural descriptions from examples. In P. Winston (Ed.), *The psychology of computer vision.* New York: McGraw-Hill.

Wirtz, R. W., Morton, B., & Sawyer, W. W., (1962). *Math workshop for children.* Level A, Teacher's Guide, Encyclopedia Britannica Press.

APPENDIX A

The Peano Axioms as they appear in Russell (1971). *Introduction to mathematical philosophy* (p. 5). New York: Simon & Schuster.

The Peano system consists of three primitives:

"0," "number," and "successor," as well as the five postulates:

p1. 0 is a number.

p2. The successor of any number is a number.

p3. No two numbers have the same successor.

p4. 0 is not the successor of any number.

p5. Any property that belongs to 0 and also to the successor of every number that has the property belongs to all the numbers.

7

Informal Reasoning and Subject Matter Knowledge in the Solving of Economics Problems By Naive and Novice Individuals

James F. Voss
Jeffrey Blais
Mary L. Means
Terry R. Greene
Ellen Ahwesh
Learning Research and Development Center
University of Pittsburgh

In recent years, a number of investigators have become interested in the question of how learning takes place in particular subject-matter domains, the research having as a major focus comparing expert and novice problem solving within the specific domains (e.g., Larkin, McDermott, Simon, & Simon, 1980; Voss, Greene, Post, & Penner, 1983). Such comparison, it generally is assumed, will help develop a better understanding of how the novice becomes an expert, that is, of how learning takes place within the particular domain. Determining how a novice becomes an expert, however, does not address the question of how those with no formal training in a particular domain, for example, naive individuals, become novices. This chapter concerns such early learning in the domain of economics and compares the performance of naive and novice individuals with respect to both their knowledge of economics and their use of informal reasoning mechanisms.

KNOWLEDGE OF ECONOMICS OF NAIVE
AND NOVICE INDIVIDUALS

Considerable evidence exists indicating that individuals having substantial prior knowledge of a particular subject matter generally perform better on domain-related tasks than do individuals who have relatively little domain knowledge (e.g., Chiesi, Spilich, & Voss, 1979). Somewhat analogously, individuals who are novices with respect to a particular domain should be able to perform domain-related tasks more readily than individuals who are naive with respect to that domain, and research in the domain of physics supports this contention. Furthermore, the physics work has indicated that naive individuals frequently have misconceptions of particular principles of physics, misconceptions that can be quite resistant to change (e.g., Caramazza, McCloskey, & Green, 1981; Champagne, Gunstone, & Klopfer, 1983). However, although novices in physics typically perform better than naive individuals, the latter nevertheless are usually able to function quite well in the physical world. They are able to hit a baseball, for example, without first solving equations related to the forces and direction of the ball and bat. The fact that naive individuals may perform accurately on "real world" tasks, while at the same time having misconceptions of physical principles, suggests that performance on domain-related tasks is a function of the task. In the physics "misconception" research, the tasks have tended to be laboratory oriented, primarily because such tasks permit assessment of a person's knowledge of physical principles. The research has not, however, been concerned with how naive individuals are able to function in the physical world without a formal knowledge of physics principles.

The present research was designed to assess knowledge of economics by employing tasks that use economic concepts to which both naive and novice individuals presumably had been exposed, for example, interest rates, unemployment, inflation, taxation, and the federal deficit. Given the use of such concepts, naive individuals were expected to perform reasonably well, although their performance was not expected to be at the level of the novices.

Although comparing the performance of naive and novice individuals with respect to economics knowledge was a central issue of the study, it was designed to take cognizance of the fact that, for both the naive individuals and the novices, there have been considerable variation in economics knowledge. Such within-class knowledge was addressed by studying two factors that were regarded as potentially important to such variation, the person's vocational and/or avocational experience, as related to economics, and the person's general intellectual history and/or educational level. An individual who has never had a course in economics may learn something about economics, if he or she is a bank loan officer or plays the stock market. Similarly, the performance of a novice who has had one or two courses in economics may be enhanced, if he or she also had vocational and/or avocational experience that is economics related. In addition, a naive individual with a relatively strong intellectual history, such as provided by a college education, may be more adept in learning about economics from everyday experience than an individual without one. (Intelligence, as well as other factors, of course, are quite likely confounded with educational level.) The design of the study thus identified naive and novice individuals who did or did not have vocational and/or avocational experience related to economics. Within the naive groups, it also identified individuals who did or did not have a college education. The college education factor was not a concern for novices, because individuals having formal training in economics generally also have had a college education.

The present study was concerned with comparison of naive and novice individuals with respect to their performance on economics-related tasks and the possible differences in their economics knowledge, as related to vocational and/or avocational experience, and, in the case of naive individuals, as related to their intellectual history.

INFORMAL REASONING MECHANISMS IN NAIVE AND NOVICE INDIVIDUALS

As noted, the present study was designed to investigate not only economics knowledge in naive and novice individuals but also to study the nature of their informal reasoning. Conceptual issues pertaining to informal reasoning are now considered.

When given a question or a problem, a solution will generally be stated immediately, if the person knows the answer or has knowledge of an algorithm that will yield the answer. For present purposes, this type of answer is termed *direct*. When not able to produce an immediate answer, however, the individual may use reasoning mechanisms to generate an answer, with such mechanisms including analogy, the conversion of the problem to another problem, and the generation of a chain of inferences. For present purposes, such answers are termed *indirect*. It was expected that, because of their presumably greater knowledge of economics and experience in solving economics problems, novices would provide more direct answers than naive individuals, and naive individuals would provide more indirect answers, employing informal reasoning mechanisms in the process.

Although the differentiation of direct and indirect answers may be loosely interpreted as indicating the absence or presence of reasoning, respectively, this distinction does not address the nature of the reasoning processes employed. In this study, the reasoning is taken to be *informal*. Like formal reasoning, informal reasoning in this discussion centers on the argument, for example, a set of propositions comprised of one or more premises and a conclusion. A major aspect of arguments is their evaluation, whether the conclusion follows from the premises (cf. Angell, 1964; van Eemeren, Grootendorst, & Kruiger, 1984). In formal logic, such evaluation typically takes place by converting the propositions to symbolic form, as in "All A are B," and determining whether the symbolic relations are in agreement with the rules of the system in question, as in categorical syllogisms or propositional logic. Formal reasoning thus may be viewed as the reasoning an individual engages in when deriving and/or evaluating arguments found in formal deduction systems, such as logic or mathematics.

Most arguments in everyday life, including those in the present study, are nondeductive in nature and are not set in terms of a formal system. Instead, such informal arguments consist of conclusions that are supported by reasons. Moreover, the validity of nondeductive arguments is considered in terms of *soundness,* with soundness based on three criteria: Whether the reason is relevant to the conclusion, whether it supports the conclusion, and whether all reasons are taken into account that could support the contradiction of the conclusion (Angell, 1964).[1] Thus, such arguments are not valid or invalid, but they are regarded as relatively sound or unsound. Informal reasoning maybe regarded as the processes of reasoning that occur when individuals generate a nondeductive argument and/or evaluate its soundness.[2] Interestingly, although the occurrence of informal reasoning is much more prominent than that of formal reasoning, the psychological study of reasoning has almost exclusively involved tasks of formal reasoning, with the two questions most frequently asked being, "Was the person's response logical?" (i.e., conforming to rules of logic) and, "If not, why not?."

To provide a detailed and coherent description of the informal reasoning mechanisms employed in the present study, a model of such mechanisms is presented. Informal reasoning has been modeled descriptively (e.g., Angell, 1964; van Eemeren, Grootendorst, & Kruiger, 1984), and a modified version of Angell's model is presented in Fig. 7.1A. The conclusion is presented at the top of the structure, and supportive reasons linked to the conclusion are presented at a subordinate level. Fig. 7.1A thus

---

[1]The description of deduction and nondeducation arguments that is presented relies heavily on the work of Angell (1964).

[2]The category of nondeductive argument is admittedly vague, but it refers to forms of reasoning including causal reasoning, reasoning by explanation, reasoning by the subjective conditional, and more traditional induction (Mill, 1879).

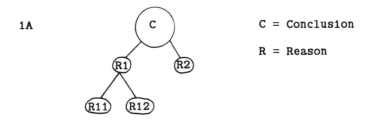

1A

C = Conclusion

R = Reason

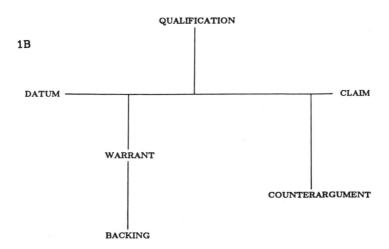

1B

FIG. 7.1.   Diagrams of argument structure adapted from Angell (1964) and from Toulmin (1958).

provides a means by which, for example, a newspaper editorial may be analyzed.

Another form of argument analysis, presented in Fig. 7.1B, is that developed by Toulmin (1958). The datum-claim, assertion, and warrant constitute the essentials of the argument. The datum consists of particular information or a premise, and the claim consists of a conclusion related to the datum. The warrant is an assertion that permits the datum-claim assertion to be made, the warrant being somewhat akin to a minor premise (Toulmin, 1958) or to Aristotle's hidden premise of the enthymeme (Cooper, 1960). Backing consists of providing support for the datum-claim relationship and the warrant. A qualifier is a statement asserting that the datum-claim relationship holds under particular conditions, and a counterargument indicates that some other datum-claim relationship could be maintained. As an example, if a person were asked how an increase in the wages of automobile workers (datum) would influence automobile prices, a person could answer that prices would go up (claim), because increases in manufacturing costs lead to increases in prices (warrant). A person could add that this had happened with previous UAW contracts (backing) and that the assertion assumes there are not massive layoffs in the industry (qualifier). An alternative claim (counterargument) might be that prices would not change because, with foreign cars on the market, manufacturers need to keep prices constant, even at the expense of profit.

The Toulmin analysis has the advantage of being more detailed, and it provides for facets of argumentation not found in the structure of Angell's model; however, in a more lengthy argument, additional assumptions are needed to provide for the necessary expansion (cf. Voss, Tyler, & Yengo, 1983). In that case, the structure may become cumbersome, and more importantly, the primary thrust of the argument may be obscured (Voss et al., 1983).

For the purpose of the study, the model of nondeductive argument structure presented in Fig. 7.2 was established. This model incorporates the most salient components of the models of Fig. 7.1A and 7.1B. Of particular importance is the modification of the conclusion structure.

The conclusion is broken down into a datum and a claim. Incorporating this facet of the Toulmin model permits a number of issues to be addressed that are not considered in the Angell model. For example, individuals in the study were asked to indicate which factors influence a particular economic effect, such as an increase in the price of automobiles. In reply, they were to furnish specific datums to the claim of increased prices. Similarly, in another part of the study, subjects were asked how a particular condition

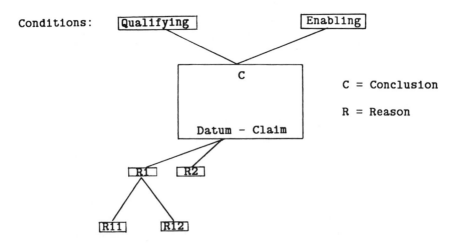

FIG. 7.2. Diagram of model of non-deductive argument used in the present study.

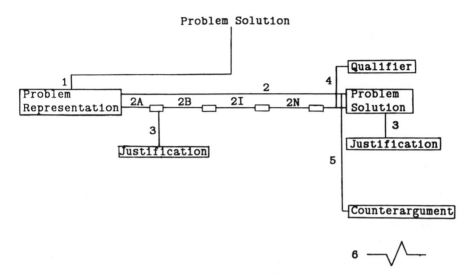

FIG. 7.3. Diagram of model of informal reasoning employed in the present study.

would influence automobile prices or, given the datum, what claim could be made.

A qualification was considered as a constraint stating a condition under which the conclusion may be stated. Similarly, an "enabling" factor represents a condition frequently observed in relation to causal reasoning that is important, or even necessary, to establish a particular relationship, even though it is not regarded as a causal factor (e.g., marriage as an enabling factor for divorce). Finally, counterarguments in the Fig. 7.2 model are regarded as reasons that lead to the contradiction of the conclusion or negate supportive reasons.

Figure 7.3 presents a diagram of the coding system used in this study, a system based on the model described in Fig. 7.2. The system is largely based on the model of ill-structured problem solving described by Voss, Greene, Post, and Penner (1983). The system assumes that the individual develops a representation of the question or problem, this step being denoted by 1. A direct solution is noted as 2, and the statement of one or more reasons justifying the solution is noted as 3. Although the representation phase typically occurs first, 2 and 3 may be interchanged. In the case of an indirect answer, 2 consists of at least two steps that denote inferences that lead to the answer. (The figure notes a total of n steps, with any step the ith step.) Justification may be stated for any of the inferences, as shown with 2A. The denotation 4 represents the use of a qualifier, and 5 denotes the use of a counterargument, generally following the description of Toulmin (1958). Both qualifiers and counterarguments may be employed with any of the inferential steps of indirect answers. The isolated line with a break, 6, represents a metastatement, an assertion made during the course of a solution that reflects an observation concerning one's own solving process. The broken line could thus be inserted anywhere in the reasoning process.

METHOD

Subjects

There were 30 subjects, 5 in each of six groups. The groups differed with respect to three factors: *Education,* in which individuals had either previously attended college or were currently enrolled or had not and were not then attending college; *Economic training,* in which individuals either had taken one or two courses in economics at the college level within the last 5 years or had no formal training in economics; and finally, *Experience in economic-related areas,* in which individuals were or were not engaging in a vocational or avocational pursuit such as banking, business, or the stock market. The three variables constituted a $2 \times 2 \times 2$ design, with two cells necessarily deleted, those involving not having a college education but taking formal economics courses. The remaining six cells are designated by a 3-column binary code representing presence or absence of college education, C and $\bar{\text{C}}$, respectively; the presence or absence of formal economics training, F and $\bar{\text{F}}$, respectively; and presence or absence of economics-related vocational or avocation experience, E and $\bar{\text{E}}$, respectively. The six groups are thus denoted by $\bar{\text{C}}\bar{\text{F}}\bar{\text{E}}$, $\bar{\text{C}}\bar{\text{F}}\text{E}$, $\text{C}\bar{\text{F}}\bar{\text{E}}$, $\text{C}\bar{\text{F}}\text{E}$, $\text{C}\text{F}\bar{\text{E}}$, and CFE.

Design, Materials, and Procedure

Pilot work was conducted to obtain a set of questions suitable for naive and novice individuals. The resulting questionnaire focused on three economic topics: automobile prices, the federal deficit, and interest rates. The questionnaire had three parts. In part I, subjects were asked to name as many factors as they could that they thought contributed to changes in each of the three economic topics. In addition, subjects were instructed to explain how or why each of the factors they named produced an effect. In part II, subjects were asked to indicate those factors that they felt were the most significant in producing changes in each of the three respective economic topics. In part III, descriptions were given of 28 specific economic situations, 9 concerning automobile prices, 9 concerning the federal deficit, and 10 concerning interest rates.

For each question, subjects were required to state an outcome and to tell why that particular outcome would occur. An example question was,

"If health care costs rise considerably, what effect, if any, do you think this would have on the size of the federal deficit and why?" The order of presentation of questions within each topic was constant, as was the topic order of automobile prices, federal deficit, and interest rates. The questions are presented in Appendix A. The questionnaire was presented to each subject individually by one of three experimenters. The experimenter read each question, and the subject responded orally. When necessary, the interviewer probed the subject for clarification of his or her responses. All interviews were tape recorded.

RESULTS

The results are presented in two parts, those related primarily to economic knowledge and those related primarily to reasoning processes.

Knowledge-Related Findings

Number and Quality of Factors.   Table 7.1 presents the mean number of economic factors generated for each group and for each economic topic in parts I and II of the questionnaire. Analysis revealed a significant difference of group, $F(5,24) = 4.70, p < .01$, topic, $F(2,48) = 19.78, p < .001$, and the group $\times$ topic interaction, $F(10,48) = 4.24, p < .001$. Additional analyses however, revealed that the significant group and group $\times$ topic effects are largely attributable to the group $C\bar{F}\bar{E}$ automobile price data. Separate analyses of the three topics indicated that group yielded a significant effect only for automobile prices, $F(5,24) = 9.03, p < .001$, (federal deficit and interest rates, $F(5,24) = 1.72, p > .05$, and $F(5,24) = 1.58, p > .05$, respectively), and a Duncan test indicated that the only significant difference for the automobile price data was that group $C\bar{F}\bar{E}$ generated

TABLE 7.1
Mean Number of Factors Generated
for Each Group and Economic Topic

Group	Automobile Prices	Federal Deficit	Interest Rates	
$\bar{C}\bar{F}\bar{E}$	4.8	2.4	2.8	3.3
$\bar{C}\bar{F}E$	3.8	2.8	3.2	3.3
$C\bar{F}\bar{E}$	13.0	4.8	5.8	7.9
$C\bar{F}E$	5.2	5.8	3.2	4.7
$CF\bar{E}$	5.2	3.8	2.8	3.9
CFE	6.6	5.4	4.2	5.4
	6.4	4.2	3.7	

more factors than each of the other groups. The data suggest that, with the exception of group CF̄Ē (for one topic), the groups generated an approximately equivalent number of factors.

Research has indicated that, as domain knowledge increases, the knowledge becomes more abstract (Chi, Feltovich, & Glaser, 1981). The data of parts I and II were examined with respect to the relative concreteness or abstractness of the factors generated, expecting that naive individuals would generate relatively concrete, real-world factors, but individuals having formal training and/or experience in economics would state more abstract factors. In scoring, a rating of 1 was given for a factor regarded as quite concrete. Examples included wages and automation for the automobile price topic, military spending and social security for the federal deficit topic, and home building and profits for the interest rate topic. A 2 was given for a factor that was more abstract, subsuming factors classified as 1. Examples included foreign competition and cost of resources for the automobile price topic, social programs and trade imbalance for the federal deficit topic, and money available for spending and deregulation for the interest rate topic. A 3 was assigned if the answer embraced a more general principle than found in 2, provided that the individual demonstrated some understanding of the concept in answering the "Why?" component of the question. Examples included supply and demand for the automobile price topic, relative balance of spending and taxation for the federal deficit topic, and supply and demand for the interest rate topic. If the answer to "Why?" did not indicate such understanding, the factor was not counted. Twenty-seven answers were eliminated. The answers distributed across groups as follows: C̄F̄Ē = 7; C̄FĒ = 1; CF̄Ē = 9; C̄FE = 0; CFĒ = 7; and CFE = 3. The most commonly unexplained factors were *the economy, inflation,* and *unemployment.* The interrater reliability of scoring the answers in terms of concreteness or abstractness was .89.

The means of the weighted factors are presented in Table 7.2. Group

TABLE 7.2
Mean Judged Ratings of Factors Generated for
Relative "Concreteness" and "Abstractness"

Group	Automobile Prices	Federal Deficit	Interest Rates	
C̄F̄Ē	1.4	1.6	1.8	1.6
C̄FĒ	1.1	1.7	1.6	1.5
CF̄Ē	1.7	2.0	2.0	1.9
C̄FE	2.1	1.8	2.7	2.2
CFĒ	1.9	2.0	3.0	2.3
CFE	1.9	2.0	2.5	2.1
	1.7	1.8	2.3	

TABLE 7.3
Economic Factors Generated: Factors Stated by at Least
Two Individuals and One Judgment of Most Important for Each Group

Group	Automobile Prices	Federal Deficit	Interest Rates
C̃F̃Ẽ	labor (2) wages (foreign vs. U.S.)(1) foreign imports (2) demand for particular cars (1)	defense spending (2)	unemployment (0) the economy (0)
C̃F̃E	cost of steel (1) labor unions (1) wages (foreign vs. U.S.)(1)	social programs (2) defense spending (2)	the economy (0) deregulation (1) housing (1)
CF̃Ẽ	material costs (2) labor costs (2) foreign competition (2) interest rates (1) automation (1) inflation (3) dealer profits (1)	govt. spending (3) defense spending (2) social programs (2) interest rates (1) balance of trade (2)	inflation (3) The Federal Reserve (3)
CF̃E	labor costs (2) material costs (2) demand (3) interest rates (1)	social programs (2) defense spending (2) special interest groups (1) taxation policy (2) govt. spending (3) vs. govt. income	supply of money (3) The Federal Reserve (3) expectation of inflation (3)
CFẼ	demand (3) material costs (2) labor costs (2) interest rates (1) employment level (3)	excessive spending (3) tax policy (reduced (2) unemployment revenue) interest rates (1)	supply of money (3) The Federal Reserve (3)
CFE	material costs (2 labor costs (2) foreign competition (2) supply (3) demand (3) import duties (1)	spending vs. taxation (3) taxation policy (2) defense spending (2)	supply of money (3) demand for money (3) The Federal Reserve (3) federal deficit (2)

Each factor is followed by the judged rating for relative concreteness or abstractness.

yielded a significant effect, $F(5,24) = 16.99$, $p < .001$, as did topic, $F(2,48) = 16.95$, $p < .001$. The group × topic interaction was not significant, $F(10,48) = 1.64$, $p > .05$. Duncan range tests indicated that groups CFE, CFẼ, and CF̃E yielded ratings significantly greater than those of groups C̃F̃Ẽ and C̃F̃E, with no significant differences occurring within clusters. The mean rating for group CF̃Ẽ did not differ significantly from either grouping. In addition, significantly higher abstract ratings were obtained for the interest rate topic than for the other two topics. Thus, individuals with a college education and formal courses and/or experience in economics stated factors that were relatively more abstract than those stated by individuals not having a college education. There were, however, no significant differences among the four college-educated groups.

To provide a sense of the factors generated and their commonality, Table 7.3 presents factors that were stated by at least two subjects and mentioned at least once as an important factor within each respective group. Each factor is listed with its rating on the "concreteness–abstractness" dimension. Remember that Table 7.2 provides a listing of only the more frequently stated factors, the data in Table 7.3 reflect the tendency for the more educated and, to some extent the more economically trained groups, to state more abstract factors, with this tendency being most apparent for the interest rate topic.

The analyses thus far indicate that there is little difference among the groups in quantity of factors stated, but factors named by college-educated individuals, especially by those who had formal economics training, were more abstract than those stated by noncollege-educated individuals.

Quality of Stated Reasons.   Each answer in parts I and II was rated for quality according to the following scale:

0 = No answer given

1 = An answer defining the stated factor rather than relating it and respective economic topic, as in "Labor, the people who put cars together" (C̄F̄Ē-2). (The number denotes the subject within the particular group.)

2 = An incomplete, partial and/or incorrect description of the relationship between the factor and topic was stated, as in, for interest rates, "Banks made bad investments to other countries they loaned money to, so how else are these banks going to get their money back?" (C̄F̄Ē-5)

3 = An acceptable description of the relationship between the factor and topic, as, in for the federal deficit, "I guess it's kind of income versus outgo. If the government takes in x dollars in tax revenue and spends y dollars, and there is a gap, that gap is the deficit. What is done with the gap is the issue, and that depends on Congress, the IRS, and numerous other factors." (CFE-1)

4 = An acceptable answer with a relatively more complete explanation than provided by a 3 answer, as, for interest rates, "Fundamentally, interest rates are determined by the supply of money and by expectations about the future value of money, that is, inflation. The supply of

TABLE 7.4
Mean Scores for Judged Quality of Justifications

Group	Economic Topic Automobile Prices	Federal Deficit	Interest Rates	
C̄F̄Ē	1.0	0.4	0.6	0.7
C̄FĒ	0.3	0.2	1.4	0.6
CF̄Ē	2.2	2.0	2.2	2.1
CF̄E	2.5	2.3	2.3	2.4
CFĒ	2.2	2.5	2.0	2.2
CFE	2.5	2.6	3.0	2.7
	1.8	1.7	1.9	

money is an issue because interest rates involve cost of money. Hence, it's supply and demand, like anything else . . . expectations about inflation, in terms of how much money will be worth, hence, the level of private savings and, therefore, the level of money available for the investment. And that determines whether rates go up or down." (C̄FĒ-2). The interrater reliability of these codings was .85.

The means of the six groups are presented in Table 7.4. The analysis indicated a significant effect of group, $F(5,24) = 10.13, p < .001$. A Duncan range test indicated that the ratings fell into two categories, groups CF̄Ē, CF̄E, CFĒ, and CFE differing significantly from groups C̄F̄Ē and C̄FĒ, with no significant differences occurring within each cluster. Topic was not significant, $F < 1$, nor was the group × topic interaction, $F(10,48) = 1.28, p > .05$. These results indicate that those subjects having a college education provided better reasons from the perspective of economic theory than those not having a college education. Significant differences were not obtained, however, between the college education having had economics training and/or experience and those without such training and/or experience.

Reasons Stated as Economic Rules.   Inspection of the data of part III indicated that, when providing a reason for their answer, subjects frequently stated a rule. The following rule categories were delineated: *no rule, institutional rule, sense rule, inappropriate economic rule,* and *generally appropriate economic rule.* In the no-rule category, the subject simply did not provide a rule. Institutional rule denoted that the effect stated was attributed to an institution or informal group acting as an agent, as in "They're still gonna keep the price up, no matter what, because the big jokers want the money in their pockets" (C̄F̄Ē-4). Sense rules consisted of vague statements providing a general notion of an economic factor, as in

"If I remember what I read in the papers, inflation makes the interest rate go up, but I really don't know why" (C̄F̄Ē-5). A generally inappropriate rule denoted an economics-related statement that was not usually in agreement with economic theory, as is "The more they sell, the lower the price should be, because you can still keep profit the same" (CF̄Ē-4). A generally appropriate rule is a statement consistent with economic theory, as in "When people look for alternative sources for money, that is, need to borrow, it may increase the interest rate. It increases the demand for money. And my view is that interest rates depend on the relationship between supply and demand for money" (CFE-2). The interrater reliability of rule classification was .85.

The mean proportion of rules stated in each category for each group over the three economic topics is presented in Table 7.5. The data indicate that Groups C̄F̄Ē and C̄F̄E had the largest proportion of no-rule cases, and only Group C̄F̄Ē used institutional rules with an appreciable frequency. Sense rules were employed with relatively low frequency, whereas five of the groups used economically inappropriate rules with a proportion of about .10. Economically appropriate rules were used more frequently by groups CFE, CF̄Ē, CF̄Ē, and CFĒ than groups C̄F̄Ē and C̄F̄E.

Due to the relatively large frequency of zero values in cells involving institutional, sense, and economically inappropriate rules, statistical analysis was limited to the no-rule and economically appropriate categories. Analysis of the no-rule data indicated group was significant, $F(5,24) = 4.72, p < .01$, with a Duncan test indicating only that group C̄F̄E did not differ significantly from groups CF̄Ē, CF̄Ē, and CFE but did differ significantly from C̄F̄E and CFE. Analysis of the appropriate rule data also yielded a significant group effect, $F(5,24) = 6.62, p < .001$, with a Duncan test indicating that the proportion of appropriate rules was significantly less in group C̄F̄Ē than in groups CFE, CF̄Ē, CF̄Ē, and CFĒ but about the same as in group C̄F̄E. In addition, groups CFE, CF̄Ē, CF̄Ē, CFĒ and

TABLE 7.5
Proportion of Rules Stated for Each
Rule Category as a Function of Group

Group	No Rule	Institutional Rule	Sense Rule	Economic Inappropriate Rule	Economic Appropriate Rule
C̄F̄Ē	.53	.13	.02	.10	.21
C̄F̄E	.40	.01	.04	.12	.42
CF̄Ē	.23	.04	.06	.11	.57
CF̄E	.15	.03	.01	.09	.73
CFĒ	.19	.02	.01	.10	.68
CFE	.17	.03	.04	.04	.71

$\bar{C}\bar{F}E$ did not differ significantly from each other. The findings of the no-rule and appropriate rule data indicate that group $\bar{C}\bar{F}\bar{E}$ generally failed to use rules as often as the other groups and employed appropriate rules less frequently. Systematic performance differences among the remaining groups, however, were not obtained.

Appropriate and Inappropriate Rules: Qualitative Differences. The analysis was conducted to determine whether there were any notable differences in the specific appropriate rules employed by the various groups. For the automobile price topic, the number of appropriate rules stated for each group was: $\bar{C}\bar{F}\bar{E}$ = 17; $\bar{C}\bar{F}E$ = 33; $C\bar{F}\bar{E}$ = 37; $\bar{C}FE$ = 49; $CF\bar{E}$ = 45; CFE = 51. Qualitatively, there was an overwhelming tendency to use a cost-price rule. For instance, as cost increases, price increases. The proportion of rules stated for each group that involved the cost-price rule was: $\bar{C}\bar{F}\bar{E}$ = .82; $\bar{C}\bar{F}E$ = .76; $C\bar{F}\bar{E}$ = .76; $\bar{C}FE$ = .74; $CF\bar{E}$ = .65; and CFE = .69. The second most frequently occurring rule for the automobile price topic related demand to price. The respective proportions using this rule were: $\bar{C}\bar{F}\bar{E}$ = .12, $\bar{C}\bar{F}E$ = .12, $C\bar{F}\bar{E}$ = .11, $\bar{C}FE$ = .18, $CF\bar{E}$ = .17, and CFE = .24. These data at least suggest that the concept of demand was used more frequently by subjects having a college education and economic experience and/or training than by subjects with no college education or with a college education but no economic training or experience. Interestingly, demand, when mentioned by group $\bar{C}FE$ subjects, involved demand for specific cars, whereas in other groups demand was viewed more as an economic principle.[3]

The number of appropriate rules stated for the federal deficit topic by the respective groups was: $\bar{C}\bar{F}\bar{E}$ = 15; $\bar{C}\bar{F}E$ = 23; $C\bar{F}\bar{E}$ = 40; $\bar{C}FE$ = 41; $CF\bar{E}$ = 37; CFE = 43. The rules fell into three categories: a relationship between taxation and deficit size, between spending and deficit size, and between spending as related to taxation and deficit size. Within each group, the proportion of rules occurring for the three categories was similar, with the exception of subjects in group $\bar{C}\bar{F}\bar{E}$, who stated no rules that depicted the importance of a balance between spending and taxation.

Appropriate rule frequencies for each group for the interest rate topic were: $\bar{C}\bar{F}\bar{E}$ = 3; $\bar{C}\bar{F}E$ = 7; $C\bar{F}\bar{E}$ = 21; $\bar{C}FE$ = 39; $CF\bar{E}$ = 31; CFE = 28. The low frequencies found for groups $\bar{C}\bar{F}\bar{E}$ and $\bar{C}\bar{F}E$, as well as the relatively low frequencies of the other groups, support the notion that interest rate was the most difficult of the three topics. Also, subjects of group $C\bar{F}\bar{E}$ tended to be less able to apply rules in the interest rate question than were

---

[3]A misconception that was observed involved not making the distinction between the supply and quantity produced and the demand and quantity sold. No subjects made either distinctions.

subjects of groups CF̄Ē, CFĒ, and CFE. The rules stated by groups C̄F̄Ē and C̄FE primarily related money supply to interest rate. The remaining four groups used a variety of rules, including relating interest rates to supply and demand, the balance of supply and demand, inflation, and the cost of money to banks.

Turning to inappropriate rule usage, the number of inappropriate rules stated varied with topic: 27 for automobile price, 7 for federal deficit, and 56 for the interest rate topic. Most of the inappropriate rules for the automobile price topic indicated price would decrease when number of sales increased because a constant profit margin could be maintained. For the interest rate topic, the frequency of inappropriate rule statements was: C̄F̄Ē = 16; C̄FĒ = 17; CF̄Ē = 9; CF̄E = 5; CFĒ = 4; CFE = 5. The majority of inappropriate rules stated by group C̄F̄Ē, C̄FĒ, and CF̄Ē involved an incorrect relationship between factors in the state of the economy and interest rates, as in "Good times are related to a decrease in interest rates" and "Bad times are related to an increase in interest rates." Most of the remaining inappropriate rules used by all the groups involved statement of an incorrect relationship between either the supply of or demand for money and interest rates.

Primary Rules.   Some individuals applied the same rule, termed a *primary rule,* to a number of questions, despite the fact that the rule was inappropriate in some cases. For example, one subject (CF̄E-4) indicated that interest rates are determined by the expectation of inflation. If he was unable to relate a particular question to the expectation of inflation, the subject claimed that there was no relationship between the question content and interest rates. To the question involving an increased use of certificates of deposit and interest rates, the subject said that there would be no effect "Because it's not whether people buy these things or invest that causes interest rates to change. Interest rates are affected primarily by inflation. If I lend you a dollar and you are going to pay me back in 10 years, I want to get some rent on my money. But if I think that the dollar is going to decrease, and you're going to pay me back a funny dollar, then I want a higher interest rate. So the main thing is expectation of what money is going to be worth." To the question of the influence of consumer income on interest rate, the subject answered, "Again, I think that is somewhat independent because of the basic thing that there is a rent on money plus expectation of inflation." To the question of how the feelings of individuals concerning the state of the economy influence interest rates, the subject answered, "It's too difficult for me to connect that with expectations. It depends on whether something is done to the current state of the economy, which would, or would not, lead to inflation." Finally, to the question involving the effect of consumer spending and business reinvestment on interest rates, the subject answered, "I can't see an effect. I don't see a direct connection just between pure economic activity and the money supply and expectation of inflation."

Two other effects of primary rule usage were noted, namely, the generation of contradictory responses and the overriding of an appropriate rule with a primary rule. One subject (CF̄Ē-4), in answering a question on interest rates, used a primary rule involving profit and/or greed: "It seems to me that as people are having to borrow more and more money that interest rates should go down because banks, or whoever's profiting from that, should be earning more and more." Later, in response to another question involving interest rates, this subject answered: "It seems that if there's more buying power that means more borrowing, more loans for the banks, and they should certainly profit. It seems that the banks would then be giving out more than they are getting in, so they should want to increase their rates for borrowing. I think banks are probably greedy." Thus, the two responses were contradictory. Another subject (CF̄Ē-4), responding to the automobile price question involving robotics, answered: "It (robotics) should stabilize the cost of them, though it probably won't. . . . It should stabilize the cost because I think longrange. . . . Or, it would be cheaper than man. Though there's maintenance still, upkeep . . . , it should still . . . I guess . . . long-range. It probably won't, because they never give you breaks on things. Things always cost more. But . . . I mean it may, but I'm not the optimist." Thus, this subject overrode an appropriate rule with a primary rule.

In summary, the primary rule data indicated that individuals may have knowledge of a particular rule and (a) overextend its usage, (b) develop contradictory responses with its usage, and/or (c) override a more acceptable rule by its application. On the other hand, these rules do provide a basis for interpreting economic events and, on a number of occasions, the usage is appropriate.

Knowledge-Related Effects: Summary

The data, when analyzed in relation to knowledge of economics, suggest the following conclusions: First, taken as a whole, performance differences were primarily obtained between those individuals having and those not having a college education. For college-educated individuals, however, little performance difference was obtained between those individuals having and those not having formal training in economics and/or economics-related experience. More specifically, although individuals in all groups stated an approximately equivalent number of economic factors, individuals with a college education tended to generate factors that were relatively more abstract, better with respect to their basis in economics. In addition, college educated also tended to utilize a larger proportion of appropriate rules than did the noncollege educated. The only hint of superior performance by those individuals having economic training or experience was suggested by the interest rate data, in which individuals having an economics background seemed to have a little better understanding of the relationships of the particular variables and interest rates. Second, only a few, well-defined misconceptions were found. The statements that could be regarded as misconceptions tended to be idiosyncratic, such as good times being associated with low interest rates, and primary rules being overextended. (See footnote three.)

Reasoning-Related Findings

Problem Representation.   The model of reasoning depicted in Fig. 7.3 indicates that the first step in developing an answer involves representing the question which, when considered in relation to the questions of part III, essentially means representing the datum. It is assumed that if an answer were provided that addressed itself in an appropriate manner to the question statement, then the individual's representation of the question would be appropriate. The data indicated that although most questions were represented appropriately, the question was on occasion converted, that is, the representation was of a question other than that stated. Two types of conversion were delineated. One consisted of modifying the question by either deleting a component or substituting one concept for another. For example, steel imports were converted to importing (deletion) or to car imports (substitution). These types of conversion were generally detrimental, yielding misinterpretations of the original question. The second type of conversion, which we termed hierarchical, consisted of interpreting the question as subordinate to a higher level concept or as superordinate to a lower level concept. For example, materials costs or wages (subordinate) were considered as production costs (superordinate), or health costs (superordinate) were considered in terms of Medicare (subordinate). Hierarchical conversions thus involved a categorization process. This type of conversion tended not to be detrimental in terms of the answer generated. The inter-rater reliability of scoring question conversion was .98.

The first column of Table 7.6 presents the frequency of deletion and substitution conversions for each group. A significant effect of group was obtained, $F(5,24) = 6.23$, $p < .001$, with a Duncan test indicating that performance fell into two clusters, groups $\bar{C}\bar{F}\bar{E}$ and $\bar{C}\bar{F}E$, and groups $C\bar{F}\bar{E}$, $C\bar{F}E$, $CF\bar{E}$, and CFE. No significant differences existed within each cluster. In addition, the interest rate topic produced more deletions and substitutions than the other two topics: automobile prices = 42; federal deficit = 31; interest rates = 77.

TABLE 7.6
Frequency of Occurrence
of Question Conversions

Group	Deletions and Substitutions	Hierarchical Conversions
C̄F̄Ē	62	0
C̄FE	50	0
CF̄Ē	13	10
CF̄E	4	9
CFĒ	9	7
CFE	12	9

The second column of Table 7.6 presents the frequency of hierarchical conversions. Because of the low frequencies, analyses were not performed. Nevertheless, the data suggest performance was again clustered, with groups C̄F̄Ē and C̄FE differing from the remaining four groups. The conversion data indicate that college-educated individuals are more likely than noncollege-educated individuals to develop an appropriate representation of the question and, if the question is converted, the former group tends to convert in terms of the concept hierarchy, but the latter group tends to modify the concept itself, by deletion or by associative substitution. Incidentally, converting a question to a more superordinate level is a highly sophisticated procedure, as demonstrated by experts in physics who classify problems in this way to solve them (Larkin et al., 1980). Naturally, one needs the knowledge base to classify in this manner.

Direct and Indirect Answers.   Following the model of Fig. 7.3, each question of part III was regarded as a datum, and the stated relationship was taken to be the claim. Also, in the data analysis, a direct answer was defined as the statement of a claim and, in most cases, a reason, stated in either order. An indirect answer denotes the subject's going through one or more intervening steps to reach the claim. The criterion used for the occurrence of an inference in an indirect answer was that the step had to be necessary to reach the claim, for example, if the inference were deleted, the subject would not have been able to state the particular claim.

Each response of part III was classified as direct or indirect. Table 7.7 presents the proportion of such answers for each group. Analysis of the proportion of direct answers indicated that group was not significant, $F(5,24) = 1.38$, $p > .05$, nor was topic $F(2,48) = 2.42$, $p > .05$, or the group $\times$ topic interaction, $F < 1$. The failure to obtain a significant difference for group with respect to the proportion of direct answers is of interest, because individuals having formal economics training did not, as

TABLE 7.7
Proportion of Direct and Indirect Responses for Each Group
and Proportion of Answers for which Reasons were Stated

| | Direct | | Indirect | |
Group	Proportion of Direct Answers	Reasons Stated (Proportion)	Proportion of Indirect Answers	Reasons Stated (Proportions)
$\bar{C}\bar{F}\bar{E}$	.80	.57	.20	.38
$\bar{C}F\bar{E}$	.77	.76	.23	.31
$C\bar{F}\bar{E}$	.61	.77	.39	.49
$C\bar{F}E$	.77	.85	.23	.39
$CF\bar{E}$	.60	.74	.40	.29
CFE	.75	.84	.25	.49

one might expect, produce more direct answers than found in the other groups.

Following the model of Fig. 7.3, the direct and indirect answer data were analyzed with respect to the number of answers for which reasons were provided. The proportion of direct answers for which reasons were stated is presented in the second column of Table 7.7. Even though the proportion for group $\bar{C}\bar{F}\bar{E}$ was below that of the other groups, group was not significant, $F(5,24) = 1.74$, $p > .05$. Topic was significant, $F(2,48) = 6.69$, $p < .01$, with a greater proportion of reasons provided for the automobile price topic, .86, than for the federal deficit, .69, and interest rate, .72, topics. The group × topic interaction was not significant, $F < 1$. With respect to indirect answers, analysis of the proportion of answers for which a reason was provided also yielded no significant effect of group, topic, or the group × topic interaction, $F < 1$ in all cases. Both the direct and indirect answer data therefore indicate that groups did not differ significantly either in the proportion of direct and indirect answers provided, or in the proportion of statements for which reasons were stated, thus showing, in terms of the Fig. 7.3 model, that the groups did not differ with respect to their providing the basic components of the informal reasoning process, data, claim, and reason. Of course, the questions specifically asked them to state the answer and indicate why.

To determine whether the groups varied in the number of steps of the inference chains generated in indirect answers, the frequency of occurrence of inference chains having two or more steps between the datum and the claim were tabulated. The frequencies were: $\bar{C}\bar{F}\bar{E} = 3$; $\bar{C}F\bar{E} = 8$; $C\bar{F}\bar{E} = 25$; $C\bar{F}E = 11$; $CF\bar{E} = 30$; and $CFE = 11$; $F(5,24) = 3.56$, $p < .02$. A Duncan test indicate that group $CF\bar{E}$ produced a greater frequency than all other groups except group $C\bar{F}\bar{E}$, and further, group $C\bar{F}\bar{E}$ performance differ significantly from that of group $\bar{C}\bar{F}\bar{E}$. Topic and the group × topic interaction were not significant, $F < 1$ in both cases. These results indicate that college-educated individuals, with or without formal economics training and without economics experience, tended to produce a greater frequency of longer indirect answers than did the other groups. In addition, group CF̄Ē produced few multiple-step inferences.

One additional result involving indirect answers was considered. A few subjects generated answers via generation of a relatively long inference chain. For example, in answer to the possible effect on interest rates when the Federal Reserve raises reserve requirements for banks, one subject (CF̄Ē-5) answered, "Ok, the Federal Reserve Board, from what I understand, is supposedly an autonomous government arm that controls interest rates. If you raise reserve requirements, that means that . . . that means that it's harder to get money. It means that, um, to whom they will lend money has become more exclusive—I assume. That's how I'm interpreting that. They will, I assume, when we say more exclusive, loan to more creditworthy customers. Now I assume these customers are banks —not you and me. So, on one hand, that means that there's a more stable population that they're lending to. On the other hand, it means that it's harder to get money. What I'm leaning to is that, if the Federal Reserve Board makes it more exclusive, if they raise their requirements on who they'll give a loan to, then that would increase interest rates because there's been, therefore, a scarcity of money. What in fact that does is that it says they may lend x million dollars to Mellon Bank, because they think they're credit worthy, but they won't lend it to First Federal of Squirrel Hill, and that means you and I, as potential loan-getters or borrowers, will find it won't be as competitive for us to get a loan. We can go to Mellon, or we might have options. Therefore, the interest rate would be higher because not as many banks have the option of lending, and there's not as much to lend. So, I think if that happens, it means that interest rates go up." Thus, even though the understanding of the tools of the Federal Reserve is open to question, this subject generated the idea that as supply decreases, interest rate increases, although the subject did not verbalize this principle per se.

Inferential Distortion.   During the course of providing an indirect answer, distortions occasionally occurred in the particular line of reasoning. Such distortions were analyzed, and two types were delineated: inference breaking and irrelevant branching. Inference breaks were defined as a lack of connectedness in the flow of the argument. For example, in response to the automobile price question on the government placing limits on steel imports, subject CF̄Ē-4 stated "Our men would be working here if we did something like that [limit steel imports], so that's why I say the prices would be up more than they are now." Irrelevant branching was noted also. In some cases, such branching constituted only a brief departure from the initial line of argument, and then the subject returned to the issue under consideration. But in other cases, irrelevant scenarios were introduced, and the subject did not return to the original argument. For example, to the steel import question subject $\bar{C}\bar{F}\bar{E}$-4 stated "Prices would come down because less cars would be imported from other countries. We would sell more, people would have to buy more American cars, and that would mean more people would be going back to work, and I think everyone would benefit."

Table 7.8 presents the frequency of argument distortion for each group. Because the frequencies differed substantially as a function of economic topic, separate analyses were performed on each topic. (Frequencies were: automobile price, 47; federal deficit, 59; interest rates, 152.) Analyses indicated group was significant for the automobile price topic, $F(5,24) = 4.55$, $p < .005$, and for the interest rate topic, $F(5,24) = 5.44$, $p < .005$, but not for the federal deficit topic, $F < 1$. Duncan tests indicated groups $\bar{C}\bar{F}\bar{E}$ and $\bar{C}\bar{F}E$ differed significantly from the remaining groups for both the automobile price and interest rate topics, with no significant differences occurring within each cluster. These results suggest that individuals having a college education produced fewer distortions in the lines of argument of their indirect answers than those not having a college education.

One more result in the argument distortion data was frequency with which a subject was able to recover from the distortion and produce an acceptable answer. The proportion of times such recovery occurred is presented in Table 7.8. Analysis indicated a significant effect of group, $F(5,24) = 6.27$, $p < .001$, with Duncan tests showing that the groups fell into two clusters, those with and those without a college education; the latter groups, when distorting a line of argument, were better able to get back on track than were individuals in groups $\bar{C}\bar{F}\bar{E}$ and $\bar{C}\bar{F}E$.

TABLE 7.8
Frequency of Argument Distortions for Each Group

Group	Argument Distortions Frequency	Proportion of Argument Distortion "Recovery"
$\bar{C}\bar{F}\bar{E}$	68	.13
$\bar{C}\bar{F}E$	63	.26
$C\bar{F}\bar{E}$	38	.29
$C\bar{F}E$	24	.50
$CF\bar{E}$	39	.54
CFE	26	.62

TABLE 7.9
Proportion of Direct and Indirect Answers for which a Qualifier was Stated

Group	Proportion of Direct Answers with Qualification	Proportion of Indirect Answers with Qualification
$\bar{C}\bar{F}\bar{E}$	.06	.07
$\bar{C}FE$	.22	.15
$C\bar{F}\bar{E}$	.44	.50
$C\bar{F}E$	.36	.44
$CF\bar{E}$	.27	.49
CFE	.33	.32

Qualifications. One component of the reasoning model of Fig. 7.3 is qualification, and the proportion of direct answers for which a qualification was stated is presented in Table 7.9. Group yielded a significant effect, $F(5,24) = 3.29$, $p <.03$, with Duncan tests indicating that group $\bar{C}\bar{F}\bar{E}$ provided a smaller proportion of qualifications than did groups $C\bar{F}\bar{E}$, $C\bar{F}E$, $CF\bar{E}$, and CFE. Group $\bar{C}FE$ performance did not differ significantly from either group $\bar{C}\bar{F}\bar{E}$ or from the remaining four groups. Topic was not significant, $F(2,48) = 2.31$, $p > .05$, nor was the group $\times$ topic interaction, $F(10,48) = 1.14$, $p > .05$. Analysis of the indirect answers for which a qualification was stated also yielded a significant effect of group, $F(5,24) = 3.38$, $p < .02$. Duncan tests indicated that group $\bar{C}\bar{F}\bar{E}$ provided a significantly smaller proportion of qualifications than all other groups except group $\bar{C}FE$, and group $\bar{C}FE$ provided a significantly smaller proportion of qualifications than did groups $C\bar{F}\bar{E}$ and $CF\bar{E}$ but not groups $C\bar{F}E$ and CFE. Topic was significant, $F(2,48) = 3.54$, $p < .04$, with the frequency of qualifier usage of 15, 42, and 24 for the automobile price, federal deficit and interest rate topics, respectively. The group $\times$ topic interaction was not significant, $F(10,48) = 1.79$, $p < .10$. These results indicate that, in general, college-educated subjects used qualifiers more frequently than did those without a college education, and that for indirect answers, qualifiers were used most frequently by the college educated who did not have formal training in economics.

Counterarguments. The frequency of occurrence of counterarguments for the respective groups was: $\bar{C}\bar{F}\bar{E} = 0$; $\bar{C}FE = 1$; $C\bar{F}\bar{E} = 9$; $C\bar{F}E = 10$; $CF\bar{E} = 10$; $CFE = 13$. Although these frequencies are relatively low, they nevertheless suggest that subjects having a college education produced more counterarguments than did individuals without a college education.

Metastatements. The frequency of metastatements for the respective groups was: $\bar{C}\bar{F}\bar{E} = 5$; $\bar{C}FE = 9$; $C\bar{F}\bar{E} = 36$; $C\bar{F}E = 20$; $CF\bar{E} = 5$; $CFE = 9$. Although not analyzed statistically, the data nevertheless indicate that metastatements were made most frequently by college-educated individuals without formal training and/or economics experience, with the second highest frequency occurring for college-educated individuals with economics experience. Because the contents of the metastatements could provide some additional information concerning the reasoning process, the metastatements were delineated with respect to qualitative differences.

Metastatements made by subjects of group C̄F̄E included: "We just answered the whole thing" (C̄F̄E-5). "I'm just answering these questions because that's what makes sense to me. Because I haven't had time to think about them" (C̄F̄E-1). "I'm not sure about that" (C̄F̄E-3). "I don't know much about the reserve bank or requirements" (C̄F̄E-5). "Of course that contradicts what I said before" (C̄F̄E-3). Group C̄FE offered metastatements including, "The deficit is not my strong point" (C̄FE-4). "Maybe I don't really understand what the federal deficit is. I know I've heard about it, I know it's out there" (C̄FE-5). "I really have no idea" (C̄FE-4). "That's just my observation. I figured it out all by myself" (C̄FE-1). "Well, I'm trying to think of what I have been hearing. This is terrible, I have not expert answers to give you" (C̄FE-1). The metastatements of Groups C̄F̄E and C̄FE generally tended to reflect a person's own awareness of his or her lack of knowledge.

Group CF̄E metastatements included "I'm not sure how gas is used in the manufacturing of cars" (CF̄E-1). "I think there's kind of a front door and a back door to this question" (CF̄E-5). "That's my personal opinion, and it may be a biased one" (CF̄E-3). "The first thing that comes to mind . . . , but no, that's not logical, . . . this is hard for me to think through, but somehow it seems to me that . . ." (CF̄E-4). "That's of course the extreme. . . . Let's see what else would happen" (CF̄E-5). "I'm wondering what proportion of government spending is of that type" (CF̄E-1). "I really don't know much about health care programs" (CF̄E-3). "I think I answered that" (CF̄E-3). "I know that . . ." (CF̄E-1). "I guess I am trying to decide what is the critical thing about circulating money. . . . I guess I was thinking" (CF̄E-1). "I sound like a Reagan fan, but I'm not" (CF̄E-5). "That's how I'm interpreting that" (CF̄E-5). "I'm trying to think of how these two things fit together" (CF̄E-4). "I mean, this is the stuff that has been going on in the past few years in the economy" (CF̄E-5). "Gosh, now I don't know if any of the answers I've given are right. But to be consistent, . . ." (CF̄E-2). Although subjects in group CF̄E made some metastatements indicating an awareness of their lack of knowledge, they made many more in reference to their progress in answering and how they were trying to develop their answer.

Group CFE subjects gave approximately five metastatements that reflected awareness of lack of knowledge. Additional metastatements included, "I really don't know how the ratio of lowering taxes—whether the government then spends less" (CF̄E-5). "Through all these questions, I could answer them like short-term or long-term, and I guess I've been answering all of them from a long-term perspective. Time is missing in these questions . . ." (CF̄E-4). "But what it would do to the overall picture, I do not know" (CF̄E-3). "Well, let me think about it. I guess you have to say as compared to what . . . then I don't know how to get a relationship. What else would corporations do with the money if they don't modernize? I'll stick with my answer" (CF̄E-4). "I guess you mean their feelings about whether the economy is doing well or doing poorly" (CF̄E-4). "I realize you're asking me the question that way . . . one doesn't seem to follow the other, unless I misunderstood the question" (CF̄E-5). "That's quantitative too" (CF̄E-1). "You said a key word there" (CF̄E-4). The metastatements of group CF̄E were similar to those of group CF̄Ē, except that they seemed to depict a greater sense of evaluation and of awareness of the economic context, as in "short-term" and "long-term."

The metastatements of group CFĒ included, "We'll zero in on one specific foreign market" (CFĒ-3). "Now I need a tie-in between the price of gasoline and the price of cars" (CFĒ-3). Although subject CFĒ-3 demonstrated an awareness of his attempt to relate concepts, more-or-less via means–ends analysis, the remaining metastatements usually involved an awareness of his progress or an evaluation of a stated answer. Group CFE's metastatements included, "That's an interesting question. . . . Then you are looking at the price per ton of steel" (CFE-1). "Maybe what I haven't said is . . ." (CFE-1). ". . . and it closes the loop holes, can I throw that in, or should I try to keep it simple?" (CFE-3). "Shouldn't it be exactly the opposite?" (CFE-3).

Taken as a whole, the metastatement analysis suggests the occurrence of general differences among groups. Specifically, groups C̄F̄Ē and C̄FĒ tended to reflect an awareness of their limited knowledge, and groups CF̄Ē and CF̄E seemed to monitoring their responses, locating their progress in answering and determining their next step. Also, these subjects tended to relate their responses to concepts beyond the question per se, as in being a "Reagan fan." Group CF̄E metastatements were also related a little more closely to economic concepts than those of group CF̄Ē. Finally, subjects in groups CFĒ and CFE, with relatively few metastatements, were apparently considering which thought followed, or they were evaluating their answers.

Reasoning-Related Effects: Summary

A summary statement of the reasoning-related results, as indicated in the Fig. 7.3 model, is as follows: First, although all groups represented most questions appropriately, individuals without a college education converted questions, which led to distortion, more often than college-educated individuals. When college-educated individuals converted a question, it generally was hierarchically, that is, the question was seen as subordinate to a higher level concept or superordinate to a lower level concept that occurred in the question. Second, groups did not differ significantly in the relative frequency of their direct and indirect answers nor in the proportion of direct and indirect answers for which reasons were provided. However, college-educated individuals provided reasons for their answers that were qualitatively superior to those of noncollege-educated individuals. Third, non-college-educated individuals distorted their line of argument in indirect answers more frequently than college-educated individuals, although the latter were better able to return to the original line of argument. Fourth, college-educated individuals used more qualifiers than noncollege-educated individuals. Fifth, college-educated individuals also produced more counterarguments. And, sixth, the analysis of metastatements suggested that noncollege-educated subjects produced metastatements depicting awareness of their own lack of knowledge, and college-educated subjects with no formal economics training who made a relatively larger number of metastatements tended to be monitoring their answers, keeping track of their progress. College-educated subjects with formal economics training, although producing relatively few metastatements, tended to be monitoring and evaluating their answers.

DISCUSSION

One objective of the present study was to compare the economics knowledge of naive and novice individuals, taking into account the different intellectual histories of naive individuals and the presence or absence of economics-related experience in both naive and novice individuals. The findings were quite consistent with respect to when differences in economic knowledge were obtained: Individuals with a stronger intellectual history, the college-educated groups, demonstrated a greater knowledge of economics than noncollege-educated groups. However, knowledge-related differences were generally not obtained between naive college-educated individuals and the novices, nor were differences generally obtained in relation to a person's having or not having vocational and/or avocational experience in economics. Given that the significant differences obtained were primarily between the college-educated and noncollege-educated groups, it is important to emphasize that a number of factors may readily be confounded with college education, for example, intelligence, and no claim is being made that a college education per se yielded the present results. What is important is that the present data demonstrate large differences in what naive individuals have learned about economic concepts.

One possible explanation for the general lack of knowledge-related performance differences between the college-educated naive individuals and the novices is that the latter in fact knew more than the naive individuals, but the questions were not sensitive to this knowledge difference. Thus, if the questionnaire had contained questions that were more technical, such as asking subjects to interpret supply and demand curves, then novices would have been expected to perform better than the college-educated naive individuals. Although this assertion may have merit, the data suggest that novice performance was not at a ceiling level on the nontechnical questions actually used. The questions, in other words, apparently provided novices with the opportunity to demonstrate knowledge gained from formal training, but they could not capitalize on this opportunity. This assertion is supported by the fact that, when an expert (an economics professor) was given the questionnaire, he provided more substantive answers than did novices, especially in terms of relating the concepts of a particular question to other economic concepts and principles.

The failure of novices to perform better in the present task situation than the college-educated naive individuals has interesting instructional implications. Specifically, the result indicates little positive transfer from the learning of economics in courses to performance on the task. This suggests that instruction in introductory economics courses is oriented toward learning the subject matter of economics requisite to majoring in economics rather than learning about the intricacies of economic operations as found in everyday life.

The finding of a lack of knowledge-related differences in economics between naive college-educated and novice individuals contrasts to the findings of two studies in physics (McCloskey, Washburn, & Felch, 1983; McCloskey & Kohl, 1983). There, the performance of naive (no physics courses) and novice (prior physics course in high school or college) college students was compared on tasks that had real-life and laboratory counterparts. In general, performance was a function of amount of training in physics. One explanation for this disparity involves the respective mapping of the tasks between the classroom and everyday life in the two domains. Specifically, the tasks used in the physics research mapped quite closely onto the physics principles studied, whereas the tasks employed in the present study mapped closely to economic issues found in everyday life, even though the concepts were, of course, part of the contents of introductory economics. Thus, both the college-educated naive individuals and the novices may have acquired a substantial amount of economics-related information from sources such as noneconomics college courses, media, and personal experience. This conclusion again suggests that the novices did not acquire a greater knowledge of the task topics in their economics courses than could be found elsewhere, or that they were unable to apply such knowledge to the tasks.

In addition to the general lack of performance differences between the college-educated naive and the novices, another knowledge-related finding requiring consideration is the sharp difference between the performances of the college-educated and noncollege-educated naive. This is a difficult question; in a sense, it is asking why college-educated individuals with training in a subject matter may learn more about it than do noncollege-educated individuals. At least two answers may be of use. College-educated individuals may have developed reasoning skills that produce considerable facility in relating new concepts to what they already know, a conclusion somewhat supported by the superior use of reasoning mechanisms by the college educated in the present study. A second, nonmutually exclusive reason is that college-educated individuals may learn how to structure information within a particular domain hierarchically, and such organization may be related to a better understanding of conceptual relationships. The generation of concrete as opposed to abstract factors and the conversion data in the present experiment lend support to this assertion. Indeed, the cross-cultural work of Cole (1985), which indicates that hierarchical structures of knowledge are not found in some societies, would at least suggest that the learning of academic-related subject matter, structured hierarchically, may produce a tendency to so organize new information even when such information is not encountered in a school context. This conjecture raises the additional question of whether it would be possible for the noncollege educated to learn a hierarchical structure of economics concepts even if briefly trained to do so in a specific domain. A negative answer would carry with it the interesting suggestion that the skill in developing such structures comes gradually with intellectual experience. Finally, the conjecture also raises the interesting question of whether college-bound individuals of junior high and high school age structure information differently from students not college bound.

In addition to investigating economic knowledge, the present study was also concerned with the use of informal reasoning mechanisms. Within the context of the Fig. 3 model, the data indicated that all groups answered the questions in the basic datum-claim and reason format, which they were essentially instructed to do, and all groups provided approximately equivalent proportions of direct and indirect answers. The college-educated groups, however, demonstrated consistently greater use of the informal reasoning mechanisms indicated in Fig. 7.3 than the noncollege-educated individuals. Thus, individuals without a college education, although on a few occasions demonstrating an awareness of their lack of knowledge (via metastatements), seemed unable to use other reasoning mechanisms to generate an answer. Indeed, although the proportion of indirect responses of groups $\bar{C}\bar{F}\bar{E}$ and $\bar{C}FE$ was not significantly different from other groups, the inferences they stated generally did not lead to substantive answers; instead, the inferences were marked by considerable distortion. The college educated, on the other hand, especially those without formal economics training, provided metastatements that seemed to reflect their attempt to generate as well as to monitor their answers. These differences are quite similar to those noted by Perkins, Allen, and Hafner (1983), in that the noncollege-educated individuals of the present study depicted a commonsense epistemology, in which they were apparently satisfied with their relatively weak answers because the answers made sense, whereas the college-educated naive individuals tended to be better reasoners in the Perkins et al. sense because, although aware of their lack of economic knowledge, they nevertheless were able to employ reasoning mechanisms to generate answers. Interestingly, this apparent difference of awareness of what constitutes an acceptable answer suggests that the college-educated individuals had a different criterion for locating an acceptable answer than did the noncollege-educated naive individuals.

How college-educated individuals develop ability to use reasoning mechanisms is not clear. A college education provides experience in using such mechanisms and individuals become skillful in this regard. However, Perkins (1985) has provided evidence indicating that whereas college students perform better than high school students on informal reasoning tasks, neither group shows much improvement in informal reasoning skill in the course of instruction over an academic year. Apart from the inference that students may develop informal reasoning skills during summer vacations, Perkins' study points to the fact that not much is known about how such skills develop.

The results of the present study, considered in terms of the knowledge of economics and use of informal reasoning mechanisms, generally indicated that those groups that demonstrated greater knowledge of economics also demonstrated greater use of informal reasoning mechanisms. A critical question therefore is how this finding should be interpreted. Caution is probably in order in drawing any conclusions about whether domain knowledge enhances reasoning skill and/or whether reasoning skill enhances the acquisition of domain knowledge. The present findings, however, indicate that the two factors work together. Indeed, the way that informal reasoning mechanisms and knowledge-based assertions were interwoven in the present data is rather striking. Instructionally, this observation at least suggests that it is desirable for classroom instruction to be sensitive not only to the learning of subject matter in the traditional sense, but also to the utilization of informal reasoning in acquiring and utilizing knowledge. Also, the findings suggest that, with respect to how naive individuals become novices, it may be enlightening to determine whether in the elementary school years, and certainly in the secondary years, individuals may be distinguished with respect to their use of informal reasoning skills. Further, it would be of interest to determine whether such use of informal reasoning mechanisms delineates, in some fashion, potentially college-bound from noncollege-bound individuals (cf. Means & Voss, 1985).

Finally, a few remarks are in order concerning the implications of the present findings for future research in social science learning. Although the results of the present study were considered in terms of knowledge and reasoning components, we do not mean to leave the impression that these processes are independent on each other. As mentioned, one of the interesting aspects of the findings is the extent to which the knowledge and reasoning components were interwoven. A reasonable approach to developing an understanding of this interaction may be to view the reasoning mechanism as operators that constrain the memory search for information related to the issue at hand. In any event, the findings suggest that developing a better understanding of social science learning will involve investigating the role of prior knowledge, including its organization and accessibility, and determining how reasoning mechanisms are related to its use.

ACKNOWLEDGMENTS

The research reported in this paper was supported by the national science foundation (BNS 8409123) and by the Learning Research and Development Center of the University of Pittsburgh. The views expressed in the chapter do not necessarily constitute the views of either organization. The authors wish to thank Drs. James Pellegrino, David Perkins, and Lauren Resnick for their helpful comments on an earlier draft of the paper.

REFERENCES

Angell, R. B. (1964). *Reasoning and logic.* New York: Appleton–Century–Crofts.

Caramazza, A., McCloskey, M., & Green, B. (1981). Naive beliefs in "sophisticated" subjects: Misconceptions about trajectories of objects. *Cognition, 9,* 117–123.

Champagne, A., Gunstone, R., & Klopfer, L. (1983). Naive knowledge and science learning. *Research in Science and Technological Education, 1,* 172–183.

Chi, M. T. H., Feltovich, P., & Glaser, R. (1981). Categorization and representation of physics problems by experts and novices. *Cognitive Science, 5,* 121–152.

Chiesi, H. L., Spilich, G. J., & Voss, J. F. (1979). Acquisition of domain-related information in relation to high and low domain knowledge. *Journal of Verbal Learning and Verbal Behavior, 18,* 257–273.

Cole, M. (1985). Education and the third world: A critical discussion and some experimental data. In E. Bol, J. P. Haenen, & M. A. Wolters (Eds.), *Education for cognitive development: Proceedings of the third international symposium on activity theory* (pp. 93–106). Gravenhage, The Netherlands Stichting voor Onderzoek van het Onderwijs S. V. O.

Cooper, L. (1960). *The rhetoric of Aristotle.* Englewood, NJ: Prentice-Hall.

Larkin, J., McDermott, J., Simon, D. P., & Simon, H. (1980). Expert and novice performance in solving physics problems. *Science, 208,* 1335–1342.

McCloskey, M., & Kohl, D. (1983). Naive physics: The curvilinear impetus principle and its role in interactions with moving objects. *Journal of Experimental Psychology: Learning, Memory, and Cognition, 9,* 146–156.

McCloskey, M., Washburn, A., & Felch, L. (1983). Intuitive physics: The straight-down belief and its origin. *Journal of Experimental Psychology: Learning, Memory, and Cognition, 9,* 636–649.

Means, M. L., & Voss, J. F. (1985). Star Wars: A developmental study of expert and novice knowledge structures. *Journal of Memory and Language, 24,* 746–757.

Mill, J. S. (1879). *A system of logic.* New York: Harper.

Perkins, D. N. (1985). Postprimary education has little impact on informal reasoning. *Journal of Educational Psychology, 77,* 562–571.

Perkins, D. N., Allen, R., & Hafner, J. (1983). Difficulties in everyday reasoning. In W. Maxwell (Ed.), *Thinking: The expanding frontier* (pp. 177–189). Philadelphia: Franklin Institute Press.

Toulmin, S. (1958). *The uses of argument.* Cambridge, MA: Cambridge University Press.

van Eemeren, F. H., Grootendorst, R., & Kruiger, T. (1984). *The study of argumentation.* New York: Irvington Publishers.

Voss, J. F., Greene, T. R., Post, T. A., & Penner, B. C. (1983). Problem solving skill in the social sciences. In G. H. Bower (Ed.), *The psychology of learning and motivation: Advances in research theory* (Vol. 17, pp. 165–213). New York: Academic Press.

Voss, J. F., Tyler, S. W., & Yengo, L. A. (1983). Individual differences in the solving of social science problems. In R. F. Dillon & R. R. Schmeck (Eds.), *Individuals differences in cognition* (pp. 205–232). New York: Academic Press.

APPENDIX A
LIST OF QUESTIONS IN PART III

Automobile Prices

1. Assume the government has decided to set limits on steel imports. What effect, if any, do you think this action would have on the price of automobiles? Why?

2. Assume that because of OPEC, the price of gasoline is expected to increase sharply in the next year. What effect, if any, do you think this would have on the price of automobiles? Why?

3. Although in the past there was limited use of robotics in assembly line automotive production, some authorities predict that over the next several years assembly line production will be accomplished almost exclusively by robotics. What effect, if any, do you think this has had on the price of automobiles? Why?

4. Due to the increase in the number of working women, there has been an

increase in the number of cars per family. What effect, if any, do you think this increase has had on the price of automobiles? Why?

5. What would be the net effect on the price of automobiles if the government set limits on steel imports, if OPEC caused an increase in gasoline prices, if the projected change to robotics occurred, and if the increase of the two-car families all took place during the next year? Why?

6. Assume the interest rates for automobile loans are expected to drop considerably in the next six months. What effect, if any, will the lower rates have on the price of automobiles? Why?

7. Assume the cost of steel and of labor in automobile production has increased dramatically over the past year. What effect, if any, do you think this has had on the price of automobiles? Why?

8. The price of material costs for automobile production has increased, and assembly line workers have been forced to agree to wage concessions. What effect, if any, will these factors have on the price of automobiles? Why?

9. Because the price of gasoline is beginning to fall slightly, assume many people are switching to larger cars again and this has resulted in the major automobile companies finding it necessary to do a considerable amount of retooling. What effect, if any, should this have on the price of automobiles? Why?

Federal Deficit

1. Assume that the United States and the Soviet Union make significant agreements with respect to arms limitations. What effect, if any, do you think this would have on the size of the federal deficit? Why?

2. If health care costs rise considerably, what effect, if any, do you think this would have on the size of the federal deficit? Why?

3. With major tax reforms, the IRS thinks that most "loop holes" can be eliminated. What effect, if any, do you think this would have on the size of the federal deficit? Why?

4. If a new tax reform bill resulted in lowering the personal income tax rate for all tax brackets, what effect, if any, do you think this would have on the size of the federal deficit? Why?

5. What do you think would be the net effect of the arms limitations agreement, rise in health care costs, elimination of "loop holes," and the lower personal income tax rate on the size of the federal deficit if all were to occur in the next year? Why?

6. If government spending were to increase substantially, what effect, if any, do you think this would have on the size of the federal deficit? Why?

7. If corporate profit taxes were to be increased significantly, what effect, if any, do you think this would have on the size of the federal deficit? Why?

8. If government policy were modified so as to increase social security benefits as well as increase personal income tax rates, what would be the effect on the size of the federal deficit, if any? Why?

9. Suppose the salaries for Armed Services personnel were to be increased, and the government also decided to lower the corporate profit tax. What effect, if any, would these changes have on the size of the federal deficit? Why?

Interest Rates

1. A number of major U.S. corporations are finding it worthwhile to reinvest a large part of their profits in order to modernize their operations. What effect, if any, should this have on interest rates? Why?

2. Many senior citizens have been using certificates of deposit (C.D.'s) as a means of keeping their life savings intact and receiving a monthly income to supplement social security benefits. What effect, if any, do you think this has on the interest rate? Why?

3. What effect, if any, do you think inflation has on the interest rate? Why?

4. What effect, if any, is there on the interest rate when the Federal Reserve Board raises reserve requirements for banks? Why?

5. When consumers' incomes rise, what effect, if any, do you think this has on the interest rate? Why?

6. What effect does an increasing rate of unemployment have on interest rates? Why?

7. What effect, if any, do the feelings of individuals concerning the "state of the economy" have on the interest rate? Why?

8. When most plants in the country are running considerably under their maximum production level, what effect, if any, do you think it has on the interest rate? Why?

9. What do you think would be the net effect on the interest rate of consumers' spending more money and business finding the need to reinvest less money back into their companies? Why?

10. What would be the net effect of consumers' incomes rising to the point that many people realize that they could begin saving again, while at the same time, businesses began to invest money in technological advances? Why?

8

Learning From Examples
Via Self-Explanations

Michelene T. H. Chi[1]
Miriam Bassok
Learning Research and Development Center
University of Pittsburgh

Numerous topics are involved in the study described here: learning, problem solving, self-explanations, the role of examples in learning, individual differences, and physics. However, three issues are overarching in our domain of inquiry and in the task and the design we used—namely, how one learns, what one learns, and how one uses what has been learned. This

---

[1]We view this chapter as an interim report of ongoing work on which Bob Glaser has been a collaborator since 1978. Hence, in describing this work, we are describing a part of Bob's research. In the first half of our decade of collaboration, Bob and I had been investigating the nature of expertise in complex problem solving. Our interest has shifted because it has become clear that we cannot understand the acquisition of expertise without first understanding *how one learns,* even the beginning novice. Most importantly, we need to understand how individuals differ in the way they learn. Any differences that we might detect could contribute to our knowledge of what enables a person to become an expert. Although the study of learning and individual differences represents a new direction for me, these topics have been a long-standing interest of Bob's (see Glaser, 1967).

chapter first describes the rationale for the particular design that we used; it then gives a brief description of the procedure of our learning study. A discussion of these three overarching issues, and of how our study can provide evidence to address them follows. In this way, we give an overview of our current state of understanding of the three issues and the degree to which the findings reported can or cannot elucidate our understanding.

RATIONALES FOR THE DESIGN OF THE STUDY

Two major goals guided the design of this study. The first was to study how one learns to solve problems, rather than to study individual differences in problem solving abilities per se. The latter approach, usually contrasting the problem-solving successes of good and poor solvers, or experts and novices, sheds light only on performance differences. By focusing instead on what students have learned *prior* to solving problems, as well as what they learn *while* solving problems, we can gain further knowledge about the transition mechanism, thus providing insights for a model of competence in problem solving.

A second concern that guided the design of this study was to approach learning as a constructive process. That is, in learning to solve problems, one must declaratively encode and store new knowledge in terms of new concepts and principles, build problem schemata, and attach procedures (or their derivations) to the problem schemata. Our interest was, thus, in the construction of this knowledge, rather than in the proceduralization of already encoded knowledge.

In the sections that follow, we elaborate on how these goals were met by the design of our study. Briefly, in order to study how one learns to solve problems, we examined the way students learned from worked-out examples in the text. The constructive aspect of their learning was then assessed via the explanations that they gave to themselves.

Contrasts With Other Approaches to Problem Solving

A customary approach to the study of problem solving is to observe how people with different skills (such as experts and novices) solve problems by collecting and analyzing their protocols and formulating models to capture their solution processes. The models of performance thus formulated constitute the knowledge of a set of procedures that each of the students possesses and can apply for solving problems. Individual differences are then explained by the differences in the knowledge possessed, as embodied by the sets of production rules or programs. The intention of these models has been to see if one could derive the knowledge of the skilled solver from the knowledge of the unskilled solver. Unfortunately, inferences about the transition to the expert's from the novice's knowledge have not been straightforward. An alternative approach—the one we have chosen—is to see what students acquire from studying, in hope of being able to represent the knowledge underlying the generation of the solution procedures for the skilled and less skilled students.

To contrast our primary interest with other researchers' contributions to the literature on problem solving, we can describe an alternative focus: how the declarative knowledge encoded from text or from the teacher's instruction becomes proceduralized into a skill. This conversion process dominates, for example, Anderson's theory (1987) of skill acquisition.

In that theory, the process of conversion is achieved by using general weak methods that can convert declarative knowledge into domain-specific procedures via the mechanism of compilation. In Anderson's theory, compilation consists of two processes: proceduralization and composition. Composition is analogous to chunking in that separate procedures can be concatenated into one larger procedure. Proceduralization, by contrast, converts declarative knowledge into a procedure. This is accomplished by applying a weak method, which takes as the condition certain declarative knowledge that has been encoded a priori as important and fundamental to the problem at hand. For instance, suppose a student is trying to solve a geometry problem that requires proving that two triangles are congruent. The student might start by applying a weak method, such as means-ends analysis, in which the goal is to transform the current state (the givens) into the goal state. To do so, the weak method sets out to reduce the largest difference between the current state and the goal state. The largest difference that the model notices is that "no corresponding sides have been proven congruent." Therefore, the model attempts to reduce this difference. However, for the model to detect that "there are no corresponding sides that have been proven congruent," it must contain the declarative knowledge that *if the corresponding sides are congruent, then one can prove the triangles to be congruent.* Thus, Anderson's theory assumes that all relevant declarative knowledge has been properly encoded. The aspect of problem solving that Anderson's theory focuses on is the compilation of the declarative knowledge in the context of a derivation of the set of actions that constitute the solution.

We are not concerned with the mechanism of compilation per se. In a complementary way, our research focuses on how students can successfully solve problems as a function of whether or not they have encoded the relevant declarative knowledge and the level to which this declarative knowledge is "understood," as revealed by the way it relates to the procedures that instantiate it. Thus, in our view, problem solving, in the sense of organizing the derivation of a set of actions, does not seem to be guided by such general heuristics as means-ends analysis (at least for the good solver). Rather, we believe that the organization of a derivation is guided by a general domain principle, which then governs the set of actions that should be derived in order to solve the problem. For example, in simple mechanics problems, if the solver knows the problem is a static one, then his set of actions (the solution) is guided by that piece of declarative knowledge and its associated consequence, namely, that the sum of all the forces acting in the system is zero. This knowledge is a specific rule that can be inferred from one of Newton's principles. The rule then guides the derivation of the set of actions, which consists of finding all the forces acting on the body, decomposing them into their respective axes, and summing the ones in the same dimension. Thus, the derivation is an implementation of the knowledge that "All the forces must sum to zero." With such a framework, the critical issues are how and to what extent students understand the declarative principles that govern the derivation of a solution.

LEARNING IN THE DOMAIN OF MECHANICS

Because we view problem solving as the organization of a derivation of a set of actions, and this derivation is guided by a general principle, we necessarily have to choose a domain in which there is a rich interrelation between the set of actions that are executed as the solution and the principles that guide the selection of the set of actions. This constraint necessarily rules out knowledge-lean puzzle-type problems. Many knowledge-rich domains, on the other hand, are still too syntactic and algorithmic in nature. Factoring algebraic expressions or subtractions, for example, are too algorithmic in that the students simply have to learn a set of procedures. The procedures can often be performed correctly only with syntactic understanding of the problems. There are many knowledge-rich domains that have a less algorithmic character, but some require diagnostic problem solving, such as troubleshooting, which is quite different from the traditional classroom-type problem solving that interests us. Simple mechanics problems, however, seem to fall in-between the two extremes. Mechanics problems satisfy our constraint in that successfully solving them demands the instantiation of principles and concepts.

Our choice of the domain of mechanics was also guided by additional considerations. First of all, mechanics problems are difficult for students to learn to solve. One major source of this difficulty, we surmise, is the fact that a mechanics problem, even the simplest one, requires that certain forces not explicitly described in the physical situation of the problem be added. Furthermore, not only must these forces be recognized, but their interrelationships must be considered. In other words, the equations or procedures that apply should not relate the entities explicit in the problem statement (the block on the incline, the angle of the incline, etc.). Rather, the equations should relate the interplay of the forces at work. (In the inclined plane case, it would be the forces that act on the block from gravity, from the string pulling on the block, and so forth.) Whether or not the block moves depends on the total sum of the forces acting on it in a given direction. Hence, a representation of the implicit relations among the forces must be constructed in order to solve such problems.

To illustrate, Fig. 8.1 shows a diagram of an inclined plane problem and the content of a *basic representation*. We propose that some students (probably the poorer ones) have only a basic representation of the problem. Such a representation consists mostly of explicit entities (the block, the inclined plane), so that the relations represented are among the explicit objects (i.e., the block is on the inclined plane, the plane is inclined at 30 degrees).

BASIC REPRESENTATION

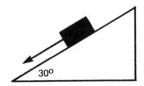

30⁰

(1)   EXPLICIT CONCRETE OBJECTS (INCLINED PLANE BLOCK)

(2)   EXPLICIT RELATIONS AMONG CONCRETE OBJECTS (BLOCK IS ON TOP OF THE PLANE; PLANE SLOPES AT 30⁰ ANGLE)

(3)   OPERATORS THAT RELATE EXPLICIT ENTITIES (F=MA)

(4)   GOAL (FIND THE MASS)

FIG. 8.1.   Content of a basic representation.

Moreover, because such a representation contains only the explicit objects and their relations, the operators necessarily act on these alone, as the following protocol excerpt from a poor solver confirms:

What is the mass of the block?   (The question posed by the problem statement.)

| Let me see. I know $F = ma$. | (Her operator is an algebraic one, embodied in the equation that F relates to m and a.) |
| What's m equal to? | (The solver is trying to find m by deriving it algebraically by dividing F by a.) |

The components of her basic representation contain entities (the force, the acceleration, and the mass of the block) that are explicitly described in the problem statement, and the operators that the poor solver has learned (algebraic ones, such as $F = ma$ can be converted to $m = F/a$) can only be applied to the explicit entities and relations.

A more successful solver, however, has a *physics representation* that includes, in addition, generated physics entities that are not explicitly described. For the same simple physical situation as depicted in Fig. 8.1, she would have, in addition, inferred implicit entities (gravity force, normal force, etc.) and their relations (the directions of these forces, and whether they oppose and cancel each other out). Figure 8.2 shows the implicit entities and relations (Items 3 and 4), as well as the explicit ones. The *macro-operator* ($\Sigma F = ma$), (Item 5 in Fig. 8.2) in this case, is really a guiding principle, and the actual proceduralized *micro-operators* are the component procedures of decomposing forces, summing forces in the same dimension, and so forth. Hence, one might even argue that the operators in the two representations (the basic and the implicit physics) are different. The necessity of generating implicit entities under the guidance of a domain principle is a fundamental difference between solving problems as algebraic expressions and doing physics. That is, to solve a mechanics problem successfully, a student must generate an implicit representation. We believe this requirement contributes largely to the difficulty in solving physics problems. In tracing the learning processes, we may be able to find out how a transition from explicit (basic) to implicit (physics) representation takes place.

Another reason for studying mechanics problems is that textbooks usually use a general problem-solving procedure as a guideline for teaching problem solving. A general procedure is not only laid out in the textbooks, but it is often taught directly by the instructor as well. It usually encompasses some set of subprocedures, as indicated in Halliday and Resnick (1981, p. 69):

1. draw a sketch of the explicit physical situation;
2. draw a free-body diagram (in other words, add the forces which are operating in the physical situation);
3. resolve the force vectors into their components (that is, calculate

PHYSICS REPRESENTATION

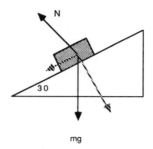

mg

(1) EXPLICIT CONCRETE OBJECTS (SUCH AS THE INCLINED PLANE AND THE BLOCK)

(2) EXPLICIT RELATIONS AMONG THE EXPLICIT OBJECTS (THE BLOCK IS ON TOP OF THE PLANE)

* (3) IMPLICIT ABSTRACT OBJECTS THAT MUST BE INFERRED (GRAVITY FORCE, NORMAL FORCE)

* (4) RELATIONS AMONG THE IMPLICIT OBJECTS (A COMPONENT OF THE GRAVITY FORCE OPPOSING THE NORMAL FORCE)

* (5) OPERATORS THAT ARE INSTANTIATED ON THE INFERRED OBJECTS AND RELATIONS ($\Sigma F=MA$)

(6) GOAL (FIND THE MASS)

FIG. 8.2. Content of a physics representation.

their projections onto the coordinate axes, which also requires selecting coordinate axes);
4. select the appropriate equation and substitute the components into the general equation to produce an instantiation corresponding to each coordinate axis;
5. solve the equations.

As one can see, such a general procedure serves only the purpose of setting subgoals, such as "draw a free-body diagram." Setting subgoals using this guideline is not very different from using a general heuristic, such as means-ends analysis, to set up subgoals. But if the problem were a static one, then one would set up the subgoals of seeking all the forces acting on the system and balancing the forces so that there is no resulting net force in any direction. A guideline that is not driven by such a domain principle can only serve the function of a syntactic heuristic that cannot be carried out without knowing the subgoal's purpose in the context of the principle. One cannot simply draw a free-body diagram unless one knows what forces to depict.

Our conjecture that a general procedure alone is not sufficient for solution can be seen in our protocol from a poor solver in our pilot study. The student would often prompt herself with these subgoals. For example, she would often say to herself, "I know I'm supposed to draw a free-body diagram here." She still, however, did not get anywhere with the solution. On the other hand, on occasions where students do succeed in solving the problems, one can consistently see a trace of this general procedure. This means that a successful solution procedure often proceeds through the steps of constructing a free-body diagram, finding and decomposing the forces, and so forth, but these steps do not necessarily serve as a guideline for finding the solution. Hence, if students are not learning problem solving by using this guideline of procedural steps, how exactly are they learning to solve problems?

Simple mechanical problems are suitable in another way. They are very tractable in the following sense: We can discriminate between procedures that are situation-specific to a particular schema (such as procedures for solving an inclined plane problem), versus the principle ($F = ma$) that underlies this solution procedure. That is, all three types of problems that we study (inclined plane, pulley, and rope problems) are instantiations of the application of Newton's Laws of Motion, especially Newton's second law. However, this particular law cannot be used in a direct syntactic way (as the poor solver mentioned earlier did) by substituting the mass of the block for m, the acceleration of the block for a, and the force of the block for F. $F = ma$ applies to the resulting net force of the whole system. Thus, we believe that mechanics problems may be particularly suitable for teasing apart different levels of understanding, both between students and at various stages of the learning process.

Finally, the most intriguing aspect of studying mechanics problems relates to the issue of *understanding*. A strict criterion of understanding requires the depiction of the knowledge that is acquired that can generate the solution procedure from deep domain principles. VanLehn (in press) refers to such knowledge as *teleological understanding*. Students who have teleological understanding could derive a procedure for solving a problem. However, one could conceive of all mechanics solution procedures as a kind of derivation. And yet, knowing (in the sense of having studied) a specific derivation that constitutes the solution to a problem may not indicate that the student understood the problem solution in a teleological sense, that is, in the sense that it is derived from some domain principle. Hence, we clearly need to distinguish teleological understanding from the issue of derivation. Problems in mechanics could conceivably provide insight into the issue.

EXAMPLES AS A SOURCE OF LEARNING

We have chosen to examine how problem-solving success is mediated by what is learned from worked-out examples. There are multiple reasons for focusing on examples. An instructional reason is that examples seem to be the primary tool which textbook writers and instructors rely upon to teach students how to solve problems. Furthermore, students themselves also prefer to rely on examples as a learning tool. In classroom findings, Van-Lehn (1986) has indirect evidence showing that 85% of the systematic errors collected from several thousand arithmetic students could be explained as deriving from some type of learning from example. In another classroom study, Zhu and Simon (1987) have shown a clear advantage (a 3-year course can be reduced to a 2-year math curriculum) if students are given only examples and problems to work on, as opposed to the standard instruction with a text and instructor's presentations.

In laboratory studies, there is also some scant evidence showing that students prefer to rely on worked-out examples. Anderson, Greeno, Kline, and Neves (1981) have claimed that students spend a considerable amount of time studying examples and that students often commit knowledge of worked-out examples to memory. Our own informal observation of two students solving problems after having read several chapters from a physics textbook confirm their claims. Upon the students' first encounter with problem solving, over 62% of the time, they either copied directly from the textbook examples or recalled a procedure from a worked-out example and used it as an analogical base. More recently, Pirolli and Anderson (1985) found that novices rely heavily on analogies to examples in the early stages of learning to program recursion. Eighteen of their 19 subjects used the example upon their first programming attempts. Not only do beginning students rely on examples, but they appear not to be able to solve problems without them. Pirolli and Anderson (1985) noted that "over the course of the four hours of protocols obtained from subject JP writing recursive functions, we saw no indication that she could write such functions without a lot of assistance from examples or the experimenter" (p. 262). Reder, Charney, and Morgan (1986) also found that the most effective manual for instructing students on how to use a personal computer are those that contain examples. Finally, LeFevre and Dixon (1986) found that subjects actually preferred to use the example information and ignored the written instruction when learning a procedural task. Hence, from an instructional point of view, worked-out examples seem to be a primary source of information from which students learn and acquire problem solving procedures. Thus, we thought it necessary that we ask what is learned from examples.

Despite the fact that examples have been shown to be a necessary tool for instructors, for textbooks, and for the students to rely upon as an instrument for learning, laboratory studies examining the usefulness of examples found severe limitations in the way that students can generalize what is learned from worked-out solutions. In almost all the empirical work to date, on the role of example solutions (Eylon & Helfman, 1982; Reed, Dempster, & Ettinger, 1985; Sweller & Cooper, 1985), a student who has studied examples often cannot solve problems that deviate slightly from the example solution.

Sweller and Cooper (1985) have clear-cut evidence showing that students who were given the opportunities to study example solutions had advantages over students who were just given opportunities to work the problems. These problems were algebraic expressions in which they had to isolate the unknown variable. The advantages were measured in terms of reduction in errors and speed. It is noteworthy that the group who was given the opportunity to study examples excelled on subsequent test problems, when these test problems were similar to the example problems. However, on dissimilar problems, there were no significant differences. These data suggest that example solutions tend to provide an algorithm for students to use and follow on similar problems; but they really have not acquired any deep understanding of the example. Similarly, in the Reed et al. (1985) study, students were able to solve only 6% of simple algebra word problems (such as mixture problems) that required a slight transformation of the original equation. For example, the mixture problem required the use of the formula:

$$(\text{Percentage}_1 \times \text{Quantity}_1) + (\text{Percentage}_2 \times \text{Quantity}_2) = \text{Percentage}_3 \times \text{Quantity}_3.$$

In the solution that the student studied, the application of this formula required that the third quantity (Quantity_3) be derived from the second quantity plus 2 ($\text{Quantity}_2 + 2$). Thus Quantity_3 can be represented as the sum of Quantity_2 and 2 quarts. In the similar test problem that the students had a great deal of difficulty solving, Quantity_1 had to be expressed in terms of 16 quarts minus Quantity_2. The point of this example is simply to show the triviality of the transformation that had to be derived from the example solution in order to solve the similar problem. The only conclusion from such findings is that the students must have learned a very syntactic structure in which they could only substitute numerical values into the unknown of the formula directly, because they had difficulty making even a slight transformation of the formula.

The pessimistic outcomes of empirical studies examining the role of examples and what can be derived from them direct our attention to the possible limitations of examples per se. One limitation seems to be that examples are inadequate at providing the rationales for the application of each of the procedural steps. That is, the solution procedure depicts a sequence of actions, without providing the specifications of the inputs that will produce such a sequence of actions (VanLehn, 1986). Simon (1980) noted that "the actions of the productions needed to solve problems in the domain of the textbooks are laid out systematically, but they are not securely connected with the conditions that should evoke them" (p. 92). We can provide a concrete example of the lack of specification of the explicit conditions under which actions should be executed by examining a worked-out solution taken from a physics textbook (Halliday & Resnick, 1981), as shown in Fig. 8.3. This is an exact solution example that we have used in our study. We can see clearly that explication of the rationale underlying the sequence of actions is often not given. It is not clear, in Statement 2, why one should "consider the knot at the junction of the three strings to be the body." This is a critical piece of information, because it implies that, at this location (as opposed to the block, for example), the sum of the forces is zero. Statement 2 also does not explain why and how other locations can be ruled out (such as the points of contact between the strings and the ceiling, etc). Such lack of specification of the explicit conditions for actions occurs throughout the example solution. In Statement 6, for example, how does the student know that $\vec{F}_A$, $\vec{F}_B$, and $\vec{F}_C$, are all the forces acting on the body and that there are no others? Statement 7 is essentially a restatement of Newton's first law, but it requires chaining several inferences together, and translating them into an equation (e.g., that because the body is at rest, there are no external forces; therefore the sum of the forces on the body must be equal to zero). Statement 8 is totally unexplained; why are the axes chosen as such? And in Statement 9, why is the vector equation translated into the scalars? (The reason is that one wants to resolve the forces so that they can be added after they are all aligned in the same x- and y- directions.) Our analysis of the example just presented strongly suggests that learning from examples is diminished if the statements in the example solution procedure are not explicit about the conditions under which the actions apply.

If students have learned only a sequence of actions, then they have basically acquired an algorithmic procedure, which is not readily amenable to transformation. This would explain why students in the empirical studies referred to earlier cannot transfer what they have learned from examples, primarily because what they have learned are syntactic or algorithmic

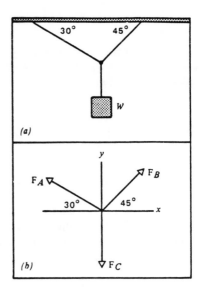

Figure 5-6 Example 5. *(a)* A block of weight W is suspended by strings. *(b)* A free-body diagram showing all the forces acting on the knot. The strings are assumed to be weightless.

1. Figure 5-6a shows an object of weight W hung by massless strings.
2. Consider the knot at the junction of the three strings to be "the body".
3. The body remains at rest under the action of the three forces shown Fig. 5-6.
4. Suppose we are given the magnitude of one of these forces.
5. How can we find the magnitude of the other forces?
6. F_A, F_B, and F_C are *all* the forces acting on the body.
7. Since the body is unaccelerated, $F_A + F_B + F_C = 0$
8. Choosing the x- and y-axes as shown, we can write this vector equation as three scalar equations:
9. $F_{Ax} + F_{Bx} = 0$,
10. $F_{Ay} + F_{By} + F_{Cy} = 0$
11. using Eq. 5-2. The third scalar equation for the z-axis is simply:
12. $F_{As} = F_{Bs} = F_{Cs} = 0$.
13. That is, the vectors all lie in the x-y plane so that they have no z components.
14. From the figure we see that
15. $F_{Ax} = -F_A \cos 30° = -0.866F_A$,
16. $F_{Ay} = F_A \sin 30° = 0.500F_A$,
17. and
18. $F_{Bx} = F_B \cos 45° = 0.707F_B$,
19. $F_{By} = F_B \sin 45° = 0.707 F_B$.

FIG. 8.3. A strings example, taken directly from Halliday and Resnick (1981).

rules, much in the way Neves's program (1981) learns. Neves (1981) constructed a program that could learn how to solve simple algebraic problems by deducing rules from consecutive statements. To illustrate, in the example solution, suppose the following steps were given:

1) $3X + 4 = 0$
2) $3X = -4$
3) $X = -4/3.$

Neves's program can detect or compute the differences between one line and the next line, and deduce the rule (for the differences between lines 1 and 2): IF there is a number on the left hand side of an equation, THEN subtract it from both sides. Such a rule does not explain why or under what conditions one would subtract a number from both sides of the equal sign. The rule is syntactic in that it applies if the structure of the given equation matches the condition of the rule exactly. Thus, in the cases where the given structure of the equation has to be derived or transformed in order for the condition of the rule to be satisfied and the action taken, students will fail, because they have not understood how the conditions of the rule can be derived from other variations of a given equation.

In sum, instructionally, the basic observation is that examples are preferred by both teachers and students as an instrument from which to learn, and yet examples are often poorly constructed (in that the rationales are often not provided for their action sequences). Perhaps because of their poor construction, students sometimes gain very little understanding from examples, other than acquiring syntactic rules, so that the knowledge gained is not transferable to related problems, as reported in the empirical studies.

Besides the value of identifying instructional dilemmas in the use of examples, there are serious theoretical reasons for studying how one learns and what is learned from examples. The important theoretical issue that is addressed by the A.I. literature concerns the ease with which a generalization can be induced from a single example or whether multiple examples are necessary. A similarity-based approach claims that generalizations are developed by inducing a principle (or a set of common features) from multiple examples. Such a principle would embody the essential features shared by all the examples. Thus, it is necessary to provide more than one example in order for such induction to take place. On the other hand, an explanation-based approach (Lewis, 1988; Mitchell, Keller, & Kedar-Cabelli, 1986) claims that generalizations can be obtained from a single example. To do so, the system must possess knowledge of both the domain from which to construct an explanation, as well as a definition of the concept which the example instantiates. That is, the induction is the construction of an explanation that justifies why the example is an instance of the concept. Thus, the method of induction in the two kinds of systems are quite different. Although the majority of psychological theories, including Anderson's ACT*, had assumed a similarity-based approach to learning, empirically, students can often generalize from single examples (Elio & Anderson, 1983; Kieras & Bovair, 1986).

This theoretical debate in the A.I. literature about the mechanism of generalization aside, we conceive of human learning in quite different terms. Students clearly are not learning principles of mechanics, such as Newton's second law, by generalizing from multiple examples, because not only might the students not know a priori the set of critical features to look for across a set of examples but further, the generality that does emerge from a set of examples must necessarily be syntactic. Suppose we mentally simulate what may be similar across a set of worked-out solutions. The kind of features that are similar may be specific procedures such as decomposing forces, imposing a reference frame, summing the forces, and so forth. The summation of these procedural components may not necessarily constitute an understanding of the principle of the second law, even though understanding it does imply that it will generate a solution that embodies these procedural components. Neither can students learn strictly via explanations in the sense of Mitchell et al.'s (1986) model because this would require that students have, by the time they encounter an example, a complete understanding of the principle or concept it instantiates. Yet empirical evidence suggests that many students can learn to solve problems by studying worked-out examples only, without any background text or lectures on the principles and concepts (Zhu & Simon, 1987). Clearly, a combined similarity-based and explanation-based approach seems necessary in order to learn from examples. (An alternative view is to propose that in some domains, such as algebra, learning can be accomplished through similarity-based generalization, whereas in less syntactic domains such as mechanics, a more explanation-based approach is necessary.)

Although our research is not addressed directly to whether generalizations can be induced from a single or multiple examples, our data can provide evidence on whether and how generalizations can emerge from learning from a single or a few examples.

ROLE OF SELF-EXPLANATIONS

We have painted a fairly pessimistic picture of the role and characteristics of textbook examples. We have noted that examples are poorly constructed, in that rationales for each of the actions required are seldom spelled out. This omission results in poor generalization and transfer, as shown in laboratory studies. But then students often prefer to rely on examples, to the exclusion of using textual elaboration of the relevant procedures and principles. Furthermore, there is also evidence showing that students often tend to ignore rationales that are given, as noted in algebra tutoring experiments (VanLehn, personal communication, December, 1987). It is also the case that some elaborations actually can disrupt students' understanding (Reder et al., 1986).

The only mediating factor that can account for these discrepant findings, we postulate, is self-explanations; which can play a significant role in effecting what can be learned from an example. We view examples as an essential instrument from which to learn because they instantiate the principles that the text aims to introduce. In other words, an example of a worked-out solution presents an interpretation of the principled knowledge presented in the text in terms of the procedural application. An example cannot be more complete without becoming redundant with the text of the chapter. When students fail to generalize from examples, perhaps we should attribute the failures not to the characteristic of the examples, but rather, to the disposition of the learners. In order to optimize learning, the students must actively construct an interpretation of each action in the context of the principles introduced in the text.

The role played by self-explanations can also explain why students sometimes ignore rationales that are provided, and why some rationales actually confuse and hurt the students' understanding. It seems likely that the explanations provided for the examples do not fit with the students' understanding. Self-generated explanations, by contrast are necessarily consistent with the students' own levels of understanding. Of course, then, the usefulness of self-generated explanations depends on the students' initial understanding of the text or principles. In any case, we can analyze students' self-explanations and the degree to which they are adequate in relating to the principles in the text. We should be able to see a relation between the adequacy of the self-explanations and successes at problem solving and transfer.

Thus, we view self-explanation as a mode of studying that can mediate learning. The degree to which self-generated explanations foster learning is a function of the accuracy and completeness of the self-explanations in interpreting the examples in terms of the principles introduced in the text.

A Brief Description of the Learning Study

The study that we conducted, which examined how students learn to solve problems by studying worked-out examples in the domain of physics, analyzed two major components: knowledge acquisition and problem solving (see Fig. 8.4 for a diagram of the experimental procedure). During the first part of the knowledge acquisition phase, students studied the necessary

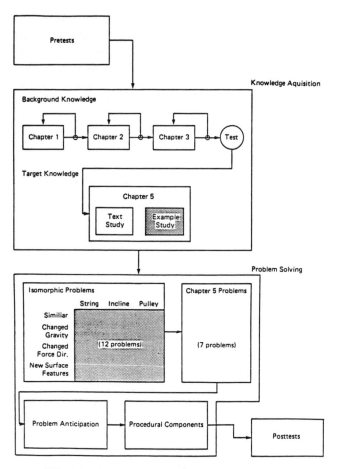

FIG. 8.4.   A diagram depicting the design of the study.

background subject matter, covering the topics of measurement, vectors, and motion in one dimension. These materials are covered in the first three chapters of Halliday and Resnick (1981), a text that is adopted by many universities as a fundamental introduction to mechanics. With each of these chapters, students studied until they reached a criterion, which was defined as the ability to correctly solve a set of declarative, qualitative, and quantitative problems.

During the second part of this phase, students studied chapter 5, the target chapter on particle dynamics. Chapter 4 was skipped because it was not essential to understanding chapter 5. We stopped at chapter 5 because the examples there elicited interesting problem-solving behavior. That is, problem solving of those materials required some understanding of phys-

Strings

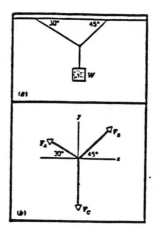

Incline

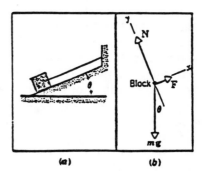

Pulley

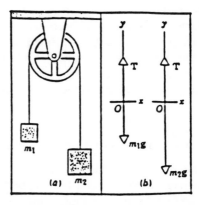

FIG. 8.5. Diagrams of the three worked-out examples used in the study.

ics, rather than merely applying algorithmic procedures. (The term understanding here is used in a general sense.) The major focus of the acquisition phase in their studying of chapter 5 was how students studied 3 worked-out examples taken directly from the text (see Fig. 8.3 for an example of a worked-out solution). Each worked-out solution represented a type of problem. There were three types, which we defined to correspond to the physical situation described: a string problem, an inclined plane problem, and a pulley problem. These are depicted in Fig. 8.5. Students talked aloud while they studied each example, and their protocols were taped. That is, they were asked to utter whatever they were thinking about as they read each statement of the example solution.

At the problem-solving stage, students solved two main sets of problems. The first set consisted of 12 isomorphic problems, with four problems corresponding to each type of example. These problems were specifically designed so that they had different degrees of similarity to the example solutions. For example, the first level of difference (the first set of isomorphs) was a problem that had fundamentally the same description and wording, except a different variable was required for the solution. To solve such a problem, one could basically follow the solution exemplified in the worked-out example, and compute the answer for a different variable than the one calculated in the worked-out example. The second level isomorphs varied only in the values of some of the variables stated in the problem statements. For example, the angle of the incline might be 60 degrees rather than 30. The third level isomorph had some dissimilarity in the surface features. For example, the orientation of the forces could be changed. The fourth level isomorphs had a completely different surface structure. For example, in the case of the strings example, instead of having two of the strings attached to the ceiling, the two strings might be attached to the floor.

The second set of problems to be solved by the students contained seven problems that were taken directly from the end of chapter 5. These problems are considerably more difficult than the isomorphic problems that we designed. Protocols were taken at all problem-solving sessions. A variety of pre- and posttests were also administered, the former before the knowledge acquisition stage and the latter at the very end of the problem-solving stage.

How One Learns From Studying Examples

In spite of the fact that all of our students successfully completed the declarative knowledge test that tapped the information presented in the text, we found substantial individual differences in their subsequent problem solving success, ranging from 28% to 100% correct. These could have resulted from differences in how students studied the examples of worked-out problems and differences in the mechanisms and techniques they used to learn the procedural instantiation of that declarative knowledge.

Our methodological approach to the study of what and how students learn from examples was to ask them to comment on each of the statements that they read in the example. All the comments that the students made can be described by the generic term "elaborations." However, there are distinct differences between the kinds of elaborations that students generated: About a third of them related to the content of the example they were studying, and we refer to these as *self-explanations.* Another third were *monitoring* statements. A final third were classified as *miscellaneous* and these contained paraphrases and mathematical elaborations, primarily.

We now discuss students' self-explanations as a mechanism of learning by which students generated tacit knowledge that links pieces of explicitly stated knowledge. In the second section we then discuss the role of cognitive monitoring, that is, how students became aware of their failure or success at understanding, and how awareness of misunderstanding led to new attempts at understanding.

THE FUNCTION OF SELF-EXPLANATIONS

Explanations are remarks that students make after reading one or several statements from the worked-out solution example. In particular, these are remarks that have some relevance to the physics content under study. We reasoned that because example-exercises, as we have analyzed, are so incomplete in providing explanations for the action sequences, the students must necessarily construct their own explanations for the sequence of actions in order to understand the material. This idea is not new. Bruner (1966) mentioned it two decades ago and Wickelgren (1974) reiterated it. Indeed, we found that good students (i.e., those who had greater success at solving problems with an average of 82% correct) generated a significantly greater number of elaboration ideas (51 ideas per example) than the poor students (18 ideas). Although the good and poor students both had a similar distribution of types of elaborations generated (explanations, monitoring statements, and miscellaneous others), the good students still generated an average of 15.9 explanations per example, whereas the poor students generated only 4.3 explanations per example. Thus, generating self-explanations seems to be an important mechanism of learning from examples, because it correlated with problem-solving successes. Besides the quantitative difference, a second important finding was that the explanations generated by the good students tended to be qualitatively better than those generated by the poor students. That is, the good students' explanations tended to infer additional tacit knowledge, whereas the poor students' explanations were often paraphrasings of the diagram, with no new information generated.

To give a flavor of what we mean by better explanations, we quote one good and one poor student's explanation of the diagram of the strings example presented in Fig. 8.4. The good student's explanation qualified the nature of the forces involved and their interrelations: "They'd just be the force, the rest mass of the thing holding it up would be the force. It could, well, actually it'd be the force of weight. Cause being upheld by . . . it's the resistance to weight W." The poor student's explanation, on the other hand, basically translated into words the surface information presented in the diagram: "Okay, so three forces are on the two strings and from the string going down to the object."[2] (Further discussions of the nature and the quality of self-explanations is presented in the section dealing with what is learned from studying examples.)

We would like to interpret the more elaborated explanation statements generated by the good students as an overt manifestation of their active processing during learning (as opposed to taking it as evidence of their articulateness). Our interpretation is consistent with the assumptions made with other types of protocol analyses, in which the verbal protocols are supposed to reflect what is being processed in working memory. Thus, longer protocols should simply indicate a greater degree of processing. This assumption is consistent, as well, with those made in analyses of eye movement protocols, in which longer fixations are taken to mean that the student is processing a particular stimulus for a longer period. Although thinking-aloud is not quite the same as elaborating on a statement presented in an example solution, many studies of this variety have shown no differences in performance between those students who were instructed to think aloud and those who were not (Klinger, 1974; Thomas, 1974). Ericsson and Simon (1984) interpreted these findings to suggest that, in response to the instruction to think-aloud or verbalize, the subjects did not change the structure of their processing, but merely expressed overtly what they otherwise would have thought covertly. Thus, we view the greater amount of elaboration produced by the good students to be the manifestations of their internal processes in trying to understand the example solution better.

Our interpretation also discounts the possibility that the good students, by taking our instruction more seriously, engaged more fully in the ac-

---

[2]In subsequent analyses, we have discounted paraphrases of a diagram as an explanation (see Chi et al., in press), and instead, categorized them in the *miscellaneous* category.

tivities of verbalizing explanations, and so achieved better understanding and thus more successful problem solving. This causality was not apparent when we analyzed the quality of the explanations. Our interpretation that explanations reflect active construction was further supported by the fact that the good students did not generate a greater number of explanations than the poor students during the problem-solving phase of the study (that is, during problem solving, many students re-read several lines of the examples, and they thus had additional opportunities to provide explanations of what they did not understand). Although they were encouraged to elaborate during problem solving as well, the good students probably did not need to. Hence, it does not seem to be the case that the good students were simply more motivated to generate explanations in order to please us.

The major support for our claim that the overt explanations reflect natural constructive processing, rather than cause more extensive processing, comes from the fact that the quality of the good students' explanations was better than the poor students'. It doesn't seem that one could obtain quality explanations by simply encouraging the poor students to generate them. The importance of the quality of the explanations generated is consistent with the results of a study by Stein and Bransford (1979). These authors asked subjects to generate their own elaborations in order to help them memorize some sentences. They found that students who generated their own elaborations, on the whole, did remember better than the control students (who were not told to elaborate), but worse than the group of students for whom the experimenter provided very precise elaborations. However, if the students were divided into those who generated precise elaborations (which is analogous to our better quality explanations) and those who generated imprecise elaborations, then those who generated precise elaborations remembered the sentences even better than the group of students who were given experimenter-generated elaborations. This result is especially consistent with our interpretation because it implies that asking students to generate elaborations per se does not necessarily produce better memory. Rather, elaborations generated were helpful only if they were precise.

There are other studies, however, that indicate that the very act of verbalization or providing justifications for solution steps while problem solving can lead to better problem solving. Gagné and Smith (1962), for example, found that by asking students to verbalize the reason for each move they made to the 2-, 3-, 4-, and 5-disk Tower of Hanoi task, they improved their performance on a subsequent 6-disk Tower of Hanoi task. However, the difference Gagné and Smith reported was a group difference: that is, the group with the instruction to verbalize performed better on the whole than the group not told to do so. They did not analyze the explanations as a function of how successful the solvers were. If we look at the content of their explanations, as did Gagné and Smith, we see that there were four types of explanations given (p. 15):

1. Those that were oriented toward single moves in the solution of the problems, with explanations such as:
   "only possible move"
   "just to try it"
   "don't know"
2. Those that anticipated to the extent of two moves, with comments such as:
   "to get at the larger disk"
   "to free up a space"
3. Reasons that anticipated sequences of moves, such as:
   "move as with a three-disk sequence"
   "if disk is odd-numbered, move to circle B"
4. Reasons that identified the principles underlying the solution, such as:
   "move odd-numbered disk in the clockwise direction"
   "move even-numbered disks in the counterclockwise direction"

It is possible that the good solvers in the Gagné and Smith study tended to give explanations that had the same characteristics as those generated by our good students, as those illustrated in Type 2 (stated subgoals), Type 3 (induced a goal from a sequence of actions), and Type 4 (relating the solution to the principle). If indeed there were such individual differences in the relation between successes at solving problems and the type of explanations given, then Gagné and Smith's result would be consistent with Stein and Bransford's and with ours. That is, giving explanations or elaborations does facilitate both problem solving and remembering in general (perhaps because it forces a person to process the material more extensively). However, individual differences in problem solving and remembering will remain as a function of the quality of the explanations and elaborations.

Students' Accuracy at Cognitive Monitoring

An important difference that was found between the good and the poor solvers was their ability to monitor their own comprehension and misunderstanding. Because a large portion of the students' elaborations (39% for the good and 42% for the poor) were monitoring statements, it seems that these statements must serve an important purpose. Even though both the good and poor students had proportionately the same amount of monitoring statements, there was a significant difference between the good and poor students in the relative proportion of statements indicating comprehension failure versus understanding. Monitoring statements that indicate comprehension failure are questions raised, usually about an example line, such as, "Why is $mgsin\Theta$ negative?" An example of a monitoring statement that indicates understanding is "Okay" or "I can see now how they did it."

In general, the good students generated a large number of statements that reflected their failure to comprehend (9.3 such statements per example), whereas the poor students claimed that they did not understand with only 1.1 statements per example. Moreover, the poor students not only did not realize that they did not understand, in fact, they thought more often that they did understand. Thus, they generated an average of 6.2 statements per example indicating that they did understand (in contrast to the 1.1 statements indicating that they did not understand). Good students, by contrast, generated an equivalent number of statements indicating that they understood (10.8 statements) and that they misunderstood (9.3 statements). Basically, this suggests that the poor students do not accurately monitor their own comprehension. Not only do they *not* realize that they have misunderstood, they in fact think that they do understand.

We do not yet have a clear conception of the underlying causes of these different monitoring accuracies between the good and the poor students. If we assume that understanding is the instantiation of cognitive structures, then, we could speculate that, when a student has barely any structures at all to correspond to the example exercise, then they might falsely believe that they understand. However, for good students who have some incomplete structure of the example exercise as derived from having read the text, they can monitor their understanding more accurately by assessing the degree to which parts of their cognitive structures are instantiated, revised, and completed. In fact, we can support this interpretation somewhat by looking at the content of what these monitoring statements say. For the good students, their monitoring statements, when referring to misunderstandings, are specific, for example: "I'm wondering whether there would be acceleration due to gravity?" or "Why does the force have to change?" Such specific queries imply that the good student has a specific schema in mind and is trying to instantiate that schema by asking a specific question that pertains to a part of the schema. Poor students, on the other hand, may not have any kind of structures in memory at all. This would predict that they cannot ask specific questions. In fact, they do ask very general questions such as: "Well, what should you do here?"

The advantage of having an accurate monitoring of one's understanding is that the realization that one does not understand should elicit attempts to understand. That is exactly what we found in both our good and poor students. That is, in the majority of the cases (85% of the time for the good students and 60% of the time for the poor students), realizations of comprehension failures triggered episodes of self-explanations. Hence, because one is more likely to resolve one's misunderstanding by engaging in self-explanation, accurate monitoring of one's understanding is crucial for learning.

WHAT ONE LEARNS WHILE STUDYING EXAMPLES

As mentioned, good students generated a significantly greater amount of self-explanations, and their explanations were qualitatively better. We decided upon two ways to further examine the nature of self-explanations that were particularly suited to those generated by the good students. First, we found that the structure of explanations often took the form of specifying the conditions of applicability for the actions, stating the consequences of actions, as well as imposing subgoals on a sequence of actions. For instance, in response to an example line which stated that: "It is convenient to choose the x-axis of our reference frame to be along the incline and the y-axis to be normal to the incline" (Halliday & Resnick, 1981, p. 71), a good student explained the conditions of the choice by saying "and it is very, umm, wise to choose a reference frame that's parallel to the incline, parallel and normal to the incline, because that way, you'll only have to split up mg, the other forces are already, component vectors for you." Thus, we can generalize that, when students explain the example actions to themselves, they basically justify the actions by inferring the additional tacit information that is not explicated in the example statements.

What is the content and the source of this tacit knowledge evident in the self-explanations? We found that the good students try to understand the example by relating the example statements to explanations and principles stated in the text. The response to Line 3 of Fig. 8.3, "So that means that they have to cancel out, only the body wouldn't be at rest," for instance, was guided by Newton's first law, that if there is no motion, then the sum of the forces must be zero. Relating the example statement to the principles previously presented in the text served the purpose of providing the rationale for the procedural steps of the example solution. Moreover, we found that through such explanations, students increased their understanding of the fundamental physics principles introduced in the text (Newton's three laws), as well as the meaning and extension of the various concepts involved (such as the relation between weight and force). It seems then, that students are able to learn a great deal from studying even a few examples. To state in a nutshell what students learned from example-exercises (these results are described in detail in Chi, Bassok, Lewis, Rei-mann, & Glaser, in press), we can say that in their explanations, by adding many linkages between the explicit statements made in the examples, as well as between the example statements and the principles in the text, they understood the rationale of the solution procedure better. That is, by specifying the conditions and consequences of various actions and inducing the goals for a set of actions, they probably constructed a more coherent representation of the entire solution procedure. The ultimate outcome of a more coherent representation was that the good students increased their understanding of the fundamental physics principles presented in the text. (This increased understanding was assessed by pre- and posttests of the physics principles, administered prior to and subsequent to the example-studying phase of the study.)

There seems to be a discrepancy between our findings, the fact that students can learn from examples and do seem to transfer their knowledge to end-of-chapter problems, and others in the literature which show that examples are of limited use and the acquired procedures seem to be rather syntactic in nature. However, there are three key differences between our study and others that seem to be responsible for this discrepancy. First, our students studied several pages of text, much as they would in a regular classroom, whereas the students in many of these other studies were not supplied with the background material (e.g., Reed, Dempster, & Ettinger, 1985). The text part of the chapters actually supplies knowledge of con-cepts and principles, which may lead to learning with understanding rather than to simply learning a syntactic procedure. The second, and perhaps the most important difference is that our students were encouraged to give explanations, and it is possible that those students who did generate self-explanations may have induced greater understanding. Finally, the suc-cessful learning we have described was characteristic only of our good students. Poor students generated very few and very impoverished expla-nations and were subsequently unsuccessful in their problem solving. Be-cause we analyzed individual differences, at least differences between the good and the poor solvers, we were able to uncover differences that may have been masked in the other studies. What students learned depended on the kind of explanations they provided.

How One Uses What is Learned

So far, we have addressed the issues of how one learns from studying examples and what one learns. Once the learning is completed, presum-ably the knowledge gained is used in solving problems. We have done some preliminary analyses that characterize how examples are used in solving problems. For example, we found that in general, *all* students liked to rely on examples in their initial attempts to solve problems, as is consistent with the findings cited earlier (e.g., Pirolli & Anderson, 1985). For example, for the 12 isomorphic problems, the good students referred to the examples in 9 out of the 12 problems, and the poor students referred to the examples in 10 out of the 12 problems. Within each problem solving protocol, however, there were pronounced individual differences in the frequency with which students used examples. Poor students used examples more often than the good students. That is, within each problem that the students had to solve, the poor solver would refer to the example about 6.6 times per problem, whereas the good solver would refer to the example only 2.7 times.

The most interesting differences between the good and poor solvers lie in the characteristics of their example-using behavior. The poor solvers, when reviewing the examples, basically reread them. Therefore, we examined the purpose of each episode of reference to an example to see how the example was being used. There were three kinds of behavior: The students could be rereading the example; they could be mapping something from the example to the problem that they were working on, such as looking to see how the frame of reference was drawn; or they could be checking for the accuracy of an equation, by looking to see what the units of weight were, for instance. The poor students predominantly spent their example-reference episodes in rereading the example. Thus, 4.1 out of their 6.6 example-referencing episodes were spent rereading, whereas only 0.6 out of the good solvers' 2.7 episodes were spent rereading.

We surmise that the poor students were rereading the examples basically because they had not gotten much out of the examples when they studied them initially. We can substantiate this interpretation by looking at the number of lines in the example that were reread, as well as the location of the line where the student began rereading. The poor students, reread, on the average, 13.0 lines for each example-referencing episode, whereas the good students reread an average of 1.6 lines. Furthermore, all the poor students, upon their first encounters with problem solving (in the first set of isomorphic problems), started rereading the examples from the very first line, whereas none of the good students did. We have thus characterized the poor students' use of examples as searching for a solution or a template from which they could map the to-be-solved problem so that they could generate a solution.

Good students, on the other hand, use examples for other purposes. The best characterization is to say that the good students used examples truly as a reference. This can be substantiated by two additional pieces of evidence. First, when they used the examples, they read only an average of 1.6 lines for each episode of use, and the 1.6 lines tended to contain a particular equation or free-body diagram that they were checking on or mapping from. This suggests that they were using the example to retrieve a particular piece of information. Thus, the good students must already have had a plan for a solution in mind. A second piece of evidence in support of this interpretation was that good students often prefaced their example-referencing episodes with the announcement of a specific goal, such as "I'm looking at the formula here, trying to see how you solve for $Force_1$, given the angle."

The kind of analyses that have been completed so far characterize, to some extent, the different ways good and poor students use examples. The kind of analyses that we need to pursue now are those that pinpoint exactly how the examples are used by each individual student. That is, in what analogical ways are examples used by the good and poor students? Do the poor students tend to notice only surface similarities, and the good students notice deeper similarities? An example of a surface similarity might be that both the example and the to-be-solved problem involve inclined planes. A deeper similarity might be noticing that both the example and the to-be-solved problem involve acceleration rather than static situations (or that the two situations are different, one involving a static situation and the other involving a dynamic case).

Likewise, we can also ask at what level is the mapping achieved? Mapping can be done at a superficial surface level. For example, a poor student might map and use an equation from the example simply because the equation contains all the variables that are stated in the to-be-solved problem. On the other hand, a good student might map a procedure from an example in a more global but deeper way. For example, a good student might know that the mapped procedure will achieve a particular result, such as decomposing the forces. Such analyses of how examples are used can also reveal the kind of understanding students have of the examples, so that the findings can validate the analyses of students' understanding as extrapolated from their explanations and their monitoring statements while studying.

INSTRUCTIONAL IMPLICATIONS

Constructing Instructional Materials: Limited Potentials

Our analyses of the limitations of example exercises, coupled with our research results, at first glance indicate that one constructive approach to improving learning might be to invest efforts in designing better example exercises. An obvious approach is to design exercises that fill in all the gaps or leaps in the current kinds of example exercises, that were pointed out earlier. For example, our results seem to indicate that example exercises should be designed to provide conditions for the actions, specify the consequences, supply goals for a sequence of actions, and relate the actions to the principles introduced in the text. Our results can further enhance the design of examples because they provide evidence about the locations of misunderstandings, as well as the kind of inferences that are needed in order to understand a particular sequence of actions in an example. In fact, we can utilize the explanations provided by the best students as a guide for constructing the justifications that are implicitly embedded between the statement lines.

Upon closer scrutiny, however, it becomes apparent that there are several reasons for the limited potential of such an approach to improving learning. First of all, it is not possible to supply all the rationales and justifications. Each example will always have some idiosyncrasies that might be perceived as inherent to the solution, and thus should not be elaborated upon, and each finite set of examples will be but a specific sample of the possible set of problems. But a more important limitation is that the justifications and explanations added have to be tailored to the individual student's understanding. For a good student who can generate his own explanations, these additional comments will be redundant. For the poor student who has little understanding, such explanations may actually confuse rather than clarify, and perhaps undercut rather than enhance performance, as Reder et al.'s (1986) results imply. And finally, as noted by VanLehn (personal communication), students can often choose to ignore the explanations provided, especially if these explanations are not tailored to their level of understanding.

Teaching Constructive Learning

Given that there are limits to the approach of improving learning by designing better—more explanatory—instructional materials, and given that students are continually encountering new domains to learn, a more sensible approach seems to be to focus on the learner, and teach the learner better learning strategies, so that he can use it in a variety of domains and learning situations. On the basis of our results, what kind of learning strategies might be good candidates? One possibility that comes immediately to mind is to teach students to monitor their comprehension more sensitively and accurately. This seems particularly important, at first sight, especially in light of our finding that for both the good and the poor students, when they do detect that they misunderstand, such misunderstanding triggers episodes of explanations. Thus, it seems important for the students to know *when* they do not understand, because such awareness potentially leads to further processing that may result in understanding. However, it is not clear that we can easily teach students to monitor their own states of comprehension. Our data show clearly that only the good students can monitor their states of comprehension accurately. The poor students are very inaccurate at monitoring their comprehension states. In order to describe what causes good students to know that they understand and poor students not to know, we need to have a better account of the mechanism underlying understanding, which we as yet know little about. One possibility is that accurate monitoring of comprehension can occur only if the statements presented in the example exercises deviate only to a small degree from the students' existing schema (the schema to which they are trying to fit the information in the example).

Regardless of what the mechanism of monitoring is, one promising instructional approach might be simply to alert the poor students to locations that the designer of the example knows might be problematic. A simple probe (such as an asterisk) at critical locations might be sufficient to serve as a prompt for students to engage in explanations. Such a prompt might be useful in eliciting relevant explanations, although not necessarily. As we noted in our results, although the poor students made very few explanation-type remarks, for the few that they did make, their contents were qualitatively poorer as compared to the explanations of the good students. However, because the poor students generated only a few explanations, the finding regarding the quality of their explanations is still tenuous. Thus, whether or not poor students can be encouraged to generate good explanations remains an open empirical question.

Besides teaching students to monitor their own understanding, and/or prodding them to generate explanations, a more promising approach might be to shape students' explanations. Given that we have identified the characteristics of good students' explanations, we can use these characteristics to develop a set of prompts that can shape students' explanations. For example, at critical problematic locations, probes can take the form of asking such questions as: "Under what condition is this action to be taken?"; or "What else may be true if this is true?" or "What is the goal of this set of actions?"; or "How does this action relate to a principle introduced in the text, and which principle does it relate to?" These kinds of more specific probes might succeed in producing explanations that are qualitatively more like those generated by good students.

CONCLUSIONS

Our research on learning from examples has uncovered several interesting phenomena. Most prominently, it has found that students who are successful at solving problems are those who learned the materials in a different way then those students who were less successful at solving problems.

More specifically, the good students' learning from examples was characterized by the generation of self-explanations. Their self-explanations had the characteristic of adding tacit knowledge about the actions of the example-solution. Moreover, these self-explanations induced greater understanding of the principles introduced in the text. It was also found that the production of these self-explanations seemed to be guided by the accuracy with which students monitored their states of comprehension. Their knowing that they misunderstood generally elicited explanations. Furthermore, the good students' self-monitoring yielded specific inquiries through which they could search for an answer, whereas the poor students' self-inquiries were general undirected questions.

There are important implications to be derived from this research. First and foremost, in terms of theories of learning from examples, our data suggest that students can learn, *with understanding,* from a single or a few examples, contrary to the other available empirical evidence. (That is, students can learn more than just syntactic rules and can transfer what they have learned to dissimilar transfer-type problems.) However, only those students who provide adequate explanations during studying are able to see the degree to which they can generalize their problem-solving skills. Hence, not only does our study resolve some of the discrepant findings in the empirical literature, but it also points to limitations in the assumptions of the existing theories of learning from examples. For instance, current theories hold that explanations serve the purpose of justifying an example as an instance of a principle, assuming that the student would have complete knowledge about the principle. Our results suggest, by contrast, that explanations can serve the additional important function of enhancing and completing students' understanding of the principles.

Our research raises more questions than it answers. Some critical ones that we need to address are: What does it mean to understand an example while studying it? How does understanding relate to cognitive monitoring? How does understanding relate to the way that examples are used? Deeper analyses of our results hinge on our potential explication of what understanding entails, how it can be represented, and how it should be assessed.

ACKNOWLEDGMENTS

We are grateful for the continued support of this research from the Office of Naval Research, under Contract No. N00014-84-K-0542. We appreciate Bob Glaser's, Lauren Resnick's, and Kurt VanLehn's comments on this chapter, as well as our lengthy (but unresolved) discussions with VanLehn about the issue of understanding.

REFERENCES

Anderson, J. R. (1987). Skill acquisition: Compilation of weak-method problem solutions. *Psychological Review, 94*, 192–210.

Anderson, J. R., Greeno, J. G., Kline, P. J., & Neves, D. M. (1981). Acquisition of problem-solving skill. In J. R. Anderson (Ed.), *Cognitive skills and their acquisition* (pp. 191–230). Hillsdale, NJ: Lawrence Erlbaum Associates.

Bruner, J. S. (1966). *Toward a theory of instruction.* Cambridge, MA: Harvard University Press.

Chi, M. T. H., Bassok, M., Lewis, R., Reimann, P., & Glaser, R. (in press). Self-explanations: How students study and use examples in learning to solve problems. *Cognitive Science.*

Elio, R., & Anderson, J. R. (1983). Effects of category generalizations and instance similarity on schema abstraction. *Journal of Experimental Psychology: Learning, Memory, and Cognition, 113*, 541–555.

Ericsson, K., & Simon, H. A. (1984). *Protocol analysis: Verbal reports as data.* Cambridge, MA: MIT Press.

Eylon, B., & Helfman, J. (1982, February). *Analogical and deductive problem-solving in physics.* Paper presented at the AERA meeting, New York.

Gagné, R. M., & Smith, E. C., Jr. (1962). A study of the effects of verbalization on problem solving. *Journal of Experimental Psychology, 63*, 12–18.

Glaser, R. (1967). Some implications of previous work on learning and individual differences. In R. M. Gagné (Ed.), *Learning and individual differences* (pp. 1–18). Columbus, OH: Merrill.

Halliday, D., & Resnick, R. (1981). *Fundamentals of physics.* New York: Wiley.

Kieras, D. E., & Bovair, S. (1986). The acquisition of procedures from text: A production system analysis of transfer of training. *Journal of Memory and Language, 25*, 507–524.

Klinger, E. (1974). Utterances to evaluate and control attention distinguish operant from respondent thought while thinking out loud. *Bulletin of the Psychonomic Society, 4*, 44–45.

LeFevre, J., & Dixon, P. (1986). Do written instructions need examples? *Cognition and Instruction, 3*, 1–30.

Lewis, C. (1988). *Why and how to learn why: Analysis-based generalization of procedures.* Cognitive Science, 2, 211–256.

Mitchell, T. M., Keller, R. M., & Kedar-Cabelli, S. T. (1986). Explanation-based generalization: A unifying view. *Machine Learning, 1*, 48–80.

Neves, D. M. (1981). *Learning procedures from examples.* Unpublished doctoral dissertation, Carnegie-Mellon University, Pittsburgh, PA.

Pirolli, P. L., & Anderson, J. R. (1985). The role of learning from examples in the acquisition of recursive programming skills. *Canadian Journal of Psychology, 32*, 240–272.

Reder, L. M., Charney, D. H., & Morgan, K. I. (1986). The role of elaborations in learning a skill from an instructional text. *Memory & Cognition, 14*, 64–78.

Reed, S. K., Dempster, A., & Ettinger, M. (1985). Usefulness of analogous solutions for solving algebra word problems. *Journal of Experimental Psychology: Learning, Memory & Cognition, 11*, 106–125.

Simon, H. A. (1980). Problem solving and education. In D. Tuma & F. Reif (Eds.), *Problem solving and education: Issues in teaching and research* (pp. 81–86). Hillsdale, NJ: Lawrence Erlbaum Associates.

Stein, B. S., & Bransford, J. D. (1979). Constraints on effective elaboration: Effects of precision and subject generation. *Journal of Verbal Learning and Verbal Behavior, 18*, 769–777.

Sweller, J., & Cooper, G. A. (1985). The use of worked examples as a substitute for problem solving in learning algebra. *Cognition and Instruction, 2,* 59–89.

Thomas, J. C. (1974). An analysis of behavior in the Hobbits-Ores problem. *Cognitive Psychology, 6,* 257–269.

VanLehn, K. (1986). Arithmetic procedures are induced from examples. In J. Hiebert (Ed.), *Conceptual and procedural knowledge: The case of mathematics* (pp. 133–179). Hillsdale, NJ: Lawrence Erlbaum Associates.

VanLehn, K. (in press). *Mind bogs: The origins of procedural misconception.* Cambridge, MA: MIT Press.

Wickelgren, W. A. (1974). *How to solve problems: Elements of a theory of problems and problem solving.* San Francisco: W. H. Freeman.

Zhu, X., & Simon, H. A. (1987). Learning mathematics from examples and by doing. *Cognition and Instruction, 4,* 137–166.

9

What Kind Of Knowledge Transfers?

Jill H. Larkin
Carnegie-Mellon University

Everyone believes in transfer. We believe that through experience in learning we get better at learning. The second language you learn (human or computer) is supposed to be easier than the first. Professors' lore has it that seniors taking Psychology 101 as a distribution requirement perform "better" than freshmen taking it as an introduction to their major. All these common beliefs reflect the sensible idea that, when one has acquired knowledge in one setting, it should save time and perhaps increase effectiveness for future learning in related settings.

But these are popular concepts of transfer. What is an operational definition of this phenomenon? Transfer does not mean merely applying old knowledge in new situations. That happens often. We frequently use our knowledge of maps to figure out the layout of unknown cities. Transfer means applying old knowledge in a setting sufficiently novel that it also requires learning new knowledge. If there were no transfer, then solving problems in a new domain would require totally mastering a set of necessary new knowledge. To the extent that transfer occurs, some of this necessary knowledge is transferred from earlier experience and need not be learned. Because necessary knowledge is transferred from earlier experience and need not be learned, the usual measure of transfer is the difference in time required to learn a new task for learners with certain prior experience as opposed to other learners who lack this experience.

This chapter first reviews some history of psychological work on transfer and then discusses current work that suggests the kind of knowledge that may transfer most often. Finally, it considers some modern models of transfer and possibilities for understanding this phenomenon more completely.

HISTORY

The Common Elements Theory

According to Thorndike (Thorndike & Woodworth, 1901) the prevailing view of transfer early in the century was a *doctrine of formal discipline*. This doctrine viewed the mind as a collection of general faculties, including observation, discrimination, and reasoning. If exercised in appropriately demanding study, these faculties, like muscles, were supposed to grow stronger and more able to acquire new knowledge. This view would explain any decrease in learning time due to prior study of a different topic by saying that the prior study strengthened faculties of the mind. According to this view, transfer can occur between domains that share no content at all. Furthermore, study of difficult subjects (e.g., Latin and geometry) should be particularly effective in decreasing learning time in any other domain.

Thorndike demonstrated in many experiments that transfer is much less broad in scope, that learning in one domain does not necessarily strengthen the mind for learning in any other domain.[1] For example, Thorndike showed that peoples' memory for numbers is uncorrelated with their memory for words. He therefore proposed a theory of "identical elements" for transfer, saying that learning time in a second domain will be decreased only if this domain shares some common elements with the domain learned earlier. Neither Thorndike nor the psychology of the time, however, had any means for better specifying what an "element" might be and in what sense it would need to be "identical" in the two domains.

---

[1]Interestingly, modern theories of athletic training also renounce universal strengthening of muscles in favor of the principle of specificity—if you want to be good at a particular sport, train in that sport (Mirkin & Hoffman, 1978).

Common Elements as General Problem-Solving Skill

If it is common elements that account for transfer, then perhaps a set of these elements might be viewed as general problem-solving skills, independent of any particular subject domain. This view lies behind research and thinking in both human and machine problem solving. For example, Ernst and Newell (1969) called their program a general problem solver (GPS) because it explicitly separated knowledge used to solve problems in a variety of domains from knowledge applicable in just one domain. They suggested that a program like GPS could potentially solve problems in a large number of domains with the addition of only a moderate amount of domain-specific knowledge. To understand this view of transferable knowledge, let us look more closely at an example from GPS.

GPS could solve problems in a collection of domains from algebra and geometry to chess and simple puzzles. But what is general in GPS is the following strategy.

1. Identify the major differences between the current situation (state) and the desired or goal state.
2. Then pick an operator that will reduce one or more of those differences.
3. If there are several such operators, choose the one with conditions that most closely match the current state.
4. If you can't apply that operator, set as subgoals achieving the conditions that would let you apply it.

A challenging problem for this strategy is a problem in integration, for example, finding a simple quantity, involving no integration, that is equal to the following:

$$\int t\, e^{t^2}\, dt$$

Figure 9.1 shows schematically how GPS solves this problem. The rounded boxes show the initial and goal states, and the expression that ultimately satisfies the goal-state criterion. The square boxes show first GPS operators and then their application to the current problem.

GPS begins by noticing the major difference (no integral in the goal state) between the current state and the goal. Figure 9.1 shows this difference (at the right) in a square box with arrows to the two states compared. This difference leads GPS to consider a set of operators (integration) that removes integrals and to find the operator (Operator 1 in Fig. 9.1) that most closely matches the current state. This operator, shown at the top of the double box labeled Operator 1 means that, if the current

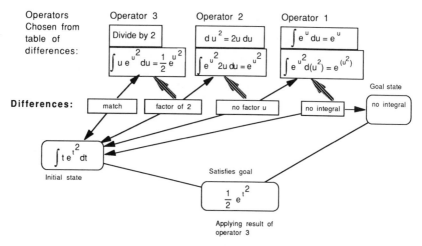

FIG. 9.1. Solution to an integration problem produced by the computer-implemented general problem solver GPS (Ernst & Newell, 1969).

expression is equal to the left-hand side, then it can be replaced by the right-hand side. GPS has the domain-specific knowledge that, in Operator 1, u can be replaced with u^2 to yield the expression in the lower box below Operator 1 in Fig. 9.1.

If the initial given state, at the left in Fig. 9.1, were identical in form to the left side of this expression in Operator 1, we could solve the problem immediately. Because it is not, GPS uses item 4 in its general strategy. It sets as a subgoal to find an operator that will reduce the difference between the left side of Operator 1 and the initial state. The major difference between the initial state and this new subgoal is that the new goal state lacks a factor u to match the factor t in the current problem state. Referring again to its table of differences, GPS now selects one of its differentiation operators because they reduce differences in the number of factors. As before, it selects among these operators the one that most closely matches the current state. The result is Operator 2 in Fig. 9.1. When applied to the left side of the result from Operator 1, it produces the expression (with an extra factor u) in the lower box labeled Operator 2. Now the difference between the current state and the left side of this operator is merely a factor of 2. Operator 3, eliminating this difference, is the algebraic operator dividing both sides of an equation by 2.

The left side of the resulting expression is now identical in form to the given equation. It can be applied to produce the result in the rounded box at the bottom of Fig. 9.1, the "answer" to the problem that matches the goal state.

What is general in the GPS process is the following strategy: (a) choosing operators according to what difference (between the goal and the current state) they will reduce, and (b) if the conditions of the current operator are not satisfied, then choosing set subgoals(s) to satisfy them. What is specific are the particular operators, differences, and the connections between them (Ernst & Newell, 1969, pp. 137–150).

Looking at this example from GPS, one has to ask about the relative importance of the general and specific knowledge. Certainly, the general strategy is powerful and useful in a variety of situations. And it is central to guiding GPS's work in many domains, just as it does in the example considered here. But this solution also involved a large amount of knowledge specific to calculus. Suppose we taught the GPS strategy in a different context—perhaps working puzzles. Would this prior learning aid in solving the calculus problem to any noticeable degree? The question is whether this simple general strategy forms a large or a small part of problem-solving knowledge. It may be that the role of such general knowledge is very small compared with the role of domain-specific knowledge, and so prior learning of the strategy would have little effect on learning a new domain.

To some extent, the importance of general problem-solving knowledge (compared with domain-specific knowledge) has been tested by a variety of popular efforts to characterize and teach "general problem-solving skills." For example, Polya (1957) says, "Take the questions: What is the unknown? What are the data? What is the condition? These questions are generally applicable, we can ask them with good effect dealing with all sorts of problems." Similarly, Wickelgren (1973) writes, "The general problem solving methods described in this book virtually guarantee that you will never again have a blank mind in such circumstances. They should also help you solve many more problems and solve them faster." Analogous comments are made by other popular authors including de Bono (1970) and Adams (1976).

These authors suggest first that there are general reasoning and problem-solving skills that form a significant core to the problem solving required in a variety of domains. Second, they believe that these skills can be taught in one setting (a problem-solving course or book) and then transferred effectively in other settings.

Lack of Success in Identifying General Problem-Solving Techniques

The lack of clear success in identifying and exploiting a common core of problem-solving techniques is evident in three areas. First, in parallel to the general computer problem solvers discussed earlier, people began to develop sophisticated programs that perform like experts in limited but intellectually challenging fields, such as diagnosis and prescription for bacterial diseases, location of mineral deposits, assembling sophisticated computers, or tutoring students in a computer language (Duda et al., 1978; Reiser, Anderson, & Farrell, 1984; Shortliffe, 1976). These programs are characterized by a large amount of detailed domain-specific knowledge and only minimal general knowledge. These expert systems, therefore, suggest that skilled problem solving uses at most minimal amounts of general knowledge, with the bulk of the knowledge being acquired in the domain. If this conclusion is true of humans as well, there would be little reason to believe that problem-solving knowledge acquired in one domain can transfer effectively to another. Furthermore, no problem-solving course can teach general skills that will have much impact on the learners abilities. Any general knowledge would form such a trivial component of the total knowledge structure required for real problem solving that teaching general skills would probably have little or no impact on ability. In this view, the only way to teach problem solving is to teach it in each individual domain.

Second, the various general problems-solving courses and books have had little demonstrable effectiveness. I searched the ERIC and Psychological Abstracts data bases for evaluations of problem-solving training programs that met the following criteria: (a) published in a journal, (b) deal with general problem solving (e.g., not "problem solving in calculus"), (c) deal with a general population (e.g., not prisoners or learning-disabled students). I assembled information on the seven studies listed in Table 9.1, a meager collection, considering the optimism expressed by the authors of general problem-solving books quoted previously. Evidently, there are not outstanding documented cases where general problem-solving instruction has produced obviously noticeable gains in learning.

Third, there are several results from basic psychological research suggesting that the nature of transferable knowledge may be less than straightforward. Reed, Ernst, and Banerji, (1974) found that subjects who had successfully solved one simple mental puzzle showed little or no decrease in the time required to solve an almost identical one, and, at most, subjects reported "occasionally" using memory of the first problem in solving the second. A variety of experiments suggest that changes in context, including physical surround, mood, and dress of the experimenter, can decrease how much is remembered. Apparently, one remembers less in a context that is different however subtly from the context in which the material was learned (Bower, 1981; Clark & Isen, 1982; Smith, Glenberg, & Bjork, 1978).

The less than spectacular success of either early information processing or popular ideas of transfer suggest that we need to understand this phenomenon in a more sophisticated way. The remainder of this chapter first speculates on some situations in which transfer seems to be effective and then discusses a more precise formulation of transfer.

TABLE 9.1
All Studies Found Reporting Results of Training
in General Problem-Solving Skills

Brumfit, C. (1984). The Bangalore Procedural Syllabus. *ELT Journal, 34* (4), 233–244.

Feldusen, J. F., & Treffinger, D. J. (1976). Design and evaluation of a workshop on creativity and problem solving for teachers. *Journal of Creative Behavior, 10*, 12–14.

Finch, C. R. (1972). The effectiveness of selected self-instructional approaches in teaching diagnostic problem solving. *Journal of Educational Research, 65*, 219–223.

Hayes, J. M., et al. (1983). Environmental impact assessment: Melding classroom instruction with problem-solving experience. *Journal of College Science Teaching, 12*, 642–645.

de Leeuw, L. (1983). Teaching problem solving: An ATI study of the effects of teaching algorithmic and heuristic solution methods. *Instructional Science, 12*, 1–48.

Lochhead, J. (1978). Teaching students how to learn. In *Proceedings of the third international conference on improving university teaching* (pp. D135–D146). College Park, MD: University of Maryland Press.

Stratton, R. P., & Brown, R. (1972). Improving creative thinking by training in the production and/or judgment of solutions. *Journal of Educational Psychology, 63*, 390–397.

WHERE ARE THE GENERAL OR COMMON ELEMENTS?

The preceding section discussed concepts of general knowledge that consist of highly general strategies. These include some exemplified by the computer program GPS (select operators on the basis of the difference between the current state and the current goal), and some suggested by writers such as Polya (What is the unknown? What are the data? What is the condition?). I have suggested that such strategies may form such a small part of the knowledge required to understand and work in a new domain, and that teaching these strategies produces relatively negligible improvement in subsequent learning. Are there then other kinds of knowledge that both comprise a larger part of problem-solving knowledge, yet are applicable to a variety of domains? This section suggests some possibilities.

Strategies That are Attached to General Features

The computer problem solver FERMI is a prototype system intended to elucidate the mechanisms of general strategies across domains in the physical sciences (Larkin, Reif, Carbonell, & Gugliotta, 1986). FERMI is *not* an entirely general problem-solving system, but it does contain general knowledge that is separate from the more specific knowledge of a domain and that the system can apply to solve problems in several domains in the physical sciences. FERMI uses two kinds of knowledge in solving problems, domain-specific knowledge that is applicable to one particular domain and separate general knowledge that is applicable to many domains.

The following example illustrates how FERMI integrates and uses these two kinds of knowledge.

Figure 9.2a shows the situation for a typical problem in fluid statics. There are two fluids of differing densities (e.g., water and oil) that form two layers. Given the densities of the two liquids and the locations of two points, the task is to compute the pressure drop from one point to the other.

FERMI's domain-specific knowledge specifies that the pressure drop along a horizontal or vertical path in a region of homogeneous density is given by the product $\rho\ g\ h$, where ρ is the density of the region, g is the gravitational acceleration (980 cm/sec^2) and h is the change in height between the points. This is knowledge specific to the domain of fluid statics. It is sufficient to solve the simpler problem of finding a pressure drop from one point to another along a horizontal or vertical path located within a single fluid; it is not sufficient to solve the problem shown in Fig. 9.2a. Therefore, FERMI applies a second kind of knowledge: general knowledge of two strategies, *decomposition*, which is applied to calculating pressure drops along component path segments and *invariance*, which is applied to calculating pressure drops computed along alternate paths.

Knowing that pressure drops are invariant under change in the path between two points, FERMI constructs the alternate path between A and B shown in Fig. 9.2a. Knowing that pressure drops can be decomposed into the sum of individual pressure drops along path segments, FERMI constructs this path as a set of segments, each being both horizontal or vertical and contained in a single fluid. Therefore FERMI can use its domain-specific knowledge to find the pressure drops along each segment [Ac: 0, cd: (1.0)(980)(7) = 6860, dB: (.9) (980)(2) = 1764]. The pressure drop from A to B is then the sum (8624 gm cm/sec^2) of these pressure drops along the segments in the decomposed path.

FERMI uses the same general knowledge but different specific knowledge in a second domain, direct-current circuits. Problem situations in this domain consist of electric resistors (like light bulbs or tape-recorder drives) and batteries connected together with wires. FERMI uses the specific knowledge that the potential drop along a path through a single resistor is the product of the resistance of the resistor and the current flowing through it, and knowledge that the potential drop through a battery is just the "voltage" printed on the battery. These two pieces of domain-specific, direct-current-circuit knowledge are sufficient to solve simple problems about the potential drops across a single-circuit element (resistor or battery). But this knowledge is not sufficient to solve a more complex problem such as finding the potential drop from a to b through resistor 1 in the circuit in Fig. 9.2b. Solving this problem requires the same general knowledge used to solve the fluid statics problem.

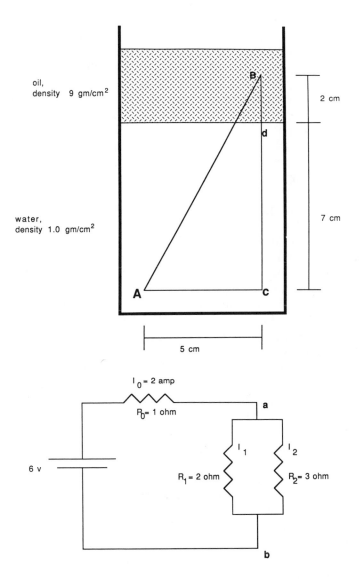

FIG. 9.2. Two problems solved with the same general knowledge by the computer-implemented problem solver FERMI: (a) finding the pressure drop from A to B in a beaker containing oil on top of water; (b) finding the potential drop from a to b in the circuit shown.

FERMI first tries to compute the potential drop along the given path. Because the current along this path is unknown, this effort fails. It therefore uses its knowledge that potential drop, like pressure drop, can be computed along any path (invariance), and the potential drop along a complete path is equal to the sum of potential drops along any set of segments making up this total path (decomposition). FERMI therefore uses exactly the same strategic knowledge that it applied to the fluid statics problem. It composes an alternate path from a to b of segments for which it knows (by means of domain-specific knowledge) how to find the potential drop. Along this alternate path shown in Fig. 9.2b, the potential drop from a to c is -2 volts (the negative sign appears because the path from a to c is opposite to the direction of current flow), and the potential drop from c to b through the battery is just 6 volts, the voltage of the battery. To get the final answer, FERMI uses again the decomposition strategy that the potential drop along a total path is the arithmetic sum of the potential drops along the set of segments making up the path. Therefore, the potential drop from a to b through resistor 1 is 4 volts.

The general strategies we call decomposition and invariance, illustrated by these two problem solutions, are not limited to these two domains. Decomposition is in the process of breaking apart a complex object into simpler components, making computations on these components, and mathematically combining the results. Invariance applies to any complex quantity that is the same in two situations—problems can then be solved by equating alternative expressions for this quantity.

For example, FERMI can find the center of mass of a complex planar object by decomposing the object into rectangular pieces of uniform density, computing the center of mass of each, and then computing the center of mass of the complete object as the weighted average (each center of mass weighted by the mass of its component) of the centers of mass of the components. (In this case the individual values are composed using a weighted average, rather than using the simple arithmetic sum as in the first examples. Also, the object decomposed is a region, not a path. But most of the strategic knowledge remains the same.) Certain quantities, associated with an object, can be computed by decomposing the object, computing the quantity associated with each of the pieces, and then combining these results with some composition function.

There are other kinds of decomposition that use some of the same strategic knowledge. For example, forces and other vectors are commonly decomposed into components along certain directions. Various results are computed, and the results combined by vector addition. Many quantities are usefully decomposed into parts associated with frequencies—Fourier decomposition. Again, computations are performed on these components that would be impossible on the whole, and then the components are combined to achieve the desired result associated with the whole.

Invariance can also be used in many different ways. For example, in more complex problems based on the circuit in Fig. 9.2b, FERMI uses input–output invariance to conclude that the current I_0 flowing into node a is equal to the sum of the currents I_1 and I_2 flowing out of node a. Invariance is also used in FERMI's application of what physicists call conservation principles. For example, the statement that energy is conserved means that the energy is invariant between two different states of a system. In all cases where invariance applies, FERMI uses a common core of strategic knowledge. It generates an expression for the invariant quantity under one set of circumstances (e.g., for one path, or for the input, or for one state) and then under another. Then these expressions are equated.

When solving a problem that is beyond its domain-specific knowledge, FERMI must have a mechanism for locating relevant general knowledge. This is achieved through a hierarchy of quantities (see Larkin et al., 1986), of which a portion is shown in Fig. 9.3. All the links, called *isa* links, mean

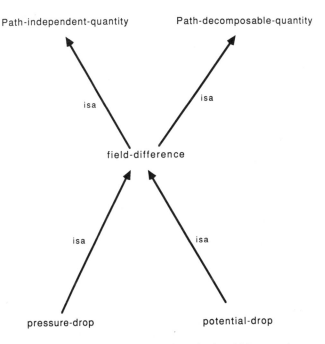

FIG. 9.3. Fragment of FERMI's quantity hierarchy in which strategies associated with general quantities are inherited by specific quantities.

that the lower quantity inherits all the properties of the higher property. As Fig. 9.3 shows, both pressure drop and potential drop have links to the general quantity we call *field difference,* which in turn has links to "path-independent quantity" and to "path-decomposable quantity." In these general quantities are stored pointers to the general strategies just described above. The knowledge about creating alternative paths is stored in a strategy pointed to by path-independent quantity. Strategic knowledge about decomposing paths is stored in a strategy pointed to by path-decomposable quantity. These pointers to strategic knowledge are inherited by every specific quantity located lower in the hierarchy and connected by isa links. Therefore, these general strategies can be applied by FERMI to a variety of specific quantities.

The quantity hierarchy with its isa links encodes what physicists call principles. Saying that pressure drop is path decomposable (i.e., is a path-decomposable quantity) is exactly equivalent to saying that pressure drop is one of those quantities to which a general path-decomposition strategy applies. The statement of the principle (i.e., the isa link) is, however, of no practical value unless the problem solver (human or computer) knows the related strategy. The important general knowledge is the strategic knowledge of general ways to work with broad categories of quantities, for example, quantities that are invariant or quantities that are decomposable.

FERMI is an example of a kind of knowledge that may generally be transferable from one domain to another, strategic knowledge within a related group of domains. Note that most of FERMI's general knowledge is strategic, not factual or conceptual. Physical scientists often point out that there are general kinds of principles, for example, conservation or invariance, that appear throughout the physical sciences. But these principles are really just statements classifying a quantity. Saying that energy is conserved is just classifying energy as one of those quantities that is invariant over change in the positions and velocities of objects in the system. This classification is useless unless one has general strategic knowledge of what one can do with any quantity that fits this classification. The important general knowledge is strategic. FERMI provides several examples of strategic knowledge applicable in a variety of settings.

Subgoal Structures

Almost all substantial problems are solved more easily if they are broken into parts by setting subgoals. The knowledge of how to set useful subgoals, like the strategies used by FERMI, may be much the same in related domains. Anderson, Boyle, Farrell, and Reiser (1987) for example, have laid out a method for constructing goals, subgoals, and alternative goals in

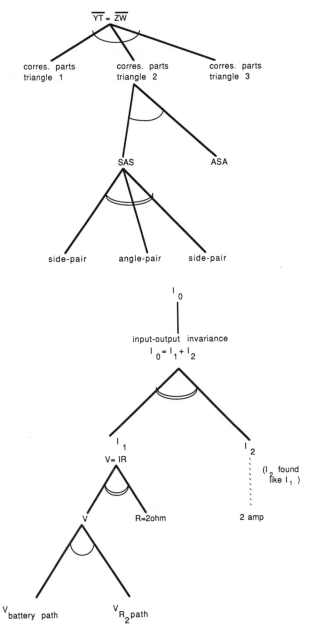

FIG. 9.4. Goal structures of the kind developed by Anderson's geometry tutor and FERMI.

geometry. As shown in Fig. 9.4a, each goal is satisfied by achieving one or more subgoals. Sometimes several subgoals must be achieved concurrently to achieve the main goal. These are called *and* goals and are labeled by double lines in Fig. 9.4a. For example, applying the side–angle–side theorem requires finding pairs of sides, angles, and sides, three "and" subgoals. Other goals can be satisfied by any one of a set of alternative "*or*" subgoals. For example, two triangles can potentially be proved congruent by applying any one of the side–angle–side, side–side–side, or angle–side–angle theorems.

The subgoals are connected by matching the results of a geometry rule (e.g., a triangle is congruent) against the current goal and then setting its conditions (e.g., three pairs of sides congruent) as "and" subgoals. If two different rules match the same goal (e.g., both the side–side–side and the angle–side–angle theorems can prove a triangle congruent), then these two sets of conditions form two sets of "or" subgoals. Satisfying either set will solve the problem.

Such a goal tree is not, however, applicable only to geometry. When doing physics, FERMI constructs a goal tree that looks very similar and that we believe uses strategic knowledge very similar to that of Anderson's geometry program. Figure 9.4b shows part of the goal tree FERMI uses to find the current I_0 in the problem in Fig. 9.2b. FERMI builds its goal tree from the top down. If there is a goal to find the value of a quantity (e.g., I_0) and there are several methods for doing so, FERMI constructs a set of "or" goals for applying each of these methods. If an equation includes one or more unknown quantities, it constructs a set of "and" goals to find the values of these quantities. For example, in Fig. 9.4b, applying the equation $V = IR$ to find the current I_1 through resistor 1 requires finding both the resistance R of resistor 1 and the potential drop V_{ac} across it.

Although physics and geometry are different domains, similar strategic knowledge can be used to build goal structures in both cases. In both domains there is some top goal, often to find the value of a quantity or to prove some result (e.g., that two objects are congruent). In each case, usually several alternative methods might be applied to achieve this top goal, forming a set of "*or*" subgoals, the success of any one of which would provide success on the top goal. Usually a method requires some ingredients, for example, the values of some currently unknown quantities, or some currently unproven results. All these ingredients must be assembled for the method to work. The ingredients therefore comprise a set of "and" goals all of which must be achieved for the supergoal to be achieved.

Much knowledge about how to use goals to set subgoals appears to be the same throughout a related set of domains involving formal inference rules.

Representations

In discussing transfer of strategic knowledge across a moderately broad range of related domains, there is an additional important factor: experts' technical problem representations. I have argued elsewhere (McDermott & Larkin, 1978; Larkin, 1983) that there are three identifiable problem representations' for scientific problem solving. The given *basic* representation contains objects that are mentioned in the problem statement and that are often observable in the real world, for example, blocks, inclined planes, and pulleys. A second *computational* representation consists of equations or other formal mathematical statements. Novices often work directly from the original base problem representation and try to construct directly a set of equations. In contrast, experts usually construct an intermediate *technical* representation. In this phase of problem solving, they talk neither about real objects (blocks and pulleys) nor computational objects (equations and substitutions), but about physics or chemistry or economics objects (forces, momenta, electrophiles, utilities).

Although this technical representation has many advantages (see Larkin, 1983; McDermott & Larkin, 1978), it seems also to facilitate use of general knowledge. For example, the powerful techniques of vector analysis apply to problems about interactions only when these problems have been redescribed in terms of forces. The general strategic knowledge associated with invariance apply when a problem has been redescribed in terms of some invariant quantity such as energy or momentum. The same comment can also apply to the computational representation. For example, an alternating circuit is a little like a pendulum until both are expressed as an identical set of differential equations.

Managerial and Metacognitive Skills

In addition to strategic knowledge, like knowledge of how to apply principles or set subgoals, a second category of knowledge that seems a plausible candidate for transfer is skill in the management of tasks, so called metacognitive skill. For example, Schoenfeld (1983) has identified managerial skills for solving problems in university-level mathematics. These include such tactics as, for example, you've been trying one approach, and you've made no progress in the last 15 minutes, then you try another approach.

Other classes of metacognitive or managerial skills include managing mood, managing time, and managing the environment. Meichenbaum (1975, 1985), for example, has improved students' ability to learn by teaching them techniques for identifying their own "negative self-talk" and for "talking back" to it. Students who "block" on a test or find it difficult to study often are discouraging themselves with internal comments like, "I'll never be able to do it. I always screw up. It's impossible. It will take forever." Meichenbaum teaches students to become aware of such thoughts and to talk back to them, saying things like, "I can do it as well as anyone else."

A variety of writers (e.g., Lakein, 1973) have dealt with the problems of managing time and concentration. These writers present potentially general skills for deciding which of a variety of tasks to do when some must be neglected and for getting started on apparently overwhelming tasks. For example, Lakein presents what he calls the *swiss cheese* approach for beating procrastination. When a large task must be done, identify small 10-minute tasks that will contribute to the whole. In writing this chapter, for example, swiss cheese tasks included making a list of papers to be reviewed before starting writing, making a file folder in which to store materials for the chapter, and spending several 10-minute slots writing random ideas for the chapter. All these tasks are easy. None requires more than 10 minutes, so they can be squeezed into a busy schedule. A sequence of these, Lakein argues, builds involvement in the project. Once a number of small tasks have been done, the project no longer seems overwhelming, some significant progress has been made, and one is often ready to sit down and engage in a serious work session on the project.

Knowledge for managing a task, knowledge for managing one's mood or time, is not specifically for doing the task but for setting things up so that task-specific knowledge can be applied. For this reason, it seems to be knowledge that has potential to be transferred across a broad range of domains.

Skills for Learning

Another class of skills that seems good candidates for transfer are skills for learning—skills for acquiring the knowledge for performing a task. There are at least two studies in the literature that have demonstrated transfer of knowledge for learning. Larkin and Reif (1976) and Reif, Larkin, and Brackett (1976) successfully trained beginning physics students to learn quantitative relations for themselves. Specifically, consider a quantitative relation, for example,

$$F = G\frac{Mm}{r^2}$$

where F is the magnitude of the gravitational force exerted on an object of mass m by an object of mass M (usually a planet or star), G is a known gravitational constant, and r is the distance between the centers of these objects. An expert learner of quantitative relations acquires a lot of knowledge from such a passage. For example, a person learns the meanings of all the symbols, units, and typical values associated with them, and any restrictions associated with applying the relation.

The training taught students the skill for independently acquiring quantitative knowledge from text. For each of 10 relations studied in a physics course, students were required to answer a set of general questions like "What are the units and typical magnitudes of the quantities in the relation?" At the end of a 6-week training period, these students studied a new text section describing an unfamiliar relation and were then tested on their knowledge of that relation. Compared to their performances on a pretest and to those for a control group who simply studied the same relations in the context of a physics course, the performances of students with systematic training showed they were better able to extract information independently. The size of this improvement was both statistically and educationally significant.

In the second study, Brown and her colleagues (Palincsar & Brown, 1984; Brown & Palincsar, chap. 13 in this volume) taught seventh graders skills for actively processing text, including summarizing, asking clear central questions, clarifying the content, and predicting new information. As in the Larkin et al. studies on physics relations, the procedure was to guide students in executing the desired skills over a period of time and with a variety of examples. Larkin's group, addressing college students and a simpler skill, used written instructional materials. Brown's training involved teachers who modeled correct behavior for students and guided them in successively improving their own behavior. With this approach, students retained the skills over time and demonstrated transfer both to other domains (e.g., classroom topics) and to related skills (e.g., detecting incongruities).

Both these studies taught learning skills systematically over a period of time during which the learners actively practiced a skill on many examples. In both cases, the learners retained the skills and were able to apply them in related areas.

A MORE DETAILED MODEL FOR TRANSFER

The preceding examples suggest that transferable knowledge may be subtly entwined with domain-specific knowledge. FERMI's invariance strategy is of no use unless the solver also knows how to construct expressions for a particular invariant quantity in a particular domain. Task management knowledge will not help without knowledge of how to perform the task. Learning skills are perhaps the single example of knowledge that may shorten learning time in appropriate new domains, independent of domain-specific knowledge.

To understand transfer, we need tools for a richer and more precise model. How can we characterize what is in the head that is used in two or more contexts, and how can that characterization allow us to understand the kinds of knowledge that can be used in many settings, and the conditions under which this occurs?

Computer-implemented, production-system models of knowledge offer a promising possibility for this characterization. In such models, knowledge is encoded as a set of condition-action rules called productions. Each possible action is stored with the conditions under which it is to be applied. The computer model than "acts" by searching its knowledge (its collection of productions) for one or more that applies to the current task situation. This task situation is stored (in some computer-coded way) in what is called a working memory. When the program finds a production with conditions that are satisfied with the current working memory, it implements the associated action(s). These actions ordinarily add, modify, or delete things that are in working memory. The resulting changes mean that new, previously inapplicable productions may become applicable. The program then again searches its collection of productions, finding any that are now satisfied by the current working memory and implementing their actions. This cycle is repeated until the task is completed, or until no production is satisfied and the system stops.

Production systems have been used to construct models that seem to capture human problem-solving behavior in a variety of domains (e.g., Anderson, 1981; Larkin, McDermott, Simon, & Simon, 1980; Newell & Simon, 1972). Their advantage is that their knowledge is encoded in small bits that seem to correspond well to the small discrete bits that are learned by human beings. By running the computer-implemented model, one can see directly the results of a complex aggregate of knowledge bits. Recently, in two cases, production system models have been used to account for knowledge transferred from one domain to another. In the discussion of these two cases, there is no need to claim that human thinking is just like a computer's, implementing production after production. But production system models have provided a good account of human reasoning in a variety of situations. Furthermore, their ability to capture the interaction of small pieces of knowledge makes them a promising tool for understanding the subtleties of how knowledge may transfer from one arena to the next. Therefore, the use of these models offers particular promise in elucidating the phenomenon of transfer.

Kieras and his co-workers (Kieras & Bovair, 1985; Polson & Kieras, 1985) had subjects solve problems in a very constrained domain—executing tasks with an artificial "control board" (for the Starship Enterprise). They modeled performance of all tasks with sets of productions. Because the tasks were related, some productions were used in more than one task. They found that, when other factors were taken into account, they could very accurately predict the learning time for a new task from the number of productions that appeared only in the new task. We can understand this result by saying that productions learned in a previous task are transferred—they are kept as part of the knowledge store. Because they need not be learned in the new domain, they do not add to learning time, which then totally depends on the number of new productions to be learned.

Singley and Anderson (1985) explored transfer in a more complex set of domains. They had subjects learn two text editors and explored how much learning one editor aided in learning a second. Like Kieras et al., Singley and Anderson modeled the tasks with sets of productions, and, again, because the tasks were related, some productions were used in models for both editors. They found that the number of productions common to the models for both was predictive of the relative time savings in learning a second editor. In other words, if one has already learned a lot of productions with the first editor, one will learn the second rather fast. Singley and Anderson's predictions of the absolute magnitudes of time savings were less precise than those of Kieras et al., probably because text editors are more complex than the artificial control panel used by Kieras.

The production-system models formulated by Kieras et al. and by Singley and Anderson have advantages for the further study of transferable knowledge. First, the production system makes it possible to capture small pieces of knowledge precisely in a formal notation. Therefore, the identification of potentially transferable knowledge is not limited to the complex knowledge integral to skills but still may include knowledge that cannot act in isolation but needs other knowledge around it. Second, the production system notation is rich. It has strong potential for replacing Thorndike's vague concept of "common elements" with detailed fine-grained representations of what those common elements are.

The precise and rich characterization of potentially transferable knowledge is a critical step toward the articulation to testable theories. We will doubtless soon move beyond the simple notions that "all productions are equal" and that savings in learning a new domain depends exactly on the number of productions that can be used from an old domain. But production-system models allow examination of such important issues as conditions of transfer as well as for testable detailed predictions like this.

CONDITIONS FOR TRANSFER

We have developed a list of knowledge types that are empirically seen either to transfer or to be good candidates for such transfer. These include: (1) strategies applicable in a limited set of related domains (e.g., physical sciences, formal logical domains), (2) methods for setting useful subgoals, (3) knowledge for task management, and (4) learning skills. Understanding transfer of any of these kinds of knowledge requires understanding, in detail, how transferable knowledge intermingles with domain-specific knowledge. Given this subtle interaction, production systems are a good tool for understanding transfer.

Our production-system model of transfer can be summarized as follows: Knowledge learned in one domain, the "base" domain, can be characterized as a set of reasoning rules called productions. If a learner can perform well on tasks for which the model uses these rules and our observations of this performance (times, intermediate steps) are consistent with the model's solutions, then we say the subject has learned these productions. This is a shorthand for saying human behavior accords with the model containing these productions. We then assume that once learned, productions are maintained in memory. When the subject turns to learning a new domain, the "target" domain, if some of the previously learned productions are applicable, these need not be acquired. Therefore, the learning times are shorter than they are for subjects without previous learning in the base domain. Using this model as a basis for reasoning, what can we say about the conditions under which knowledge can transfer?

Obviously, the learner must know the base domain well. There cannot be use of "old" productions in the target domain, if the old productions were never learned. Some of the failure of transfer in the literature (e.g., Gick & Holyoak, 1983 and Reed et al., 1974) may simply reflect that nothing was learned in the base domain. Everyone has had the subjective experience (especially with a completely novel task) of managing to solve a problem; but with the feeling of having learned nothing. Subjects in the Reed et al. study solving the missionaries and cannibals puzzle managed with considerable effort to achieve a solution, using their existing knowledge, but they added nothing to that knowledge that could possibly transfer to a second problem. The Gick and Holyoak example is more complex but might yield to the same explanation. When solving the base problem, subjects may consider the solution an isolated clever trick, with nothing learned that could be relevant to other situations.

Even if something is learned from the base, for transfer to occur, this knowledge must be encoded in such a way that it can be used in the target domain. This means that general knowledge from the base domain must not be intermingled with specific knowledge in a way that prevents it from being separated and applied in the target domain. In a production-system model, this separation of general from specific knowledge means that general knowledge must appear in separate productions, and items that have one referent in the base domain and a different referent in the target domain must be represented appropriately by variables, rather than by constants. For example, as in FERMI, for transfer to occur, path-invariant quantity must be represented internally by something like a variable, <path-invariant-quantity>, rather than by pressure-drop, or whatever the specific quantity is in the base domain.

Production-system models suggest several reasons why the general problem-solving courses have not had great success. First, these courses (e.g., Wickelgren, 1973) often teach extremely general strategies, which do not seem to play a large role in the real-world of the problem-solving domains that have been analyzed (e.g., Duda et al., 1978; Shortliffe, 1976). Hill-climbing and means–ends analysis, extremely general problem-solving methods discussed by Wickelgren, for example, play at most a small role in models of transferable knowledge discussed previously (text editing, control-board task). Our most detailed models of human problem solving do not seem to make extensive use of such strategies. Singley and Anderson (1985) also suggest that, to the extent general "weak" methods do play a role, they are relatively unimportant in transfer, because most adult human solvers have long ago learned such strategies.

The work with FERMI suggests that general strategies often come in several more specific varieties that must be learned for the allegedly general knowledge to be applied. For example, invariance is a very general concept, and some of FERMI's knowledge about invariance applies to all invariant quantities. However, most of FERMI's strategic knowledge applies to specific cases. Although in all cases invariance is exploited by generating alternatives across which the invariance holds, these alternatives can be different paths, different states, or different directions. This does not contradict the points made earlier—these invariance varieties are each general in that they apply to many specific situations in many domains. But these observations from FERMI do suggest that general strategies in themselves can be quite complex and presumably are difficult to learn.

CONCLUSION

Although attractive, the notion that transferable knowledge is a core of general problem-solving skills has been historically unproductive. There is not good evidence that instruction in such skills improves performance. Computer programs based around general reasoning skills have turned out to have limited abilities. There is evidence of varying kinds and of varying strengths that skills that are somewhat domain specific may transfer. These include strategies that apply to a moderately broad range of domains, skills for managing the surround of a task, and skills for learning. None of these kinds of knowledge, however, forms a complete routine that can be executed in the absence of other knowledge; all are intermingled with other more domain-specific knowledge.

Production systems, which encode small bits of knowledge separately, have proven a useful means of modeling how transferrable knowledge interacts with more specific knowledge. Instruction in skills is most effective if we can understand in detail what we want to teach and focus instruction accordingly. Detailed models of strategies for related domains, methods for setting subgoals, knowledge of task management, and learning skills seem a promising road to this end. Although the transferable knowledge may be intermingled with other knowledge in subtle ways, if we can begin to separate it, we have a basis for teaching it more reliably.

ACKNOWLEDGMENTS

This work was supported in part by grants from the Office of Naval Research (under contract No. N00014-82-C-50767, Contract Authority Identification Number, NR No. 667-494), and from the National Science Foundation Program for Education in Mathematics, Science and Technology #1-49-147. Lauren Resnick contributed substantially through extensive comments on an earlier draft. The manuscript was completed under support from the John Simon Guggenheim Foundation and an NSF Visiting Professorship for Women.

REFERENCES

Adams, J. L. (1976). *Conceptual blockbusting: A guide to better ideas*. New York: Norton.

Anderson, J. R. (1981). *Tuning of search of the problem space for geometry proofs* (Tech. Rep.). Department of Psychology, Carnegie–Mellon University, Pittsburgh.

Anderson, J. R., Boyle, C. F., Farrell, R., & Reiser, B. J. (1987). Cognitive principles in the design of computer tutors. In P. Morris (Ed.), *Modelling cognition*. New York: Wiley.

Bower, G. H. (1981). Mood and memory. *American Psychologist, 36,* 129–148.

Clark, M. S., & Isen, A. M. (1982). Toward understanding the relationship between feeling states and social behavior. In A. Hastorf & A. M. Isen (Eds.), *Cognitive social psychology*. New York: Elsevier.

de Bono, E. (1970). *Lateral thinking: Creativity step by step*. New York: Harper Colophon Books.

Duda, R. O., Hart, P. E., Barrett, P., Gashnig, J. G., Konolige, K., Reboh, R., & Slocum, J. (1978). *Development of the PROSPECTOR consultation system for mineral exploration* (Tech. Rep. 5821 & 6415). SRI International.

Ernst, G. W., & Newell, A. (1969). *GPS: A case study in general problem solving*. New York: Academic Press.

Gick, M. L., & Holyoak, K. J. (1983). Schema induction and analogical transfer. *Cognitive Psychology, 15,* 1–38.

Kieras, D. E., & Bovair, S. (1985). *The acquisition of procedures from text: A production system analysis of transfer of training,* (Tech. Rep. No. 16, TR-85/ONR-16). Ann Arbor: University of Michigan.

Lakein, A. (1973). *How to get control of your time and your life.* New York: Signet.

Larkin, J. H. (1983). The role of problem representation in physics. In D. Gentner & A. L. Stevens (Eds.), *Mental models.* Hillsdale, NJ: Lawrence Erlbaum Associates.

Larkin, J. H., & Reif, F. (1976). Analysis and teaching of a general skill for studying scientific text. *Journal of Educational Psychology, 68*(4), 431–440.

Larkin, J. H., McDermott, J., Simon, D. P., & Simon, H. A. (June, 1980). Expert and novice performance in solving physics problems. *Science, 208,* 1335–1342.

Larkin, J. H., Reif, F., Carbonell, J. G., & Gugliotta, A. (1986). FERMI: *A flexible expert reasoner with multi-domain inferencing* (Tech. Rep.) Department of Psychology, Carnegie-Mellon University, Pittsburgh.

McDermott, J., & Larkin, J. H. (1978). Representing textbook physics problems. In *Proceedings of the 2nd national conference.* The Canadian society for computational studies of intelligence.

Meichenbaum, D. (1975). Enhancing creativity by modifying what subjects say to themselves. *American Educational Research Journal, 12,* 129–145.

Meichenbaum, D. (1985). A cognitive-behavioral perspective. In S. F. Chipman, J. W. Segal, & R. Glaser (Eds.), *Thinking and learning skills.* Hillsdale NJ: Lawrence Erlbaum Associates.

Mirkin, G., & Hoffman, M. (1978). *The sports medicine book.* Boston: Little, Brown.

Newell, A., & Simon, H. A. (1972). *Human problem solving.* (pp. 28–30) Englewood Cliffs, NJ: Prentice-Hall.

Palincsar, A. S., & Brown, A. L. (1984). Reciprocal teaching of comprehension-fostering and comprehension-monitoring activities. *Cognition and Instruction, 1*(2), 117–176.

Polson, P. G., & Kieras, D. E. (1985). A quantitative model of the learning and performance of text-editing knowledge. In M. Mantei & P. Orbeton (Eds.), *Proceedings of CHI, 1985* (pp. 207–212). New York: ACM.

Polya, G. (1957). *How to solve it* (2nd ed., p. 2). Princeton, NJ: Princeton University Press.

Reed, S. K., Ernst, G. W., & Banerji, R. (1974). The role of analogy in transfer between similar problem states. *Cognitive Psychology, 6,* 436–450.

Reif, F., Larkin, J. H., & Brackett, G. C. (1976). Teaching general learning and problem-solving skills. *American Journal of Physics, 44,* 212–217.

Reiser, B. J., Anderson, J. R., & Farrell, R. G. (1984). *Dynamic student modelling in an intelligent tutor for LISP programming* (Tech. Rep.). Department of Psychology, Carnegie-Mellon University, Pittsburgh.

Schoenfeld, A. H. (1983). Beyond the purely cognitive: Belief systems, social cognitions, and metacognitions as driving forces in intellectual performance. *Cognitive Science, 7,* 329–363.

Shortliffe, E. H. (1976). *Computer-based medical consultations: MYCIN.* New York: American Elsevier.

Singley, M. K., & Anderson, J. R. (1985). The transfer of text-editing skill. *International Journal of Man–Machine Studies, 22,* 403–423.

Smith, S. M., Glenberg, A., & Bjork, R. A. (1978). Environmental context and human memory. *Memory & Cognition, 6,* 342–353.

Thorndike, E. L., & Woodworth, R. S. (1901). The influence of improvement in one mental function upon the efficiency of other functions. *Psychological Review, 8,* 247–261.

Wickelgren, W. A. (1973). *How to solve problems.* San Francisco: W. H. Freeman.

10

There are Generalized Abilities and One of Them is Reading

Charles A. Perfetti
Learning Research and Development Center
University of Pittsburgh

It must be the complexity of mental life that causes the rapid changes in the intellectual breezes that blow across the cognitive sciences. Nowhere are such changes more evident than in descriptions of human abilities. The approach to cognition that sought discrete components of information processing is being replaced by one that sees cognitive life determined by complex interactions among cognitive components. Yesterday's search for components of general intelligence is replaced by today's search for specialized domain expertise. Old assumptions that learners are served by general adaptive strategies are replaced by new assumptions that learning is dominated by specific knowledge. And so it goes. Of course, such generalizations are misleading because such changes meet resistance, and the study of cognition is all the richer for the confrontation.

In the context of changing conceptions of human abilities, my aim is to present a case for the existence of *restricted domain-general human abilities*. Such abilities are simultaneously restricted in their prohibition against unbridled interactionism and general in their applicability across knowledge domains. Their restricted nature arises from constraints on the mental processes that underlie them. In particular, at least some of these processes are free of influences from information outside their "speciality." The generality of these abilities, their applicability across different domains, arises because various task domains make use of the same restricted processes, for example, language processes. In this chapter, I try to demonstrate that reading is an ability of the restricted-general type.

The first step is to stipulate a realistic domain of performance. It would be relatively easy, although theoretically nontrivial, to define reading so that its restricted and general characteristics are salient. Defining reading as written word recognition will promote this outcome. Although this is a reasonable definition of reading, the more challenging course is to allow reading ability to include comprehension. In general, the course I adopt here is to accept the comprehension definition, although word recognition and decoding necessarily receive some attention. Thus, the question is whether comprehending texts and even learning from them can be understood as reflections of a restricted-generalized reading ability. An affirmative answer to this question means that reading comprehension ability is essentially dependent on restricted language processes that are not influenced by domain knowledge.

GENERAL READING ABILITY REQUIRES MORE THAN KNOWLEDGE

Because one of my central claims is that reading ability cannot be identified with knowledge, it is important to stipulate that knowledge indeed has a large role in reading, as it does in other human abilities, and then to show its limits. The demonstrations that specific knowledge makes a critical contribution to reading comprehension are well known. My favorite example comes not from an experiment but from a *Los Angeles Times* newspaper column that was reprinted in the international edition of the *New York Herald Tribune* (Catran, 1982).

> LOS ANGELES—The latest fallout of the space program is an astonishing data-recording system developed by scientist E. T. Seti.
>
> The brain of the machine, located on one end, is known as the Data Stream Imprint System, or DSIS, a NASA-copyrighted graphite linear feed designed to perform a message-recording function. Protection against the hostile environment of space is provided by a cellulose-fiber, reinforced-resin protection layer.
>
> The opposite end of the machine incorporates an ingenious solution to

error-correction problems, an abrasive data character erase module. In the erase mode, the module is briskly rubbed across the characters to be deleted and, by the phenomenon known in physics as "lift-off," the undesired characters may easily be expunged.

Reliability tests, conducted under rigid National Aeronautics and Space Administration test parameters, revealed an extremely low failure rate, with the graphite fracturing only once in every 1,000 performances. (A peripheral product has been devised, to be used in the rare event of such a failure, that incorporates the use of a clever device called the Linear Feed Maintenance System. The LFMS literally "sharpens" the recording implement by removing the cellulose-fiber protection layer, exposing a fresh length of graphite.)

When I called Dr. Seti to ask him about the instrument, he conceded that each time it is "sharpened" it shortens, which limits its effective half-life to the operator's ability to handle short stubs. That problem is elegantly solved, however, by the interchangeable "throwaway" concept, enabling the operator to select, at his option, the manual override mode provided. This allows him to discard the stub and replace it with a brand new data-recording instrument from the box of spares provided.

These devices cost NASA $237.50 each. They will be offered to the public at 49 cents, including an instruction booklet, a fully equipped LFMS and a 90-day warranty.

When I show this column in a classroom or at a research talk, I ask people to raise their hands when they understand what the text is about. A few hands go up on the third paragraph, but most people do not catch on until they read the strong clues at the end of paragraphs four and five. A few read the whole column, which runs 14 paragraphs, without ever figuring it out.

This example is especially revealing because, unlike the examples from the experimental literature, it is well written. It has specific references, containing neither referential vagueness nor ambiguity, and it has local coherence. It appears to be referentially opaque only because of its pseudotechnical vocabulary. Once some text clue triggers the appropriate knowledge, comprehension falls into place, for example, the sentence in paragraph four asserting that some device "literally 'sharpens' the recording implement by removing the cellulose—fiber protection layer . . ."

It is instructive to compare this text with those better known from the literature on comprehension. For example, consider Bransford and Johnson's (1973) classic research testing comprehension and recall failure for vaguely worded passages. The "washing clothes" passage from their experiment contains referentially vague phrases as "First you arrange things into different groups" that rapidly cascade into an impossibly impenetrable text. Its comprehension ratings and recall were dramatically improved by a prior presentation of the title "Washing Clothes," which serves as an organizing scheme to activate specific referents from referentially vague phrases. A demonstration by Dooling and Lachman (1971) was similar in its use of metaphonical phrases to avoid referential specificity. Such research demonstrates that knowledge is critical to the comprehension of passages that are low in referential specificity and local coherence.

As the newspaper column shows, however, it is also true that specific knowledge is critical to the comprehension of texts that do not have obvious referential vagueness. Furthermore, the research of Voss's group on the understanding of baseball texts shows that comprehension depends on individual knowledge (Chiesi, Spilich, & Voss, 1979; Spilich, Vesonder, Chiesi, & Voss, 1979). Thus, there are two general routes for a contribution of knowledge to text understanding: (1) differences in texts' explicitness and coherence—in extreme examples inexplicit and incoherent texts will fail to trigger appropriate mundane knowledge required for comprehension (or perhaps learning); (2) individual differences in specific domain knowledge—comprehension of texts in a domain will be heavily influenced by the extent of an individual's knowledge.

Having granted knowledge a critical role in comprehension, I now argue that this role is very limited in general reading ability. Indeed, the concept of general reading ability requires that specific knowledge has no role— reading ability is what remains after specific domain knowledge is taken into account. Nevertheless, this is partly an empirical issue as well as a definitional one. It may be that the concept of general reading ability is a mirage formed by otherwise unobserved domain-specific abilities. By the mirage account, there would be an ability to read baseball, an ability to read nuclear physics, and an ability to read gothic romances but no ability to read. The precedence for trying to identify specialized reading abilities comes from the study of intelligence, where faith in a generalized intellectual ability waxes and wanes. (Compare Spearman's 1924, general "g" with Guilford's, 1967, specialized structures of intellect.) If it is possible that there is no general intelligence, then it certainly ought to be possible that there is no general reading ability.

There is, however, no reason yet to accept the specialized view of reading. Until there is evidence to the contrary, the assumption that reading ability is general can be taken as more nearly correct than the assumption that reading skill is specialized. There are two reasons for this claim. First, the hypothesis that reading ability is the application of domain-specific knowledge to texts—the knowledge of hypothesis—can be shown to rest in part on a failure to distinguish between two components of comprehension, *meaning* and *interpretation*. If this distinction is made, there is less reason to give knowledge a central role in comprehension. Second, certain reading processes are relatively uninfluenceable by knowledge. The existence of such processes places constraints on the contribution of domain knowledge to reading comprehension. These arguments are expanded in the next two sections.

MEANING VERSUS INTERPRETATION

Bransford and Johnson (1973) reported an experiment in which subjects recalled sentences such as: *The haystack was important because the cloth ripped.* Recall was relatively poor when subjects were given the subject noun *haystack* as a recall cue, but recall was improved when a context cue, *parachute,* was provided—despite the fact that *haystack* but not *parachute* was actually in the sentence. From this, one might say that comprehension depends on linking sentences to knowledge of the world and that *parachute* provides the needed knowledge to understand the connection between the haystack and the ripped cloth.

The claim that knowledge affects comprehension in this case, however, conflates two different aspects of comprehension. "Comprehension" is an equivocation between two possibilities: achieving a meaning for a text and achieving an interpretation for a text. Although a clear boundary between the two is not easily drawn, the essence of the difference is readily captured: Meaning is more restricted, more text based, more symbol driven, and less inferential. Interpretation is less restricted, less text based, less symbol driven, and more inferential. In combination, these constrasting characteristics give knowledge a large role in interpretation but a small role in meaning. Implicitly identifying comprehension only with interpretation leads to the claim that comprehension depends on knowledge. Identifying comprehension with meaning leads to a different perspective—that comprehension depends on a symbol-based meaning process, whereas interpretation depends on that process plus additional knowledge.

By this account, there is no problem in comprehending The haystack was important because the cloth ripped. Its meaning is exhausted by the intensional meanings of its words plus the elementary propositions in which the words participate. Thus, the sentence presupposes the existence of two conceptual objects (x = haystack, y = cloth), asserts a predication for each concept (*important* and *ripping*), and asserts a predication (*because*) that links these two predications. The symbol values of the words (their intensional meanings) and the propositions are the meaning of the sentence. This meaning can be paraphrased roughly as follows: *There was some cloth such that it ripped and some haystack such that it was important because of the ripping of the cloth.* The word meanings and propositions that underlie this paraphrase exhaust the meaning of the sentence. The inference that the cloth was part of a parachute—indeed the existence of a parachute and the specific referents for haystack and cloth—is a matter of interpretation, not meaning.

The distinction between meaning and interpretation seems to parallel the distinction between a propositional text model and a situational model made by van Dijk and Kintsch (1983). (See also Kintsch, chap. 2 in this volume.) The meaning of a text can be identified with the restricted propositional base of the text, whereas the interpretation may require the model of the situation described by the text. Another kindred distinction is that between meanings and mental models (Johnson-Laird, 1983). Whether these distinctions, including the one between meaning and interpretation, can sustain analysis as clearly principled dichotomies is not altogether clear. It is clear, however, that there is a critical issue shared among these dichotomies. The critical issue, the one that really divides meaning from interpretation, is the richness of inference. Text meaning is an inference-restricted representation, and text interpretation is an inference-rich representation. On this point, the distinction between meanings and interpretations, that between propositional models and situational models, and that between meanings and mental models are identical.

It is unwise and unnecessary to claim that inferential processes represent binary possibilities, either occurring or not occurring; thus, on the *process* level meanings and interpretations may not be clearly divided. With enough inferencing (or *particularization*) comprehension moves from meaning to interpretation. Thus, at a representation level we have a principled dichotomy, whereas at the process level we have a continuum of inferential processing: Meanings are linguistic and propositional, determined by symbol values and syntax plus limited inferencing; interpretations are nonlinguistic, symbol–world mappings, determined by meanings plus unrestricted inferencing.

Word Meaning

The meaning–interpretation distinction seems to place a significant burden on the concept of word meaning. Word meanings present a deeply rooted problem of longstanding, and there is little new that can be contributed to it here. It is useful, however, to examine one dispute in the analysis of meaning in its psychological context, namely, the *context* approach versus the *symbol* approach.

The context tradition, as represented by the later Wittgenstein (1953), holds that there are no necessary and sufficient conditions for word meaning, that meaning is a matter of language use. The symbol tradition, as represented by Katz and Fodor (1963) and by Katz (1966) among many others, holds that there are systematic meaning components that comprise word meaning. Critical to the symbol tradition is the distinction between sense and reference (Frege, 1892). Accepting this distinction allows a focus on the analysis of conventional symbol components—on senses rather than references. The context approach emphasizes many different aspects of language use but often implies emphasis on reference.

In the psychological literature, the *context* approach is represented by the classic Bransford and Johnson work (1973) and by a number of other important studies of comprehension. A good representative of the contextual approach is a study by Anderson and Ortony (1975), who report a cued recall experiment for such sentences as: (1) *The accountant pounded the stake;* (2) *The accountant pounded the desk.*

The key result of the experiment concerned the effectiveness of words that did not appear in the sentence as recall cues. For the first sentence *hammer* but not *fist* was an effective cue. For the second sentence *fist* but not *hammer* was effective.

Anderson and Ortony (1975) observed that "sentence comprehension and memory involve constructing particularized and elaborated mental representations (p. 167). Thus, a reader is apt to understand "pounded the stake" as a particular action that is different from "pounded the desk." The mental representations, certainly the mental images, are not the same in the two cases. Thus we might reasonably conclude that a single word, *pound*, has two different interpretations in two different contexts. It is also possible, however, that these different interpretations arise not during comprehension but during retrieval.

This general question of whether inferences are drawn as a routine part of comprehension has some significance for the argument that reading ability is a restricted but general skill whose main characteristic is the construction of restricted (inference-poor) linguistic representations. If "on-line" comprehension typically includes a rich inference process, then this argument, even if correct, would leave a large portion of comprehension unaccounted for. If on-line comprehension typically does not include a rich inference process, then identifying reading ability with the construction of restricted meanings accounts for a good deal of comprehension. Notice that this is a question of the practical implications of the argument, not the merit of the argument itself. Even if comprehension is inference rich, so the argument goes, it depends on the construction of meanings.

The literature on on-line inferences does not provide an unequivocal answer to this question of whether comprehension routinely includes rich inferences. However, it appears that many routine inferences that could be made during comprehension are not made. They are triggered by retrieval operations, if at all. McKoon and Ratcliff (1986), for example, have reported experiments that seem to show that readers make inferences on-line only when they are demanded by text coherence. In their study, there was no evidence that readers made inferences that were strongly invited pragmatically but not strictly necessary for coherence. Other research indicates a similar lack of evidence for rich inference processes specifically in the comprehension of verbs. Corbett and Dosher (1978) found no evidence for on-line inferences of instruments of verbs, and McKoon and Ratcliff (1980) found such evidence only for instruments highly related to the verb. These verb results are especially relevant for the *pound* example and for the interpretation of the Anderson and Ortony (1975) results: Do readers immediately encode *pound* as *pound with hammer* in sentence (1) and as *pound with fist* in sentence (2)? Perhaps not.

However, to advance the argument, let us grant an inference-rich comprehension process, despite its possible incorrectness. To return to the "pounding" example, let us agree that a different representation is constructed on reading sentence (1) *The accountant pounded the stake,* compared with sentence (2) *The accountant pounded the desk.* The stronger position that the words only loosely constrain the mental representation, however, must be rejected. Whatever representation the reader constructs for "pounding," it will be consistent with the semantic constraints of *pound: pound* (AGENT, OBJECT, INSTRUMENT). The difference between sentences (1) and (2) is how the reader is apt to fill in the instrument role, which is not explicit in either sentence. Of course, it is possible that *no* instrument role is filled in until some retrieval-related event causes the reader to do so. In any case, the core meaning of *pound* constrains the possibilities for semantic role and hence the range of inferences that might be drawn.

There are additional constraints that word meaning places on interpretation. For example, *The accountant pounded the stake* cannot be used to mean that the accountant pounded the desk. Nor can it be used to mean that the accountant pulled up the stake, nor that the bartender pounded the desk. The fact is that interpretations generally are constrained by meanings. One cannot use any sentence to carry any interpretation. There is a range of likely interpretations, and there may be an interpretation prototype, based on semantic defaults, but there are constraints imposed by both symbol meaning and syntax.

A counter claim to this argument is sometimes heard, roughly that anything can "mean" anything in the right context. On the contrary, it seems correct only to say that words can be used to refer to anything, and any sentence can be given a certain interpretation both in just the right context. There is nothing gained by this claim. Interpretation is indeed a matter of context, and reference can be assigned by convention or whim. However, the distinction between meaning and interpretation makes context stretching an idle exercise.

Finally, it is important to note that nothing in this argument requires the *fixed-meaning* view of language, the view that word meaning consists of necessary and sufficient components. It is perfectly possible to accept the Wittgenstein analysis of meaning as family resemblance and simultaneously hold to a distinction between meaning and interpretation. Many concepts, particularly natural categories, can be understood as organized around prototypical instances (Rosch, 1973), rather than as sets of necessary and sufficient features. Others may include family resemblance features and fuzzy set probabilities. Indeed, no strong assumption about the mental representation of word meaning is necessary. The only necessary assumption is that word meanings, however represented, place significant constraints on sentence meanings and hence on interpretations.

Knowledge Affects Interpretation

The meaning–interpretation distinction places the effects of context and world knowledge in general on interpretation, not meaning. By this view, the many studies that have shown knowledge effects in text processing have demonstrated such effects on how a reader interprets a passage. In some cases, vagueness of reference and/or low-text coherence fail to adequately constrain interpretations and passages are incomprehensible and poorly recalled (Bransford & Johnson, 1973). In other cases, referential vagueness causes low consensus about interpretations and allows readers to build interpretations that reflect individual backgrounds (Anderson, Reynolds, Schallert, & Goetz, 1976). These demonstrations are dramatic because the texts are contrived to weaken relationships between meaning and interpretation. When texts are more mundane and less obfuscatory, meaning has a more perceptible overlap with interpretation. However, in all texts, the effect of knowledge is to influence the interpretation constructed by the reader. The meaning is given by the text.

An additional point must be addressed. The argument does not require a sharp distinction between linguistic and "real-world" knowledge. This distinction can be made in the case of syntax but has proved difficult in the case of word meanings. Katz and Fodor (1963) held to a sharp distinction between a finite set of systematic (linguistic) meaning features that grouped concepts and an indefinitely large set of nonsystematic (real-world) features that distinguished concepts. The distinction itself turned out to be insupportable in principle (Bolinger, 1965).

It may seem that the claim that some kinds of knowledge affect interpretations whereas other kinds of knowledge affect meaning comprehension is in the same jeopardy as that of Katz and Fodor (1963). However, the important fact is that no sharp distinction between linguistic and world knowledge is required by the claim that world knowledge has its effects on interpretation. Consider again the example of *pound the desk*.

Pound is a verb that links three semantic roles—a pounder, a thing pounded, and a pounding instrument. This is the basic action of pounding and constitutes the core meaning of the verbs. Assigning values to the variables—who pounded what in what manner—is the process of *particularization*. Particularization is the essential process of interpretation in many instances of language comprehension. The degree of particularization varies. The lowest degree (zero degree) corresponds to generic schema instantiation as exemplified by *The accountant pounded the desk* when it appears with no other context. This zero-degree context-poor particularization in fact is at the meaning level, not the interpretation level. As context triggers more knowledge, true interpretation comes in; we know both the accountant and the desk in question and map the semantic roles of agent and object onto these specific real-world entities.

The claim here is that the semantic role structure constitutes part of the core meaning of a verb. Learning the core meaning is a matter of extracting case properties from pounding instances observed in the world. The verb itself, of course, has important linguistic properties, some of which map, although very imperfectly, onto semantic roles (subject noun—agent, direct object—semantic object). The existence of dual levels, one linguistic and one "real world," invites an attempt to hold to a sharp distinction between them. Indeed, this distinction *is* sharp for some purposes; grammars must make use of linguistic categories exclusively. However, for meaning, this distinction between linguistic and real-world knowledge is not the relevant one, because word meanings derive, in part, from experience with the world. Instead, the relevant distinction is between the knowledge that comprises the core meaning and the knowledge that comprises the particularization of the concept in context. The comprehension of core meaning, in contrast to its interpretation, is minimally affected by knowledge.

The force of the argument so far is that the knowledge effects seen in comprehension are restricted. They may be localized to processes of interpretation, e.g., particularization. By contrast, the substantial portion of comprehension that is driven by symbol meaning and syntax may be less influenced by knowledge. The argument rests mainly on a distinction between meaning comprehension, relying mainly on symbol manipulation with reduced inferential processes, and interpretation, building on meaning with rich inferential processes. An empirical implication of the argument is that we might observe two distinct components to global comprehension that differ in the richness of their inferential processes. The correctness of this implication is not clear at present. On the other hand, the underlying principle that comprehension, as a global process, includes a component that is relatively impervious to knowledge influence is made plausible by a distinction between meaning and interpretation. The next section argues further for this impenetrable stage of comprehension.

SOME MEANING COMPREHENSION PROCESSES ARE IMPENETRABLE

Certain processes of comprehension are not easily penetrated by "outside" sources of information. Thus, comprehension occurs within a processing system that has constraints on how its components interact. The strong form of this claim is that a language processor consists of noninteracting autonomous components (Forster, 1979).

This claim has taken on added life recently in the form of the modularity thesis (Fodor, 1983). (See also Pylyshyn, 1980, who argues specifically for the cognitive impenetrability of some processes.) The modularity thesis is quite compatible with the present argument; on the other hand, it has some entailments that go beyond what I wish to argue. For example, the assumption that modular cognitive systems are innate is stronger than needed for the argument here, although it may be correct. What is important for my purpose is to demonstrate that some processes of comprehension do not have much access to knowledge, expectation, beliefs, or any other source of imported information. Such a comprehension process would be "informationally encapsulated" (Fodor, 1983), rapidly executing, and driven by data structures for which it is specialized.

Although a modular process may reflect specialized innate structures, as Fodor would have it, its critical characteristic, impenetrability, can be acquired from extended practice. Understood as an acquired characteristic, modularity results from the gradual specialization of the data structures that are necessary and sufficient to trigger a given computation. For example, in word reading, extended practice with a specific stimulus input brings about increasingly rapid activation of a specific word representation. Although there are probably important differences between them, acquired modularity and innate modularity do share the critical functional characteristic of impenetrability. Indeed, it may be more descriptive to speak of acquired impenetrability than of acquired modularity, a process that has acquired modularity will have become impenetrable by knowledge, beliefs, and expectations.

For reading comprehension, there are two processes that can acquire some impenetrability. One process is printed word identification, and the second is sentence parsing. Word identification, or lexical access generally, if it is modular in any sense, will acquire impenetrability. The modularity of sentence parsing might result jointly from innate structures that constrain parsing preferences and from specific language experience. In both cases, however, the critical claim is that these processes are immune from serious influences of knowledge and expectations.

Word Identification

In the case of skilled word reading, the identification of a printed word is triggered by a stimulus letter string through connections with mental representations of words. This lexical activation process is impenetrable. The information in the letter string is sufficient to activate the word representation, and the activation process is so rapid that there is little possibility for knowledge to penetrate.

This observation was developed by Perfetti and Roth (1981) to help account for individual differences in reading skill. A result in the literature on children's reading is that high-skill readers' word identification is less facilitated by context than is low-skill readers' (Perfetti, Goldman, & Hogaboam, 1979; Perfetti & Roth, 1981; Stanovich & West, 1981; West & Stanovich, 1978). The studies showing this result have used latencies in naming and lexical decision tasks, with sentence and discourse contexts to facilitate or inhibit the recognition of a word. It is significant here that Perfetti and Roth (1981) showed that the degree of context facilitation for word identification is a function of the word's identification time in isolation. In their analysis, the time to identify a word in isolation was variable either because of the perceptual quality of the word—it varied in its degree of visual degrading—or because of the speed of a particular reader in identifying the word in isolation. It did not matter which of these determined the time for the word's basic identification. In either case, the word's basic identification time determined the degree of context facilitation. A word that was identified slowly in isolation showed greater context facilitation than a word identified rapidly. This is exactly the result one would expect according to the impenetrability argument. The penetration of the word identification process by knowledge, belief, or expectations is possible only to the extent that the identification process is slowly executing. In skilled reading with a high-quality perceptual input, word identification is too rapid for penetration. With a reader of low skill or a perceptual input of low quality, word identification is not too rapid for penetration, and context effects become more likely.

This raises the question of whether a rapidly executing impenetrable process differs fundamentally from a slower penetrable process or whether it is merely faster. Qualitative differences appear likely. According to this view, the impenetrable process triggers when a stimulus pattern, a letter string, activates the word representation that contains that pattern. The slower penetrable process seems to take whatever incomplete output it obtains from this initial process and adds outside information to it. Word identification may have some of the characteristics of problem solving in such a case. This is the work of an executive central processor rather than a word recognition module.

This account appears to overlook the fact that there are facilitative effects in word recognition that do not depend on slow recognition processes. Priming effects have been observed in lexical decision tasks in which the interval between a priming word and a target word is under 250 milliseconds (DeGroot, 1983; Neely, 1976), probably too short a span to allow any facilitating expectation processes. Furthermore, priming effects have been observed under conditions in which the prime itself was not perceived because of a brief-exposure-plus-masking procedure (Fowler, Wolford, Slade, & Tassinary, 1981). Such cases suggest a very fast-acting context effect and are consistent with a two-process theory of context effects, one operating quickly and automatically and the other operating slowly and only with attention shifts (Neely, 1977; Posner & Snyder, 1975; Stanovich & West, 1981).

A quickly executing contextual priming process is consistent with the impenetrability hypothesis, especially if this process is restricted to superficial lexical links; that is, activation may spread locally through a memory network from one word to a related neighbor. If the neighboring word is then quickly presented visually, it will be "recognized" more quickly than otherwise. The usual way of thinking about this quicker recognition is to assume that recognition is a decision process relative to some threshold value. The threshold is reached more quickly following priming because the word's representation already has some activation from the priming connection (Morton, 1969). This facilitation is consistent with the impenetrability hypothesis because the effect does not involve imported knowledge or expectations. It involves only a very local lexically based effect that occurs, in modularity terms, within the lexical module.

It is interesting in this regard that the evidence suggests that activation may be even more local than is usually implied by the concept of "spreading activation." DeGroot (1983) has shown that within 240 milliseconds (SOA) priming of a lexical decision occurs across one associative link but not across two links. Thus, the word *bull* can prime *cow* and *cow* can prime *milk*, but *bull* does not seem to prime *milk*. Based on DeGroot's results, the spread of activation is very restricted, perhaps to immediate lexical neighbors.

Stronger support for the impenetrability hypothesis comes from the well-known experiments of Swinney (1979) and Onifer and Swinney (1981). Swinney (1979) used a cross-modal priming paradigm in which subjects heard an ambiguous prime word as part of a sentence. The priming word triggered a visual presentation of a word for lexical decision. For example, the auditory prime *bug* was presented in a biasing sentence, "The man was not surprised when he found several spiders, roaches, and other *bugs.*" A lexical decision was required immediately for *ant* or *spy,* each related to one sense of *bug,* or a control word. The result was a priming effect for both related words and a faster lexical decision for *ant* and *spy* compared with that for the control word even though context should have biased only one word, *ant* in this case. Thus, we have a case in which a contextually based expectation does not penetrate lexical processing. We get the basic lexical priming effect but no effect based on what the word means in context. After a longer interval, however, the priming is selective, only *ant* and not *spy* showing an effect. This result suggests a two-process account of semantic encoding, a preliminary short-lived stage in which the multiple meanings represented by a word are activated and a second slower stage in which the contextually appropriate meaning is selected. The first stage is impenetrable, the second is penetrable.

There is an important additional result from the cross-model paradigm for impenetrability. Kintsch and Mross (1985) replicated the Swinney experiment, but, in addition, included a condition of *thematic* priming. Thematic primes derive from the model of the text presumably being constructed by the reader. For example, in a text about a man who is in danger of missing a very important plane, the word "gate" would be presented for lexical decision (at the asterisk) as the subject heard this sentence: . . . *so he hurried down to his plane***. Plane* and *gate* are not highly associated words. If processing of *gate* is facilitated, it is due to the theme of the story. However, the result was no priming effect. By contrast, a lexical decision on *fly* was facilitated following plane because of the strong association between the two words. This result supports the hypothesis that knowledge does not penetrate word identification, specifically meaning activation.

An obvious question deserves some attention. Is the proposal of acquired modularity nothing more than the concept of *automaticity?* Certainly, practice can cause some processes to take on the characteristics of attention free or automatic processes (LaBerge & Samuels, 1974; Posner & Snyder, 1975;Schneider & Shiffrin, 1977). At least two characteristics of automatic processing are relevant: (1) Automatic processes occur without a shift of attention (or without allocation of resources); (2) automatic processes are not easily inhibited. Both characteristics are important for skilled word reading. First, the skilled reader can be said to identify words (automatically) while his attention is directed to text interpretation. Second, the skilled reader can be said to (automatically) identify words unavoidably. The demonstrations of the attention-free aspect of automaticity have tended to come from experiments using divided attention or dual-task methodology. The uninhibitable characteristic of automaticity comes mainly from experiments requiring selective attention, for example, the

Stroop task. Acquired impenetrability seems to be more closely allied with this second characteristic of automaticity, its resistance to inhibition. Impenetrability suggests that word identification occurs without any knowledge influences. It is unmodifiable once triggered.

If there is a practical difference between acquired modularity and automaticity, it is in their entailments as they are applied specifically to reading: Automaticity in reading entails practice at word identification that causes it to become less demanding of resources. Acquired modularity entails practice at word identification that causes it to become impenetrable to knowledge, belief, and expectations.

Sentence Parsing

The second component of comprehension that may show relative impenetrability is sentence parsing. Although sentence parsing, properly understood, is a process that operates on a specialized linguistic vocabulary and thus lends itself to strong claims about syntactic modules, a weaker assumption is again sufficient here. I assume that an early stage of comprehension involves a preliminary attachment of words and phrases to other words and phrases. Parsing is the process by which these attachments are made. The output of parsing is the basis for a semantic analysis of the sentence and, in particular, it is *preliminary* to the propositional representation of sentences.

When a reader or listener encounters *The beer is in the refrigerator next to the tomatoes,* the parsing process readily attaches the phrase *next to the tomatoes* to *beer* rather than to *the refrigerator.* However, an attachment to *the refrigerator* is possible, given, for example, the context of a restaurant kitchen with several refrigerators, one of which sits next to a large container of tomatoes. However, it appears that the parse required by this interpretation—attaching the final prepositional phrase to the immediately preceding noun phrase—is not the preferred parse. It requires that an intermediate noun phrase node be constructed above the noun phrase node that represents "by the refrigerator," in violation of what Frazier (1979; Frazier & Rayner, 1982) calls the *minimal attachment* strategy.

Minimal attachment is a principle of parsing based on syntactic complexity. Of two possible syntactic trees, the one with fewer phrase structure attachments is minimally attached. For example, the minimal attachment reading of the refrigerator sentence links constituents within the verb phrase somewhat as follows: PREPOSITIONAL PHRASE (*in the refrigerator*) + PREPOSITIONAL PHRASE (*next to the tomatoes*), with no additional structural level. In contrast, the nonminimal attachment reading involves an additional structure, one that embeds the second prepositional phrase in the noun phrase of the first prepositional phrase: PREPOSI-

TIONAL PHRASE (*in* (NOUN PHRASE (*the refrigerator* (PREPOSITIONAL PHRASE (*next to* the tomatoes)))))). Thus, in this latter parse an extra layer of structure is created between the prepositional phrase (*next to the tomatoes*) and the verb phrase that includes it. Cognitively, the simpler structure is preferred.

Of course, what's interesting about minimal attachment, or any other syntactically defined parsing principle, is exactly its lack of reference to nonsyntactic information. In the refrigerator example, however, semantics and pragmatics add their weight to the syntactic principle of minimal attachment; that is, normal expectations might place the beer and the tomatoes next to each other in a single refrigerator, which is the minimal attachment reading. By contrast, in a sentence such as *The beer is in the refrigerator next to the wall*, the influence of pragmatic expectations is in the opposite direction. On syntactic grounds (minimal attachment), the preference is the same as before, *next to the wall* with *the beer;* however, this interpretation does not work as well here as the alternative nonminimal attachment, in which the refrigerator, not the beer, is next to the wall. Nevertheless, there is evidence that the preference for the minimal attachment is strong enough that readers take longer to read a sentence that requires the nonminimal attachment (Frazier & Rayner, 1982). Furthermore, even when story contexts bias the nonminimal reading, the preferred reading may still be the minimal attachment reading, at least for some sentence types (Ferreira & Clifton, 1986).

The basis for syntactic preferences is a matter not easily resolved. They may reflect constraints on syntactic tree building that in turn reflect psychological processing principles, for example minimal attachment, or they may reflect knowledge about environments associated with lexical items, especially verbs (Ford, Bresnan, & Kaplan, 1982). For the present argument, the ultimate source of parsing principles is not critical, except that it cannot lie in a general knowledge component. Parsing principles reflect linguistic knowledge that is *essentially*—as opposed to "under all conditions"—independent of general knowledge. Most important is the possibility, now demonstrated for at least some sentence constructions, that these principles are not overridden by knowledge, context, and expectations; that is, they are impenetrable.

WHY KNOWLEDGE IS INADEQUATE:
A RECAPITULATION

Knowledge is critical to skilled performance in complex tasks. The research in such domains as physics (Chi, Feltovich, & Glaser, 1981; Larkin, McDermott, Simon, & Simon, 1980) and chess (Chase & Simon, 1973) demonstrates situations in which domain knowledge dominates performance. Language comprehension usually has seemed to be different—a domain—general ability. However, some artificial intelligence approaches to language have found it necessary to build very rich knowledge representations into text understanding programs (e.g., Shank & Abelson, 1977) and have argued that human language comprehension must be similarly knowledge-rich (Winograd, 1977). At the same time, research has demonstrated that knowledge is an important influence in the comprehension of texts (Bransford & Johnson, 1973) and produces specific individual differences (Anderson et al., 1976; Spilich et al., 1979). Thus there has been a coupling of comprehension with problem solving—both have been shown to depend on specific knowledge in critical ways. Given this emphasis on specific knowledge, it is possible to believe that general abilities are illusions and that the substance of mental abilities lies in rich knowledge representations. Reading ability then would consist of specific knowledge structures that allow comprehension of many specific domains.

Instead, I have argued that reading is a restricted-general ability. It is restrictive, rather than permissive, of knowledge influence, and it is general in its application across diverse knowledge domains. Two related arguments make the case for this claim. First, notions of "comprehension" often conflate at least two separable components, meaning comprehension and interpretation. Meaning comprehension is driven by the text in accord with constrained principles of symbol meaning and syntax. Interpretation is unconstrained and inference rich. The effects of knowledge are largely on interpretation through such processes as particularization and inference building. Meaning comprehension is relatively free of knowledge influences.

Second, some comprehension processes, at least some that comprise meaning comprehension, can acquire impenetrability. Such processes are resistant to knowledge penetration, rapidly executing, and computationally autonomous. Lexical access and sentence parsing are both candidates for impenetrable modular processes. Word identification becomes impenetrable with increasing reading skill, and parsing seems to follow structural principles. The implication of this argument is that skilled reading is a general ability that is free of specific knowledge influences in the processes of (a) word identification and (b) syntactic parsing. Because these are early occurring processes that enable the assembly of propositions from sentences, there are grounds for identifying general reading ability with the reader's ability to encode propositions.

SPECULATION ON EMPIRICAL IMPLICATIONS

If the arguments for reading as a restricted-general process are correct, there are some implications for characterization of reading ability. The most important concerns the basic nature of reading ability: Ability in reading depends on linguistically based processes that control word identification and proposition encoding. It depends much less on abilities to draw inferences, to make elaborations, and more generally to apply interpretative schemata to the outcome of meaning comprehension. A definitional retreat—to define reading ability so that the preceding claim is necessarily true—is avoided, in principle, by the following hypothetical experiment. In an ideal world of valid and error-free measures of cognitive abilities, we identify a group of low-ability readers who do poorly at answering inference-demanding questions about what they are reading. The empirical question is what cognitive deficit causes their problem? In principle, the possibilities are: (a) Specific knowledge deficits and no other problem; (b) No specific knowledge deficits, but an unspecified inability to make inferences in texts, and no other problem; (c) No specific knowledge deficits, but a systematic failure to apply knowledge to text reading, and no other problem; (d) A reduced ability to encode propositions and no other problem.

The strong form of the knowledge hypothesis, the one that forces the conclusion that general ability is a mirage, must predict the first outcome. Given any sample of low-skilled readers tested with certain texts, it can predict that further test sampling will cause a change of classification—some low-ability readers will become average ability readers and vice-versa. If further text sampling does not change the classification, this only can be a reflection of true individual differences in knowledge across domains. In either case, reading ability is merely an artifact of knowledge variance.

A strategy deficit hypothesis predicts alternatives (b) and (c). However, a weak form of the knowledge hypothesis and a strategy-deficit hypothesis would be indistinguishable. They both permit the explanation that low-ability readers fail to use the knowledge they have to make inferences. However (b) suggests more clearly some general procedural deficit; that is, there are general inference procedures that operate on all kinds of knowledge and it is these procedures that are defective in low-ability readers.

The fourth alternative is that the cause of low-comprehension performance lies in basic meaning comprehension processes. Observed difficulties in inferential comprehension, by this hypothesis, do not lie in knowledge or strategy deficits but in meaning comprehension. Alternative (d) is based on the assumption of a restricted-general reading ability. Low-ability readers will have linguistic processes that are ineffective in word identification and/or proposition encoding. (Perfetti, 1985, contains a more detailed account of these general possibilities.)

In reality, it is likely that many, perhaps most, subjects would show combinations of problems—strategy, knowledge, and encoding deficits.

But this reality merely reflects the difficulty or the impossibility of assessment of specific abilities in isolation. In an ideal experiment, the fate of the alternative theories is fairly clear. The hypothesis that reading ability is centrally based on restricted-general processes implies that results for many subjects will indicate the fourth alternative. A serious knowledge-deficit hypothesis would claim that many subjects' performances indicate the first possibility. These predictions are necessarily relative: A knowledge hypothesis does not require that knowledge is the only factor in performance, nor does the restricted-general hypothesis preclude possibility for failures outside the restricted-general processes it asserts are at the heart of reading.

Actually, there is very little research on reading that can be brought to bear on the specific knowledge hypothesis. Studies that have shown low-ability readers to have inference problems have not assessed processes of more basic meaning comprehension. Similarly, the studies that have shown reading ability to be linked to such processes as word identification, sentence memory, and comprehension have not assessed knowledge related factors.

A study by Oakhill (1982) does seem to separate inferential abilities from certain reading abilities. Along with a study by Garnham, Oakhill, and Johnson-Laird (1982), this study has been interpreted by Johnson-Laird (1983) as showing critical skill differences in readers' abilities to construct mental models. Oakhill (1982) identified two groups of 7- and 8-year-old children whose performances were equal on a test of word-identification accuracy but unequal on a test of text comprehension. Importantly, the experimental task involved *spoken* language, not reading. Recognition memory was assessed for sentences from aurally presented three sentence "stories." For example: *The car crashed into the bus. The bus was near the crossroads. The car skidded on the ice.* The key result was the rate of false recognitions to foils that were semantically congruent with the text as a whole compared with foils that were not congruent. For the example, *The car was near the crossroads* is congruent and *The bus skidded on the ice* is incongruent. Although the pattern of recognition errors was the same for the two groups of readers, with more errors to semantically congruent foils than to incongruent ones, the magnitude of the difference was larger for the skilled comprehenders. This result indicates that skilled comprehenders are more likely to construct an integrated model of the text than are less skilled comprehenders. On the other hand, the data show a difference, nonsignificant, of comparable magnitude in their recognition of actually occurring sentences; skilled comprehenders made fewer errors. Overall, the data are quite consistent with both the hypothesis that skilled comprehenders establish a more accurate propositional representation of the text and the hypothesis that they make more inferences.

The problem, of course, is a unifying processing explanation of such results. The simplest explanation, favored by Johnson-Laird (1983), would be to say that it is a processing characteristic of skilled readers to construct a mental model from a text. Thus, they construct *interpreted* representations that are referentially and inferentially rich. Less skilled readers, for some reason, fail to construct a mental model, at least a coherent one. However, to the extent that the interpreted representation (mental model) is built from a less interpreted representation, then the process of encoding basic propositions must have a role. Thus, the explanation for observed differences in inference ability in such studies remains elusive.

Another study, by Garnham, Oakhill, and Johnson-Laird (1982) was carried out on subjects comparable to those in Oakhill's (1982) study discussed earlier. Subjects read scrambled versions of short stories and recalled them. Normally in research, scrambling of sentences within a story produces two effects. First, the event structure is altered because sentences are out of order. Second, the referential coherence of the text is altered, because, after scrambling, a sentence with a pronoun or some other anaphoric term may appear prior to mention of its antecedent. These two problems were illustrated in one of the scrambled stories used by Garnham et al. (1982), which originally appeared in Rumelhart (1975): "She had just won it and was hurrying home to show her sister. Suddenly, the wind caught it and carried it into a tree. Jenny was holding on tightly to the string of her beautiful new balloon. Jenny cried and cried. The balloon hit a branch and burst." (p. 41)

The story is fairly incomprehensible because of bizarre event sequences and lack of antecedents for "she" and "it." In Garnham et al. (1982) the referential problem was solved by switching antecedents and anaphora where appropriate: "Jenny had just won a beautiful new balloon and was hurrying home to show her sister. Suddenly the wind caught it and carried it into a tree. Jenny was holding on tightly to the string of her balloon. She cried and cried. It hit a branch and burst." (p. 42)

The results of interest were the recall of the original text, the random text (fully scrambled), and the referentially revised text. The key result was that only skilled readers showed an advantage for the referentially revised text over the random text. Indeed, skilled readers showed a fairly dramatic gain for the referentially revised text compared with the random text, whereas less skilled readers showed no gain at all.

It is possible to attribute this result to a greater inferential ability on the part of skilled readers. This was Garnham's explanation and also Johnson-Laird's (1983). However, the likelihood of more basic meaning comprehension differences would be suggested by evidence of a nonsignificant difference between the two groups for the random passage and a significant difference for the original nonscrambled passage. Nevertheless, the most straightforward explanation is that the recall of both the original and the referentially revised text was based on an interpreted representation. This representation depends more on inference abilities in scrambled texts, and such abilities may be especially characteristic of skilled comprehenders.

One serious reservation should be held: The inferential processes triggered by normal texts probably are unlike those required by scrambled texts. Indeed, texts with scrambled events, even those with some referential coherence, probably do not trigger inferences at all. Instead, the reader has to become a problem solver. If so, it is not clear that the parsimonious explanation that assumes inference building to be the central comprehension process can be made on the basis of scrambled texts. It is quite possible that skilled comprehenders are indeed better problem solvers for text problems than less skilled readers, just as they are better at phonetic segmentation. Whether either process serves their comprehension of ordinary texts is another question.

On the other side of the issue, the fact that much research on children's reading ability suggests a pervasive role for lower level processing factors seems to support the restricted-general hypothesis. In my research, high-ability readers, as defined by comprehension texts, consistently show certain processing advantages over low-ability readers: (1) faster and/or more accurate word identification; (2) Word identification latencies less affected by intrinsic stimulus variables—length, frequency, lexicality loss difference between words and pseudowords, both in accuracy and latency; (3) Word identification latencies *less* affected by context; (4) A greater working memory capacity, as assessed in linguistic memory tasks in both visual or aural modalities; (5) Shorter times to understand simple sentences.

The skilled reader's performance is characterized by rapidly executing context-free word-recognition processes that can be hypothesized to enable rapid and accurate meaning comprehension from simple sentences, and by an effective general modality-independent linguistic memory. There may be something missing in this characterization, perhaps an ability to use knowledge to arrive quickly at interpretations. However, these lower level factors are very pervasive; that is, they are readily found in studies comparing readers of different ability (see Perfetti, 1985, for example).

We have recently begun an experiment that addresses knowledge versus reading ability more directly. Because the research is still in progress, the conclusions are very tentative. Still, the results to date suggest the contributions of both knowledge and general reading ability to learning from text.

Subjects in the experiment were assessed for their domain-specific knowledge and their reading-comprehension ability. Results of this assessment produced four groups, as defined by the four combinations of reading skill and knowledge. The domain is football as a rule-structured game. Subjects read both football and nonfootball texts and produced data on reading times and comprehension, the latter assessed by comprehension questions targeted to specific structural levels of the story as well as by recall. (The nonfootball text is a story about a fire in a school, for which we assumed all subjects had the necessary knowledge.) In addition, the subjects' latencies to identify simple isolated words unrelated to the texts were obtained in a separate session. A reader's mean identification latency is taken to reflect his general word-processing efficiency, an important component of general reading ability. Some of the words are football related.

If specific knowledge drives text comprehension, then we should find, as other studies have, (e.g., Spilich et al., 1979) that high-knowledge subjects comprehend more of the football text. However, if there is a general reading ability, we should find that high-skill readers outperform low-skill readers; that is, in general, we should find that comprehension of even a knowledge-rich text depends on general abilities that are observable even after specific knowledge is accounted for. Finally, to the extent that knowledge plays its role by adding to meaning comprehension rather than short-circuiting it, we would expect to find reading times for football texts, as contrasted with comprehension, less related to football knowledge than to basic textual and linguistic features.

Thus far, we have preliminary results from about 40 subjects representing distinct levels of reading ability and of football knowledge. First, with respect to reading times, low-skill subjects took longer to read a text, regardless of whether it was a football or nonfootball text. Knowledge was related to reading time only for the football texts, with low-knowledge subjects taking longer than high-knowledge subjects. It was particularly interesting that high-skill subjects with low knowledge took longer on the football text than the nonfootball text, but low-skill subjects with low knowledge were equally slow on both texts. This last result suggests that the skilled readers slowed their reading rates in response to the knowledge demands of the text, whereas the less skilled ones did not.

With respect to comprehension, football knowledge made a difference with the football story but not with the nonfootball story, as one would expect. High-knowledge subjects showed better performance on comprehension questions than low-knowledge subjects for both levels of reading skill. Further analysis, based on the types of information in the stories, suggests that the knowledge effect is general. High-knowledge subjects were not only more successful in recalling the high-level content of the story, for example, the progression of scoring and failure to score that comprises the goal structure of the game, but also the lower level content on specific game events that are important to the game's progress, as well as story setting information.

Given the issues raised in this chapter, perhaps the most important result is that reading ability showed a strong influence on the comprehension of both stories and in fact was an equivalent factor in the football and nonfootball texts. Interestingly, two groups, these were the low-skill high-knowledge group and the high-skill low-knowledge group, showed virtually identical comprehension performance on the football text. Thus, a reader could achieve a respectable level of comprehension of the football text either by knowing a lot about football or by being a skilled reader. (This level was, of course, lower than that achieved by the high-knowledge high-skill group.) In this situation at least, a reader could compensate for lack of domain knowledge with basic reading skill and compensate for lack of reading skill with domain knowledge. Presumably, there are minimum levels for both knowledge and reading skill that are required before this compensation can occur.

Another perspective on the knowledge-ability issue was obtained by examining the text variables that predict reading times. To predict per-line reading time we used three classes of text variables corresponding roughly to three linguistic levels, lexical (number of words per line), syntactic (occurrence of sentence boundaries and fragments), and discourse (the paragraph number and "page" number). The data are easily summarized. By far the best predictor of reading time was the number of words per line ($r = .64$). This was true when data from all 40 subjects were taken on the nonfootball text, and it remained true for the football text and for all subgroups of subjects. The discourse variables and syntactic variables were moderately correlated with reading time, with lines from later paragraphs requiring less time than lines from earlier paragraphs and lines ending in sentence fragments taking longer to read than lines that did not. The important point is that there was no obvious shift in the pattern of correlations when the control text was compared with the football text, nor when subgroups of subjects were compared. Thus, there is no evidence in the data yet that knowledge-demanding texts produced drastic alterations in what controls reading speed, although supporting this conclusion will depend totally on the selection of predictor variables.

Finally, the data on word identification bear on the argument. Skilled readers showed faster word identification times than less skilled readers, as is always the case. Times to identify a block of football-related words (e.g., *fumble, touchdown*) were compared with times for control words for the different subject subgroups, controlling for frequency and length factors. High-knowledge subjects showed no advantage over low-knowledge subjects in this comparison. This result, of course, is consistent with the assumption that lexical access is relatively uninfluenced by knowledge beyond the lexical knowledge necessary to establish and maintain the lexical entry.

The results of this incomplete experiment are no more than suggestive for the issues raised in this chapter. The experiment does, however, illustrate one empirical approach to identifying a general reading ability component that is relatively free of knowledge influences. As more research of this kind and of the kind reported by Oakhill (1982) and Garnham et al. (1982) is completed, the distinction between relatively uninterpreted and relatively inference-rich interpreted representations will become increasingly important and will require more careful examination than in the past. High-ability readers may more readily construct an interpreted representation than low-ability readers. But to interpret such a fact, we must know more about how such representations are tied to basic meaning representations. There are at least two issues here. First, the extent to which rich interpretations are constructed "on line" is not clear. If interpretations are relatively impoverished during reading, then reading ability must be understood by basic meaning processes rather than by interpretative processes. This is not to suggest that inferential and interpretative processes are not important, only that they are *necessarily* dependent on basic meaning construction processes. The second issue follows: Differences in observed inference abilities cannot be clearly interpreted without careful assessment of basic meaning construction abilities.

What remains is to develop a fuller account of the nature of restricted-general ability. It is, by hypothesis, an essentially linguistic ability. Its component parts are abilities in context-free lexical access and elementary meaning construction. The latter includes sentence parsing and context-sensitive word-meaning assignment. However, these abilities will probably not account for a skilled reader's compensation for deficient knowledge. The skills that allowed our skilled readers to achieve some interpretation of the football text in the absence of adequate domain knowledge undoubtedly included reasoning skills that go well beyond word identification and parsing. These skills require detailed identification, even if they are shown to depend on success in basic meaning construction.

INSTRUCTIONAL IMPLICATIONS

I have tried to suggest that the richer inferential processes required for an interpreted representation are peripheral reading abilities that are very dependent on an earlier more fundamental meaning comprehension process. However, this claim should not be confused with stronger and probably incorrect claim that a boundary between meaning comprehension and interpretation can be easily seen in every text comprehension situation or the claim that reading education should somehow not attend to knowledge processes. It is likely, as Glaser (1984) has suggested, that learning can be promoted best in environments that emphasize domain-specific knowledge.

Learning to read, of course, is different from reading to learn, and the implications of the restricted-general hypothesis are different in the two cases. If reading is essentially a meaning construction process that depends on word identification, parsing, and proposition encoding, then children must acquire these skills to be good readers. However, these processes, except for written word identification, are not specifically reading skills but general language skills. Learning to read depends on linguistic skills that have developed outside the school environment, a fact that is obvious enough to be the basis for vaguely "linguistic" approaches to reading instruction.

However, to accept the linguistic basis of reading is to accept the need to build on basic linguistic skills by improving them. The assumption that all children enter school with language competence is too facile. What a child brings to school does include basic grammatical competence, a universal but primitive ability in the context of literacy demands. The child also has a high degree of pragmatic linguistic competence, implicitly understanding conditions on communication, conversational turn taking, and so on. This competence is of little value in literacy, however, because reading demands exactly that competence that pragmatic competence excludes and even conspires to suppress, the ability to get meaning from symbols rather than out of contexts.

Reading requires of the child a significant addition to and departure from his or her general language skill. This "schooled language competence" (Perfetti & McCutchen, 1987) develops in the context of literacy acquisition, both promoting it and depending on it. The beginning reader has the basic linguistic competence to understand words and sentences. Instruction for beginning reading needs to build on this competence. The key principle that follows from the restricted-general hypothesis is that the student must learn to achieve meaning from print. This requires learning to decode print in meaningful contexts. *Phonics* approaches single out the decoding part of this principle for early emphasis, and *look–say* approaches single out the meaning part for early emphasis. As others (e.g., Feitelson, 1980) have pointed out, this divorce of meaning and decoding is unnecessary. Indeed, programs in beginning reading instruction have been based on materials designed to be simultaneously meaningful and engineered to reveal the regularities of the sound–symbol system that the student will learn. In such conditions a student is learning what has to be learned, the code, in the context in which it is to be used. Of course, in some orthographies it may seem difficult to compose simple sentences and simple stories that reflect an optimal ordering of letter–sound regularities and are interesting at the same time. However, this is merely a challenge for talented writing. The only real excuse for not doing it is adherence to a particular instructional dogma.

The outcome of successful reading instruction is that a student acquires the decoding principles of the orthography, creates a large "sight" vocabulary, and increases his basic ability to use symbols rather than context to construct meaning. These skills continue to develop with meaningful practice in reading. A particularly important example of continued skill increase is the growth of the orthographic lexicon. This growth is a word-by-word process as individual words become represented and eventually fully "modular." At any given point in development, the child has a functional lexicon and an autonomous lexicon (See Perfetti, in prep.) The autonomous lexicon has acquired impenetrability and its size continues to increase with practice at reading. Notice that by this account the question of when word recognition becomes "automatic" is not very meaningful.

The implications of the restricted-general hypothesis for reading to learn are different. It is important to realize that practice in reading, which is critical to achieving high-skill levels, is occasioned by subject-matter texts. Reading history or science in the sixth grade remains important for learning how to read, but the critical demands made on knowledge and the ultimate need for rich interpretation—i.e., deep understanding—are new. Here, instruction needs to take special notice of the specific knowledge demands of a text and the reader's deficiencies in knowledge. Direct encouragement for the student to construct a mental model of what he or she is reading may also be important. This implies procedures to get the student reasoning about the content of a text.

Glaser (1984) has suggested that skills for thinking develop generality only as individuals use them in a variety of literacy tasks and knowledge domains. Reading ability is similar; only through reading in a number of domains can reading ability attain its maximum generality. The restricted-general hypothesis is consistent with this claim. In addition, it helps to make clear that there is an essential component to reading ability that allows this variety of domains to be read at all.

REFERENCES

Anderson, R. C., & Ortony, A. (1975). On putting apples into bottles—a problem of polysemy. *Cognitive Psychology, 7,* 167–80.

Anderson, R. C., Reynolds, R. E., Schallert, D. L., & Goetz, E. T. (1976). *Frameworks for comprehending discourse* (Tech. Rep. No. 12). Urbana: University of Illinois Laboratory for Cognitive Studies in Education.

Bolinger, D. (1965, Oct.–Dec.). The atomization of meaning. *Language, 41,* 4.

Bransford, J. D., & Johnson, M. K. (1973). Considerations of some problems of comprehension. In W. G. Chase (Ed.), *Visual information processing* (pp. 383–438). New York: Academic Press.

Catran, J. (1982, Sept.). *Newspaper column.* Reprinted in *The New York Herald Tribune.*

Chase, W. G., & Simon, H. A. (1973). The mind's eye in chess. In William G. Chase (Ed.), *Visual information processing* (pp. 215–281). New York: Academic Press.

Chi, M. T. H., Feltovich, P., & Glaser, R. (1981). Categorization and representation of physics problems by experts and novices. *Cognitive Science, 5,* 121–152.

Chiesi, H. L., Spilich, G. J., & Voss, J. F. (1979). Acquisition of domain-related information in relation to high- and low-domain knowledge. *Journal of Verbal Learning and Verbal Behavior, 18,* 257–274.

Corbett, A. T., & Dosher, B. A. (1978). Instrument inferences in sentence encoding. *Journal of Verbal Learning and Verbal Behavior, 17,* 479–491.

DeGroot, A. M. B. (1983). The range of automatic spreading activation in word priming. *Journal of Verbal Learning and Verbal Behavior, 22,* 417–436.

Dooling, D. J., & Lachman, R. (1971). Effects of comprehension on retention of prose. *Journal of Experimental Psychology, 88,* 216–222.

Feitelson, D. (1980). Relating instructional strategies to language idiosyncracies in Hebrew In J. K. Kavanagh & R. L. Venezky, *Orthography, reading and dyslexia.* Baltimore: University Park Press.

Ferreira, F., & Clifton, C., Jr. (1986). *The role of context in resolving syntactic ambiguity.* Amherst: University of Massachusetts.

Fodor, J. (1983). *Parsing, constraints and the freedom of expression.* Montgomery, VT: Bradford Press.

Ford, M., Bresnan, J. W., & Kaplan, R. M. (1982). A competence-based theory of syntactic closure. In J. W. Bresnan (Ed.), *The mental representation of grammatical relations* (pp. 727–795). Cambridge, MA: MIT Press.

Forster, K. I. (1979). Levels of processing and the structure of the language processor. In W. E. Cooper & E. C. T. Walker (Eds.), *Sentence processing: Psycholinguistic studies presented to Merrill Garrett* (pp. 27–85). Hillsdale, NJ: Lawrence Erlbaum Associates.

Fowler, C. A., Wolford, G., Slade, R., & Tassinary, L. (1981). Lexical access with and without awareness. *Journal of Experimental Psychology: General, 110,* 341–362.

Frazier, L. (1979). *On comprehending sentences: Syntactic parsing strategies.* Doctoral dissertation, Bloomington: Indiana University Linguistics Club.

Frazier, L., & Rayner, K. (1982). Making and correcting errors during sentence comprehension: Eye movements in the analysis of structurally ambiguous sentences. *Cognitive Psychology, 14,* 178–210.

Frege, G. (1892). Uber Sinn und Bedeutung. *Zeitschrift fur Philosphie und philosophische Kritik, 100,* 25–50. Translated in P. T. Geach & M. Black (Eds.), *Philosophical writings of Gottlob Frege.* Oxford: Blackwell, 1952.

Garnham, A., Oakhill, J., & Johnson-Laird, P. N. (1982). Referential continuity and the coherence of discourse. *Cognition, 11,* 29–46.

Glaser, R. (1984). Education and thinking: The role of knowledge. *American Psychologist, 39,* 93–104.

Guilford, J. P. (1967). *The nature of human intelligence.* New York: McGraw-Hill.

Johnson-Laird, P. N. (1983). *Mental models.* Cambridge, MA: Harvard University Press.

Katz, J. (1966). *The philosophy of language.* New York: Harper & Row.

Katz, J., & Fodor, J. (1963). The structure of a semantic theory. *Language, 39,* 170–210.

Kintsch, W., & Mross, F. (1985). Context effects in word identification. *Journal of Memory and Language, 24,* 3.

LaBerge, D., & Samuels, S. J. (1974). Toward a theory of automatic information processing in reading. *Cognitive Psychology, 6,* 293–323.

Larkin, J. H., McDermott, J., Simon, D. P., & Simon, H. A. (1980). Expert and novice performance in solving physics problems. *Science, 80,* 1335–1342.

McKoon, G., & Ratcliff, R. (1986). Inferences about predictable events. *Journal of Experimental Psychology: Learning, Memory, & Cognition, 12,* 82–91.

Morton, J. (1969). Interaction of information in word recognition. *Psychological Review, 76,* 165–178.

Neely, J. H. (1976). Semantic priming and retrieval from lexical memory: Evidence for facilitatory and inhibitory processes. *Memory & Cognition, 4,* 648–654.

Neely, J. H. (1977). Semantic priming and retrieval from lexical memory: The roles of inhibitionless activation and limited-capacity attention. *Journal of Experimental Psychology: General, 106,* 1–66.

Oakhill, J. (1982). Constructive processes in skilled and less skilled comprehenders' memory for sentences. *British Journal of Psychology, 73,* 13–20.

Onifer, W., & Swinney, D. A. (1981). Accessing lexical ambiguities during sentence comprehension: Effects of frequency of meaning and contextual bias. *Memory & Cognition, 9,* (6), 225–233.

Perfetti, C. A. (in preparation). *The representation problem in reading acquisition.* In P. B. Gough (Ed.), *Reading acquisition.* Hillsdale, NJ: Lawrence Erlbaum Associates.

Perfetti, C. A. (1985). *Reading ability.* New York: Oxford University Press.

Perfetti, C. A., Goldman, S. R., & Hogaboam, T. W. (1979). Reading skill and the identification of words in discourse context. *Memory & Cognition, 7,* 273–282.

Perfetti, C. A., & McCutchen, D. (1987). Schooled language competence: Linguistic abilities in reading and writing. In S. Rosenberg, *Advances in applied psycholinguistics* (Vol. 1) (pp. 105–141). New York: Cambridge University Press.

Perfetti, C. A., & Roth, S. F. (1981). Some of the interactive processes in reading and their role in reading skill. In A. M. Lesgold & C. A. Perfetti (Eds.), *Interactive processes in reading* (pp. 269–297). Hillsdale, NJ: Lawrence Erlbaum Associates.

Posner, M. I., & Snyder, C. R. R. (1975). Attention and cognitive control. In R. Solso (Ed.), *Information processing and cognition: The Loyola symposium* (pp. 55–85). Hillsdale, NJ: Lawrence Erlbaum Associates.

Pylyshyn, Z. W. (1980). Computation and cognition: Issues in the foundations of cognitive science. *The Behavioral and Brain Sciences, 3,* 111–169.

Rosch, E. (1973). On the internal structure of perceptual and semantic categories. In T. M. Moore (Ed.), *Cognitive development and the acquisition of language* (pp. 111–144). New York: Academic Press.

Rumelhart, D. E. (1975). Notes on a schema for stories. In D. Bobrow & A. Collins (Eds.), *Representation and understanding: Studies in cognitive science.* New York: Academic Press.

Schneider, W., & Shiffrin, R. M. (1977). Controlled and automatic human information processing. I: Detection, search, and attention. *Psychological Review, 84,* 1–66.

Schank, R. C., & Abelson, R. P. (1977). *Scripts, plans, goals, and understanding: An inquiry into human knowledge structures.* Hillsdale, NJ: Lawrence Erlbaum Associates.

Spearman, C. (1924). *The nature of 'intelligence' and the principles of cognition.* London: Macmillan.

Spilich, G. J., Vesonder, G. T., Chiesi, H. L., & Voss, J. F. (1979). Text-processing of domain-related information for individuals with high and low domain knowledge. *Journal of Verbal Learning and Verbal Behavior, 18,* 275–290.

Stanovich, K. E., & West, R. F. (1981). The effect of sentence context on ongoing word recognition: Tests of a two-process theory. *Journal of Experimental Psychology: Human Perception and Performance, 7,* 658–672.

Swinney, D. A. (1979). Lexical access during sentence comprehension: Reconsideration of context effects. *Journal of Verbal Learning and Verbal Behavior, 18,* 645–659.

van Dijk, T. A., & Kintsch, W. (1983). *Strategies of discourse comprehension.* New York: Academic Press.

West, R. F., & Stanovich, K. E. (1978). Automatic contextual facilitation in readers of three ages. *Child Development, 49,* 717–727.

Winograd, T. (1977). A framework for understanding discourse. In M. Just & P. Carpenter (Eds.), *Cognitive processes in comprehension* (pp. 63–88). Hillsdale, NJ: Lawrence Erlbaum Associates.

Wittgenstein, L. (1953). *Philosophical investigations.* Translated by G. E. M. Anscombe. New York: Macmillan.

11

Toward Intelligent Systems
for Testing

Alan Lesgold
Joyce Ivill-Friel
Jeffrey Bonar
Learning Research and Development Center
University of Pittsburgh

The concept of criterion-referenced testing (Glaser, 1963), has been a significant contribution to psychology and education. Unlike norm-referenced testing, which supports decisions that involve choosing among people or comparing them, criterion-referenced testing can tell us what people know or what they can do. Such knowledge is central to *adaptive* education, to shaping education to each student's current competences rather than shaping it to serve only the people who score well on general tests.

Although adaptive education has been a recurring theme in the past two decades (cf. Corno & Snow, 1986), most work on criterion-referenced testing (cf. Hambleton, 1984) has focused on issues of certification, of setting standards for educational outcomes, and of tracking; that is, tests are still seen more as tools for selection than for adaptation, and for good reason. Criterion-referenced tests can tell us about each student's knowledge and skills; but knowing this is not the same as knowing how to steer a course of learning or how to adapt an educational process.

This chapter explores one way the technologies of testing might combine with certain cognitive science techniques to provide an adaptive form of instruction. Its focus is a computer system that combines testing with instruction on the basis of successive models of student performance. (The approach can be generalized to other instructional forms, however, including such reactive environments as exploratory microworlds and, perhaps, even conventional classroom instruction.) This form of diagnostic testing, used often, in small amounts, provides continuous assessment and instruction as opposed to relatively standard pretest-treatment-posttest designs for individualizing training and instruction. The testing process is individualized, making it more efficient in steering instruction.

PROBLEMS OF DIAGNOSTIC TESTING

In any test, including a diagnostic or steering test, the test subject carries out some performance on each of the items, and those performances are assigned scores that are aggregated to arrive at an evaluation. Steering tests require test items and procedures for scoring performance that are relevant to the decisions that must be made about a particular student in a particular context. They must be efficient to administer because steering requires frequent, but not necessarily precise, feedback. (Given the inertia of teaching and learning, the steering error produced by an imprecise test will probably be canceled out by subsequent course corrections.)

Standard psychometric methods are not designed for steering tests. They are designed to assure that different forms of a test are equivalent and that the scores on that test are reliable. Because steering tests must be brief so that testing does not take too much time from learning, they are less likely to be reliable, yet steering requires at least some reliability of feedback to be successful.

There are two ways a test can be made more reliable. The first is to increase the extent to which performance on its items directly reflects the skills to be assessed. This can be done statistically or substantively. Statistical approaches, such as item-response theory (Lord, 1980), help assure that different items measure the same thing, and thereby increase the reliability of scores, but not necessarily their validity. It is also possible, however, to develop a microtheory of the target competences that can help specify items that test particular subsets of the target skills.

The second way to make a test more reliable is to use knowledge about the student's performance on prior items to limit the information each new test item must provide. Adaptive testing algorithms that use such a sequential strategy have been developed. After the student completes an item, an estimate of performance based upon the items so far completed is used to select the most informative next item to administer, and then the score on that next item is used to update the estimate. The adaptive testing approach, which almost always requires a computer for the real-time estimates just mentioned, can be applied even when nothing more than the difficulty ordering of items is known. But it is especially powerful if more detailed information about the items is available. Again, a theory that relates performance on various test items to underlying competences and their acquisition can be helpful, even if it is incomplete.

In at least one case, adaptive testing techniques were applied to diagnostic testing. Spineti and Hambleton (1977) used learning hierarchies specified by rational task analysis (Gagné, 1965) to help constrain the estimation process. That is, they selected items by analyzing the material being learned and making some theoretical predictions about the order of acquisition for parts of that material, and in this way reduced by 50% the number of items required to achieve a given level of score reliability.

Our approach is somewhat different. It uses very simple heuristics for reasoning about the level of a student's competence in particular subskills. Its power derives primarily from its ability to intelligently manufacture practice opportunities (test items) for the student that will reveal current competences. We believe, although it remains to be proven, that these practice opportunities are generally appropriate learning vehicles as well as test items. In that sense, we are pursuing steering as a unified system in which testing and learning are combined.

In our view, a cognitive theory of diagnostic testing should have two characteristics. First, it should permit logical as well as purely statistical constraint on diagnosis. Second, it should be based on a representation of the knowledge that is needed to exercise the skill it purports to measure. The use of logic in diagnosis is not at all foreign to our experience. Diagnosis in medicine requires that the physician develop a hypothesis about a specific patient's pathology. This hypothesis is rooted in theories of disease mechanisms and not just in unexplained statistical relationships. When we go to a physician, we are not satisfied with probabilistic statements about our ailments. We expect a diagnosis constrained by the physician's reasoning on the basis of his or her knowledge of disease.

The diagnostic process is dynamic. For example, to test the hypothesis that a patient has heart disease, the physician may probe for more explicit detail about certain symptoms or order a test. A teacher may combine prior knowledge about a student with current observations, to hypothesize that grammatical errors in the student's paper are attributable either to inexperience with written language, or to use of nonstandard dialect, or to a mistaken sense of when formal conventions are needed.

The good teacher's diagnosis differs from a physician's in one respect. We come to a physician to get a diagnosis when something is wrong— he/she does not generally shape continuing decisions about how we should act (except perhaps in developing special regimens, e.g., diets for control of diabetes). A teacher, in contrast, is carrying out an active, goal-directed activity—teaching—which needs only small course corrections. Consequently, it seems reasonable to conduct the testing, at least in part, from a teacher's point of view.

We would like to produce tests that capture some of the capabilities of the most perceptive and observant teachers. We want them to be driven mostly by the teacher's goal structures, but also to respond to knowledge of the expertise the teacher is trying to convey, and the treatments available to the teacher for effecting learning. We also want them to be responsive to more global teacher concerns, such as adapting to general aptitude differences and general characteristics of competence at different levels of learning.

In the next section, we examine the different kinds of knowledge needed to adapt teaching to an individual student's course of learning. We take the viewpoint of intelligent tutoring system design, but the same concerns arise in all approaches to instruction. This is followed by sections that discuss a specific approach to the generation of diagnostically and educationally useful problems.

COMPONENTS OF TEACHING
AND TESTING KNOWLEDGE

When designing computer systems to teach or to test, it is important to clarify the different kinds of knowledge or competence that are involved. We have categorized that knowledge into four[1] types: *domain expertise, curriculum knowledge, instructional and test planning knowledge,* and *treatment knowledge.* Each type has a different structure, different generalized methods, and a different purpose and applicability. Further, there are a variety of connections from one type to another. Figure 11.1 shows these four categories, with examples of the kinds of knowledge they contain, for an electricity tutoring/testing system under development at the Learning Research and Development Center.

---

[1]In Lesgold (in press) a three-category model was presented. Since then, we have become convinced that the curriculum and treatment categories should be separated.

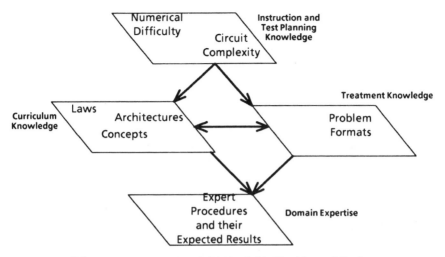

FIG. 11.1.   Types of Knowledge Needed in Teaching and Testing.

Domain Expertise

Domain expertise is always embodied in instructional decision making, either explicitly or implicitly. Deep diagnosis of student difficulties may require an explicit representation of the knowledge required for the performances that are the goals of instruction. For example, the ability of a computer-based tutor to diagnose bugs (systematic errors) in children's arithmetic performances requires a model of the algorithms that experts use in executing those performances. Also, feedback on test performance and advice to the student may have to be expressed as procedures for acting rather than as criteria for outcomes specified in the curriculum. Nonetheless, the performances that constitute the goals of a curriculum derive from information about the competences that constitute expertise.

Another aspect of domain expertise that is important in instruction and testing is knowledge of the targeted task environment. When we speak of what we want people to do, we are referring not only to the knowledge they need to perform successfully but also to the circumstances under which that knowledge must be employed. Again, knowledge of these circumstances might be the basis for curricular objectives, but those objectives rest upon domain expertise. If we have the objective that, given situation X, the student can do Y, it rests upon knowledge of what kind of situation X is and how Y can be done in X. For example, a student might be able to solve a proportion problem at the time a lesson on proportion is presented but not be able to use that knowledge later in solving a word problem or even to solve the same problem as one of a set on mixed topics.

When testing or teaching is done by a computer program, the underlying domain knowledge must sometimes be made explicit in order for the program to function adequately.

Curriculum Knowledge

Curriculum knowledge is the specification of the goal structure that guides the teaching of a body of expertise. Educational researchers and developers often treat the procedures that constitute expertise and the instructional goals that constitute curriculum as more or less the same. They assume that expertise can be split apart easily "at its joints" (to use Plato's phrase) and that curriculum is a natural hierarchy of goals and subgoals to teach the natural units of expertise. There appear, however, to be many different plans for splitting apart expertise, especially when it involves complex performances.

Consider, for example, the curricular issues involved in teaching simple electrical principles. Given some basic concepts—voltage, current, and resistance; some basic laws—Kirchhoff's Laws and Ohm's Law; and different types of circuits—series and parallel; the subject matter could be broken down in several different ways. One legitimate decomposition might first teach the behavior of voltage in series and parallel circuits, then teach about resistance in the two types of circuits, and finally treat current. Another decomposition might, with equal legitimacy, build the entire curriculum on Kirchhoff's current laws. Yet another view might treat parallel circuits as being quite distinct from series circuits and redevelop the concepts of voltage, resistance, and current separately for each.

We need to capture all these multiple viewpoints if they correspond to different curricular goals about which steering information may be needed. For this reason, the various subgoals of knowledge that the teacher or curriculum writer has are best represented by multiple hierarchical goal structures. These goal structures overlap in the components of expert performance to which they refer.

Once we concede that instructional goals are not really a simple decomposition of the expertise being taught into discrete sets and subsets, we are in a position to understand why some testing that is part of a curriculum may not be sufficiently diagnostic. Specifically, we can understand why a student might demonstrate clear competence on a curricular goal that is prerequisite to some other goal but still appear, from the standpoint of the teacher of that second goal, not to have mastered the first. For example, a student may demonstrate understanding of Kirchhoff's current law but later fail to apply it where relevant. Separating expertise from curriculum allows us to understand such occurrences better.

Suppose that we consider domain expertise to be represented by a surface. Expert knowledge is, after all, highly interconnected. Even if it is properly represented as some kind of network, it can be approximated by a continuous surface (specifically, a manifold of unspecified dimensionality). We start by assuming that each curricular subgoal corresponds to a region of the expertise continuum. The expertise subset corresponding to a curricular goal will likely be convex, in the sense that if two pieces of knowledge are part of the same curricular goal, then any strong relationship that directly ties them together should also be part of that goal. On the other hand, a curriculum goal's corresponding expertise is not a completely closed set, because concepts it subsumes may well have connections to other knowledge. That is, the expertise subsets corresponding to different curricular subgoals do not necessarily meet at clean edges.

The untargeted knowledge lying between the clusters of expertise directly addressed by the curriculum can be important in remediating lack of transfer from a curriculum goal's prerequisites to the final target capability.[2] Ordinarily, instruction is directed at the center of the expertise subset corresponding to a curricular goal (see Fig. 11.2). This helps keep the new knowledge to be taught simple enough to be learned. This approach can sometimes backfire, however. For example, if two bundles of expertise are both curricular goals, their centers may be well taught but their peripheries ignored. I may teach you how to compute the joint resistance of two resistors in series, for example, and this may satisfy an instructional objective. Later, if you need to find the joint resistance of three resistors to solve a problem, you may be able to do that or you may not. In either case, simply reteaching the two-resistor algorithm will be insufficient.

If a higher order curricular goal happens to depend upon the integration of the two lower order subgoals, it will likely depend exactly on the edges of their domain knowledge subsets. For decisions about what to teach when remediation seems necessary and also for decisions about how to interpret apparent inconsistencies in diagnosing whether a curricular subgoal has been achieved, domain expertise may be needed.

Planning Knowledge

In addition to specific curricular goals, there are some other higher order curricular issues that need to be addressed in planning testing or teaching. Often, these are abstractions from, or specialized viewpoints on, the curricular goal structure. These may include learning skills, problem solving heuristics, general aptitudes, and even preferences. These concerns, for example, the more general inquiry skill goals in a science course, overlap

---

[2]This issue is addressed more completely in Lesgold (in press).

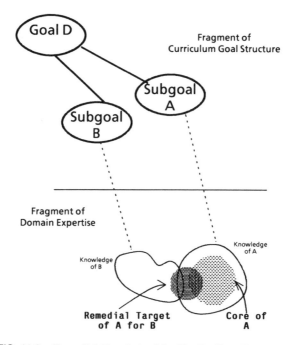

FIG. 11.2.   Remedial Knowledge May Not Be Core Knowledge.

some of the higher level goals in the curriculum. It could even be argued that these concerns really are part of the curriculum, but we retain the distinction because planning issues often color the exact form that goal-specific instruction might take.

For example, we would treat as a planning issue the complexity of arithmetic computation that is required to solve a word problem in a math course. The metagoal is for the student to be able to advance through the problem-solving part of the curriculum, even if his arithmetic skills are developing more slowly than his problem-solving skills. The arithmetic required in a word problem might be adjusted to keep it simple enough to let new problem-solving skills develop. Later, when problem-solving skills are strong, the situation might reverse, and increasingly tough arithmetic might be required whenever the student is expected to find the problem solving tasks easy. Note that the issue of arithmetic skills getting in the way of problem solving could also arise in the electrical networks curriculum sketched in Figs. 11.1 and 11.3. For this reason especially we choose to treat the matter as a metacurricular planning issue. Sometimes capability in skills that are not the focus of instruction requires alteration of instructional and testing strategies for target skills. This is why instruction and testing systems need planning and metacurricular knowledge.

The planning of teaching must also take into account the long-term, higher order aspects of education: metacognitive skills, mature and flexible preferences, and fundamental principles that apply in many domains. From the point of view of the steering test developer, these higher order issues, for the most part, represent variables to be controlled. We really cannot understand whether a student knows how to solve electrical network problems, for example, if his capability is hidden by slow arithmetic performance. We have to take account of metacurricular issues in selecting problems for instructional or measurement use. That is, problems can be selected not only to require domain-specific skills but also to assure that the student answering a given problem will not be troubled by weakness on general basic skills that are not the current focus of measurement or instruction. If a student is weak in arithmetic, a problem might be generated that required only small-integer arithmetic. If a different student finds it easier to receive information in graphical form, the information given for a problem might be presented via a diagram, graph, or even photographic image.

Treatment Knowledge

We turn now to educational treatments and test-item development. Even when we know what to teach or what to measure, there remains a separate

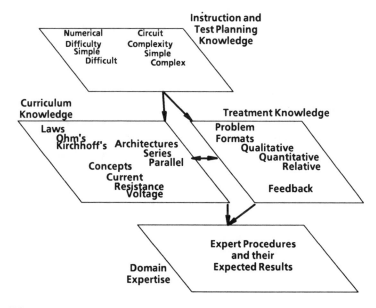

FIG. 11.3.   Examples of Different Knowledges Needed for Steering Testing.

form of expertise involved in successfully generating a situation in which a piece of knowledge can be exercised. For example, several different types of problems can be created to test understanding of electrical network principles (or to provide opportunities for coached practice): they can be quantitative or qualitative; they can deal with unchanging situations or focus on relative changes in different measurements of a circuit. Because electricity knowledge must be applied in slightly different ways for each type of problem, we could treat problem type as a curriculum issue. However, the knowledge that an intelligent system needs about problem categories is different in form from knowledge about curricular goals. This is especially the case when we want to develop problems for practice or for steering tests that require integrated use of several different skill components that are separate curricular goals. The knowledge needed to develop such problems is specific to electricity and to the teaching of electricity and is what we define as treatment knowledge.

Practice and testing that require combining multiple skills are important goals of our work. Some formal instructional development methodologies, such as the Defense Department's Instructional Systems Design (ISD) (Merrill & Tennyson, 1977) take a contrasting approach. This approach consists of complete development and elaboration of the curriculum, followed by the development of tests and treatments corresponding to each curricular goal. This seems entirely sensible, an extension of a management-by-objectives approach. If this method is applied superficially, however, difficulties can arise. We have already discussed the problem of focusing too narrowly on core concepts without adequate elaboration and qualification, but there are other related problems as well. For example, a variety of apprenticeship situations involve simultaneous practice of a wide range of skill components, only some of which may be the current targets of instruction. When practice is provided on each skill component separately, without attention to when each should be used and how they all tie together, fragmentary learning results. The instructor can show, on academic-style tests, that the student learned each subskill, but the student cannot put the subskills together to solve real-world problems.

The holistic approach is not a new one. It has been prevalent in the field of reading instruction, for example, and underlies case study approaches to the teaching of medicine and business. There is, of course, some evidence against it. Chall (1967) surveyed a number of reading curricula and found that, on average, weaker students benefited from a phonics approach, in which recognition of each individual grapheme was the focus of separate instruction. In medicine, critics question whether a student who took a case study course really learned everything he should have. What if a patient has a disease that was not one of the cases discussed?

We can be a bit more formal about this problem if we view subskills as productions–actions to be performed under specific conditions. When subskills are taught in isolation, the conditions under which they should apply cannot be specified because those conditions relate to the broader context of holistic performances. Also, there may be specific productions that are not represented as subgoals for instruction but that combine the productions that were direct curricular targets.

An instructional synthesis of the holistic and componential approaches requires several things, including an understanding of the circumstances under which new subskills or concepts should be introduced in isolation, even if they are later to be practiced more holistically. Of course, the missing productions that hold together the targeted subskills cannot be taught adequately *in vitro;* they require holistic instruction. They also must be assessed. We may need to help students attend to gluing their fragmentary knowledge together if they have trouble doing so on their own. Further, hoping that they will be inferred through rich domain experience, we may not always choose to introduce new pieces of knowledge formally and explicitly. If we take this approach, which may be very efficient, we need to be able to assess later whether there are any subgoals that were not well attained.

Our basic approach is to generate test items (and instructional treatments, for that matter) in the course of testing. That is, at any given point in the course of testing, if a question arises about achievement of a specific curricular goal, a test item is generated by an intelligent subsystem of the tutoring program. The item can also be shaped by metacurricular considerations. Further, if multiple skills are required for any realistic performance within the domain, sets of items can be developed for which particular subskill requirements are systematically varied.

Given a family of cognitive analyses (of expertise, metacurricular issues, and problem environments in which the expertise can be manifested or practiced), our approach is to generate the equivalent of a controlled experiment that systemically varies target pieces of knowledge. If the student fails to perform items requiring a piece of knowledge but performs other items that do not require it, we infer that work is needed on that knowledge. Further, we ask only about pieces of knowledge that are in the part of the curriculum we are steering through. Finally, rather than make statistical decisions about whether a piece of knowledge is present or absent, we assume that knowledge can be present at various strength levels and use experience about the reliability with which a particular piece of knowledge manifests itself to specify the level of learning of that knowledge.

Summary.   Perhaps the best way to illustrate the ideas just presented is to refer to Fig. 11.3, which elaborates the knowledge categories, in part, for our system to teach and test basic electricity principles. The curriculum knowledge includes three sets of goals: laws, concepts, and architectures. Under each of these are subgoals. For example, the architectures being considered are series and parallel circuits (i.e., no bridge circuits). The planning knowledge includes two sets of planning concerns: the arithmetic difficulty of problems that are presented to the student and the circuit complexity. Both apply with respect to a variety of curricular subgoals. For example, circuit complexity may affect whether a student can handle parallel circuits, whether he can apply Kirchhoff's current law, and so forth. Arithmetic difficulty could also affect these subgoals, especially if quantitative problems are presented to the student. The treatment knowledge includes information on problem formats and feedback to the student. Finally, the domain expertise contains specific details of expertise in handling electrical networks that are referenced by the curriculum specification.

GENERATING TEST ITEMS FROM A STUDENT MODEL

Having described the architecture of the knowledge in a steering-testing system, we turn now to applying that knowledge in an assessment driven by a cognitive model of the capabilities being taught. We offer as a first approximation an approach that has been tested in prototype form in an intelligent tutor. It assumes additional knowledge that we have not yet discussed: a student model, that is, some sort of knowledge structure specifying which subskills the student is thought to know and not know.

We currently specify the student model by embedding it in the curricular goal structure of an intelligent tutor. For each curricular subgoal, there must be some sort of notation about the student's assumed competence. In one tutor that Lesgold and his colleagues are building (Lesgold, Lajoie, et al., 1986), there are only four notations—*unlearned, perhaps* acquired, *probably* acquired, and reliably *strong*. These notations relate to an underlying cognitive model of learning derived from John Anderson's (1983) work. The rules currently used to change a subskill notation from one state to another are quite rough, but they are principled.

Movement to the *probably learned* state assumes that a correct production, or set of productions, has been developed by the student. The *perhaps* state indicates that the student has been observed to perform the target skill component, but that there is insufficient evidence to conclude that he knows the conditions as well as the actions for the subskill. The *perhaps* state is unstable. Either further correct performances will occur, prompting classification to the *probably* state, or we assume that the single correct performance observed was accidental relative to the problem ecology for the curriculum, and the student will be moved back to the *unlearned* state.

Recurrent reliable performance will move a student from *probably* to *strong*. We can imagine other approaches in which the notations might include indicators of misconceptions as well. The important point is that if we look in on a student who is in the midst of learning a skill, some of the subskills will be clearly demonstrated already, some will be manifesting obvious problems, some will be unlearned, and some will be in an unknown status.

If we consider how to diagnose student progress in a holistic practice environment given a current model of the student's state, we see that a first issue to be addressed is what to test. In principle, the student could have learned anything since the last test. For that matter, any prior demonstration of competence might have been a fluke, so all positive entries in the model of the student are tentative. Nonetheless, the model would be useless if we merely tested for every skill component at every opportunity. The model enables testing for selected skill components efficiently and in realistic performance contexts. It is the equivalent for steering testing of the patient's chart for medical diagnosis.

We use the model of the student to generate constraints on the test item problems posed. These constraints make the items maximally informative in tuning the student model to changes in the student's capabilities. What can guide our choices of curricular goals to test? There are several possibilities. We discuss them in terms of the four-level model of acquisition mentioned above (*unlearned, perhaps* learned, *probably* learned, and *strong*). The *perhaps* stage may be the most volatile. Suppose a curricular goal is the attainment of a specific production (carrying out a particular action when appropriate). When the action is initially performed successfully, there is a considerable chance that the student may not notice the most important cues about the circumstance of the moment. So, he may be unable to demonstrate the production in other circumstances. For all practical purposes, it was never really learned at all. Until we have several demonstrations of the attainment of a curricular goal, we must assume that our assessment of the student is unstable. Once we see multiple successful performances, we will reclassify the student's competence to the *probably* level. Thus, a first principle in selecting current curricular goals to test is to check up on goals in the *perhaps* state.

A second issue has to do with prerequisite skills. If *skill A* depends upon *skill B,* then there is no point in regularly testing for *A* until *B* is demonstrated. Put another way, if there is ordering information about the curricular goals, we may want to concentrate testing on the ordering between the goals in the *strong* state and those in the *unlearned* state, testing most often the *perhaps* goals, checking for progress on the next few *unlearned* goals, and checking occasionally to see if any goals have gone from *probably* to *strong.* (Operationally, we check to see if problems requiring this subgoal's skills are answered correctly for several consecutive occasions with varying requirements.)

The next issue involves metacurricular concerns, especially those relating to extraneous sources of difficulty, such as a need for complicated arithmetic performance or information presented in a medium known to be difficult for the student. The basic rule of thumb we propose is to adapt these difficulty variables to the current student model level. For example, if the goal is to detect a movement from *unlearned* to *perhaps* for some curricular goal, then we want to set the metacurricular difficulty levels low so that the initial weak acquisition of that subgoal's knowledge is not masked by too many other demands for processing capacity. For movement from *perhaps* to *probably,* an appropriate problem constraint is to have some situational changes from the problem in which the initial appearance of the relevant knowledge was first noted, because the theoretical motivation for the distinction is the possibility of the correct actions having been linked to imprecise conditions. For validating movement to *strong* on some goal, there should be a demonstration of the relevant capability under more difficult circumstances, because the question is whether the relevant knowledge is robust enough to occur even under adverse conditions.

The Concept of Constraint Posting

The basic approach is to begin each cycle of diagnosis by sweeping through the curricular goal structure, noting which subskills are ripe for testing. When the sweep is completed, we try to build one or more problems that maximize our chances for accurately noting changes in the student's current knowledge state, using some of the rules of thumb just described. We then use performance on these made-to-order problems to model the student's level of competence—we make a diagnosis.

Critical to the approach is the concept of *constraint posting* (Stefik, 1980). Rather than building test items as we sweep through the curricular goal structure, we simply add to a list of item constraints as we proceed. Each time we see an issue that we would like clarified, we post that concern as a constraint on the test-item generation process. When the sweep through the curriculum is complete, we take the bundle of constraints and try to build items that satisfy them. Stefik has shown that in many complex problem-solving tasks involving multiple sources of complexity and interactions between problem aspects (e.g., designing recombinant DNA experiments), this constraint posting approach is much more efficient than piecemeal search processes.

Constraint Posting Applied to Problem Generation

The item generation process, then, can work as follows. We first consider the model of the student. Some of the subskills may be marked as reliably strong. These represent beachheads in the conquest of ignorance. From these beachheads, as we venture out toward related subskills, we find some whose status is uncertain (subskills that may or may not have been acquired yet and acquired subskills that may or may not be reliable yet). We can make this search process more efficient if we know, for some subgoals, which others are prerequisite and which are subsequent. A subgoal for which a just attained subgoal is prerequisite is likely to be a testing target, but we will also give some weight to all subgoals, using the rules of thumb discussed earlier. Because we are making steering decisions, we focus on the area of the curriculum that is currently the object of instruction. For each subgoal that is a current target of testing, at least one constraint is posted: A test problem must address that subgoal. For example, if we want to find out whether the student's capabilities in applying Ohm's Law to series circuits have improved, we post constraints that the problem must require Ohm's Law and must involve a series circuit.

We must also consider metacurricular planning issues. For example, a part of the system's planning component may question whether a physics student has adequate math facility, or the ability to learn information from graphical presentations. Constraints can also be posted based on metacurricular aspects of the student's model. Essentially, we say to the test generator, "Because this student is poor in arithmetic, we can't find out if he has learned (moved from *unlearned* to *perhaps*) how to use Ohm's Law to compute the current in a circuit, if the arithmetic comes out messy, so make the numbers simple."

Once the sweep through the curricular and planning structures is complete, the posted constraints must be analyzed before test items are generated. Are there too many to handle at once? If so, we might partition them into several clusters. Are the constraints inconsistent, in the sense that a problem embodying some of them cannot, in principle, embody the others? For example, if we constrain an electricity problem to be simple and we want to know both whether a student knows how to deal with two resistors in series and whether he knows how to deal with two in parallel, this cannot all be done with one problem. So, again, we might partition the constraints into bundles that can comfortably be handled.

Finally, one or more holistic problems that satisfy the constraints posted must be posed. From performance on a problem, either a diagnosis can be made immediately or a more focused problem can be specified for further testing. In essence, we are dealing with a qualitative process that has many of the properties of one of psychometrics' most important quantitative processes—adaptive testing.

An Example From a Tutor for Basic Electricity Principles

To illustrate some of these ideas, we describe MHO, a tutor that teaches basic electrical principles (current, voltage, and resistance; Kirchhoff's Laws and Ohm's Law). MHO is designed to work in both a problem-posing and an exploration mode. In the exploratory mode, the student can make measurements on circuits and even build his own circuit. In the didactic mode, MHO must decide what problem to present. Thus, it faces the same problem that a testing program would face: to examine the model of the student's competence and determine which problem to pose to optimize the information value of the student's answer.

MHO's student model is a specialized form of checklist: a goal structure for teaching the specific knowledge it wants to teach. The checklist derives from the curriculum and planning issues shown in Fig. 11.3. For each subgoal, the student is marked as being in one of the four states described earlier, as shown in Table 11.1. Quantitative scores could be entered as well. What is critical is that some student knowledge levels are considered to indicate potential for change, but others are not. For example, a student

TABLE 11.1
Example Student Model

Metacurricular Issues	
Numerical Difficulty	Simple vs. Difficult
Circuit Complexity	Simple vs. Complex

Curricular Subgoals	Current Student State
Laws	
Ohm's	Unlearned
Kirchhoff's	Perhaps
Architecture	
Series	Perhaps
Parallel	Unlearned
Concepts	
Current	Perhaps
Resistance	Unlearned
Voltage	Unlearned

Treatment Issues	
Problem Formats	
Qualitative	
Quantitative	
Relative	

who knows certain material is not likely to stop knowing it suddenly, but a student who has yet to learn some material is in a more changeable state.

From the subgoal scores and other knowledge, such as curricular sequencing and prerequisite relationships, it is possible to define a set of subgoals that are most unstable. These are the subgoals that may require more frequent measurement in order for instruction to be steered well. As discussed earlier, they represent the front along which instruction is progressing through the curriculum goal structure. The task of a test item generator, then, is to generate a test item that will be especially informative about this front. MHO does this by posting a set of constraints for the test problem. In the student model in Table 11.1, the Series, Kirchhoff's Law, and Current subgoals are at this front. Each constraint helps adapt the steering feedback to the student's current state. To see how this is done, we need to consider MHO's architecture and the subject matter that it teaches and tests.

Architecture

At this time, MHO teaches and tests several levels of DC circuits. It poses problems such as that shown in Fig. 11.4. We call its architecture the *Bite-Size Architecture.* It is an object-oriented architecture for intelligent tutoring systems.[3] An object is a semiautonomous piece of computer program that can be called upon to achieve particular goals. It includes both data structures and procedural capabilities. Object-oriented programming involves designing sets of objects that can efficiently interact to solve problems. Each curriculum subgoal (and also each metacurricular planning issue and each problem format) is represented by an object called a "bite." Within the computer program, a bite contains a record of the student's performance on a subgoal and the knowledge needed to post a constraint for that subgoal.

Voltage, for example, is represented by a bite in MHO. That bite has

---

[3]See Bonar, Cunningham, and Schultz, 1986, for a description of "An Object-Oriented Architecture for Intelligent Tutoring Systems." MHO is implemented in Loops, Xerox's proprietary object-oriented specialization of the standard artificial intelligence language Lisp. The graphics and student interface are handled via an interface package called *Chips. Chips* is a program developed at the Learning Research and Development Center, primarily by John D. Corbett and Robert E. Cunningham, with some contribution by Andrew D. Bowen. The *Chips* tools allow circuit displays to be designed so the student can click the mouse (a pointing device that causes a marker to move on the screen as the device is moved on a table top; it often contains buttons as well, so that the computer user can point to an object on the screen by moving the marker over that object and then pressing a button) on any of the components and thereby cause a menu of query options to appear. Each object can behave differently: when a student clicks on a meter, a question is asked; when he clicks on a resistor, a special menu of options is presented.

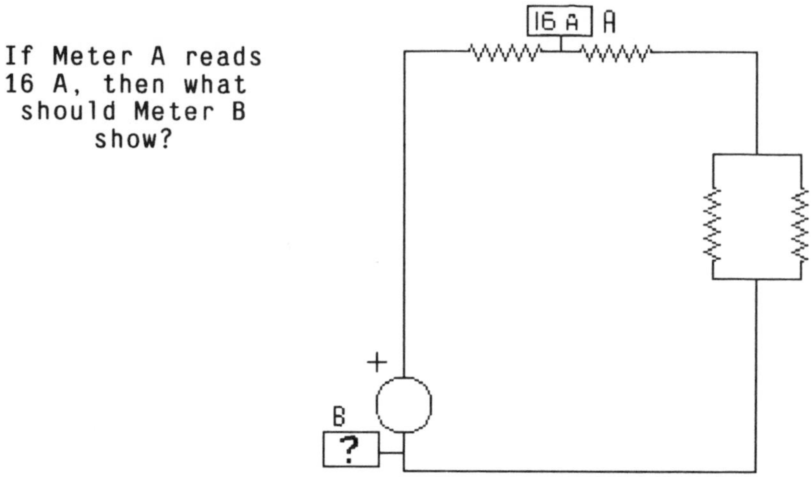

If Meter A reads
16 A, then what
should Meter B
show?

FIG. 11.4.   Example Problem from MHO Test Generator.

rules for teaching about voltage. It contains information pertinent to developing an understanding of what voltage represents, including the constraints it should post to create relevant problems. Also, it can update the student model by noting how the student does on problems relevant to its subgoal. One byproduct of this architecture and the curricular model on which it is based is that a tutoring program's knowledge is modular and can easily be expanded by adding additional curricular objects along with their pointers to the other knowledge components (which may involve additions to those components as well). For example, MHO's designers are now expanding it to include curricular goals involving simple alternating current circuits.

Problem Generation

MHO poses problems by presenting a circuit diagram and asking a question about it. The machinery used in problem generation chooses most of the circuit components randomly, but it is constrained by both general and specific curricular subgoals (bites) that the student has not yet mastered. Some of the choices represented by these constraints are the following:

1. A problem can be posed in qualitative, quantitative, or relative form.
2. The problem can vary in the complexity of the arithmetic it requires

and the complexity of the circuit diagram to which it refers. This is determined by a global assessment of how much of the curriculum the student has mastered.

3. The problem can require knowledge of Ohm's Law or either of Kirchhoff's Laws.

4. The problem can focus on voltage, current, or resistance.

5. The problem can focus on series or parallel circuit topologies. (MHO also worries about where the meters are placed in circuit diagrams, because students have particular difficulty handling some placements, but we ignore that matter to make presentation of the basic approach more straightforward.)

The product of constraint posting is stored as a list structure (see Footnote 3) to be used as the basis for problem generation and problem solving. This list structure contains information that specifies how to create a circuit and a problem based on that circuit, what the circuit should look like, and what electronic concepts are relevant. An example of such a list, derived from the student model shown in Table 11.1, is:

$$((((Rel\ Simple)\ (\$\ Kirchhoff))\ (\$\ I{=}Series))\ (UninterruptedS))$$
$$Series). \qquad [1]$$

This list represents the constraints that have been posted in sweeping the model shown in Table 11.1 and is the starting point for automatic generation of a problem. *Rel* stands for a relative problem that will pose a simple question asking if two areas of the circuit have the same measurement (in this case, current). *Simple* specifies the student's level of general understanding and will cause the circuit to be very simple in structure. *Kirchhoff* is the law this problem centers around. *I = Series* is a specialization of Kirchhoff's Law, that current is equal at all points in a series array. *UninterruptedS* informs the problem generator that one meter should appear next to another, with no other components between them (this is the simplest form for a problem looking at Kirchhoff's Law). Constrained by this information, the problem generator can develop many different circuits and pose many different problems about them, so it is quite plausible to do as much steering testing as any student requires and also to give students sets of appropriate problems as homework.

At the next, more elaborated, level of representation, the circuit is designated as a network of resistors, a combination of series and parallel subnets with a power source. A more detailed list breaks this circuit into four nodes, each representing a side of a rectangular circuit. The nodes are created separately and then put together to make up a circuit. One at a time, the nodes are passed into a recursive function called **MakeCircuit-String** to be elaborated further. **MakeCircuitString** makes decisions about how many resistors are placed on a node and whether these resistors should appear in a parallel or series net. These decisions are based on the information from the first list.

Simple instructs **MakeCircuitString** to limit the number of resistors that appear and to otherwise make the circuit conform to the specifications of a simple circuit. The *Simple* specifications keep the components that will be drawn to a minimum. *Simple* also informs **MakeCircuitString** that, depending on what net we are working with, all nodes should be of this kind. $I = Series$ specifies the net to be used: All sides are series arrays. If this were a *Difficult* problem, some sides might have parallel subnets and other series. An example of a simple circuit, [1], that has passed through **MakeCircuit-String** is

$$((VoltageSource)\ (Series\ (Resistor)\ (Resistor))\ (Parallel\ (Resistor)\ (Resistor))\ (Wire)).\qquad [2]$$

Figure 11.5 shows the circuit designated by [2].

The final specifications development step is determining what problem should be posed about the circuit, where meters should be placed, and what question should be asked about them. This step requires some information from the first list, [1]. $I = Series$ reveals whether current or voltage is the target concept; *UninterruptedS* holds information pertaining to how many problems and where problems should appear. Several recursive func-

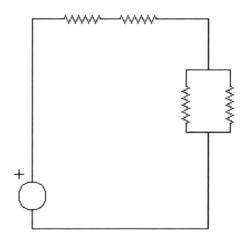

FIG. 11.5.   Circuit described by Eq. 2.

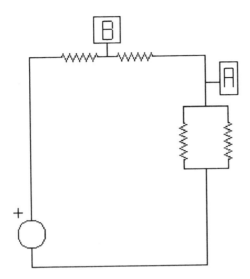

FIG. 11.6.   Circuit described by Eq. 3.

tions tear apart the second list and insert problem information (mainly meters) where it is best suited. Using the present example and placing several meters into the list, one example of the next stage is

((Problem Rel current after on (VoltageSource)) (Series (Resistor)
(Problem Rel current before off (Resistor)) (Parallel (Problem
Rel current after on (Resistor) (Resistor)) (Wire)).   [3]

This list is then passed to an intelligent problem developer, which composes and draws the circuit. Figure 11.6 shows a display corresponding to [3]. The question posed to the student will end up being, *"Is the current at Meter A higher, lower, or the same as the current at Meter B?"*

The Simulator assigns values to the components, for example, resistance and voltage, and then finds the dependent values, like current, voltage drops over resistors, and so forth. It can, for simple problems, ensure that all the values for current and voltage will be integral, and also determine whether resistors and voltage sources should be displayed. If the circuit were more complex, an iterative propagation would occur next. Resistance for a subnet of a complex circuit, for example, would be calculated by asking each subnet component its resistance and then adding the resistances. Parallel structures are handled recursively as well, using the appropriate formulae.

THE SOFTNESS OF STUDENT CLASSIFICATIONS

We conclude by reconsidering more broadly the issue of diagnostic assessment of cognitive skills to steer instruction. Fundamentally, cognitive skill, like physical skill, often requires substantial practice of its basic components in the contexts in which they are applied. Actions can be learned without learning the exact conditions for which they are appropriate. Newly learned, and consequently weak, knowledge can fail to be used because stronger but incorrect knowledge is overgeneralized from related situations. The processing capacity demands of one subskill may be so great as to make impossible the execution of another newly formed subskill. Thus, for most of the course of learning, the following fundamental principle is true: *One cannot be sure a subskill has not been learned just because it was not demonstrated on an occasion where it should have been.*

On the other hand, cognitive skill, like physical skill, is partly redundant. Weak methods can sometimes make up for a lack of appropriate domain knowledge. Sometimes a problem that, in theory, should require a particular subskill can be solved correctly by accident. The correct action may be taken with incorrect knowledge of the conditions in which it is appropriate, or an incorrect action may work once only. Thus, we note a second fundamental principle: *One cannot be sure a subskill is completely learned just because it has been demonstrated.*

These two principles suggest that the steering approach to diagnostic testing, in which local microtesting is embedded in the curriculum to steer instruction, is a more valid approach than the broader diagnostic testing that has become part of many current monitoring programs in our schools. By asking broad, generic questions (e.g., "What can I diagnose knowing nothing about the student in advance and giving only a general test?") we can get only broad, generic answers. That is, we can know how well, in general, learning is proceeding, but we can't steer specific children's education with such broad indicators, any more than we could steer a ship if all we had was an hourly account of how close to the correct path we were.

Empirical experience and cognitive theory indicate that cognitive performance is unreliable unless substantial practice has occurred, and that success can come for multiple reasons. These factors have to be taken into account in diagnosis. Ironically, perhaps, the less statistically reliable steering-testing approach provides better steering capability than the highly refined approaches used in current psychometric diagnostic efforts. Continuously knowing approximately where you are affords better steering capability than occasionally knowing how well you are steering in general.

The field of testing has become remarkably efficient at making precise estimates from inherently unreliable data. Approaches such as item-response theory and adaptive testing have helped sharpen the broad and vague measures that tests provide. Further progress, especially progress in steering testing (as opposed to certification and selection testing), will depend on better use of information we already have, or can readily obtain, about the cognitive requirements of the performances and student competences relative to those performances that interest us. Like the physician, we will, in steering the course of a child's education, be better guided by sketchy data tied to specific theoretical analysis than by precise, but general, indicators.

Our approach can be seen as an outgrowth of the steering forms used in the curricula that grew from work on individualized instruction (Glaser, 1977). However, the technology of the time did not permit more than a short, uniform mastery test after each lesson. This allowed adequate teaching of the higher aptitude student, but did not handle the remediation problem. That is, it suffered from having to treat each curricular goal and its corresponding student capability as separable from every other, and it could not handle the problem of core learning without fringe transfer. There was much discussion during that period about having remediation that was more than repetition of practice. The present approach to steering testing permits adaptation that is grounded in cognitive analysis of the instructional domain. It moves toward the goal for educational research established when criterion referenced testing and individually prescribed instruction made clear the possibility of reliable, systematic approaches to serving the full range of students in our schools.

ACKNOWLEDGMENTS

This research was supported by a contract from the Office of Naval Research, Personnel and Training Branch, for which the first author is Principal Investigator. The methodology derives from work done under a subcontract from Universal Energy Systems, Inc., for the Air Force Human Resources Laboratory. The contents of this chapter have not been reviewed by either organization and no endorsement by them should be inferred. Arlene Weiner, Ronald Hambleton, and Lauren Resnick provided many helpful comments on an earlier draft.

REFERENCES

Anderson, J. R. (1983). *The architecture of cognition*. Cambridge, MA: Harvard University Press.
Bonar, J. G., Cunningham, R., & Schultz, J. (1986). An object-oriented architecture for

intelligent tutoring systems. In N. Meyrowitz (Ed.), *OOPSLA '86: Object-oriented programming, systems, languages and applications. Conference Proceedings* (pp. 269–276). New York: The Association for Computing Machinery.

Chall, J. (1967). *Learning to read: The great debate.* New York: McGraw-Hill.

Corno, L., & Snow, R. E. (1986). Adapting teaching to individual differences among learners. In M. C. Wittrock (Ed.), *Handbook of research on teaching, Third Edition.* New York: Macmillan.

Gagné, R. M. (1965). *The conditions of learning.* New York: Holt, Rinehart and Winston.

Glaser, R. (1963). Instructional technology and the measurement of learning outcomes. *American Psychologist, 18,* 510–522.

Glaser, R. (1977). *Adaptive education: Individual diversity and learning.* New York: Holt, Rinehart and Winston.

Hambleton, R. K. (1984). Criterion-referenced measurement. In T. Husen & T. N. Postlethwaite (Eds.), *International encyclopedia of education,* (pp. 1108–1113). New York: Pergamon Press.

Lesgold, A. M. (in press). Toward a theory of curriculum for use in designing intelligent instructional systems. In H. Mandl & A. Lesgold (Eds.), *Learning issues for intelligent tutoring systems.* New York: Springer-Verlag.

Lesgold, A. M., Lajoie, S. P., Eastman, R., Eggan, G., Gitomer, D., Glaser, R., Greenberg, L., Logan, D., Magone, M., Weiner, A., Wolf, R., & Yengo, L. (April, 1986). *Cognitive task analysis to enhance technical skills training and assessment.* Technical report. Learning Research and Development Center, University of Pittsburgh, Pittsburgh, PA.

Lord, F. M. (1980). *Applications of item response theory to practical testing problems.* Hillsdale, NJ: Lawrence Erlbaum Associates.

Merrill, M. D., & Tennyson, R. D. (1977). *Teaching concepts: An instructional design guide.* Englewood Cliffs, NJ: Educational Technology Publications.

Spineti, J. P., & Hambleton, R. K. (1977). A computer simulation study of tailored testing strategies for objective-based instructional programs. *Educational and Psychological Measurement, 37,* 139–158.

Stefik, M. J. (1980). Planning with constraints. *Artificial Intelligence, 16,* 111–139.

12

Intentional Learning As A Goal of Instruction

Carl Bereiter
Marlene Scardamalia
Ontario Institute for Studies in Education

Contemporary cognitive psychology has only recently begun to make contact with an important set of everyday intuitions about learning. These intuitions have to do with the role of intentions, plans, and mental effort in learning. It is not that intentions, plans, and mental effort have been ignored in accounts of cognitive behavior—quite the contrary (see, for instance, Dennett, 1983, on intentions; Sacerdoti, 1977, on plans; Kahneman, 1973, on mental effort). But we have yet to do justice to what folk psychology treats as their role in learning itself.

Informal educational talk is full of idioms that are applied to learning and intentions. Teachers will voice the opinion that one student is not trying hard enough, that another may be trying too hard, and that a third is "working up to capacity." The extent to which such notions are internalized by students is suggested by the fact that even among severely learning-disabled students a substantial number attribute their problems to insufficient effort (Schneider, 1984). Yet, such references to effort are ambiguous. It is not clear whether *trying* refers to overt matters such as doing homework and getting assignments in on time or whether it refers to internal, specifically mental efforts. One of the weaknesses in everyday psychologizing is a tendency to leave the concept of effort dangling, without indicating what the effort is applied to. A less ambiguous but more deeply puzzling reference to intentionality and learning is suggested by the expression, "a *serious* student." Here, something is implied beyond efforts involved in getting good grades. The word *serious* seems to refer to a special relationship between the student and the subject matter. But what kind of relationship is it? Suffice it to say, at this point, that the relationship does not seem to be adequately represented by available scientific terms. Finally, we may note the somewhat overused term, *lifelong learner*. As the term is used by educators, it refers to more than the obvious fact that people continue to learn throughout their lives. It seems to refer to someone who has a lifelong *commitment* to learning, that is, someone whose top-level goals, the goals that govern major life plans, include learning goals. Thus, the lifelong learner appears to have more than a lively curiosity and a willingness to study, more even than a serious involvement in some subject matter. The lifelong learner treats learning itself as a valued part of life and structures other activities in life so that they will serve learning.

Clearly, folk notions about intentions, plans, and effort in learning touch on some of the very deepest concerns of the educational enterprise. In instructional research, however, these deeper concerns have tended to fall into the gap between two divergent research traditions. One tradition has been concerned with *opportunities* for students to exercise their intentions in learning. Its focus has been the learning situation, especially the relative amounts of external direction versus self-direction. Representative research has been concerned with evaluations of open education (Giaconia & Hedges, 1982), with classroom management styles (Doyle, 1985), and with self-direction in programmed learning (Steinberg, 1977). Such research has tended to focus on external manifestations or avowals of student effort and therefore has not contributed to an understanding of what, internally, might distinguish the serious student from the less serious one or the student who is trying to learn from the student who is not. A more far-reaching limitation of such research is that, in focusing on observable behavior, it has tended to foster the impression that students are intentionally involved in learning only when they are visibly engaged in independent learning activities. Yet it is obvious on introspection that this cannot be the case. We know that we can be actively pursuing learning goals while listening to a lecture or doing assigned problems, just as surely as we can engage in the same overt behavior without any active effort at learning. Indeed, as a first approximation, we might characterize the serious student as one who maintains pursuit of learning goals under external conditions that can be satisfied without doing so.

The contrasting research tradition has examined what students do to advance their learning, often in cases where remedial supports are required. We refer to research on study skills, as summarized for instance in Anderson (1979). Although research in this tradition yields results of both theoretical and practical interest, its remedial emphasis has meant that it has tended to concentrate on learning goals of a circumscribed nature. The goals that might be associated with being a serious student, a lifelong learner, or a liberally educated person are thus little accounted for in the study skills literature.

In recent years, however, a cognitive science approach has begun to penetrate both of these research traditions, with the resulting promise of closing the gap between them (see, e.g., the collection of papers in Chipman, Segal, & Glaser, 1985, and in Segal, Chipman, & Glaser, 1985). Research on classroom conditions has begun to pay attention to what is going on in students' minds and to the procedural knowledge that they bring to classroom processes (Doyle, 1983; Winne & Marx, 1982). At the same time, research on learning and study skills has begun to attend to higher order learning objectives—for instance, to what is involved in achieving an organized knowledge of a domain as contrasted with achieving the knowledge required to pass a test on a particular unit of text (e.g., Chi, 1985).

We use the term *intentional learning* to refer to cognitive processes that have learning as a goal rather than an incidental outcome.[1] All experience, we assume, can have learning as an incidental outcome, but only some cognitive activity is carried out according to procedures that contain learning goals. Whether intentional learning occurs is likely to depend on both situational and intrinsic factors—on what the situation affords in goal-attainment opportunities and on what the student's mental resources are for attaining those goals. Thus, focusing on intentional learning provides a natural way of coordinating the two relevant research traditions—the tradition dealing with learning situations and the tradition dealing with learning skills. As a step toward such coordination, this chapter looks at learning situations and at children's beliefs about learning from the standpoint of how they support or deter intentional learning.

---

[1]Thomas and Rohwer (1986) propose the term *autonomous learning* with much the same meaning. We prefer *intentional learning,* however, because *autonomous* unfortunately suggests freedom from external direction. We think it is important to be clear (and in their discussion of the topic Thomas and Rohwer are clear) that the kind of learning we are talking about can occur, and indeed should occur, in both self-directed and teacher-directed learning situations.

LEARNING AS PROBLEM SOLVING

In the study of cognitive processes it has often proved productive to see activities as forms of problem solving, even activities that are not normally thought of in that way. This has been done with processes as diverse as writing (Hayes & Flower, 1980), reading (Olshavsky, 1976–1977), scientific theory building (Laudan, 1977), and syllogistic reasoning (Newell, 1980). Newell (1980), in fact, has argued that all symbolic activity can profitably be treated as operation within a problem space. Accordingly, there is some a priori justification for treating learning itself as a form of problem solving.

An initial formulation of this approach to learning was offered by Resnick and Glaser (1976) as part of an effort to develop an information-processing conception of intelligence. They defined intelligence as the ability to learn under problematic conditions—that is, under conditions of indirect or incomplete instruction. Learning under such conditions they saw as requiring invention, and invention in turn they interpreted as a variety of problem solving. Leinhardt (1986) has since shown how much problem solving may be involved even in what by ordinary standards would be judged to be very direct and complete instruction. In trying to elaborate a conception of intentional learning, however, it is important to recognize that learning varies in the kind and difficulty of problems it presents to the learner. Much learning in daily life is incidental to other activities and goes on without awareness or intent to learn (consider, for instance, the learning that takes place while watching a movie that has an exotic setting). Also, some kinds of learning can be achieved by well-practiced routines. This might be the case, for instance, when an experienced computer user learns to use a well-documented new software package (whereas poorly documented software might require problem-solving effort in addition to routine learning procedures). Another example of relatively nonproblematic learning would be the improvement in skill that comes through practice; problem solving may well be involved only in the initial stage of skill learning, when declarative knowledge is being converted into procedures (Anderson, 1982).

Another important distinction is more difficult to pin down: learning *through* problem solving as opposed to learning *as* problem solving. Problem solving always implies the lack of a known route to the goal, which necessitates some search through a space of possibilities.

In learning *through* problem solving, learning results from operations applied to knowledge states, in search of a state that satisfies or constitutes an advance toward the goal state. This was the kind of learning examined by Resnick and Glaser (1976) and pursued farther by Pellegrino and Glaser (1982). The latter endeavored to show how both knowledge of a domain and general problem-solving strategies may be acquired through solving domain-relevant problems. Pellegrino and Glaser (1982) stated: "Learning skill ensues as the content and concepts of a knowledge domain are attained in learning situations that constrain this knowledge to serve certain purposes and goals. The goals are defined by uses of this knowledge in procedural schemes such as those required in analogical reasoning and inductive inference" (p. 341).

Learning *as* problem solving, on the other hand, implies that the goal itself is a learning goal and that there is something problematic about achieving this goal. The contrast to learning through problem solving is illustrated in instructional research reported by Resnick and Neches (1984), where both kinds of learning are noted. The instructional tasks required children to devise operations with blocks that correspond to symbolic operations in arithmetic (e.g., carrying and borrowing) or, conversely, to show symbolic operations corresponding to operations with the blocks. These activities represent an effort to promote learning *through* problem solving that is common at all levels of mathematics instruction; it is expected that through solving assigned problems students will discover or acquire a deeper understanding of mathematical concepts. As Owen and Sweller (1985) have shown, however, solving problems that embody certain mathematical concepts does not necessarily lead to learning those concepts. Resnick and Neches (1984) noted this as well but observed that certain children do "make great advances in understanding through such instruction and come to construct elegant explanations of why the written arithmetic procedures work as they do" (p. 288). Such children, they say, were "*trying* to learn," which is to say that, over and above efforts to accomplish the assigned tasks, they were actively trying to construct mathematical knowledge that would make sense of what they were doing. Resnick and Neches (1984) stated:

> When one learns, one is always putting in extra current effort in the interest of later improvements in power or efficiency. This includes the extra work of keeping track of one's own procedural actions so as to be able to reflect on and modify them, or of storing representations of recurring events and patterns in the environment that may eventually become the basis for formulating a rule or applying a strategy transformation. It would seem reasonable to posit differences in the extent to which individuals are likely to engage in this kind of work. (p. 318)

As we interpret it, the children who were "*trying* to learn" were not simply investing extra effort in trying to solve the problems they were presented. Instead, they were dividing their effort between solving those problems and solving other, unassigned problems, which were problems having to do with the state of their own understanding of the phenomena. These latter were learning problems. The learning that resulted was not an incidental consequence of solving mathematics problems but rather a goal to which the children's problem-solving efforts were directed.

As Resnick and Neches cautioned us, the protocol data are not yet sufficient to support strong assertions about what was actually going on in the minds of children working on these mathematical tasks. At present, the observations serve purposes of a conceptual clarification that distinguishes trying to learn from, for instance, trying to earn a good grade in school. The distinction is frequently expressed as between intrinsic and extrinsic motivation. But that distinction is too crude to be of much service in studying the intentional aspects of learning. In the distinction we are trying to draw between learning through problem solving and learning as problem solving, both kinds of learning may be intrinsically motivated. In the first case the learner may be motivated out of intellectual curiosity to solve a mathematical problem, but this is distinct from and may exist independently of motivation to learn the mathematical principles underlying the problem solution. In the latter, what Resnick and Neches referred to as the "extra current effort" is dedicated to more long-term goals of competence and understanding, which we label *intentional learning*. This conception of intentional learning seems to bring us closer to what is connoted by the expressions "serious student" and "lifelong learner."

LEARNING SKILLS, METAKNOWLEDGE, AND THE INSTRUCTIONAL SITUATION

Most of the applied research relevant to intentional learning is found catalogued under the heading of *learning* or *study skills*. A large collection of recent work appears in volumes edited by Chipman et al. (1985) and Segal et al. (1985). An interpretive review of research on the development of learning skills in children and adolescents is given in Brown, Bransford, Ferrara, and Campione (1983). This research has dealt mainly with self-regulatory or self-management procedures that make up the strategic repertoire of the intentional learner—rehearsal and review, monitoring and checking, unpacking implicit implications, relating new information to old, summarizing, considering alternatives, and the like. Because this aspect of intentional learning has been so thoroughly dealt with elsewhere, we bypass it here, pausing only to note two conclusions that have general implications for work on intentional learning.

First, it is clear that intentional learning is an achievement, not an automatic consequence of human intelligence. This is shown by developmental trends in every aspect of learning skill and by the effects of training students in learning strategies. Although evidence is presently scanty about the durability and generalizability of such training, the immediate effects are sufficient to show that there are a variety of strategies for achieving learning that many students do not normally apply. In fact, the very existence of the study skills training enterprise, which is typically aimed at helping college students, testifies to the fact that many students reach young adulthood with inadequately developed strategies for managing their own cognitive behavior in learning (see also Anderson, 1980; Brown & Day, 1983).

Second, there is some indication that students learn to cope with school tasks by means of strategies that actually have the effect of subverting learning (Bereiter & Scardamalia, 1985; Brown & Day, 1983; Scardamalia & Bereiter, 1984). These strategies meet the short-term goals of school activities (producing a summary, completing a writing assignment, preparing to answer comprehension questions) but fail to address long-term goals (learning to integrate information in reading and writing or to build knowledge of long-term value). A representative strategy, the copy-delete strategy (Brown, Day, & Jones, 1983), consists of processing a text one statement at a time and retaining or by-passing each fact according to its independently judged importance. Such a strategy economizes on mental effort and is reasonably effective in sorting out information likely to be required for later school activities, but it lacks the sorts of more effortful moves that skilled readers make in abstracting the main ideas from a text (cf. Johnston & Afflerbach, 1985).

Two further aspects of intentional learning that have received rather less attention than learning skills are treated in this chapter, students' conceptions or theories of learning and knowledge and the instructional situation, insofar as it relates to students' efforts to learn.

To the extent that students take an active role in learning, their own theories of what knowledge consists of and how it is acquired can be expected to matter. To take a simple example, even though the teacher may conceive of learning as consisting of much more than the memorization of facts, the student might nevertheless conceive of it that way, and this can be expected to have an influence on learning (Marton & Säljö, 1976). If, furthermore, the teacher handles classroom activities and testing so that memorizing facts turns out to be a successful way of getting along, this can be expected to further influence how students learn. Thus, the interaction between situational factors and student theories merits investigation. The conventional view is that free-learning environments encourage intentional learning, whereas teacher-prescribed activities discourage it, but this is surely an oversimplification. In any classroom situation there are goals of the students (which may or may not include learning goals), goals of the teacher regarding the students (which also may or may not include learning goals), and situational constraints (which may favor or disfavor any of these goals). To design effective environments we must understand how these three factors interact. We turn to this issue now. In the final section of the chapter we sketch a model of interactive instructional processes and make an effort to diagnose the major block to fostering intentional learning in schools.

CHILDREN'S IMPLICIT THEORIES OF KNOWLEDGE AND LEARNING

The effect of students' own conceptions of educational processes has begun to receive attention at all levels from preschool (Pramling, 1985) to university (van Rossum & Schenk, 1984). According to Pramling's interview findings, knowledge is largely "invisible" to the preschooler. Even with considerable probing, few children below the age of eight could identify any knowledge they had learned. They saw learning as an outcome of the teachers' actions but not of their own actions in the classroom. Among older students a major split seems to develop between those who see learning primarily as memorization and those who see learning as having its basis in understanding. Reported learning strategies reflect this split: Low-achieving students report the same use of memorization strategies as high-achieving ones, but high-achieving students report the use of comprehension strategies in addition (Biggs, 1979, 1984).

In the following discussion we look in more detail at children's conceptions of the nature of knowledge and learning as revealed in three recent studies in which we collected interview, observational, and thinking-aloud protocol data. Rather than summarize findings from each study in turn, we briefly describe them and then discuss several emerging themes, drawing data and examples from whichever studies were pertinent.

1. Free-Learning Study.   Two sixth-grade[2] classes were informed that they would have an hour a day on two successive days to learn anything they wished, and that they were responsible for planning the learning and obtaining materials. They were interviewed beforehand about their learning goals and plans and were observed and questioned during the two free-learning periods. The interest here was to see how children would go about planning and pursuing learning goals, given hardly any constraints or guidance.

---

[2]These and other classes referred to as sixth grade were actually split grade classes containing some fifth graders as well.

2. Long-Term Learning Goals Interview. The free learning study allowed the possibility of students' relating immediate activities to long-term cognitive goals but did nothing to elicit such behavior. (We could not find any previous research that even suggested whether students could think in terms of long-term cognitive goals.) Thus, in our second study, students in one third-grade and one sixth-grade class were questioned about their long-term goals in life and about what they could do in a free-learning hour a day to advance toward their long-term goals. They were also asked more directly how they would use a free hour a week to learn anything they wished. These questions were also posed to six adults possessing graduate degrees, to provide a kind of expert–novice comparison in the formulation of learning goals and plans.

3. New Learning Study. This was the first phase of a longitudinal study concerned with children's changing perceptions of what they know, do not know, and have just learned about a topic. Students in Grades 1, 3, and 6 were read informative texts. After each segment of approximately 25 words, the experimenter stopped and asked them to report what they were thinking. Prior to the reading, half the students were questioned on what they knew about the topic (which was either germs or dinosaurs). The other half were questioned about what they did not know. After the reading, the students were tested on both free and cued recall of the text, were asked to summarize it in a sentence, and to report anything new they had learned from it.

LEARNING AS PROBLEM SOLVING VERSUS LEARNING AS AN ACTIVITY

In expert–novice comparisons, it is common to find novices applying means–end analysis and other problem-solving strategies, whereas experts retrieve already-learned scripts or schemata that permit them to handle the tasks in a more routine manner (Glaser, 1984). It would not be surprising if learning itself showed this effect. There are, after all, various routines of study, analysis, rehearsal, checking, and the like that are applicable to a variety of learning tasks and that more experienced learners should have more readily at their command.

An analysis of protocols from our long-term learning goals interview suggested, however, that it was the adults who more frequently took a problem-solving approach to learning. Raters coded all the interview statements dealing with how people would make use of an hour a week that they could devote to learning anything they liked. Statements were first sorted into categories according to what aspect of learning they referred to, and then they were rated on a 5-point scale that represented, for the category chosen, a continuum running from a low to a high degree of problem-solving orientation. Age differences appeared only minimally in the categories used, but differences were highly significant in ratings on problem-solving orientation. The mean rating for third graders on the 5-point scale was 1.44; for sixth graders, 1.85; and for adults, 4.03.

Data for the three most frequently used categories of statements are summarized in Fig. 12.1. In the category labeled *Purpose,* statements were rated on a continuum having endpoints defined as "learning organized around topics and activities" (low end, level 1) and "learning organized around goals" (high end, level 5). For adults, most of the statements of purpose specified learning goals as some state of knowledge or skill that they hoped to attain: One wanted to study yoga "to learn how to relax," another to study Cantonese to understand the linguistic structures that might be causing difficulties for his Chinese students. Children, on the other hand, generally indicated only a topic or activity, without an objective. Among the third graders, about half only indicated a school subject, such as math or spelling, others identified a topic, such as an animal, or a skill, such as a sport, that they wanted to work on. Children in Grade 6 more frequently chose specific topics or skills of personal interest and identified subtopics, components, or stages to focus on. Thus, they had

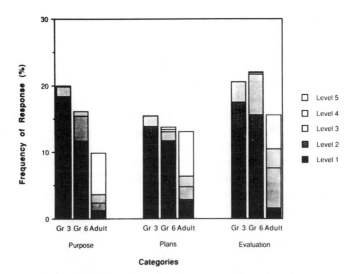

FIG. 12.1. Distribution of learning interview statements of children and adults in three categories, scaled according to level of problem-solving orientation. Other less frequently used statement categories are not shown but reflect the same distribution of levels of problem-solving orientation.

more articulated purposes, although they still did not specify goals that could serve as endpoints for their problem-solving efforts.

In the category labeled *Plans,* the endpoints of the continuum were "use of routine procedures (practice, rehearsal, etc.)" (low end) and "Means to an end arrived at through problem solving" (high end). Even third graders showed a familiarity with all the common ways of achieving learning, and they chose means appropriate to their purposes. Thus, if the purpose was to learn about some topic, they would mention reading, taking notes, rehearsing, and the like, whereas if the purpose was to learn a skill, they would mention practice. Children in Grade 6 showed awareness of a greater variety of learning activities and were more tentative about which procedures they would use as learning proceeded. Adults also referred frequently to familiar procedures, but in addition they would cite means–end plans aimed at achieving some particular subgoal: For instance, an adult planning to study weaving proposed that she might get different kinds of wool and experiment to see how different textures could be achieved.

In the Evaluation category, the continuum ranged from "backward-looking evaluation" (low end) to "forward-looking evaluation" (high end). The distinction here was between evaluation carried out merely to see what one had accomplished and evaluation carried out to make decisions about future action, the latter taken to be an aspect of means–end operations in problem solving. Again, children showed awareness of the typical means and generally chose methods of evaluation that were appropriate to the kind of knowledge being acquired—for instance, checking against an authoritative source in the case of declarative knowledge, testing against a practical criterion in the case of procedural knowledge. Almost completely absent from the children's protocols, however, although common in the adults' protocols, was any intention to use feedback to influence goals or plans.

It is not difficult to think of explanations for these age differences. One obvious advantage the adults had in elaborating goals and plans was that they already knew more about what they intended to learn, and, where they lacked direct knowledge, they could make use of analogies. For instance, the person who planned to take up weaving already knew how to knit, and she used this knowledge to infer appropriate subgoals, to anticipate problems, and generally to get a sense of what learning to weave would be like. In their naivete, children often showed limited awareness of what needed to be learned, and by the same token, unrealistic expectations about how rapidly they would learn it. What was more telling about children's implicit theories of learning was their showing hardly any awareness of a need to find out what needed to be learned.

These findings add up to the view that children see learning as an *activity,* whereas sophisticated adults see it as a *goal.* Children see the activity as taking various forms, and, through their school experiences, they have become familiar with many of these forms and know how to choose them appropriately. Learning itself, however, is not something they conceive as an intentional pursuit; they see it as a natural consequence of carrying out appropriate learning activities. This belief is correct, of course, as far as it goes, and it was also seen reflected in the adult interviews. It is probably also safe to surmise that many teachers regard school learning as a natural result of learning activities and, thus, do not treat it as problematic (cf. Bromme, 1980).

In regarding learning as a goal, the adults in our study may be said to have treated learning as inherently problematic. This does not mean they saw it as fraught with difficulties; some anticipated very little difficulty in achieving their learning goals. But, by treating learning as inherently problematic, they approached it within a problem-solving framework. Within this framework, learning is seen as converting one's present state of knowledge into some desired future state, and progress consists of attaining various intermediate states. Learning may, in fact, turn out to be nonproblematic, attainable by engaging in well-practiced routines. But if blocks or diversions do occur, one is able to bring problem-solving resources to bear. Also, by approaching learning within a problem-solving framework, the learner is in a position to elaborate and revise goals, to make practical decisions about the allocation of time and resources to various subgoals, and generally to pursue a more planful course. Intentional learning, viewed from this perspective, is learning carried out within a problem-solving framework.

Theory Versus Practice in Children's Learning

Findings from the three studies reported thus far were all based on people's speculative statements about how they would go about a learning project. In the free learning study, after the interviews, the Grade 6 children actually planned and devoted two class periods to carrying out independent learning. To facilitate comparison, the same coding and rating scheme that was used in the interview study was applied to children's planning statements and to observations made during the two class periods of independent learning. Each child was checked four or five times during these sessions by an experimenter who asked what the child was doing and why.

Statements the children made while planning their learning projects were almost identical in distribution to those made during the long-term learning goals interview, which suggests that the hypothetical nature of the learning task in that interview did not unduly distort the findings. We may therefore properly ask whether the children's activities during their free-learning periods reflected a more or a less sophisticated approach to learning than was revealed in their interviews.

Overall, there was no significant difference between the interview data and observational data, when individual statements or observations were scored on the 5-point scales indicating amount of problem orientation. The mean score for interviews was 1.88 and the mean for observations was 2.03. One interesting shift appeared, however. In the interview data it was noted that most children simply named global topics or skills as learning goals, but that some of the children in Grade 6 identified subtopics or components, thus providing a basis for a more planful approach to learning. This tendency was stronger still in practice. Whereas 59% of the relevant interview statements were rated at the lowest level, indicating learning organized around simple topics and activities, only 35% of the relevant process observations were so rated. Thus, it seemed that children's approach to learning was somewhat more complex in practice than in their prospective accounts, but there was still no indication of an approach to learning generally more problem-oriented than had been revealed in the interviews.

Implicit Theories of Knowledge

Having a learning goal presupposes that one can prefigure a state of knowledge that one does not currently possess. Thus, one's knowledge about different kinds of knowledge is relevant to intentional learning, determining the kinds of learning goals that one can envision. There is a body of interview data indicating that many students conceive of knowledge as consisting solely of memorized facts (van Rossum & Schenk, 1984). On the basis of our recent findings, however, we need to modify this conclusion in at least one important respect. The children we interviewed made a clear tacit distinction between declarative and procedural knowledge (or what are more familiarly referred to as "knowing that" and "knowing how"). This was shown by their selection of learning activities. It would have been strange if children did not make this distinction, but if we are to try to characterize their knowledge about knowledge, it is well to note at the outset that their implicit understanding encompasses a distinction that many philosophers as well as cognitive scientists treat as fundamental (Anderson, 1983; Ryle, 1949).

The question remains, however, whether students see declarative knowledge as consisting of anything more than memorizable discrete facts. The new learning study provides some clues from the initial round of data collection—more definite information will unfold in longitudinal data on children's awareness of changes in their knowledge. Different kinds of verbal reports give different kinds of indications about children's conceptions of knowledge. When children were asked what they already knew or what they had just learned about germs or dinosaurs, they almost invariably listed discrete facts. But when they were commenting freely on text statements or when they were reporting on what they did not know about a topic, indications began to appear of more sophisticated intuitions. We simply note and give examples of some of these intuitions here, because we are not yet in a position to comment on their prevalence or developmental course.

Schema-Based Notions of Knowledge.   One kind of abstract characterization of knowledge that seemed available to all children reflects high-level schemata or scripts. With reference to an animal, for instance, children might say they want to learn what it eats, where it lives, or what size it is. In other words, they can identify categories of knowledge and not just particular instantiations of those categories. This may not seem like much of an advance over conceiving of knowledge as discrete facts, but it does suggest an awareness that different *kinds* of facts are relevant to different topics. Such awareness is obviously an asset for the articulation of learning goals, because learning goals necessarily refer to categories of knowledge that have not yet been instantiated.

Knowledge as Having Structure.   A realization that knowledge has structure, that it is not just a collection of facts, was sometimes shown by students in their plans for long-term learning, typically, by their breaking a large topic down into subtopics to be studied separately. It also showed up in their identifying components or subskills of some general skill. One student advanced a more explicit structural notion, proposing that in studying writers she would produce a chart that listed each writer and the main facts about each one. Even here, however, structure appears to be conceived simply as a way of arranging or sorting elements of knowledge.

Knowledge as Transformative.   Some new learning does more than add a fact or alter a specific prior belief. By providing a new perspective, by connecting previously unrelated facts, or by calling into question a central belief, it sets off a reflective process that may lead to the overhaul of a substantial portion of one's knowledge (Maria & MacGinitie, 1982). For indications of whether children are aware of such an effect, in the new learning study we examined responses to a segment of a text on germs that stated:

"Harmful germs are not trying to be bad when they settle down in your body. They just want to live quietly, eat, and make more germs."

This passage contradicts the whole popular image of germs as aggressors, which we have seen vividly dramatized in television commercials and children's cartoons. Responses to the passage varied widely. Some children dismissed the new information as wrong or stupid. Some missed the point, thinking the passage was representing germs as lazy. Some reacted emotionally with a diatribe: "Why do they want to come in us? Why don't they go in some other place, like bears? Because we don't want to die. . . ."

Others, however, recognized that a different way of thinking about the topic had been advanced:

"That's hard to believe. Let's see. Then I always thought [of] germs moving around or fighting with us. I didn't think that they would just settle down and raise a family. That's not exactly my idea of a germ."

A few not only recognized the conflict between the new perspective and the old but tried in some way to reconcile the two:

"Well, they don't really know that they're bad, but they're just living their normal way, but everybody else thinks they're bad."

"Well, I guess they don't know they're hurting you or something. . . . I'm not too sure. . . . They are killed by other cells in your body. I wonder what they think. If they knew that they were doing something, so they could prevent it or something, or if scientists could find a way that bacteria or viruses could live in your body without hurting you."

One child appeared to have begun reconstructing his knowledge from a larger perspective:

"I wonder if germs are intelligent. I guess not. Maybe there's a whole new world, like . . . there is fighting going on between the good and the bad . . . . It's kind of neat when you think about it, 'cause to think of a whole new world inside your body."

These examples indicate that some children responded to new information in a knowledge-transforming manner. But they do not indicate whether the children had any implicit or explicit conception of knowledge transformation as a goal. That is a matter for more pointed experimentation. Comparison of the emotional diatribe responses to those that clearly recognized the knowledge conflict suggests, however, that those who reacted emotionally must have been responding to more than an isolated discrepancy, that they somehow felt that their hold on a piece of reality was being threatened, but they were unable to recognize why. The child who said, "That's not exactly my idea of a germ," on the other hand, clearly did see what was at issue. This suggests a better developed implicit notion of how one item of information can affect a whole knowledge structure.

Awareness of Knowledge Lacks

Knowing what one does not know is a vital part of intentional learning. Without it, the only kind of learning goal one can set is to learn more about a topic—which is typically the goal that we found children setting. Suradijono (1988) examined children's responses in the new learning study to being asked what they do not know or are puzzled about concerning the topic of germs or dinosaurs. Responses were rated on a scale of increasingly complex formulations of knowledge needs. At the lowest level, a single-known fact is involved (e.g., dinosaurs were big). It is transformed to a question, perhaps by a turn of phrase (e.g., why were dinosaurs big or how big were dinosaurs?). At the other extreme, a hypothesis is formulated, representing an attempt to make sense of two or more facts, but requiring verification.

Students' mean level of rating on "Don't know" questions was related to their subsequent thinking-aloud responses to items of text information. These responses were also rated according to the amount of constructive knowledge-processing that appeared to be involved, ranging from simple associations to isolated words and phrases, up through coherent restatement of the gist, and on to statements like those cited in the previous section, which indicate efforts to reconstruct knowledge on the basis of new information. Level of "Don't know" questions was significantly related with the level of response to subsequent text information, whether or not the text information had anything to do with the don't know questions. More interesting, however, is that students' responses to text information relevant to their "Don't know" questions was at a higher level than their average response to other items of text information. Thus, having previously recognized a knowledge lack of a specific sort appeared to result in deeper processing of information relevant to remedying that lack.

Metaknowledge Needed for Intentional Learning

The several issues touched on in these recent studies can be brought under the general heading of *metaknowledge*—knowledge about knowledge, access to one's own knowledge, and skills, which take that knowledge as an object to operate upon. Although it is obvious that sophisticated adults are better equipped with metaknowledge than children, the purpose of these inquiries has not been to distinguish the haves from the have-nots, but to identify more clearly what kinds of metaknowledge may be significant for intentional learning.

The major metaknowledge needs that have turned up may be characterized as follows:

1. A Problem-Solving Framework for Approaching Learning. As we emphasize, this does not mean that learning must always involve means–end or other effortful procedures. Rather, it means that learning should be approached within an executive structure that makes it possible to apply effort effectively, insofar as it is needed to pursue a learning goal, to contend with obstacles, to allocate mental resources appropriately, and so on.

2. Awareness of the Functional Potential of Knowledge.   Awareness that knowledge can enable the acquisition of other knowledge, can bring about the revision of other knowledge, and can be conjoined in various ways to play various roles is critical to intentional learning. Naive learners seem instead to regard knowledge as basically inert *stuff* that can be accumulated and sorted and arranged. Without some more lively conception of what knowledge is about, students would seem to be poorly equipped to overcome the tendency of conventional schooling to produce what Whitehead (1929) condemned as "inert knowledge."

3. Strategies for Identifying Deficits in Knowledge.   When learning is approached within a problem-solving framework, identifying what one does not know becomes a variety of *problem-finding* (Getzels, 1979). As such, it is an active, strategically guided process and not simply a matter of spontaneous curiosity.

THE DEGENERATION OF LEARNING
INTO SCHOOLWORK

The preceding discussion has suggested that children have little conception of learning as a goal-directed process, so that, when they try to direct their own learning, they can do little except assign themselves some kind of school-like work. One is immediately tempted to say that the children are simply acting as accustomed (Lancy, 1976a,b). Lancy (1976a) concluded from his participant observation studies of elementary school classrooms: "Working is the principal business of the school from the pupils' (and undoubtedly others') point of view. Even pupils who say they do not like to work agree that working is what school is for" (p. 40).

Studying is work, of course, but that is not the point. The work that characterizes classroom life may have originally been conceived with learning goals in mind, and it may even achieve some learning objectives, but from the standpoint of the students, doing schoolwork is what school is about. It is their job, not attaining learning goals. As Lancy (1976b) observed, the school day also included times for play and "fooling around," but even these existed within an overall structure of work; they were, respectively, permitted and nonpermitted respites from work. Basically, the description of activities that Lancy produced for elementary classrooms would fit any informally organized workplace. We could find nothing in Lancy's detailed descriptions of childrens' talk and behavior to suggest that the children thought of themselves as learners.

The tendency of schools to resemble factories has often been noted. Frequently, a Marxist explanation is offered, according to which the schools are dedicated to preserving capitalist structures and conditioning students to their future roles as workers (Apple, 1979). A somewhat more useful explanation can be derived, however, by considering the factory model as a solution to the problems inherent in trying to sustain goal-directed learning activity in schools.

From the child's standpoint, learning goals are undoubtedly difficult to get hold of, and so more concrete and tangible features of school activities are likely to be seized on as indicating the point of the activities. It is interesting to see how the language of the children studied by Lancy (1976b) subtly transformed learning activities into activities with some more material objective. The science curriculum included self-initiated, independently conducted experiments. But in the language of the children, experimenting became transformed into "making an experiment." For instance, one fourth grader reported, "Well, sometimes I make an experiment. Like my girlfriend and I once made an experiment. We put 1/3 dixie cup of lemon juice and sugar in it, and we stirred it, and then we put it in the freezer. . . . Then, in three days, we came back and it was frozen" (p. 18).

Similar concretization has been observed by Carlson (1982).

Observer: Tell me about your work.
Pupil 1: We're just working on this page on maps (points to an open workbook). We're both in D-3 (a skill level), and on Friday we're going to take the test, so we have to finish up through all of this (flips through a few pages).
Observer: What happens then?
Pupil 1: I don't know. You think I'm the teacher or something?
Pupil 2: We'll start new classes again, and get workbooks like this, only they won't be the same. I mean instead of maps we'll do something else.

By interpreting learning activities as jobs to be done, students not only concretize them but assimilate them to the rich knowledge structure that surrounds work in industrialized societies. Even young children know something about what it means to have a job, to be a good worker, to take pride in a job well done, and so on. All this knowledge can immediately be brought to bear on schoolwork, making what might otherwise be an incomprehensible enterprise something easy to understand and adjust to. The drawback, however, is that schoolwork rather than learning becomes the object of effort.

From the standpoint of the teacher, there are also incentives to concretizing learning as schoolwork. Learning goals are often vague and progress toward them is hard to monitor, at least over the time spans that individual teachers have to work with. This is particularly true of so-called higher order skills of comprehension, planning, composing, and problem solving. Schoolwork goals provide a handy and satisfying substitute for such elusive learning goals.

Although it is difficult to ascertain whether students are learning composition skills, it is not so difficult to ascertain (to one's own satisfaction) whether students have written good compositions. So attention shifts from the goal of teaching composition skills to the goal of getting students to do good written work. Strategies that produce good work—certain topics, certain ways of introducing a writing assignment—can be distinguished from ones that do not. Sometimes the feedback is instantaneous, as when students apply themselves eagerly to one writing task but act confused or bored by another. If the quality of written work improves, the teacher has the rewarding sense that the students are learning to write better. This could, of course, be true; but all that has actually been observed is improvement in the quality of schoolwork, and this could be due to improved management on the part of the teacher rather than to the acquisition of new skills by the students.

By a similar transformation, the goal of teaching comprehension skills turns into the goal of getting students to comprehend the daily reading. The goal of teaching problem-solving skills turns into the goal of getting students to do well on workbook problems. The goal of teaching independent learning skills turns into the goal of getting students to produce laudable "projects." By a fortunate confluence, these transformations mesh with those carried out by the students. The result, if things are handled skillfully, is a busy and happy workplace in which the students exhibit a high level of "time on task." But, to the extent that schoolwork goals have taken the place of learning goals, whatever learning goes on is incidental.

This point is crucial to defining the role of intentional learning in school contexts. As we note, much everyday learning is incidental to activities that do not have learning as a goal. Naturally, many of these activities involve work; and the amount of effort invested in the work is not irrelevant to what is learned.

We see learning from schoolwork as essentially no different from learning from any other kind of work. If the student's goals are schoolwork goals, then whatever is learned is incidental to the schoolwork activities. Again, effort is by no means irrelevant. Trying harder to do a good job on a schoolwork assignment is likely to result in learning more of something, and if the assignment is well conceived, what is learned will likely be worthwhile and congruent with the purposes of the person who designed the assignment. Thus it is that "time on task" and other work-related variables prove to be predictive of school learning.

What, then, is wrong with transforming learning into schoolwork. There are at least three serious drawbacks. First, instruction carried out via schoolwork is necessarily indirect. The task must elicit certain efforts from the students, and these efforts are then expected to produce the intended learning. As the examples from classroom interview studies indicate, however, there is substantial risk that schoolwork will elicit something quite different from the intended kind of effort. This uncertainty, combined with lack of firm knowledge about which kinds of effort lead incidentally to which kinds of learning, makes instruction via schoolwork an unreliable venture.

Second, as we saw in the case of children learning about the correspondence between concrete and symbolic operations in arithmetic, the kinds of cognitive operations that can be required by a task are limited. Generally speaking, schoolwork can require students to produce a certain product or result but cannot require them to carry out the sense-making efforts that generate meaningful, integrated knowledge. That students have to do for themselves.

Third, insofar as the focus of schooling is activities and tasks, there is little support for students in developing knowledge about knowledge or skills that are applicable to knowledge (as contrasted with skills applicable to school tasks). Perhaps these kinds of metaknowledge are beyond the grasp of young children, so that in the early school years the best that can be hoped for is to involve them in engrossing activities and work that will indirectly produce learning. It would follow, however, that an important goal of schooling in the ensuing years should be to upgrade children's conceptions of what they are doing—from seeing it as work, evaluated according to its execution and its material products, to seeing it as learning, in which they themselves have a major stake (Pramling, 1985).

INSTRUCTION AS A JOINT COGNITIVE PROCESS

Cognitive science provides a variety of ways to model the cognitive behavior of an individual—flow charts, production systems, scripts, strategy descriptions, and the like. Thus, it should be possible to represent cognitive activities of a learner that distinguish intentional learning from less intentionally guided activity. Similarly, it should be possible to represent the cognitive behaviors that distinguish teaching focused on the attainment of learning goals from teaching focused on the execution of work routines (Leinhardt & Greeno, 1986, provide a problem-oriented model that could serve as a framework for such distinctions). Lacking, however, is a way to encompass cognitive behavior of the teacher and of the student within a single coherent description that shows their relationships and generates predictions about the resulting learning of the student.

The kind of model that seems to be needed is a model of a *joint cognitive process.* A joint cognitive process is a single coherent process, with different parts carried out by different people. An example would be the writing of a feature article, as it is done by news magazines. The overall process is the same as a single person's composing (see, for instance, Flower & Hayes, 1981), but the person who does the planning is not necessarily the person who does the initial writing, that person is not necessarily the one who does the revising, and so on. The model will differ from a model of a solitary process in that it must deal with (a) the partitioning of the process among different agents, (b) the passage of control from one agent to another, and (c), most importantly, the possibility that different goals may be operating simultaneously in different parts of the process.

We sketch such a model for a common instructional process known as the directed reading lesson. The directed reading lesson is a common instance of a schoolwork goal (comprehending a reader selection) taking the place of a more remote learning goal (the development of reading comprehension skills). The directed reading lesson is a well established activity in elementary schools that includes (a) prereading activities, designed to arouse interest and to supply or activate knowledge required for comprehending a text, (b) reading of the text, often aloud, and (c) discussion and questioning after the whole text or a segment of it has been read (Beck, 1984). Such activities are commonly referred to as "teaching reading comprehension," and it is reasonable to suppose that teachers have in mind some goal of helping children become better comprehenders. It seems unlikely that the children would have a parallel goal in mind however, because nothing in the activity itself suggests that the development of skills and strategies is at issue. The goals active in the minds of the children are likely to be more immediate, the instructionally relevant ones being to understand a particular point in the text or to provide acceptable answers to the teacher's questions.

Apart from the various goals represented in the minds of participants, however, we may speak of the *point* of an activity (Heap, 1985b). The point of an activity is not necessarily represented in the mind of any participant, but it may be said to exist in the sense that it must figure in any coherent process model of the activity. This may be recognized as an ethnomethodological way of looking at social activities, and it is to ethnomethodological research on reading instruction that we may turn for insights into the point of the directed reading lesson.

From the research of James Heap (1985a,b), we infer that the point of the directed reading lesson is to arrive at a set of propositions that constitute the agreed-upon meaning of the text. Indications that this is the point of the activity are that procedures tend to iterate until it has been achieved and to terminate thereafter, and that alternative procedures for attaining the point are used in the event that initial procedures fail. For instance, the preferred procedure seems to be for the propositions to be generated by the students in response to teacher questioning, but if this fails the teacher will often conclude by providing a summary of the text (Pearson & Gallagher, 1983). Viewed in this way, the directed reading lesson is a joint comprehension process, resulting in the public construction of a semantic macrostructure assignable to the text (cf. van Dijk & Kintsch, 1983).

Figure 12.2 presents a much simplified model of this joint comprehension process. The model represents the joint behavior of a teacher and one student; we say a word at the end about elaborating the model to include multiple students. The first thing to notice about this model is its partitioning of the process into parts carried out by the teacher and parts carried out by the student. The student's part of the process is limited to reading a text segment, constructing some kind of mental representation of the text segment (the provisional textbase), and then drawing on the provisional textbase to answer questions posed by the teacher. The crucial part played by the teacher is posing questions that will elicit from the students statements that can serve as macropropositions in the approved textbase—the final macrostructural representation that constitutes comprehension of the text and therefore attainment of the goal of the activity.

The working of the model can be illustrated using material from a lesson transcript analyzed by Heap (1985b). (To avoid complications not germane to the model, we extract and paraphrase transcript segments rather than present them verbatim.) The text segment the student had just read told of a boy nursing an injured sea bird back to health. The student's reading resulted in a provisional mental representation. The teacher posed a question: "Why do you think the bird didn't fly away?" The student, drawing on his or her provisional textbase, inferred an answer: "It couldn't."

The teacher evaluated this answer, not only for correctness, but for its adequacy as a jointly endorsed statement of text meaning. In this case the answer, although correct, did not at all represent the proposition the teacher had in mind, so the teacher reformulated the question: "Why didn't the bird try to get away?" After several cycles of attempts and reformulations of questions, the answer was "Because Jimmy feeds it every day."

This was evidently still not the proposition the teacher had in mind, but it is close enough that, instead of continuing the cycle of questioning, the teacher opted to give up and to state the desired macroproposition (incidentally, as if the proposition had come from the student): "Right. So the bird knows Jimmy, doesn't he? Good for you."

The macroproposition, *The bird knows Jimmy,* was then entered into the approved textbase, which presumably constituted the mental representation of the text jointly held by teacher and student.

On the face of it, the model shows only how a student came to arrive at an understanding of the text that was approved by the teacher. But if that were all that was at issue in a reading lesson, then the teacher might as well

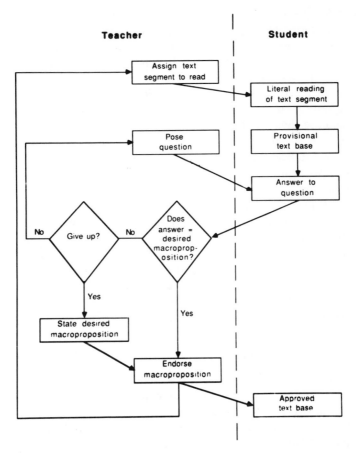

FIG. 12.2.   Model of the directed reading lesson as a group cognitive process, parts of which are carried out by the teacher and parts by the student.

have stated the intended interpretation of the text at the outset and have been done with it. But, of course, the assumption was that the student was also learning or practicing comprehension skills. The model in Fig. 12.2 allows us to identify what the student is doing cognitively in the context of an instructional interaction.

We propose the following working hypothesis:
The skills a student will acquire in an instructional interaction are those required by the student's role in the joint cognitive process.

Let us see how this hypothesis applies to the development of comprehension skills in the directed reading lesson. According to the model presented, students read, construct a semantic representation of the text, and consult this representation to answer questions. Obviously, therefore, they are in some fashion practicing important comprehension skills. But by looking more closely at the student's role in the joint cognitive process, we can be more specific about the skills being practiced and the strategies likely to be learned.

Because the student's role, as represented by the model, is primarily that of question–answerer, we conclude that the skills and strategies being developed are those that produce answers to questions. These would not necessarily be a well-rounded set of comprehension skills. Skills in identifying what is significant in a text, in identifying difficulties and uncertainties, in judging what inferences are relevant, and in evaluating the correctness of interpretations are all comprehension skills that, according to the model, are practiced by the teacher but not by the student. It is little wonder, then, if question-and-answer approaches to comprehension produce little gain in these skills when compared to approaches that involve students directly in the exercise of them (Bereiter & Bird, 1985; Brown & Palincsar, chap. 13 in this volume). It is even reasonable to suspect that the kind of textbase the student learns to construct will be adapted to retrieval for question-answering purposes rather than to the construction of a coherent body of world knowledge (Scardamalia & Bereiter, 1984).

Elaborations of the Model

To describe classroom instruction, the model shown in Fig. 12.2 would of course have to incorporate multiple students. Insofar as the interaction is between the teacher and one student at a time, no interesting new principles are introduced. Interactions among students in such forms as helping or competing with one another might be significant in determining whether or how efficiently the goal of the joint cognitive process is achieved, but it seems likely that, except in cases where students bring sharply conflicting goals into the instructional interaction, a reduced model like that shown in Fig. 12.2 is sufficient to capture the essential definition of the learner's role within the instructional activity. And it is from this role that hypotheses about what skills will and will not be learned can be derived.

The more important thing that is missing from Fig. 12.2 is a representation of the student's personal goals, and of cognitive actions in pursuit of those goals. We have tacitly assumed that the student's only operative goal is to provide acceptable answers to the teacher's questions. This does not seem an unreasonable assumption to apply to an ordinary student who is trying to do what is expected; it is on this basis that we infer the very limited educational benefit of the reading lesson. But suppose we are dealing with our "serious" student. In such a student, reading the story about the injured sea bird might activate a variety of personal goals or learning agendas—goals of literary appreciation or criticism, goals related to understanding bird behavior, and so on. These goals might influence the provisional textbase constructed and thence the answers given to questions. They might furthermore lead the student to ask questions, to challenge the teacher's interpretation, or at least mentally to link information brought out in the class to other information in memory rather than passively assimilate the publicly endorsed text base.

Thus, to understand the function of intentional learning in classroom instruction, we need an elaborated model that shows how pursuing personal learning goals relates to the student's role in the joint cognitive processes of instruction. The present model is too simple for this purpose. It does, however, suggest why, in the absence of intentional learning, ordinary classroom instruction is likely to produce limited learning of academic skills. Being assigned a circumscribed role in the joint cognitive process, the student is encouraged to develop skills limited to that narrow role.

BEYOND LEARNING SKILLS

By several different routes we arrive at the same conclusion: *In order to learn what is ostensibly being taught in school, students need to direct mental effort to goals over and above those implicit in the school activities.* Without such intentional learning, education degenerates into the doing of schoolwork and other activities. Learning results, of course, but it is not learning commensurate with educational objectives. It seems that to learn mathematics well, the student must do more than strive to work problems correctly. The student must actively try to understand the principles involved (Davis & McNight, 1979; Resnick & Neches, 1984). To develop high-level skills of learning from text, the student must do more than try to answer assigned questions. The student must actively try to grasp the central messages of the text and try to relate them to his or her own knowledge.

This pursuit of cognitive goals, over and above the requirements of tasks, is what we have labeled *intentional learning.* In preceding sections of this chapter, we have considered some of the less obvious constituents of intentional learning and have analyzed school instruction to suggest why it is unsuccessful unless the student brings intentional learning to bear. The question remains of how intentional learning can be promoted.

To date, the main contribution of instructional psychology to the promotion of intentional learning has been research on the teaching of learning skills and strategies (Brown et al., 1983; Pressley, Forrest-Pressley, Elliott-Faust, & Miller, 1985). Strategies are undoubtedly important in that they empower students to pursue cognitive goals of their own and thus to be less dependent on schoolwork procedures. But it also seems likely that strategy instruction alone is insufficient to develop children into successful intentional learners.

A crucial issue is what goals the strategies are harnessed to. As we have seen, students tend to treat learning as an activity rather than a goal. Accordingly, strategies are likely to be applied to accomplishing the activity rather than to achieving the cognitive objectives for which the activity was designed. We ran up against this difficulty repeatedly in trying to teach students strategies for written composition. Whereas the strategies were intended to promote a more problem-oriented approach to composition, the students would often find ways to divert them to the more immediate goal of generating sufficient content to complete a writing assignment. For instance, in one instructional condition, videotaped modeling and direct cuing were used to direct students to think about the goals of their composition, their knowledge of the topic, the audience, the organization, and any potential problems. Thinking-aloud protocols showed no evidence that this training promoted the intended kinds of thinking. There was evidence that students were using the suggestions as prompts for retrieving content from memory, and so were incorporating into their texts material having to do with goals, audience, potential problems, etc. (Burtis, Bereiter, Scardamalia, & Tetroe, 1983).

What about open education and other attempts to give students more autonomy in learning? Evidence suggests that students in open education learn to take more initiative in learning (Giaconia & Hedges, 1982). Following Leinhardt, Walker, and Bar-tal's (1976) analysis of autonomy in learning, we may consider open education and learning skills instruction as standing in a complementary relationship: One provides the opportunity but not necessarily the abilities to carry out autonomous learning; the other seeks to provide the abilities but not the opportunities. This would suggest that a combination of the two should work wonders.

Certainly, there is no reason why learning skills instruction cannot profitably be combined with greater opportunities for students to pursue learning independently. But such a simple combination leaves several important factors out. The opportunity to pursue learning goals does not ensure that learning goals will be pursued, even if students have the necessary skills. Nothing in the open education setting itself prevents the degeneration of learning into schoolwork (or perhaps into games or other activities) that students may pursue without having learning as an objective. In fact, a line of progressive educational thought descending from John Dewey (1916, p. 169) is explicitly opposed to intentional learning, holding that all learning should be an incidental consequence of action directed toward other ends. An open classroom pervaded by such a philosophy may provide a rich environment for incidental learning experiences but is not likely to nurture the deliberate pursuit of learning goals.

In addition to opportunities for independent learning and instruction in learning skills, at least four other elements are suggested by the issues considered in this chapter:

1. Teaching Relevant Types of Metaknowledge.   As previously enumerated, this would include teaching students a problem-solving framework for approaching learning, making students aware of the functional potential of knowledge, and teaching strategies for identifying knowledge lacks.

2. Progressive Turnover of Higher Level Parts of Instructional Processes to Students.   In our analysis of the directed reading lesson it was evident that most of the high-level skills were exercised by the teacher rather than by the student. It was the teacher who decided what the main ideas were, who framed questions to direct students' attention to these ideas, and who evaluated the fit between text and interpretation. The essence of reciprocal teaching (Palincsar & Brown, 1984) is that these high-level functions are gradually turned over to the students, with the teacher helping them gain the ability to handle them. Within the directed reading model shown in Fig. 12.2, for instance, this would entail getting students to the point where they could take over the question-asking function. We see this turnover of functions as essentially distinct from the teaching of learning strategies (which may or may not accompany it). It is, rather, a gradual restructuring of the joint cognitive process between teacher and student.

3. Modeling the Setting of Cognitive Goals.   In most cognitive strategy instruction, the goal is presupposed. A major difficulty in intentional learning is the goal setting itself. In trying to teach higher level cognitive processes in writing, Scardamalia, Bereiter, and Steinbach (1984) used thinking aloud to model not only the solving of composition problems but the identification of problems and goals. Modeling of thinking might also be used to convey to students the idea of transcending schoolwork goals—showing the process of setting a higher level and personally meaningful learning goal that subsumes (and therefore satisfies) the externally imposed schoolwork goals (cf. Scardamalia & Bereiter, 1982).

4. Self-Assessment of Level of Constructive Effort.   Intentional learning, conceived of as mental effort directed toward learning goals, cannot be distinguished by the onlooker from other kinds of "on task" behavior. Therefore, if feedback is to play a role in the development of intentional learning skills, it will have to come from students' self-assessments. Rella (1985) gave first graders training in distinguishing *easy ideas* from *learning ideas* in stories (these were the terms taught to the children). Trained children significantly increased the thought content of their verbalized responses to text. It appears therefore, that even at an early age children can make some subjective assessment of their mental effort in learning.

A list of ingredients fails, however, to convey the sense of a whole educational environment geared to the pursuit of learning goals. Such an environment is sometimes referred to as a community of scholars. Partial realizations undoubtedly exist in many exemplary classrooms. In a community of scholars, there must exist not only a body of knowledge but also a dedication to further development of that body of knowledge at both the individual and the corporate level. Shared support of knowledge growth distinguishes a community of scholars from an unconnected assortment of knowledge seekers on one hand and from groups that do not have knowledge growth as a communal goal on the other hand.

A community of scholars differs from the conventional school in important ways. The degeneration of knowledge building into schoolwork or other routines, although it inevitably occurs, is actively resisted. Knowledge keeps being reasserted as the central goal. When scholars say that they want to get back to their work, they mean getting *away* from the job-defined routines so that they can devote themselves to knowledge construction. To the extent that the scholars are a community, there is mutual responsibility for each individual's growth in knowledge. It seems to us that, with appropriate adjustments for level of sophistication, all these characteristics could be realized in a school setting.

Some may doubt whether such a community of scholars ever actually exists outside commencement addresses and other flights of academic fancy. Granted that this ideal seldom is more than crudely approximated, it nevertheless contrasts favorably with the equally unrealized ideal images of the common school. These ideal images have been expressed through a variety of metaphors—the home, the garden, the factory, the democratic community. Although each of these images captures something important of what schooling is about, they fail to capture the essential fact that schooling is about knowledge. Knowledge is not just one of the consequences of growth, one of the possible products of a manufacturing enterprise, or one of the outcomes of participation in the life of a democratic community. It is a metagoal of schooling—over and above, not merely additional to the other outcomes—and it is a goal easily lost sight of. A cognitively based educational theory, it seems, must start by establishing knowledge construction as the communal enterprise that schooling is essentially about.

ACKNOWLEDGMENTS

Prepared on the basis of talks given at the July, 1985 symposium on Cognition and Instruction at the Learning Research and Development Center,

University of Pittsburgh, which was held in celebration of LRDC's 20th Anniversary and to honor Robert Glaser. The research discussed in this chapter was supported by a grant from the Social Sciences and Humanities Research Council of Canada and by the Ontario Ministry of Education through its block transfer grant to the Ontario Institute for Studies in Education. The authors gratefully acknowledge the research assistance of Valerie Anderson, Clare Brett, Jud Burtis, Carol Chan, Linda Mainwaring, Wanda Malcolm, Denise Mumford, Pamela Paris, Mary Rella, Rosanne Steinbach, and Earl Woodruff.

REFERENCES

Anderson, J. R. (1982). Acquisition of cognitive skill. *Psychological Review, 89,* 369–406.

Anderson, J. R. (1983). *The architecture of cognition.* Cambridge, MA: Harvard University Press.

Anderson, T. H. (1979). Study skills and learning strategies. In H. F. O'Neill, Jr. & C. D. Spielberger (Eds.), *Cognitive and affective learning strategies* (pp. 77–98). New York: Academic Press.

Anderson, T. H. (1980). Study strategies and adjunct aids. In R. J. Spiro, B. C. Bruce, & W. F. Brewer (Eds.), *Theoretical issues in reading comprehension* (pp. 483–502). Hillsdale, NJ: Lawrence Erlbaum Associates.

Apple, M. (1979). *Ideology and curriculum.* Boston: Routledge & Kegan Paul.

Beck, I. (1984). Developing comprehension: The impact of the directed reading lesson. In R. C. Anderson, J. Osborn, & R. J. Tierney (Eds.), *Learning to read in American schools: Basal readers and content texts* (pp. 3–20). Hillsdale, NJ: Lawrence Erlbaum Associates.

Bereiter, C., & Bird, M. (1985). Use of thinking aloud in identification and teaching of reading comprehension strategies. *Cognition and Instruction, 2,* 131–156.

Bereiter, C., & Scardamalia, M. (1985). Cognitive coping strategies and the problem of "inert knowledge." In S. F. Chipman, J. W. Segal, & R. Glaser (Eds.), *Thinking and learning skills: Vol. 2. Research and open questions* (pp. 65–80). Hillsdale, NJ: Lawrence Erlbaum Associates.

Biggs, J. B. (1979). Individual differences in study processes and the quality of learning outcomes. *Higher Education, 8,* 381–394.

Biggs, J. B. (1984). Learning strategies, student motivation patterns and subjectively perceived success. In J. R. Kirby (Ed.), *Cognitive strategies and educational performance* (pp. 111–134). Orlando, FL: Academic Press.

Bromme, R. (1980). Die alltagliche Unterrichtsvorbereitung von Mathematiklehrern [Daily preparation of lessons by mathematics teachers]. *Unterichtswissenschaft, 8,* 142–156.

Brown, A. L., Bransford, J. D., Ferrara, R. A., & Campione, J. C. (1983). Learning, remembering, and understanding. In J. H. Flavell & E. M. Markman (Eds.), *Handbook of child psychology: Vol. 3. Cognitive development* (4th ed., pp. 77–166). New York: Wiley.

Brown, A. L., & Day, J. D. (1983). Macrorules for summarizing texts: The development of expertise. *Journal of Verbal Learning and Verbal Behavior, 22,* 1–14.

Brown, A. L., Day, J. D., & Jones, R. S. (1983). The development of plans for summarizing texts. *Child Development, 54,* 968–979.

Burtis, P. J., Bereiter, C., Scardamalia, M., & Tetroe, J. (1983). The development of planning in writing. In G. Wells & B. M. Kroll (Eds.), *Explorations in the development of writing* (pp. 153–174). Chichester, England: Wiley.

Carlson, D. (1982). "Updating" individualism and the work ethic: Corporate logic in the classroom. *Curriculum Inquiry, 12,* 125–160.

Chi, M. T. H. (1985). Interactive roles of knowledge and strategies in the development of organized sorting and recall. In S. F. Chipman, J. W. Segal, & R. Glaser (Eds.), *Thinking and learning skills: Vol. 2. Research and open questions* (pp. 457–483). Hillsdale, NJ: Lawrence Erlbaum Associates.

Chipman, S. F., Segal, J. W., & Glaser, R. (Eds.). (1985). *Thinking and learning skills: Vol. 2. Research and open questions.* Hillsdale, NJ: Lawrence Erlbaum Associates.

Davis, R. B., & McNight, C. C. (1979). Modelling the processes of mathematical thinking. *Journal of Children's Mathematical Behavior, 2,* 91–113.

Dennett, D. C. (1983). Intentional systems in cognitive ethology: The "Panglossian paradigm" defended. *Behavioral and Brain Sciences, 6,* 343–390.

Dewey, J. (1916). *Democracy and education.* New York: Macmillan.

Doyle, W. (1983). Academic work. *Review of Educational Research, 53,* 159–199.

Doyle, W. (1985). Classroom organization and management. In M. C. Wittrock (Ed.), *Handbook of research on teaching* (3rd ed., pp. 392–431). New York: Macmillan.

Flower, L., & Hayes, J. R. (1981). A cognitive process theory of writing. *College Composition and Communication, 32,* 365–387.

Getzels, J. W. (1979). Problem-finding: A theoretical note. *Cognitive Science, 3,* 167–171.

Giaconia, R. N., & Hedges, L. V. (1982). Identifying features of effective open education. *Review of Educational Research, 52,* 579–602.

Glaser, R. (1984). Education and thinking: The role of knowledge. *American Psychologist, 39,* 93–104.

Hayes, J. R., & Flower, L. (1980). Writing as problem solving. *Visible Language, 14,* 388–399.

Heap, J. L. (1985a, August). *Applied ethnomethodology: Looking for local rationality in reading and writing activities.* Paper presented at the meeting of the Seventh International Institute for Ethnomethodology and Conversation Analysis, Boston University, Boston.

Heap, J. L. (1985b). Discourse in the production of classroom knowledge: Reading lessons. *Curriculum Inquiry, 15,* 245–280.

Johnston, P., & Afflerbach, P. (1985). The process of constructing main points from text. *Cognition and Instruction, 2,* 207–232.

Kahneman, D. (1973). *Attention and effort.* Englewood Cliffs, NJ: Prentice–Hall.

Lancy, D. F. (1976a). *The beliefs and behaviors of pupils in an experimental school: Introduction and overview.* LRDC Publication 1976/3. Pittsburgh: Learning Research and Development Center, University of Pittsburgh.

Lancy, D. F. (1976b). *The beliefs and behaviors of pupils in an experimental school: The science lab.* LRDC Publication 1976/6. Pittsburgh: Learning Research and Development Center, University of Pittsburgh.

Laudan, L. (1977). *Progress and its problems.* Berkeley: University of California Press.

Leinhardt, G. (1986, April). *The skill of learning from classroom lessons.* Paper presented at the meeting of the American Educational Research Association, San Francisco.

Leinhardt, G., & Greeno, J. G. (1986). The cognitive skill of teaching. *Journal of Educational Psychology, 78,* 75–95.

Leinhardt, G., Walker, A., & Bar-Tal, D. (1976). *Autonomy in education: A research approach.* LRDC Publication 1976/22. Pittsburgh: Learning Research and Development Center, University of Pittsburgh.

Maria, K., & MacGinitie, W. H. (1982). Reading comprehension disabilities: Knowledge structures and nonaccommodating text processing strategies. *Annals of Dyslexia, 32,* 33–59.

Marton, F., & Säljö, R. (1976). On qualitative differences in learning. II. Outcome as a function of the learner's conception of the task. *British Journal of Educational Psychology, 46*, 115–127.

Newell, A. (1980). Reasoning, problem solving, and decision processes: The problem space as a fundamental category. In R. S. Nickerson (Ed.), *Attention and performance VIII* (pp. 693–718). Hillsdale, NJ: Lawrence Erlbaum Associates.

Olshavsky, J. N. E. (1976-1977). Reading as problem solving: An investigation of strategies. *Reading Research Quarterly, 12*, 654–674.

Owen, E., & Sweller, J. (1985). What do children learn while solving mathematics problems? *Journal of Educational Psychology, 77*, 272–284.

Palincsar, A. S., & Brown, A. L. (1984). Reciprocal teaching of comprehension-fostering and monitoring activities. *Cognition and Instruction, 1*, 117–175.

Pearson, P. D., & Gallagher, M. C. (1983). The instruction of reading comprehension. *Contemporary Educational Psychology, 8*, 317–344.

Pellegrino, J. W., & Glaser, R. (1982). Analyzing aptitudes for learning: Inductive reasoning. In R. Glaser (Ed.), *Advances in instructional psychology* (Vol. 2, pp. 269–345). Hillsdale, NJ: Lawrence Erlbaum Associates.

Pramling, I. (1985). *Entrance into the "world of knowledge."* Paper presented at the meeting of the Research Seminar on the Written Code and Conceptions of Reality, Sydkoster, Sweden.

Pressley, M., Forrest-Pressley, D. L., Elliott-Faust, D., & Miller, G. (1985). Children's use of cognitive strategies, how to teach strategies, and what to do if they can't be taught. In M. Pressley & C. J. Brainerd (Eds.), *Cognitive learning and memory in children* (pp. 1–47). New York: Springer-Verlag.

Rella, M. (1985). *Modelling higher levels of thought in order to elevate the constructive mental effort in six-year-olds.* Unpublished honors thesis, York University, Downsview, Ontario, Canada.

Resnick, L. B., & Glaser, R. (1976). Problem solving and intelligence. In L. B. Resnick (Ed.), *The nature of intelligence* (pp. 205–230). Hillsdale, NJ: Lawrence Erlbaum Associates.

Resnick, L. B., & Neches, R. (1984). Factors affecting individual differences in learning ability. In R. J. Sternberg (Ed.), *Advances in the psychology of human intelligence* (Vol. 2, pp. 275–323). Hillsdale, NJ: Lawrence Erlbaum Associates.

Ryle, G. (1949). *The concept of mind.* London: Hutchinson.

Sacerdoti, E. (1977). *A structure for plans and behavior.* New York: Elsevier North-Holland.

Scardamalia, M., & Bereiter, C. (1982). Assimilative processes in composition planning. *Educational Psychologist, 17*, 165–171.

Scardamalia, M., & Bereiter, C. (1984). Development of strategies in text processing. In H. Mandl, N. Stein, & T. Trabasso (Eds.), *Learning and comprehension of text* (pp. 379–406). Hillsdale, NJ: Lawrence Erlbaum Associates.

Scardamalia, M., Bereiter, C., & Steinbach, R. (1984). Teachability of reflective processes in written composition. *Cognitive Science, 8*, 173–190.

Schneider, B. H. (1984). Learning disability as they see it: Perceptions of adolescents in a special residential school. *Journal of Learning Disabilities, 17*, 533–536.

Segal, J. W., Chipman, S. F., & Glaser, R. (Eds.). (1985). *Thinking and learning skills: Vol. 1. Relating instruction to research.* Hillsdale, NJ: Lawrence Erlbaum Associates.

Steinberg, E. R. (1977). Review of student control in computer-assisted instruction. *Journal of Computer-Based Instruction, 3*, 84–90.

Suradijono, Sri Hartati. (1988). *The relation of self-reported knowledge lacks to understanding.* Unpublished master's thesis, The Ontario Institute for Studies in Education, Toronto.

Thomas, J. W., & Rohwer, W. D., Jr. (1986). Academic studying: The role of learning strategies. *Educational Psychologist, 21*, 19–41.

van Dijk, T. A., & Kintsch, W. (1983). *Strategies of discourse comprehension.* New York: Academic Press.

van Rossum, E. J., & Schenk, S. M. (1984). The relation between learning conception, study strategy and learning outcome. *British Journal of Educational Psychology, 54*, 73–83.

Whitehead, A. N. (1929). *The aims of education.* New York: Macmillan.

Winne, P., & Marx, R. (1982). Students' and teachers' views of thinking processes for classroom learning. *Elementary School Journal, 82*, 493–518.

13

Guided, Cooperative Learning and Individual Knowledge Acquisition

Ann L. Brown
University of California at Berkeley

Annemarie S. Palincsar
Michigan State University

The recent spurt of interest in children learning in groups stems from several different research traditions including Piagetian (Doise & Mugny, 1984) and Vygotskian (1978) theories in developmental psychology; philosophical examinations of the nature of argument and explanation (Grize, 1982; Kneupper, 1978; Toulmin, 1958; Von Wright, 1971); as well as observations of classroom dialogues (Barnes & Todd, 1977; Cazden, 1984; Mehan, 1979), and of a variety of cooperative learning environments (Aronson, 1978; Johnson & Johnson, 1975; Sharan, 1980; Slavin, 1983). However, fundamental questions about group learning remain unanswered: Does participation in a group problem-solving setting influence individual learning? If so, in what way? What essential functions of groups encourage learning? What role, if any, does an explicit instructional goal play in such settings?

In the first section of this chapter, we discuss theoretical claims concerning a variety of group-learning procedures and the evidence for their efficacy. In the second section, we concentrate on reciprocal teaching, an expert-led cooperative learning procedure developed to improve children's understanding of complex text (Brown & Palincsar, 1987; Palincsar & Brown, 1984). We describe how reciprocal teaching was designed to incorporate many of the best features of group learning, notably modeling and expert scaffolding within a cooperative learning environment. Similarly, the ways in which reciprocal teaching mimics apprenticeship methods of instruction are discussed.

LEARNING AND UNDERSTANDING

Learning: A Question of Degree

Learning is a term with more meanings than there are theorists; however, most would agree on some basic distinctions. For example, the addition of a new fact to the knowledge base is a very different phenomenon from a conceptual upheaval in understanding the kind that resembles theory change in the history of science (Carey, 1985; Kuhn, 1962).

Learning clearly admits of degrees. One traditional criterion of learning is that a certain body of information can be recovered sometime after it has been read, heard, or discussed; indeed, school examinations often use this criterion of learning. Unfortunately, preparation for tests that emphasize retention of facts often leads to the acquisition of "inert" knowledge (Whitehead, 1916), encapsulated information that is rarely accessed again unless a specific cue to activation is given, such as an expected examination question (Brown & Campione, 1981, 1984). The information fails to become part of a usable store of knowledge. In a very real sense, the learner has not established *ownership* of that knowledge that would afford him or her flexible access to it, access that would enable him or her to adapt, apply, update, or modify it at will.

A qualitatively different kind of knowledge acquisition requires the assimilation of new knowledge so that it is owned by the learner, readily accessible, and potentially applicable to related but novel situations. Here the new information becomes part of a workable knowledge base and can be applied widely, for better or worse.

Yet another kind of learning involves modification or adaptation of this usable knowledge in the face of new experiences. When a generalizable body of knowledge proves incompatible with new experience alteration, modification, refinement, or *restructuring* may occur. If the incompatibility is striking and persistent, it must lead to true *theory change,* in which a stage-like shift in fundamental modes of thinking radically restructures knowledge throughout the system. Controversial as such radical restructuring notions may be (Carey, 1985; Case, 1985; Fischer, 1980; Flavell, 1971), most agree that this kind of learning is fundamentally different from the mere acquisition of new facts. Determining whether or not group problem-solving experiences influence individual learning depends on what kind of change we examine.

Understanding and Conceptual Change

One of the most common claims about group settings is that they force learning with understanding and therefore are likely to foster conceptual change. They are regarded by their proponents as ideal for encouraging consideration of underlying reasons and principles. In contrast are situations that encourage automatization, ritualization, or routinization of skill, in which speed is emphasized at the expense of thought. We argue that conceptual change is more likely to result where the purpose of procedures is emphasized rather than blind drill and practice, even when that drill and practice is devoted to appropriate procedures (Brown, 1978; Brown & Campione, 1986). Moreover, conceptual understanding and adaptive change are presumed to be fostered in situations that encourage dissatisfaction with the existing state of knowledge; change is unlikely when the status quo is unquestioned. Environments that encourage questioning, evaluating, criticizing, and generally worrying knowledge, taking it as an object of thought, are believed to be fruitful breeding grounds for *restructuring*. In group problem solving, evaluation leads often to uncertainty; insecurity is accentuated by questioning and criticism, and dissatisfaction leads to mental experimentation. Change is more likely when one is required to explain, elaborate, or defend one's position to others, as well as to oneself; striving for an explanation often makes a learner integrate and elaborate knowledge in new ways.

Self-Directed Learning

A well-respected tradition in the developmental psychology of learning accords a very minor role to social agents. It is argued that, short of supplying a source of imitation, social agents play little part in inducing conceptual change. In the extreme, this position holds that all "meaningful" conceptual change is *self-directed*. There can be little doubt that human beings, even the youngest, maybe especially the youngest, are intrinsically motivated to understand the world around them. Some argue that learning is guided by systems of *internal* structures, principles, or constraints that seek support in the environment for their growth and development. In addition, children come equipped with a propensity to extend knowledge by systematically monitoring naturally occurring variations and the results of their own active experimentation (Gelman &

Brown, 1985a,b). Herein lies the foundation of such metaphors as the tireless explorer (Chukovsky, 1968) or the child as scientist (Piaget, 1950) central to many conceptions of childhood thought. The child is seen as essentially a self-directed learner seeking data to test and modify his or her current theories and hypotheses about how things work (Carey, 1985; Gelman & Brown, 1985a; Inhelder, Sinclair, & Bovet, 1974; Karmiloff-Smith & Inhelder, 1974/1975).

Social Genesis of Individual Understanding

At the opposite extreme from theories of self-directed learning are theories of cognitive development that emphasize *other-direction* almost exclusively. According to such theories, conceptual development has an essentially social genesis. Conceptual change in children is a process of their internalizing cognitive activities originally experienced in the company of others.

We argue that a coordination of the two positions, self-directed and social learning, comes somewhat nearer the truth (Brown & Reeve, 1987; Gelman & Brown, 1985a). In fact, Vygotsky and Piaget, who are usually blamed for the extremes, acknowledged both social and individual learning in their theories, although each chose to focus primarily on one. For example, in his early work, Piaget (1967) considered the role of social experience in cognitive development, noting "that human intelligence develops in the individual as a function of social interaction is too often disregarded" (pp. 224–225). In particular, he regarded peer interactions as an ideal forum for helping children take the leap to a higher level of understanding. A group of peers, who not only fail to accept one's own view but actually hold opposing opinions, must cause reflection in a reasonable child. Such experiences help children "decenter" their thinking, shift it away from an egocentric perspective, thereby enabling them to consider multiple perspectives. Group discussions reveal opposing egocentric views and enable a more comprehensive mature conception to emerge. According to this view, Piaget (1976a) states: "social interaction is a necessary condition for the development of logic" (p. 80). The process (the group interactions), as well as the product (the solution to the problem), are internalized as part of the child's emergent thinking repertoire.

Although Vygotsky (1978) paid considerable attention to self-directed learning, notably in his treatment of play and tool use, clearly he has been the developmental theorist who most emphasized the essentially social nature of individual cognition. Vygotsky argued that thinking is a social activity, initially shared between people but gradually internalized to reappear again as an individual achievement. For Vygotsky, individual thinking is essentially the re-enactment by the individual of cognitive processes that were originally experienced in society. The fundamental process of development is the gradual internalization and personalization of what was originally a social activity.

Thus, Piaget and Vygotsky, not to mention Binet (Binet, 1909; Brown, 1985) and Dewey (1910), all emphasized guided learning as an impetus to developmental change. The key explanatory concept in their theories is some form of internalization; that which is witnessed in social settings becomes harnessed as individual cognition. These theories are seductive, but progress demands more exact specification of the processes that are implicated and how they are internalized. Although certain social activities must be prime candidates for translation to the internal world, everything the child witnesses is not internalized. Social interactions do not always create new learning; peer interactions vary enormously; only some teaching environments actually create ideal learning experiences. We need a great deal more examination of such questions as: (a) What kinds of interactions are maximally effective at inducing cognitive growth? (b) To what extent do social collaborations lead to independent competence? (c) What are the mechanisms underlying internalization? (d) Can optimal interactions be orchestrated deliberately in instructional settings? Although theories provide a blueprint for research, the variables embodied in the concept of supportive social contexts need to be delineated in far greater detail (Brown & Reeve, 1987). In the next section, we discuss research on group problem solving that helps provide some of the necessary specification.

COOPERATIVE LEARNING

The term, cooperative learning, is most closely associated with research in educational psychology concerned with alternatives to traditional classroom organizational structure. Although the term has been used to refer to cooperative behavior, or the division of labor within tasks, the primary interest has been in motivation and incentive (Slavin, 1983); cooperative, competitive, and individualistic incentive structures are compared and contrasted (Johnson & Johnson, 1974, 1975). In-depth consideration of the actual thinking processes affected by such settings is rare. Researchers have been mainly concerned with whether or not cooperative settings result in better products or learning outcomes, than competitive and individualistic environments. Sharan (1980) has argued that even these products tend to tap rote learning of the content of the interacted-on material, rather than higher level thinking such as "elaboration of ideas, analysis and problem solving" (p. 255), the type of thinking processes that are supposed to be exercised in group discussions.

The main findings from this literature indicate that cooperative settings do result in significant improvement in outcome measures (Sharan, 1980). We know, for example, that giving explanations is positively correlated with achievement. But we must be cautious in interpreting this finding. Even when care is taken to partial out starting ability, ability is not synonomous with knowledge. It could be that those giving explanations already know the relevant content and, therefore, it is scarcely surprising that they score well on subsequent tests of that content. Receiving help is also related to achievement; one would like to know, however, if the presence of an effect is influenced by the type of help and accuracy of information that is received, surely important factors. Finally, it comes as no surprise that receiving no answer to one's questions is firmly related to poor outcomes (Swing & Peterson, 1982; Webb, 1984). This pattern of findings is intriguing and brings into high relief the importance of *explanation* in group learning. What is needed is a more fine-grained examination of the explanation process itself.

In conversations, discussions, and debates, participants must offer explanations, interpretations, and resolutions to problems. In addition to requesting elaborations and corroborations, group members may call on discussion leaders to "back" their arguments, not only with additional data, but also with warrants attesting to the pertinence, credibility, or legitimacy of the data already proferred. According to Toulmin (1958), "Rules, principles, inference-licenses are required that show that given the data provided, the step to the original claim or conclusion is an appropriate or legitimate one" (p. 98). The group demands both corroborative data on the one hand, and warrants or backings for that data on the other. Structurally, the argument progresses from statements of factual data, statements of the warrants or authority for that data, to backings for those warrants that can be expressed in the form of categorical statements of facts to support the warrant (Toulmin, 1958). Group members force discussion leaders to provide warrants and backings that attest to the legitimacy of their arguments, thereby elaborating, extending, and providing them with coherence. In so doing, the group offers both support for the arguments of its members and conflict in the form of opposing arguments. In the next section, we consider in some detail these two aspects of group explanation and discussion, the role of support and the role of conflict, particularly in reference to discussions among children.

The Role of Support

Groups are said to provide social support for the efforts of their members. Studies of group discussion often report that more work goes into motivational factors, such as providing encouragement, rewards, and camaraderie than into actual problem solving (Barnes & Todd, 1977). But a great deal of cognitive support is provided in group settings. We now review the main evidence to support this claim.

Culturally Appropriate Participant Structures. Microethnographic studies of group constellations in the classroom have examined the participant structures that modulate interaction. Erickson and Schultz (1977) describe participant structures as constantly changing, interactionally constituted environments that are marked by specific sets of rules for speaking, listening, turntaking, and so forth. Some participant structures are more hospitable to young children than others, and this is especially true when they come from ethnic groups other than the dominant white culture. For example, the most typical participant structure in grade schools is that of "simple reciprocation" (Dunkin & Biddle, 1974; Mehan, 1979)—the teacher asks a question to which he or she clearly knows the answer, a student is called on, and the teacher evaluates the response explicitly or implicitly (by turning to another respondant). These teacher-directed discussions are awkward at best because they put an individual child on the spot and are culturally inappropriate at worst, clashing with accepted norms of social interaction. Studies with native Hawaiian (Au, 1980; Boggs, 1972), Odawa (Philips, 1972), Cherokee (Dumont, 1972), and Athabascan (Van Ness, 1982) Indian children have all shown these interaction patterns to be culturally unsuitable.

Simple reciprocation routines result in considerably depressed student participation, even apathy, among those children who prefer activities based on collective rather than individual performance. For example, teachers experienced with native Hawaiian children capitalized on a culturally well-practiced routine to direct reading groups (Au, 1980). The participant structure that emerged closely resembled "talk-story," a common Hawaiian group activity of collectively telling jokes and stories. In talk-story, two or more speakers collaboratively produce the narrative, overlapping and intermingling turns at will. The resultant classroom reading ritual, which permitted shared construction and elaboration, resulted in far greater academic engaged time (Au, 1980) and has been cited as a primary reason for the success of the Kamehameha Early Education Program.

Certain participant structures have been amply demonstrated to be culturally inappropriate for a variety of ethnic groups. But it has not been proven that simple reciprocation is culturally appropriate to the dominant group. Indeed, many have argued against this claim (Mehan, 1979), particularly when the children in question are young, poor, or academically delayed (Brown, Palincsar, & Purcell, 1985). Collaboration may be the preferred mode for many children. Again, we need to "unpack" exactly what we mean by collaboration.

Shared Responsibility for Thinking. In group problem-solving situations, collaboration distributes the thinking load among the members, with both cognitive and emotional consequences. Pontecorvo (1985) states:

> What happens at the emotional level is that the group sustains the general emotive tension because it shares out the effort of thinking and reduces the anxiety produced by having to keep the argument going; each person has to think and say only one piece of the discourse, which can be used to construct another. This piece then comes back in more elaborated form in someone else's statement,—and can be used later at a level of greater complexity. (p. 3)

For example, consider a group of English 13-year-old working-class children helping each other establish a point about littering, each providing a piece of the argument (Barnes & Todd, 1977, p. 33):

David: I think bigger fines should be imposed for the people who don't obey the country laws and thereby spoil the countryside.
Jonathan: Yeah
Marianne: . . . by leaving . . .
Jonathan: . . . by dropping litter . . .
Marianne: . . . and broken glass.

Or a group of Italian 10-year-olds discussing why bread gets stale (Pontecorvo, 1985, p. 3):

Sa: Because, because it is closed.
Ma: Because it is too closed.
Val: If you leave it . . .
Ric: If it is closed, it keeps because . . .
Sa: All the soft parts . . .
Val: Actually, if you leave it on the sideboard, it gets hard because the air hardens it.
Sa: It absorbs its softness.

Through collaboration, argument construction can be jointly managed. Furthermore, it is possible within group settings to share potential argument roles and strategies that an individual would need to perform for her or himself. Group members spontaneously adopt a variety of clearly identifiable thinking roles (Bales, 1950; Dashiell, 1935; Kelley & Thibaut, 1954; Shaw, 1932), such as those of: (a) the *executive* or doer, who designs plans for action and suggests solutions; (b) the *skeptic* or *critic,* who questions premises and plans, usually those of others; (c) the *instructor* or educator, who takes on the burden of explanation and summarization for less involved members of the group; (d) the *record keeper,* who keeps track of what has passed; and (e) the *conciliator,* who resolves conflicts and strives to minimize interpersonal stress. One of these roles might be appropriated by an individual member (Pontecorvo, 1985), or role assumption might fluctuate over time. In both cases, however, the roles are separated so that each participant need play only one of them, thus reducing the cognitive load for upgrading the level of problem solving for any one individual.

Not only are such spontaneous role assumptions naturally occurring outcomes of setting people the tasks of combining their talents to solve problems, but the division of labor can be artificially legislated to good instructional effect. Many successful adult dyadic-learning procedures require that one member of the learning pair acts as executive, thinker, or planner, while the other acts as critic or evaluator (Bloom & Broder, 1950; Frase & Schwartz, 1975; Whimbey & Lochhead, 1978). And separating the role of learning leader from learning listeners works well in group problem solving with young children in classroom settings (Yager, Johnson, & Johnson, 1985).

Models of Cognitive Processes.   Another advantage of learning in social settings is that the roles of executive, skeptic, bookkeeper, educator, and so forth are executed overtly. Not only do individuals have less of the thinking burden placed on their shoulders, but they also witness others' enactment of each of the roles, roles that correspond to thinking strategies that they must subsequently perform independently and silently. In the course of group argument and explanation, the individual member is likely to witness a whole variety of epistemic operations, such as defining the problem, isolating important contributing variables, referring to context, past knowledge, data, or general principles, and evaluating progress.

Even children observe some basic rules of formal argument in group problem-solving settings. For example, Barnes and Todd (1977) identified 12 recurrent cognitive strategies that their working-class British 13-year-olds routinely used in group discussions of physical and social science problems. These included an elaborated set of causal reasoning activities, such as proposing and evaluating causal explanations by asking such questions as "Why necessary?" and "How possible?" "Answers to questions of the first type can be used for making predictions; answers to questions of the second type for making retrodictions" (Von Wright, 1971). Barnes and Todd also report frequent recourse to arguments concerning the (in)validity of a premise; attempts to justify premises with warrants and backings (Toulmin, 1958); application of general principles to cases, elaboration, restatement in different terms, negation, and evaluation. Often the premises are weak, and the logical progression of the argument ill formed, but primitive precursors of argument structure can be seen even in quite young children (Bos, 1937; Paley, 1981). Sharing the burden not only permits a collaborative level of functioning far in advance of the individuals' ability to maintain discourse cohesion, but it also provides important modeling of essential argument forms.

Shared Expertise.   It has often been argued that a major advantage of group over individual learning is that any group will benefit from the increased range of expertise of its members' combined knowledge. Shared expertise is the underlying concept of cooperative learning procedures such as Aronson's (1978) Jigsaw method where children are divided into groups of five or six, each group held responsible for a large body of material on which they will later be tested individually. The material is also divided into five or six parts. For example, the life history of Thomas Edison might be broken into sections covering childhood, first accomplishments, major setbacks, later life, and world events during his lifetime. Each member of the team is assigned just'one section to study. Members with the same assignment (across groups) meet first in expert groups to discuss their common responsibility. Now expert, the subject-matter specialists return to their cooperative learning groups and pass on their information. Each child is expert in one area. The learning groups are responsible for covering all the material.

Unfortunately, the written reports on the outcomes of Jigsaw leave us somewhat in the dark about the learning process. Although we are told that children are given training to improve communication and tutoring skills, and that the groups monitor their own interpersonal interactions, we are given little detail on the actual group mechanisms, or on the cognitive consequences of participation in such discussions. Furthermore, tests of independent achievement following Jigsaw participation have tended to be multiple-choice questions of content retention rather than tests of improved thinking skills, such as argumentation and elaboration (Sharan, 1980). A further look at Jigsaw and other cooperative learning methods, such as Student Team Achievement Division (Slavin, 1983), Teams–Games–Tournaments (DeVries, Slavin, Fennessey, Edwards, & Lombardo, 1980), Group Investigation (Sharan & Sharan, 1976), and the Learning Together Model (Johnson & Johnson, 1975), should concentrate on what the students actually do in these groups. This would help us pinpoint which thinking processes are practiced and, therefore, what type of improvement in higher order skills might be expected. Improved retention of the content of a particular set of materials, although desirable, may not be the primary benefit of group participation. Practice discussing, defending, and evaluating one's opinions and those of others may result in improved ability to learn about future text content, a learning to learn effect that would be far more beneficial than gains on any one set of factual material (Brown, 1985; Brown, Campione, & Day, 1981).

The Role of Conflict

Confrontation causes change, or at least developmental psychologists of varied theoretical persuasions agree that confrontation, especially conflict, is the great catalyst of change. In this section, we consider the subject of confrontation in groups.

Elaboration. Social settings provide an audience for an individual's attitudes, opinions, and beliefs, and audiences can request clarification, justification, and elaboration. The skeptic or critic role in group discussion has been accorded special status, some arguing that by forcing the group to defend or elaborate solutions, a more mature resolution will emerge. Pontecorvo (1985) reported repeated examples of grade school children playing this positive role of demanding a better understanding. For example, 10-year-old En would not accept the mere fact that pasta put in water explained why it expands. *En:* "Yes, but the explanation of being in the water is not a logical one. I want to know *how* it [the water] gets in [the pasta]." Similarly, on the same topic, *En* demanded, "Yes, they say it gets softer, but they must have some idea in order to say it gets softer; how does it get softer?" And again, *En:* "But what does the water do to spaghetti to make it soft." Finally, in a telling judgment of the level of answers he was getting, *En* contends, "It is possible for everyone to speak of their ideas without giving an explanation!" En wanted elaboration, justification, warrants, and backing, and he would not be satisfied with less. En's persistence forced the group to be more specific about causal mechanisms. In addition, En provided an ideal role model of the skeptic who needs justification of opinions.

In the Barnes and Todd (1977, p. 30) dialogues between 13-year-olds, requests for causal mechanism were frequent. In the following excerpt, a group was considering how bird eggs are fertilized:

Louise: But how's it fertilized?
Donald: It's fertilized in the body; it must be. Of course it's fertilized in the body.
Louise: What makes you think so?
Helen: It must be.
David: 'Cos it wouldn't get back through.
Helen: It can hardly get through the damn shell, can it?

Teresa, in another group, followed up on Nicola's description of why a cork will be ejected from a bottle placed in a bell jar with the following requests for causal explanation:

Teresa: So what made it possible for the cork to come out then?
Nicola: Well, it didn't actually come out, it were sort of forced out really.

Teresa:	Yeah? (sounding unconvinced)
Nicola:	And there were all pressure, all the way round it, all them little particles floating about.
Teresa:	Yeah? (still unconvinced)
Nicola:	They were forcing the cork to come out anyway.
Teresa:	Mm! (still unconvinced)

Justifications, Warrants, and Backings.   Adults' argument structure follows certain identifiable sequences. For example, an argument is usually supported by data; these data are then supported by warrants for their pertinence and credibility, and finally further backing is provided in terms of recourse to general law (Toulmin, 1958). At a very simple level, children follow these argument structures in their dialogues. Consider first a group of American kindergarten children discussing a black Santa (Paley, 1981, pp. 91–92):

Rose:	I saw a black Santa Claus.
Kenny:	He can't be black. He has to be only white [questions fact].
Rose:	I saw him at Sears [factual support].
Warren:	Santa Claus is white [support with general law].
Wally:	If you're black, Santa Claus is black, and if you're white, Santa Claus is white. But I think he's white [general principle and personal experience].
Teacher:	But aren't you black, Wally?
Wally:	I know. But I see Santa Claus, and he's white [personal experience].
Tanya:	I haven't seen a black Santa Claus, but I know he could be there, because everything comes in black and white. (*She looks around.*) Or Japanese. Or Chinese [questions personal experience with recourse to general principles].
Eddie:	No. I know only one color he should be. White. I saw him in the store [personal experience].
Teacher:	But Rose *saw* a black Santa.
Eddie:	He could have been dressing up like a black Santa [justification for exception].
Wally:	Did he talk, Rose? Maybe he had wires [request for backing].
Rose:	He said, "Ho, ho, ho!"
Wally:	I think he was real.
Tanya:	See, someone must be dressed up to be a certain kind of Santa Claus. If they need a white one, *he* comes out. If they need a black one, *he* comes out [resolution of conflict].

Next, consider a group of Italian 7-year-olds discussing where tap water comes from. They had already established that in Florence, where they live, the water comes from the river Arno. In this excerpt, they requested and discussed warrants and backings for the inference they have drawn that all tap water comes from the Arno (Pontecorvo, 1985, pp. 9–10):

And: But there isn't just one Arno in the whole world? [questions warrant for assumption].

Gin: How does he know there is not just one Arno? . . . There are a lot of rivers; he hasn't been everywhere. [questions factual backing].

Bar: He imagines them. He didn't need to go everywhere to find out how many rivers there are [appeal to general principles to provide foundation for the emerging many rivers hypothesis].

Bar: In Florence there is only one [limits the general principle].

T: But near where I live there is another [antithesis to limitation].

Be: It must be the one I have seen [brings in corroborating personal experience].

Ef: He knows there are many rivers in the world. There are many rivers in the world because the world is large enough for there to be many rivers, so there are many rivers [appeal to general principle ad rem which provides further backing for many rivers hypotheses].

Alternative Points of View.   The classic case of confrontation involves conflicting points of view. For example, let us return to the American kindergarten children who are having a disagreement about the size of the classroom rugs they are using as props to act out "Jack and the Beanstalk" (Paley, 1981, pp. 13–14):

Wally: The big rug is the giant's castle. The small one is Jack's house.

Eddie: Both rugs are the same.

Wally: They can't be the same. Watch me. I'll walk around the rug. Now watch—walk, walk, walk, walk, walk, walk, walk, walk, walk— count all these walks. OK. Now count the other rug. Walk, walk, walk, walk, walk. See? That one has more walks.

Eddie: No fair. You cheated. You walked faster.

Wally: I don't have to walk. I can just look.

Eddie: I can look too. But you have to measure it. You need a ruler. About six hundred inches or feet.

Wally: We have a ruler.

Eddie: Not that one. Not the short kind. You have to use the long kind that gets curled up in a box.

Wally: Use people. People's bodies. Lying down in a row.

Eddie: That's a great idea. I never even thought of that.

Eddie and Wally readily settled their disagreement by agreeing to an impartial method of proof. Similarly, the children, after reading "Stone Soup" and missing the point of the story, demanded proof that stones melt by actually boiling some. Some argued that the stones were smaller (have melted), others that they were just the same.

Ellen: They're much smaller.
Fred: Much, much. Almost melted.
Mickey: Draw a picture of them.
Teacher: And cook them again? All right.

The children then compared the picture (large) and the stones (small) and declared them to be melted. The teacher intervened (Paley, 1981, pp. 17–18):

Teacher: I know they seem smaller, but it's very hard to match stones and patterns. Is there another way to prove whether the stones have melted?
Teacher: Let's weigh them on this scale. How much do they weigh?
Everyone: Two.
Teacher: Two pounds.
Lisa: Do we have to cook them again? They'll just keep melting.
(*After a short period of boiling, they weight the stones again.*)
Eddie: Still two. But they *are* smaller.
Teacher: They weigh the same. Two pounds before and two pounds now. That means they didn't lose weight.
Eddie: They only got a *little* bit smaller.
Wally: The scale can't *see* the stones.

The issue of conflicting points of view in children has been studied most rigorously by Genevan psychologists (Doise & Mugny, 1984; Inhelder, Sinclair, & Bovet, 1974), who have extended Piaget's concern with peer group learning. Their model experiment consists of dyads or small groups of children trying to solve classic Piagetian tasks. The majority of studies concern various forms of perspective-taking or conservation tasks designed for children transitional between preoperational and concrete operational thought (5 to 7 years of age). In the more recent studies (Perret-Clermont, 1980), fairly strict measures of reliability and generalization are taken as posttest measures of individual learning. Such studies show that collaboration leads to enhanced performance and is particularly beneficial for children entering the experiment with partial understanding; collaboration pushes them over the edge, as it were (but see Russell, 1981, 1982a for an alternative explanation). The research agenda, given these findings, becomes one of systematically establishing what in the group setting accelerates learning.

We can summarize an extensive literature (see review by Doise & Mugny, 1984; Perret-Clermont, 1980) by saying that the superiority of collaborative cognition cannot be accounted for simply in terms of the less informed children imitating those who already know. It appears that group experiences result in "fundamental cognitive restructuring," not mere temporary compliance or imitation. Furthermore, not all social interactions automatically lead to individual cognitive growth. The facilitating effect of collaborative cognition depends on a number of key factors, the first being the initial competence of the child; only when a child has a partial grasp of the concept in question will peer interactions be effective. Second, the social status of the children is important. One member of the group must not be so dominant that the result is pseudoconsensus, with a weaker child giving way to a dominant one without considering the alternative view (Russell, 1982b). Indeed, problems with compliance and pseudoconsensus led Piaget to believe that adults are less effective catalysts of change than peers. Third, children must be faced with a view that not only conflicts with their own but is also one that they can take seriously. Serious opposition is consistent, reasonable, and backed by data and warrants. It forces children to question their own position, to recognize the opposition as a "valid centration," and to compare it with their own. Sometimes, before it will be taken seriously, two out of three members of a triad must press the opposing view; one against one is not enough.

Change does not occur when pseudoconsensus or juxtaposed centrations are tolerated (Russell, 1982b). For example, in a typical conservation of length task, two identical sticks are placed parallel with their ends aligned. The children judge that they are equal. One stick is then displaced to the side, and the children are again asked if they are the same length. Two children may disagree, one claiming that they are still the same length, the other that now one is longer. Pseudoconsensus that would resolve this disagreement could take the following form, "When you are looking at it, it is bigger, but when I'm looking, they are just the same." Similarly, the children might agree that one stick is now longer but not which one it is" . . . where you are looking, that stick looks very big, but from where I'm standing, it's not so big." These tendencies toward conciliation and pseudoagreement are exacerbated by defensive attributional styles, wherein a child attributes differences to his or her own ineptitude or to his or her partner's supposed expertise.

Although conflict may be an essential trigger, it has been argued that change is more readily the result of processes of co-elaboration and co-construction (Bryant, 1982; Russell, 1982a,b). Confrontation provides a vantage point from which the children come to challenge both points of view. Together they elaborate, modify, and restructure, thereby producing a new theory that takes into account their individual differences.

The importance of co-construction is not limited to Piagetian tasks but has been documented on games such as Mastermind (Glachan, 1982; Glachan & Light, 1982). Because these tasks result in a great deal of spontaneous argument, systematic examination of relations between discourse form and the type of posttest improvement should be possible. Such fine-grained analyses of what happens in group discussions and what type of learning occurs are badly needed.

In summary, change is not the automatic outcome of group problem solving. It is not the result of social qua social, motivational qua motivational, or even conflict qua conflict; it is the result of certain social settings that force the elaboration and justification of various positions. Groups, peers, and adults can cause change, if they set into motion the appropriate processes. By extension, experienced learners can cause change on their own by adopting these process roles in thought experiments, or by "internalizing" role models from their experiences of group discussion in later intrapersonal dialogues.

Internalization

Both the support and conflict aspects of cooperative learning settings can be gradually removed from the social plane as they are individualized, internalized, or adopted as independent cognition. Indeed, both Piaget and Vygotsky visualized a form of internal dialogue where the mature thinker plays all the roles, the function of such inner dialogues being that of planning, guiding, and monitoring thought and action. Vygotsky (1978) states: "The greatest change in children's capacity to use language as a problem solving tool takes place somewhat later in development, when socialized speech (which has previously been used to address an adult) *is turned inward*. Instead of appealing to the adult, children appeal to themselves; language thus takes on an *intrapersonal function* in addition to its *interpersonal use*" (p. 27).

Piaget (1926) adds:

> The adult, even in his most personal and private occupation, even when he is engaged on an inquiry which is incomprehensible to his fellow-beings, thinks socially, has continually in his mind's eye his collaborators or opponents, actual or eventual, at any rate members of his own profession to whom sooner or later he will announce the result of his labours. This mental picture pursues him throughout his task. The task itself is henceforth socialized at almost every stage of development . . . the need for checking and demonstrating calls into being an inner speech addressed throughout to a hypothetical opponent whom the imagination often pictures as one of flesh and blood. When, therefore, the adult is brought face to face with his fellow beings, what he announces to them is something already socially elaborated and therefore roughly adapted to his audience. (p. 59)

THE ZONE OF PROXIMAL DEVELOPMENT, EXPERT SCAFFOLDING, AND SOCRATIC DIALOGUES

Three theories of guided learning that share a family resemblance are the zone of proximal development adapted from Vygotsky's theory (Vygotsky, 1978), expert scaffolding most commonly associated with Wood and Bruner (Bruner, 1978; Wood, 1980; Wood, Bruner, & Ross, 1976; Wood & Middleton, 1975), and Socratic dialogues (Collins & Stevens, 1982; Davis, 1966).

The Zone of Proximal Development. Vygotsky (1978) intended the notion of a zone of proximal development to capture the fact, widely recognized then and now, that "learning should be matched in some manner with the child's developmental status" (p. 85). But he went farther, by arguing that one cannot understand the child's developmental level unless one considers two aspects of it: the *actual developmental level* and the *potential development level.* "The zone of proximal development is the distance between the actual developmental level as determined by independent problem solving and the level of potential development as determined through problem solving under adult guidance, or in collaboration with more capable peers" (p. 86). Vygotsky (1978) argues that what children can do with the assistance of others is "even more indicative of their mental development than what they can do alone" (p. 85).

By observing learners operating within a zone of proximal development, we are able to mark bandwidths of competence (Brown & Reeve, in press) within which a child can navigate. At the lower boundaries are those "fruits" of "developmental cycles already completed," a conservative estimate of the child's status. At the upper bound are the estimates of just emerging competence that are actually *created* by the interactions of a supportive context. According to Vygotsky (1978), social interaction creates zones of proximal development that operate initially only in collaborative interactions. But, gradually, the newly awakened processes "are internalized, they become part of the child's *independent developmental achievement*" (p. 90). The upper bound of today's competence becomes the springboard of tomorrow's achievements (Brown & Reeve, in press).

It is important to note that, without any explicit instructional goal, social settings can provide learning zones for novices. Group problem-solving settings of the kind discussed earlier provide a learning forum for their members, even though the guiding activity is successful problem solution, regardless of individual contributions or the potential for personal development. Similarly, many situations examined by those interested in the zone of proximal development involve informal apprenticeships, where the teaching function is a minor part of the total activity. Typical of learning in informal settings is a reliance on *proleptic teaching* (Rogoff & Gardner, 1984; Wertsch & Stone, 1979). Proleptic means "in anticipation of competence" and refers to situations where novices are encouraged to participate in a group activity before they are able to perform unaided, the social context supporting the individual's efforts. The novice carries out simple aspects of the task while observing and learning from an expert, who serves as a model for higher level involvement.

In many cultures children are initiated into adult work activities such as weaving (Greenfield, 1980, 1984), tailoring (Lave, 1977), marketing (Lave, Murtaugh, & de la Rocha, 1984), and so forth, without explicit formal instruction (Cole & Bruner, 1971; Cole & Scribner, 1975). The expert members of the group have as their main agenda the task (of weaving, tailoring, etc.) and are only secondarily concerned with initiating the novice, or overseeing the progress of the apprentice. It is the adult who is responsible for getting the task done, with the child participating first as a spectator, then as a novice responsible for very little of the actual work (Laboratory of Comparative Human Cognition, 1983). As the apprentices become more experienced and capable of performing more complex aspects of the task, aspects that have been modeled by adults time and time again, they are ceded greater and greater responsibility until they become experts themselves. Within these systems of tutelage, novices learn about the task at their own rate, in the presence of experts, participating only at a level they are capable of fulfilling at any point in time.

Note the role of children or novices in such enterprises. They join in, often on their own initiative or with seemingly little pressure from the adults; they participate only at the level they are currently able to perform, or just beyond. They are rarely allowed to fail because errors are costly to production of a concrete product, the major task at hand. There is rarely any demand for solo performance on the part of children; indeed, it is often difficult to measure any child's individual contribution because everyone is participating at the same time. Children perform well within their range of competence; rarely are they called on to perform beyond their capacity; the adults do not expose the children's ignorance but jointly benefit from their increasing competence. Collaborative learning environments, through a nexus of social support, shared goals, modeling, and incidental instruction, create new levels of competence in the young.

Expert Scaffolding.   A closely related theory is that of expert scaffolding, which was also developed to deal with the instructional role assumed by an expert, implicitly or explicitly, in guiding children's learning. Most commonly studied have been mother–child interactions within the context of problem solving (Wertsch, 1978; Wood, 1980), language acquisition (Cazden, 1979; Greenfield, 1984; Scollon, 1976), and apprenticeship systems (Greenfield, 1984). The expert acts as a guide, shaping the learning efforts of novices, providing support for their inchoate learning until it is no longer needed. The metaphor of a scaffold captures the idea of an adjustable and temporary support that can be removed when no longer necessary. For example, Wood has shown that parental tutorial interventions are inversely related to the child's level of competence—so the more difficulty a particular child has, the more directive the intervention of the adult would be (Wood, 1980). In more detail, Greenfield (1984) sets out the common structure of scaffolded instruction in two quite disparate informal guided learning settings, language acquisition and learning to weave. The structure consists of six elements: (a) the extent of aid, or scaffolding, is adapted to the learner's current state; (b) the amount of scaffolding decreases as the skill of the learner increases; (c) for a learner at any one skill level, greater assistance is given if task difficulty increases, and vice versa; (d) scaffolding is accompanied by shaping—local correction and aid are given in response to the child's current performance; (e) the aid or scaffolding is eventually internalized, permitting independent skilled performance; and finally (f) in both the language and weaving contexts, the teacher appears to be generally unaware of her teaching function.

Socratic Dialogues.   A third theory of instruction with obvious family resemblance to the preceding is the Socratic dialogue (Collins & Stevens, 1982) or discovery teaching method (Davis, 1966). These are classic examples of expert-guided group discussions. Central to these methods is the tripartite goal of teaching: (a) the facts and concepts; (b) a rule or theory to account for these concepts; and (c) a method for deriving rules or theories in general. Socratic teachers achieve this end by a variety of standard questioning activities that force students to elaborate, justify, and provide warrants and backings for their statements.

Teachers routinely use five main discussion ploys: (a) *systematic variation of cases,* selected to help students focus on relevant facts; (b) *counterexamples and hypothetical cases* are suggested to question the legitimacy of students' conclusions; (c) *entrapment strategies* are used to lure students into making incorrect predictions or premature formulations of general rules based on faulty reasoning; (d) *hypothesis identification strategies* are aimed at forcing students to specify their working hypotheses; and (e) *hypothesis evaluation strategies* are used to make students evaluate predictions and hypotheses critically.

Throughout the discussions, which often seem free ranging, even rambling, the teacher has a consistent *agenda* of goals and subgoals; higher order goals aim at eventual understanding, opportunistic lower level goals aim at diagnosing and correcting local misconceptions. Teachers have consistent priorities for organizing their goal hierarchies; they tend to take up errors before omissions, easy misconceptions before fundamentally wrong thinking, prior steps in theory before later steps, important factors before less important ones, and so on. In group settings, teachers tend to address students who have not participated recently before those who are more engaged. There is also order in the teacher's method for selecting teaching examples and analogies—ones that exemplify important factors and cases are stressed and grouped together so that significant generalizations can be reached. Finally the teacher fields questions based on his or her model of the students' knowledge, skipping topics assumed to be known (too simple) or beyond their existing competence (too advanced), and concentrating on what students can assimilate now. Given the continual growth in knowledge, such models of student understanding must be constantly adjusted.

The advantage claimed for Socratic methods is that they model modes of scientific thought, thereby teaching students how to think, rather than merely conveying a particular set of content material. Furthermore, Socratic teachers can interact with individual students within their own levels of (mis)understanding. Such teachers are able to gauge how well each student has learned the material by probing for generalized and novel applications of the principles involved. Claims of increased student engagement and motivation are also common.

On the negative side, such discovery methods are associated with low-information transfer rate, extensive discussion focuses on a limited set of material. And perhaps for this reason, it has been suggested that the method is no more, perhaps even less, effective than lectures (Anderson & Faust, 1974). This is true if tests of effectiveness cover only content retention. Yet to be proven are general improvements in thinking skills, an important item on the agenda for future research.

Internalization.   The learning theories underlying the related notions of a zone of proximal development, expert scaffolding, and Socratic dialogues all rely heavily on the mechanism of *internalization* to fuel individual conceptual development. The hope is that Socratic-like methods will be internalized in such a way that individuals can self-test, self-question, and eventually provide entrapment arguments for their own hypotheses and generalizations. These activities of "knowledge worrying" (Brown, 1985; Brown & Campione, 1981) would then become part of an individual's own hypothesis-testing mental activities, feeding directly into the young child's propensity to conduct thought experiments with more and more sophisticated and systematic ways of doing so. The mature learner is capable of autocriticism and mental experimentation, which Binet singled out as the hallmark of intelligence (Binet, 1909; Brown, 1985) and Piaget (1976b), in the notion of reflective abstraction, regarded as the central pillar of formal thought.

RECIPROCAL TEACHING OF COMPREHENSION STRATEGIES

Theoretical Rationale

In this section we focus on our own work on cooperative learning and expert scaffolding as embodied in a procedure known as reciprocal teaching. (See Brown & Palincsar, 1982, 1987; Palincsar & Brown, 1984, 1985 for details.) Reciprocal teaching was designed to provide a simple introduction to group discussion techniques aimed at understanding and remembering text content. The group provides social support, shared expertise, and role models. Within this context, the teacher provides expert scaffolding when he or she attempts to modulate the children's discussion. We believed that, if we could establish a very simple routine that could be handled by average teachers and less-than-average students, it would be possible later to build on it and provide practice in more complicated argument structures of premises, justifications, warrants, and backings.

Reciprocal teaching takes place in a cooperative learning group that features guided practice in applying simple concrete strategies to the task of text comprehension. The basic procedure is simple. An adult teacher and a group of students take turns leading a discussion on the contents of a section of text that they are jointly attempting to understand. The discussions are free ranging, but four strategic activities must be practiced routinely: *questioning, clarifying, summarizing,* and *predicting.* The dialogue leader begins the discussion by asking a question on the main content and ends by summarizing the gist. If there is disagreement, the group rereads and discusses potential candidates for question and summary statements until they reach consensus. Summarizing provides a means by which the group can monitor its progress, noting points of agreement and disagreement. Particularly valuable is the fact that summarizing at the end of a period of discussion helps students establish where they are in preparation for tackling a new segment of text. Attempts to clarify any comprehension problems that might arise are also an integral part of the discussions. And, finally, the leader asks for predictions about future content. Throughout, the adult teacher provides guidance and feedback tailored to the needs of the current discussion leader and his or her respondents.

The procedure was designed to create a zone of proximal development for learners and to embody expert scaffolding and a cooperative learning environment. The group is jointly responsible for understanding and evaluating the text message. All members of the group, in turn, serve as learning leaders, the ones responsible for orchestrating the dialogue, and as learning listeners (Yager, Johnson, & Johnson, 1985) or supportive critics (Binet, 1909; Brown, 1985), those whose job it is to encourage the discussion leader to explain the content and help resolve misunderstandings. The goal is joint construction of meaning: The strategies provide concrete heuristics for getting the procedure going, the reciprocal nature of the procedure forces student engagement, and the teacher modeling provides examples of expert performance.

The deceptively simple reciprocal teaching procedure is based on several theoretical principles involving the strategies taught, the environment in which they are taught, and the role of the instructor in guiding learning.

Strategies.   First consider the strategies: questioning, clarifying, summarizing, and predicting were not randomly chosen activities. They are examples of strategic activities that good students routinely bring to the task of studying texts but poor students rarely report using, either during on-line attempts to study or in retrospective reports (Brown & Lawton, work in progress). Furthermore, they serve an interesting dual function, if used intelligently; they both improve comprehension and afford the alert reader an opportunity for monitoring understanding. For example, if one attempts to paraphrase a section of text and fails, this is a sure sign that comprehension and retention of main points is not proceeding smoothly and that some remedial action, such as rereading, is called for. The strategies are *self-testing mechanisms,* and there is ample evidence that such self-testing improves comprehension (Brown, Armbruster, & Baker, 1986).

In reciprocal teaching, the strategies are practiced in an *appropriate context,* during studying, not as isolated skill exercises to be mastered individually and then used whenever the students see fit. Each strategy is called into play in response to a concrete problem of text comprehension. For example, the students learned that summarizing was a test to see if they understood what had happened in the text. If they could not summarize a section, it was regarded as an important indication that comprehension was not proceeding as it should, not as a failure to perform a particular skill. Similarly, clarifying occurred only if misunderstandings were generated by some unclear aspect of the text or by a student's interpretation of the content. The strategies were introduced as tools to provide a backbone for the discussion and to achieve the acknowledged goal of understanding and remembering. The main goal was *not* refining the strategies but understanding the text; of course, improvement in strategy use was a much-welcomed side benefit.

The discussions focused on both the text content and the student's *understanding of the strategies* they were practicing. For example, discussion of the aptness of a particular summary statement in capturing the essential gist taught students about the strategies and helped them to understand the particular content of any one text.

Another interesting feature of these particular strategic activities is that they can serve to structure intrapersonal as well as social dialogues. Reviewing content (summarizing), attempting to resolve misunderstandings (clarifying), anticipating possible future text development (predicting), and assessing the state of one's gradually accumulating knowledge (questioning) are all activities that the experienced learner engages in while studying independently, by means of an internal dialogue. The reciprocal teaching procedure renders such internal attempts at understanding *external*. Reciprocal teaching provides social support during the inchoate stages of the development of internal dialogues. In the course of repeated practice such meaning-extending activities, first practiced socially, are gradually adopted as part of the learner's personal repertoire of learning strategies.

Finally, these particular strategies are *readily taught,* at least to the extent that the novice can begin participating early. Closing one's eyes (metaphorically) and retelling what one has just read is the first step towards more and more sophisticated attempts to state the gist in as few words as possible. Similarly, asking about the meaning of unknown words is a clarification exercise that lays the ground for more subtle comprehension monitoring of unknown or unclear ideas or referents. Practically, it is very important that the students can handle an easy version of the strategies quickly, thus providing them with entree into the discussions. Refinement in strategy use, however, is gradual and takes considerable practice.

The Learning Environment. Reciprocal teaching was designed to provide a zone of proximal development within which novices could take on greater responsibility for more expert roles. The group cooperation ensures that mature performance is maintained, even if each individual member of the group is not yet capable of full participation. It embodies a form of proleptic teaching that can best be understood by comparison to what it is not. Consider tried and true educational procedures such as easy-to-hard sequences and fading. In such procedures, the novice learner is introduced to a skill by starting out on a decontextualized easy version of it. On success, often after errorless learning on the easy task, a more difficult version is "faded in," and this step is repeated through gradually incrementing levels of difficulty until the learner is confronted with the "mature" version of the target task. The easy versions, however, are often pale shadows of the real task; indeed, the early forms are often unrecognizable as facsimiles of the target task. Thus, one way of making the task easier is to divide it into manageable subcomponents and to provide practice on these in isolation until they are perfected. This increases the likelihood that the easy tasks will not resemble the complex target, and it is often the case in educational settings that the role of recombining the subcomponents (vertical transfer) or using them flexibly in tasks of which they are elements (lateral transfer) is left up to the student with disastrous results (Gagné, 1965).

In proleptic teaching, by contrast, the integrity of the target task is maintained; components are handled in the context of the entire task; skills are practiced in context. The aim of understanding the texts remains as undisturbed as possible, but the novice's *role* is made easier by the provision of expert scaffolding and a supportive social context that does a great deal of the cognitive work until the novice can take over more and more of the responsibility. The task, though, remains the same, the goal the same, the desired outcome the same. There is little room for confusion about the point of the activity, thus finessing to some extent problems of metacognition and transfer (Brown, 1978; Brown & Campione, 1984).

The cooperative feature of the learning group in reciprocal teaching, where everyone is trying to arrive at consensus concerning meaning, relevance, and importance, is an ideal setting for novices to practice their emergent skills. All the responsibility for comprehending does not lie on their shoulders, only part of the work is theirs, and even if they fail when called on to be discussion leaders, the others, including the adult teacher, are there to keep the discussion going. The group shares the responsibility for thinking and thus reduces the anxiety associated with keeping the argument going singlehandedly (Pontecorvo, 1985). Because the group's efforts are externalized in the form of a discussion, novices can contribute what they are able and learn from the contributions of those more expert than they. In this sense, the reciprocal teaching dialogues create a zone of proximal development (Brown & Ferrara, 1985; Vygotsky, 1978) for their participants, each of whom may share in the activity to the extent that he or she is able. Collaboratively, the group, with its variety of expertise, engagement, and goals, gets the job done; the text gets read and understood. What changes over time is who has the responsibility for strategic activities.

This notion of a social setting creating a zone of proximal development for its members in which they can exercise cognitive activities that are just emerging should not be equated with the notion of expert scaffolding, which it closely resembles (Griffen & Cole, 1984). For the activities of the group members are not explicitly designed to tutor the needy. Just by being privy to the group activities allows the novice to witness comprehension strategies that might not have been understood before, thereby opening up wider and wider potential zones of development.

Within reciprocal teaching, however, one member of the group does have an explicit instructional goal. The teacher does engage in deliberate scaffolding techniques when he or she directs attention to the current discussion leader in an attempt to improve his or her level of participation. Thus, reciprocal teaching is *both* a cooperative learning group jointly negotiating the understanding task *and* a direct instruction forum wherein the teacher attempts to provide temporary scaffolding to bolster the learning leader's inchoate strategies. As such, it embodies the main features thought to make *apprenticeship learning* so successful.

The Role of the Instructor.   The adult teacher in reciprocal teaching plays many roles. First, she provides a model of expert behavior. When it is her turn to be the teacher, and when she is shaping the teacher role playing of the students, she is able to model mature comprehension activities, thus making them *overt, explicit,* and *concrete.* Comprehension-fostering and -monitoring activities are difficult to observe as expert learners usually execute them covertly. In reciprocal teaching, the teacher can engage in the strategies overtly and hence provide a model of what it is that experts do when they try to understand and remember texts. This repetitive modeling serves to demonstrate to the students concrete ways of monitoring their own learning through methods they can readily understand. Instead of being told to "be strategic" and "monitor your comprehension," the students can emulate the teacher by retelling content in their own words, by asking what something means, and by posing questions about main points.

Second, the teacher has a *clear instructional goal.* In many forms of cooperative learning, the students are left to construct learning goals for themselves; the goals change over time as the interests of the group change (Griffen & Cole, 1984), and groups sometimes concoct goals far different from those envisaged by the authorities (Barnes & Todd, 1977). In reciprocal teaching, membership in the group is not democratic; the adult teacher is definitely a first among equals. Her goal is clearly one of keeping the discussion focused on the content and directing the group's efforts towards cognitive economy, seeing that enough discussion takes place to ensure a reasonable level of understanding but no more.

Third, the adult teacher closely monitors the learning leaders, giving them room to control the discussions when they can. But she is always ready to provide feedback and, if necessary, to take back the leader role when things go awry. The adult teacher provides *feedback that is tailored to the students' existing levels,* encouraging them to progress gradually toward full competence. Note that students must participate when it is their turn to be the teacher, or when they answer the questions of the learning leaders, even if they are not yet expert. Because the students do participate, the teacher has an opportunity to gauge their competence, competence that is often masked in other settings by weaker students' tendency not to volunteer until they are sure of themselves, which may be never.

The responsibility for the comprehension activities is *transferred to the students as soon as they can take charge of their own learning*. The idea is for the teacher to take control only when needed and to hand over the responsibility to the students whenever they are ready. Through interactions with the supportive teacher, the students are guided to perform at an increasingly mature and challenging level. In response, the adult teacher gradually fades into the background and acts as a sympathetic coach, leaving the students to handle their own learning. Like a coach, the teacher is always monitoring the discussions and is ready to step back and relinquish control or step forward to take up the reins again when necessary.

Main Findings: The Reading Setting

The original development of the reciprocal teaching procedures took place in the context of reading groups consisting of seventh and eighth graders. Subsequently, however, we have adapted the procedures for use with first- and second-grade children in a listening comprehension setting. We give some of the key results from the reading program before turning to the newer work with listening comprehension.

Several features are common to many of the studies we have conducted with reading comprehension: (a) the students were selected from junior high schools on the basis of their low scores on reading comprehension tests; (b) the intervention was fairly extensive (by experimental standards) consisting of never fewer than 10 days of discussions and usually continuing for 4 weeks, or approximately 20 days; (c) progress was measured not only by observable changes in the students' participation in the discussions but also by daily independent tests of their reading and retention of novel passages (this is a conservative test of progress; most studies of group learning estimate individual retention of the discussed material only, *not* the application of the learned processes to novel materials); (d) long-term maintenance, transfer, and generalization were all measured with improvements in standardized test scores.

Participation in the Discussion.   Independent raters were quite able to rate the sophistication of the discussions by correctly assigning the transcripts to the first, second, and third phase of the intervention. Individual students' scores on the four strategies of summarization, question formulation, clarification, and prediction all showed large and reliable improvement (Brown & Palincsar, 1982; Palincsar & Brown, 1984). But these numerical facts do not begin to illustrate what actually happened to the students' participation—they progressed from relatively passive answerers of others' questions to quite adequate discussion leaders. Only by looking at the dialogues can one really grasp the extent of these changes.

As an example, consider a teacher interacting with a group of seventh-grade remedial readers. Excerpts from their discussions are shown in Tables 13.1 and 13.2 (taken from Palincsar & Brown, 1984). The dialogues are from early (Day 3) and later sessions (Day 13) with the same group of five students. In the early sessions (Table 13.1), the adult teacher is very much the learning leader, even though a student (A) has been assigned that responsibility. In this example, one segment of silent reading is followed by an extensive discussion, where the students interact with one another only once (statements 1–3); the remaining interactions follow a typical teacher-directed classroom format, simple reciprocation (Mehan, 1979), where the teacher is followed by a student repeatedly.

The same group is seen again, 10 instructional days later, in the dialogue shown in Table 13.2. Here, three reading–discussion sets are included in 29 statements, rather than only one as on Day 3. And now the majority of the interactions are student controlled, with the teacher interspersing praise, encouragement (4, 10, 12), and management (4, 14, 21). The teacher intercedes with advice and modeling only when a student misses the point and the others do not catch it (18, 26, 28). The teacher has moved from the pivotal role of responding individually to each student to that of a coach who sits in the background, offers encouragement, and occasionally pushes for a better interpretation of the text. The teacher provides just the degree of structure necessary for the discussion to remain on track, leaving the students to take over as much responsibility as they can.

In Table 13.3 (taken from Palincsar & Brown, 1984), we provide selected excerpts of a teacher interacting over time with one member of the group. This particular seventh grader began the group discussions quite unable to take his part as dialogue leader because, quite simply, he could not formulate a question. He began as by far the weakest member of the group. The excerpts in Table 13.3 provide excellent examples of the expert scaffolding role of the teacher as she gradually shapes the student's question-asking ability. Within the context of the group activity, the teacher is able to provide individual help geared to each student's special needs.

Independent Learning.   The changes seen in the discussions were reflected in the students' independent studying behavior. Collapsing findings from across several replications of the intervention, we have found that students in general begin by scoring 30%–40% correct and reach a stable level of 70%–80% correct within 4 to 15 days. When the teachers are

TABLE 13.1
Reciprocal Dialogue from an Early Session (Day 3)

TEXT: CAN SNAKES STING WITH THEIR TONGUES?
No—snakes' tongues are completely harmless. They're used for feeling things and for sharpening the snakes' sense of smell. Although snakes can smell in the usual way, the tongue flickering in the air picks up tiny particles of matter. These particles are deposited in two tiny cavities at the base of the nostrils to increase the snakes's ability to smell.

1. A: Do snakes' tongues sting?
2. K: Sometimes.
3. A: Correct.
    This paragraph is about do snakes sting with their tongue, and different ways that the tongue is for and the senses of smell.
4. *T: Are there any questions?
5. C: Snakes' tongues don't sting.
6. *T: Beautiful! I thought, boy, I must have been doing some fast reading there because I missed that point. A_____, could you ask your question again?
7. A: Do snakes' tongues really sting?
8. *T: Now, A_____, since you have asked the question, can you find in that paragraph where the question is answered?
9. A: No, snakes' tongues are completely harmless.
10. *T: So we'll try it again. Can you generate another question that you think a teacher might ask?
11. A: What are the tongues used for?
12. *T: Good!
13. L: The sense of smell.
14. *T: Is that correct? A_____, do you disagree? Yes.
15. A: That answer was right, but there are other things that the tongue can do.
16. L: But she only said tell one, she didn't say tell all of them.
17. *T: OK.
18. B: It is used to pick up tiny particles.
19. *T: OK. I think that this is an important point. You have the basic concept which is correct, OK., but what the question really is saying is, is it used for smell? OK?
20. B: They are used for feeling things for sharpening snakes' sense of smell.
21. *T: OK. They are used for sharpening the snakes' sense of smell. Are they used for smelling? That's the point we aren't clear on.
22. L: In my answer I said it is for the sense of smell.
23. *T: This is fine; this is what the technique is all about. What it means is not that you are right or wrong or good or bad. What is says is that we have just read something and have had a disagreement about what it says. We need to work it out.
24. A: My prediction is that they will now talk about the different things about snakes. Where they live, and what they eat and stuff like that.
25. *T: OK. Good. What do you think they eat?
26. A: Animals.
27. A: Deserts.
28. C: I challenge. Snakes, all of them, don't live in the desert. They live in the woods and in swamp areas.

*Indicates turns taken by adult teacher

TABLE 13.2
Reciprocal Dialogue from a Later Session; Study 2, Group 3, Day 13

TEXT: In the United States salt is produced by three basic methods: solar (sun) evaporation, mining, and artificial heat evaporation. For salt to be extracted by solar evaporation, the weather must be hot and dry. Thus, solar salt is harvested in the tropic-like areas along our southern ocean coasts and at Great Salt Lake.

1.   C: Name three different basic methods how salt is produced.

2.   A: Evaporation, mining, evaporation . . . artificial heat evaporation.

3.   C: Correct, very good. My summary on this paragraph is about ways that salt is being produced.

4.   *T: Very good. Could you select the next teacher?
     (Student selects another student)

Text: The second oldest form of salt production is mining. Unlike early methods that made the work extremely dangerous and difficult, today's methods use special machinery, and salt mining is easier and safer. The old expression "back to the salt mine" no longer applies.

5.   L: Name two words that often describe mining salt in the old days.

6.   K: Back to the salt mines?

7.   L: No. Angela?

8.   A: Dangerous and difficult.

9.   L: Correct. This paragraph is all about comparing the old mining of salt and today's mining of salt.

10. *T: Beautiful!

11. L: I have a prediction to make.

12. *T: Good.

13. L: I think it might tell when salt was first discovered, well, it might tell what salt is made of and how it's made.

14. *T: OK. Can we have another teacher?

Text: Table salt is made by the third method—artificial evaporation. Pumping water into an underground salt bed dissolves the salt to make a brine that is brought to the surface. After purification at high temperatures, the salt is ready for our tables.

15. K: After purification at high temperatures the salt is ready for what?

16. C: Our tables.

17. K: That's correct. To summarize: After its purification, the salt is put on our tables.

18. *T: That was a fine job, Ken, and I appreciate all that work, but I think there might be something else to add to our summary. There is more important information that I think we need to include. This paragraph is mostly about what?

19. A: The third method of artificial evaporation.

20. B: It mainly tells about pumping water from an underground salt bed that dissolves the salt to make a brine that is brought to the surface.

21. *T: Angela hit it right on the money. This paragraph is mostly about the method of artificial evaporation and then everything else in the paragraph is telling us about that process. OK. Next teacher.

Text: For thousands of years people have known salt—tasting it, using it for their lives' needs. Sometimes it has been treasured as gold; other times it has been superstitiously tossed over the shoulder to ward off bad luck. Somehow people and salt have always been together, but never is the tie more complete than when the best people are called "the salt of the earth."

(continued)

TABLE 13.2 *(Continued)*

22.	C:	My question is, what are the best people called?
23.	L:	The salt of the earth.
24.	C:	Why?
25.	L:	Because salt and the people have been together so long.
26.	*T:	Chris, do you have something to add to that? OK. It really isn't because they have been together so long; it has to do with something else. Brian?
27.	B:	(reading) "People and salt have always been together but never has the tie been so complete."
28.	*T:	All right, but when we use the expression, "That person is the salt of the earth," we know that means that person is a good person. How do we know that?
29.	B:	Because we treasure salt, like gold.

seasoned volunteers, 98% of the students reach such a criterion (Palincsar & Brown, 1984).

Reciprocal Teaching is Instructionally Viable. In studies conducted by nonvolunteer, unselected teachers, the success rate was not quite so dramatic but still impressive, if we consider that the instructional period was only 4 weeks. For example, the results shown in Fig. 13.1 come from six teachers who were assigned to the program under conditions that were not exactly ideal, for 150 students were also assigned to the study, with the group size ranging from 8 to 18! And the teachers varied in their enthusi-

TABLE 13.3
The Acquisition of Question Asking
by a Weak Seventh-Grade Student (Charles)

Day 1:		
TEXT:		The water moccasin, somewhat longer than the copperhead, is found in the southeastern states. It lives in swampy regions. It belongs, as do also the copperhead and the rattlesnakes, to a group of poisonous snakes called pit vipers. They have pits between their eyes and their nostrils which, because they are sensitive to heat, help the snakes tell when they are near a warm-blooded animal. Another name for the water moccasin is "cottonmouth." This name comes from the white lining of the snake's mouth.
1.	S:	What is found in the southeastern snakes, also the copperhead, rattlesnakes, vipers—they have. I'm not doing this right.
2.	T:	All right. Do you want to know about the pit vipers?
3.	S:	Yeah.
4.	T:	What would be a good question about the pit vipers that starts with the word "why?"
5.	S:	(No response)
6.	T:	How about, "Why are the snakes called pit vipers?"
7.	S:	Why do they want to know that they are called pit vipers?
8.	T:	Try it again.

(continued)

TABLE 13.3 (*Continued*)

9.	S:	Why do they, pit vipers in a pit?
10.	T:	How about, "Why do they call the snakes pit vipers?"
11.	S:	Why do they call the snakes pit vipers?
12.	T:	There you go! Good for you.

Day 4:

TEXT: Spinner's mate is much smaller than she, and his body is dull brown. He spends most of his time sitting at one side of her web.

13.	S:	(No question)
14.	T:	What's this paragraph about?
15.	S:	Spinner's mate. How do spinner's mate . . .
16.	T:	That's good. Keep going.
17.	S:	How do spinner's mate is smaller than . . . How am I going to say that?
18.	T:	Take your time with it. You want to ask a question about spinner's mate and what he does, beginning with the word "how."
19.	S:	How do they spend most of his time sitting?
20.	T:	You're very close. The question would be, "How does spinner's mate spend most of his time?" Now, you ask it.
21.	S:	How does spinner's mate spend most of his time?

Day 7:

TEXT: Perhaps you are wondering where the lava and other volcanic products come from. Deep within our earth there are pockets of molten rock called magma. Forced upward in part by gas pressure, this molten rock continually tries to reach the surface. Eventually—by means of cracks in the crustal rocks or some similar zone of weakness—the magma may break out of the ground. It then flows from the vent as lava, or spews skyward as dense clouds of lava particles.

22.	S:	How does the pressure from below push the mass of hot rock against the opening? Is that it?
23.	T:	Not quite. Start your question with, "What happens when?"
24.	S:	What happens when the pressure from below pushes the mass of hot rock against the opening?
25.	T:	Good for you! Good job.

Day 11:

TEXT: One of the most interesting of the insect-eating plants is the Venus's flytrap. This plant lives in only one small area of the world—the coastal marshes of North and South Carolina. The Venus's flytrap doesn't look unusual. Its habits, however, make it truly a plant wonder.

26.	S:	What is the most interesting of the insect eating plants, and where do the plants live at?
27.	T:	Two excellent questions! They are both clear and important questions. Ask us one at at time now.

Day 15:

TEXT: Scientists also come to the South Pole to study the strange lights that glow overhead during the Antarctic night. (It's a cold and lonely world for the few hardy people who "winter over" the polar night.) These "southern lights" are caused by the Earth acting like a magnet on electrical particles in the air. They are clues that may help us understand the Earth's core and the upper edges of its blanket of air.

28.	S:	Why do scientists come to the South Pole to study?
29.	T:	Excellent question! That is what this paragraph is all about.

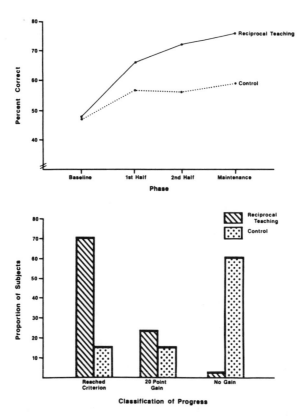

FIG. 13.1.   Independent learning scores of the junior high school students ($N = 150$) taking part in a reading conducted by regular classroom teachers.

asm, experience, and teaching skill, which ranged from barely adequate to outstanding. The teachers taught one reciprocal teaching group and another group in their regular fashion, thus serving as their own controls. Or at least this was the design; however, two of the better teachers unconsciously introduced more and more of the reciprocal teaching features into their control classes, which also began to improve, a desired outcome for the students but not for the experimenters. On the top half of Fig. 13.1, averaged data reveal the significant improvement of the reciprocal teaching group compared with the control classes. On the bottom half of Fig. 13.1 are the number of students reaching criterion or maintaining better than a 20 percentage point gain. Reciprocal teaching procedures result in significant individual student achievement, even under less than ideal circumstances (Palincsar & Brown, 1986; Palincsar, Brown, & Samsel, work in progress).

The reciprocal teaching procedure can be modified so that the essential features can be used in whole-class discussion. For example, seventh-grade teachers have introduced the discussion techniques into their science classes, where the number of students make the strict oral turn taking of reciprocal teaching unwieldy. In its place they substituted a procedure whereby the students and teacher read approximately four paragraphs silently, during which time they individually composed two questions and a summary statement in preparation for group discussions. After several segments had been covered, the teacher asked students to volunteer their responses and wrote several candidate summaries and questions on the board. Then, the students as a group debated the merits of each until they reached a degree of consensus on the most appropriate version. Requests for clarifications were also handled at this point. Over the semester, the students showed marked improvement on their written questions and summaries and on their classroom participation; in addition, they improved significantly (from 30%–70% correct) on daily independent tests of comprehension (Palincsar, Brown, & Samsel, work in progress).

In determining who can conduct reciprocal teaching, we have had some success in training peer tutors. We asked three adult teachers, experienced with reciprocal teaching, to supervise nine tutors, who were selected because, though they were classified as remedial readers, they scored well on our baseline assessments (70% correct). The teachers trained the tutors in the reciprocal teaching procedure and then assigned them one or more tutees who were performing poorly (40% or below) on baseline measures. The teachers supervised the initial tutoring sessions, giving aid and answering questions when needed. By the second half of the intervention, the tutors were able to bring the independent scores of their tutees up to 78% correct and, in so doing, reached a level of 87% correct themselves (Palincsar, Brown, & Dunn, in press).

Reciprocal Teaching is More Than the Sum of its Parts. These reliable improvements in reading comprehension scores do not come easily to the poor learning students who are our main clients. For example, to further test the effectiveness of the reciprocal teaching procedure, we have conducted a series of comparison studies where the method is pitted against a variety of control groups. We give just two examples here. In the original set of studies (Brown & Palincsar, 1982; Palincsar & Brown, 1984), we included obvious control conditions where, for example, students took all the daily tests but received no training. We also included a group of students who took the daily tests and had an equal number of instructional days devoted to a procedure, locating information, where the teacher guided the students in finding the answer to the questions in the text. These results are shown in Fig. 13.2. Only the reciprocal teaching

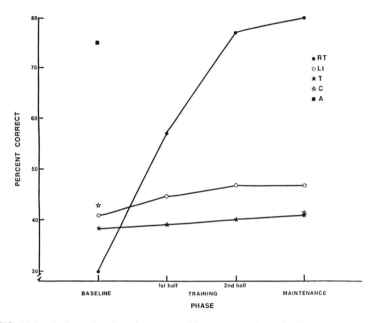

FIG. 13.2.   Independent learning scores of four groups of matched junior high school students. RT = students taught by volunteer teachers using the reciprocal teaching procedures; LI = students taught in a procedure that provided guided practice locating information to answer text questions; T = students who took all the independent tests but received no training; and C = an untreated control group. A refers to the level of performance set by average and above-average students on the test passages (Palincsar & Brown, 1984).

group showed reliable improvement, reaching the level set by average junior high school students.

One could legitimately argue that training on locating information, although it provided extensive practice in test taking, did not provide appropriate strategy training. Thus, the results from the initial control groups rule out explanations of the reciprocal teaching students' improvement in terms of practice, teacher attention, time-on-task, etc., but they do not separate the strategy training from the reciprocal teaching element. A great deal of research now suggests that explicit instruction in strategy use is necessary before significant improvement in students' independent performance is seen (Brown, Bransford, Ferrara, & Campione, 1983; Brown, Campione, & Day, 1981). Hence, we decided that it was not the most stringent test of the reciprocal teaching procedure to compare it to practice conditions only, or to an intervention that does not include appropriate strategy training. Therefore, in other studies (Brown, Palincsar, Samsel, & Dunn, work in progress), we contrasted reciprocal teaching to other training procedures that included instruction in the *identical strategies* of questioning, clarifying, summarizing, and predicting.

The results of one illustrative study are shown in Fig. 13.3. Groups of closely matched junior high school students, all with reading comprehension problems, were assigned to one of three training conditions or to a control group. Students in each of the training conditions received 12 sessions involving group instruction and independent daily tests. The three instructional groups were reciprocal teaching (RT), modeling (M), and explicit instruction (EI). In the modeling group, the teacher modeled how to use the four strategies on each segment of the passages and the students' role was to observe and answer the teacher-posed questions. In the explicit instruction group, the teacher demonstrated and discussed each strategy for the first half of the session; and in the second half, the students completed pencil and paper exercises in applying the strategies to the remaining text segments. Thus, modeling consisted of an expert talk-aloud procedure in which the teacher used the strategies for the students to see (Bereiter & Bird, 1985). Explicit instruction was based on normal classroom demonstration and practice routines. In both cases, however, the explicit teaching in the modeling and demonstration procedures was focused on the strategies themselves, not a common classroom practice (Durkin, 1984).

Not all methods of training comprehension strategies are equal. In Fig.

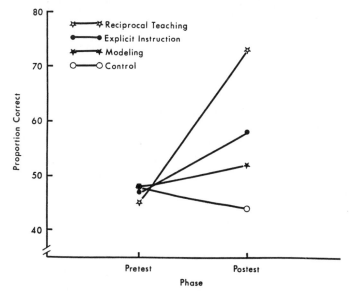

FIG. 13.3   Independent learning of three groups of matched junior high school students receiving strategy training and an untreated control.

13.3, all groups improved except the untreated control. But the reciprocal teaching students' performance was significantly better than that of the other two instructional groups. Reciprocal teaching, where the students receive instruction, modeling, and practice, gradually taking charge of their own learning, is by far the most effective form of intervention (Brown, Palincsar, Samsel, & Dunn, work in progress).

Generalization of the Effect.   We would like to emphasize that these improvements in individual learning scores were maintained over time, for up to 6 months in the one study where we were able to test after such a delay (Brown & Palincsar, 1982), and always after 2 months, the time span of our routine maintenance check (Palincsar & Brown, 1984).

Perhaps a more dramatic indication of the effects of reciprocal teaching instruction is the extent to which the students improved in settings other than those orchestrated by our project personnel. In general, we have found three types of transfer of training: (1) generalizations to the classroom, (2) improved performance on posttests that tap the trained skills, and (3) improvement in standardized test scores. Representative transfer data, taken from the original Palincsar and Brown (1984) studies, are shown in Fig. 13.4. Entries 1 and 2 present data taken from classroom generalization probes. Following a traditional practice in the cognitive behavior modification literature (Meichenbaum, 1977), tests identical to our daily independent learning assessments were administered in the classroom setting. The students read science and social studies content passages and answered comprehension questions on them from memory. No mention was made that these tasks formed part of the study and, to maintain the cover, all seventh graders ($N = 130$) took the tests as part of their regular classroom activity. In the top part of Fig. 13.4, the performance over time of the reciprocal teaching group is compared with that of matched control students. The reciprocal teaching group showed steady improvement, whereas the control students did not. Perhaps of more interest are the data shown in the second part of Fig. 13.4; this is the reciprocal teaching students' improvement in percentile rankings compared with all the seventh graders in the school (students drawn from the full range of ability). Whereas the control group showed only random fluctuations in their rankings, the reciprocal teaching students improved dramatically, bringing their level to *above* the average for their age.

The third set of statistics shown in Fig. 13.4 are the reciprocal teaching students' improvements on standardized tests of reading comprehension. Again, the improvement was dramatic; one third of the students tested at or *above* grade level. Similar findings were found when nonselected teachers conducted the program, with students in reading groups improving 11

Classroom Generalization Data

1) <u>Classroom Probes</u>

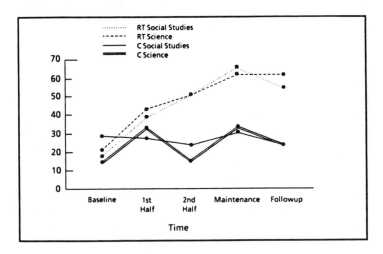

2) <u>Changes in Percentile Rankings</u>

		Pretest	Posttest
Reciprocal Teaching:	Social Studies	25	78
	Science	5	69
Control Groups:	Social Studies	13	11
	Science	20	18

3) <u>Standardized Tests</u>

	(Gates-McGinitie)	
	Comprehension	Vocabulary
Reciprocal Teaching:	+ 20 month	+ 4 months
Control Groups:	+ 1 month	+ 3 months

4) <u>Laboratory Transfer</u>

Significant transfers to novel tests of summarizing, questioning, and clarification.

FIG. 13.4. Transfer measures taken from reciprocal teaching students taught by volunteer teachers (Palincsar & Brown, 1984).

months and those in the science classes 15 months, after a few weeks of instruction (Palincsar, Brown & Samsel, work in progress).

Finally, reciprocal teaching students, but not the controls, showed significant improvement on laboratory tests that differed in appearance from the training tasks but could be said to tap the same underlying processes. This improvement was sufficient to bring them up to the level set by average junior high students. Reciprocal teaching students showed reliable improvement in their ability to apply macrorules to writing summaries (Brown & Day, 1983), to invent appropriate comprehension questions to accompany a text, and to detect (clarify) anomalous sentences (Harris, Kruithof, Terwogt, & Visser, 1981).

Main Findings: The Listening Setting

Over the past 4 years, we have been working on an adaptation of the reciprocal teaching procedure to be used with younger and more severely impaired learners, those whose lack of decoding skill compounds their comprehension difficulties. It is entirely possible that the child with problems of listening in the first few grades will become the student with reading comprehension difficulties and inadequate study skills in the later grades. Can the reciprocal teaching training procedure be adapted to the needs of these younger children? Our aim was to train and test the identical strategies and procedures in both listening and reading. If we can diagnose and treat the comprehension problem early in a child's academic career, we might be able to alleviate some of the problems associated with extensive failure experiences, with all the attendant problems such failure portends (Brown, Palincsar, & Purcell, 1985; Dweck, 1989).

In this discussion we concentrate on the listening training only. Our work with listening comprehension followed the same route as that with reading. We began by developing, refining, and establishing the details of the procedure in a laboratory setting where the teaching was undertaken by experts. Only then did we test the procedures in the regular classroom, recruiting average teachers to see if we could obtain reasonable results under the normal pressures of the classroom. We discuss only the classroom studies here. (See Brown & Palincsar, 1986 for details of the laboratory studies.)

In a representative classroom study, 17 first-grade teachers were assigned to the project, 8 in the first year, 3 in the second, and 6 in the third. As the data are not yet fully analyzed, we report the findings from the first 2 years only, and hence the data are from 11 teachers. Each teacher received 3 days of in-service training and then interacted with groups consisting of 6 first graders. Each group met for 20 days of instruction. As each teacher instructed 2 groups per year, the data from 132 experimental children (and 66 controls) are reported.

Each group of six consisted of four high-risk children, each in need of individual educational programs (IEPs) and awaiting more permanent special education placement testing. The remaining two children per group were selected as teacher supporters. The nonvolunteer teachers were more than dubious that the weaker students could participate in the discussions and, as a safeguard against total disaster, wanted to include children who they felt could handle the procedure. These children supposedly had no learning problems; however, in this particular district all the children, including the teacher supporters, performed at or below the median on standardized scores.

Participation in the Discussion.   Look first at one group in detail. The group consisted of Mara and Charlie, the teacher supporters, and Daryl, Susan, Reggie, and Justin, the high-risk children. The examples we have selected primarily feature Daryl, a slow learner with both speech and hearing problems that caused some concern about his ability to participate in the group. Daryl had a full-scale IQ of 82, and his individual listening scores before instruction averaged 44%. During training, he showed steady improvement, scoring 60% during the first half and 80% during the second half of the intervention.

Daryl failed to contribute spontaneously for the first 6 days, and the teacher did not call on him. Daryl stuttered, and when he did begin to contribute, the teacher tended to come to his aid too quickly to spare him embarrassment. By the last few days, however, Daryl had improved dramatically.

Let us pick up the group on Day 18. They are halfway through a long passage about Daddy Long Legs. In Table 13.4 are two teacher statements, only one of which (20) is a clarification of a major misunderstanding. Daryl, *without help,* came up with an excellent question, albeit clumsily phrased, led the discussion, and composed a reasonable summary. He was in total charge of the dialogue until statement 11, when Mara asked for clarification of the ambiguous *it* (10) that gives out its bad smells. Daryl knew the answer (21) but could not quite deal with the confusion, so the teacher cleared it up for him (20). The teacher only spoke up when needed; she had the children settle the dispute if they could.

Table 13.5 begins with an interruption for a vocabulary clarification and a long segment follows on the features of Daddy Long Legs that are not spider like. Note that Daryl offered a question (9), even though it was not his turn because he, later echoed by Charlie, was confused by how a Daddy Long Legs catches its food if it doesn't bite. Evidently, Daryl must have been monitoring both the content read by the teacher and the ensuing dialogue. Again the teacher intervened to dispel this confusion (23). Even though 20 utterances have followed her original question, Susan, the leader, still remembers her responsibility and summarizes (24, 26, 31), with some help from the teacher (27).

As shown in Table 13.6, Daryl again asked a question (10) when it was not his responsibility, a better question than Susan's original request for detail (1). He went on to evaluate Justin's answer (13). Daryl had to be

TABLE 13.4
First-Grade Listening Comprehension, Day 18

READING

> Behind the front legs there are two odor glands. They look like two extra eyes. To protect itself a Daddy Long Legs can give off a smelly liquid from these glands. Birds, toads, and large insects don't like it at all. It makes them feel too sick or too weak to try to catch the Daddy Long Legs.

1. D: [QUESTION] What does the Daddy Long Legs do when something comes around it. Justin?
2. J: Use that odor gland . . . (not audible)
3. D: Yeah. Charlie.
4. C: When a animal comes along, he puts out his odor and they get too sick to catch him.
5. D: Yeah. Mara.
6. M: Or too weak.
7. R: They feel too weak and too sick.
8. D: Everybody gave me good answers.
9. *T: Very good.
10. D: [SUMMARY] I will summarize. When a animal comes around, it gives out its bad smell, and they get too weak and too old to catch it.
11. M: [CLARIFICATION] Who does?
12. D: That's the Daddy Long Legs.
13. M: [CLARIFICATION] Who does?
14. D: The animals.
15. M: [CLARIFICATION] Which animals?
16. D: All kinds of animals.
17. R: Yeah, different kinds.
18. D: Different kinds of animals put out a spray?
19. R: [CLARIFICATION] Om, it might be the same kind of animal as tries to catch the Daddy Long Legs.
20. *T: OK, I think you are talking about two different things. He's talking about the animals that come around to the spider, and he's trying to get you to say who puts out the odor. Is it all animals?
21. D: No (emphatic). It's the Daddy Long Legs—Sigh (exasperated)

---

listening to the text, remembering its content, and monitoring the dialogue to be able to make these contributions. Susan remembered to summarize (17, 19), with help from the teacher, even though other questioners, notably the intrusive Daryl, have interrupted her role as teacher. The adult teacher's turns were mainly management, reinforcement, feedback, and attempts to involve nonparticipating children, in this case, Charlie.

Daryl was legitimately the leader, responsible for questions and summaries, in the excerpt shown in Table 13.7. He formulated a question (1), but it was one that Mara rejected (2); so he tried again (3), hitting on one detail from a passage of many details. Daryl was then interrupted by a long clarification sequence about how Daddy Long Legs can stand on water. Thirty utterances later, *with no reminder,* he summarized quite adequately

TABLE 13.5
First-Grade Listening Comprehension, Day 19

READING

Daddy Long Legs are related to spiders.

1.	S:	[CLARIFICATION] What does related mean?
2.	*T:	What do you think, Charlie?
3.	C:	Sort of like, they're the same kind of animal, sort of like. Like, tigers are related to cats.
4.	*T:	Very good. They may not be in the same family, but they are similar.

READING

Daddy Long Legs are related to spiders, but they are not true spiders. Daddy Long Legs don't spin webs to trap insects for food the way spiders do. Daddy Long Legs go out hunting for their food. Daddy Long Legs never bite people and they are never poisonous.

5.	S:	[QUESTION] Are the spiders ever poisonous or not? Mara.
6.	M:	They aren't.
7.	D:	I did have a different question.
8.	*T:	OK.
9.	D:	[QUESTION AND CLARIFICATON] If the spiders didn't spin a web for their food, how did they get their food?
10.	M:	Oh, that's a terrific question.
11.	*T:	It sure is, isn't it?
12.	D:	Justin.
13.	J:	They went out hunting.
14.	D:	Yeah.
15.	*T:	And you said you even had a different question.
16.	C:	[QUESTION AND CLARIFICATION] If they didn't catch them and the spider didn't bite them, what did he do?
17.	*T:	I'm a little confused.
18.	S:	I think he was talking about how they catch their food without biting them.
19.	*T:	Does the story really tell us? It just says they go hunting for it, doesn't it? I think, does it say that a Daddy Long Legs never bites its food?
20.	ALL:	No.
21.	*T:	What did it say it never bites?
22.	M:	It never bites people.
23.	*T:	All right. So, I imagine if it is going out hunting, Charlie, if it wants to eat it has to bite, doesn't it?
24.	S:	I forgot to summarize.
25.	*T:	Oh, I don't think you did, we just haven't gotten there. Now you can do it for us.
26.	S:	[SUMMARY] We learned that the Daddy Long Legs aren't poisonous.
27.	*T:	Great. Anything else you think it's important to remember. Did we learn anything about how they eat? How they get their food, or how they are different from spiders?
28.	J:	They don't spin webs. They hunt for their food.
29.	*T:	Very good. All right. So, what you might want to do is remember, if you see a Daddy Long Legs are you going to call it a spider.
30.	ALL:	NO
31.	S:	[SUMMARY] No, because it doesn't spin a web. And it hunts for its food, and it's not poison.

TABLE 13.6
First-Grade Listening Comprehension, Day 20

READING

Ten to twenty Daddy Long Legs can live together in this cage. It is fun to watch them at night. They are more active then. They rest during the day. If you look into your Daddy Long Legs cage when they are resting, your shadow will wake them suddenly. Then they will scamper around the cage, bouncing up and down in their funny dance. A few minutes later, they will all be resting quietly again.

1. S: [QUESTION] How many spiders can fit in a cage?
2. R: It didn't tell.
3. S: Yes it did.
4. J: Reggie doesn't think it told us.
5. S: Charlie?
6. C: About ten or so.
7. S: Mara?
8. M: Ten to twenty.
9. *T: Ten to twenty. Daryl, do you have a different one? What question would you ask?
10. D: [QUESTION] If you came by and looked, if you came by and looked in the Daddy Long Legs cage, what would the Daddy Long Legs do? Justin?
11. J: Your shadow would wake him up and then they would start scampering around and . . .
12. M: And in a little bit all of them will lay down and go back to sleep again.
13. D: He kind of left some out.
14. *T: What did he leave out?
15. D: When they bounce up and down.
16. *T: In a funny dance, right. That was a good question, Daryl. And, Justin, I like the way you brought in the use of shadow. That's good too. All right.
17. S: [SUMMARY] I learned that over ten to twenty Daddy Long Legs could fit in a cage.
18. *T: And can you include the information that Daryl brought with his question?
19. S: [SUMMARY] If your shadow goes on the Daddy Long Legs, it moves around. And they do a funny dance and scamper around.
20. *T: Good job, Susan. I might have also asked the question, when is the best time to watch your Daddy Long Legs if you catch one? Mara?
21. M: When it's night?
22. *T: Do you remember why? Charlie, do you?
23. C: They're more active.
24. *T: What does that mean? More active.
25. C: It means they move more than they do in the day.

(32), given that this segment is one from which it was quite difficult to extract a single main idea. Note, we are not claiming that Daryl's summary was perfect, far from it; the adult teacher continued by shaping up Daryl's ideas. We claim that Daryl had advanced from a noncontributer in the early sessions to a fully participating member of the group—able to do his best as learning leader (with considerable help from the teacher), contributing questions and clarification requests, evaluating the answers he re-

TABLE 13.7
First-Grade Listening Comprehension, Day 20 (cont'd)

READING

> Keep the cage in a cool, shady place, so the sand won't dry out. Daddy Long Legs need a lot of moisture. They are always thirsty. Their second legs help them find water. Daddy Long Legs can't swim, but they can stand on water. They often stand on top of the water to drink. If direct sun ever shines on the cage, the Daddy Long legs will curl up and die. They don't mind the cold so long as it is damp. After you have watched your Daddy Long Legs for a few days, set them free outside. You can catch more any time you like.

1.	D:	[QUESTION] What does it do when you watch it too long.
2.	M:	It didn't tell anything about it.
3.	D:	[QUESTION] What can, what can the Daddy Long Legs do with water?
4.	C:	He can stand up and drink.
5.	D:	Yeah.
6.	S:	[CLARIFICATION] Does it stand up and drink?
7.	*T:	You don't think it stands up? What would you say?
8.	S:	It stands in the water and drinks.
9.	*T:	I thought it was something very interesting about that water and the spider. Do you remember?
10.	*T:	Daddy Long Legs can't do something.
11.	M:	Swim.
12.	*T:	They couldn't swim. I'm glad you remembered that. But they can stand . . . on the water! Do you think that's unusual?
13.	ALL:	Yeah!
14.	M:	Nobody can stand on the water.
15.	*T:	People can't.
16.	C:	Not even people could because we're too heavy to stand on water.
17.	*T:	Do you have a different question that you would have asked, Reggie? What's your question that you would have asked?
18.	R:	[QUESTION] What would hurt the Daddy Long Legs?
19.	*T:	That's a good question.
20.	R:	[QUESTION] Or kill the Daddy Long Legs?
21.	C:	[CLARIFICATION] I don't understand that.
22.	*T:	Charlie didn't understand your question. would you say it one more time?
23.	R:	[QUESTION] What kills the Daddy Long Legs? Charlie?
24.	C:	The water.
25.	R:	Nope.
26.	R:	Susan?
27.	S:	The sun.
28.	R:	Yeah.
29.	S:	But um, and you got to let it go so you could catch more Daddy Long Legs.
30.	*T:	All right, is that sort of what you meant by your first question, Daryl? What would happen if you watched it too long?
31.	D:	Yeah. It curls up and dies.
32.	D:	[SUMMARY] I would summarize that the Daddy Long Legs, it can stand on the water and drink it. And it can't swim. And if you, the sun kills it—And you have to let it go, so you can catch more.

---

ceived, and remembering his responsibility to summarize the text and dialogue, even after considerable interruption.

In contrast, consider Mara, clearly the teacher's favorite, one nominated by her to be a supporter. Actually, Mara's independent performance differed little from Daryl's, but because of the teacher's expectations of her ability, Mara was called on often in the early sessions. By the latter sessions, she was very much in evidence as a teacher's helper.

In Table 13.8, the discussion centers around the notion of camouflage and the meaning of the word "dull." Reggie, a quiet child, was the learning leader. The teacher was very much in evidence, however, in leading the discussion as Reggie could not yet handle the responsibility alone. Of interest here was Mara's role after the first part of the dialogue, when the critical issue of the meaning of the word "dull" came up. Mara alternated with the teacher in keeping the dialogue going. She argued with the teacher that there is no clue as to why Daddy Long Legs can't be seen (12), asked for a fix-up strategy, in this case rereading (14), noted the clue word, dull, on rereading (16), and came up with the first definition (22), "like dark paint," which she never relinquishes, even in the face of Justin's championing of green [(Mara, 22, 27, 30, 37, 47; Dull = Black, Blackish, Dark Paint) (Justin, 24, 28, 32, 34, 46; Dull = Green)]. Pseudoconsensus was reached, as Mara stuck to black or dark, and Justin still insisted on green. Mara alternates with the teacher, and indeed, by the last few days of discussions, the teacher has some difficulty repressing Mara sufficiently to

TABLE 13.8
First-Grade Listening Comprehension (Day 19)

READING

The dull coloring of the Daddy Long Legs is another way it is protected from its enemies. Daddy Long Legs are awfully hard to see as they wobble along in the grass.

1.   R: [QUESTION] Can you see them very good? Justin.
2.   J: No.
3.   R: Right, Justin.
4.   *T: And as the teacher you might want to know a little bit more.
5.   R: But you could see him in the light, but you can't really see them in the dark when they wobble along.
6.   J: Om, cause they already have black on them.
7.   *T: What makes you think they have black on them?
8.   R: Because they have hair.
9.   *T: Was there a clue here that I gave you that made you know that they were not easy to see?
10. ALL: Yeah.
11.   *T: What was it?

(interruption clarifying the word wobble)

(continued)

TABLE 13.8 *(Continued)*

12.	M:	[CLARIFICATION] We can't tell why it's hard to see.
13.	*T:	There's a clue
14.	M:	[CLARIFICATION] Read it again.
15.	*T:	All right. [REREADING] "The dull coloring of the Daddy Long Legs is another way that it is protected from its enemies."
16.	M:	Dull! It's dull.
17.	*T:	Reggie, what does dull mean?
18.	R:	Protected.
19.	*T:	Does it mean that it's protected? How is it protected?
20.	D:	By its spray (referring to text content covered on the previous day).
21.	*T:	Well, we know it is protected by its odor, but that's not what it's talking about here. Maybe you should have asked me to clarify what dull means? I'm not saying doll, like a doll you play with. A DULL coloring. Mara.
22.	M:	It means it's sort of like, dark paint.
23.	*T:	It you were a spider walking along on the top of the grass or a Daddy Long Legs and you didn't want to be seen, what kind of coloring would you have? A bright orange?
24.	J:	Green.
25.	*T:	Bright red or yellow.
26.	J:	No.
27.	M:	I would be black.
28.	J:	Black and green.
29.	*T:	Oh, when you said it probably was black, I thought maybe you were thinking of this part of the story.
30.	M:	A dark black.
31.	*T:	A dark color, or you said another color would be good.
32.	J:	Green.
33.	*T:	Green would be a good color?
34.	J:	Cause the grass is green.
35.	*T:	Right, all right. So, dull just means it's sort of dim and dark and not real bright and noticeable. It sort of blends in. OK, it's not a very exciting color at all. And those of you that have really seen Daddy Long Legs?
36.	D:	It's sort of brownish.
37.	M:	It's sort of blackish.
38.	*T:	All right, would you be teacher for this part, Susan?
39.	R:	I need to summarize.
40.	*T:	Oh, you didn't summarize, thank you. How are you going to summarize?
41.	R:	[SUMMARY] I summarize that we learned that Daddy Long Legs wobbles on top of the grass.
42.	*T:	Was that the most important part on what you asked about? You're right, but we learned something very important.
43.	R:	[SUMMARY] It blends in with the grass, so you can't see it. That's part of its protection.
44.	*T:	All right.
45.	J:	He could have put it might be green or black.
46.	*T:	He could have put that in, but did the story really tell us the colors?
47.	M:	It said dull, dull like black paint.
48.	*T:	Well, that's what we thought, wasn't it? But what Reggie said was right, it blends in so that it is hard to see. That was an excellent summary.

give other children equal time. Nonetheless, Mara was an excellent role model for this group.

Although the first graders became quite efficient contributers to the discussions, they did not take over the learning leader role as quickly or as completely as did the junior high school students. Compare, for example, the late (Day 20) first-grade dialogues shown in Table 13.9 with the somewhat earlier (Day 13) seventh-grade dialogue shown in Table 13.2. Even though the excerpt in Table 13.9 forms part of the last day of instruction, the first-grade teacher reverted to the pivotal teacher role. She modeled vocabulary clarification, one of the simplest and earliest activities mastered. Here, (36) she was working on the clarification of regionally inappropriate words, for example, rain spouts and cellars for gutters and basements, pointing out lost opportunities for clarification requests. She was also closely involved with keeping Reggie on the track of his question, despite the constant interruptions (Teacher, 15, 17, 27, 29, 32; Reggie, 16, 18, 23, 30, 33). In contrast, in Table 13.2, the seventh-grade teacher rarely took over the dialogue from the students, and it was a reflection of this transfer of responsibility that a great deal of text was covered by the students in one day. Two-thirds of the segments were covered efficiently, with little discussion, as in statements 1–4 in Table 13.2, which consist of a question, an answer, a summary, and teacher praise. The younger children needed more teacher direction for a longer period of time.

TABLE 13.9
First-Grade Listening Comprehension (Day 20)

READING
　　　To learn more about Daddy Long Legs, you could go out and catch some. Early fall is the best time. Look on dark, damp walls, outside cellar windows, or near rain spouts.
1.　R: [CLARIFICATION] What are rain spouts?
2.　*T: All right, does anyone know what a rain spout is?
3.　D: Rain spouts?
4.　*T: It says to look near rain spouts. Do you know what a rain spout is—remember the song we sang? (singing) "I'm a little teapot, short and stout. Here's my handle, here's my spout."
5.　M: It's the thing you pour.
6.　*T: Right, that's where the tea poured out of the teapot. Well, then, what would a rain spout be?
7.　M: Oh, I know.
8.　*T: Mara?
9.　M: It's a tube that rain falls through—instead of falling inside of your house.
10.　D: [CLARIFICATION] Do you mean they're on your houses?
11.　*T: What would you call the tube that goes round your house and collects the rain so it doesn't go into your house? But it takes it out to the yard.

(continued)

TABLE 13.9 *(Continued)*

12. C: Rain spouts.
13. *T: Have you heard of gutters?
14. R: Yeah.
15. *T: Well, some people call them rain spouts. All right. Now, have we made you forget your question, Reggie? Or do you still have one in mind?
16. R: I forgot.
17. *T: All right, this was a short part, so I'll reread it. [REREAD] "To learn more about Daddy Long Legs, you could go out and catch some. Early fall is the best time. Look on damp, dark walls, outside cellar windows, or near rain spouts."
18. R: [QUESTION] Why was fall the best time to look for the Daddy Long Legs?
19. D: Where the sun is out.
20. M: No!—and he said why.
21. *T: You don't think he should say why? Or you mean Daryl didn't answer why?
22. M: He didn't answer why.
23. R: Mara, when?
24. M: In the fall. Oh, early fall.
25. *T: What else did it tell us then?
26. M: Where to find them.
27. *T: Where to find them. Good. So, instead of saying when, you could have asked a question starting with where. What would that have been, Reggie?
28. R: Where to find them.
29. *T: Okay, make up a question using all the information.
30. R: [QUESTION] Where could you find all them spiders?
31. D: [CLARIFICATION] Spiders?
    (interruption centered on an argument between Daryl, Mara and Reggie concerning whether Daddy Long Legs are true spiders. This discussion referred back to text content covered two days earlier.)
32. *T: Do you want to try it again? I bet you can do it this time. Let's have one last try at your question, Reggie.
33. R: [QUESTION] Where could you find the Daddy Long Legs?
34. D: That's much better.
35. J: Near water spouts.
36. *T: [CLARIFICATION] All right, I want you to listen to this one sentence once more, and I want you to help me with a word that I don't quite understand. Look on dark, damp walls outside cellar windows—
37. M: Oh! Oh! I know. What does cellar mean?
38. *T: Too late, I'm asking you, what does cellar mean, Daryl?
39. D: It's sort of like a jail where you take people when they did something wrong.
40. *T: That might have happened in olden days. Now, where is the cellar usually located?
41. S: In southern states.
42. *T: We call them by other names . . . (pause) . . . You have to go down the stairs.
43. D: Oh, basements.
44. M: Dark and damp, dark and damp.
45. D: That's it, basements.
46. *T: We call them basements. Yes. Now that would have been a good thing to have asked me earlier. If you didn't understand what cellar windows were, you should have asked. That would have been a good question, clarification question.

One point of concern with all dialogue teaching procedures, and reciprocal teaching is no exception, is the leisurely pace of the reading. Because of the demands of the procedure, discussing content until everyone understands, very little text is covered until the students become more skilled in using the strategies. This is seen as a problem by teachers who assess progress in reading lessons by the number of pages covered each day. However, the relatively slow rate of information exchange can be defended; the main agenda is to teach methods of *understanding* any text, not just to assist in the *acquisition of the content of one particular text*. Very important, then, is the additional evidence that students are acquiring facility with the processes of learning; this comes from the independent learning scores.

Independent Learning. Shown in Fig. 13.5 are the independent learning scores of the six first-grade children who featured in the dialogues of Tables 13.4–13.9. These are the results of the daily assessments where the children listened to novel texts and answered questions on them from memory. On the right-hand side are the averaged data of these children when they were in an untreated control condition (20 days) and subsequently when they received 20 days of instruction. The improvement in the

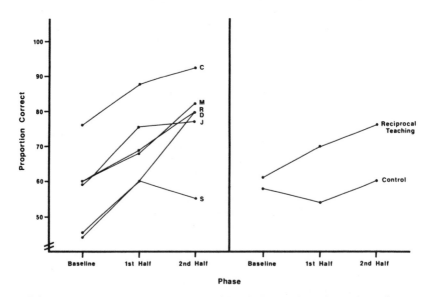

FIG. 13.5. Independent learning scores of the six first-grade students whose discussions are featured in Tables 4-9. The left-hand panel contains individual learning curves. The data in the right-hand panels are the average performance of the six children when they served as an untreated control and when they were taught by the reciprocal teaching procedure.

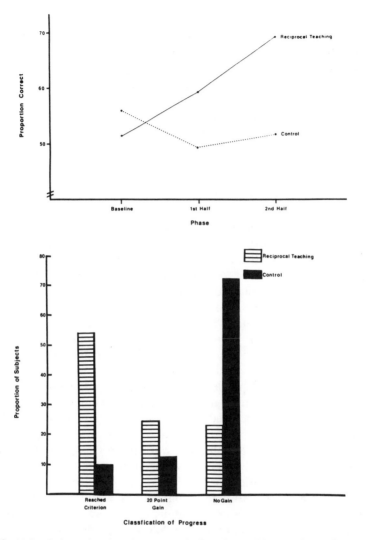

FIG. 13.6. Independent learning scores of all students taking part in the first-grade classroom listening study (132 students in reciprocal teaching and 66 control students).

reciprocal teaching condition is steady and reliable. On the left-hand side are the children's individual learning curves. Five of the six reached a criterion of 75%; only one, Susan, did not show a 20% gain. One, Charlie, started and finished well; the remaining children all show the typical gain pattern of reciprocal teaching students. Daryl's progress was particularly dramatic, from 44 to 80% correct.

In Fig. 13.6 we have plotted the averaged data for all the children in the study so far, 132 reciprocal teaching students and 66 control subjects. Students performing at ceiling (like Charlie) were dropped. For the remaining children, we again see the reliable gain for reciprocal teaching students and the steady state of the control (practice) condition. On the bottom half, we have plotted the number of children reaching criterion of 70% or maintaining a 20 percentage point gain, compared with those showing no reliable gain. Comparing this pattern to that shown in Fig. 13.1 illustrates the difference between the success of the reading and listening interventions. The nonvolunteer reading teachers who provided the data in Fig. 13.1 helped 71% of the seventh-grade students to reach criterion (compared with 98% reaching criterion when expert teachers ran the program), and 24% achieved a 20% gain. In contrast, only 53% of the listening students reached criterion, and 24% maintained a 20 percentage point gain. We believe that the differences indicate that 20 days was not quite long enough for the very young children to take over the learning leader role fully and consistently, a hypothesis we are testing in the third year of project, when the first graders will be in the program for the whole year. Nonetheless, the 22% failure to show reliable independent learning in the reciprocal teaching group compares very favorably with the 72% failure rate in the control condition. The difference between reciprocal teaching and control conditions is large and reliable. Remember, we demand a stringent test of progress when we ask the children to improve their performance on independent tests of novel material.

In addition to the independent comprehension and retention questions centered on the text content, in our more recent studies of both reading and listening, we have included application questions where the children are asked, at a very simple level, to apply what they have just learned (Brown, Ryan, Slattery, & Palincsar, work in progress). In other words, these questions test whether the knowledge gained from the text is represented in usable form rather than merely retained inertly for a subsequent test. As texts for the reciprocal teaching sessions, we used sets of analogous materials that differed in surface details but covered shared underlying topics, such as camouflage, biological deterrents, animal survival, and so on. For example, under the biological deterrent theme the children heard about the manatees, large sea mammals that were forced to move inland, where they took to eating the water irises that had previously clogged Florida's inland waterways. The manatees were thus welcomed by the residents because they provided a biological (rather than chemical) solution to an environmental problem. Immediately after discussing this example of a biological deterrent, or natural pest control, the students read and answered questions on a text that contained the analogous problem of how to rid a garden of mosquitos, where they were told that purple martins eat mosquitos and purple martins like to live in man-made bird houses. This crucial information was buried under other facts about the life-style of these birds. An observant child would respond like Jeremy did: "The house-owner could build a home for purple martins at the bottom of the garden . . . but I think Raid is best—but it's just like the manatees we talked about . . . and the ladybugs eating the farmer's a- a- [Teacher— 'aphids'] Right, aphids. We talked about that last week."

So far we have found that regular practice greatly improves ability to use analogy to answer the questions; that is, guided practice creates a mind set to reason by analogy. Children begin by noting few of the analogies, but, during the later part of the intervention, they are able to solve the analogies with an 80% success rate. Not only do they show the typical improvement in answering short-term tests of content retention on our test passages, but they also show long-term improvement in their understanding of the biological themes to such an extent that they can classify novel exemplars of a theme. Repeated experience noting the analogy between texts and problem solutions leads to quite different methods of reading and discussing than does practice on questions that examine only content retention. We are currently testing this hypothesis in greater detail.

RECIPROCAL TEACHING, ARGUMENT STRUCTURE, AND SYSTEMATIC KNOWLEDGE ACQUISITION

In this final section, we discuss what we have accomplished with reciprocal teaching and what still remains to be done. As currently practiced, reciprocal teaching is a form of guided, cooperative learning featuring a collaborative learning environment of learning leaders and listeners; expert scaffolding by an adult teacher; and direct instruction, modeling, and practice in the use of four simple strategies that serve to prop up an emergent dialogue structure.

The strategies featured so far have been very simple activities, serving primarily as checks that the children can use to test whether they have understood the main content. The strategies also serve as tools to launch a discussion among students who are not accustomed to engaging in "knowledge-worrying" (Brown, 1985). Questions, for example, initiate each piece of dialogue, giving the teacher some indication of whether the learning leader has understood and providing a starting point for the learning listeners' discussion. Clarification takes care of obvious points of confusion. The younger children use this device almost exclusively to resolve problems of pronominal reference and unknown vocabulary but older students become quite sophisticated at catching misunderstanding. Summarization takes place at the end of each discussion episode, serving as a means by which progress can be monitored, points of agreement and conflict checked, and ideas from many sources combined into one statement. It serves as a form of place holder, a method of rounding off conversation in preparation for the next interaction with the text (Barnes & Todd, 1977).

But these activities are only primitive precursors of potential argument forms. In future work, we intend to build on this simple beginning and examine more elaborate argument devices and epistemic roles. Profiting from information gained from naturally occurring dialogues (Barnes & Todd, 1977; Paley, 1981; Pontecorvo, 1985) and theoretical analyses of argument (Toulmin, 1958) and explanation structures (Von Wright, 1971), we can modify our guided learning instruction to introduce students to premise, supporting/conflicting data, warrants, and backing, albeit in simple forms. Will these shared experiences enable children to deal with more extensive and substantive texts?

Which brings us to the issue of knowledge accumulation. So far we have concentrated primarily on children's learning of naturally occurring grade-appropriate expository texts of a vaguely scientific nature (such as snakes, Daddy Long Legs, and so forth, see Tables 13.1–13.9). These materials have several drawbacks, if one is interested in the accumulation of knowledge, as well as process. First, they encourage encapsulated knowledge acquisition; topic follows topic with little opportunity for cumulative reference. Second, the material affords little room for emotional engagement, controversy, opinion, conflict, or dispute. This choice of material has been accompanied by another practice modeled on school routine; tests of learning have been primarily measures of fact and simple inference. Such measures positively encourage the child to build up encapsulated "inert" knowledge (Whitehead, 1916), rarely used again after the test hurdle has been surmounted. If one is interested in reading as a process of decoding text and grasping the meaning, any text will do, and any test of encapsulated short-term retention will serve to ascertain whether the child has read and comprehended. But if one is interested in learning with understanding, in the sense of acquiring a usable, flexible body of knowledge, such procedures are unsatisfactory.

Having established that academically marginal children can readily handle short-term tests of encapsulated knowledge, an outcome by no means predicted by many colleagues and teachers who deal with similar populations, we are eager to see if we can make headway on helping such children accumulate usable, coherent, and connected knowledge structures. Our initial work with the obvious analogies contained in the biological themes passages (Brown, Ryan, Slattery, & Palincsar, work in progress) is a first step in this direction. Within the miniature world of these passages, repetitive cases can be recognized and general principles of camouflage, biological deterrants, and so on extracted. Such small "knowledge bundles" are potentially applicable to a wide variety of situations, and we see this as a first step toward the really difficult problem of examining the accumulation of systematic bodies of knowledge, such as basic biological principles. If one is interested in learning, in the sense of the acquisition of generative knowledge structures, it will be necessary to examine various procedures, like reciprocal teaching, the jigsaw method, and other programs, in situations where children are asked to learn principled bodies of knowledge over time.

Finally, the key notion of internalization needs careful consideration. How does process (argument and discussion roles) and knowledge (cases, generalized rules, and principles) become part of a learner's usable knowledge base? If internalization is a prime mechanism of conceptual change, it is little understood. Again, we see no alternative but to study learning taking place within individuals over time. With regard to process, one might want to teach children rudimentary argument structures and see them practiced extensively in guided oral discussions. Next, one might "fade out" the teacher by replacing her with cue cards of the type used by Barnes and Todd (1977) and Scardamalia, Bereiter, and Steinbach (1984) to provide temporary concrete supports for children's arguments. If the prompt cards can maintain the discussion, perhaps the next step would be to see if the students can apply their knowledge of argument devices, first with and then without prompts, to the task of written composition. Kneupper (1978) has succeeded in helping college students improve their written composition using Toulmin's (1958) analysis of argument. It remains to be seen whether children can also benefit from systematic instruction, such as a form of reciprocal teaching, in which modeling and support is given for the acquisition of complex argument rules.

Of equal interest is the internalization of knowledge that gives the learner ownership over it, that is, allows him or her to access it at will and to use it to interpret new knowledge, or to provide justification, backing, and warrants in discussions and written compositions. Mechanisms of internalization are central to an understanding of how ownership of knowledge is established and how processes for acquiring knowledge in general are formed. These are the building blocks, the structure and process, of conceptual change. Observing and assisting children learning in groups will provide important insight into the mechanisms of change.

ACKNOWLEDGMENTS

Preparation of this chapter was supported by PHS Grants HD-05951 and HD-06864 from the National Institution of Child Health and Human Development, and OSE Grant G008400648 from the Department of Education. Funds from the Spencer Foundation supported the first author's fellowship at the Center for Advanced Study in the Behavioral Sciences at Stanford in 1984–1985, where the argument in the first half was developed, greatly influenced by discussions with Jacqueline Goodnow. The authors would like to thank Joseph Campione and Robert Reeve for useful discussions of various sections. Special thanks are due to Katherine Ranson, Reading Coordinator, School District 186, Springfield, Illinois; her enthusiasm and support for reciprocal teaching has contributed enormously to its success. Indeed, it would have been impossible to undertake such an extensive research program in the schools without her aid. Thanks are also due to Deborah Dunn and Melinda Samsel for conducting the laboratory studies, to the teachers of reading studies, and the teachers of Lincoln and Sandburg elementary schools for conducting the listening studies. Finally, we would like to thank Marilyn Ryan for her patient transcription of audio taped classroom discussions and Paul Eccher and Becky Davison for their painstaking work compiling the Reference section.

REFERENCES

Anderson, R. C., & Faust, G. W. (1974). *Educational psychology: The science of instruction and learning*. New York: Dodd Mead.

Aronson, E. (1978). *The jigsaw classroom*. Beverly Hills, CA: Sage.

Au, K. H. (1980). *A test of the social organizational hypothesis: Relationships between participation structures and learning to read*. Unpublished doctoral dissertation, University of Illinois.

Bales, R. F. (1950). *Interaction process analysis: A method for the study of small groups*. Cambridge, MA: Addison–Wesley.

Barnes, D., & Todd, F. (1977). *Communication and learning in small groups*. London: Routledge & Kegan Paul.

Bereiter, C., & Bird, M. (1985). Use of thinking aloud in identification and teaching of reading comprehension strategies. *Cognition and Instruction, 2*, 131–156.

Binet, A. (1909). *Les idees modernes sur les infants*[Modern ideas on children]. Paris: Ernest Flammarion.

Bloom, B., & Broder, L. (1950). *Problem-solving processes of college students*. Chicago: University of Chicago Press.

Boggs, S. T. (1972). The meaning of questions and narratives to Hawaiian children. In C. Cazden, V. John, & D. Hymes (Eds.), *Functions of language in the classroom*. New York: Teachers College Press.

Bos, M. C. (1937). Experimental study of productive collaboration. *Acta Psychologica, 3*, 315–426.

Brown, A. L. (1978). Knowing when, where, and how to remember: A problem of metacognition. In R. Glaser (Ed.), *Advances in instructional psychology* (Vol. 1, pp. 77–165). Hillsdale, NJ: Lawrence Erlbaum Associates.

Brown, A. L. (1985). Mental orthopedics: A conversation with Alfred Binet. In S. Chipman, J. Segal, & R. Glaser (Eds.), *Thinking and learning skills: Research and open questions* (Vol. 2, pp. 319–337). Hillsdale, NJ: Lawrence Erlbaum Associates.

Brown, A. L., Armbruster, B. B., & Baker, L. (1986). The role of metacognition in reading and studying. In J. Orasano (Ed.), *Reading comprehension: From research to practice* (pp. 49–75). Hillsdale, NJ: Lawrence Erlbaum Associates.

Brown, A. L., Bransford, J. D., Ferrara, R. A., & Campione, J. C. (1983). Learning, remembering, and understanding. In J. Flavell & E. M. Markman (Eds.), *Handbook of child psychology* (4th ed.). *Cognitive development* (Vol. 3, pp. 515–629). New York: Wiley.

Brown, A. L., & Campione, J. C. (1981). Inducing flexible thinking: A problem of access. In M. Friedman, J. P. Das, & N. O'Connor (Eds.), *Intelligence and learning* (pp. 515–529). New York: Plenum Press.

Brown, A. L., & Campione, J. C. (1984). Three faces of transfer: Implications for early competence, individual differences, and instruction. In M. Lamb, A. Brown, & B. Rogoff (Eds.), *Advances in developmental psychology* (Vol. 3, pp. 143–192). Hillsdale, NJ: Lawrence Erlbaum Associates.

Brown, A. L., & Campione, J. C. (1986). Psychological theory and the study of learning disabilities. *American Psychologist, 41*(10), 1059–1068.

Brown, A. L., Campione, J. C., & Day, J. D. (1981). Learning to learn: On training students to learn from texts. *Educational Researcher, 10,* 14–21.

Brown, A. L., & Day, J. D. (1983). Macrorules for summarizing texts: The development of expertise. *Journal of Verbal Behavior, 22,* 1–14.

Brown, A. L., & Ferrara, R. A. (1985). Diagnosing zones of proximal development. In J. Wertsch (Ed.), *Culture, communication and cognition: Vygotskian perspectives* (pp. 273–305). Cambridge, MA: Cambridge University Press.

Brown, A. L., & Palincsar, A. S. (1982). Inducing strategic learning from texts by means of informed, self-control training. *Topics in Learning and Learning Disabilities, 2*(1), 1–17.

Brown, A. L., & Palincsar, A. S. (1987). Reciprocal teaching of comprehension strategies: A natural history of one program for enhancing learning. In J. D. Day & J. Borkowski (Eds.), *Intelligence and exceptionality: New directions for theory, assessment and instructional practice* (pp. 81–132). Norwood, NJ: Ablex.

Brown, A. L., Palincsar, A. S., & Purcell, L. (1985). Poor readers: Teach, don't label. In U. Neisser (Ed.), *The academic performance of minority children*. Hillsdale, NJ: Lawrence Erlbaum Associates.

Brown, A. L., Palincsar, A. S., Samsel, M. S., & Dunn, D. (work in progress). *Bringing meaning to text: Early lessons for high-risk first graders.*

Brown, A. L., & Reeve, R. A. (1987). Bandwidths of competence: The role of supportive contexts in learning and development. In L. S. Liben (Ed.), *Development and learning: Conflict or congruence?* (pp. 173–223). Hillsdale, NJ: Lawrence Erlbaum Associates.

Bruner, J. (1978). The role of dialogue in language acquisition. In A. Sinclair, R. J. Jarvella, & J. M. Levelt (Eds.), *The child's conception of language* (pp. 241–256). Berlin: Springer–Verlag.

Bryant, P. (1982). The role of conflict and of agreement between intellectual strategies in children's ideas about measurement. *British Journal of Psychology, 73,* 243–251.

Carey, S. (1985). Are children fundamentally different kinds of thinkers and learners than adults? In S. F. Chipman, J. W. Segal, & R. Glaser (Eds.), *Thinking and learning skills* (Vol. 2, pp. 485–517). Hillsdale, NJ: Lawrence Erlbaum Associates.

Case, R. (1985). *Intellectual development: A systematic reinterpretation.* New York: Academic Press.

Cazden, C. B. (1979). Peekaboo as an instructional model: Discourse development at home and at school. In *Papers and reports on child development* (No. 17 pp. 1–19). Stanford, CA: Department of Linguistics, Stanford University.

Cazden, C. B. (1984). Classroom discourse. In M. C. Wittrock (Ed.), *Handbook of research and teaching.* New York: Macmillan.

Chukovsky, K. (1968). *From 2 to 5.* Berkeley: University of California Press.

Cole, M., & Bruner, J. S. (1971). Cultural differences and inferences about psychological processes. *American Psychologist, 26,* 867–876.

Cole, M., & Scribner, S. (1975). Theorizing about socialization of cognition. *Ethos, 3,* 249–268.

Collins, A., & Stevens, A. L. (1982). Goals and strategies of inquiry teachers. In R. Glaser (Ed.), *Advances in instructional psychology* (Vol. 2, pp. 65–119). Hillsdale, NJ: Lawrence Erlbaum Associates.

Dashiell, J. F. (1935). Experimental studies of the influence of social situations on the behavior of individual human adults. In C. Murchison (Ed.), *Handbook of social psychology.* Worcester, MA: Clark University Press.

Davis, R. B. (1966). Discovery in the teaching of mathematics. In L. S. Shulman & E. R. Keisler (Eds.), *Learning by discovery: A critical appraisal.* Chicago: Rand McNally.

DeVries, D. L., Slavin, R. E., Fennessey, G. M., Edwards, K. J., & Lombardo, M. M. (1980). *Teams-Games-Tournament: The team learning approach.* Englewood Cliffs, NJ: Educational Technology Publications.

Dewey, J. (1910). *How we think.* Boston: Heath. (2nd ed., Heath, 1933).

Doise, W., & Mugny, G. (1984). *The social development of the intellect.* New York: Pergamon Press.

Dumont, R. V. (1972). Learning English and how to be silent: Studies in Sioux and Cherokee classrooms. In C. Cazden, V. John, & D. Hymes (Eds.), *Functions of language in the classroom.* New York: Teachers College Press.

Dunkin, M. J., & Biddle, B. J. (1974). *The study of teaching.* New York: Holt, Rinehart & Winston.

Durkin, D. (1984). Do basal manuals teach reading comprehension? In R. C. Anderson, J. Osborn, & R. J. Tierney (Eds.), *Learning to read in American schools: Basal readers and content texts* (pp. 29–38). Hillsdale, NJ: Lawrence Erlbaum Associates.

Dweck, C. S. (1989). Motivation. In A. Lesgold & R. Glaser (Eds.), *Foundations for a Psychology of Education* (pp. 87–136). Hillsdale, NJ: Lawrence Erlbaum Associates.

Erickson, F., & Schultz, J. (1977). When is a context? Some issues and methods on the analysis of social competence. *Quarterly Newsletter of the Institute for Comparative Human Development, 1,* 5–10.

Fischer, K. W. (1980). A theory of cognitive development: The control and construction of hierarchies of skills. *Psychological Review, 87,* 477–531.

Flavell, J. H. (1971). Stage-related properties of cognitive development. *Cognitive Psychology, 2,* 421–453.

Frase, L. T., & Schwartz, B. J. (1975). Effect of question production and answering on prose recall. *Journal of Educational Psychology, 67,* 628–635.

Gagné, R. M. (1965). *The conditions of learning.* New York: Holt, Rinehart & Winston.

Gelman, R., & Brown, A. L. (1985a). *Early foundations of cognitive development.* The 1985 Annual Report for Center for Advanced Study in the Behavioral Sciences, Stanford, CA.

Gelman, R., & Brown, A. L. (1985b). Changing views of cognitive competence in the young. In N. J. Smelser & D. R. Gerstein, (Eds.), *Knowledge in the social and behavioral sciences: Discovery and trends over fifty years* (Proceedings of a Commemorative Symposium on the Fiftieth Anniversary of the Ogburn Report, *Recent social trends in the United States*). New York: Academic Press.

Glachan, M. (1982). *Peer interaction: Its role in cognitive development.* Unpublished doctoral dissertation, University of Southamptom, England.

Glachan, M., & Light, P. H. (1982). Peer interaction and learning. In G. E. Butterworth & P. H. Light (Eds.), *Social cognition: Studies of the development of understanding.* Brighton: The Harvester Press.

Greenfield, P. M. (1980). Toward an operational and logical analysis of intentionality: The use of discourse in early child language. In D. R. Olson (Ed.), *The social foundations of language and thought*. New York: Norton.

Greenfield, P. M. (1984). A theory of the teacher in the learning activities of everyday life. In B. Rogoff & J. Lave (Eds.), *Everyday cognition: Its development in social context* (pp. 117–138). Cambridge, MA: Harvard University Press.

Griffen, P., & Cole, M. (1984). Current activity for the future: The Zo-ped. In B. Rogoff & J. V. Wertsch (Eds.), *Children's learning in the "zone of proximal development."* San Francisco: Jossey-Bass.

Grize, J. B. (1982). *De la logique à l'argumentation* [From logic to argumentation]. Paris–Genevè.

Harris, P. L., Kruithof, A., Terwogt, M. M., & Visser, P. (1981). Children's detection and awareness of textual anomaly. *Journal of Experimental Child Psychology, 31,* 212–230.

Inhelder, B., Sinclair, H., & Bovet, M. (1974). *Learning and the development of cognition.* Cambridge, MA: Harvard University Press.

Johnson, D. W., & Johnson, R. T. (1974). Conflict in the classroom: Controversy and learning. *Review of Educational Research, 49,* 51–70.

Johnson, D. W., & Johnson, R. T. (1975). *Learning together and alone.* Englewood Cliffs, NJ: Prentice-Hall.

Karmiloff-Smith, A., & Inhelder, B. (1974/1975). If you want to get ahead, get a theory. *Cognition, 3,* 195–212.

Kelley, H. H., & Thibaut, J. W. (1954). Experimental studies of group problem solving. In G. Lindzey (Ed.), *Handbook of social psychology* (Vol. 2). Reading, MA: Addison-Wesley.

Kneupper, C. W. (1978). Teaching argument: An introduction to the Toulmin model. *College Composition and Communication, 29,* 237–241.

Kuhn, T. S. (1962). *The structure of scientific revolutions.* Chicago: University of Chicago Press.

Laboratory of Comparative Human Cognition. (1983). Culture and cognitive development. In P. H. Mussen (Ed.), *Handbook of child psychology (Vol. 1): History, theory, and methods* (pp. 295–356). New York: Wiley.

Lave, J. (1977). Tailor-made experiences in evaluating the intellectual consequences of apprenticeship training. *Quarterly Newsletter of Institute for Comparative Human Development, 1,* 1–3.

Lave, J., Murtaugh, M., & de la Rocha, O. (1984). The dialectic of arithmetic in grocery shopping. In B. Rogoff & J. Lave (Eds.), *Everyday cognition: Its development in social context* (pp. 67–94). Cambridge, MA: Harvard University Press.

Mehan, H. (1979). *Learning lessons: Social organization in the classroom.* Cambridge, MA: Harvard University Press.

Meichenbaum, D. (1977). *Cognitive behavior modification: An integrative approach.* New York: Plenum Press.

Paley, V. (1981). *Wally's stories.* Cambridge, MA: University of Harvard Press.

Palincsar, A. S., & Brown, A. L. (1984). Reciprocal teaching of comprehension-fostering and monitoring activities. *Cognition and Instruction, 1*(2), 117–175.

Palincsar, A. S., & Brown, A. L. (1985). Reciprocal teaching: Activities to promote "reading with your mind." In E. J. Cooper (Ed.), *Reading, thinking, and concept development: Interactive strategies for the class.* New York: College Board.

Palincsar, A. S., & Brown, A. L. (1986). Interactive teaching to promote independent learning from text. *The reading teacher, 39*(8), 771–777.

Palincsar, A. S., Brown, A. L., & Dunn, P. (in press). Exploration of mediated peer interaction in reading comprehension instruction. *Educational Psychologist.*

Palincsar, A. S., Brown, A. L., & Samsel, M. S. (in preparation). *From skill "builders" to building skills: The adoption of reciprocal teaching by a school district.*

Perret-Clermont, A. N. (1980). *Social interaction and cognitive development in children.* London: Academic Press.

Philips, S. (1972). Participant structures and communicative competence. In C. Cazden, V. John, & D. Hymes (Eds.), *Function of language in the classroom.* New York: College Press.

Piaget, J. (1926). *The language and thought of the child.* London: Routledge & Kegan Paul.

Piaget, J. (1950). *The psychology of intelligence.* London: Routledge & Kegan Paul.

Piaget, J. (1967). *Biologie et connaissance* [Biology and knowledge]. Paris: Gallimard.

Piaget, J. (1976a). Postscript. *Archives de Psychologie, 44,* 223–228.

Piaget, J. (1976b). *The grasp of consciousness: Action and concept in the young child.* Cambridge, MA: Harvard University Press.

Pontecorvo, C. (1985, June). *Discussing for reasoning: The role of argument in knowledge construction.* Paper presented at the European Association for Research on Learning and Instruction. Leuven, Belgium.

Rogoff, B., & Gardner, W. P. (1984). Adult guidance of cognitive development. In B. Rogoff & J. Lave (Eds.), *Everyday cognition: Its development in social context* (pp. 95–116). Cambridge, MA: Harvard University Press.

Russell, J. (1981). Dyadic interaction in a logical reasoning problem requiring inclusion ability. *Child Development, 52,* 1322–1325.

Russell, J. (1982a). Cognitive conflict, transmission, and justification: Conservation attainment through dyadic interaction. *Journal of Genetic Psychology, 140,* 283–297.

Russell, J. (1982b). Prepositional attitude. In M. Beveridge (Ed.), *Children's thinking through language.* London: Edward Arnold.

Scardamalia, M., Bereiter, C., & Steinbach, R. (1984). Teachability of reflexive processes in written composition. *Cognitive Science, 8,* 173–190.

Scollon, R. (1976). *Conversations with a one-year-old.* Honolulu: University Press of Hawaii.

Sharan, S. (1980). Cooperative learning in small groups: Recent methods and effects on achievement, attitudes, and ethnic relations. *Review of Educational Research, 50,* 241–271.

Sharan, S., & Sharan, Y. (1976). *Small-group teaching.* Englewood Cliffs, NJ: Educational Technology Publications.

Shaw, M. E. (1932). A comparison of individual and small groups in the rational solution of complex problems. *American Journal of Psychology, 44,* 491–504.

Slavin, R. E. (1983). *Cooperative learning.* New York: Longman.

Swing, S., & Peterson, P. L. (1982). The relationship of student ability and small-group interaction to student achievement. *American Educational Research Journal, 19,* 259–274.

Toulmin, S. (1958). *The uses of argument.* Cambridge: Cambridge University Press.

Van Ness, H. (1982). Social control and social organization in an Alaskan Athabascan classroom: A microethnography of getting ready for reading. In H. T. Trueba, G. P. Guthrie, & K. H. Au (Eds.), *Culture in the bilingual classroom.* Rowley, MA: Newbury House.

Von Wright, G. H. (1971). *Explanation and understanding.* New York: Cornell University Press.

Vygotsky, L. S. (1978). *Mind in society: The development of higher psychological processes* (M. Cole, V. John-Steiner, S. Scribner, & E. Souberman, Eds.). Cambridge, MA: Harvard University Press.

Webb, N. (1984). Peer interaction and learning in cooperative small groups. *Journal of Educational Psychology, 76,* 333–344.

Wertsch, J. V. (1978). Adult–child interaction and the roots of metacognition. *Quarterly Newsletter of the Institute for Comparative Human Development, 1,* 15–18.

Wertsch, J. V., & Stone, C. A. (1979, February). *A social interactional analysis of learning disabilities remediation.* Paper presented at the International Conference of the Association for Children with Learning Disabilities, San Francisco.

Whimbey, A., & Lochhead, J. (1978). *Problem-solving and comprehension: A short course in analytical reasoning.* Philadelphia: Franklin Institute Press.

Whitehead, A. N. (1916). *Address to the British Mathematical Society.* Manchester, England.

Wood, D. J. (1980). Teaching the young child: Some relationships between social interaction, language, and thought. In D. R. Olson (Ed.), *The social foundations of language and thought.* New York: Norton.

Wood, D., & Middleton, D. (1975). A study of assisted problem solving. *British Journal of Psychology, 66,* 181–191.

Wood, P., Bruner, J., & Ross, G. (1976). The role of tutoring in problem solving. *Journal of Child Psychology and Psychiatry, 17,* 89–100.

Yager, S., Johnson, D. W., & Johnson, R. T. (1985). Oral discussion, group to individual transfer, and achievement in cooperative learning groups. *Journal of Educational Psychology, 77,* 60–66.

14

Cognitive Apprenticeship: Teaching the Crafts of Reading, Writing, and Mathematics

Allan Collins
BBN Laboratories

John Seely Brown
Xerox Palo Alto Research Center

Susan E. Newman
Xerox Palo Alto Research Center

Only in the last century, and only in industrialized nations, has formal schooling emerged as a widespread method of educating the young. Before schools appeared, apprenticeship was the most common means of learning and was used to transmit the knowledge required for expert practice in fields from painting and sculpting to medicine and law. Even today, many complex and important skills, such as those required for language use and social interaction, are learned informally through apprenticeship-like methods—that is, methods not involving didactic teaching, but observation, coaching, and successive approximation.

The differences between formal schooling and apprenticeship methods are many, but for our purposes, one is most important. Perhaps as a by-product of the relegation of learning to schools, skills and knowledge have become abstracted from their uses in the world. In apprenticeship learning, on the other hand, target skills are not only continually in use by skilled practitioners, but are instrumental to the accomplishment of meaningful tasks. Said differently, apprenticeship embeds the learning of skills and knowledge in their social and functional context. This difference is not academic; it has serious implications for the nature of the knowledge that students acquire. This chapter attempts to elucidate some of those implications through a proposal for adapting apprenticeship methods for the teaching and learning of cognitive skills. Specifically, we propose the development of a new cognitive apprenticeship to teach students the thinking and problem-solving skills involved in school subjects such as reading, writing, and mathematics.

In the first section, we briefly discuss some key shortcomings in current curricular and pedagogical practices. We then present some of the structural features of traditional apprenticeship and discuss, in general, the requirements of adapting these characteristics to the teaching and learning of cognitive skills. In the second section, we consider in detail three recently developed pedagogical "success models" that exemplify aspects of apprenticeship methods in teaching the thinking and reasoning skills involved in reading, writing and mathematics. We attempt to show how and why these methods are successful, with regard to the development of not only the cognitive but also the metacognitive skills required for true expertise.

In the final section, we organize our ideas about the purposes and characteristics of successful teaching into a general framework for the design of learning environments, where "environment" includes the content taught, the pedagogical methods employed, the sequencing of learning activities, and the sociology of learning. This framework emphasizes how cognitive apprenticeship goes beyond the techniques of traditional apprenticeship. We hope it will be useful to the field in studying, designing, and evaluating pedagogical methods, materials, and technologies.

TOWARD A SYNTHESIS OF SCHOOLING AND APPRENTICESHIP

Schooling and the Acquisition of Expert Practice

Although schools have been relatively successful in organizing and conveying large bodies of conceptual and factual knowledge, standard pedagogical practices render key aspects of expertise invisible to students. Too little attention is paid to the processes that experts engage in to use or acquire knowledge in carrying out complex or realistic tasks. Where processes are addressed, the emphasis is on formulaic methods for solving "textbook" problems or on the development of low-level subskills in relative isolation. Few resources are devoted to higher order problem-solving activities that require students to actively integrate and appropriately apply subskills and conceptual knowledge.

As a result, conceptual and problem-solving knowledge acquired in school remains largely unintegrated or inert for many students. In some cases, knowledge remains bound to surface features of problems as they appear in textbooks and class presentations. For example, Schoenfeld (1985) has found that students rely on their knowledge of standard textbook patterns of problem presentation, rather than on their knowledge of problem-solving strategies or intrinsic properties of the problems themselves, for help in solving mathematics problems. Problems that fall outside these patterns do not invoke the appropriate problem-solving methods and relevant conceptual knowledge. In other cases, students fail to use resources available to them to improve their skills because they lack models of the processes required for doing so. For example, students are unable to make use of potential models of good writing acquired through reading because they have no understanding of the strategies and processes required to produce such text. Stuck with what Bereiter and Scardamalia (1987) call "knowledge-telling strategies," they are unaware that expert writing involves organizing one's ideas about a topic, elaborating goals to be achieved in the writing, thinking about what the audience is likely to know or believe about the subject, and so on.

To make real differences in students' skill, we need both to understand the nature of expert practice and to devise methods appropriate to learning that practice. To do this, we must first recognize that cognitive and metacognitive strategies and processes are more central than either low-level subskills or abstract conceptual and factual knowledge. They are the organizing principles of expertise, particularly in such domains as reading, writing, and mathematics. Further, because expert practice in these domains rests crucially on the integration of cognitive and metacognitive processes, it can best be taught through methods that emphasize what Lave (in preparation) calls successive approximation of mature practice, methods that have traditionally been employed in apprenticeship to transmit complex physical processes and skills.

Traditional Apprenticeship

To give an idea of these methods and why they are likely to be effective, let us first consider some of the crucial features of traditional apprenticeship, as practiced in a West African tailoring shop (Lave, in preparation).

First and foremost, apprenticeship focuses closely on the specific methods for carrying out tasks in a domain. Apprentices learn these methods through a combination of what Lave calls observation, coaching, and practice, or what we, from the teacher's point of view, call modeling, coaching, and fading. In this sequence of activities, the apprentice repeatedly observes the master executing (or modeling) the target process, which usually involves some different but interrelated subskills. The apprentice then attempts to execute the process with guidance and help from the master (i.e., coaching). A key aspect of coaching is the provision of scaffolding, which is the support, in the form of reminders and help, that the apprentice requires to approximate the execution of the entire composite of skills. Once the learner has a grasp of the target skill, the master reduces (or fades) his participation, providing only limited hints, refinements, and feedback to the learner, who practices by successively approximating smooth execution of the whole skill.

The interplay between observation, scaffolding, and increasingly independent practice aids apprentices both in developing self-monitoring and -correction skills and in integrating the skills and conceptual knowledge needed to advance toward expertise. Observation plays a surprisingly key role; Lave hypothesizes that it aids learners in developing a conceptual model of the target task or process prior to attempting to execute it. Provision of a conceptual model is an important factor in apprenticeship's success in teaching complex skills without resorting to lengthy practice of isolated subskills, for three related reasons. First, it provides learners with an advanced organizer for their initial attempts to execute a complex skill, thus allowing them to concentrate more of their attention on execution than would otherwise be possible. Second, a conceptual model provides an interpretive structure for making sense of the feedback, hints, and corrections from the master during interactive coaching sessions. Third, it provides an internalized guide for the period of relatively independent practice by successive approximation. Moreover, development of a conceptual model that can be continually updated through further observation and feedback encourages autonomy in what we call reflection (Collins & Brown, 1988). Reflection is the process that underlies the ability of learners to compare their own performance, at both micro and macrolevels, to the performance of an expert. Such comparisons aid learners in diagnosing difficulties and incrementally adjusting their performances until they reach competence.

Another key observation about apprenticeship concerns the social context in which learning takes place. Apprenticeship derives many cognitively important characteristics from being embedded in a subculture in which most, if not all, members are participants in the target skills. As a result, learners have continual access to models of expertise-in-use against which to refine their understanding of complex skills. Moreover, it is not uncommon for apprentices to have access to several masters and thus to a variety of models of expertise. Such richness and variety, helps them to understand that there may be multiple ways of carrying out a task and to recognize that no one individual embodies all knowledge or expertise. And finally, learners have the opportunity to observe other learners with varying degrees of skill; among other things, this encourages them to view learning as an incrementally staged process, while providing them with concrete benchmarks for their own progress.

From Traditional to Cognitive Apprenticeship

This chapter proposes a rethinking of these aspects of apprenticeship for subjects such as reading, writing, and mathematics. We call this rethinking of teaching and learning in school "cognitive apprenticeship" to emphasize two issues. First, the method is aimed primarily at teaching the processes that experts use to handle complex tasks. Where conceptual and factual knowledge are addressed, cognitive apprenticeship emphasizes their uses in solving problems and carrying out tasks; that is, in cognitive apprenticeship, conceptual and factual knowledge are exemplified and situated in the contexts of their use. Conceptual and factual knowledge thus are learned in terms of their uses in a variety of contexts, encouraging both a deeper understanding of the meaning of the concepts and facts themselves and a rich web of memorable associations between them and problem-solving contexts. It is this dual focus on expert processes and situated learning that we expect to help solve the educational problems of brittle skills and inert knowledge.

Second, our term, cognitive apprenticeship, refers to the focus of the learning-through-guided-experience on cognitive and metacognitive, rather than physical, skills and processes. Although we do not wish to draw a major theoretical distinction between the learning of physical and cognitive skills, there are differences that have practical implications for the organization of teaching and learning activities and teacher–learner interactions. Most importantly, traditional apprenticeship has evolved to teach domains in which the process of carrying out target skills is external and thus readily available to both student and teacher for observation, comment, refinement, and correction and bears a relatively transparent relationship to concrete products. The externalization of relevant processes and methods makes possible such characteristics of apprenticeship as its reliance on observation as a primary means of building a conceptual model of a complex target skill. And the relatively transparent relationship, at all stages of production, between process and product facilitates the learner's recognition and diagnosis of errors, on which the early development of self-correction skills depends.

Applying apprenticeship methods to largely cognitive skills requires the externalization of processes that are usually carried out internally. At least as most subjects are taught and learned in school, teachers cannot make fine adjustments in students' application of skill and knowledge to problems and tasks, because they have no access to the relevant cognitive processes. By the same token, students do not usually have access to the cognitive problem-solving processes of instructors as a basis for learning through observation and mimicry. Cognitive research, through such methods as protocol analysis, has begun to delineate the cognitive and metacognitive processes that comprise expertise, which heretofore were inaccessible. Cognitive apprenticeship teaching methods are designed to bring these tacit processes into the open, where students can observe, enact, and practice them with help from the teacher and from other students.

Cognitive apprenticeship also requires extended techniques to encourage the development of self-correction and -monitoring skills, as we cannot rely on the transparent relationship between process and product that characterizes the learning of such physical skills as tailoring. We have identified two basic means of fostering these crucial metacognitive skills. First, cognitive apprenticeship encourages reflection on differences between novice and expert performance by alternation between expert and novice efforts and by techniques that we have elsewhere called *abstracted replay* (Collins & Brown, 1988). Alternation between expert and novice efforts in a shared problem-solving context sensitizes students to the details of expert performance as the basis for incremental adjustments in their own performance. Abstracted replay attempts to focus students' observations and comparisons directly on the determining features of both their own and an expert's performance by highlighting those features in a skillful verbal description or, in some domains, through use of recording technologies such as computers or videotapes.

A second means of encouraging the development of self-monitoring and -correction skills is based on the insight that these skills require the problem solver to alternate among different cognitive activities while carrying out a complex task. Most notably, complex cognitive activities involve some version of both generative and evaluative processes. However, both types of processes are complex and can be difficult to learn in tandem. Thus, cognitive apprenticeship involves the development and externalization of a producer–critic dialogue that students can gradually internalize. This development and externalization are accomplished through discussion, alternation of teacher and learner roles, and group problem solving.

Some Caveats

In addition to the emphasis on cognitive and metacognitive skills, there are two major differences between cognitive apprenticeship and traditional apprenticeship. First, because traditional apprenticeship is set in the workplace, the problems and tasks that are given to learners arise not from pedagogical concerns but from the demands of the workplace. Cognitive apprenticeship, as we envision it, differs from traditional apprenticeship in that the tasks and problems are chosen to illustrate the power of certain techniques or methods, to give students practice in applying these methods in diverse settings, and to increase the complexity of tasks slowly, so that component skills and models can be integrated. In short, tasks are sequenced to reflect the changing demands of learning. Letting the job demands select the tasks for students to practice is one of the great inefficiencies of traditional apprenticeship.

On the other hand, the economic bias in apprenticeship has useful as well as less-than-ideal effects. For example, apprentices are encouraged to quickly learn skills that are useful and, therefore, meaningful within the social context of the workplace. Moreover, apprentices have natural opportunities to realize the value, in concrete economic terms, of their developing skill: Well-executed skills result in saleable products. Cognitive apprenticeship must find a way to create a culture of expert practice for students to participate in and aspire to, as well as devise meaningful benchmarks and incentives for progress.

A second difference between cognitive and traditional apprenticeship is the emphasis in cognitive apprenticeship on decontextualizing knowledge so that it can be used in many different settings. Traditional apprenticeship emphasizes teaching skills in the context of their use. We propose that cognitive apprenticeship should extend situated learning to diverse settings so that students learn how to apply their skills in varied contexts. Moreover, the abstract principles underlying the application of knowledge and skills in different settings should be articulated as fully as possible by the teacher, whenever they arise in different contexts.

We do not want to argue that cognitive apprenticeship is the only way to learn. Reading a book or listening to a lecture are important ways to learn, particularly in domains where conceptual and factual knowledge are central. Active listeners or readers, who test their understanding and pursue the issues that are raised in their minds, learn things that apprenticeship can never teach. To the degree that readers or listeners are passive, however, they will not learn as much as they would by apprenticeship, because apprenticeship forces them to use their knowledge. Moreover, few people learn to be active readers and listeners on their own, and that is where cognitive apprenticeship is critical—observing the processes by which an expert listener or reader thinks and practicing these skills under the guidance of the expert can teach students to learn on their own more skillfully.

Even in domains that rest on elaborate conceptual and factual underpinnings, students must learn the practice or art of solving problems and carrying out tasks. And to achieve expert practice, some version of apprenticeship remains the method of choice. Thus, apprenticeship-like methods are widely used in graduate education in most domains. Students are expected to learn how to solve problems that arise in the context of carrying out complex tasks and to extend and make use of their textbook knowledge by undertaking significant projects guided by an expert in the field.

We argue that the development of expert practice through situated learning and the acquisition of cognitive and metacognitive skills is equally if not more important in more elementary domains. This is nowhere more evident than in the foundational domains of reading, writing, and mathematics. These domains are foundational not only because they provide the basis for learning and communication in other school subjects, but also because they engage cognitive and metacognitive processes that are basic to learning and thinking more generally. Unlike school subjects such as chemistry or history, these domains rest on relatively sparse conceptual and factual underpinnings, turning instead on students' robust and efficient execution of a set of cognitive and metacognitive skills. Given effective analyses and externalizable prompts for these skills, we believe that these domains are particularly well suited to teaching methods modeled on cognitive apprenticeship. In the next section, we discuss a set of recently developed and highly successful models for teaching the cognitive and metacognitive skills involved in reading, writing, and mathematics in terms of the key notions underlying our cognitive apprenticeship model.

THREE SUCCESS MODELS FOR COGNITIVE APPRENTICESHIP

Palincsar and Brown's Reciprocal Teaching of Reading

Palincsar and Brown's (1984, this volume) method of teaching reading comprehension, which exemplifies many of the features of cognitive apprenticeship, has proved remarkably effective in raising students' scores on reading comprehension tests, especially those of poor readers. The basic method centers on modeling and coaching students in four strategic skills: formulating questions based on the text, summarizing the text, making predictions about what will come next, and clarifying difficulties with the text. The method has been used with groups of two to seven students, as well as with individual students. It is called *Reciprocal Teaching* because the teacher and students take turns playing the role of teacher.

The procedure is as follows: Both the teacher and the students read a paragraph silently. Whoever is playing the role of teacher formulates a question based on the paragraph, constructs a summary, and makes a prediction or clarification, if any come to mind. Initially, the teacher models this process, eventually turning it over to the students. When students first undertake the process, the teacher coaches them extensively on how to construct good questions and summaries, offering prompts and critiquing their efforts. In this way, the teacher provides scaffolding for the students, enabling them to take on whatever portion of the task they can. As the students become more proficient, the teacher fades, assuming the role of monitor and providing occasional hints or feedback. Table 14.1 shows the kind of scaffolding and group interaction that occurs with children during Reciprocal Teaching.

Reciprocal Teaching is extremely effective. In a pilot study with individual students who were poor readers, the method raised subjects' reading comprehension test scores from 15% to 85% accuracy after about 20 training sessions. Six months later the students were still at 60% accuracy, recovering to 85% after only one session. In a subsequent study with groups of two students, the scores increased from about 30% to 80% accuracy, with very little change 8 weeks later. In classroom studies with groups of four to seven students, test scores increased from about 40% to 80% correct, again with only a slight decline 8 weeks later. These are very dramatic effects for any instructional intervention.

Why is Reciprocal Teaching so effective? In our analysis, which reflects in part the views of Palincsar and Brown (Brown & Palincsar, chap. 13 in this volume; Palincsar & Brown, 1984) its effectiveness depends on the co-occurrence of a number of factors.

First, the method engages students in a set of activities that helps them form a new conceptual model of the task of reading. In traditional schooling, students learn to identify reading with the subskills of recognizing and pronouncing words and with the activities of scanning text and saying it aloud. Under the new conception, students recognize that reading requires constructive activities, such as formulating questions and making summaries and predictions, as well as evaluative ones, such as analyzing and clarifying the points of difficulty. Moreover, carrying out these activities by repeatedly reviewing the text helps students realize that reading for understanding is often more than a one-pass operation; it provides them with a more realistic expectation about the requirements of reading increasingly difficult texts.

Second, these activities involve the student in using the reading strategies and metacognitive skills necessary for expert reading. In particular:

Formulating questions is an important strategic activity for understanding difficult texts (Collins, Brown, & Larkin, 1980) because it provides the basis for checking whether the text makes sense (self-monitoring). Formulating questions that capture the main ideas of the text sometimes leads to questions that the text raises but does not answer.

Summarizing, like formulating questions, provides a general test of

TABLE 14.1
Sample Reciprocal Teaching Dialogue (from Palincsar, 1986)

Text from which students are working:

Crows have another gift. They are great mimics. They can learn to talk and imitate animal sounds. Some have been known to learn 100 words, and even whole phrases. They can imitate the squeak of a chicken, the whine of a dog, or the meow of a cat.

Games have a certain fascination to crows. In a game of hide-and-seek, a crow hides in the hollow of a tree and then sounds a distress caw. The others rush to the spot, look around, then flap away. This may be done over and over, after which the young crow pops out of its hiding place and caws gleefully. Far from being annoyed at this, the flock bursts into loud cawing themselves. They seem to like the trick that has been played on them.

T: Chantel, you're our teacher, right? Why don't you summarize first? Remember, just tell me the most important parts.

S1: Crows have a hundred words they can learn by imitation. They can imitate chickens, the whine of a dog, and cats.

T: Okay. We can shorten that summary a bit.

S2: You could say they can imitate other animals.

T: Oh! Good one! There's a list there, Chantel, did you notice that? It says they can imitate the squawk of a chicken, the whine of a dog or the meow of a cat; and you could call that "animal sounds." Can you ask us a question?

S1: Ain't no questions in here.

S3: The words (sic.) that need to be clarified are (sic.) "mimics".

S4: That means imitate, right?

T: Right. How did you figure that out, Shirley?

S4: The paragraph.

T: Show us how somebody could figure out what "mimic" means.

S5: They are great mimics. They can learn to talk and imitate animal sounds.

T: Yes, so the next sentence tells you what it means. Very good. anything else need to be clarified?

All: No.

T: What about that question we need to ask?
     (pause)
     What is the second paragraph about, Chantel?

S1: The games they play.

S3: They do things like people do.

S4: What kinds of games do crows play?

S3: Hide and seek. Over and over again.

T: You know what, Larry? That was a real good comparison. One excellent question could be, "How are crows like people?"

S4: They play hide and seek.

T: Good. Any other questions there?

S2: How come the crows don't get annoyed?

S5: What does annoyed mean?

T: Irritated, bothered.

S5: Because they like it, they have fun. If I had a crow, I'd tell him he was it and see what he'd do.

T: Let's summarize now and have some predictions.

S1: This was about how they play around in games.

T: Good for you. That's it. Predictions anyone?

S2: Maybe more tricks they play.

S4: Other games.

T: Maybe. So far, they have told us several ways that crows are very smart; they can communicate with one another, they can imitate many sounds, and they play games. Maybe we will read about another way in which they are smart. Who will be the next teacher?

comprehension and so forms the basis for comprehension monitoring: it is a preliminary phase of self-diagnosis. Students learn that if they cannot form a good summary, then they do not understand the text and had better either reread or try to clarify their difficulties (Collins & Smith, 1982).

Clarification is a key activity in comprehension monitoring that involves detailed self-diagnosis, in which students attempts to isolate and formulate their particular difficulties in understanding a text. Although summarizing is a fairly global test of comprehension, usually applied at the paragraph level, clarification attempts to narrow points of difficulty by focusing on word and phrase levels of meaning. Skill at clarifying difficulties provides students with the basis for using evidence from subsequent text to disambiguate the meaning of problematic words or phrases, a key strategy employed by expert readers.

Prediction involves formulating guesses or hypotheses about what the author of a text is likely to say next and, as such, promotes an overall reading strategy of hypothesis formation and testing. The inclusion of prediction as an explicit strategic activity for beginning readers reflects the fact that skilled reading involves developing expectations and evaluating them as evidence accumulates from the text (Collins & Smith, 1982).

The third factor critical for the success of Reciprocal Teaching is that the teacher models expert strategies in a problem context shared directly and immediately with the students. This organization of teacher–learner interaction encourages students first to focus their observations and then to reflect on their own performance relative to that of the teacher during subsequent modeling. Here is how it works: Both teacher and students read a paragraph. The teacher then performs the four activities: She articulates the questions she would ask about the paragraph, summarizes it, makes predictions about what will be next, and explains what part of the paragraph gave her difficulty. She may try to explain why she generated a particular question or made a particular prediction. What is crucial here is that the students listen in the context of knowing that they will soon undertake the same task, using that expectation to focus their observations on how those activities are related to the paragraph. After they have tried to do it themselves and perhaps had difficulties, they listen to the teacher with new knowledge about the task. As they read subsequent passages, they may try to generate a question or summary for themselves, noticing later what she does differently; that is, they can compare their own questions or summaries with the questions or summaries she generates. They can then reflect on any differences, trying to understand what led to those differences. We have argued elsewhere that this kind of reflection is critical to learning (Collins & Brown, 1988).

Fourth, the technique of providing scaffolding is crucial in the success of Reciprocal Teaching for several reasons. Most importantly, it decomposes the task as necessary for the students to carry it out, thereby helping them to see how, in detail, to go about it. For example, in formulating questions, the teacher might first want to see if the student can generate a question on his or her own; if not, she might suggest starting a question with "Why" or "How." If the student still cannot generate a question, she might suggest formulating a simple "Why" question about the agent in the story. If that fails, she might generate one herself and ask the student to reformulate it in his or her own words. In this way, it gets students started in the new skills, giving them a "feel" for the skills and helping them develop confidence that they can do them. Scaffolding is designed to help students when they are at an impasse (Brown & VanLehn, 1980). With successful scaffolding techniques, students get as much support as they need to carry out the task, but no more. Hints and modeling are then gradually faded out, with students taking on more and more of the task as they become more skillful. These techniques of scaffolding and fading slowly build students' confidence that they can master the skills required.

The final aspect of Reciprocal Teaching that we think is critical is having students assume the dual roles of *producer* and *critic*. They not only must produce good questions and summaries, but they also learn to evaluate the summaries or questions of others. By becoming critics as well as producers, students are forced to articulate their knowledge about what makes a good question, prediction, or summary. This knowledge then becomes more readily available for application to their own summaries and questions, thus improving a crucial aspect of their metacognitive skills. Moreover, once articulated, this knowledge can no longer simply reside in tacit form. It becomes more available for performing a variety of tasks; that is, it is freed from its contextual binding and can be used in many different contexts.

Scardamalia and Bereiter's Procedural Facilitation of Writing

Scardamalia and Bereiter (1985; Scardamalia, Bereiter, & Steinbach, 1984) have developed an approach to the teaching of writing that relies on elements of cognitive apprenticeship. Based on contrasting models of novice and expert writing strategies, the approach provides explicit procedural supports, in the form of prompts, that are aimed at helping students adopt more sophisticated writing strategies. Like other exemplars of cognitive apprenticeship, their approach is designed to give students a grasp of the complex activities involved in expertise by explicit modeling of expert processes, gradually reduced support or scaffolding for students attempting to engage in the processes, and opportunities for reflection on their own and others' efforts.

According to Bereiter and Scardamalia's (1987) analysis of expert–novice differences, children who are novices in writing use a *knowledge-telling* strategy. When given a topic to write on, they immediately produce text by writing their first idea, then their next idea, and so on, until they run out of ideas, at which point they stop. This very simple control strategy finesses most of the difficulties in composing. In contrast, experts spend time not only writing but also planning what they are going to write and revising what they have written (Hayes & Flower, 1980). As a result, they engage in a process that Scardamalia and Bereiter call *knowledge transforming,* which incorporates the linear generation of text, but is organized around a more complex structure of goal setting and problem solving. Scardamalia and Bereiter (1985) argue that for experts writing is a "compositional" task in which goals are emergent, that is, "your knowledge of what you are after grows and changes as part of the process" (p. 563). Emergent goals are products of the fact that "there is a wealth of potentially applicable knowledge and potential routes to the goals" (p. 563).

To encourage students to adopt a more sophisticated writing strategy, Scardamalia, Bereiter, and colleagues have developed a detailed cognitive analysis of the activities of expert writers. This analysis provides the basis for a set of prompts, or *Procedural Facilitations,* that are designed to reduce students' information-processing burden by allowing them to select from a limited number of diagnostic statements. For example, in their analysis, planning is broken down into five general processes or goals: (a) generating a new idea, (b) improving an idea,(c) elaborating an idea, (d) identifying goals, and (e) putting ideas into a cohesive whole. For each process, they have developed some specific prompts, designed to aid students in their planning, as shown in Table 14.2. These prompts, which are akin to the suggestions made by the teacher in Reciprocal Teaching, simplify the complex process of elaborating and reconsidering one's plans by suggesting specific lines of thinking for students to follow. A comparable analysis and set of prompts has been developed for the revision process as well (Scardamalia & Bereiter, 1983b, 1985).

Scardamalia and Bereiter's teaching method, like Reciprocal Teaching, proceeds through a combination of modeling, coaching, scaffolding, and fading. First, the teacher models how to use the prompts, which are written on cue cards, in generating ideas about a topic she is going to write on. Table 14.3 illustrates the kind of modeling done by a teacher during an early phase of instruction. Then the students each try to plan an essay on a new topic using the cue cards, a process the students call *soloing.* As in Reciprocal Teaching, students have the opportunity to assume both producer and critic roles. While each student practices soloing, the teacher as

TABLE 14.2
Planning Cues for Opinion Essays
(From Scardamalia et al., 1984)

New Idea

An even better idea is . . .
An important point I haven't considered yet is . . .
A better argument would be . . .
A different aspect would be . . .
A whole new way to think of this topic is . . .
No one will have thought of . . .

Improve

I'm not being very clear about what I just said so . . .
I could make my main point clearer . . .
A criticism I should deal with in my paper is . . .
I really think this isn't necessary because . . .
I'm getting off the topic so . . .
This isn't very convincing because . . .
But many readers won't agree that . . .
To liven this up I'll . . .

Elaborate

An example of this . . .
This is true, but it's not sufficient so . . .
My own feelings about this are . . .
I'll change this a little by . . .
The reason I think so . . .
Another reason that's good . . .
I could develop this idea by adding . . .
Another way to put it would be . . .
A good point on the other side of the argument is . . .

Goals

A goal I think I could write to . . .
My purpose . . .

Putting It Together

If I want to start off with my strongest idea I'll . . .
I can tie this together by . . .
My main point is . . .

TABLE 14.3
Example of Teacher Modeling in Response to a Student-Suggested
Writing Assignment

Assignment

Write an essay on the topic, "Today's Rock Stars are More Talented Than Musicians of Long Ago."

Thinking-Aloud Excerpt

I don't know a thing about modern rock stars. I can't think of the name of even one rock star. How about, David Bowie or Mick Jagger . . . But many readers won't agree that they are modern rock stars. I think they're both as old as I am. Let's see my own feelings about this are . . . that I doubt if today's rock stars are more talented than ever. Anyhow, how would I know? I can't argue this . . . I need a new idea . . . An important point I haven't considered yet is . . . ah . . . well . . . what do we mean by talent? Am I talking about musical talent or ability to entertain—to do acrobatics? Hey, I may have a way into this topic. I could develop this idea by . . .

Note: Underlined phrases represent selection from planning cues similar to those shown in Table 14.2.

well as other students evaluate the soloist's performance, by noticing, for example, discrepancies between the soloist's stated goals (for example, to get readers to appreciate the difficulties of modern dance) and their proposed plans (to describe different kinds of dance). Students also become involved in discussing how to resolve problems that the soloist could not solve. As in the Reciprocal Teaching method, assumption of the role either of critic or producer is incremental, with students taking over more and more of the monitoring and problem-solving process from the teacher, as their skills improve. Moreover, as the students internalize the processes invoked by the prompts, the cue cards are gradually faded out as well.

Scardamalia and Bereiter, (1983a) have also developed a specific technique, called *co-investigation,* aimed at encouraging students to reflect on both their existing strategies and the new ones they are acquiring. In co-investigation, Scardamalia and Bereiter try to have students think aloud as they carry out some task, such as writing a paragraph linking two sentences together. They propose to the students that together they try to examine their own thinking as they carry out the task. This motivates the students to consider their reflections as data from an experiment. When students have learned how to reflect on their own thinking, Scardamalia and Bereiter provide the procedural supports shown in Table 14.2, so that children can carry out writing tasks in more expert ways. The scaffolding provided by the cue cards thus enables them to reflect on how their normal writing methods differ from these more expert methods.

Scardamalia and Bereiter have tested the effects of their approach on both the initial planning and the revision of student compositions. In a series of studies (Bereiter & Scardamalia, 1987), procedural facilitations were developed to help elementary school students evaluate, diagnose, and decide on revisions for their compositions. Results showed that each type of support was effective, independent of the other supports. And when all the facilitations were combined, with modeling and co-investigation, they resulted in superior revisions for nearly every student and a tenfold increase in the frequency of idea-level revisions, without any decrease in stylistic revisions. Another study (Scardamalia et al., 1984) investigated the use of procedural cues to facilitate planning. Students gave the teacher assignments, often ones thought difficult for her. She used cues like those shown in Table 14.2 to facilitate planning, modeling the process of using the cues to stimulate her thinking about the assignment (Table 14.3). Pre and postcomparisons of think-aloud protocols of a randomly selected portion of the subjects showed significantly more reflective activity on the part of experimental-group students, even when prompts were no longer available to them. Time spent in planning increased tenfold. And when students were given unrestricted time to plan, the texts of experimental-group students were judged significantly superior in thought content.

Clearly, Scardamalia and Bereiter's methods bring about significant changes in the nature and quality of student writing. In addition to the methods already discussed, we believe there are two key reasons for their success. First of all, as in the Reciprocal Teaching method for reading, their methods help students build a new conception of the writing process. Students initially consider writing a linear process of knowledge telling. By explicitly modeling and scaffolding expert processes, they are providing students with a new model of writing that involves planning and revising. Most children found this view of writing entirely new and showed it in their comments during co-investigation ("I don't usually ask myself those questions," "I never thought closely about what I wrote," and "They helped me look over the sentence, which I don't usually do."). Moreover, because students rarely if ever see writers at work, they tend to hold naive beliefs about the nature of expert writing, thinking that writing is a smooth and easy process for "good" writers. Live modeling helps to convey that this is not the case. The model demonstrates struggles, false starts, discouragement, and the like. Modeling also demonstrates for students that in evolving and decomposing a complex set of goals for this writing, expert writers often treat their own thoughts as objects of reflection and inquiry. These reflective operations underscore the fact that writing is not a linear, but an iterative, process—another new idea for students.

Second, because writing is a complex compositional task, a key component of expertise is the control structure by which the writer organizes the numerous subactivities or lines of thinking involved in producing high-quality text. A clear need of student writers, therefore, is to develop a more useful control structure and related processes than are evidenced in *knowledge telling*. Scardamalia and Bereiter's methods encourage this development in an interesting way: The cue cards act to externalize not only the basic cognitive processes involved in planning but also to help students to keep track of the higher order intentions (such as generating an idea, elaborating or improving an idea, and so on) that organize these basic processes. This externalization aids students in monitoring their own (and others') progress in the writing task, so that they can determine what general activity is required before moving on to specific prompts. This explicit hierarchical decomposition of general goals and process into more locally useful subprocesses aids students in building an explicit internal model of what might otherwise seem a confusing or random process.

Schoenfeld's Method for Teaching Mathematical Problem Solving

Our third example is Schoenfeld's (1983, 1985) method for teaching mathematical problem solving to college students. Like the other two, this method is based on a new analysis of the knowledge and processes required for expertise, where expertise is understood as the ability to carry out complex problem-solving tasks in a domain. And like the other two, this method incorporates the basic elements of a cognitive apprenticeship, using the methods of modeling, coaching, and fading and of encouraging student reflection on their own problem-solving processes. In addition, Schoenfeld's work introduces some new concerns, leading the way toward articulation of a more general framework for the development and evaluation of ideal learning environments.

One distinction between novices and experts in mathematics is that experts employ heuristic methods, usually acquired tacitly through long experience, to facilitate their problem solving. To teach these methods directly, Schoenfeld formulated a set of *heuristic strategies*, derived from the problem-solving heuristics of Polya (1945). These heuristic strategies consist of rules of thumb for how to approach a given problem. One such heuristic specifies how to distinguish *special cases* in solving math problems: For example, for series problems in which there is an integer parameter in the problem statement, one should try the cases $n = 1, 2, 3, 4$ and try to make an induction on those cases; for geometry problems, one should first examine cases with minimal complexity, such as regular polygons and right triangles. Schoenfeld taught a number of these heuristics and how to apply them in different kinds of math problems. In his experiments, Schoenfeld (1985) found that learning these strategies significantly increased students' problem-solving abilities.

But as he studied students' problem solving further, he became aware of other critical factors affecting their skill, in particular what he calls *control strategies* and *belief systems*. In Schoenfeld's analysis, control strategies are concerned with executive decisions, such as generating alternative courses of action, evaluating which will get you closer to a solution, evaluating which you are most likely to be able to carry out, considering what heuristics might apply, evaluating whether you are making progress toward a solution, and so on. Schoenfeld's notion of belief systems includes beliefs about oneself (e.g., math phobia), about the world (e.g., "physical phenomena have physical causes, not psychic causes"), and about the domain (e.g., "mathematical proof is of no use in geometry construction problems"). Schoenfeld found that it was critical to teach control strategies and productive beliefs, as well as heuristics.

As with the reading and writing examples, explicit teaching of these elements of expert practice yields a fundamentally new understanding of the domain for students. To students, learning mathematics had meant learning a set of mathematical operations and methods, what Schoenfeld calls *resources*. Schoenfeld's method is teaching students that doing mathematics consists not only in applying problem-solving procedures but in reasoning about and managing problems using heuristics, control strategies, and beliefs.

Schoenfeld's teaching (1983, 1985) employs the elements of modeling, coaching, scaffolding, and fading in a variety of activities designed to highlight different aspects of the cognitive processes and knowledge structures required for expertise. For example, as a way of introducing new heuristics, he models their selection and use in solving problems for which they are particularly relevant. In this way, he exhibits the thinking processes (heuristics and control strategies) that go on in expert problem solving but focuses student observation on the use and management of specific heuristics. Table 14.4 provides a protocol from one such modeling.

Next, he gives the class problems to solve that lend themselves to the use of the heuristics he has introduced. During this collective problem solving, he acts as a moderator, soliciting heuristics and solution techniques from the students, while modeling the various control strategies for making judgments about how best to proceed. This division of labor has several effects. First, he turns over some of the problem-solving process to students by having them generate alternative courses of action, but he provides major support or scaffolding by managing the decisions about which course to pursue, when to change course, etc. Second, significantly he no longer models the entire expert problem-solving process but a por-

TABLE 14.4
An Example of Expert Modeling
in Mathematics (from Schoenfeld, 1983)

Problem

Let $P(x)$ and $Q(x)$ be two polynomials with "reversed" coefficients:

$$P(x) = a_n x^n + a_{n-1} x^{n-1} +$$
$$\ldots + a_2 x^2 a_1 x + a_0,$$
$$Q(x) = a_0 x^n + a_1 x^{n-1} +$$
$$\ldots + a_{n-2} x^2 a_{n-1} x + a_n,$$

where $a_n \neq 0 \neq a_0$. What is the relationship between the roots of $P(x)$ and those of $Q(x)$? Prove your answer.

Expert Model

What do you do when you face a problem like this? I have no general procedure for finding the roots of a polynomial, much less for comparing the roots of two of them. Probably the best thing to do for the time being is to look at some simple examples and hope I can develop some intuition from them. Instead of looking at a pair of arbitrary polynomials, maybe I should look at a pair of quadratics: at least I can solve those. So, what happens if

$$P(x) = ax^2 + bx + c$$

and

$$Q(x) = cx^2 + bx + a?$$

The roots are

$$\frac{-b \pm \sqrt{b^2 - 4ac}}{2a}$$

and

$$\frac{-b \pm \sqrt{b^2 - 4ac}}{2c}$$

respectively.

That's certainly suggestive, because they have the same numerator, but I don't really see anything that I can push or that'll generalize. I'll give this a minute or two, but I may have to try something else. . . .

Well, just for the record, let me look at the linear case. If $P(x) = ax + b$ and $Q(x) = bx + a$, the roots are $-b/a$ and $-a/b$ respectively.

They're reciprocals, but that's not too interesting in itself. Let me go back to quadratics. I still don't have much of a feel for what's going on. I'll do a couple of easy examples, and look for some sort of a pattern. The clever thing to do may be to pick polynomials I can factor; that way it'll be easy to keep track of the roots. All right, how about something easy like $(x + 2)(x + 3)$?

Then $P(x) = x^2 + 5x + 6$, with roots -2 and -3. So,
$Q(x) = 6x^2 + 5x + 1 = (2x + 1)(3x + 1)$, with roots $-1/2$ and $-1/3$.
Those are reciprocals too. Now that's interesting.
How about $P(x) = (3x + 5)(2x - 7) = 6x^2 - 11x - 35$? Its roots are $-5/3$ and $7/2$;
$Q(x) = -35x^2 - 11x + 6 = -(35x^2 + 11x - 6) = -(7x - 2)(5x + 3)$.

(continued)

TABLE 14.4 (Continued)

All right, the roots are 2/7 and −3/5. They're reciprocals again, and this time it can't be an accident. Better yet, look at the factors: they're reversed! What about
$$P(x) = (ax + b)(cx + d) = acx^2 + (bc + ad)x + bd? \text{ Then}$$
$$Q(x) = bdx^2 + (ad + bc)x + ac = (bx + a)(dx + c).$$
Aha! It works again, and I think this will generalize. . . .

At this point there are two ways to go. I hypothesize that the roots of $P(x)$ are the reciprocals of the roots of $Q(x)$, in general. (If I'm not yet sure, I should try a factorable cubic or two.) Now, I can try to generalize the argument above, but it's not all that straightforward; not every polynomial can be factored, and keeping tract of the coefficients may not be that easy. It may be worth stopping re-phrasing my conjecture, and trying it from scratch:

Let $P(x)$ and $Q(x)$ be two polynomials with "reversed" coefficients. Prove that the roots of $P(x)$ and $Q(x)$ are reciprocals.

All right, let's take a look at what the problem asks for. What does it mean for some number, say r, to be a root of $P(x)$? It means that $P(r) = 0$. Now the conjecture says that the reciprocal of r is supposed to be a root to $Q(x)$. That says that $Q(1/r) = 0$. Strange. Let me go back to the quadratic case, and see what happens.

Let $P(x) = ax^2 + bx + c$, and $Q(x) = cx^2 + bx + a$. If r is a root of $P(x)$, then $P(r) = ar^2 + br + c = 0$. Now what does $Q(1/r)$ look like?

$$Q(1/r) = c(1/r)^2 + b(1/r) + a = \frac{c + br + ar^2}{r^2} = \frac{P(r)}{r^2} = 0$$

So it works, and this argument will generalize. Now I can write up a proof.
Proof:

Let r be a root of $P(x)$, so that $P(r) = 0$. Observe that $r \neq 0$, since $a_0 \neq 0$. Further,
$Q(1/r) = a_0(1/r)^n + a_1(1/r)^{n-1} + \ldots + a_{n-2}(1/r) + a_n = (1/r^n)(a_0 + a_1r + a_2r^2 + \ldots + a_{n-2}r^{n-2} + a_{n-1}r^{n-1} + a_nr^n) = (1/r^n)P(r) = 0$, so that $(1/r)$ is a root of $Q(x)$.

Conversely, if S is a root of $Q(x)$, we see that $P(1/S) = 0$. Q.E.D.

All right, now it's time for a postmortem. Observe that the proof, like a classicial mathematical argument, is quite terse and present the results of a thought process. But where did the inspiration for the proof come from? If you go back over the way that the argument evolved, you'll see there were two major breakthroughs.

The first had to do with understanding the problem, with getting a feel for it. The problem statement, in its full generality, offered little in the way of assistance. What we did was to *examine special cases* in order to look for a pattern. More specifically, our first attempt at special cases—looking at the quadratic formula—didn't provide much insight. We had to get even more specific, as follows: *Look at a series of straightforward examples that are easy to calculate, in order to see if some sort of pattern emerges. With luck, you might be able to generalize the pattern.* In this case, we were looking for roots of polynomials, so we chose easily factorable ones. Obviously, different circumstances will lead to different choices. But that strategy allowed us to make a conjecture.

The second breakthrough came after we made the conjecture. Although we had some idea of why it ought to be true, the argument looked messy, and we stopped to reconsider for a while. What we did at that point was important, and is often overlooked: *we went back to the conditions of the problem, explored them, and looked for tangible connections between them and the results we wanted.* Questions like "what does it mean for r to be a root of $P(x)$?", "what does the reciprocal of r look like?" and "what does it mean for $(1/r)$ to be a root of $Q(x)$?" may seem almost trivial in isolation, but they focused our attention on the very things that gave us a solution.

tion of it. In this way, he shifts the focus of student observation during modeling from the application or use of specific heuristics to the application or use of control strategies in managing those heuristics.

Like Scardamalia and Bereiter, Schoenfeld employs a third kind of modeling that is designed to change students' assumptions about the nature of expert problem solving. He challenges students to find difficult problems, and at the beginning of each class offers to try to solve one of their problems. Occasionally, the problems are hard enough that the students see him flounder in the face of real difficulties. During these sessions, he models not only the use of heuristics and control strategies, but the fact that one's strategies sometimes fail. In contrast, textbook solutions and classroom demonstrations generally illustrate only the successful solution path, not the search space that contains all the dead-end attempts. Such solutions reveal neither the exploration in searching for a good method nor the necessary evaluation of the exploration. Seeing how experts deal with problems that are difficult for them is critical to students' developing a belief in their own capabilities. Even experts stumble, flounder, and abandon their search for a solution until another time. Witnessing these struggles helps students realize that thrashing is neither unique to them nor a sign of incompetence.

In addition to class demonstrations and collective problem solving, Schoenfeld has students participate in small-group problem-solving sessions. During these sessions, Schoenfeld acts as a "consultant" to make sure that the groups are proceeding in·a reasonable fashion. Typically, he asks three questions: What they are doing, why they are doing it, and how will success in what they are doing help them find a solution to the problem? Asking these questions serves two purposes: First, it encourages the students to reflect on their activities, thus promoting the development of general self-monitoring and -diagnosis skills; second, it encourages them to articulate the reasoning behind their choices as they exercise control strategies. Gradually, the students, in anticipating his questions, come to ask the questions of themselves, thus gaining control over reflective and metacognitive processes in their problem solving. In these sessions, then, he is fading relative to both helping students generate heuristics and, ultimately, to exercising control over the process. In this way, they gradually gain control over the entire problem-solving process.

Schoenfeld (1983) advocates small-group problem solving for several reasons. First, it gives the teacher a chance to coach students while they are engaged in semi-independent problem solving; he cannot really coach them effectively on homework problems or class problems. Second, the necessity for group decision making in choosing among alternative solution methods provokes articulation, through discussion and argumentation, of the issues involved in exercising control processes. Such discussion encourages the development of the metacognitive skills involved in, for example, monitoring and evaluating one's progress. Third, students get little opportunity in school to engage in collaborative efforts; group problem solving gives them practice in the kind of collaboration prevalent in real-world problem solving. Fourth, students are often insecure about their abilities, especially if they have difficulties with the problems. Seeing other students struggle alleviates some of this insecurity as students realize that difficulties in understanding are not unique to them, thus contributing to an enhancement of their beliefs about self relative to others.

Another important reason why small-group problem solving is useful for learning is the differentiation and externalization of the roles and activities involved in solving complex problems. Successful problem solving requires that one assume at least three different, though interrelated, roles at different points in the problem-solving process: that of moderator or executive, that of generator of alternative paths, and that of critic of alternatives. Small-group problem solving differentiates and externalizes these roles: Different people naturally take on different roles, and problem solving proceeds along these lines. Thus, group discussion and decision making models the interplay among processes that an individual must internalize to be a successful problem solver. And here, as in Reciprocal Teaching, students may play different roles, so that they gain practice in all the activities they need to internalize.

In its use of the techniques of modeling, coaching, and fading, and its promotion of a new understanding of the nature of expertise, Schoenfeld's methods bear important similarities to our other two "success models." Perhaps because of the requirements both of the domain and of the stage of learning that his students have achieved, Schoenfeld's work introduces some new issues into our discussion of pedagogical methods. First, Schoenfeld places a unique emphasis on the careful sequencing of problems. He has designed problem sequences to achieve four pedagogical goals: motivation, exemplification, practice, and integration. He first tries to show students the power of the heuristics he is teaching by giving them problems they will fail to solve without the heuristics. He then presents a few heuristics that enable students to solve the problems. The change in their ability to solve problems convinces the students that the heuristics are worth learning.

As he introduces each new heuristic, he tries to exemplify it with problems that are particularly "interesting," by which he presumably means problems in which the heuristic is especially effective. Over the next week, he assigns extensive practice problems for which the new heuristic is helpful; he estimates that perhaps one-third of the week's problems involve use of the new heuristic. Finally, after the heuristic has been introduced and practiced, problems involving that heuristic continue to be assigned, but less frequently. As the course progresses, the problems involve use of multiple heuristics, so that students are learning to integrate the use of different heuristics to solve complex problems.

By selection and sequencing of examples and problem sets, Schoenfeld is trying to ensure that students will learn when to apply the heuristics as well as how to apply them. Initially, instruction focuses on how to apply each heuristic; thus, the first problems all involve the heuristic. What varies is the problem context: A given problem might be a series problem or a geometry problem or an algebra problem, but the same heuristic always applies. Once the students know how to apply the heuristic, they must learn to recognize those situations in which the heuristic applies. Therefore, it is important to include problems for which the heuristic does not apply, forcing students to differentiate problems for which the heuristic applies from problems for which it does not. This problem-differentiation ability is critical to transfer of skills. The final phase, during which problems requiring the heuristic are assigned occasionally, is aimed at preventing students from learning to apply the heuristic only to those problems assigned while the heuristic is being taught. (This is typical of the strategies that students derive from school courses.) Unless the need for the heuristic recurs, it will drop out of their repertoire.

There is one final aspect of Schoenfeld's method that we think is critical and that is different from the other methods we have discussed: what he calls *postmortem* analysis. As with other aspects of Schoenfeld's method, students alternate with the teacher in producing postmortem analyses. First, after modeling the problem-solving process for a given problem, Schoenfeld recounts the solution method, highlighting the generalizable features of the process (see Table 14.4). For example, he might note the heuristics that were employed, the points in the solution process where he or the class engaged in generating alternatives, the reasons for the decision to pursue one alternative before another, and so on. He thereby provides what we (Collins & Brown, 1988) have labeled an *abstracted replay,* that is, a recapitulation of some process designed to focus students' attention on the critical decisions or actions. Postmortem analysis also occurs when individual students explain the process by which they solved their homework problems. Here students are required to generate an abstracted replay of their own problem-solving process, as the basis for a class critique of their methods. The alternation between expert and student postmortem analyses enables the class to compare student problem-solving processes and strategies with those of the expert; such comparisons provide the basis for diagnosing student difficulties and for making incremental adjustments in student performance. Moreover, generating abstracted replays involves focusing on the strategic as well as the tactical levels of problem solving; this aids students in developing a hierarchical model of the problem-solving process as the basis for self-monitoring and -correction, and in seeing how to organize local (tactical) processes to accomplish high-level (strategic) goals.

A FRAMEWORK FOR DESIGNING LEARNING ENVIRONMENTS

In our discussion, we have described an apprenticeship-like approach to teaching the skills necessary for expert practice in cognitive domains and considered in detail three recently developed teaching methods, viewed as "success models" of cognitive apprenticeship. Our discussion of these teaching methods has introduced numerous pedagogical and theoretical issues that are important to the design of learning environments generally. To facilitate considerations of these issues, we have developed a framework, outlined in Table 14.5. The framework describes four dimensions

TABLE 14.5
Characteristics of Ideal Learning Environments

Content

Domain knowledge
Heuristic strategies
Control strategies
Learning strategies

Methods

Modelling
Coaching
Scaffolding and fading
Articulation
Reflection
Exploration

Sequence

Increasing complexity
Increasing diversity
Global before local skills

Sociology

Situated learning
Culture of expert practice
Intrinsic motivation
Exploiting cooperation
Exploiting competition

that constitute any learning environment: content, method, sequence, and sociology. Relevant to each of these dimensions is a set of characteristics that should be considered in constructing or evaluating learning environments. We now consider these characteristics in detail, giving examples from reading, writing, and mathematics.

Content

Recent cognitive research has begun to differentiate the types of knowledge required for expertise. In particular, researchers have begun to distinguish between the explicit conceptual, factual, and procedural knowledge associated with expertise and various types of *strategic* knowledge. We use the term strategic knowledge to refer to the usually tacit knowledge that underlies an expert's ability to make use of concepts, facts, and procedures as necessary to solve problems and carry out tasks. This kind of expert problem-solving knowledge involves problem-solving strategies and heuristics, and the strategies that control the problem-solving process at its various levels of decomposition. Another type of strategic knowledge, often overlooked, includes the learning strategies that experts have about how to acquire new concepts, facts, and procedures in their own or another field.

Within our framework, the appropriate target knowledge for an ideal learning environment is likely to include all four categories of expert knowledge, only one of which is often the current focus in schools.

1. *Domain knowledge* includes the conceptual and factual knowledge and procedures explicitly identified with a particular subject matter; these are generally explicated in school textbooks, class lectures, and demonstrations. As we argued earlier, this kind of knowledge, although certainly important, provides insufficient clues for many students about how actually to go about solving problems and carrying out tasks in a domain. Moreover, when it is learned in isolation from realistic problem contexts and expert problem-solving practices, domain knowledge tends to remain inert in situations for which it is appropriate, even for successful students. And finally, although at least some concepts can be formally described, many of the crucial subtleties of their meaning are best acquired through applying them in a variety of problem situations. Indeed, it is only through encountering them in real problem solving that most students will learn the boundary conditions and entailments of much of their domain knowledge.

Examples of domain knowledge in reading are vocabulary, syntax, and phonics rules; the standard procedure for reading is scanning text, either silently or aloud, and constructing an interpretation. For writing, domain knowledge includes much of the same vocabulary and syntactic knowledge and in addition, knowledge about rhetorical forms and genres and about writing drafts and revising. In mathematics, most of the domain knowledge, other than number facts and definitions, consists of procedures for solving different kinds of problems, from addition algorithms to procedures for solving problems in algebra and constructing proofs in geometry.

2. *Heuristic strategies* are generally effective techniques and approaches for accomplishing tasks that might be regarded as "tricks of the trade"; they don't always work, but when they do they are quite helpful. Most heuristics are tacitly acquired by experts through the practice of solving problems: however, there have been noteworthy attempts to address heuristic learning explicitly. The literature is replete with examples of heuristics for mathematical problem solving, beginning with Polya (1945); though less widely formalized, useful problem-solving heuristics and strategies can also be identified for more open-ended task domains, such as reading and writing.

For example, a standard heuristic for writing is to plan to rewrite the introduction to a text (and therefore to spend relatively little time crafting it); this heuristic is based on the recognition that a writer's initial plan for a text is likely to undergo radical refinement and revision through the process of writing and, therefore, that the beginning of a text often needs to be rewritten to "fit" the emergent organization and arguments of the main body and conclusion. Another strategy, designed to help a writer maintain momentum and "flow of ideas," is to avoid getting bogged down in syntax or other presentational details while getting one's ideas down. In reading, a general strategy for facilitating both comprehension and critical reading is to develop an overview and set of expectations and questions about a text before reading line by line; one can achieve this by looking through tables of contents and reading section headings in chapters to get a sense of the overall organization of the text. Certain kinds of text, for example, experimental psychology articles, have a standard format corresponding to a paradigmatic argument structure; one can read the introduction and conclusions to understand the major claims being made before attempting to assess whether they are supported by evidence presented in other sections.

3. *Control Strategies,* as the name suggests, control the process of carrying out a task. As students acquire more and more heuristics and strategies for solving problems, they encounter a new management or control problem: how to select among the various possible problem-solving strategies, how to decide when to change strategies, and so on. The knowledge that experts have about managing problem solving can be formulated as control strategies. Control strategies require reflection on the problem-solving process to determine how to proceed. Control strategies operate at many different levels. Some are aimed at managing problem solving at a global level and are probably useful across domains; for example, a simple control

strategy for solving a complex problem might be to switch to a new part of a problem, if one is stuck on another part. Other strategies control selection of domain-specific problem-solving heuristics and strategies for carrying out parts of the task at hand.

Control strategies have monitoring, diagnostic, and remedial components; decisions about how to proceed in a task generally depend on an assessment of the current state relative to one's goals, on an analysis of current difficulties, and on the strategies available for dealing with difficulties. Monitoring strategies can be represented as activities that help students to evaluate their progress in a general way by providing a simple criterion for determining whether or not a given goal is being achieved.

For reading, these strategies are called *comprehension monitoring* strategies (Baker & Brown, 1980; Collins & Smith, 1982). For example, a comprehension monitoring strategy might be to try to state the main point of a paragraph one has just read; if one cannot do so, then one has not understood the text. Monitoring strategies lead either to diagnosis or directly to remedial actions. For example, if one does not understand a given paragraph, one may proceed to analyze the source of one's difficulties or simply reread the text. Diagnosis refers to those processes whereby the problem solver arrives at a useful analysis of the nature or cause of his difficulties. The level of diagnostic analysis required depends on a number of factors, for example, how important understanding the current difficulty is to achieving the overall goals of the activity or what level of diagnosis is necessary to determine corrective action. In the diagnostic activity for reading that Palincsar and Brown call *clarifying difficulties* with the text, students attempt to isolate the particular word or phrase that they do not understand. To be useful, diagnoses must point to remedial strategies, that is, to problem solving or learning activities that will lead out of the difficulty by introducing new knowledge or providing an alternate tack on the problem. Having recognized that their difficulties in understanding a passage lie with a particular word or phrase, readers can employ various strategies, such as looking up words or continuing to read, with the plan of coming back to the difficult passage to see if subsequent evidence from the text resolves the difficulty (Collins & Smith, 1982).

4. *Learning strategies* are strategies for learning any of the other kinds of content just described. Like the other types of process knowledge we have described, knowledge about how to learn ranges from general strategies for exploring a new domain to more local strategies for extending or reconfiguring knowledge as the need arises in solving problems or carrying out a complex task. Inquiry teachers, in fact, model effective learning strategies for students (Collins & Stevens, 1982, 1983).

For example, if students want to learn to read better on their own, they have to know how to pick texts that expand their vocabulary but are not too demanding. They also have to know how to check their understanding against other people's, by reading critical reviews of the texts they have read or by discussing the text with someone. If students want to learn to write better, they need to find people to read their writing who can give helpful critiques and explain the reasoning underlying the critiques (most people cannot). They also need to learn to analyze others' texts for strengths and weaknesses. To learn to solve math problems better, it helps to try to solve the example problems presented in the text before reading the solution, to provide a basis for comparing one's own solution method to the solution method in the book. These are just a few of the more general strategies that expert learners acquire. Just as it is possible to teach heuristic and monitoring strategies by apprenticeship, it is possible to teach such learning strategies by apprenticeship.

Method

As we have discussed, a key goal in the design of teaching methods should be to help students acquire and integrate cognitive and metacognitive strategies for using, managing, and discovering knowledge. It is our belief, however, that the way these strategies are acquired and, once acquired, brought to play in problem solving, is both subtle and poorly understood. In general, it seems clear that both the acquisition and the use of these strategies depend crucially on interactions between the individual's current knowledge and beliefs, the social and physical environment in which the problem solving takes place, and the local details of the problem solving itself as it unfolds. A major direction in current cognitive research is to attempt to formulate explicitly the strategies and skills underlying expert practice, to make them a legitimate focus of teaching in schools and other learning environments. Indeed, all three success models we have discussed are based on explicit formulations of cognitive and metacognitive strategies and center their teaching around activities designed to convey these explicitly to students. We believe, however, it is also important to consider the possibility that, because of the nature of the relationship between these strategies and the overall problem context, not all the necessary—and certainly not all the possible—strategies involved in complex cognitive activities can be captured and made explicit. It is worth noting that these strategies and skills have tended to remain tacit and thus are lost to formal education precisely because they arise from the practice of solving problems, in situ, in the domain. Moreover, even given explicit formulation of strategies, understanding how to use them depends crucially on understanding the way they are embedded in the context of actual problem solving.

For these reasons, we believe that teaching methods should be designed to give students the opportunity to observe, engage in, and invent or discover expert strategies in context. Such an approach will enable students to see how these strategies fit together with their factual and conceptual knowledge and how they cue off and make use of a variety of resources in the social and physical environment. This is the essence of what we mean by situated learning (as we point out later in discussing Sociology) and the reason why the cognitive apprenticeship method, with its modeling–coaching–fading paradigm, is successful and perhaps indispensable.

The following six teaching methods fall roughly into three groups: the first three (modeling, coaching, and scaffolding) are the core of cognitive apprenticeship, designed to help students acquire an integrated set of cognitive and metacognitive skills through processes of observation and of guided and supported practice. The next two (articulation and reflection) are methods designed to help students both focus their observations of expert problem solving and gain conscious access to (and control of) their own problem-solving strategies. The final method (exploration) is aimed at encouraging learner autonomy, not only in carrying out expert problem-solving processes, but also in defining or formulating the problems to be solved.

1. *Modeling* involves an expert's carrying out a task so that students can observe and build a conceptual model of the processes that are required to accomplish the task. In cognitive domains, this requires the externalization of usually internal (cognitive) processes and activities—specifically, the heuristics and control processes by which experts make use of basic conceptual and procedural knowledge. For example, a teacher might model the reading process by reading aloud in one voice, while verbalizing her thought processes (e.g., the making and testing of hypotheses about what the text means, what the author intends, what she thinks will happen next, and so on) in another voice (Collins & Smith, 1982). Tables 14.3 and 14.4 give examples of teacher modeling of expert processes in the domains of writing and mathematics.

2. *Coaching* consists of observing students while they carry out a task and offering hints, scaffolding, feedback, modeling, reminders, and new tasks aimed at bringing their performance closer to expert performance. Coaching may serve to direct students' attention to a previously unnoticed aspect of the task or simply to remind the student of some aspect of the task that is known but has been temporarily overlooked. Coaching focuses on the enactment and integration of skills in the service of a well-understood goal through highly interactive and highly situated feedback and suggestions; that is, the content of the coaching interaction is immediately related to specific events or problems that arise as the student attempts to

carry out the target task. In reading, coaching might consist of having students attempt to give summaries of different texts. The teacher in the role of coach might choose texts with interesting difficulties, might remind the student that a summary needs to integrate the whole text into a sentence or two, might suggest how to start constructing a summary, might evaluate the summary a student produces in terms of how it could be improved, or might ask another student to evaluate it. Similarly, the description of Scardamalia and Bereiter's classes, and of Schoenfeld's classes provides examples of how the teacher can function as a coach while students try to carry out tasks in writing and mathematics.

3. *Scaffolding* refers to the supports the teacher provides to help the student carry out a task. These supports can either take the forms of suggestions or help, as in Palincsar and Brown's (1984) Reciprocal Teaching, or they can take the form of physical supports, as with the cue cards in Scardamalia et al.'s (1984) procedural facilitation of writing or the short skis used to teach downhill skiing (Burton, Brown, & Fischer, 1984). When scaffolding is provided by a teacher, it requires the teacher to carry out parts of the overall task that the student cannot yet manage. It involves a kind of cooperative problem-solving effort by teacher and student in which the express intention is for the student to assume as much of the task on his own as possible, as soon as possible. A requisite of such scaffolding is accurate diagnosis of the student's current skill level or difficulty and the availability of an intermediate step at the appropriate level of difficulty in carrying out the target activity. *Fading* consists of the gradual removal of supports until students are on their own. The three models described employed scaffolding in a variety of way.

4. *Articulation* includes any method of getting students to articulate their knowledge, reasoning, or problem-solving processes in a domain. We have identified several different methods of articulation. First, inquiry teaching (Collins & Stevens, 1982, 1983) is a strategy of questioning students to lead them to articulate and refine "prototheories" about the four kinds of knowledge enumerated. For example, an inquiry teacher in reading might systematically question students about why one summary of the text is good but another is poor, to get the students to formulate an explicit model of a good summary. Second, teachers might encourage students to articulate their thoughts as they carry out their problem solving as do Scardamalia et al. (1984). Third, they might have students assume the critic or monitor role in cooperative activities, as do all three models we discussed, and thereby lead students to formulate and articulate their knowledge of problem-solving and control processes.

5. *Reflection* (Brown, 1985a, b; Collins & Brown, 1988) enables students to compare their own problem-solving processes with those of an expert, another student, and ultimately, an internal cognitive model of

expertise. Reflection is enhanced by the use of various techniques for reproducing or "replaying" the performances of both expert and novice for comparison. For example, an expert's skillful postmortem of the problem-solving process, as Schoenfeld (1983) showed, can serve as a target for reflective comparison, as can the students' postmortems of their own problem-solving process. Alternately, various recording technologies, such as video or audio recorders and computers, can be employed to reproduce student and expert performance. The level of detail for a replay may vary depending on the student's stage of learning, but often some form of "abstracted replay," in which the determining features of expert and student performance are highlighted, is desirable. For reading or writing, methods to encourage reflection might consist of recording students as they think out loud and then replaying the tape for comparison with the thinking of experts and other students.

6. *Exploration* involves pushing students into a mode of problem solving on their own. Forcing them to do exploration is critical, if they are to learn how to frame questions or problems that are interesting and that they can solve. Exploration is the natural culmination of the fading of supports. It involves not only fading in problem solving but fading in problem setting as well. But students do not know a priori how to explore a domain productively. So exploration strategies need to be taught as part of learning strategies more generally.

Exploration as a method of teaching sets general goals for students and then encourages them to focus on particular subgoals of interest to them or even to revise the general goals as they come upon something more interesting to pursue. For example, in reading, the teacher might send the students to the library to find out which president died in office as a result of a trip to Alaska or to investigate theories about why the stock market crashed in 1929. In writing, students might be encouraged to write an essay defending the most outrageous thesis they can devise or to keep a diary of their best ideas or their most traumatic experiences. In mathematics, students might be given a data base on teenagers detailing their backgrounds and how they spend their time and money; the students' task might be to analyze the data base to devise and test hypotheses about how different groups of teenagers spend their time or money. The goal is to find general tasks that students will find interesting and to turn them loose on them, after they have acquired some basic exploration skills.

Sequencing

Lave (in preparation) has suggested that research emphasis on early skill acquisition has resulted in a failure to recognize the changing learning needs of students at different stages of skill acquisition and, consequently, to sequence and structure materials and activities appropriately for those stages. In particular, designers need to understand how to support both the phases of integration and of generalization of knowledge and complex skills. We have identified some dimensions or principles that should guide the sequencing of learning activities to facilitate the development of robust problem-solving skills.

1. *Increasing complexity* refers to the construction of a sequence of tasks and task environments or microworlds where more and more of the skills and concepts necessary for expert performance are required (Burton, Brown, & Fischer, 1984; VanLehn & Brown, 1980; White, 1984; White & Frederiksen, in press). We doubt it is possible to sequence skills and tasks so they undergo a monotonic increase in complexity. Instead, there are more likely to be jumps in complexity as learners are required not only to learn and integrate the interrelated set of skills or activities necessary to carry out an interesting task (even a relatively simple one) but also to manage and direct these activities. For example, in the tailoring apprenticeship described by Lave, apprentices progress over a series of ordered steps from practicing very simple rudimentary skills, such as wielding scissors and needle and sewing scraps, to actually putting together a garment, which requires the integration of sewing skill with a conceptual understanding of the structure of the garment.

There are two mechanisms for helping students manage increasing complexity. First, efforts should be made to control task complexity. As an example, in the tailoring apprenticeship described by Lave (in preparation), apprentices first learn to construct drawers, which have straight lines, few pieces, and no special features, such as waistbands or pockets. They then learn to construct blouses, which require curved lines, patch pockets, and the integration of a complex subpiece, the collar. The second key mechanism for helping students manage complexity is the use of scaffolding, which enables students to handle, at the outset, with the support of the teacher or other helper, the complex set of activities needed to carry out any interesting task.

Presumably, in most domains, task complexity can vary along a variety of dimensions. For example, in reading, texts can vary in complexity along the dimensions of syntax, vocabulary, conceptual abstractness, and argumentation. Increasing task complexity might consist of progressing from relatively short texts, employing straightforward syntax and concrete description, to texts in which complexly interrelated ideas and the use of abstractions make interpretation difficult.

2. *Increasing diversity* refers to the construction of a sequence of tasks in which a wider and wider variety of strategies or skills are required. Although it is important to practice a new strategy or skill repeatedly in a sequence of

(increasingly complex) tasks, as the skill becomes well learned, it becomes increasingly important that tasks requiring a diversity of skills and strategies be introduced so the student learns to distinguish the conditions under which they do (and do not) apply. Moreover, as students learn to apply skills to more diverse problems and problem situations, their strategies become freed from their contextual bindings (or perhaps more accurately, acquire a richer net of contextual associations) and thus are more readily available for use with unfamiliar or novel problems. For reading, task diversity might be attained by intermixing reading for pleasure, reading for memory (studying), and reading to find out some particular information in the context of some other task. Varying task diversity in writing might be achieved by posing different rhetorical problems, such as writing to persuade an audience of some point of view versus writing descriptive or instructional text, or by introducing specific constraints, such as writing for a particular audience (say the school board) or under different time constraints. We described earlier how Schoenfeld systematically increases diversity in teaching mathematics.

3. *Global before local skills.* In the tailoring apprenticeship described by Lave, apprentices invariably learn to put together a garment from precut pieces before learning to draw and cut out the pieces themselves. This sequencing of activities provides learners with the opportunity to build a conceptual model of how all the pieces of a garment fit together before attempting to produce the pieces. For cognitive domains, this implies sequencing of lessons so students have a chance to apply a set of skills in constructing an interesting problem solution before they are required to generate or remember those skills. This requires some form of scaffolding (see Methods section). Scaffolding can be applied to different aspects of a problem-solving process, for example, to management and control of the problem solving or to the subprocesses that are required to carry out the task. Global before local skills means that in the sequencing of lessons there is a bias toward supporting the lower level or composite skills that students must put together to carry out a complex task. In algebra, for example, students may be relieved of having to carry out low-level computations in which they lack skill to concentrate on the higher order reasoning and strategies required to solve an interesting problem Brown (1985b).

The chief effect of this sequencing principle is to allow students to build a conceptual map, so to speak, before attending to the details of the terrain. In general, having students build a conceptual model of the target skill or process (which is also encouraged by expert modeling) accomplishes two things: First, even when the learner is able to carry out only a portion of a task, having a clear conceptual model of the overall activity both helps him make sense of the pieces that he is carrying out and provides a clear goal toward which to strive as he takes on and integrates more and more of the pieces. Second, the presence of a clear conceptual model of the target task acts as a guide for the learner's performance, thus improving his ability to monitor his own progress and to develop attendant self-correction skills. We also suspect that having such a model helps crucially to prevent students from developing bugs in the acquisition of individual composite skills; having an understanding of the purpose of various skills can help clarify the conditions under which they are applicable, their entailments, their relationships to other processes, and so on.

Sociology

The final dimension in our framework concerns the sociology of the learning environment, a critical dimension that is often ignored in decisions about curriculum and pedagogical practice. In her analysis of tailoring apprenticeship, Lave (in press) discusses some of the determining features of the embedding social context and the ways they affect learning. For example, she notes that apprentices learn tailoring not in a special, segregated learning environment but in a busy tailoring shop. They are surrounded by both masters and other apprentices, all engaged in the target skills at varying levels of expertise. And they are expected, from the beginning, to engage in activities that contribute directly to the production of actual garments, advancing quickly toward independent skilled production. As a result, apprentices learn skills in the context of their application to realistic problems, within a culture focused on and defined by expert practice. They continually see the skills they are learning being used in a way that clearly conveys how they are integrated into patterns of expertise and their efficacy and value within the subculture. And by advancing in skill, apprentices are increasing their participation in the community, becoming expert practitioners in their own right. These characteristics—the ready availability of models of expertise-in-use, the presence of clear expectations and learning goals, and the integration of skill improvement and social reward—help motivate and ground learning.

Furthermore, we believe that certain aspects of the social organization of apprenticeship encourage productive beliefs about the nature of learning and of expertise that are significant to learners' motivation, confidence, and, most importantly, their orientation toward problems that they encounter as they learn. For example, the presence of other learners provides apprentices with calibrations for their own progress, helping them to identify their strengths and weaknesses and thus to focus their efforts for improvement. Moreover, the availability of multiple masters may help learners realize that even experts have different styles and ways of doing things and different special aptitudes. Such a belief encourages learners to understand learning as using multiple resources in the social context to obtain scaffolding and feedback.

We believe that structuring the social context to encourage the development of these productive beliefs sets the stage for the development of cooperative learning styles, such as those found by Levin (1982) in contemporary computer clubs, and of collaborative skill generally. In his study, Levin found that nonexperts were able successfully to bootstrap their knowledge about computers without regular access to high-level expertise by pooling their fragments of knowledge and using other learners as a source of scaffolding for carrying out their tasks. This decoupling of the experience of learning from the availability of an "authority" encourages independent and self-directed learning. Moreover, awareness of the distributed nature of expertise and insight is at the foundation of successful collaboration in all domains. Partly because of this key belief—that knowledge is not concentrated in any single person—skilled collaborators are more likely to be open to and seek help and input from others. As a result, they are better able to take advantage of interactions with others to construct better and more satisfactory solutions to complex problems.

From our consideration of these general issues, we have abstracted five critical characteristics affecting the sociology of learning.

1. *Situated Learning.* A critical element in fostering learning is to have students carry out tasks and solve problems in an environment that reflects the multiple uses to which their knowledge will be put in the future. Situated learning serves several different purposes. First, students come to understand the purposes or uses of the knowledge they are learning. Second, they learn by actively using knowledge rather than passively receiving it. Third, they learn the different conditions under which their knowledge can be applied. As we pointed out in the discussion of Schoenfeld's work, students have to learn when to use a particular strategy and when not to use it (i.e., the *application conditions* of their knowledge). Fourth, learning in multiple contexts induces the abstraction of knowledge, so that students acquire knowledge in a dual form, both tied to the contexts of its uses and independent of any particular context. This unbinding of knowledge from a specific context fosters its transfer to new problems and new domains.

The reason that Dewey (see Cuban, 1984), Papert (1980), and others have advocated learning from projects rather than from isolated problems is, in part, so that students can face the task of formulating their own problems, guided on the one hand by the general goals they set, and on the other hand by the "interesting" phenomena and difficulties they discover through their interaction with the environment. Recognizing and delineating emergent problems, that is, problems that arise while students are carrying out complex tasks in a rich problem-solving context, is a crucial skill. Emergent problems encountered in projects are ones for which they cannot use knowledge about the instructional designer's goals to help solve the problem, as students do in working textbook problems (Schoenfeld, 1985). Instead, problems emerge from interactions between the overall goals and the perceived structure of the environment. Thus, in projects students learn first to find a problem and then, ideally, to use the constraints of the embedding context to help solve it. They are learning the processes of "problem finding" identified by Getzels and Csikszentmihalyi (1976) while studying artists, and of pursuing "emergent goals" identified by Scardamalia and Bereiter (1985) in the writing process.

Reading and writing instruction might be situated in the context of an electronic message system, where students are sending each other questions and advice, as in the computer club described by Levin (1982). Dewey created a situated learning environment in his experimental school by having the students design and build a clubhouse (Cuban 1984), a task that emphasizes arithmetic and planning skills.

2. *Culture of expert practice* refers to the creation of a learning environment in which the participants actively communicate about and engage in the skills involved in expertise, where expertise is understood as the practice of solving problems and carrying out tasks in a domain. A culture of expert practice helps situate and support learning in several ways. First, a culture focused on expert practice provides learners with readily available models of expertise-in-use; as we have discussed, the availability of such models helps learners build and refine a conceptual model of the task they are trying to carry out. However, a learning environment in which experts simply solve problems and carry out tasks, and learners simply watch, is inadequate to provide effective models for learning, particularly in cognitive domains where many of the relevant processes and inferences are tacit and hidden. Thus, if expert modeling is to be effective in helping students internalize useful conceptual models, experts must be able to identify and represent to students the cognitive processes they engage in as they solve problems. Drawing students into a culture of expert practice in cognitive domains involves teaching them how to "think like experts." The focus of much current cognitive research is to understand better what is really meant by such a goal and to find ways to communicate more effectively about the processes involved. Even without a thorough theoretical understanding and formulation of expert processes, such mechanisms as group problem solving are helpful in externalizing relevant processes and reasoning, so that students can observe and enact them. Thus, the creation of a culture of expert practice for learning should be understood to include focused interactions among learners and experts for the purpose of solving problems and carrying out tasks.

Activities designed to engender a culture of expert practice for reading might engage students and teacher in reading and discussing how they interpret and use what they read for a wide variety of purposes, including the variety of learning needs that arise in other classes or domains.

3. *Intrinsic motivation.* Related to the issue of situated learning and the creation of cultures of expert practice is the need to promote intrinsic motivation for learning. Lepper and Greene (1979) and Malone (1981) discuss the importance of creating learning environments in which students perform tasks because they are intrinsically related to an interesting or at least coherent goal, rather than for some extrinsic reason, like getting a good grade or pleasing the teacher. There is some evidence that when an extrinsic reward is provided for performing a task like reading, students are less likely to perform the task on their own. In general, the methods of modeling–coaching–fading, insofar as they promote acquisition of integrated skills in the service of a coherent overall activity, are supportive of intrinsic motivation. But equally important is that students attempt to carry out realistic tasks in the spirit and for the purposes that characterize adult expert practice. In reading, for example, intrinsic motivation might be achieved by having students communicate with students in another part of the world by electronic mail (Collins, 1986; Levin, 1982) or by playing a game that requires a lot of reading.

4. *Exploiting cooperation* refers to having students work together in a way that fosters cooperative problem solving. Learning through cooperative problem solving is both a powerful motivator and a powerful mechanism for extending learning resources. As we discussed earlier, cooperative learning and problem solving provides students with an additional source of scaffolding, in the form of knowledge and processes distributed throughout the group. One crucial aspect of distributed knowledge concerns the multiple roles that a problem solver must play to carry out a complex task successfully and one students may have difficulty integrating. For example, to write effectively, students must alternate between the roles of producer and critic. By taking turns writing and reading each other's writing, students can get practice in both roles. Moreover, as students learn complex processes, they will grasp different aspects of a problem and of the methods needed to solve it. Cooperative problem solving enables them to share their knowledge and skills, giving students additional opportunities to grasp the relevant conceptual aspects of an overall process. In addition, students are often able to help each other grasp the rationale for or distinguishing characteristics of some new concept or skill because they are closer to the problem of learning about it. Students may have a better internal model of other students' difficulties and how to address them because they have recently had the same or a similar difficulty themselves.

Finally, cooperative learning helps foster the situated articulation of processes and concepts, thus helping students to gain conscious access to and control of cognitive and metacognitive processes and the ways these employ conceptual and factual knowledge.

In reading, activities to exploit cooperation might pair up students, where one student articulates his thinking process while reading, and the other student questions the first student about why he made different inferences.

5. *Exploiting competition* refers to the strategy of giving students the same task to carry out and then comparing what each produces. One of the important effects of comparison is that it provides a focus for students' attention and efforts for improvement by revealing the sources of strengths and weaknesses. However, for competition to be effective, comparisons must be made not between the products of student problem solving, but between the processes, and this is rarely the case. Moreover, although competition is a powerful motivator and organizer of learning for some students, it presents a number of thorny issues for educators. For example, there is evidence that many students are inhibited rather than motivated by competitive situations. Competition raises difficult emotional issues for some students, thus introducing potentially confusing or confounding factors into classroom interactions. And some people feel that competition encourages behavior and attitudes that are socially undesirable and even unethical.

At least some of the ill effects of competition have to do with attitudes toward and beliefs about errors (Brown & Burton, 1978). If students believe that making errors or being wrong about some process makes them "dumb," then comparative, competitive situations will be profoundly discouraging to weaker students. Another factor that makes competition seem problematic is that, under many forms of teaching, students lack the means, in the form of an understanding of the underlying processes, strategies, and heuristics involved in solving problems, for improving their performance. In these cases, the motivation to improve that might be engendered by competition is blocked, leaving students frustrated and discouraged.

It may be that at least some of these ill effects can be reduced by blending cooperation and competition; for example, individuals might work together in groups to compete with other groups. In such cases, students can take advantage of the scaffolding provided by the group to learn and strengthen their performance. For example, in reading, different groups might compete in trying to find some obscure information by searching through the library.

This completes our framework for the design of learning environments. The framework was evolved partly through a close consideration of the three "success models" discussed in the first sections of the chapter, as well as other models of apprenticeship learning, for example, in tennis (Braden & Bruns, 1977; Galwey, 1974), in skiing (Burton, Brown, & Fischer, 1984), in computational skills (Lave, Murtaugh, & de la Rocha, 1984), and Dewey's experimental school (Cuban, 1984). The framework provides a critical lens for evaluating the strengths and weaknesses of different learning environments and teaching methods.

CONCLUSION

Apprenticeship is the way we learn most naturally. It characterized learning before there were schools, from learning one's language to learning how to run an empire. We now have three very successful models of how apprenticeship methods, in all their dimensions, can be applied to teaching the school curriculum of reading, writing, and mathematics.

These models, and the framework we have developed, help point the way toward the redesign of schooling so students may better acquire true expertise and robust problem-solving skills, as well as an improved ability to learn throughout life. Perhaps less obviously, we believe that the core techniques of modeling, coaching, and fading can be formalized and embedded in tomorrow's powerful personal computers, thereby fostering a renewal of apprenticeship-style learning in our schools. Obviously, a number of advances in research are required before this dream can become a widespread reality. Current work on developing explicit, cognitive theories of domain skills, metacognitive skills, and tutoring skills is making the crucial first steps in the right direction.

We believe the thrust toward computer-aided learning is an important development in education for several reasons. First, computers make it possible to give more personal attention to individual students, without which the coaching and scaffolding of apprenticeship-style learning are impossible. It is precisely in human-resource-intensive settings, such as tennis coaching, learning foreign languages at Berlitz, or receiving training in medical diagnosis, that apprenticeship methods are still used. Appropriately designed computer-based modeling, coaching, and fading systems can make a style of learning that was previously severely limited, cost effective and widely available. Of course, apprenticeship-based computer systems need not take on the total responsibility. Instead, they only need to *augment* the master teacher in a way that amplifies and makes her efforts more cost effective.

Second, and perhaps more importantly, research aimed at building computer-based apprenticeship learning environments can encourage the more precise formulation, not only of the processes and knowledge that students require for expertise, but also of the knowledge that we as teachers require to effectively diagnose student difficulties, give useful hints, sequence learning activities, and so on. This type of knowledge can obviously have fruitful implications, not only for the design of electronic learning environments but also for teacher training, curriculum design, and educational policy generally.

ACKNOWLEDGMENTS

Prepared on the basis of talks given at the July, 1985 symposium on Cognition and Instruction at the Learning Research and Development Center, University of Pittsburgh, which was held in celebration of LRDC's 20th Anniversary and to honor Robert Glaser.

This research was supported by the National Institute of Education under Contract No. US-NIE-C-400-81-0030 and the Office of Naval Research under Contract No. N00014-85-C-0026. We thank Marlene Scardamalia, Frank Fisher, Lauren Resnick, Alan Schoenfeld, Annemarie Palincsar, Tom Malone, and Andee Rubin for comments and editing help on this manuscript.

REFERENCES

Baker, L., & Brown, A. L. (1980). Metacognitive skills of reading. In D. Pearson (Ed.), *Handbook of reading research* (pp. 353–394). New York: Longman.

Bereiter, C., & Scardamalia, M. (1987). *The psychology of written composition.* Hillsdale, NJ: Lawrence Erlbaum Associates.

Braden, V., & Bruns, W. (1977). *Vic Braden's tennis for the future.* Boston: Little Brown.

Brown, J. S. (1985a). Process versus product; A perspective on tools for communal and informal electronic learning. *Journal of Educational Computing Research, 1,* 179–201.

Brown, J. S. (1985b). Idea-amplifiers: New kinds of electronic learning. *Educational Horizons, 63,* 108–112.

Brown, J. S., & Burton, R. (1978). Diagnostic models for procedural bugs in basic mathematical skills. *Cognitive Science, 2,* 155–192.

Brown, J. S., & VanLehn, K. (1980). Repair theory: A generative theory of bugs in procedural skills. *Cognitive Science, 4,* 379–426.

Burton, R., Brown, J. S., & Fischer, G. (1984). Skiing as a model of instruction. In B. Rogoff & J. Lave (Eds.), *Everyday cognition: Its development in social context* (pp. 139–150). Cambridge, MA: Harvard University Press.

Collins, A. (1986). Teaching reading and writing with personal computers. In J. Orasanu (Ed.), *A decade of reading research: Implications for practice* (pp. 171–187). Hillsdale, NJ: Lawrence Erlbaum Associates.

Collins, A., & Brown, J. S. (1988). The computer as a tool for learning through reflection. In H. Mandl & A. Lesgold (Eds.), *Learning issues for intelligent tutoring systems* (pp. 1–18). New York: Springer-Verlag.

Collins, A., Brown, J. S., & Larkin, K. M. (1980). Inference in text understanding. In R. J. Spiro, B. C. Bruce, & W. F. Brewer (Eds.), *Theoretical issues in reading comprehension* (pp. 385–407). Hillsdale, NJ: Lawrence Erlbaum Associates.

Collins, A., & Smith, E. E. (1982). Teaching the process of reading comprehension. In D. K. Detterman & R. J. Sternberg (Eds.), *How much and how can intelligence be increased?* (pp. 173–185). Norwood, NJ: Ablex.

Collins, A., & Stevens, A. L. (1982). Goals and strategies of inquiry teachers. In R. Glaser (Ed.), *Advances in instructional psychology* (Vol. 2, pp. 65–119). Hillsdale, NJ: Lawrence Erlbaum Associates.

Collins, A., & Stevens, A. L. (1983). A cognitive theory of interactive teaching. In C. M. Reigeluth (Ed.), *Instructional design theories and models: An overview*. Hillsdale, NJ: Lawrence Erlbaum Associates.

Cuban, L. (1984). *How teachers taught*. New York: Longman.

Galwey, W. T. (1974). *The inner game of tennis*. New York: Random House.

Getzels, J., & Csikszentminhalyi, M. (1976). *The creative vision: A longitudinal study of problem finding in art*. New York: Wiley.

Hayes, J. R., & Flower, L. (1980). Identifying the organization of writing processes. In L. W. Gregg & E. R. Steinberg (Eds.), *Cognitive processes in writing* (pp. 1–32). Hillsdale, NJ: Lawrence Erlbaum Associates.

Lave, J. (1988). *The culture of acquisition and the practice of understanding* (Tech. Rep. No. 88-0007). Palo Alto, CA: Institute for Research on Learning.

Lave, J. (in preparation). *Tailored learning: Education and everyday practice among craftsmen in West Africa*.

Lave, J., Murtaugh, M., & de la Rocha, O. (1984). The dialectic of arithmetic in grocery shopping. In B. Rogoff & J. Lave (Eds.), *Everyday cognition: Its development in social context* (pp. 67–94). Cambridge, MA: Harvard University Press.

Lepper, M. R., & Greene, D. (1979). *The hidden costs of reward*. Hillsdale, NJ: Lawrence Erlbaum Associates.

Levin, J. A. (1982). Microcomputer communication networks for education. *The Quarterly Newsletter of the Laboratory of Comparative Human Cognition, 4*, No. 2.

Malone, T. (1981). Toward a theory of intrinsically motivating instruction. *Cognitive Science, 4*, 333–369.

Palincsar, A. S. (1986). Metacognitive strategy instruction. *Exceptional Children, 53*, 118–124.

Palincsar, A. S., & Brown, A. L. (1984). Reciprocal teaching of comprehension-fostering and monitoring activities. *Cognition and Instruction, 1*, 117–175.

Papert, S. (1980). *Mindstorms: Children, computers, and powerful ideas*. New York: Basic Books.

Polya, G. (1945). *How to solve it*. Princeton, NJ: Princeton University Press.

Scardamalia, M., & Bereiter, C. (1983a). Child as co-investigator: Helping children gain insight into their own mental processes. In S. Paris, G. Olson, & H. Stevenson (Eds.), *Learning and motivation in the classroom* (pp. 83–107). Hillsdale, NJ: Lawrence Erlbaum Associates.

Scardamalia, M., & Bereiter, C. (1983b). The development of evaluative, diagnostic, and remedial capabilities in children's composing. In M. Martlew (Ed.), *The psychology of written language: A developmental approach* (pp. 67–95). London: Wiley.

Scardamalia, M., & Bereiter, C. (1985). Fostering the development of self-regulation in children's knowledge processing. In S. F. Chipman, J. W. Segal, & R. Glaser (Eds.), *Thinking and learning skills: Research and open questions* (pp. 563–577). Hillsdale, NJ: Lawrence Erlbaum Associates.

Scardamalia, M., Bereiter, C., & Steinbach, R. (1984). Teachability of reflective processes in written composition. *Cognitive Science, 8*, 173–190.

Schoenfeld, A. H. (1983). Problem solving in the mathematics curriculum: A report, recommendations and an annotated bibliography. *The Mathematical Association of America*, MAA Notes, No. 1.

Schoenfeld, A. H. (1985). *Mathematical problem solving*. New York: Academic Press.

VanLehn, K., & Brown, J. S. (1980). Planning Nets: A representation for formalizing analogies and semantic models for procedural skills. In R. E. Snow, P. A. Federico, & W. E. Montague, (Eds.), *Aptitude learning and instruction, Vol. 2: Cognitive process analyses of learning and problem-solving* (pp. 95–137). Hillsdale, NJ: Lawrence Erlbaum Associates.

White, B. Y. (1984). Designing computer games to help physics students understand Newton's laws of motion. *Cognition and Instruction, 1,* 69–108.

White, B. Y., & Frederiksen, J. (in press). Progressions of qualitative models as a foundation for intelligent learning environments. *Artificial Intelligence.*

Author Index

Subject Index